# Adult Development and Aging

THIRD EDITION

JOHN M. RYBASH
Hamilton College

PAUL A. ROODIN
State University of New York, Oswego

WILLIAM J. HOYER
Syracuse University

Madison Dubuque, IA Guilford, CT Chicago Toronto London
Caracas Mexico City Buenos Aires Madrid Bogota Sydney

**Book Team**

Editor *Steven Yetter*
Developmental Editor *Ted Underhill*
Production Editor *Patricia A. Schissel*
Designer *Anna Manhart*
Art Editor *Miriam Hoffman*
Permissions Coordinator *Karen L. Storlie*
Visuals/Design Developmental Specialist *Janice M. Roerig-Blong*
Production Manager *Beth Kundert*
Visuals/Design Freelance Specialist *Mary L. Christianson*

WCB Brown & Benchmark
A Division of Wm. C. Brown Communications, Inc.

Executive Vice President/General Manager *Thomas E. Doran*
Vice President/Editor in Chief *Edgar J. Laube*
Vice President/Production *Vickie Putman*
National Sales Manager *Bob McLaughlin*

**Wm. C. Brown Communications, Inc.**

President and Chief Executive Officer *G. Franklin Lewis*
Senior Vice President, Operations *James H. Higby*
Corporate Senior Vice President and President of Manufacturing *Roger Meyer*
Corporate Senior Vice President and Chief Financial Officer *Robert Chesterman*

The credits section for this book begins on page 585 and is considered an extension of the copyright page.

Cover photo © Ron Chappel/FPG International

Interior photo research by Gail Meese/Meese Photo Research

Copyedited by Laurie McGee



A Times Mirror Company

Library of Congress Catalog Card Number: 94–72190

ISBN 0–697–10503–2



Printed in the United States of America by Wm. C. Brown Communications, Inc., 2460 Kerper Boulevard, Dubuque, IA 52001

10 9 8 7 6 5 4 3 2

*To my wife Vinnie, a continual source of encouragement, understanding, patience, and love.*

*J. R.*

*To my children Neal and Pamela whose constant love, joy, and thoughtfulness make each day of my life a delight.*

*P. R.*

*To Joan, for your love and friendship.*

*W. J. H.*

# Brief Contents

# Expanded Contents

3

## *INDIVIDUAL DIFFERENCES: BIOLOGICAL, PHYSICAL, AND SENSORY PROCESSES* 51



4

## *INFORMATION PROCESSING: PERCEPTION, ATTENTION, AND MEMORY* 91

## *INTELLIGENCE AND CREATIVITY* 125

# 8

## Work, Leisure, and Retirement 239



# 9

## Personality and Moral Development 291



# 10

## Coping, Adaptation, and Mental Health 335

## *APPLICATIONS AND THE CONTEXTS OF AGING 385*



12

## *HOW WE DIE 443*

*Appendix*

## *Developmental Research Methods 493*



*Appendix*

## *Careers in Basic and Applied Gerontology 523*

# List of Research Focus Boxes

# *Preface*

## *To the Student*

The field of adult development and aging is an exciting one. For many years, the prevailing view of adult development was that it was a time of steady decline and little, if any, positive psychological change. It was generally believed that an individual's intelligence, creativity, and personality were cast in cement by the end of adolescence. To be sure, childhood and adolescence have important effects on psychological functioning. But the next five, six, or seven decades are just as complex and just as important as the first two decades of life.

As you read this book, you most likely will find yourself thinking about your own development. What will you be like as you grow older? This book provides an accurate picture of the awesome, complex unfolding of development during the adult years. Not only will you learn important facts about the nature of adult development, you should be able to apply these facts to your own life as you grow older. What you learn can be a guide to your future growth and development and make you aware of the significant challenges that all of us must face as we age.

## *To the Instructor*

An instructor faces a difficult task in deciding which textbook to adopt for a course in adult development and aging. The book you are about to read, *Adult Development and Aging,* presents a unique blend of up-to-date, cutting-edge research and theory. We tried to present the material in a way that would engage and motivate students. In this third edition, we offer you and your students a clear, comprehensive, and current account of the salient issues and concerns that dominate the field. After reading this text, your students will have a keen understanding of where the field of adult development and aging has been in the past, where it is right now, and where it will be headed in the future.

We tried to present a balanced view of the gains *and* losses that characterize psychological development throughout the adult years. Also, we gave special attention to how different aspects of psychological development may be *optimized* throughout adulthood.

Virtually all textbook authors try to accomplish the difficult task of maintaining academic excellence while avoiding a stuffy, didactic style that is likely to turn students off. We believe that the third edition of *Adult Development and Aging* accomplishes this task better than the dozen or so other adulthood and aging texts that are now on the market. First, the writing itself is clear, lively, logical, and communicative. Second, a number of pedagogical help-to devices make the book interesting as well as informative. Each chapter opens with a chapter outline and also includes a number of boxed Research Focus inserts containing supplementary, high-interest, discussion-provoking material. A comprehensive glossary appears at the end of the text; we have also made certain that all key terms are highlighted, defined, and thoroughly explained the first time they are mentioned in the text. These are just some of the pedagogical and organizational features that make the third edition of *Adult Development and Aging* not only the most current and informative text available but the most interesting and enjoyable to read as well.

## *Audience*

This text is appropriate for students taking an introductory or advanced course in adult development and aging. Such courses are titled Adult Development, Adult Development and Aging (or the Psychology of Adult Development and Aging), Adult Psychology, Psychology of Adulthood, or simply Aging. The typical student in such a course is likely to be a sophomore, junior, or senior undergraduate who has completed a general introductory-level psychology course. However, the text assumes no prior detailed knowledge of psychology and is written in a style that allows the student to build a conceptual structure of the field from the ground up.

*Adult Development and Aging* would also be useful to instructors who teach a course in lifespan development and want to use two books—one on child and adolescent development and another on adult development and aging. The text is equally appropriate for faculty at two-year and four-year colleges and universities. Finally, *Adult Development and Aging* is most suitable for individuals teaching in the departments of psychology, human services, gerontology, sociology, social work, nursing, and education.

## *Content and Organization*

*Adult Development and Aging* presents the basic views, principles, research findings, and ideas about adulthood from an interdisciplinary, process-oriented perspective. The adoption of such a perspective allows students to understand the developing individual through an analysis of the biological, social, and cultural contexts in which aging occurs. The text consists of twelve chapters, each concerned with a major theme or aspect of adult development and aging. (See the Contents for more detailed information.) Also included are two detailed appendixes. The first offers an in-depth analysis of the research methods used to investigate psychological development over the entire adult lifespan. The second presents an overview of different career paths within the fields of adult developmental psychology and gerontology.

## *Additional Textual Learning Aids*

This text has been written with the student in mind. We have already mentioned some of the unique pedagogical aids in the text, including the chapter outlines, research focus sections, and extensive glossary. In addition, all of the terms contained in the glossary are printed in **boldface** type when they first appear in the text. This will alert your students to the importance of basic terms and provide them with a concise definition of each of these terms when needed. Graphs, tables, and figures illustrate the findings of important research studies, compare and contrast different theoretical perspectives, and summarize important issues. Photographs and line drawings give visual emphasis to key concepts and events and to those people, present and past, who have advanced our knowledge of adult development and aging. Finally, each chapter ends with a detailed summary, and a list of review questions. Separate indexes for authors and subjects appear at the end of the book.

## *Instructor's Manual and Test Bank*

An *Instructor's Manual and Test Bank* is available to adopters. This manual contains an introductory essay to the instructor for each chapter, followed by several essay questions and multiple-choice items, and a film/videotape list. The multiple-choice items are also available on *Testpak,* Brown & Benchmark's computerized testing service.

## *Acknowledgments*

Special thanks go to Brown & Benchmark Publishers for the special attention given this book. Michael Lange and Sheralee Connors, Psychology Editors, have provided support and encouragement throughout this project. Production editor Pat Schissel has competently overseen the swift and accurate production of this book. Anna Manhart, the designer, has made *Adult Development and Aging* very attractive and readable. And Shirley Lanners deserves credit for her work on the photographs. We also thank Laurie McGee and Karen Storlie for their assistance in copyediting and permissions, and art editor Miriam Hoffman. Also, we are very appreciative of the efforts of LunShan Liao for checking references.

Janet Simons deserves special thanks as well. She has prepared an *Instructor's Manual and Test Bank* that will greatly enhance the use of this text.

The third edition of this text benefited greatly from the assistance provided by colleagues through user reviews of the first and second editions. For their countless good ideas and helpful suggestions, we would like to thank the following:

**Frederic Agatstein** Rhode Island College
**Denise R. Barnes** University of North Carolina–Chapel Hill
**Janet E. Bitzan** University of Wisconsin–Milwaukee
**F. H. Blanchard-Fields** Louisiana State University
**Don C. Charles** Iowa State University
**Philip Compton** Ohio Northern University
**Elton C. Davis** Pasadena City College
**Rodney Dennis** Kennesaw College
**Joan T. Erber** Florida International University
**Shirlee Fenwick** Augustana College
**Oney D. Fitzpatrick, Jr.** Lamar University
**J. Steven Fulks** Utah State University
**Ernest Furchtgott** University of South Carolina
**Robert J. Gregory** University of Idaho
**Kristine L. Hansen** University of Winnipeg
**Bert Hayslip, Jr.** North Texas State University
**Mary W. Lawrence** University of Toronto
**Robert Bruce McLaren** California State University–Fullerton
**Marcia Mosh** Ryerson Polytechnical Institute
**Carmen H. Owen** York College of Pennsylvania
**Suzanne Prescott** Governors State University
**Irene McVay Staik** University of Montevallo
**Marcia Summers** Ball State University
**Mary Jane S. Van Meter** Wayne State University

Finally, we would like to thank our wives, Vinnie Rybash, Marlene Roodin, and Joan Hoyer for their patient support and understanding during the preparation of this manuscript.

1

# *Adult Development and Aging*
## *An Introduction*

*At first we want life to be romantic; later to be bearable; finally to be understandable.*
—Louise Bogan

*Life is what happens when you're busy making other plans.*
—John Lennon

## *Introduction*

The goal of this chapter is to provide a foundation for the study of adulthood and aging. We introduce you to some of the different ways that developmental scientists describe and explain the adult part of the human life span. We also call your attention to the fundamental concerns and controversies that underlie the study of adult development and aging.

## *Why Study Adult Development and Aging?*

People study adult development and aging for many reasons. The reasons range from wanting to understand the processes of development to wanting to directly improve the quality of life for older persons. More specifically, these reasons can be categorized as: (1) scientific or factual, (2) personal, and (3) altruistic. The philosopher Habermas (1971) suggested that human action is largely motivated by precisely these kinds of concerns. First, in terms of *factual interest,* there is a desire to have an objective understanding of what happens to people as they grow older. We pursue factual knowledge because we are curious about how and why people change. How does personality or intelligence change with aging? Over the course of adulthood, is a person more likely to become wise and creative, or foolish and forgetful? Why is it that some people experience declines in cognitive function or major changes in their personality while others do not? Is aging an inherently pathological process? Can some of the negative changes associated with aging be reversed or modified? Are there some very positive aspects of psychological functioning (wisdom, for example) that only emerge during the later years of life? Questions such as these need to be examined through precise scientific inquiry.

Second, in terms of *personal interest,* we are motivated to learn about adult development and aging because we have a selfish stake in becoming prepared for the changes, challenges, risks, and opportunities that face us as we move through adulthood and grow older. What can this field tell us about our own future development and aging? Do we have any control over how we age? How can we become our best self? Knowledge of adult development and aging can be applied to one's own development. This is especially important when one considers that significant developmental change occurs throughout the entire adult life span—from the twenties onward.

A third reason for wanting to study adult development and aging is *altruistic.* Knowledge within this domain is directly relevant in helping others to live better lives throughout the life span. We can be helpful to others in the various roles of spouse, friend, confidant, adult-child, grandchild, parent, or professional. There are things we can do to help others to negotiate the tasks and challenges of adult development and aging. For example, we may face the challenge of helping a close friend adjust to a new job or a divorce. Or, we may have to know how to be effective as a caregiver for a parent with dementia. We may even want to pursue a career in psychology, medicine, or social work that involves direct service to aged individuals. Changes in the American health care system, combined with the fact that the numbers and proportions of older adults will continue to rise, have created needs within families and many employment opportunities in various health and human service professions. It is also important to mention that accurate knowledge about the myths and realities of adult development and aging provides an essential basis for helping others and for helping individuals within our society to relinquish oppressive and negative stereotypes associated with old age and aging.

## *What Is Developmental Psychology?*

Developmental psychology has two aims. First, developmental psychology is concerned with understanding the origins and development of behavior within the individual; this focus is referred to as **ontogeny** or **intraindividual change.** Although the intensive study of individual development is a primary goal of developmental psychology (Burchinal & Applebaum, 1991; Hoyer & Rybash, 1994; Hooker, 1991), really there are relatively few studies of individual development. Most of the research in developmental psychology is conducted by comparing groups of individuals of different ages. Studies comparing different age groups are intended to have implications for "average" individual development. Second, developmental psychology is concerned with the study of age-related **interindividual differences.** Developmental psychologists study how different individuals develop and change, and the factors that account for individual differences in development. Thus, developmental psychologists are primarily interested in how individuals develop and change as they grow older, and in how different people show different patterns of development and change.

With these aims in mind, we can define **developmental psychology** as the study of age-related interindividual differences, and age-related intraindividual change. The main goals of developmental psychology are to describe, explain, predict, and improve or optimize age-related behavior change. We use the term *age-related* because age (or time) by itself does not give us a satisfactory explanation for development. The specific events or processes that occur during an interval of time, whether measured in hours, days, years, or decades, are the real determinants of development or aging. We should also mention that *nonevents,* or the events that are not personally or directly experienced, can also determine the paths of development. That is, we might have developed entirely differently if we had lived in a different neighborhood or country, attended different schools, participated in other activities, or had other friends or teachers. Or, we might have developed differently if we had not learned how to read, if we had not been physically injured as a result of a car accident, or if we had not been victimized by sexual abuse. We have been changed by what we have experienced, and we are different from others in part because of the developmental consequences of the events we have and have not experienced.

In our definition of developmental psychology, *behavior* is the focus of study, because psychology is the study of behavior. Psychologists conceptualize behavior broadly to include just about everything that people do. For example, social interactions, thoughts, memories, emotions, attitudes, and physical activities are all topics of study within the psychology of adult development and aging. Particular kinds of behavior are selected for study because they may be important in their own right, or because that behavior is thought to be a reliable measure of an important concept or process that cannot be measured directly.

The term **development** is reserved for changes in behavior that are known to vary in an orderly way with age. Developmental change must be relatively durable and distinct from temporary fluctuations in behavior that are due to mood, short-term learning, or other factors (Nesselroade, 1991). We would not identify an infant's one-time utterance of someone's name as evidence of language development. Nor would we identify a one-time failure to recall someone's name as evidence of age-related memory deficit. Development is reversible, and the term refers to increases as well as decreases in behavior, but the changes must be relatively durable to be considered developmental change.

## *Theoretical Issues in the Study of Adult Development and Aging*

The major theoretical issues in the study of adult development and aging are summarized in table 1.1. As can be seen in the table, those who study adult development and aging generally take the view that development takes place throughout the entire adult life span. In general usage, the term *development* refers to growth, such as physical maturation during the early years of childhood and adolescence; developmental psychologists who study the adult years recognize that there is development or change throughout the human life span.

### Development as Gains and Losses

Although the types of changes that occur between birth and 20 years of age, and the kinds of changes that occur after one's 20th birthday, are quite different, development in the form of *gains,* and *losses,* continues to occur throughout life (e.g., Baltes, 1987; Hoyer & Rybash, 1994).

Those who study adult development and aging take the view that no age period is any more important than any other period of development (Baltes, 1987). The changes that occur during the adult years are just as significant as those that occur

**TABLE 1.1**

| *A Summary of Theoretical Issues in the Study of Adult Development and Aging* |
|---|
| Development is a lifelong process. |
| No age or period of development is any more important than any other age or period of development. |
| Development refers to both increases and decreases, and gains and losses, in behavior. |
| Development is modifiable or reversible; the individual is active in determining the course of development, and there is plasticity in how an individual develops and changes throughout the life span. |
| Development can take many different paths, as reflected by age-related interindividual differences. |
| Development is multidirectional, in that there are different rates and directions of change for different characteristics within the individual and across individuals. |
| Developmental change can be gradual and continuous, or qualitative, relatively abrupt, and stagelike. |
| Developmental changes are considered to be relatively durable, to distinguish them from temporary fluctuations due to motivation, short-term memory, or other nondevelopmental processes. |
| Development is contextual in that it can vary substantially depending on the historical and sociocultural conditions in which it takes place. |
| Development is an outcome of the interactive effects of nature and nurture; the contributions of environmental and biological influences vary for different aspects of development and for different points in the life span. |
| The study of development is multidisciplinary in that it involves combining the perspectives of anthropology, biology, psychology, sociology, and other disciplines. |

during childhood or adolescence. For example, large changes in social maturity occur during the college years. One's choice of vocation has a strong impact on how we develop socially and intellectually during the adult years, and on our health and happiness. Whether or not we marry or become a parent has a substantial effect on many aspects of development. Perhaps we notice large changes in the attitudes, motivations, and capabilities of our parents, or grandparents, as they grow older. The point is that there are many important changes throughout the life span.

## Qualitative versus Quantitative Change

It is also mentioned in table 1.1 that developmental change can be characterized as either **qualitative** or **quantitative.** Are you basically the same person that you were five years ago, or are you basically a different person? Developmental change can appear to be qualitative, abrupt, and stagelike. Or it can appear to be quantitative, gradual, and continuous.

For example, developmental change can be considered to be qualitative when there are dramatic changes in the way the individual thinks about interpersonal relationships. Quantitative change refers to differences in amount rather than differences in kind. For example, throughout adulthood, the speed of retrieval of information from memory may gradually become slower.

Whether adult development is essentially qualitative or quantitative is both an empirical and theoretical issue. It is likely that developmental change is *both* qualitative and quantitative (Lerner, 1984).

## Stagelike versus Nonstagelike Change

Some researchers and theorists maintain that there are identifiable stages of adult development and aging. Others maintain that no universal markers distinguish one stage of development from any other. The notion of stages of development is controversial; researchers disagree about whether distinct stages of development occur during the adult years, and they argue about the criteria that indicate the presence of stages.

A **stage theory** is a description of a sequence of qualitative changes. Stage 1 must always precede Stage 2. Additional criteria for a stage theory are that (1) each successive stage consists of the integration and extension of a previous stage, (2) the transition from one stage to another is abrupt, and (3) each stage forms an organized whole that is characterized by the occurrence of several particular behaviors or competencies. Thus, if an entire set of organized behaviors appeared rather suddenly in the course of development for most if not all individuals at a particular point in the life span, and if each new stage incorporated and extended the competencies of the previous stage, then we would have clear evidence for a developmental stage. Evidence for stages of development is quite rare, however, leading some investigators to doubt the stage concept (Flavell, 1985) and others to want to relax the criteria for defining stagelike development (Fischer, 1980; Wohlwill, 1973).

## Continuity versus Discontinuity of Functioning

Stage theories imply an abruptness or developmental **discontinuity** between stages, and **continuity** within stages. Nonstage theories imply that development is always *continuous.* This means that the same processes control psychological functioning throughout the life span. According to social learning theory, for example, the same principles operate throughout the life span. An individual's behavior is continually shaped over the course of development through imitation, reward, and punishment. The influence of these mechanisms results in an increase, a decrease, or stability in behavior over the life span. For example, because of changes in reinforcement contingencies, we can expect that some adults will display increases in depressive symptomatology and feelings of helplessness as they age.

The study of adult development and aging is primarily concerned with the understanding of continuities as well as the gains and losses that can be observed at many points during the life span. Researchers are interested in understanding the nature of the consistencies and continuities that are evident in observations of adults across time. Although, traditionally, adulthood is characterized as a period of long-lasting continuity relative to earlier and later periods (e.g., Shanan, 1991), it is obvious that there is substantial diversity or interindividual differences among adults, as well as substantial variability within the same person across time (i.e., intraindividual change) and across tasks or situations (i.e., intraindividual differences).

It is also important to point out that despite the appearance of stability and continuity, it may be the case that a considerable amount of change is necessary in various underlying mechanisms and processes for the maintenance of behavior during the adult years.

## Plasticity versus Nonplasticity of Change

Another issue in the study of adult development and aging is the extent to which there is **plasticity** in behavior (Baltes, 1987; Baltes & Baltes, 1990; Fries, 1990). Baltes and his colleagues, in particular, have been active proponents of the notion of developmental **reserve capacity,** and they have provided a number of thoughtful discussions of the relevance of the concepts of plasticity and reserve capacity to the study of adult development and aging (e.g., Baltes & Kliegl, 1992; Baltes & Lindenberger, 1990; Kliegl, Smith, & Baltes, 1990). There is evidence to suggest that many kinds of age-related deficits can be remediated through appropriate intervention.

Although the reversibility of some aspects of adult development is an exciting possibility to explore, research evidence appears to support the position that reserve capacity is diminished with age in late life. That is, older adults are less able to benefit from training designed to optimize performance on cognitive tasks (e.g., Baltes & Kliegl, 1992). The significance of the notions of plasticity and reserve is in terms of the mechanisms that underlie competence and performance. Analogous to cardiovascular function, muscular efficiency, and other biological systems, age differences in behavioral efficiency arise when systems that are critical to maintaining performance are challenged by stress or other externally or self-imposed factors (Fries & Crapo, 1981; Rodin, 1986; Rowe & Kahn, 1987). Fries and Crapo (1981) reviewed evidence to suggest that reserve capacity is reduced with age across many biological systems. The concept of reserve is useful for describing adult cognitive function under stressed situations, but it may be of limited usefulness in accounting for developmental variability in everyday behavior.

Developmental psychologists are also confronted by the fact that the same individual performs differently at different times, and that any theory of adult development and aging must take account of variability in adaptive competencies. Such an approach gives emphasis to what the individual can do or is capable of doing under some conditions, some of the time.

## Multidirectional versus Unidirectional Change

Another theoretical issue in the study of adult development and aging has to do with the directionality of development. **Multidirectionality** refers to the observation that there are intraindividual differences in the patterns in aging. That is, individuals show stability for some types of behavior, declines in others, and improvements in still others. The developing individual might show an increase in creativity or wisdom and a decrement in some memory functions with advancing age.

In contrast to research and theory in adult development and aging, child-focused views of development, such as those of Piaget and Freud, generally assumed a **unidirectional** view of development in that all abilities were thought to show the same trend with maturation.

## *Determinants of Adult Developmental Change*

Why do individuals change and develop as they do? Some aspects of development are universal in that they are the same for everyone. Some aspects of development are culture-specific, cohort-specific, or specific to a segment of historical time. Some aspects of development are gender-specific, and some aspects of development are entirely unique to individuals because of their particular experiences. In this section we identify three general categories of determinants of developmental change. These are: **normative age-graded factors, normative history-graded factors,** and **nonnormative life events.** Development occurs as the result of the interaction of these factors. Usually it is an error to attribute developmental change to only one of these factors.

### Normative Age-Graded Factors

When we study young children, development appears *normative,* or similar across individuals and even cultures. It also appears that development is determined largely by a variety of normative age-graded factors. For example, the maturation and deterioration of the brain and nervous system occur at roughly the same ages in all individuals. There are also reliable age-graded changes in the speed of information processing and predictable changes in vision and hearing with aging.

### Normative History-Graded Factors

Some developmental influences are closely related to specific historical eras or events rather than to age. These events, called normative history-graded factors, occur at certain times in history. They produce dramatic effects on individuals who experience them—effects that may persist for a lifetime (see Research Focus 1.1). Normative history-graded factors include the pervasive and enduring effects of societal events such as wars and economic depressions on individual lives. Think of the personality differences that exist between different-aged adults. People in their thirties and forties may have different attitudes and personalities than individuals in their seventies and eighties. Why do these differences exist? Is it simply because of the different ages of these two groups of adults? Or is it because the different age groups grew up in different circumstances? In today's world, for example, the AIDS epidemic or the tough job market may have different effects on different-aged individuals.

Normative history-graded influences can be observed by comparing different cohorts of individuals. The term **cohort** refers to a group of individuals born at a particular time. History-graded or cohort factors have been shown to affect the level of intellectual abilities in different-aged individuals. Consider the results of the Seattle Longitudinal Study. This study began as a doctoral dissertation by K. Warner Schaie in 1956. Careful planning and design has allowed Schaie and his colleagues to distinguish the influences of age-related changes and history-graded changes over six waves of testing (1956, 1963, 1970, 1977, 1984, and 1991). For each wave of data collection, individuals ranging in age from 22 to 70 years and older were tested on measures of verbal meaning, spatial orientation, inductive reasoning, number, and word fluency from the Primary Mental Abilities (PMA) test (Schaie, 1993, 1994; Schaie & Willis, 1993). As expected, there were age-related declines for most of the measures of intellectual performance at each of the testing occasions. Considering these cross-sectional data by themselves, it appears that cognitive ability declines with age. However, when the results of different-aged individuals are examined across the six measurement occasions from 1956 to 1991, the results conclusively demonstrate that there are substantial history-graded differences in intellectual performance. These results suggest that both age and history-graded factors are responsible for differences in intellectual ability. In Schaie's study, for example, individuals born in 1910 performed worse on all of the measures of mental ability when compared with individuals born in 1917 and later. Generally, subsequent cohorts of individuals experience better schooling, greater educational opportunities, and intellectually more stimulating environments. History-graded factors influence many other aspects of psychological functioning, and the importance of distinguishing age effects and history-graded or cohort effects in developmental research cannot be overemphasized. Schaie's research design for disentangling age and cohort effects is described in detail in Appendix A.

## Nonnormative or Idiosyncratic Life Events

One of the most important aspects of the developmental study of the adult years is that change is idiosyncratic, presumably due to variations associated with a wide range of environmental opportunities and demands (e.g., Featherman, 1983; Lerner, 1991; Riley, 1985). Age-ordered normative change is much less evident during the adult years than during the childhood and adolescent years. Many of the individual changes and interindividual differences in adult development can be attributed to nonnormative or idiosyncratic influences rather than to general or universal patterns of adult developmental change. It is generally the case that there is a high degree of interindividual variability among adults. Thus, during adulthood, age-ordered, biological, or maturational processes are only one source of interindividual and intraindividual variability, leaving room for a wide range of environmental influences and experiences (e.g., Rybash, Hoyer, & Roodin, 1986).

Many influences on adult development are nonnormative or unique to the individuals who experience them. Some nonnormative life events are common to a small proportion of same-age individuals; others affect only a single individual. Furthermore, nonnormative life events do not happen at any predictable time in a person's life. For example, winning first prize in a multimillion-dollar state lottery is an event that would profoundly influence a person's behavior. However, it is only likely to happen to a small number of individuals and cannot be predicted to occur at any particular point in a person's life. Nonnormative life events, then, are usually chance occurrences.

Other examples of nonnormative events include accidents, illnesses, business failures, or the death of a loved one. Albert Bandura (1982) reminds us that nonnormative life events also include unintended meetings of people unfamiliar to one

## How Have Historical Events and Life Experiences Influenced Middle-Aged Adults?

One of the most elaborate longitudinal studies—the California Longitudinal Study—provides data on individual lives over a period of almost fifty years (Eichorn, Clausen, Haan, Honzik, and Mussen, 1981). The individuals in the California Longitudinal Study, who are now in later adulthood, were born in 1920–21 and 1928–29. Thus their birthdates preceded the depression. As Glenn Elder (1981) comments:

> . . . [the] forces set in motion by the swing of boom and bust—the economic growth and opportunity of the predepression era, the economic collapse of the 1930s, and recovery through wartime mobilization to unequaled prosperity during the 1940s and 1950s—influenced the life histories of these study members in ways that have yet to be fully understood. (p. 6)

Elder describes how individuals from these two cohorts (those born in 1920–21 and those born in 1928–29), although they experienced the same historical conditions of the 1920s and 1930s, underwent these experiences at different points of development and thus were affected in very different ways. The earlier-born subjects, those in the Oakland Growth Study, were children during the prospering 1920s. This was a time of unusual economic growth, particularly in the San Francisco area. The members of this cohort entered the depression after a reasonably secure early childhood, and they later avoided joblessness because of wartime mobilization. Most of them married and started families by the mid-1940s. This historical timetable minimized their exposure to the hardship of the depression.

For the group of adults born in 1928–29, the same historical events and circumstances occurred at a different point in their development as children. Members of this group, who formed the Guidance Study, grew up in Berkeley, California. During their early childhood years, they and their parents experienced the hardship of the depression; then again, during the pressured period of adolescence, they encountered the unsettling experience of World War II. According to Elder, the hardships they experienced increased their feelings of inadequacy during the war years and reduced their chances for higher education.

Recent analyses of these data by Elder, Shanahan, and Clipp (1994) provide new insights into the potential health consequences of social disruption and social breakdown.

Table 1.A shows the ages of the Oakland and Berkeley subjects at the time of various historical events. How might some of these events and circumstances influence the lives of people—in terms of generational differences, the employment of women, and childbearing, for example? As we consider such life events and circumstances, we can see how social history shapes the lives of adults.

---

another. It is sobering to reflect that chance encounters may become critically important determinants of many aspects of our lives, including career choice and marriage. How many college students settle on an academic major because of an enthusiastic and inspiring professor they encounter by chance in an elective course? How many young men and women receive their first job offers through an unanticipated meeting at a party? These are important and interesting questions that have yet to be explored in the scientific literature. The role of scientific research in this area is not to count the frequency of occurrence of chance encounters. Instead, we need to learn about how much choice and control we really do have over the events that affect our future development.

As shown in figure 1.1, the relative importance of normative age-graded factors, normative history-graded factors, and nonnormative life events varies across the life span. Figure 1.1 reveals that normative age-graded factors, for example, are most likely to influence development at the beginning and end of the life span. Most of the behavioral hallmarks of infancy (e.g., crawling, walking, talking, etc.) and very old age (e.g., generalized decrements in vision and attention) are probably due, to a great

TABLE 1.A

**Age of Oakland Growth and Guidance Study Members by Historical Events**

| Date | Event | Age of Study Members | |
|---|---|---|---|
| | | OGS* | GS** |
| 1880–1900 | Birth years of OGS parents | | |
| 1890–1910 | Birth years of GS parents | | |
| 1921–22 | Depression | Birth (1920–21) | |
| 1923 | Great Berkeley Fire | 2–3 | |
| 1923–29 | General economic boom; growth of "debt pattern" way of life; cultural change in sexual mores | 1–9 | Birth (1928–29) |
| 1929–30 | Onset of Great Depression | 9–10 | 1–2 |
| 1932–33 | Depth of Great Depression | 11–13 | 3–5 |
| 1933–36 | Partial recovery, increasing cost of living, labor strikes | 12–16 | 4–8 |
| 1937–38 | Economic slump | 16–18 | 8–10 |
| 1939–40 | Incipient stage of wartime mobilization | 18–20 | 10–12 |
| 1941–43 | Major growth of war industries (shipyards, munitions plants, etc.) and of military forces | 20–23 | 12–15 |
| 1945 | End of World War II | 24–25 | 16–17 |
| 1950–53 | Korean War | 29–33 | 21–25 |

*From G. Elder, "Social History & Life Experience" in* Present and Past in Middle Life. *Copyright © 1981 Academic Press. Reprinted by permission.*
**OGS = Oakland Growth Study*
***GS = Guidance Study*

extent, to age-related biomaturational changes. Normative history-graded factors are most likely to produce developmental change during adolescence and young adulthood. Adolescence and young adulthood are times when an individual first constructs an understanding of society and his or her relationship to it. It seems obvious, for example, that living through the Vietnam War and the civil rights movement in the United States would have the least effect on extremely young and old individuals and the greatest effect on adults entering the mainstream of societal life. Finally, nonnormative life events may take on a gradually more powerful role in promoting developmental changes as an individual ages. This idea may account for the observation that with increasing age, individual differences become progressively more identifiable. A group of 60-year-olds, for example, is generally more heterogeneous among themselves than a group of 40-year-olds. As we grow older, the continued emergence and accumulation of unique nonnormative life events helps to shape our personal lives, making individual differences more and more apparent.

Thus, we can distinguish three types of influences on adult development. These include the normative age-graded factors that have been emphasized in traditional

*Many people now choose to marry or begin parenting responsibilities at a later age. Medical advances and increased opportunities for family planning allow for a wider range of individual choices in many aspects of development. The timing of marriage and family decisions is also affected by career demands and financial limitations.*

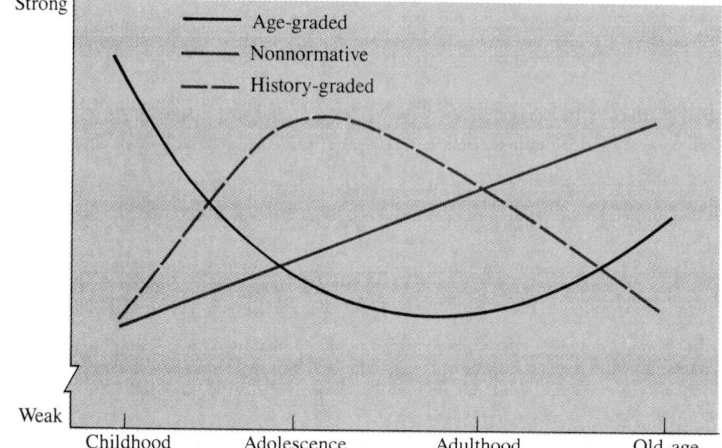


**Figure 1.1** The relative influence of normative age-graded factors, normative history-graded factors, and nonnormative life-event factors in promoting developmental change at different times across the human life span. *Source: Data from P. B. Baltes et al.,* Annual Review of Psychology, *Volume 31, Annual Reviews, Inc. Palo Alto, CA, 1980.*

*Both women in these photos are 80 years old. Biological, psychological, and functional aging occur at different rates for different individuals.*

developmental research; nonnormative life-event influences (such as winning a lottery or being abducted by a terrorist); and normative history-graded factors (such as the Great Depression of the 1930s or the Vietnam War) (Baltes, Reese, & Lipsitt, 1980; Elder, Shanahan, & Clipp, 1994).

## *The Concept Of Age*

What is age? Can it be considered a *cause* of development? Note that the concept of age is *multidimensional* in nature. In the following paragraphs, we describe the different meanings that Birren and Birren (1990) have attached to the concept of age.

### Chronological Age

**Chronological age** refers to the number of years that have elapsed since a person's birth. Several psychologists (e.g., Baer, 1970) have argued that chronological age per se is *not* relevant to an understanding of psychological development; that is, a person's age in and of itself does not cause development. Age is merely a marker for the processes that change over time and influence behavior.

### Biological Age

The concept of **biological age** has been defined as an estimate of the individual's present position with respect to his or her potential life span (Schroots & Birren, 1990). This concept of age involves measuring the functional capacities of an individual's vital organ system. From this perspective, age can be viewed as an index of biological health. An individual's vital capacities may be better or worse than those of other persons of comparable chronological age. The younger a person's biological age, regardless of chronological age, the longer we would expect the individual to live.

## Psychological Age

**Psychological age** refers to the adaptive capacities of an individual—that is, an individual's ability to adapt to changing environmental demands as compared to the adaptability of other individuals of identical chronological age. Individuals adapt to their environments by drawing on various psychological characteristics: learning, memory, intelligence, emotional control, motivational strengths, coping styles, and so on. Therefore, individuals who display a greater amount of such psychological characteristics than their chronological agemates are considered "psychologically young;" those who possess such traits to a lesser degree are "psychologically old."

## Functional Age

**Functional age** is a measure of a person's ability to function effectively within a given environment or society. For example, an individual needs a number of skills and abilities (both psychological and physical) to function effectively as the sole occupant of an apartment—the individual has to be mobile and active to be able to shop, clean, cook, and wash as well as be able to efficiently plan and remember pertinent information. It is not surprising that some 75-year-olds are more self-sufficient than some 25-year-olds. Given the fact that chronological age is not perfectly related to functional age, psychologists find it increasingly important to develop valid and reliable measures of a person's functional abilities.

## Social Age

**Social age** refers to the social roles and expectations that people have for themselves as well as those imposed by other members of society. Consider the role of "mother" and the behaviors that accompany that role. It is probably more important to know that she is the mother of a 3-year-old child than to know whether she was born twenty or thirty years ago. Furthermore, individuals are often aware of being on-time or off-time with regard to social age. Some older adults, for example, act like perpetual teenagers because they consider themselves "young."

## Age Profiles

Given these different dimensions of age, we can develop an overall age profile for any individual. For example, a 70-year-old man (chronological age) might be in very good physical health (biological age), yet be experiencing a number of problems remembering and focusing attention (psychological age). The same man might be coping exceptionally well with the new demands placed on him by his wife's recent hospitalization (functional age) and might consider himself more a "retired businessman who likes to play golf" than a "grandfather" (social age).

*Social age refers to the age-graded prescriptions people have for themselves and others. Although definitions of social age are changing by becoming more flexible in American Culture, we still take notice of individuals who are atypical of traditional age prescriptions. Musical artist and performer, Mick Jagger, at age 49.*

## *Conceptual Paradigms for the Study of Adult Development*

**Paradigms** or "world views" enable researchers to construct meaningful patterns for what would otherwise be a collection of unrelated observations. Scientific activity is guided by paradigms that determine what is important to study, how it should be studied, and what kinds of theoretical ideas can be advanced on the basis of such study (Kuhn, 1962).

Paradigms are not directly testable; they are too abstract to be objectively verified or falsified. Paradigms serve to stimulate ideas, issues, and questions that *can* be tested. Thus, paradigms are *not* the same as theories. Paradigms provide a framework for generating theories, and theories generate research. Paradigms are useful if they serve this purpose, not in terms of whether they are right or wrong. Historically, psychologists have used mechanistic, organismic, and contextual paradigms to understand human development.

### The Mechanistic Paradigm

According to the **mechanistic paradigm,** the individual's development is a product of environmental forces. The mechanistic model assumes that human behavior is machinelike. Machines are passive. From this view, behavior is reactive to events in life.

## The Organismic Paradigm

According to the **organismic paradigm,** development is qualitative. From this view, the individual is active, planful, and strategic. The organismic paradigm shifted the emphasis from the study of simple stimulus-response relationships and quantitative change to the study of internal processes and qualitative change. Individual development unfolds in a universal, orderly sequence of stages.

## The Contextual Paradigm

In recent years, the **contextual model** has become the predominant paradigm. The metaphor underlying the contextual paradigm is the historical event. This paradigm suggests that adults, like historical events, are ongoing, dynamic, and not directed toward an ideal goal or end-state. Furthermore, the meaning and interpretation of historical events may change, depending on the *context* or perspective from which such events are viewed. A war may be viewed as "moral" from one historical context and "immoral" from another. Similarly, the contextual model takes neither a purely passive nor a purely active view of the individual. The basic conception of this model is that an adult individual continuously influences and is influenced by the different contexts of life.

It is important to understand that *context* is an open-ended term that may apply at different levels of analysis. For example, the environmental context pertains to one's physical environment. The social, historical, or cultural context pertains to influences such as societal norms and the expectations of friends and relatives. Further, the biological context pertains to an individual's health and physical skills. In all of these examples, not only do the contexts have an effect upon the individual, but also the individual has an effect upon the context. To take a simple example, one's family might make unreasonable demands. When the individual begins to refuse these demands more often, it might alter the family's subsequent demands, which in turn alters the individual's responsiveness to further demands.

The contextual model serves as the foundation for a broad range of theories that address various aspects of adult development. For example, an adult's ability to remember an event depends on (1) the psychological, social, and physical contexts in which the person initially experienced the event, (2) the unique skills, abilities, knowledge, and motivation that the individual brings to the context in which he must remember, and (3) the special characteristics of the context in which the person attempts to remember. As the individual changes, and as the contexts in which she is asked to remember change, we would expect the person's memory to change as well. Thus, we could say that memory is a dynamic process involving the continual *reconstruction* of past events and experiences. Adults, therefore, seem to serve as their own "historians." They constantly revise their pasts from the perspective of the present.

One version of the contextual paradigm is the **dialectical view.** Riegel (1976) argued that individuals and the contexts of their lives are always in a state of flux; that is, adults are constantly changing organisms in a constantly changing world.

*TABLE 1.2*

*Overview of the Three Life-Span Models of Adult Development*

| *Questions for Distinguishing Among Developmental Models* | *Models* | | |
|---|---|---|---|
| | *Mechanistic* | *Organismic* | *Contextual* |
| What is the underlying metaphor? | machine | cell, embryo | historical event |
| What is the relationship between the person and the environment? | active environment; passive person | passive environment; active person | active environment; active person |
| What is the focus of developmental psychology? | quantitative changes in observable behavior | qualitative changes in internal structures | person/environment transactions |

From Riegel's view, the individual and society are never at rest. Riegel also believed that contradiction and conflict are an inherent part of development and that no single goal or end point in development is ever reached. The dialectical perspective stresses the inherent multidirectionality of developmental change and the wide-reaching interindividual variability observed with increasing chronological age.

New ways of thinking about a wide variety of topics in adult development and aging have emerged in recent years, and these views are largely contextual (e.g., see Baltes & Baltes, 1990; Dannefer & Perlmutter, 1990; Lerner, 1991; Sinnott & Cavanaugh, 1991). These views are partially motivated by dissatisfaction with the mechanistic and organismic preoccupation with the negative aspects of aging. There is also some dissatisfaction with the overemphasis on chronological age as the measure of development, and the lack of emphasis on such concepts as resiliency, vitality, and adaptation in adult development and aging.

New contextual approaches to development try to take into account individual differences, gains as well as losses in function during the adult years, and the role of social interaction and contradiction or conflict in adult development. Another characteristic of new work in adult development and aging is that there is a greater emphasis than ever before on practical aspects of development. Many everyday activities in adulthood and old age are contextually based. Thinking, reasoning, and other aspects of everyday function in adulthood are not so much constrained by biological aging as they are by the contexts in which these activities take place. Primary interest is in the investigation of contextual factors that enable individuals to function effectively during the adult life span.

## *PARADIGMS AND ISSUES IN ADULT DEVELOPMENT*

It is useful to compare the mechanistic, organismic, and contextual paradigms with respect to the issues considered earlier in this chapter. As table 1.2 shows, the organismic model is distinguished by the emphasis it places on qualitative change, distinctive stages of development, and continuity of change. It also is unique in

### TABLE 1.3

**Models and Characteristics of Adult Development**

| Degree of Emphasis on Different Characteristics of Human Development | Models: Mechanistic | Organismic | Contextual |
|---|---|---|---|
| Qualitative change | Low | High | Medium |
| Stages of change | Low | High | Medium |
| Continuity of change | Low | High | Medium |
| Multidirectionality of change | Medium | Low | High |
| Reversibility of change | Medium | Low | Medium |
| Multiple determinants of change | | | |
| Normative age-graded factors | Low | High | Medium |
| Normative history-graded factors | Low | Low | High |
| Nonnormative life-event factors | High | Low | High |
| Chronological age as a useful variable | Low | High | Medium |

emphasizing the importance of age-graded influences on development. One of the main differences between the mechanistic and contextual models is that the contextual model places greater emphasis on the multidirectional nature of developmental change. Another difference is the importance of history-graded influences in the contextual model. The mechanistic model emphasizes nonnormative life-event influences at the expense of all other aspects of development. The contextual model also emphasizes nonnormative influences but not exclusively; it considers history-graded influences as well as individual differences. Indeed, as indicated in table 1.3, the contextual model stresses all aspects of development. From the perspective of the contextual model, development is multifaceted and multidetermined. The contextual model, more than the others, recognizes the individual as producer of his or her own development.

## OVERVIEW OF THE TEXT

One of the challenges for those who study adult development and aging is to construct a useful and accurate framework for describing and explaining the experiences of adult development. Some researchers have found it useful to concentrate on the factors that *constrain* development at different ages. For example, some social and cultural influences, such as restrictive sex roles and stereotypes of ageism, sexism, and racism, serve to limit opportunities for growth during the adult years and constrain individual development. Of course, there are also biological and health influences that constrain the range or nature of development during the adult years. In this text we emphasize not only the constraining factors but also the factors that are associated with *optimization* of development at different points throughout the adult life course. Furthermore, we stress the ideas that development throughout the adult years consists of a complex interplay of gains *and* losses, and that adult development and aging is characterized by a great deal of intraindividual change and interindividual variability. Throughout the text we illustrate how sociocultural, biological, and experiential factors influence functioning within different domains that are of primary interest to developmentalists.

## Domains of Development

The *biological and physical domain* refers to changes that range from simple alterations in size, weight, and other anatomical features, to the genetic blueprint that places constraints on our development from conception to death. The genes we were born with still influence our adult development. Scientists are looking closely at the role genetics plays in such adult disorders as schizophrenia, dementia, alcoholism, and depression. Hormones are yet another aspect of biological makeup that play an important part in the understanding of adult development; for example, the onset of menopause in women is accompanied by significant hormonal change. Furthermore, we will pay close attention to age-related changes in the brain and nervous system. And we will describe how these changes influence psychological functioning.

The *cognitive domain* refers to the age-related series of changes that occur in mental activity—thought, memory, perception, and attention. As part of our study of cognitive development, we will explore how adults process information; how intelligence and creativity change over time; and how qualitatively new styles of thinking emerge during adulthood. We will look carefully at declines in memory during adulthood, paying special attention to the issue of how "normal" memory deficits may be distinguished from "pathological" memory deficits in older adults.

The *personality domain* in adult development usually refers to the properties distinguishing one individual from another individual. But as we will see, some experts believe that there are also commonalities that characterize individuals at particular points in adult development. One's sex-role orientation, perception of self, moral values, and sociability represent some of the aspects of personality we will discuss. You will find that it often is impossible to meaningfully present personality development in adulthood without frequently looking at the individual's interactions with and thoughts about the social world.

The *social domain* involves an individual's interactions with other individuals in the environment. Two elderly people consoling each other, a mother hugging her daughter for bringing home a good report card, two sisters arguing, and a boss smiling at a secretary are all examples of interaction in the social world. Social development focuses on how these different aspects unfold as the individual grows. We also will study contexts in the section in which we discuss social processes and development. As we have seen in this chapter, the contexts in which adult development occurs are a very important factor in determining what people are like. Some of the most important social contexts of adult development are families, relationships, and work.

Although it is helpful to study adult development within different domains, keep in mind while reading this text that you are an integrated human being. Biological, physical, cognitive, social, and personality development are inextricably woven together. For example, in many chapters, you may read about how social experiences shape cognitive development, how cognitive development restricts or promotes social development, and how cognitive development is tied to physical development.

## Summary

Developmental psychology is the study of age-related interindividual differences, and age-related intraindividual change. The main goals of developmental psychology are to describe, explain, predict, and improve or optimize age-related behavior change. Some of the guiding principles of developmental psychology are:

1. Development is a lifelong process.
2. No age or period of development is any more important than any other age or period of development.
3. Development refers to both increases and decreases, and gains and losses, in behavior.
4. Development is modifiable or reversible; the individual is active in determining the course of development, and there is plasticity in how an individual develops and changes throughout the life span.
5. Development can take many different paths, as reflected by age-related interindividual differences.
6. Development is multidirectional, in that there are different rates and directions of change for different characteristics within the individual and across individuals.
7. Developmental change can be gradual and continuous, or qualitative, relatively abrupt, and stagelike.
8. Development is contextual in that it can vary substantially depending on the historical and sociocultural conditions in which it takes place.
9. The study of development is multidisciplinary in that it involves combining the perspectives of anthropology, biology, psychology, sociology, and other disciplines.

It is important to study development during the adult life span for many reasons. These reasons can be categorized as: scientific or factual; personal; and altruistic.

There are multiple determinants for development during the adult years. In addition to the normative age-graded influences emphasized by traditional developmental theory, nonnormative life events (e.g., accidents and chance encounters) and normative history-graded influences (e.g., wars and depressions) also affect development.

Although chronological age may not be useful in explaining change, age is an important descriptive variable in developmental research. Also, it is possible to construct a useful age profile based not only on chronological age, but on biological, psychological, functional, and social age.

Paradigms (models) are useful for generating ideas, issues, and questions for research. Models also suggest appropriate methodological approaches for exploring these ideas, issues, and questions. In contrast to the mechanistic and organismic models, the contextual model is unique in its broad attention to all types of change and all determinants of change. Indeed, the contextual model actually seems to encompass the mechanistic and organismic models.

Development takes place within different domains. Thus, to achieve an integrative view of adult development, it is necessary to understand how the biological/physical, cognitive, personality, and social dimensions of individuals change (or remain stable) over time.

## Review Questions

1. Give some examples of scientific, personal, and altruistic reasons for studying adult development and aging.
2. What are the primary goals of developmental psychology?
3. Explain what is meant by intraindividual change and interindividual variability.
4. What is meant by the term "development"? Is development characterized by gains *or* losses? Is development reversible? What does the "optimization" of development refer to?
5. Contrast the life-span perspective of adulthood with a traditional child-focused perspective.
6. Discuss the importance of idiosyncratic factors, normative history-graded factors, and normative age-graded factors in adult development.
7. Why is the concept of age a controversial variable in the study of adult development?
8. Explain the difference between the concepts of chronological, biological, psychological, functional, and social age. Why is it useful to make distinctions between these various dimensions of age?
9. Develop an age profile for yourself and other salient individuals (e.g., family members) in your life.
10. What are the purposes and functions of a paradigm? What is the relationship between a paradigm and a theory?
11. Describe the mechanistic, organismic, and contextual paradigms. Which paradigm, at present, is generating the most important impact on research and theory on adult development and aging?
12. Give examples of the different "domains" in which adult development and aging takes place.

## For Further Reading

Abeles, R. P., Gift, H. C., & Ory, M. G. (1994). *Aging and quality of life.* New York: Springer.

Baltes, P. B., & Baltes, M. M. (Eds.). (1990). *Successful aging.* New York: Cambridge University Press.

Birren, J. E., & Birren, B. A. (1990). The concepts, models, and history of the psychology of aging. In J. E. Birren & K. W. Schaie (Eds.), *Handbook of the psychology of aging* (3d ed., pp. 3–20). San Diego: Academic Press.

# *INDIVIDUAL DIFFERENCES*
## *Social and Cultural Influences*

*Is a dream a lie if it don't come true, or is it something worse?*
—Bruce Springsteen, The River

*We breathe the air of our times.*
—Anonymous

## *Introduction*

This chapter underscores the wide range of diversity that is evident in adult populations. The influences of norms and expectations associated with age, cohort, gender, and ethnicity on individual development and on individual differences during the adult years are discussed. A main focus of this chapter is to consider the effects of social and cultural factors on individual development and individual differences during the adult years. We begin with a description of the demographic characteristics of the population in the United States, and projected changes in the numbers and proportions of older adults. Next we turn our attention to the increasing diversity within and across age groups in the United States. The experience of adult development and aging is different in different cultures and countries, for different cohorts, and different for men and women. Age roles serve as organizers and filters for social interaction and for other aspects of development during the adult years.

## *Characteristics of the Adult Population in the United States*

People change and cultures change—each influences the other continuously. Many changes in the composition of the American population have occurred throughout the history of the United States. In recent years, the most striking changes have to do with the size and distribution of age groups within the population, and changes in the ethnic composition of the population. In terms of age distributions, the number and percentage of older adults in the United States is growing at an unprecedented rate. For example, the number of adults over age 65 in American society is expected to double in the next forty years. In terms of ethnic composition, there is greater diversity of race and ethnicity in the United States than ever before. Ethnic and cultural diversity is evident throughout the country. For example, more foreign-born residents than nonimmigrants live in Miami and Miami Beach, Florida; in Huntington Park, Santa Ana, and Monterey Park, California; and in Union City, New Jersey. In 1990, the American population was 76 percent Anglo, 12 percent Black, 9 percent Latino, 3 percent Asian. By 2050, the population will be 52 percent Anglo, 16 percent Black, 22 percent Latino, and 10 percent Asian. We describe these trends in the sections that follow. We first consider the "graying of America," then we discuss trends toward ethnic diversity and the implications of these trends on individual development and on changes in social institutions such as the family and the educational system. We begin by describing changes in the size of the older population in the United States.

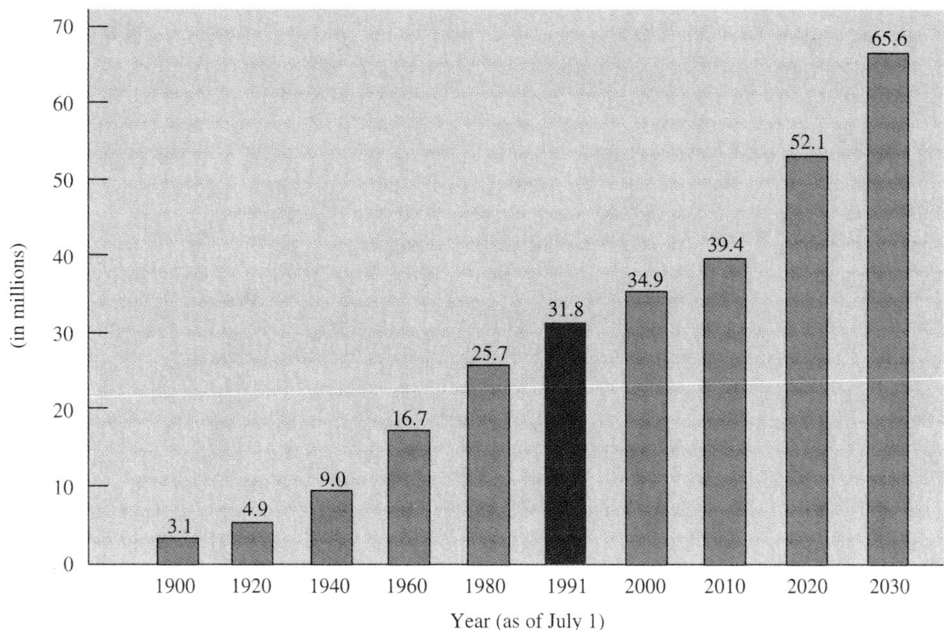


**Figure 2.1** Number of persons 65+ : 1900 to 2030. *Source: Data from the U.S. Bureau of the Census.*

## *The Graying of America*

The phrase "Graying of America" aptly describes the trend toward greater numbers and proportions of older adults in the United States population. As shown in figure 2.1, there were about 3.1 million Americans aged 65 and over in 1900. In 1991, there were more than ten times as many older adults — 31.8 million. Older adults also represent a much greater proportion of the American population than ever before. Since 1900, the percentage of Americans aged 65 and over has tripled. In 1991, 12.6 percent of the population was age 65 and over, compared with 4.1 percent in 1900.

It is projected that the older population will continue to grow at a faster rate than other age groups. Since 1980, the older population increased by 6.1 million or 24 percent, compared with an increase of 9 percent for the under-65 population. By 2030, there will be 66 million older adults in the United States, approximately twice the present number. Older adults will comprise 21 percent of the population by 2030 (Kasper, 1988; U.S. Bureau of Census, 1990).

The older population is getting older. The most rapidly growing segment of the American population is the *old-old,* defined as those who are aged 85 years and older. The old-old constitute nearly 10 percent of the population over age 65. By 2050, the old-old will represent 25 percent of the population (U.S. Bureau of the Census, 1990). Between 1960 to 1990 the population of the United States 85 and over increased by 232 percent (U.S. Bureau of the Census, 1990).

It is also noteworthy that the number of *centenarians,* individuals who reach their 100th birthday, has increased substantially in this century, and the number of centenarians is expected to continue to increase. In 1990, there were 36,000 centenarians (U.S. Bureau of the Census, 1990). By the year 2080, it is expected that there will be more than 1 million centenarians.

## Age Structure

One of the ways to show how we have become an aging society is to examine changes in the **age structure.** Age structure refers to the percentages of men and women grouped by age decades. The first two graphs in figure 2.2 show the age structure of the United States in 1850 and 1950. Figure 2.2 also shows the projected age structure of the United States for the year 2030 (U.S. Bureau of the Census, 1990). The shapes of the age distributions are quite different for different years. One of the graphs resembles a pyramid. One of the graphs looks like a rectangle. That is, comparing the age structures in 1850 and 2030, there is a trend toward equalization of the percentages of Americans within various age intervals. By the year 2030, the percentages of individuals in each period of the life course will be approximately equal.

## Life Expectancy

**Life expectancy** refers to the predicted chronological length of one's life. Life expectancy varies from country to country and has changed over time. A person born in 1900 had an average life expectancy of 48 years, whereas a person born in 1990 has an average life expectancy of 75.4 years. In this century, average life expectancy in the United States increased by twenty-eight years. This increase in average life expectancy is greater than that seen during all of human history.

Until about 1970, most of the change in life expectancy came from improved health care in infancy and early childhood. Life expectancy for those who reached 50 years of age, in contrast, remained unchanged. More recently, however, life expectancy at age 50 has witnessed some remarkable changes. This is primarily due to improvements in the quality of health care available to today's adults. For example, during the last decade, fewer males in middle adulthood and the early part of late adulthood seem to be dying because of heart attack or stroke (National Center for Health Statistics, 1992). However, projections must be cautiously interpreted, since changes in infant mortality, immigration, and social-environmental conditions will influence the health and life expectancy of tomorrow's older adults. Research Focus 2.1, for example, describes how being overweight in adolescence affects health in later life.

The changes in average life expectancy are not uniform across race. The National Center for Health Statistics (1992) reported that between 1984 and 1986, life expectancy for blacks dropped to 69.4 years, the lowest it has been since 1982. At the same time, corresponding data for whites (males and females combined) increased to 75.4 years. This is the first time that blacks' life expectancy has declined while whites' life expectancy has risen. Whites generally have shown a pattern of living nearly six years longer than blacks, with both groups increasing in life expectancy at

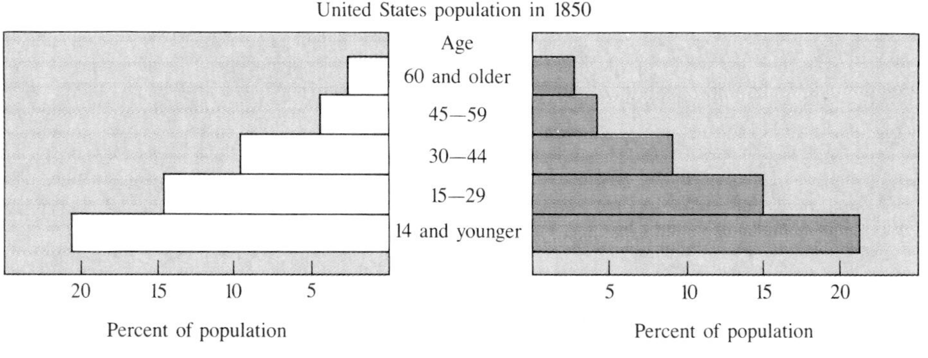


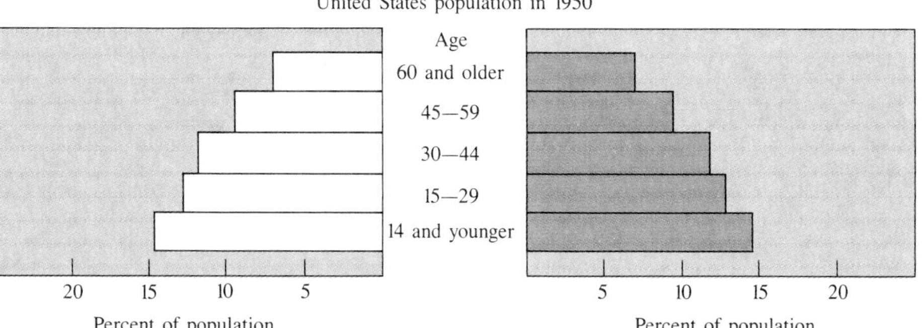


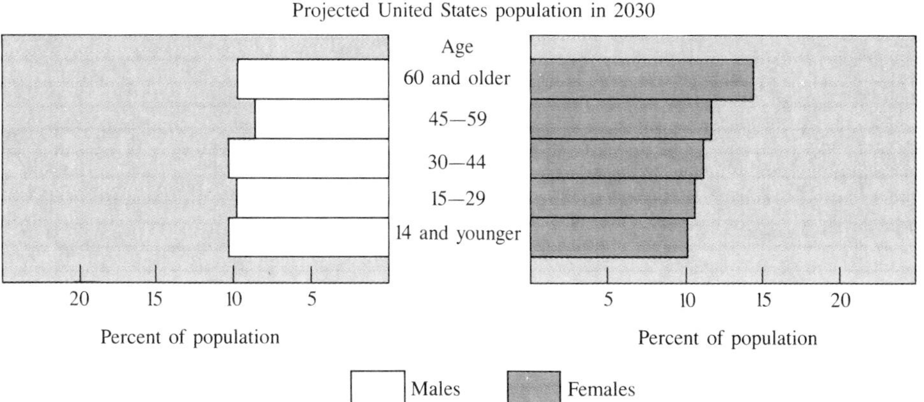


**Figure 2.2** The changing age structure of the U.S. population. *Source: The 1850 and 1950 figures are from the United Nations Department of Economic and Social Affairs,* The Aging of Populations and its Economic and Social Implications *(Population Studies, No. 26), United Nations, New York, NY, 1956; the 2030 figures are from the U.S. Bureau of the Census,* Household and Family Characteristics *(Current Population Reports, Series P-20, No. 326), Government Printing Office, Washington, DC, 1977.*

roughly the same rate (one year added every two and a half years since the turn of the century). A key to understanding the differential life expectancy for black men and women is to recognize that blacks are dying far earlier in young and middle adulthood. Black children and adults are victims of murder and violence in the streets; black males are victims of drug abuse; and blacks are more likely than whites to face limited access to medical care, poor nutrition, and substandard housing.

##### *Research Focus 2.1*

### *Health in the Later Years Is Affected by Being Overweight in Adolescence*

One of the major research issues in the study of adult development and aging is to understand the relationships between earlier and later development. Behavior in adolescence and early adulthood affects health in many ways throughout the adult life span.

Researchers at Harvard University have documented what people have suspected about the consequences of early obesity on health across the life span. Adverse health in the later years is associated with being overweight in adolescence. Being overweight in adolescence affects both morbidity and mortality in later life. **Morbidity** refers to the percentage or rate of disease in a group of people. **Mortality** refers to the death rate in a population group. In a recent follow-up to the Harvard Growth Study of the three thousand children who were first measured in 1922, adolescents between the ages of 13 and 18 years who were overweight had increased *morbidity* and *mortality* fifty-five years later when they were old (Must, Jacques, Dallal, Bajema, & Dietz, 1992). The adolescents who were overweight when the first weight and height measurements were taken between 1922 and 1935 were more likely to experience a broad range of adverse health effects when they reached later adulthood. To make the connection between being overweight in adolescence and increased morbidity and mortality in later life, the researchers needed to take into account the more immediate adverse effects of being overweight as adults. The research showed that adult weight was a less powerful predictor of morbidity and mortality than being overweight in adolescence. Thus, being overweight in adolescence is a powerful predictor of adverse health in later life.

## Sex Differences in Life Expectancy

According to 1990 Census Bureau data, females begin to outnumber males at age 25. This gap widens with increasing age. By age 75, about 61 percent of the population is female. By age 85 and over, 70 percent of the population is female.

Sex differences in longevity are due to a combination of social, biological, and genetic factors. Social factors include health behavior and attitudes, habits, lifestyles, and occupational styles. For example, the major causes of death in the United States, such as lung cancer, motor vehicle accidents, suicide, cirrhosis of the liver, emphysema, and coronary heart disease are more likely to strike men than women. Such causes of death are associated with habits or lifestyles. For example, the sex difference in deaths caused by lung cancer and emphysema is linked to the fact that historically men have been heavier smokers than women.

To the extent that life expectancy is influenced strongly by stress at work, we would expect the sex difference in longevity to begin narrowing since so many more women have entered the work force in the last forty years. Actually, it seems that different factors are associated with longevity and physical functioning for older men and women. Income level, educational level, and marital status were strongly associated with changes in physical functioning for men. For women, control of health was strongly associated with changes in physical functioning (Strawbridge, Camacho, Cohen, & Kaplan, 1993). Results of this study suggested that older men would do better in terms of staying healthy if encouraged to participate in structured exercise programs, and older women would do better by keeping active by going out on a regular basis and doing the things they enjoy.

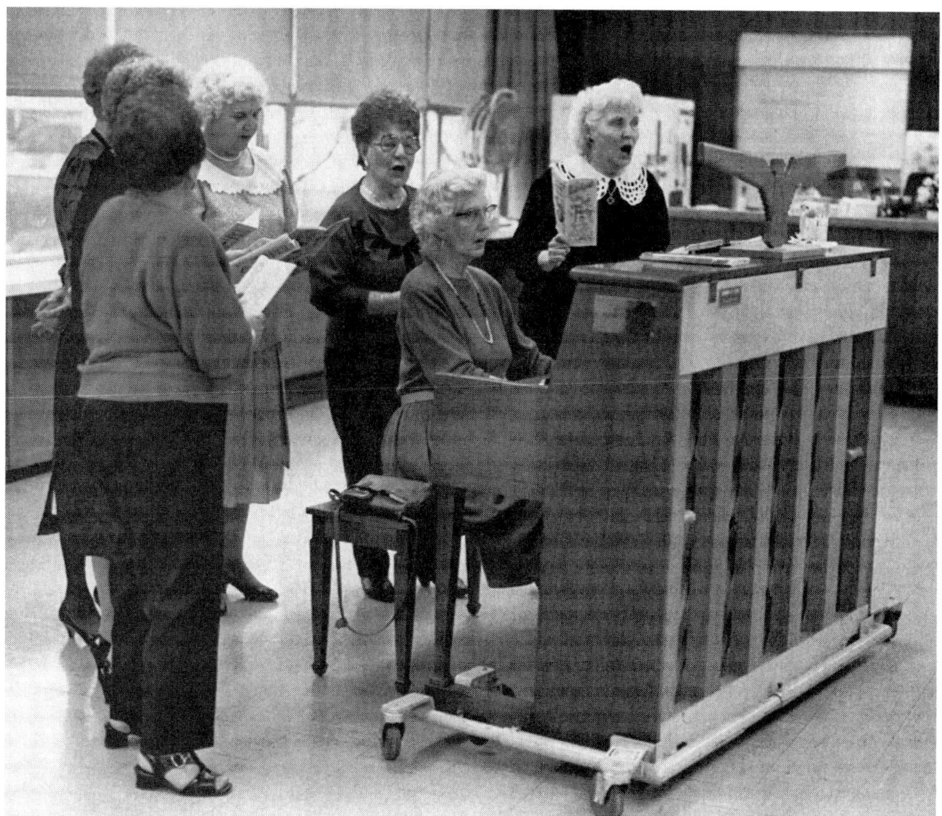

*Sex differences in longevity account for the increasingly higher percentage of females in the older population.*

Sex differences in longevity are also influenced by biological factors. In practically all animal species, females have longer life spans than males (Franceschi & Fabris, 1993). Women have more resistance to infectious and degenerative diseases. For instance, the female's estrogen production helps to reduce the risk of atherosclerosis (hardening of the arteries). Further, the two X chromosomes women carry may be linked with the production of more antibodies to fight disease (Franceschi & Fabris, 1993).

## Longevity and Life Expectancy

How long will you live? The term **longevity** refers to the number of years an individual actually lives. Longevity can be contrasted with average **life expectancy,** which refers to demographic projections regarding the length of life. Although life expectancy has increased dramatically in recent decades, the actual upper limit of the human life span has not changed much since the beginning of recorded history.

The upper limit, or the **potential life span,** refers to the maximum age that could be attained if an individual were able to avoid the consequences of all illnesses and accidents. It has been estimated that the maximum potential human life span is

**Figure 2.3** The rectangularization of the human life span. This graph shows human survivorship trends from ancient times to the present. These idealized curves illustrate the rapid approach to the rectangular survivorship curve that has occurred during the last 180 years. *Source: Strehler, 1975; Hayflick, 1980; and Cote, 1981.*

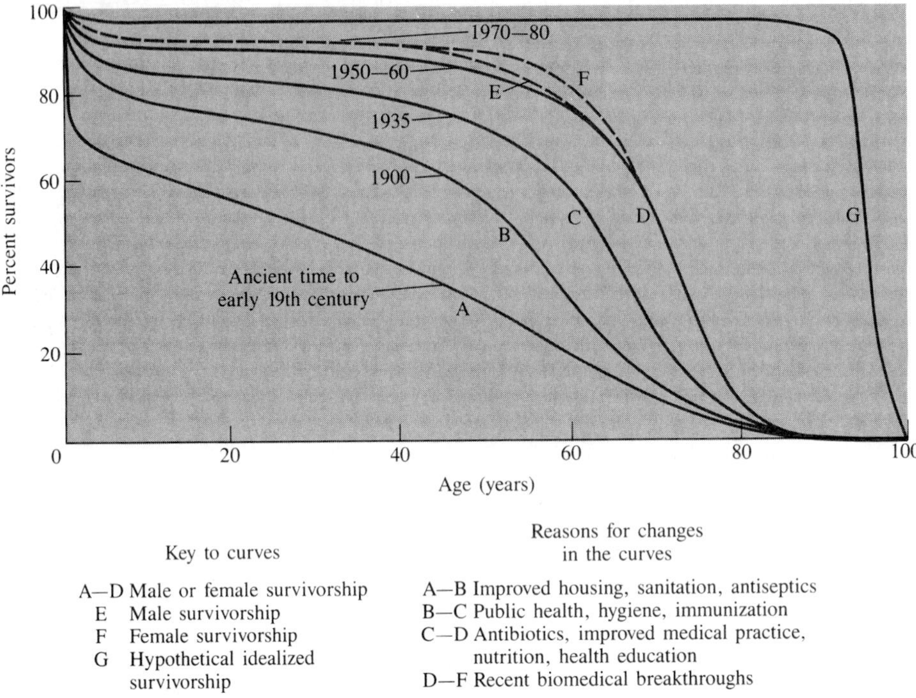


| Key to curves | |
|---|---|
| A—D | Male or female survivorship |
| E | Male survivorship |
| F | Female survivorship |
| G | Hypothetical idealized survivorship |

| Reasons for changes in the curves | |
|---|---|
| A—B | Improved housing, sanitation, antiseptics |
| B—C | Public health, hygiene, immunization |
| C—D | Antibiotics, improved medical practice, nutrition, health education |
| D—F | Recent biomedical breakthroughs |

approximately 110 to 120 years of age (Cristofalo, 1986; Hayflick, 1980). This means that the benefits of improved medicine, nutrition, and public health on our longevity have a biological limit.

Improved health care, coupled with the fact that there is a fixed upper limit on the potential human life span, has produced changes in the survivorship curve, as shown in figure 2.3. From ancient times to the present, the curve has become increasingly more rectangular as more people reached to the fullest extent of their potential life span. Further, it is generally expected that the survivorship curve will become increasingly more rectangular in the future with continued advances in public health, nutrition, and medicine, and as more people live longer, healthier lives.

In light of some new and largely unanticipated concerns, some researchers are beginning to question whether the increasing rectangularization of the life curve will become fact. When medical researchers and demographers put forward the notion of rectangularization of the life curve, they were optimistic that medical science would soon succeed in its quest to conquer diseases that shorten the length of the human life span. Remarkable medical achievements, such as the eradication of smallpox, polio, and other childhood diseases by widespread vaccination, boosted optimism. Further, the potential for the universal availability of effective antibiotics, combined with national trends toward healthier lifestyles, served to support the view that people would be more likely to live to the fullest extent of their life spans.

Heart disease is the leading cause of death in the United States, and cancer is the second cause. Great strides have been made to reduce the risk and improve the treatment of these diseases. These kinds of advances have enabled many adults who have experienced heart disease and cancer to live longer than they would have in the past.

But new diseases are emerging, and "old" diseases are reemerging (Berkelman & Hughes, 1993). Certainly, by now everyone is aware of the devastating effects of human immunodeficiency virus (HIV). HIV, infection, pneumonia, and influenza are now ranked among the ten leading causes of death in the United States. Diseases such as tuberculosis and measles, which not long ago were considered to have been practically eradicated, have reappeared as major diseases in the United States. Further, new strains of tuberculosis and other infectious diseases have developed for which there are no effective treatments. Infectious diseases are the leading cause of death worldwide, and they are the leading cause of serious illness in the United States (Berkelman & Hughes, 1993).

## Predicting Longevity

What factors can be used to predict longevity? One of the most well-known studies designed to identify the predictors of life expectancy is the *Duke Longitudinal Study of Aging*. In this study, 270 volunteers were examined for the first time between 1955 and 1959 by means of a series of physical, mental, social, and laboratory tests (Palmore, 1982). At that time the adults ranged in age from 60 to 94, with a median age of 70. All were noninstitutionalized, and although it was not a random sample, the group was a mixture of males and females, blacks and whites, and different socioeconomic groups. The investigators analyzed these individuals again in 1981, some twenty-five years after their initial testing. Only twenty-six participants were still alive, and estimates of their life expectancy were made.

In the early analysis of the Duke Longitudinal data, the strongest predictors of life expectancy (when age, sex, and race were controlled) were physical function, being a nonsmoker, work satisfaction, and happiness (see, e.g., Palmore, 1982). More recent analyses of the Duke data allowed for a more precise determination of life expectancy because (1) some of the individuals alive in 1981 later died, so that their exact life span is now known, and (2) in addition to the original factors tested, a number of new ones were added to allow for more complex evaluation.

Palmore (1982) developed a mathematical model that predicted the **longevity difference** for the participants in the Duke study. The longevity difference is the difference between the number of years individuals live after initial testing and the expected number of years remaining in their lives based on age, sex, and race. Palmore's model took into consideration both the direct and indirect effects of the variables that influence life expectancy. The variables within this model include *parents' longevity, intelligence, activities, sexual relations, tobacco and alcohol abuse, life satisfaction,* and *health.* Parents' longevity was believed to have a direct effect on longevity through genetic transmission and an indirect

*Physical activity throughout the adult years is one of the predictors of longevity.*

effect through environmental experience. Intelligence was thought to have a direct effect on survival through problem-solving and adaptive ability. Activities were thought to have a direct effect on longevity through increased physical, mental, and social stimulation and an indirect effect by means of their contribution to life satisfaction and improved health. Sexual relations were thought to have a direct effect through psychosomatic processes as well as an indirect effect through their influence on life satisfaction and health. Tobacco and alcohol abuse were predicted to have a direct effect on longevity through their effects on lung cancer, cardiovascular diseases, and other health problems and indirect effects through a reduction of life satisfaction and general health. Life satisfaction was also predicted to have a direct effect through psychosomatic processes and an indirect effect through its influence on general health. And finally, health factors were believed to have a direct effect on longevity.

Of the various predictors of longevity, the following were most important:

1. In terms of parents' longevity, only the father's age at death was significant.
2. Scores on the performance component of the Wechsler Adult Intelligence Scale were better predictors than were scores on the verbal part of this test, but intelligence predictors were significant.

3. Three socioeconomic predictors were significant: education, finances, and occupation.
4. Several activity factors were significant in predicting longevity: the number of activities requiring physical mobility; the number of organizations the individual belonged to; the number of meetings attended; the time spent reading; the number of leisure activities; and the amount of time given to daily activities and hobbies.
5. Three indicators of sexual relations were significant predictors of longevity: frequency of intercourse per week, enjoyment of intercourse in the past, and present enjoyment of intercourse.
6. Tobacco use, as measured by the daily use of cigarettes, cigars, or pipes, was a significant negative predictor.
7. Four satisfaction factors predicted longevity: work satisfaction, religious satisfaction, usefulness, and happiness.
8. Three health predictors were significantly linked with longevity. A physical-function rating was based on the individual's medical history, physical and neurological examinations, audiogram, electroencephalogram, electrocardiogram, and laboratory evaluation of blood and urine. A health self-rating was based on each individual's *own* ratings of his or her health. And a health satisfaction score was determined by an individual's agreement or disagreement with six statements, including, "I feel just miserable most of the time" and "I am perfectly satisfied with my health."

## Social and Economic Impact of an Aging Population

The age structure of a society determines, in part, the allocation of its resources. Over the next several decades, larger sums will be needed to meet the needs of a progressively more aged population. One way to understand how the young members of a society support the old members of a society is to calculate the **old-age dependency ratio.** The old-age dependency ratio is defined as the number of retired people 65 years and older for every one hundred people of working age—that is, between 18 and 64. The **young-age dependency ratio,** on the other hand, is the number of individuals 17 years of age and younger for every one hundred people of working age. Table 2.1 shows how these dependency ratios are expected to change between the years 1960 and 2060. In 1960, the old-age dependency ratio was 16.4 (there were 16.4 retired adults for every 100 workers). The young-age dependency ratio was 65.1 (there were 65.1 youths for every 100 workers). By the year 2040, the old-age dependency ratio will have more than doubled to 38.7; and the young-age dependency ratio will be approximately 38.1.

In all societies, it is difficult to obtain and to fairly distribute the economic resources needed to support the young and old (Chen, 1987; Palmore, 1990). It is only recently that the United States has made strides toward developing a health-care system that provides for all individuals.

**TABLE 2.1**

| Year | Young-age dependency ratio | Old-age dependency ratio |
|---|---|---|
| *Changing Dependency Ratios in the United States between 1960 and 2060* | | |
| 1960 | 65.1 | 16.4 |
| 1970 | 60.7 | 17.1 |
| 1980 | 45.9 | 18.1 |
| 1990 | 41.0 | 20.2 |
| 2000 | 38.6 | 20.9 |
| 2020 | 37.1 | 29.5 |
| 2040 | 38.1 | 38.7 |
| 2060 | 38.3 | 38.9 |

*Adapted from Chen, 1987.*
*Source: Data from Y. P. Chen, "Making Assets Out of Tomorrow's Elderly" in* The Gerontologist, *27:410–416, 1987.*

## SOCIAL CLASS, POVERTY, AND HOUSING

In the United States, the experience of growing older is different for individuals from different social classes, races, and economic levels. One of the reasons is that if people can't afford to pay for routine dental checkups, eye exams, or physical exams, it is less likely that a health problem will be detected at an early stage. Also, economic and educational factors affect health attitudes and exposure to health information. In this section, we examine how the effects of social class, race and ethnicity, and economic level impact on individual development and individual differences.

### Social Class

In every culture, there is stratification by social class. Cultures differ in terms of the strictness or specificity of the prescriptions as well as the nature of the roles. In every culture, occupations vary in pay structure, prestige, and power to influence others. Thus, different individuals possess different economic resources, and individuals have different educational and occupational opportunities. Cultural differences in the methods of distribution of the rewards of society often produce inequities for different ethnicities (racism), for men and women (sexism), and for different-aged individuals (ageism). **Ageism** refers to unequal opportunities for individuals as they grow older (Atchley, 1983).

### Poverty

In 1991, of the nearly 31.8 million citizens in the United States aged 65 and over, more than 3.8 million, or 12.4 percent, of the elderly were classified as poor (AARP, 1992). The definition of poverty is determined by examining the minimum income needed to sustain families of various sizes (Bould, Sanborn, & Reif, 1989). For example, in 1991 the federal poverty level for an elderly person living alone was $6,532; for an elderly couple it was $8,241. The median income of older persons in 1991 was $14,357 for men and $8,189 for women.

These figures compare dramatically to those elderly defined as affluent whose income is at least five times higher than the poverty level (Duncan, & Smith, 1989). Affluent elderly couples have incomes of $41,205, while affluent single elderly individuals earn at least $32,660 (Bould et al., 1989). Women currently represent 2.3 million or 71 percent of the elderly poor in our society (Church, Siegel, & Foster 1988).

The percentage of elderly poor would probably be much greater than statistics indicate if it included the *near poor* and the **hidden poor.** The near poor refers to individuals with incomes between the poverty level and 125 percent of this level. In total, 20 percent of the older population was poor or near poor in 1991. The *hidden poor* refers to those individuals who could be classified as poor on the basis of their own incomes but who are supported by relatives who are not poor. Recent estimates place the number of hidden poor at nearly double the rate determined by official census statistics (Bould et al., 1989). The hidden poor are cared for in the homes of family members or friends and listed in census data as part of that household. About 92 percent of those 85 years of age and older are women who live under such arrangements and are not classified as poor.

One of the socioeconomic concerns of individuals in late adulthood is the decrease in income they usually experience. Many older adults are simply unprepared for the consequences of reduced income associated with retirement from paid work. (Hardy, 1985). Many people expect their Social Security benefits to provide the support necessary to live comfortably in retirement, but Social Security is seldom sufficient. Yet in 1990 the major source of income for those 65 years of age and older was Social Security. Social Security accounted for 36 percent of the income of older Americans, with additional income from assets representing 24 percent, from pensions representing 18 percent, and from earnings another 18 percent, and all other assets representing 3 percent (U.S. Department of Health and Human Services, 1992). For those who are poor and living alone, Social Security represents a far more sizable percentage of income than it does for those with moderate or high incomes.

Very few older adults are prepared to handle the financial impact of long-term health-care (Branch, Friedman, Cohen, Smith, & Socholitzky, 1988). Among those 75 years of age and older and living alone, 46 percent would reach poverty levels within thirteen weeks of institutionalization in a skilled nursing facility. For married couples, poverty level would be reached for 25 percent of the sample in thirteen weeks and for 47 percent of the sample in one year (Branch et al., 1988). Elderly couples, when compared to younger couples, have more out-of-pocket health expenditures (Rubin & Koelln, 1993).

Race is a significant predictor of poverty among the elderly. In 1991, blacks comprised 34 percent of those living at poverty levels and Hispanics comprised 21 percent, while whites represented 11 percent of the total population of elderly living at or below poverty levels (AARP, 1992). The best predictors of poverty in old age continue to be race (black), education (no high school degree), gender (female), marital status (divorced or widowed), and city living environment (Jackson, 1988; Taylor & Chatters, 1988).

Although some older Americans have the benefit of having accumulated substantial assets over a lifetime, for many of these individuals, their assets are not available or liquid (Church et al., 1988). It is difficult for elderly people with fixed incomes to sell their homes or assume sizable home equity loans to meet current expenses for medical care, food, clothes, and taxes.

The young-old, have lower poverty rates than the old-old (Bould et al., 1989). The difference is largely due to the willingness and ability of the young-old to continue to work at either full- or part-time jobs. Among elderly Americans 65 to 71 years of age, there was only a 4 percent risk of poverty if they had been employed in any capacity for any length of time in the previous twelve months (U.S. Bureau of the Census, 1990). For those over 75, poverty rates increase substantially as disability, the physical self-care routine, medical visits, and housekeeping demand increased time and leave minimal chances to work (Bould et al., 1989).

## Housing

Although the bulk of research concerned with the living environments of the elderly has focused on special situations such as nursing homes, public housing, mobile home parks, welfare hotels, or retirement communities, the proportions of older Americans in these special living conditions are small. In 1991, approximately 20.1 million older adults lived in family homes while 9.4 million lived alone (AARP, 1992). Home ownership represents a sign of achievement among all adults, particularly the elderly (National Center for Health Statistics, 1987a).

However, the data concerned with housing quality are less positive. The U.S. Senate Special Committee on Aging estimated that 30 percent of the elderly occupy housing that is deteriorating or substandard.

Suitable living environments directly influence the morale, adjustment, sociability, and intellectual abilities of the elderly (Beland, 1987; Lawton, 1977). The immediate impact of housing is far greater for the elderly because their lifestyle centers so much more on activities in the home. Among the elderly the overwhelming preference is to maintain ownership of their own homes, assuming they are physically, mentally, and economically able to do so. Beland (1987) reported that 57 percent of an elderly sample preferred to live independently either alone or with a spouse. The remaining elderly who preferred to live with someone else and had already moved into the home of a child, relative, or friend usually had done so because of an emergent problem that prevented their independent living (Beland, 1987). Scheidt (1985), in a study of rural elderly, found that housing quality was a powerful predictor of overall mental health.

One attempt to deal with some of the problems faced by older Americans is to provide subsidized housing. The elderly currently comprise more than 27 percent of people who reside in subsidized housing nationwide. Experts continue to debate issues such as whether housing arrangements for the elderly should be age-segregated or integrated (Cohen, Bearison, & Muller, 1987). Age segregation helps provide a defense against social rejection and social comparison. Age integration provides the opportunity for growth, insight, and understanding of different perspectives. Those older people living in single family dwellings show a distinct preference (80%) to have people of all ages in their neighborhood; however, for those living in multiunit apartments, less than 50 percent prefer age-integrated groups in such buildings, and among those living in retirement homes, communities, or attached dwellings, age-integrated neighborhoods are even less popular (AARP, 1993b). Subsidized housing will continue to be a crucial issue for those examining public policies for the elderly. As we have seen previously, race and ethnicity are factors highly predictive of which elderly adults will experience less than adequate housing.

The homeless elderly provide a grim reminder that statistics summarize human lives. Though most elderly are able to meet their housing needs in some fashion, there is a segment of our population that is not so fortunate. It is estimated that at least 27 percent of the homeless are over 60 years of age. Cohen, Teresi, Holmes, and Roth (1988) suggest that this figure is an underestimate, since many elderly homeless do not compete for shelter space, fearing beatings, abuse, and the loss of independence in such institutionalized programs. In a recent analysis of elderly homeless men in New York City, the use of an informal peer information and social support network helped some homeless elderly men to cope. Those who were unable to develop a support network displayed poor physical health, emotional depression, and high levels of stress (Cohen et al., 1988).

For those who are unable to live independently, those who have higher income have many more options with regard to living conditions. For example, some elderly can afford to insure themselves against long-term costs and escalating inflation, taxes, and home maintenance by enrolling in *Continuity Care Retirement Communities* (Branch, 1987; Cohen, Tell, Batten & Larson, 1988; Tell, Cohen, Larson, & Batten, 1987). They pay a substantial initiation or entrance fee as well as a monthly fee. The fees remain constant regardless of the medical and nursing care a resident may require in the future. Unfortunately, only a small percentage of the population can afford to consider such options.

Nursing homes may be the only alternative for older adults with serious, chronic health problems. About 5 percent (or 1.4 million adults) over 65 were residents of nursing homes in 1987 (AARP, 1992). Percentages in nursing homes increase dramatically as age increases. For example, about 1 percent of those between the ages of 65 and 74 live in nursing homes, whereas 25 percent of those who are age 85 and over reside in nursing homes.

## *Ageism*

Stereotypes of the elderly as nonproductive are inaccurate. Ageism, like sexism and racism, describes the prejudiced behavior of a society. Ageism refers to prejudice against or negative stereotyping of older adults (Palmore, 1990). Many older adults in the United States face painful discrimination. Older adults may not be hired for new jobs or may be eased out of old ones because they are perceived as incapable. Elders are sometimes avoided because they are presumed to be verbose or boring. Infirm elders are sometimes perceived as "babies with wrinkles," without sensitivity,

*TABLE 2.2*

| Common Misperceptions About the Elderly That are Based on Stereotypes |
|---|
| ***Examples of Misperceptions Based on Negative Stereotypes*** |
| 1. Most older persons are poor. |
| 2. Most older persons are unable to keep up with inflation. |
| 3. Most older people are ill-housed. |
| 4. Most older people are frail and in poor health. |
| 5. The aged are impotent as a political force and require advocacy. |
| 6. Most older people are inadequate employees; they are less productive, efficient, motivated, innovative, and creative than younger workers. Most older workers are accident-prone. |
| 7. Older people are mentally slower and more forgetful; they are less able to learn new things. |
| 8. Older persons tend to be intellectually rigid and dogmatic. Most old people are set in their ways and unable to change. |
| 9. A majority of older people are socially isolated and lonely. Most are disengaging or disengaged from society. |
| 10. Most older persons are confined to long-term care institutions. |
| ***Examples of Misperceptions Based on Positive Stereotypes*** |
| 1. The aged are relatively well off; they are not poor, but in good economic shape. Their benefits are generously provided by working members of society. |
| 2. The aged are a potential political force that votes and participates in unity and in great numbers. |
| 3. Older people make friends very easily. They are kind and smiling. |
| 4. Most older persons are mature, experienced, wise, and interesting. |
| 5. Most older persons are very good listeners and are especially patient with children. |
| 6. A majority of older persons are very kind and generous to their children and grandchildren. |

*From S. Lubomudrov, "Congressional Perceptions of the Elderly: The Use of Stereotypes in the Legislative Process" in* Journal of Gerontology, *27:77–81, 1987.* 

and without regard for who they are and who they once were. The elderly are sometimes pushed out of their families by children who see them in negative ways rather than in terms of their potential to family dynamics.

One of the most serious problems facing the elderly in the United States is stereotyping. Misperceptions of aging and the elderly may be positive (idealizing old age) or negative (viewing the elderly as useless and inadequate). Table 2.2 lists some of the stereotypes.

According to Covey (1988), since the last part of the nineteenth century older people have been labeled with increasingly negative and debilitative terms. Covey found terms that clearly separated old men from old women: Labels for older men included old-fashioned, feeble, and conservative, and labels for older women included bad-tempered, repulsive, and mystical. Animal terms such as "old buzzard" or "old goat" were associated with old men, while "old bird" and "old crow" were reserved for women.

## *AGING IN OTHER CULTURES*

The cultural milieu—that is, the physical and social setting in which adults develop—has many dimensions. There is tremendous variety across cultures in terms of how aging occurs. We examine cross-cultural differences in adult development and aging.

The term *culture* refers to the behaviors, attitudes, values, and products of a particular group of people. For example, the culture of the United States, China, and the Caribbean represent different belief systems, languages, and dialects, and rituals of daily life. Always, within each culture, there are many subcultures, each with its own distinct set of behaviors and values.

As a child, you began to learn the values of your community. You may have learned that some values seemed relatively constant across individuals and families, and other values were quite varied, or that your family was the same as some other families, all other families, or no other families.

In the United States, there is considerable variation in how families view parents, grandparents, and other older relatives, in part related to ethnic diversity (Bastida, 1987).

In China and Japan, older persons are venerated and encouraged to be active in family contexts and in other social roles (Kinoshita & Kiefer, 1993). Intergenerational relations are reciprocal rather than linear. **Filial piety** runs high in China; respect and homage to family and community elders is a way of life. For example, one custom permits parents to send weekly or monthly stipends to a married child. This money is not to be spent, even though it is a gift. Rather, the stipend is to be saved and safely invested so that it can be returned to the parents when they reach old age. In Japan, the elderly are more integrated into their families than the elderly in most industrialized countries. More than 75 percent live with their children, and very few single older adults live alone. Respect for the elderly in Japan is evidenced in a variety of everyday encounters: The best seats on public transportation are usually reserved for the elderly, cooking caters to the tastes of the elderly, and people bow respectfully to the elderly. However, such respect appears to be more prevalent among rural than urban Japanese and among middle-aged than young adult Japanese (Palmore & Maeda, 1985).

It is clear that, with modernization, the status and integration of elders in Japan has declined in recent years (Palmore and Maeda, 1985). Tobin (1987) suggested that Western observers have idealized Japan's approach to old age. The idealization conforms to our own society's ambivalence toward the dependency experienced in old age versus that experienced at other points in the life course. Tobin noted that our idealized view of Japanese old age is exaggerated, stereotyped, limiting, and one-dimensional. Tobin suggests that there are negative aspects to Japanese aging often overlooked by experts. The observance of Respect for Elders Day and the designation of subway seats as "silver seats" for the elderly and handicapped may mean that such policies are needed to ensure respect and honor toward the elderly. Similarly, although it appears that in Japan more older people live with their children than is true in the United States, the elderly may yet experience loneliness and emotional distance. Living together does not ensure reverence, respect, and belongingness. Finally, Tobin (1987) suggested that the overall percentage of parents living with children in Japan has declined steadily over the past fifty years as modernization, housing space, and population changes have occurred. Japan is actually far behind the United States in providing housing options for elders (Kinoshita & Kiefer, 1993). The language used to refer to Japanese old age has also evolved dramatically. Current usage gives a negative connotation to the traditional term *rojin* or *ecstasy years.* It has been replaced with the more preferable *jitsunen,* translated as *the age of harvest* or *the age of fruition* (Loveridge-Sanbonmatsu, 1994).

In earlier times, when fewer individuals reached old age, the elders were granted high status in many cultures. Members of the culture may have believed that elders were imbued with special powers and wisdom. Jay Sokolovsky (1986), drawing upon the work of Cowgill and Holmes (1972), identified seven different factors that seem to be universally associated with high status for the elderly. Specifically, high status should be accorded the elderly in cultures where:

Older people possess valuable knowledge.
Older persons control key family and community resources.
Older persons are allowed to perform useful and valued functions as long as possible.
There are fewer role shifts and a greater sense of role continuity throughout the life span.
Age-related role changes involve gains in responsibility, authority, or advisory capacity.
The extended family is an important residential and/or economic unit and the elderly are integrated into it.
Less emphasis is placed on individual ego development.

Some cultures do not remove elders from their homes, friends, and family to place them in a hospital or nursing home. In Hindu tradition, for example, there are four life stages (ashrams). Each stage, though distinct, produces a totality, a balance and harmony between person, nature, life forces, and one's duty (dharma). These stages apply to all but the menial caste and are centered on males. The first stage consists of the *celibate student* in adolescence and early adulthood. This is a time when a teacher provides both a home and a mentor relationship in transmitting religious knowledge. The second stage of life consists of marriage and the special obligations of a *householder,* which include bringing children into the world and involvement in family life. In traditional Hindu marriages, sons bring their wives into the paternal home, creating an extended family from which religious and cultural practices can be preserved by direct transmission to the next generation.

After the stage of householder and the establishment of family, a man is to voluntarily begin to remove himself from his family. The third life stage is that of a *hermit in the forest.* This is a time for meditating, studying, and totally absorbing Hindu religious thought and ideas. It involves living a life devoted to asceticism, self-control, and the acquisition of inner spiritual power. A man is ready for this third stage when he sees "his skin wrinkled, his hair white, and the son of his sons." The final stage is complete separation from all worldly concerns; the elderly man abandons all ties to family, possessions, and home. He wanders unencumbered, free to seek harmony between himself and the universe, free to find the common cord between his existence and the existence of others, both animate and inanimate. The goal of the fourth stage is to eliminate the need for spirituality, sensuality, psychological bonds, or social dimensions. The individual has no selfish needs, no real-world

*TABLE 2.3*

| Masculine Items | Feminine Items |
|---|---|
| *Examples of Masculine and Feminine Items From Bem's Sex-Role Inventory* | |
| Acts as a leader | Affectionate |
| Analytical | Compassionate |
| Competitive | Feminine |
| Forceful | Gullible |
| Individualistic | Sensitive to the needs of others |
| Self-reliant | Sympathetic |
| Willing to take a stand | Warm |

*Reproduced by special permission of the publisher, Consulting Psychologists Press, Inc., from the Bem Sex Role Inventory by Sandra Bem, Ph.D., copyright 1978.*

concerns; he waits to die. Death is blissful liberation. It is the deserved attainment of one who has led a perfect life: having committed time to religious study, having married and produced children, and having offered support and help to those in need. Given these accomplishments, his life should be in total harmony.

In India, even among the highest caste (Brahmins), few people practice or attain the goals of each of the four stages. Yet, these stages provide a culturally prescribed path to follow for successful aging. They provide a direction to life, a target for maturity. Other cultures prescribe different paths. In modern technological societies, for example, productive personal achievements in the workplace are emphasized (Valliant, 1977).

## *Age-Related Changes in Sex Roles*

The term **sex role** refers to the characteristics that individuals display because of their gender. Spence and Helmreich (1978) defined sex roles as the behaviors *expected* of individuals because they are either male or female. An important aspect of being male or female is gender identity, which refers to the extent to which individuals actually take on as part of their personalities the behaviors and attitudes associated with either the male or female role. The development of sex-appropriate sex roles results in "masculine" males and "feminine" females. Although in past years researchers assessed the sex roles of masculinity and femininity as distinct categories, current researchers usually take a continuous view that is based on Bem's (1974) concept of androgyny.

### Androgyny

By the mid-1970s, work by Sandra Bem (e.g., Bem, 1974) and others was helping to make clear that it was inaccurate to consider masculinity and femininity as polar opposites on a continuum. Bem (1974) reported that 30 to 40 percent of men and women have an **androgynous** sex-role identity. That is, when given a list of masculine and feminine attributes (see Table 2.3), and asked to indicate how well each describes themselves, androgynous individuals score high on both sets of attributes. Bem (1974, 1977, 1981) suggested that masculinity and femininity involve separate attributes, and that people with an androgynous identity are advantaged in psychological adjustment. The androgynous person endorses having both male traits (e.g., achievement orientation) and female traits (e.g., warmth). Having a broad range of personal attributes enables individuals to adapt competently to a wide variety of tasks and interpersonal situations.

The notion of androgyny has some limitations as it applies to the understanding of sex-role identity throughout the adult life span. Traditional sex-typed traits and behaviors are usually more characteristic of young adulthood than of middle or later adulthood, and there are several ways of interpreting *how* and *why* individuals become more androgynous as they become older (Huyck, 1990).

Several researchers have studied longitudinal changes in personality and sex-role (e.g., Chiriboga, 1982a, 1982b; Eichorn, Clausen, Haan, Honzik, & Mussen, 1981; Lowenthal, Thurnher, & Chiriboga, 1975; Neugarten, 1973; York & John, 1992). In the Kansas City Longitudinal Study, Neugarten (1973) reported that sex-role differences between the sexes appear with age. Older men were more receptive to their own affiliative and nurturant behavior than younger men; whereas older women were more receptive than younger women to their own aggressive and egocentric behavior. Coming to terms with the emerging dimensions of one's personality (e.g., nurturance or aggressiveness) may be one of the most important challenges of midlife development. With self-acceptance and integration of masculine and feminine dimensions of personality, individuals may become more adaptable in facing the challenges of growing older (Huyck, 1990).

## David Gutmann's View of Sex-Role Changes During Adulthood

Gutmann (1977, 1987, 1992) suggested that a critical difference in men's and women's **ego mastery styles** is dominant in the early adult years, but that this difference shifts as adults reach middle age. *Ego mastery* refers to the style adopted in coping with self and others. It is more, however, than just how we respond or behave; ego mastery style is the underlying organization of values and beliefs that govern external behavior. Two ego mastery styles have been associated with age-related personality changes for men and women: active mastery and passive accommodative mastery. **Active mastery** is typified by striving for autonomy, control, and personal competence. One shapes the external environment to fulfill one's own needs and desires. To accomplish active mastery, individuals may employ strategies centered on achievement. **Passive accommodative mastery,** in contrast, is an ego mastery style in which individuals gain control over their environments by accommodating others perceived to be in power. By accommodating the needs and desires of others, the individual gains a sense of ego mastery and control. Passive accommodation implies social sensitivity.

These two styles of ego mastery, while present in both men and women, appear to wax and wane at particular periods in the life course. According to Gutmann, active mastery generally overshadows passive accommodative mastery in younger men. By middle age, however, the two styles have shifted; passive

*Gutmann has suggested that men and women change the ways that they express mastery after the parenting years. New research suggests that individuals seek to master new "possible selves" throughout their lives.*

accommodative mastery becomes the more predominant male orientation. Interestingly, Gutmann suggests that the situation is frequently reversed for women. Passive accommodative ego mastery style generally predominates women in young adulthood, whereas active mastery predominates by middle age. Gutmann's conclusions are based on observations of adults in a variety of cultures (Mayan Indian, Navajo Indian, and Middle-Eastern Druze).

Gutmann offers a socio-evolutionary model for age changes in mastery style among men and women. His theory emphasizes the concept of the **parental imperative.** To ensure the biological and social survival of our species, it is essential that parents develop effective divisions of labor so as to manage the demands and responsibilities of childrearing. One division of labor, which has evolved over thousands of years, has given rise to the two ego mastery styles. A passive accommodative style is uniquely suited to the nurturing tasks of parenting, while the active mastery style is suited to providing the necessary economic and material support necessary for family survival. After parenting is over, middle-aged adults begin a process of sex-role reversal. The shift or transition identified by Gutmann is gradual, not abrupt. Individuals slowly recognize dimensions of their egos that have been unfulfilled and unrecognized. By middle age, men frequently become more aware of their inner selves, their dependency, social needs, nurturant dispositions, and underlying emotional lives. Corresponding changes in women are also evident by middle age.

Critics of Gutmann's theory have questioned whether the observed changes in ego mastery style in middle age are reflective of sex-role reversal or are simply a description of emergent socialization. Cool and McCabe (1983) analyzed research on a number of Mediterranean cultures and observed that women display a shift in mastery styles consistent with Gutmann's theory. However, they attributed this shift to socialization, the increased opportunity for women to control their own lives and the lives of others around them.

## Carl Jung's View of Sex-Role Development in Adult Life

Carl Jung broke with traditional Freudian psychoanalytic theory to create a theory of personality development, that focused on adulthood. (Jung, 1933). In Jung's view, a healthy adult personality involves an equilibrium among various components, including the polarities of masculinity and femininity. The period of early adulthood is marked by a decided imbalance between the two, so that one of these components dominates to the exclusion of the other. Masculinity or femininity predominates at this time because of society's coercive sex-role stereotyping or modeling. Usually, the dominant orientation to masculinity or femininity matches one's biological sex. By middle age, however, masculinity and femininity become more balanced as males become more expressive of their feminine characteristics (e.g., nurturance), and females become more expressive of their masculine attributes (e.g., aggression). By old age, Jung suggested, a healthy equilibrium often exists in the personality components of masculinity and femininity. Older males and females see this balance in themselves and recognize their personalities as consisting of *both* masculine and feminine features.

## Jeanne Brooks's View of Sex-Role Behavior and Social Maturity

Jeanne Brooks (1981), in examining data from the Berkeley Growth study (see Research Focus 1.1), identified a pattern of sex-role behavior in adulthood analogous to those suggested by Gutmann and Jung. Brooks suggested that, beginning in middle age, the distinction between male and female personality characteristics becomes progressively blurred. In fact, social maturity emerges from middle age onward. *Social maturity* consists of three essential components. First is the recognition of how to live easily and comfortably with all people, both men and women. Second is the capacity to develop one's own standards and values, regardless of social stereotypes. Third is the ability to respond humanely, appropriately, and sensitively to those who, like ourselves, experience stressful life circumstances and need help coping. It is Brooks's contention that from middle age onward men and women appear far more alike than different in their articulated sense of social maturity.

## Conclusions about Sex-Role Changes in Later Life

Some data suggest that by middle age, males and females become increasingly aware of new or hidden aspects of their personalities and identities. Neugarten (1977), for example, highlights this change as an increase in the incorporation of opposite-sex characteristics. Bengtson, Reedy, & Gordon, 1985, Gutmann (1987, 1992) and others find a greater expression and acceptance of nurturance for both older men and women.

It seems that both men and women become more aware of personality components they have not fully recognized, fostered, or expressed as they grow older. According to Bengtson, Reedy, and Gordon (1985), age-related social forces may have a profound impact on personality and sex roles.

## *Social Theories of Aging*

For some years, two perspectives dominated the thinking of social scientists on the social basis of aging: **disengagement theory** and **activity theory.** Each of these theories sought to explain how people derive well-being and life satisfaction as they age. **Life satisfaction** is a complex construct with various operational definitions. Some investigators assume life satisfaction reflects the assessment of "life in general" or "life as a whole," whereas other researchers argue that there are separable domains or areas of life satisfaction.

### Disengagement Theory

Developed by Cumming and Henry (1961), disengagement theory argues that as people age, they slowly give up specific roles, interests, and activities and gradually withdraw from society. Disengagement is viewed as a mutual activity; the individual disengages from society at the same rate that society disengages from the individual. According to the theory, an older individual develops increasing self-preoccupation, reduces emotional ties with others, and shows a decreasing interest in the affairs of the world. Such a reduction of social interaction and increased self-preoccupation was considered adaptive to maintain life satisfaction in late adulthood.

Disengagement theory has been criticized on several grounds. First, the hypothesis that low morale is characteristic of elders who maintain high activity is not supported by research. Second, no empirical evidence supports the prediction that social withdrawal will be inevitable and welcomed by adults as they grow older. Third, there is no support for the idea of mutual withdrawal from activities and roles. The disengagement process is rarely mutual; usually, others withdraw from the older person. From loss of significant work roles, to loss of friends and spouse, to loss of good health, the loss of active roles and activities is seldom welcomed (George, 1990a).

### Activity Theory

Bernice Neugarten and her colleagues (Neugarten, Havighurst, & Tobin, 1968) found that *activity and involvement* rather than disengagement were often associated with life satisfaction. Neugarten et al. (1968) categorized individuals in late adulthood as having four different personality styles: *integrated* (engaged, involved people); *armored-defended* (holding on, particularly to middle-adulthood roles); *passive-dependent* (medium to low activity level, sometimes passive and apathetic); and *unintegrated* (disorganized, deteriorated cognitive processes, weak emotional control). The life satisfaction of the more active personality types, the integrated and armored-defended individuals, was greater than the less involved passive-dependent and unintegrated types.

*Many older adults still enjoy and benefit from exercise, especially if they were physically active earlier in life. Dr. Patricia Peterson, shown here, holds a number of world running records in her age group.*

According to activity theory, then, the more active and involved older people are, the more likely they will feel life satisfaction. Activity theory suggests that it is often healthy for individuals to continue their middle-adulthood roles through late adulthood and that if these roles are taken away (e.g., through retirement), it is important to find substitute roles that keep people active and involved in the world. Yet continued activity and involvement alone will not bring about positive adjustment to aging and high life satisfaction in all individuals.

## Life Satisfaction

A consistent pattern seems to appear in the lives of older people who report they are making good adjustments to aging and deriving high life satisfaction. Those with particular personality styles, for example, may find that disengagement produces the kind of aging that brings them the greatest satisfaction. For instance, disengagement may be desirable for a person who has felt unfulfilled in an occupation and for whom retirement is eagerly anticipated as a chance to be distanced from a career ("I don't have to get up any longer to go to work"). On the other hand, activity may be singularly important for an armored-defended person who clings to an identity in which one's career remains as central in old age as in young adulthood.

Are there other variables that predict positive adjustment to aging and high life satisfaction? Perhaps the most important one is the person's sense of control and mastery from which life satisfaction derives. The importance of a sense of control over one's life emerges in the work of Neugarten (1977), Bandura (1989), Hooker & Kaus (1994), and Lachman (1986).

Obviously a host of other variables are also predictive of positive life satisfaction and healthy adjustment to aging. Studies of subjective well-being identified the best predictors of life satisfaction to be income, health, degree of social interaction, marital status, independent living arrangements, and availability of transportation (Schultz, 1985). Furthermore, Paul Costa and Robert McCrae (1985) suggest that basic personality traits and life satisfaction remain stable from a person's early thirties to their seventies and eighties. In keeping with Costa and McCrae's theme of continuity and stability, George (1980) noted that subjectively experienced well-being does not show any appreciable age-related changes across the adult portion of the life span. Those with positive outlooks in middle age remain generally positive, whereas those with negative views remain so throughout the second half of life.

## Conclusions about the Social Dimensions of Aging

Because of the tremendous variation in cultural and ethnic backgrounds among the aged in the United States, social integration must be considered within the context of cultural value systems. One lifestyle and set of activities may suit people from one ethnic background better than another. For example, social interaction with family members tends to be more frequent and important for older people of French-American background than for their Scandinavian counterparts. The Scandinavian elderly have adapted to an individualized lifestyle and may seek social integration through organizational participation.

There are many ways for adults to experience high morale and positive life satisfaction, and many pathways toward successful aging in American society. Some age successfully by being active, and some by striking a unique balance among a variety of roles and responsibilities.

### Summary

America is "graying." In 1900 about 3.1 million Americans were aged 65 and over. In 1991, the number rose to 31.8 million. By 2030, there will be 66 million older adults in the United States. Older adults, especially the old-old, represent the fastest growing segment of our population.

Although our life expectancy has increased substantially in recent years, the potential human life span has remained remarkably stable, with an upper limit of approximately 110 to 120 years. Until recently, the increase in life expectancy was mostly due to a reduction in deaths during infancy and early childhood. But in the last few decades, improved nutrition and health care have increased the chances that those reaching older adulthood will live longer. In the future, older adults are expected to have healthier, more productive, and longer lives. For reasons that are still unknown, women will probably continue to live longer than men. Furthermore, substantial differences in life expectancy are associated with social class, race, and ethnicity.

The aging of the United States will have profound economic and social ramifications. As our population ages and the old-age and young-age dependency ratios equalize, we will have to develop a system that equitably distributes the resources of our society to both young and old.

Aging takes place within a cultural context. One important aspect of a culture is social class. One of the major concerns of individuals in late adulthood is the decrease in income they are likely to experience. The elderly have a higher poverty rate than any other age group.

Aging in America carries with it a number of negative stereotypes. Ageist stereotypes are evident in young children who often view the elderly as inactive, lonely, and bored.

Some cultures, such as China's and Japan's, appear to hold positive attitudes toward the elderly. However, recent social, economic, and demographic changes in these cultures have led to more negative attitudes toward the elderly. Examining various cultural definitions of aging and the treatment of the elderly in diverse cultures gives us important insights into our own values and attitudes toward aging. There are many views of aging across many different cultures. By increasing our knowledge and awareness of other cultures, we can become less ethnocentric and more tolerant and accepting of diversity within American culture and across cultures.

Aging, within our own culture as well as several other cultures, may be very different for men and women. The nature of sex roles and how they change over the life span is highly complex. Many researchers have focused on the concept of androgyny—the belief that every individual's personality has both masculine and feminine dimensions and that adults who portray positive aspects of both roles may be more flexible and better adjusted. The degree to which an adult with a masculine, feminine, or androgynous sex-role orientation shows better adjustment may depend, in part, on cultural-historical context. Gutmann's work indicates an increase in sex-typed feminine traits in the personality profiles of older men and a corresponding tendency for older women to display an increase in sex-typed masculine traits.

Two major theories have been developed to explain the social basis of aging: disengagement theory and activity theory. Each theory attempts to explain how some people derive life satisfaction from and make a positive adjustment to aging. An individual's ability to derive life satisfaction may depend not only on relating personality to disengagement and/or activity, but also on demographic, social, and psychologically relevant factors.

## Review Questions

1. What is the difference between life expectancy, potential life span, and longevity?
2. Who are the old-old? Why are they an important group to study?
3. Outline the changing age structure of our population. What effects will the changing old-age and young-age dependency ratios have on our society?
4. What factors seem to contribute most to longevity?
5. Discuss how sex, race, ethnicity, and social class affect life expectancy. What factors account for these differences?
6. Describe the economic hardships that many of today's elderly must endure.
7. What is ageism? Trace the historical background of ageist attitudes toward the elderly in the United States.
8. How do attitudes about the aged in countries like China, Japan, and India compare to the attitudes held by Americans?
9. How do sex roles affect adults? What is androgyny?
10. Explain the meaning of the following terms: active mastery, passive accommodative mastery, and the parental imperative.
11. Describe three different explanations for the sex-role reversal that seems to occur during adulthood.
12. Describe three different theories concerning the social basis of aging.
13. From a social perspective, is there an optimal way to age? What evidence supports your position?

## For Further Reading


Elder, G. H., Shanahan, M. J., & Clipp, E. C. (1994). When war comes to men's lives: Life-course patterns in family, work, and health. *Psychology and Aging, 9,* 5–16.

Greer, G. (1992). *The change: Women, aging, and menopause.* New York: Knopf.

Huyck, M. H. (1990). Gender differences in aging. In J. E. Birren & K. W. Schaie (Eds.), *Handbook of the psychology of aging* (3d edition, pp. 124–132). San Diego: Academic Press.

Riley, M. W. (1985). Age strata and social systems. In R. H. Binstock & E. Shanas (Eds.), *Handbook of aging and the social sciences* (Vol. 3, pp. 369–411). New York: Van Nostrand Reinhold.

Riley, M. W., & Riley, J. W. (1994). Age integration and the lives of older people. *The Gerontologist, 34,* 110–115.

3

# *Individual Differences*

## *Biological, Physical, and Sensory Processes*

*You have made your way from worm to man, and much in you is still worm.*
—Friedrich Nietzsche, *Thus Spoke Zarathustra*

## *Introduction*

In this chapter, we describe the physical, neural, and sensory changes that occur during the adult years. In reading this material, it is important to distinguish the processes of *normal* aging from the consequences of particular diseases and poor health in later life. Normal aging, or **senescence,** refers to the time-related biological processes that affect all persons, whereas diseases, such as heart disease and Alzheimer's disease, affect some individuals and not others. Some diseases are more common in later life than in earlier periods of development, but their effects are distinct from normal aging. In this chapter, we try to distinguish the characteristics of normal aging from diseases such as Alzheimer's disease and other dementias that affect subgroups of older adults. Although some aspects of effective biological functioning are impaired in later life, the declines associated with normal aging are relatively mild and occur more gradually compared with the nature and extent of impairment associated with disease and poor health in late life.

It is also important to distinguish between *normal* aging and *successful* aging. For many individuals, the period of later adulthood is a time of continued good health (Rowe & Kahn, 1987). As mentioned in chapter 1, there are both gains and losses in physical functioning throughout life (Baltes, 1987). Age-related losses occur in sensory function and in the basic biological processes. Some caution is needed in interpreting the substantial amount of research on the physical aspects of aging. Since most of the available research is based on cross-sectional comparisons between young adults and elderly adults, it is impossible to distinguish between the effects of age and the effects of a wide range of cohort factors that affect health and vitality in the later years.

## *Biological Theories of Aging*

Birren (1988) defined aging as "the orderly or regular changes that occur with time in mature, genetically representative organisms living under representative environmental conditions" (p. 160). If everyone lived exactly to age 85 regardless of environmental conditions and lifestyle factors, we would conclude that aging is entirely genetically controlled. The fact is that some aspects of aging seem to closely follow a genetically prescribed timetable, whereas other aspects of aging are largely determined or influenced by a complex interplay between environmental "wear and tear" and time-sensitive biological factors.

Biologists and biopsychologists who study aging have advanced a number of general theories about aging. One type of theory is referred to as *wear and tear.* In a very real way, the human body "wears out" or "wears down" as it ages. The goal of researchers who take this approach is to determine how and why the body wears out. Early theorists viewed the body as a kind of machine that becomes less efficient and requires more repairs because of use and stress. One of the difficulties for wear-and-tear theories is that some kinds of exertion or activity, such as challenging work and vigorous exercise, are predictive of continued vitality and are essential to long life, whereas other kinds of stressful activities may be detrimental to longevity (Cristofalo, 1986).

Biological aging researchers also give emphasis to the role of cellular, metabolic, or genetic mechanisms in accounting for aging. **Cellular theories** propose that aging is caused by various processes or malfunctions that take place within the cells of the body. For example, Hayflick (1980) demonstrated that cells can divide only a limited number of times. Hayflick found that connective tissue cells extracted from human embryonic tissue doubled only about fifty times.

**Genetic theories** suggest that aging is caused by damage to the genetic information that regulates cellular functioning. Genetic information is represented in the structure of a complex molecule called *deoxyribonucleic acid* (DNA). DNA controls the formation of life-sustaining proteins. The information contained in DNA must be transmitted to other locations within a cell where the formation of proteins actually occurs. The molecule that does this work is *ribonucleic acid* (RNA). RNA is sometimes called messenger-RNA because of its transportation function. There is good evidence to suggest that the effects of aging are related to some type of breakdown, or error, that develops in the DNA-RNA communication system.

Such errors could occur in several ways (Williamson, Munley, & Evans, 1980). According to the **mutation theory,** aging is caused by changes, or mutations, in the DNA of the cells in vital organs of the body. In cells that continue to divide throughout the life cycle, these mutations are likely to be passed on to new cells. Eventually, the number of mutated cells in a vital organ would increase to the point that the cell's functioning is significantly reduced. Possible sources for these mutations may be intrinsic factors in cell division, such as chance errors in DNA replication or genes that specifically cause mutations in other genes. These mutations may be beneficial in evolutionary terms but might also hasten the aging process. Other possible sources of mutations are extrinsic factors such as toxins in the air, in water, and in food.

According to the **genetic switching theory,** certain genes cease to operate or switch off, and this causes aging. Information needed to produce DNA is no longer available, and so the cells atrophy (Selkoe, 1992). Eventually, genetic switching leads to cell death and the loss of organ functioning. According to this theory, there is a kind of genetic blueprint in each of the body's cells.

According to the **error catastrophe theory,** aging is caused by damage to RNA, enzymes, and certain other proteins rather than by errors in DNA. For example, if an error occurs in the RNA responsible for the production of an enzyme essential to cell metabolism, the result will be a marked reduction in cell functioning and possibly cell death. The escalating impact of the original error in the RNA is the "error catastrophe" (Orgel, 1973).

Another theory-driven line of research, the **free radical theory,** emphasizes the role of free radicals as an explanation of biological aging (Selkoe, 1992). *Free radicals* are chemical components of cell metabolism that exist for only one second or less before they react with other substances such as fats. Free radicals can damage cells through their reactions with other substances, and they can cause chromosome damage. It has been suggested that vitamins C and E reduce the collisions of free radicals with other cell substances, but further evidence is needed to substantiate the effects of vitamins, such as antioxidants, on health and longevity.

**Physiological theories** of aging focus on the nature of breakdowns in the functioning of a particular organ system, or on the impairment of particular physiological control mechanisms. Two of the most important physiological control systems are the immune system and the endocrine system.

The *immune system* protects our body from foreign substances such as viruses, bacteria, and mutant cells (e.g., cancer). The immune system may generate antibodies that react with the proteins of foreign organisms, and it may form cells that literally eat up the invading cells. The efficiency of the immune system gradually declines with aging. Also, as an individual ages, errors in the operation of the immune system may cause it to attack and destroy normal, healthy body cells, possibly because immune mechanisms mistakenly identify normal cells as pathological. Support for an **autoimmune theory** of aging comes from the findings that diseases of the immune system such as rheumatoid arthritis and maturity-onset diabetes are age-related. Furthermore, recent evidence has shown that the human immunodeficiency virus associated with the disease of AIDS progresses more quickly in older adults (Kendig & Adler, 1990).

Important new research in the area of *psychoneuroimmunology* has demonstrated that stressful environmental situations serve to impair the operation of the immune system in adults. For example, suppression of the immune system as a result of chronic stress has been found in persons with disrupted social networks, including the bereaved (Schleifer, Keller, Camerino, Thornton, & Stein, 1983), people in troubled marriages (Kiecolt-Glaser, Fisher, Ogrocki, Stout, Speicher, & Glaser 1987), and caretakers of Alzheimer's disease victims (Kiecolt-Glaser, Glaser, Shuttleworth, Dyer, Ogrocki, & Speicher, 1987). Further, increased immune function as a result of supportive situations has been found among persons reporting strong social networks (e.g., Baron, Cutrona, Hicklin, Russel, & Lubaroff, 1990), and feelings of belonging (Kennedy, Kiecolt-Glaser, & Glaser, 1990).

We also may age because of the changes in the efficiency of the endocrine system. The glands of the *endocrine system* secrete hormones that travel to different points in the body. Hormonal changes are controlled by the brain, particularly by the pituitary gland and the hypothalamus. Finch (1991) suggested that aging pacemakers in these control centers of the brain stimulate a series of hormonal changes that cause us to age. This is the basis of the **hormonal theory** of aging.

Changes in the hormonal activity of the hypothalamus and pituitary play a role in biological aging. The hypothalamus periodically stimulates the pituitary gland to release antithyroid or "blocking" hormones that travel in blood cells throughout the body. These blocking hormones begin releasing shortly after puberty. They keep the body's cells from absorbing an adequate supply of *thyroxine,* a hormone produced in the thyroid gland that is required for normal cell metabolism. A number of metabolic imbalances result when thyroxine is not available in adequate quantities. According to this view, it is these imbalances that produce an excess of free radicals, mutations, toxins, and **autoimmunity,** which together cause aging (Selkoe, 1992).

Yet another kind of explanation of biological aging has to do with reserve capacity. In early adulthood, the functional capacity of human organs is four to ten times that needed to respond successfully to stressful conditions. The existence of this *organ reserve* enables the stressed organism to restore homeostasis, or balance, when it is challenged by an external threat. The amount of organ reserve shows a linear decline beginning at about the age of 30 (e.g., Fries, 1990; Fries & Crapo, 1981). As organ reserve decreases, so does the ability to restore homeostasis. Eventually, in the absence of sufficient reserve capacity, even a small external stress would inevitably result in death. Although exposure to a particular disease or type of stressor may seem to be the cause of death, the actual cause is an age-related depletion in reserve capacity. Importantly, the reserve capacity of many or most biological systems can be increased though appropriate interventions (Fries, 1990).

## *Biological Clocks*

Scientists acknowledge that aging takes place at many different levels. Some researchers give emphasis to cellular mechanisms, others emphasize genetic factors, and still others emphasize reserve capacities, which are to some extent modifiable by exercise, diet, and lifestyle factors. That some biological systems show change or decline sooner than other systems suggests that there must be more than one genetic timing mechanism or *biological clock* that sets the pace for physical aging. Biological clocks run at different rates for different systems and for different individuals.

Miriam, who is 75 years old, looks and acts much younger than other women who are her age. Tom, her husband, looks and acts much older than his 75 years. Like most aspects of adult development, there are noticeable individual differences in biological aging. Despite such differences in the rates of aging for different individuals and for different biological systems, the consequences of physical aging are inevitable, if life is not prematurely shortened because of disease or accident (Fries, 1990). As can be seen in figure 3.1, many of the major biological systems begin to show decline as early as the twenties or thirties.

Senescence is the term used to mark the point in the life cycle where degenerative processes begin to overtake regenerative processes. Finch (1991) suggested that it is useful to describe three types of senescence: *rapid, gradual,* and *negligible.* Although these terms do not indicate different biological mechanisms, many studies show that diet, exercise, and other environmental variables can shift the rate of senescence from rapid to gradual, or vice versa. With regard to diet, for example, there is a growing literature to suggest that dietary restriction is a predictor of increased longevity in laboratory animals (Levine, Janda, Joseph, Ingram, & Roth, 1981; Masoro, 1988) and humans (e.g., Rodin, 1986; Walford, 1986). Although the onset and rate of senescence is different for different biological systems and for different individuals, senescence ultimately affects all individuals. The rate of senescence is relatively gradual compared with disease processes.

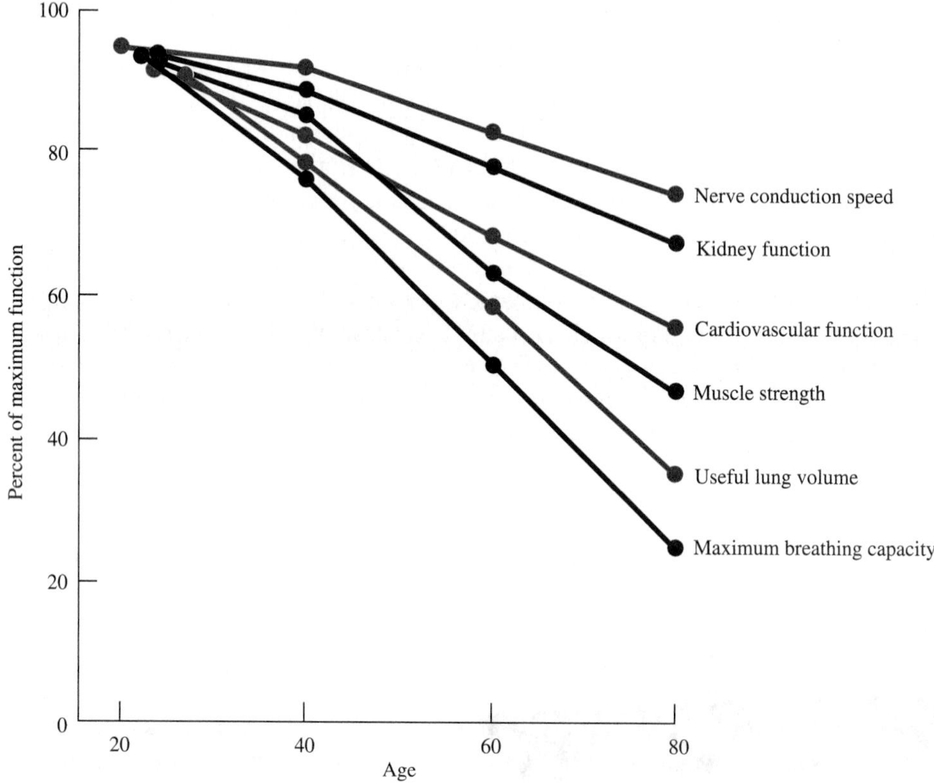


**Figure 3.1** Average declines in major biological systems. *Source: Data from J. F. Fries and L. M. Crapo,* Vitality and Aging, *W. H. Freeman and Company, New York, NY, 1981.*

Senescence is largely genetically programmed although external factors may affect the onset and time-course of senescence.

Senescent changes can be accelerated by extrinsic factors, such as exposure to toxic substances. The terms *primary aging* and *secondary aging* are used to distinguish the intrinsic or internal processes of senescence from the extrinsic sources of physical change in the later years. Primary aging refers to senescent changes that are inevitable, universal, and genetically programmed. Secondary aging refers to the processes that serve to affect the rate at which primary aging occurs. Prolonged work-related stress is an example of a secondary aging factor that accelerates the rate of primary aging processes.

*Biomarkers* are measures of individual differences and system differences in the rate of senescence (Birren & Birren, 1990). For example, Sophie might have the cardiovascular system of a typical 60-year-old, or an overall biological age of 60 even though she is really 50 years old. Such functional age measures have been developed for a variety of biological, social, and psychological measures, and presumably are useful for predicting longevity. Just as there is a **social clock** that gives us a sense of where we think we should be in terms of a family timeline, there are other functional age measures against which we compare our physical appearance and health to our expectations for being "on time" or "off time" (Featherman & Petersen, 1986; Neugarten, 1977).

*Give up the chips. Health in late life will be affected by the choices we make in young adulthood. Healthy eating habits are associated with increased longevity and reduced risk of heart disease.*

*Unquestionably, our physical appearance continues to change as we grow older, and some changes bring on other changes—gains as well as losses. Will changes in our physical appearance affect how we see ourselves? Clint Eastwood at ages 35 and 63.*

## *Physical Changes and Aging*

Sometimes, within a period of just a few months, you can see large changes in the physical appearance of an older relative or friend. Although individual differences prevail, frequently there are predictable changes in physical appearance and function with aging. As we grow older, our appearance changes, perhaps as quickly as it did when we were children. The difference is that we probably welcomed the changes that brought us to maturity, and we are sometimes less enthusiastic about some of the physical changes that take place during maturity.

### Changes in Physical Appearance with Age

One of the physical manifestations of aging has to do with changes in the appearance of the skin. Facial wrinkles and age spots become more apparent as we age. Age-related changes in the skin are largely cosmetic, since the primary functions of the skin, which involve protection of the internal organs and body temperature regulation, are relatively unaffected by aging.

Facial structure also changes with age. The cartilage in the nose and ears continues to grow with age, although the bones of the face do not enlarge after young adulthood. Scalp hair also grays and thins. Some men experience a form of hair loss that is genetically based. This type of hair loss, called *male pattern baldness,* begins at the temples, proceeds to the top of the head, and continues until the entire top of the head is bare (the "monk's spot").

For men, there is a decrease in height by about a half inch between 30 and 50 years, and a decrease in height by about three-fourths inch between 50 and 70 years. The height loss for women is slightly greater and may be as much as two inches between 25

**Figure 3.2 Osteoporosis: Reducing the risk.** After age 30, and especially after menopause in women, bone loss begins. Osteoporosis is an extreme form of the bone loss and mineralization that ordinarily occur with age. As bones become more brittle, fractures in the wrist, spine, and hip become more likely. Back pain, a bent spine, and loss of height also occur.

In fact, osteoporosis can first be detected by a loss of height. A decrease of more than one inch from the baseline height at age twenty is a sign that significant bone loss is taking place. The likelihood of osteoporosis can be minimized by starting as a young adult to maintain a good calcium intake, to engage in weight-bearing exercise, and to get a moderate amount of sun (in order to manufacture vitamin D), as well as by restricting alcohol intake and not smoking. After menopause, women should consult a doctor about estrogen replacement theory and calcium supplements. *Adapted from Stevens-Long and Comman (1992).*

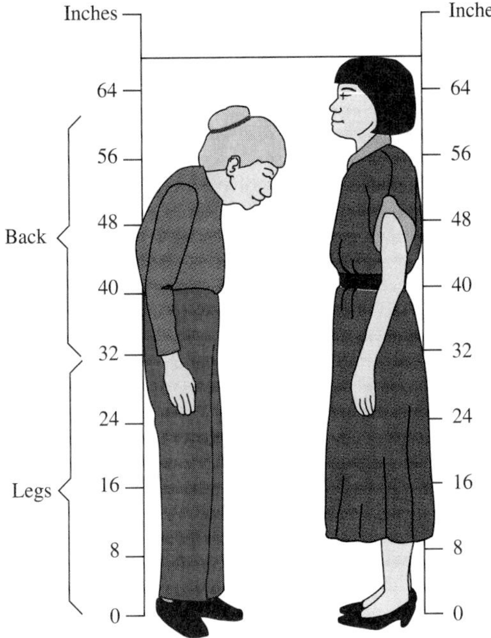


and 75 years. These changes in height are associated with postural change, compression of the cartilage in the spine, and loss of bone calcium with age (Whitbourne, 1985).

Loss of bone calcium occurs at a faster rate for women after menopause. **Osteoporosis** is the term for the disease that involves extreme losses in bone calcium and increased brittleness. Individuals with osteoporosis are at risk for breaking bones, if they fall. Osteoporosis can be detected early by a loss in height of more than one inch from one's height at age 20 (see figure 3.2). Postmenopausal women are advised to consult a physician regarding the benefits and disadvantages of estrogen replacement therapy. Risk of osteoporosis can be minimized by maintaining a properly balanced diet including daily requirements for calcium, and engaging in exercise on a regular basis (Nordin & Need, 1990).

With regard to height changes, it is likely that improved nutrition has had a major effect on different cohort groups. Young adults today are generally taller than young adults of just a decade ago, and part of this cohort difference is probably due to improved nutrition. The potential effects of nutrition on height are illustrated in figure 3.3 for middle-aged and older adults. This figure shows the estimated mean height for groups of middle-aged and older adults measured in 1995. The solid line

**Figure 3.3** This figure shows the estimated mean height for groups of middle-aged and older adults measured in 1995. The solid line indicates age differences in height. The dashed line indicates age change for this cohort. These data illustrate two important points about physical aging. First, some part of the difference we observe between different age groups for any measure is due to cohort factors rather than age. With regard to height, improved nutrition has had a major effect on height and other physical characteristics. Second, there is a large degree of stability for individuals along some physical dimensions or for some characteristics.

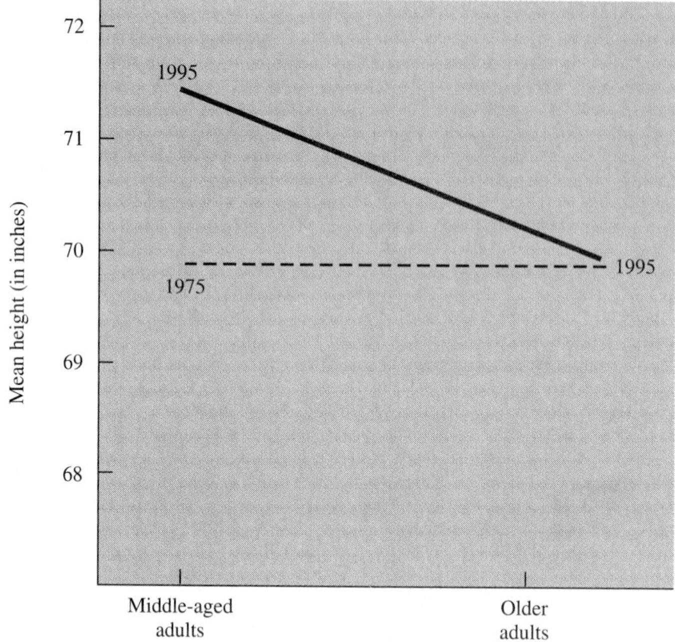


indicates *age differences* in height. The open circle represents the mean height of the older adults when they were middle-aged in 1975. The dashed line indicates *age change* for this cohort. Although these data are estimations of actual heights for these groups, they illustrate that some part of the difference we observe between different age groups for any physical measure is due to cohort factors. Methods for disentangling age and cohort influences are described in detail in Appendix A.

Studies of age differences and age changes also suggest that muscle tissue gradually declines in strength, size, firmness or tone, and flexibility (Whitbourne, 1985). Age-related changes in strength and muscle tone can be attributed to tissue changes, but the extent of decline in strength depends largely on one's level of activity and exercise (Horvath & Davis, 1990; Schulz & Curnow, 1988).

## Changes in Circulation

For the cells of the body to survive and to function properly, they must receive oxygen and nutrients and they must have a way of disposing of waste products. The circulatory system provides for these needs. Figure 3.4 shows the four chambers of the

**Figure 3.4 Circulation in the heart.** The heart is a four-chambered muscle, about the size of a fist. Each side of the heart contains two separate spaces separated by a valve. The thin-walled upper chamber is called the atrium, and the thick-walled lower chamber is called the ventricle.

Used blood returns to the heart via the vena cava, the body's largest vein, and enters the right atrium. It then flows down into the right ventricle. The ventricle contracts, forcing the blood through the pulmonary artery into the lungs, where carbon dioxide is removed and oxygen is added. The clean, oxygenated blood returns to the heart via the pulmonary veins into the left atrium and then down into the left ventricle. The powerful muscular wall of the left ventricle forces the blood up through the aorta, the body's largest artery, and into the systemic circulation. The familiar "lub-dub" sound of the heartbeat is caused by the alternating contraction (systole) and relaxation (diastole) of the chambers of the heart.

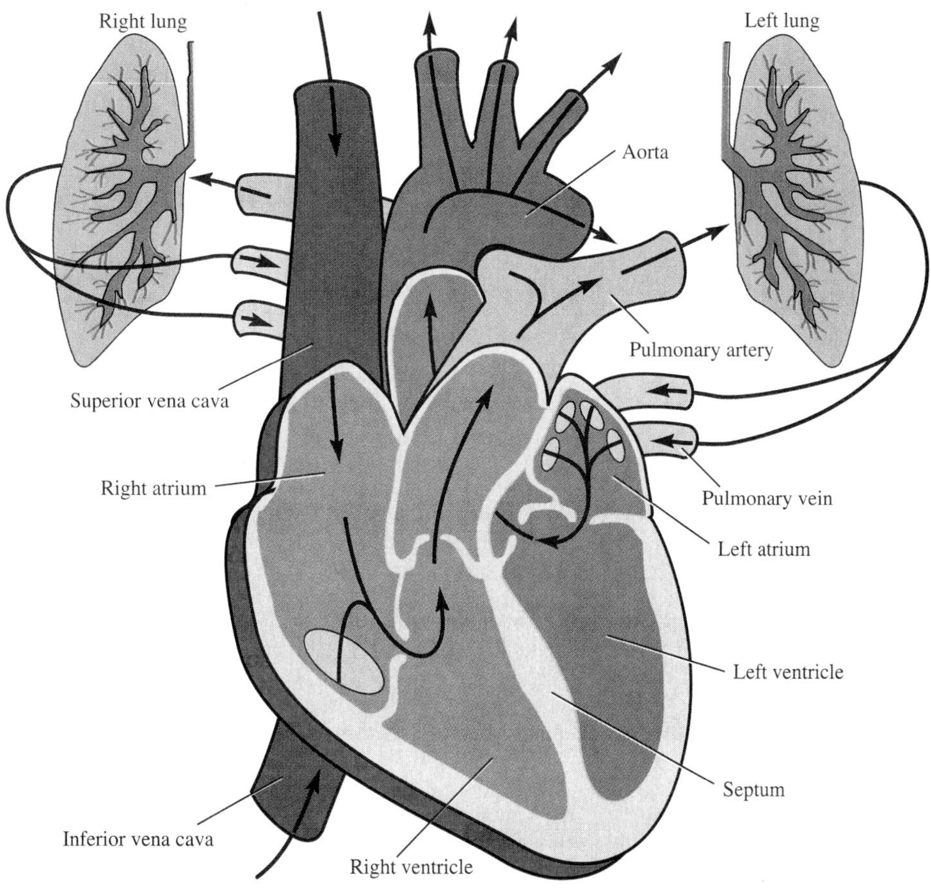


heart, and the pattern of circulation. Although muscles of the heart become less efficient, and the arteries become less flexible and narrower, normal aging of the circulatory system does not pose a problem for most older adults. However, diseases of the circulatory system, such as heart disease, hypertension, and atherosclerosis, are serious problems for a large number of middle-aged and older adults (Elias, Elias, & Elias, 1990). Although the incidence of heart disease is decreasing, it is still the leading cause of death in the United States.

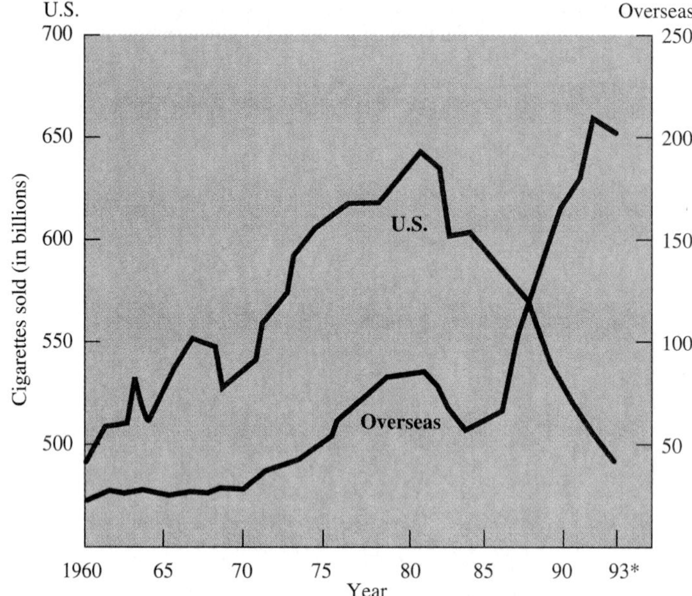


**Figure 3.5** U. S. cigarette sales. Annual domestic cigarette sales have plummeted by 140 billion cigarettes since 1981.
*Source: Tobacco Institute, U.S. Dept. of Agriculture.*

Changes in health behavior as well as medical advances have helped to reduce the consequences of heart disease. There is evidence to suggest that many people are more concerned about their own health behavior than ever before. From 1982 to 1992, tobacco sales dropped 22 percent (see figure 3.5).

## Hormone Regulation and Reproduction

There are age-related changes in hormonal regulation, due to changes in secretion patterns and in the effects of secretions on target tissues. One of the most important systems that exhibits the consequences of hormonal change with aging is the female reproductive system. The transition from the comparative regularity of the menstrual cycle during young adulthood to increased variation in the menstrual interval in middle age is due to increased variation in the length of the follicular and luteal phases of the cycle. Changes in the function of the ovaries determine the timing of the events leading to irregular cycles (Wise, 1993). Changes in anterior pituitary function are also likely to occur with aging. Age-related change in levels of *follicle stimulating hormone* (FSH) is one of the earliest hallmarks of reproductive aging in women. In regularly cycling women over age 45, FSH concentrations are elevated during the early follicular phase. Subsequently, FSH levels fall to normal during the late follicular phase. The mean number of follicles in the ovaries of women who are still menstruating is ten-fold higher than it is in postmenopausal women of the same age. Over the entire life span, there is a continuous, exponential reduction in ovarian oocytes and follicles. By the time of menopause, there is less than 1 percent of the original reserve of oocytes and primordial follicles.

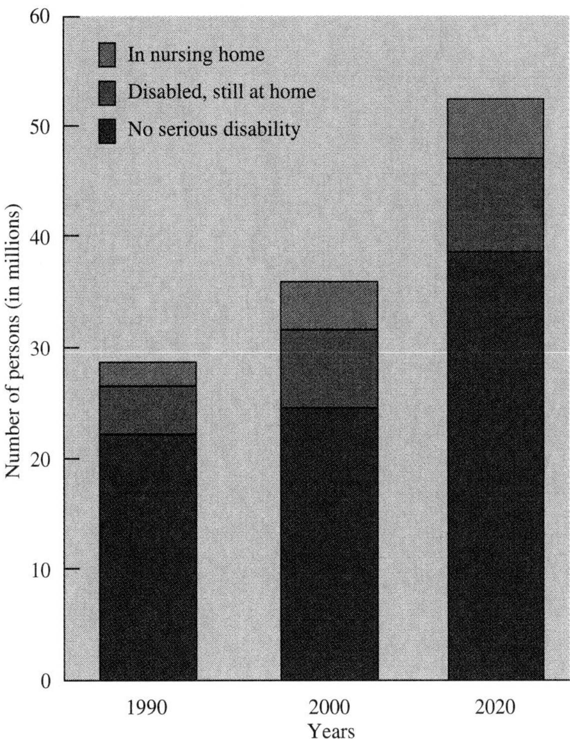


**Figure 3.6** Disabled versus healthy adults over age 65. *Source: Manton, Corder, & Stallard, 1993; Riley & Riley, 1994.*

Men do not generally experience abrupt changes in fertility or other sexual functions. However, during the later adult years, reproductive impairments become more likely for men. The incidence of impotence increases, testosterone concentrations decrease, and the diurnal rhythm in testosterone levels disappears (Wise, 1993).

## *Health and Aging*

"I don't want to live to be 100 years old if I have to be mentally or physically impaired or a burden to family members or others." Most everyone agrees with this statement. It is generally the case that aging is accompanied by declines in health. As can be seen in figure 3.6, most older adults are healthy, not disabled (Manton, Corder, & Stallard, 1993). In 1990, 28 percent of older persons assessed their health as fair or poor, compared with 7 percent for persons under 65 years old. There was no difference between men and women in health self-ratings, but there were race differences. Older blacks are much more likely to rate their health as fair or poor (40%), compared with older whites (27%).

The number of days in which usual activities are restricted because of illness or injury increases with age. Older persons averaged thirty-one days per year in 1990. Despite these findings, recent studies by Lentzner, Pamuk, Rhodenhiser, Rothberg, & Powell-Griner, (1992), and Manton, Corder, and Stallard (1993) have shown that

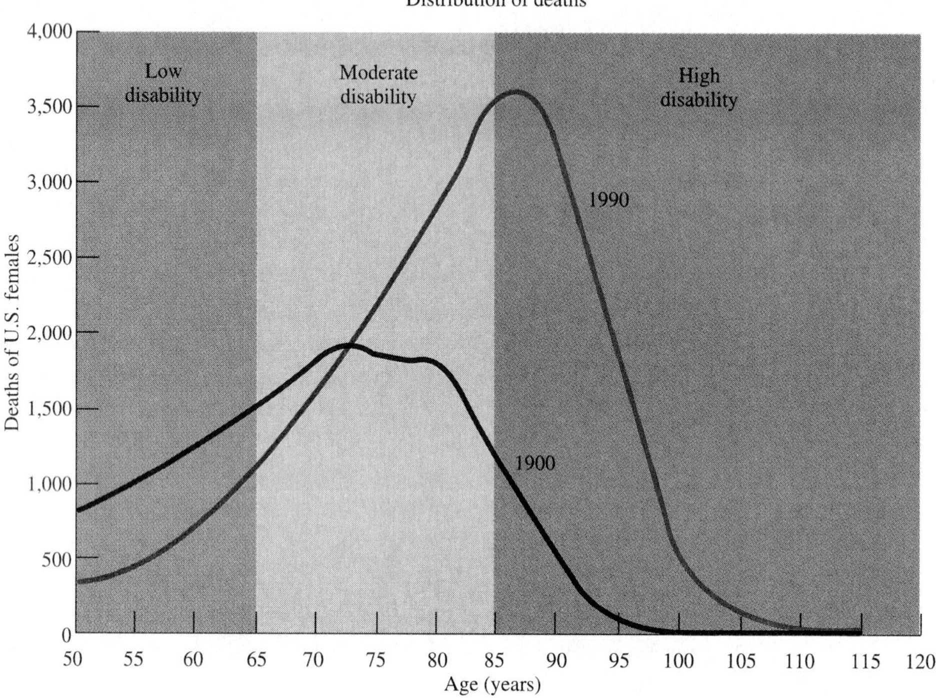


**Figure 3.7** Patterns of disability and death are shifting. With healthier lifestyles and improved medical care, people are surviving longer than ever before with heart disease, stroke, and cancer. Because of extended survival, those who are 85 years and older may live with a high level of disability. *From "The Aging of the Human Species" by S. Jay Olshansky, Bruce A. Carnes, and Christine K. Cassel. Copyright © 1993 by Scientific American, Inc. All rights reserved.*

older adults today are healthier than ever before. Older adults today report fewer sick days compared with previous generations of older adults, they spend fewer weeks in the hospital, and they have fewer disabilities and limitations of physical and mental competence. Functional health is usually measured in terms of activities of daily living (ADL), such as the extent to which help is needed with eating, bathing, dressing, walking, and toileting.

Although women live longer than men, women are more likely to be in poor health than men in their later years. In Lentzner et al.'s (1992) study, for example, women were 40 percent less likely than men to have been fully functional and were 70 percent more likely to have been severely restricted in the last year of life. It should also be mentioned that although women are more likely to be in poor health than men, women take greater care than men in responding to their illness symptoms (Hickey, Akiyama, & Rakowski, 1991).

In Lentzner's study, being unmarried doubled the chances of being severely restricted for both men and women. The older adults who were most functional were less likely to have smoked or to have abused alcohol.

One implication of these findings is that health care costs will increase substantially in the future because greater numbers of adults will reach old age and will require costly medical services. In Lentzner et al.'s study, for example, it was estimated that 50 percent of those age 85 and over will be severely restricted in their last year of life. As can be seen in figure 3.7, disability levels are higher in older adults over age 85 than previously, because people with heart disease, cancer, and other diseases are living longer than ever before (Olshansky, Carnes, & Cassel, 1993). However, some recent evidence also suggests that disability rates among the elderly are actually declining (Manton et al. 1993). Manton and his colleagues at Duke University have reported that while the population of those past their 65th birthday increased by 15 percent between 1982 and 1989, the chronically disabled elderly population increased by 9 percent during this period.

In considering the consequences of the graying of America for the economics of health care, it should be noted that the bulk of the increase in health care costs in the United States can be attributed to the increased costs per patient visit associated with more thorough testing and the provision of more comprehensive care and services, rather than to increasing numbers of older adults requiring care.

Most people are healthiest and reach their level of peak physical performance during early adulthood. Nine out of ten people between the ages of 17 and 44 view their own health as good or excellent. Relative to older adults, young adults have few chronic health problems. If young adults are hospitalized, it is usually because of an accident or for childbirth (National Center for Health Statistics, 1992).

The fact that physical functioning and health are at their peak in early adulthood is in some ways a risk. Because young adults do not notice any direct negative consequences of poor diet, alcohol abuse, stress, smoking, and other insults, they often see little need to take better care of themselves or to modify their behaviors, even though these behaviors will have substantial negative effects on their health when they reach middle age and later life.

In terms of diet, for example, it has been reported that proper nutrition combined with dietary restriction produces beneficial effects with regard to life expectancy, biological integrity, and behavioral ability (Masoro, 1988; Walford, 1986). It should also be emphasized that diets high in cholesterol and fat are associated with heart disease, and diets lacking adequate amounts of such nutrients as vitamin $B_{12}$, folic acid, and niacin are associated with mental impairment in elderly adults (Zarit, Eiler, & Hassinger, 1985).

Health becomes a major concern in middle adulthood. Middle adulthood is characterized by an increasing awareness of gradual losses in optimal physical functioning and health. The three health concerns that have received the greatest attention in middle adulthood are heart disease, cancer, and obesity. Cardiovascular disease is the number one killer in the United States, followed by cancer (National Center for Health Statistics, 1992).

## Breast Cancer

Perhaps the most serious health threat for middle-aged and older women is breast cancer. If all women lived to age 85, recent statistics indicate that one in nine women could expect to have a diagnosis of breast cancer. Statistics also indicate that 1.6 million women have the disease, and that there may be as many as 1 million undiagnosed cases. Among women age 50, one in fifty will get breast cancer. At that point in the life span, the probability of the disease increases with aging. Overall mortality rates have remained the same, but have recently decreased for women under age 50, and increased for women over age 50. Depending on the study, between 70 percent and 85 percent of women who get breast cancer have no known risk factors. Only 5 percent of all breast cancers are inherited.

Although incidence of breast cancer is less in black women than in white women, more blacks die of breast cancer. Though mammogram screening may not have much predictive value prior to age 50, regular mammographic examinations have been shown to reduce mortality from breast cancer by 20 percent to 39 percent in women aged 50 years and older (Kerlikowske, Grady, Barclay, Sickles, Eaton, & Ernster 1993). At all ages, early diagnosis is critical to surviving breast cancer (Kerlikowske et al., 1993).

## Human Immunodeficiency Virus and AIDS

Another threat to the health of middle-aged individuals is AIDS. Health-care professionals are concerned with the growing number of older individuals (50 years of age and older) who suffer from AIDS. There is neither a vaccine nor a cure for AIDS. Therefore, preventing the transmission of the virus that causes AIDS, the Human Immunodeficiency Virus (HIV), is the primary goal of public health programs.

Joseph Catania and his associates (Catania et al., 1989) have noted three reasons why older adults may be more likely than younger adults to become HIV-infected and to develop the symptoms of AIDS. First, the efficacy of the immune system declines with age. Older adults have a shorter HIV incubation period than younger adults (5.8 years versus 7.3 years, respectively). Second, older adults—more so than younger adults—are likely to be the recipients of blood transfusions, which increases the risk of infection through contaminated blood. Third, postmenopausal women are likely to experience the thinning of the cells of the vaginal wall. Since AIDS is transmitted by sexual contact, the deteriorating vaginal wall of the older woman provides more potential sites for HIV infection. Although AIDS is generally thought of as a young adult disease that affects mainly males, there are more than 125,000 HIV-infected middle-aged and older adults (Stall, Catania, & Pollack, 1988).

## Weight Control and Physical Activity

Being overweight is a critical health problem in middle adulthood. For people who are 30 percent or more overweight, the probability of dying in middle adulthood increases by 40 percent. Furthermore, **obesity** increases the likelihood that an individual will suffer a number of other ailments, including hypertension and digestive disorders (Lew & Garfinkel, 1979).

Recent studies have demonstrated the long-term benefits of avoiding obesity and being physically active on health and longevity (e.g., Paffenbarger, 1993; Sandvik & Erikssen, 1993). Paffenbarger and his colleagues showed that avoiding obesity and making other healthy lifestyle choices (such as quitting smoking and being physically active) were associated with lower mortality for middle-aged and older men. Sandik and his colleagues showed that physical fitness was a predictor of lower mortality among healthy middle-aged Norwegian men.

## Heart Disease and Lifestyle

In the California Longitudinal Study (Livson & Peskin, 1981), good health ratings at ages 34 to 50 were positively associated with several personality measures that reflect emotional stability and good control of stress. Most strongly associated with health at middle age was a calm, self-controlled, and responsible personality, a pattern that appeared at least by early adolescence. Health status at midlife was linked with this early adult personality pattern.

The heart and coronary arteries undergo change in middle adulthood. Under comparable conditions of stress, the heart of a 40-year-old can pump a much smaller number of liters of blood per minute (23) than the heart of a 20-year-old (40). The coronary arteries that supply blood to the heart narrow during middle adulthood, and the level of cholesterol in the blood increases with age (average at age 20, 180 mg; at age 40, 220 mg; at age 60, 230 mg). The cholesterol begins to accumulate on the artery walls, which are themselves thickening. The net result is that arteries are more likely to clog, increasing the pressure on the arterial walls, which in turn pushes the heart to work harder to pump blood and makes a stroke or heart attack more likely. Actually, heart attacks are more common in middle adulthood than in old age.

Lifestyle, as well as diet, physical condition, and family history, is a risk factor for heart disease. One intriguing theory relates individual behavior styles to either a high risk (Type A) or a low risk (Type B) of heart disease (Friedman & Rosenman, 1974). The **Type A behavior style** is excessively competitive, accelerates the pace of ordinary activities, is impatient with the rate at which most events occur, often thinks about doing several things at the same time, shows hostility, and cannot hide the fact that time is a struggle in his or her life. By contrast, the **Type B behavior style** is typified by the absence of these behavioral tendencies. About 10 percent of the subjects studied were clearly Type A or Type B styles, although most people were various mixtures of the two. It is interesting to note that high achievement and Type A behavior style seem also to be related (Friedman & Rosenman, 1974).

Stephanie Booth-Kewley and Howard Friedman (1987) reviewed eighty-three different studies conducted between 1945 and 1984 investigating the relationship between behavioral lifestyle (Type A versus Type B) and coronary heart disease. Their analysis revealed that Type A behavior is reliably related to the incidence of heart disease. However, they discovered a somewhat different profile of the Type A behavioral style than the one originally outlined by Friedman and Rosenman (1974). Specifically, they concluded that "the true picture seems to be one of a person with one or more negative emotions: perhaps someone who is depressed, aggressively competitive, easily frustrated, anxious, (or) angry . . ." (Booth-Kewley & Friedman, 1987, p. 358).

## Health and the Old-Old

As we approach old age, the probability that we will contract some disease or illness increases. A majority of individuals who reach the age of 80 will likely have some type of health impairment. Normal or *usual aging* can be distinguished from *unusual aging* or *successful aging* with regard to health (Rowe & Kahn, 1987), since it is very rare to find anyone over the age of 80 or 85 who is completely free from disease or illness.

Heart disease and cancer are the most serious health concerns in late adulthood. Other diseases and illnesses, such as arthritis, can severely limit physical functioning, mobility, and the quality of life of older adults. Almost two of every five people between the ages of 65 and 75 have some impairment of physical functioning. After age 75, the rate rises to three of five. Some of the most prevalent chronic conditions that impair the health of the elderly are arthritis (38%), hearing impairment (29%), vision impairment (20%), and heart condition (20%). Studies of sex differences in health indicate that elderly women are more likely to have a higher incidence of arthritis, hypertension, and visual problems but are less likely to have difficulty with hearing than men.

## Coping with Disease

People have always been interested in preventing or postponing the negative consequences of illness and aging. Some have looked for the fountain of youth, others have tried special potions and diets, but the best approach for optimizing health throughout the adult years has to do with our own behavior with regard to nutrition and diet, exercise, stress management, and lifestyle (Rodin, 1986).

Individuals differ in how they cope with the effects of disease and aging. Taylor (1983) emphasized the importance of meaning, mastery, and self-enhancement in adapting to life-threatening illnesses. Taylor found that women who had breast cancer adapted more successfully if they were somehow able to create an explanation for their cancer, if they were able to have or perceive some control over their disease, and if they were able to maintain or restore their self-esteem. Recently, Taylor and colleagues have demonstrated how optimism affects coping, psychological distress, and the high-risk sexual behavior of men at risk for AIDS (Taylor, Kemeny, Aspinwall, Schneider, Rodriguez, & Herbert, 1992).

Howard Leventhal and his colleagues (Leventhal, Leventhal, & Schaefer, 1991) have studied individual differences in how people think about their illnesses. These investigators examined the cognitive factors that are involved in how people represent or understand illness. A person's representation of illness, whether accurate or not, will affect the emotional reactions to the illness and the coping and appraisal process (Folkman & Lazarus, 1980; Folkman, Lazarus, Gruen, & DeLongis, 1986; Lazarus & DeLongis, 1983; Lazarus & Folkman, 1984). It has been reported in a number of studies that individuals who are more optimistic cope more effectively with disease.

## Brain Aging

There are considerable individual differences in how the brain ages. The structural and chemical changes that typify brain aging in the absence of disease are heterogeneous, like the brain itself.

## Major Components of the Brain

The major structures or parts of the human brain are shown in figure 3.8. The **brain stem** is the oldest part of the brain. It begins as a swelling of the spinal cord and extends into the middle of the brain. It controls basic biological functions such as breathing and heart rate. The **ascending reticular activation system (ARAS),** a structure that originates within the brain stem and extends to the other portions of the brain, regulates an individual's state of consciousness and level of arousal. Attached to the brain stem is the **cerebellum.** This structure helps maintain balance and posture and coordinate body movements. Memories for simple learned responses may be stored in the cerebellum, and age-related declines in the strength of classical conditioning, both in humans and animals, may be affected by age-related changes in the cerebellum (Woodruff-Pak, 1993).

The **limbic system** is a border area between the oldest part of the brain (the brain stem and cerebellum) and the newest part of the brain (the cerebrum). One part of the limbic system, called the hypothalamus, which is about the size of a pea in the adult brain, controls eating, drinking, body temperature, and sexual activity. It also regulates the activity of the master gland of the endocrine system, the pituitary gland. For many years, psychologists have known that the limbic system exerts a powerful influence on emotional behavior. Damage to certain areas of the limbic system can result in episodes of extreme rage or anger.

Of primary interest to developmental psychologists and gerontologists is a component of the limbic system called the **hippocampus.** A great deal of evidence suggests that the hippocampus plays a crucial role in memory processes (Squire, 1992). Patients who suffer from amnesia and Alzheimer's disease, disorders in which memory failure is readily apparent, display significant damage to the hippocampus (Kolb & Whishaw, 1992). Furthermore, it has been suggested that biological changes in the hippocampus that accompany normal aging may be responsible, in part, for the declining memory abilities of older animals and humans (Moscovitch & Winocur, 1992).

The **cerebrum** is the largest, and evolutionarily the most recent, part of the brain. It totally covers the limbic system as well as significant portions of the brain stem and cerebellum. The cerebrum has several important features. First, it is divided down the middle into two halves or **hemispheres**—the right hemisphere and the left hemisphere. Second, the cerebral hemispheres are connected by a tract of nerve fibers called the **corpus callosum.** Third, the top covering of the cerebrum is called the **cortex.** The cortex, from the viewpoint of a psychologist, is one of the most important, if not *the* most important part of the brain. In fact, it may be argued that it is the cortex which makes us "human" (Ornstein & Thompson, 1984). The cortex has been identified as the source of personality, cognition, perception, communication, and creativity.

The cortex may be divided into four different regions called **lobes,** where various psychological functions are housed. In the **frontal lobe** are basic aspects of personality and social behaviors, planning and execution of complex behavioral sequences, and control of motor movements. In the **temporal lobe** we find

**Figure 3.8** Brain structures.
*From "Aging Brain, Aging Mind" by Dennis J. Selkoe, Copyright © 1992 by Scientific American, Inc. All rights reserved.*

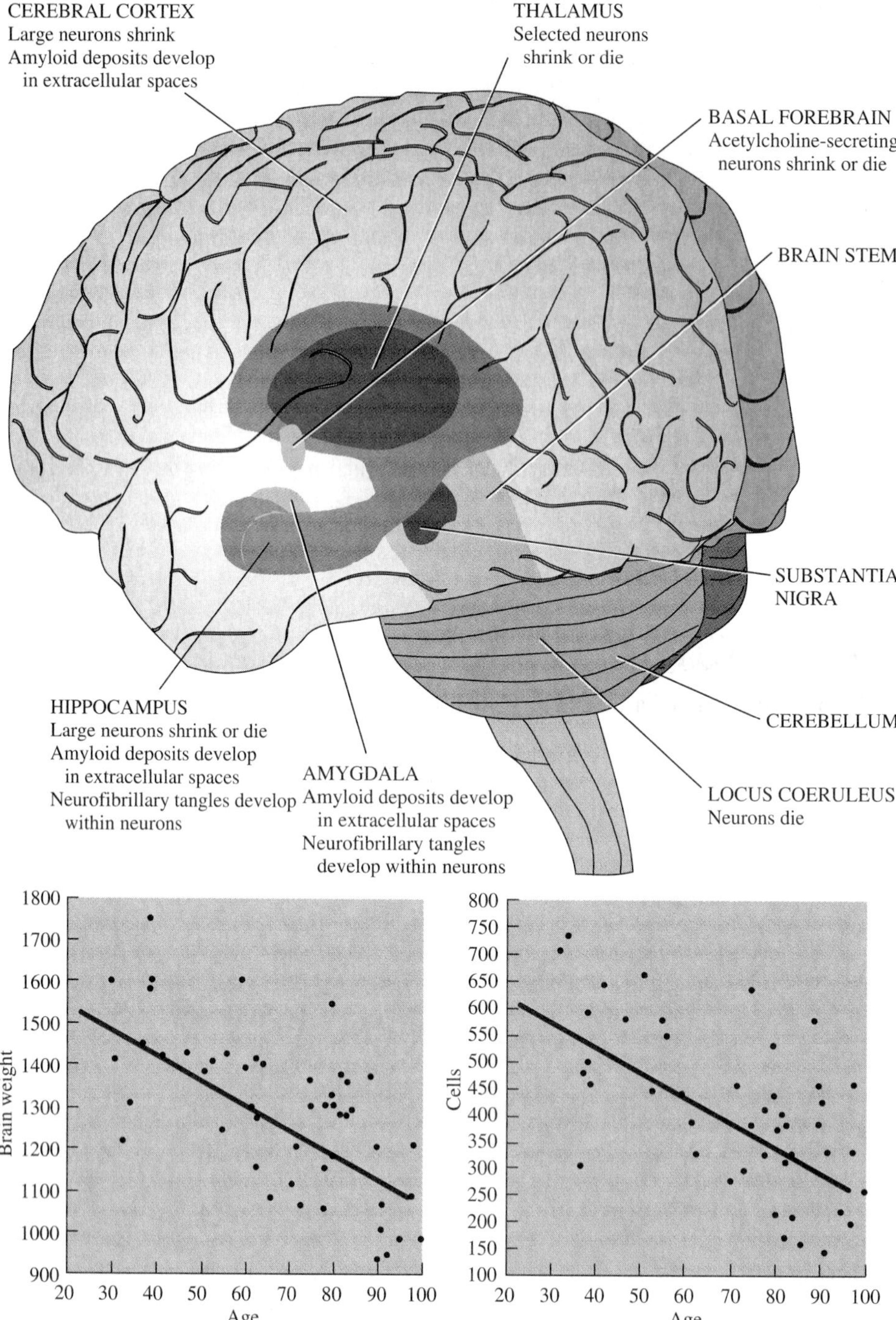

consolidation of long-term memories, the assigning of emotional properties to incoming experiences, and simple auditory sensation. The **parietal lobe** controls processing of short-term memories and the construction of a spatial representation of one's body. Finally, the **occipital lobe** controls basic visual processing (Kolb & Whishaw, 1992). Despite its importance in human psychological functioning, the cortex is amazingly delicate, fragile, and thin. In fact, the cortex only consists of the top *one-eighth inch* covering the cerebrum.

As individuals age, they are more likely to suffer from damage or injury to the cortex. Also with aging, the brain becomes less plastic. This means that uninjured parts of the cortex are less likely to take over the functions of injured cortical areas. Damage to the elderly brain usually results from a stroke or a brain tumor. Strokes occur when brain tissue is deprived of oxygen. This deprivation may occur when a blood vessel in the brain becomes clogged, plugged, or broken. In general, damage to the left hemisphere results in **aphasia,** a breakdown or loss of an individual's language abilities. Damage to the right hemisphere, on the other hand, typically results in visual-spatial disorders (e.g., Kosslyn, 1987). Adults with right hemisphere damage may fail to recognize familiar objects or faces **(agnosia),** become lost in familiar environments (even their own homes or neighborhoods), and may not be able to form a visual representation of all of the objects (including their own bodies) in the left half of their visual field.

## Neuronal Aging

The brain consists of a diverse array of *neurons, glial cells,* and *blood vessels.* The neurons carry the signals, and the glial cells support and repair neurons. Neurons have one axon that relays signals to other neurons that are often a good distance away. Neurons usually have many **dendrites,** which are found in large branching arbors, and which receive signals from other neurons. A sketch of a neuron is shown in figure 3.9. Figure 3.10 is a photo of the dendrites of neurons in the hippocampus for different-aged individuals. Some groups of neurons and areas of the brain are more prone to age-related damage than others. The extent of the damage and the time of onset of the alterations differ from person to person.

With aging, brain weight decreases and the number of large neurons decreases. However, neurons are not lost in a uniform fashion throughout the brain. Very few neurons disappear from the *hypothalamus,* the area of the brain that regulates the secretion of hormones by the pituitary gland. In contrast, many more nerve cells are lost from the **substantia nigra** and *locus coeruleus,* which are specialized populations of cells in the brain stem that manufacture **neurotransmitters** for transport to other areas of the brain.

With aging there is also a substantial amount of cell loss in the limbic system, including the hippocampus. The limbic system is central to learning, memory, and emotion. Researchers have estimated that about 5 percent of the neurons of the hippocampus are lost with each decade after age 50. For the neurons in the hippocampus that survive, there are age-related changes in the **soma** or cell body and in the **axons** and dendrites. At the cortical level, neuronal loss is least likely in sensorimotor areas

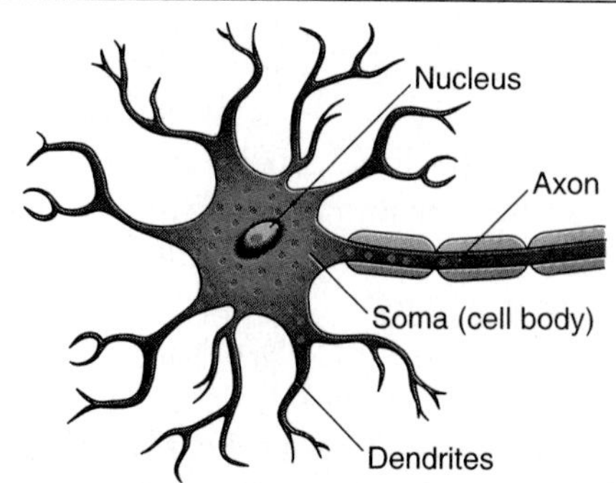


**Figure 3.9** A typical neuron.

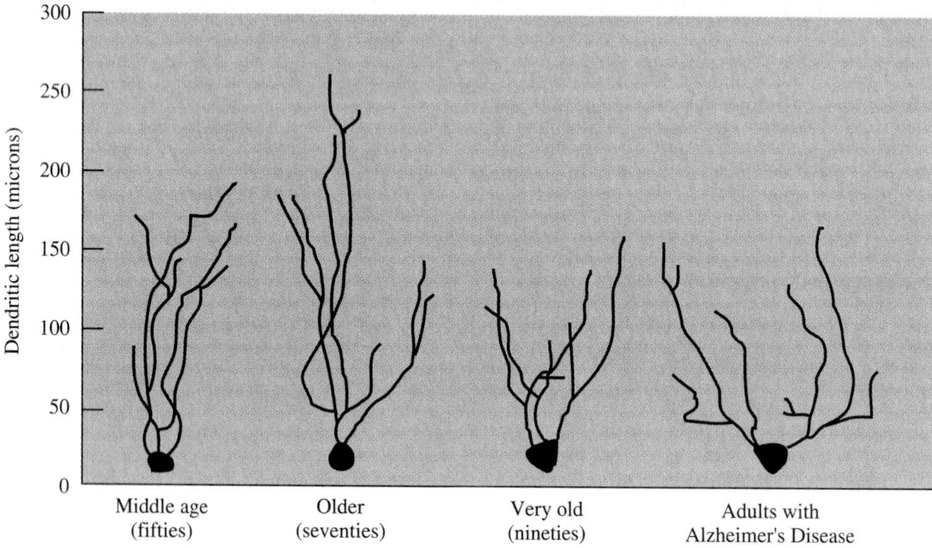


**Figure 3.10** Illustration of age differences in dendritic branching for healthy adults from middle age to very old age, and for an Alzheimer's patient. The illustrations are drawn from photographs of neurons from the hippocampus. *From "Aging Brain, Aging Mind" by Dennis J. Selkoe. Copyright © 1992 by Scientific American, Inc. All rights reserved.*

(e.g., occipital and parietal lobes) and is most likely in those areas that control intelligence, memory, and abstract thinking (e.g., frontal and temporal lobes).

There are also structural changes in the cell bodies and the dendrites and axons of neurons that secrete **acetylcholine.** These neurons extend from the basal forebrain to the hippocampus and other areas of the cortex. Acetylcholine is one of the neurotransmitters that enables neurons to convey signals to one another.

Not all neuronal changes with aging are detrimental. Coleman and Flood, (1987) observed a net growth in the number of dendrites in some regions of the hippocampus and cortex between the forties and the early seventies, followed by a reduction in the number of dendrites in the eighties and nineties. One explanation for this increase in dendrites is that healthy neurons compensate for losses of neighboring neurons by generating additional dendrites.

Neurons undergo changes in their internal architecture with aging. For example, the *cytoplasm* of particular cells of the hippocampus can begin to fill with tied or

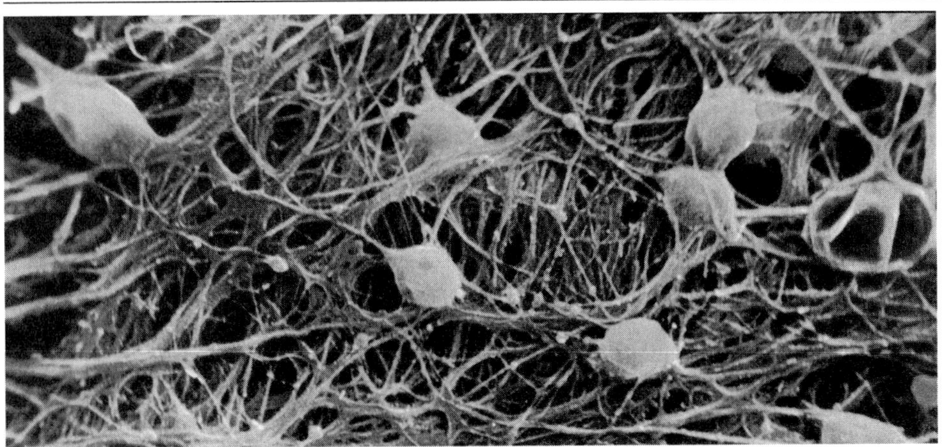

**Figure 3.11** A 3-d photomicrograph of the interneuronal structure.

tangled bundles of protein filaments known as *neurofibrillary tangles.* The development of tangles during aging seems to indicate that certain proteins, particularly those of the *cytoskeleton,* or the internal walls of the cell, have been chemically modified in ways that impair the signaling efficiency of these neurons (Selkoe, 1992). An abundance of such tangles in these and other areas of the brain contributes to the memory deficits associated with Alzheimer's disease.

Another internal alteration is that neural cytoplasm in many parts of the brain becomes increasingly dotted with innumerable granules containing **lipofuscin.** Lipofuscin is a fluorescent pigment that is thought to derive from lipid-rich internal membranes that have been incompletely digested. Investigators disagree about whether lipofuscin has harmful effects on cell function.

Glial cells serve a supporting role in neural function. Some types of glial cells, called *fibrous astrocytes,* increase in size and number after age 60. These cells are capable of releasing substances that promote neuronal growth. The effects of the proliferation of these cells on brain function are not known, but it has been suggested that glial activity represents a compensatory response to neuronal decrements.

As can be seen in figure 3.11, there is a massively complex network of interconnections among neurons, and there are large open spaces between neurons. With normal aging, the extracellular spaces of the hippocampus, cerebral cortex, and other brain regions gradually accumulate spherical deposits called **senile plaques.** These plaques are aggregates of a small molecule known as beta-**amyloid** protein. These plaques also accumulate in blood vessels in these regions of the brain.

As we have already mentioned, one of the theories of biological aging is that cells atrophy and die because defects slowly accrue in their DNA. DNA, or deoxyribonucleic acid, is the material from which genes are constructed. Genes carry the chemical instructions that inform cells about how to reproduce themselves and how to specifically synthesize proteins. DNA damage lowers the quality or quantity of critical proteins in cells and increases the amount of undesirable proteins such as those that promote cancer. The enzymatic machinery that is responsible for repair of faulty DNA in the nucleus of cells becomes less efficient with aging and in the presence of some brain diseases, such as dementia.

The DNA in the *mitochondria* of cells plays a major role in brain aging (Finch, 1991). The mitochondria are oval-shaped intracellular structures that provide cells with critically needed metabolic energy for cellular activity. Mitochondria contain enzymes that serve to break down carbohydrates, fats, and proteins into energy, carbon dioxide, and water. There are DNA instructions within the mitochondria for the duplication and manufacture of thirteen proteins needed for giving energy to cells. If the manufacture of DNA within the mitochondria becomes defective with time, mitochondrial proteins are eliminated or defective proteins are produced.

The long strands of helical DNA serve to store the genes for virtually all the proteins made in cells. The efficiency of mitochondrial DNA is impaired by the accumulation of free radicals. Free radicals are a continual by-product of the reactions through which mitochondria produce energy. They oxidize, or add, oxygen atoms to molecules, thereby altering molecular structure. Researchers have identified specific errors in stretches of mitochondrial DNA in aged brains, and in patients with particular brain disorders such as **Parkinson's disease.** Some researchers have suggested that the rate of primary aging and of certain diseases can be slowed by preventing oxidative injury.

Even if the DNA in the nucleus and mitochondria is unaffected by aging, and continues to produce the proper blend of healthy proteins, other modifications of the proteins can occur with aging. Proteins undergo distinct chemical modifications, including oxidation of certain of the component amino acids, and *cross-linking.* Cross-linking refers to the formation of strong chemical connections or bridges between proteins. Such modifications occur normally and help proteins to carry out their functions, but harmful modifications also occur with aging. For example, the level of oxidized proteins in skin cells of humans increases progressively with age. Further, researchers have also found that oxidized proteins can account for 30 to 50 percent of the total protein content of the brain cells of very old laboratory rats (Selkoe, 1992). It is also known that cells from young adults with *progeria,* a rare and remarkable disease that causes premature aging of many body tissues, contain levels of oxidized proteins that approach those found in healthy 80-year-olds.

Many important nonprotein molecules in the brain also change with aging. The long chains of carbon atoms that comprise the lipids in membranes that enclose cells undergo oxidation by free radicals. Small changes in the composition of the membrane can have major effects on the efficiency of cell functions. There are age-related changes in the fluidity of membranes making up *synaptosomes,* the tiny neuronal vesicles involved in the storage and release of neurotransmitters. And age-related changes occur in the lipid composition of the myelin that sheathes and insulates axons. Alteration of the **myelin sheath** has measurable effects on the speed and efficiency of neural transmission.

It is well known that there is irreplaceable neuronal loss in various regions of the human brain. Overall, the degree of neuronal loss is 5 to 30 percent compared with young adults (Coleman & Flood, 1987). Similarly, there are age-related neurochemical deficits, such as declines in the activity of particular enzymes or proteins or in RNA molecules

(Finch & Morgan, 1990). However, the brain has considerable physiological reserve, and there is continuous adaptation to gradual changes in neural structures and function.

## Measuring Brain Activity

Recent advances in brain imaging allow a noninvasive examination of the structure and function of the human brain. For example, the technique of computerized axial tomography, or the **CT scan,** allows a two- or three-dimensional representation of the human brain. The CT scan has revealed that the ventricles—the four cavities within the brain containing cerebrospinal fluid—enlarge with normal aging. CT scans have shown that from the first through the seventh decades of life there is a gradual increase in the size of the ventricles and, importantly, in the eighth and ninth decades comes a sharper increase (Barron, Jacobs, & Kirkei, 1976). Whether the age-related changes observed in the CT scan actually correspond to cognitive deficits is a matter of debate. Albert and Stafford (1988) have reported that CT changes are related to both changes in electroencephalogram recordings (EEGs) and decrements in cognitive abilities.

Similar to the CT scan, but more informative and safer, is the technique of **magnetic resonance imaging** or **MRI** (Cohen, 1988). In this procedure, various regions of the brain are surrounded by a strong magnetic field and exposed to a specific radio-frequency pulse. Under these circumstances the stimulated brain tissue emits a signal that is transformed into a two-dimensional image by a computer. The MRI technique is so powerful that it can identify structural abnormalities in the brain that are as small as 1 millimeter.

Unlike the CT scan and MRI, which depict brain anatomy, the PET scan **(positron–emission tomography)** reveals the brain's actual metabolic activity (Cohen, 1988). PET measures the radioactive emissions from the brain and produces an image revealing which regions are metabolizing the most glucose (i.e., which are the most active). Using the PET scan, researchers have found different patterns of activity in the brains of individuals engaging in different mental activities (e.g., reading versus solving math problems). PET scans have shown that the metabolic activity of older healthy adults' brains is very similar to that of younger adults. It has also been reported that glucose metabolism is reduced in certain areas of the brains of Alzheimer's disease patients (Albert & Moss, 1988).

It is also possible to measure the general electrical activity of the brain by means of an **electroencephalogram (EEG).** Despite some limitations, research involving the EEG has yielded a number of important findings. For example, several different patterns of rhythmical electrical activity (i.e., brain waves) have been detected in the brain by using the EEG. Each of these waves has been related to a particular level or state of consciousness. The **alpha rhythm** is the dominant rhythm displayed by the brain and is linked with alert wakefulness. The alpha rhythm contrasts with the faster **beta rhythm,** which characterizes an individual during a period of focused thinking and problem solving. The **delta rhythm** is the slowest of all of the different brain waves. It appears when individuals enter the deepest, most restful component of the sleep cycle.

There are several important ways in which various brain rhythms, as measured by the EEG, change with age (Bashore, 1993). Bashore examined age-related changes in the brain by measuring *event-related responses* (ERPs). Changes in ERPs have been linked to changes in basic perceptual and cognitive processes. A typical ERP experiment might involve embedding a novel stimulus in a series of common stimuli and determining the extent of electrical change in the brain when the infrequent stimulus is detected. For example, an individual might be presented with a series of similar tones in which a small number of extremely different tones is inserted on a random basis. The person's task is to count the irregular tones.

The **P300 brain wave** is a late-occurring ERP. This brain wave occurs somewhere between 300 to 500 milliseconds after a stimulus has been presented. The onset of the P300 seems to signify that the person has recognized a stimulus and has evaluated the psychological significance of the stimulus. A number of investigations have shown a shift toward longer latency (the amount of time it takes a person to respond) of the P300 brain wave with advancing age (e.g., Bashore, 1993). Also, it has been discovered that reaction time, but *not* P300 latency, is related to the response strategies that participants employ in an experiential task. Remember that older adults adopt a more conservative response strategy than younger adults do. The adoption of a conservative strategy by older adults would lead them to show longer reaction times than younger adults. Bashore (1993) and others have shown that older and younger groups of adults differ much more on measures of reaction time than on P300 latency. This means that reaction-time tasks may lead researchers to overestimate the extent to which behavioral slowing in late adulthood is caused by changes in central processes. An inspection of the P300 data suggests that the age-related slowing of reaction time is due to decrements in peripheral processes (e.g., slower response output) in combination with the adoption of a conservative response bias (putting greater emphasis on accuracy than speed).

## *Aging and Sensory Processes*

We make contact with the world around us through our five primary senses—vision, hearing, touch, taste, and smell. **Sensation** refers to the reception of information by the ears, skin, tongue, nostrils, eyes, and other specialized sense organs. When we hear, for example, waves of pulsating air are sensed by the outer ear, transmitted through the bones of the middle ear to the cochlear nerve, and sent to the brain. When we see, waves of light are collected by the eyes, focused on the retina, and travel along the optic nerve to the brain. We now consider the effects of aging on vision, hearing, and other sensory processes.

### Vision

Figure 3.12 shows a diagram of the human eye. Although there is relatively little change in visual function during the early adult years, very noticeable changes in vision occur during the middle and later years. In the middle adult years, most or all

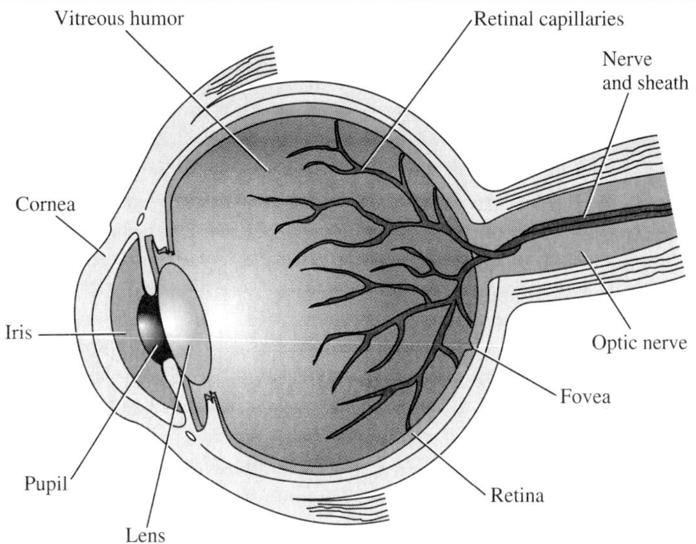


**Figure 3.12** Major structures of the eye.

individuals will experience difficulties in near vision tasks such as reading. There is a substantial decline in the processes of **accommodation,** the ability of the lens to focus and maintain an image on the retina (Schieber, 1992). The lens gradually loses its capacity to accommodate to near and far objects, and you can observe middle-aged adults holding newspapers and books at greater distances from their eyes as they try to read without the aid of glasses. The reduction of near vision in middle adulthood is termed **presbyopia**.

Although visual acuity is the most common measure of accommodation, measures of **contrast sensitivity** provide a more accurate assessment of visual function (see Research Focus 3.1).

Another problem associated with the middle-aged years is an increased sensitivity to **glare.** This change in sensitivity is usually noticed after age 45. Age-related changes in glare sensitivity are largely due to changes in the lens; and indeed, the lens becomes progressively thicker, less flexible, and more opaque with age (Weale, 1986). Also, the lens takes on a yellowish tint with increasing age. All of these changes in the lens mean that less light reaches the retina. It has also been shown that the number of cones (color receptors) on the fovea (the center of the retina) markedly decreases between 40 and 60 years of age. Such a change has a negative influence on visual acuity (Schieber, 1992).

Third, as we grow older, the processes involved in adjusting to changes in illumination take longer (Weale, 1986). The term **dark adaptation** refers to the adjustment involved in going from a brightly lit to a dimly lit environment.

As we grow older, the area of the effective visual field becomes smaller with advancing age. This means that the size or intensity of stimuli in the peripheral area of the visual field must be increased if the stimuli are to be seen. As we grow older, events occurring away from the center of the visual field are less likely to be detected

## RESEARCH FOCUS 3.1

# Age Changes in Contrast Sensitivity

Contrast sensitivity refers to an individual's ability to perceive visual stimuli that differ in both contrast and spatial frequency. **Contrast** refers to the difference in brightness between adjacent areas of a visual stimulus. A black line on a white piece of paper possesses a great deal of contrast; a light grey line on a white piece of paper possesses a smaller amount of contrast. **Spatial frequency** refers to the number of cycles of bars of light (one cycle consisting of both a light bar and a dark bar of the same width) imaged within a specific area on the retina. This means that very wide bars of light have low spatial frequencies, while very narrow or fine bars of light have high spatial frequencies. Psychologists have constructed simple visual stimuli called **gratings** that differ in spatial frequency. See figure 3.A for an example of two simple gratings. If held at arm's length, grating *A* has a spatial frequency of 1 (each cycle of one light bar and one dark bar takes up one degree of visual angle on the retina); grating *B* has a spatial frequency of 3 (three cycles of light and dark bars are needed to take up one degree of visual angle). In other words, there are three times as many bars of light in grating B as in grating A.

It is possible to conduct an experiment in which we present adults of varying ages with a number of gratings differing in both contrast and spatial frequency. By doing such a study we can determine the **contrast threshold** for different-aged adults. This refers to the minimal amount of contrast needed to perceive gratings that differ in spatial frequency. Owsley, Sekuler, and Siemsen (1983) have discovered that the contrast threshold changes in a predictable manner from twenty to eighty years of age. Figure 3.B summarizes the results of this study as well as other research dealing with the topic of age-related changes in contrast sensitivity.

**Box Figure 3.A** Two gratings illustrate the concept of spatial frequency.

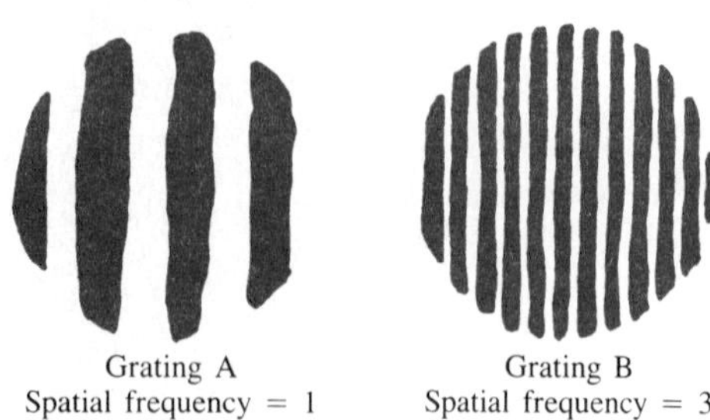


In figure 3.B the area below the curve represents combinations of contrast and spatial frequency that individuals can see. The area above the curve represents combinations of contrast and spatial frequency that are invisible to humans. In general, this figure shows that humans need a great deal of contrast to see gratings with very low or very high spatial frequencies, but relatively little contrast to see gratings of moderate spatial frequency. Furthermore, this figure also shows that, with increases in age, adults (1) need more and more contrast to see gratings with high spatial frequencies, (2) become progressively blind to higher spatial frequencies regardless of the amount of contrast inherent in a grating, and (3) display no alteration in their ability to see low spatial frequencies.

Why do you think that scientists are so concerned with the concept of contrast sensitivity in general and age-related changes in the contrast threshold in particular? To answer this question we need to consider the concept of **visual acuity.** When an adult goes to an optometrist for a routine

(Cerella, 1985). Changes in the size of the visual field are due, in part, to an age-related reduction in the amount of blood reaching the eye (Weale, 1986).

Age-related declines in visual function have also been traced to reductions in the quality or intensity of light reaching the retina. This is due to several factors, including the progressive yellowing of the lens, an increased waviness and irregularity of the cornea, and a reduction in the diameter of the pupil. It has been determined that the retina of a 60-year-old receives only approximately one-third of the light received by the retina of a 20-year-old (Weale, 1986).

Although changes in visual function are quite substantial and unavoidable, it is important to note that there are ways to compensate for such changes so as to not limit mobility and quality of life. In a recent study, Kosnik, Winslow, Kline, Rasinski, and

**Box Figure 3.B** Changes in human contrast sensitivity from 20 to 80 years of age. *Source: Data from C. Owsley, R. Sekuler, and D. Siemsen, "Contrast Sensitivity Throughout Adulthood" in* Vision Research, *23: 689–699, 1983.*

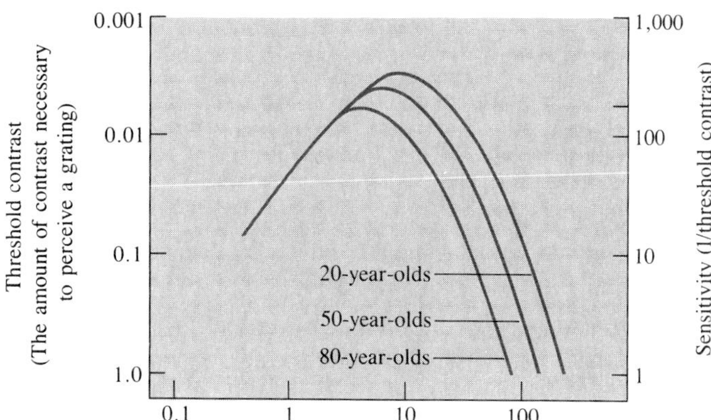


eye exam she is typically given a test of visual acuity. Visual acuity refers to a person's ability to perceive objects under maximum amounts of contrast. When you take your eye exam, you are placed in a dark room and the optometrist projects an eye chart consisting of black letters against a white background. Your task is to identify the letters. Alternatively, the contrast threshold is a measurement of the minimum amount of contrast necessary to see an object. This means that a test of visual acuity would be a very liberal estimate of an adult's visual ability—it would likely overestimate the individual's visual ability. For example, suppose that several older adults complain of poor vision. But when they are administered a test of visual acuity, they appear to have normal vision. This does not mean that old people are "faking it" or that they are complaining because they want attention. Instead, it means that under conditions of reduced contrast (for example, driving at dusk or reading in a dimly lit room), older adults may experience a pronounced difficulty in seeing. But when high levels of contrast are available, as in a test of visual acuity, they experience less difficulty in seeing. Put somewhat differently, it is possible for two adults (one older and one younger) to test out at the same level of visual acuity while the contrast sensitivity of the younger adult greatly exceeds that of the older adult.

Contrast sensitivity is a more sensitive and more meaningful measure of a person's visual ability than is visual acuity. For example, a person's contrast sensitivity seems to be a better predictor of one's ability to drive a car under conditions of reduced visibility than a person's visual acuity.

Sekuler (1988) surveyed a large number of adults ranging from 18 to 100 years of age. These participants provided information about their ability to perform everyday visual tasks. The participants reported that five different aspects of vision declined with age: *visual processing speed* (the time necessary to read a passage or recognize an object); *light sensitivity* (trouble seeing at dusk or sorting dark colors); *near vision* (inability to read small print); *dynamic vision* (inability, e.g., to read the moving credits at the end of a movie); and *visual search* (e.g., difficulty in locating a particular type of cereal at the supermarket). The reports of the participants in this study suggested that dynamic vision, visual search, and the time necessary to adjust to dim environments declined very gradually with age, whereas visual processing speed, near vision, and the ability to see in dim environments declined rapidly with age. Adjusting to glare and brightly lit environments was the most frequent complaint of middle-aged adults.

Two of the most common pathologies of the aging eye are **cataracts** and **glaucoma** (Schieber, 1992). A person with a cataract suffers from a lens that is completely opaque—light cannot travel through the lens to project onto the retina. Cataracts can be surgically treated by removing the lens and inserting an artificial lens. Glaucoma results from increasing pressure inside the eye, which leads to irreparable damage to the retina and the optic nerve. Glaucoma affects 2 percent of individuals over the age of 40. Glaucoma is easily detected by a simple optometric test.

## Hearing

Hearing remains fairly constant during much of early adulthood and starts to decline during middle adulthood. By age 40, a specific decline in hearing can sometimes be detected. By age 50, we are likely to have problems hearing high-pitched sounds. Why? The reduction in the ability to hear high-pitched sounds seems to be caused by a breakdown of cells in the **organ of corti**, the organ in the inner ear that transforms the vibrations picked up by the outer ear into nerve impulses. Sensitivity to low-pitched sounds, on the other hand, does not decline very much in middle adulthood. The need to increase the treble on stereo equipment is a subtle sign of this age-related hearing change. Men are more likely than women to lose their auditory acuity for high-pitched sounds (Schieber, 1992). This sex difference may be due, in part, to the greater exposure of men to noise in occupations such as construction work and factory work.

Hearing impairment becomes more serious in the later years. About 20 percent of the individuals between 45 to 54 years of age experience some hearing difficulty, but for those between 75 and 79, the percentage rises to 75 (Fozard, 1990). It has been estimated that 15 percent of the population over 65 is legally deaf. Such hearing loss is usually due to degeneration of the **cochlea**, the primary neural receptor for hearing. **Presbycusis**, which is a decline in the ability to hear high-pitched sounds, is the general term used to describe the most common age-related problems in hearing. Another specific hearing disorder of late life is **tinnitus**. This is a constant high-pitched "ringing " or "whistling " sound in the ears. It has been reported in nearly 11 percent of those between 65 and 74 years of age (Rockstein & Sussman, 1979). Though not unknown among middle-aged adults (9%) or younger adults (3%), tinnitus is a problem the elderly find most difficult to accept. It is distracting, virtually constant, and nearly impossible to "tune out."

With increasing age, it is more and more difficult to hear speech sounds. This effect becomes especially noticeable when processing speech sounds under *noisy* conditions. It is not clear why older adults are greatly affected by noise when processing speech sounds. Corso (1981) argued that the degeneration of certain areas within the brain, as well as within the ear, may be responsible for this phenomenon. Whatever the cause, it is certain that this deficit can have a negative effect on the older adult's ability to communicate with others (Souza & Hoyer, 1994).

Hearing aids are used by many older adults. Recent technological improvements in hearing aids have made them more comfortable and effective, especially if they are properly fitted by a professional. Some older adults must wear two hearing aids to correct for different degrees of hearing loss in each ear. If the aids are not

*Ronald Reagan, in order to compensate for his hearing loss, used a small canal-style hearing aid while he was president.*

properly balanced or if only one is used, the subtle differences in phase and intensity at the two ears, which enable sounds to be localized and identified, are lost. Localization of sounds helps us to attend to one conversation while ignoring another. When we don't do this well, both wanted and unwanted sounds combine and produce noise or confusion. Some adults who wear a single hearing aid complain that all it does is bring in noise. Individuals may make other attempts to compensate for hearing losses, such as learning to read lips or by relying on normal scripts or expectations in conversation as a way of filling in what was not heard.

Deficits in hearing often lead individuals to choose patterns of physical and social isolation. This may contribute to reductions in intellectual enrichment, social functioning, and perhaps even life satisfaction.

## Taste, Smell, and Touch

There are age-related declines in taste, smell, and tactile sensitivity (Engen, 1977; Schiffman, 1977), although declines in these senses are not as dramatic or noticeable as those observed for vision and hearing. Declines in the sense of taste and smell affect one's enjoyment and intake of food (Whitbourne, 1985) and can also affect one's choice of diet. For example, some older adults suffer from nutritional deficiencies because of an increased desire for highly seasoned but nonnutritious "junk food."

The human tongue contains specialized receptors that detect four different tastes: sweet, salty, bitter, and sour. Bartoshuk, Rifkin, Marks, and Bars (1986) found that older adults (averaging 82.8 years of age) were less sensitive than younger adults (24.4 years of age) to all of the basic tastes. Wiffenbach, Cowart, and Baum (1986) found no basic differences in taste sensitivity for those between 40 and 70 years of age. However, the youngest age group (20- to 39-year-olds) in this study displayed greater taste sensitivity than the over-40 group. Other researchers have suggested that sensitivity to all tastes remains stable until the late fifties, when a steep decline in the ability to detect all tastes occurs (Whitbourne, 1985). Researchers agree that age-related changes in

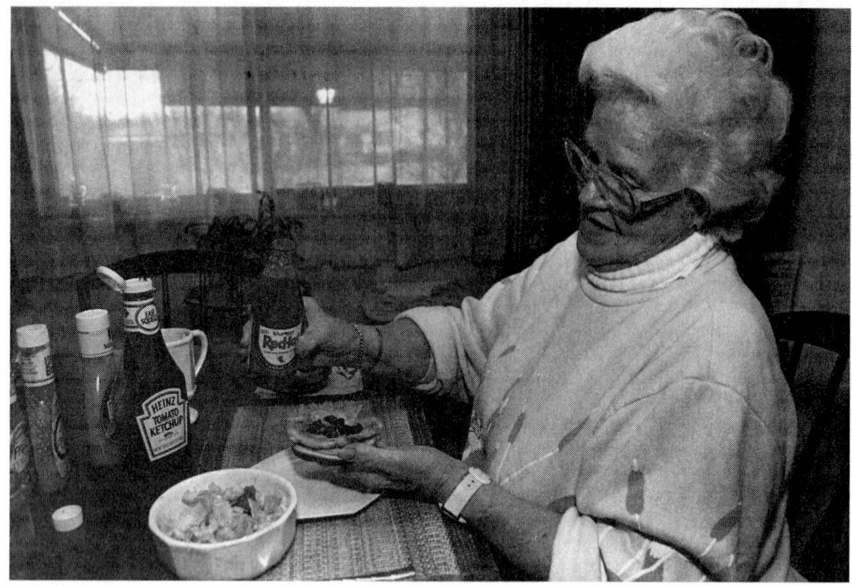


*Age-related changes in sensitivity to taste and smell affect dietary preferences, and may affect how much "hot sauce" we use.*

taste sensitivity occur. But there seems to be some disagreement about when the changes first occur and how rapidly the changes occur.

Changes in taste sensitivity are *not* responsible for all changes in eating behavior during older adulthood. Older adults may eat less because they don't want to bother to cook, shop, and clean up, or for other reasons (such as loneliness) independent of their level of taste sensitivity (Schieber, 1992).

Information about age-related changes in *smell* have been very difficult to reliably document (Engen, 1977; Whitbourne, 1985). This is because smell is one of the last senses to decline with age, and because smell is affected by a number of variables (e.g., health) that are correlated with age. For example, Chalke, Dewhurst, and Ward (1958) examined how well two different groups of adults (a healthy group and a group of inpatients and outpatients in a hospital) could detect the smell of natural gas. Results showed that as many as 30 percent of adults over age 65 were not sensitive to lower concentrations of gas.

Age-related changes have also been reported in *touch.* Verrillo (1980), for example, examined vibrotactile sensitivity (i.e., the ability to detect vibrations on the surface of the skin) in individuals between 8 and 74 years of age. He found age-related declines for high-frequency but not low-frequency stimulation. Corso (1977) has observed that, with aging, the touch sensitivity of the lower extremities (ankles, knees, and so on) is more impaired than that of the upper extremities (wrists, shoulders, and so forth).

## Temperature, Pain, and Kinesthetic Senses

Older adults are less sensitive to *temperature* changes than are young adults, but the changes are quite minor (Schieber, 1992). Because older adults may be less able to detect changes in temperature, they are more susceptible to hypothermia, heatstroke, and frostbite.

One of the age-related losses in sensory sensitivity, the sensitivity to *pain,* may have an advantage. Earlier studies have shown that older people are less sensitive to and suffer less from pain than do their younger counterparts (see, e.g., Kenshalo, 1977; Whitbourne, 1985). More recent research has revealed that older adults tend to underreport low levels of pain and overrate higher-intensity pain (Harkins, Price, & Martinelli, 1986). Nevertheless, Harkins et al. (1986) reported that there were more similarities than differences between younger and older participants. Although decreased sensitivity to pain may help the elderly cope with disease and injury, it can be harmful if it masks injuries and illnesses that need to be treated. Importantly, a vast array of personality and cultural factors influence the reporting and experience of pain.

Ochs, Newberry, Lenhardt, and Harkins (1985) reviewed evidence that shows that the elderly are likely to have impaired **kinesthesis.** Kinesthesis refers to a person's ability to know where his or her body parts are as he or she moves through space. For example, being able to touch your nose when your eyes are closed. A reduced kinesthetic sense would make elderly adults more susceptible to falls (see Research Focus 3.2).

## *Aging and Physical Ability*

The physical skills of an individual usually peak between the early twenties and the midthirties. One of the major reasons for a decrease in physical performance during adulthood is a reduction in muscle strength. Muscular strength and the ability to maintain maximum muscular effort have both been found to decline steadily during middle adulthood. By age 30, about 70 of a man's 175 pounds are muscle. Over the next forty years, he loses ten pounds of that muscle as cells stop dividing and die. By age 45, the strength of a man's back muscles declines to approximately 96 percent of its maximum value, and by age 50, it declines to 92 percent. Most men in their late fifties can only do physical work at about 60 percent of the rate achieved by men who are 40. Much of this decline appears to be linked with such physiological changes as the thickening of the walls of the air sacs in the lungs, which hinders breathing, and the hardening of connective sheaths that surround muscles, which is linked with decreases in both oxygen and blood supply. All these age-related changes, because they have been identified for the most part by cross-sectional research, are confounded with a variety of other potent variables, such as changes in lifestyle, and cohort differences in exercise habits. With exercise and training, individuals can reduce the rate of decline in various psychomotor and physical functions (Adrain, 1981; Rikli & Busch, 1986).

Simple actions that entail little, if any, strength and endurance are just as likely to slow down with aging as are complex behaviors that demand strength, endurance, and skill. For example, finger tapping and handwriting have been found to slow dramatically with age (Dixon, Kurzman, & Friesen, 1993) Salthouse (1985) noted that **psychomotor slowing** is probably the most reliable finding in the study of human aging. Older adults, because of the slowing of their motor performance, may be less able to adapt to the demands of a changing world than younger adults. According to Salthouse (1985):

> If the external environment is rapidly changing, the conditions that lead to the initiation of a particular behavior may no longer be appropriate by the time the behavior is actually executed by older adults. This could lead to severe problems in operating

## *Falling: The Leading Cause of Accidental Injury among the Elderly*

Among those over the age of 65, falling is the leading cause of accidental injury. For example, of the 200,000 hip fractures each year in the United States, more than 170,000 occur to those over the age of 65. The rate of mortality from falling increases directly with increased age and represents the seventh leading cause of death in those over 75, surpassing even causes such as automobile accidents (Ochs, Newberry, Lenhardt, & Harkins, 1985). About 25 percent of older people require intensive medical intervention and hospitalization from falls. Severe falls are associated with broken bones (fractures of the hip, wrist, and vertebrae), head injury, and multiple facial, skin, and hand lacerations.

Most falls occur in the homes of older people (Ochs et al., 1985), especially in the living room or bedroom during the regular daytime routine, or while going downstairs. The institutionalized elderly are also at high risk of falling due to the many predisposing medical conditions that require institutional placement (Ochs et al., 1985). Institutional falls are more common at night, as older people perhaps become disoriented and confused in unfamiliar surroundings. Newly admitted patients in institutions are particularly vulnerable (Ochs et al., 1985).

The causes of falling among the elderly represent a burgeoning area of research. Many studies suggest that the elderly who are most likely to experience severe injury or death from a fall are those who are just beginning to undergo physical and psychological decline and have not yet recognized their limitations. On the other hand, those elderly who are frequent fallers and have identified their problem are less likely to be seriously injured in a fall. The risk of falling has been found to be related to poor illumination, dark staircases, and loose rugs. Some of the physical conditions that contribute to falling are arthritis, loss of balance and equilibrium **(presbystasis),** weakness in the muscles that control coordination of the knees and ankles, impaired vision, impaired hearing (hearing provides critical feedback for walking), and diabetes (leading to reduced sensation in the legs). Neurological disorders can increase the likelihood of falling, and medications can increase the risk of falling.

Why do falls lead to such severe injury in the elderly? First, because of the generalized age-related slowing of behavior, older people may not be as able as younger people to prepare themselves to break a fall. Second, the age-related phenomenon of osteoporosis, or thinning and weakening of the bones, may cause the spontaneous shattering of brittle, thinning bones (especially in the pelvis) in older people. This sudden breakage can actually cause a fall. Thus, falls can cause broken bones, and brittle or broken bones can cause falls.

One of the most profound consequences of falling is that falling may unnecessarily restrict the range of activities selected by an older person. This type of self-limiting lifestyle, focused on self-protection rather than freedom, may lead to isolation and depression.

---

vehicles, controlling equipment, or monitoring displays. Despite some claims to the contrary . . . it appears that the speed of decision and response can be quite important in our modern automated society, and, consequently, the slowness of older adults may place them at a great disadvantage relative to the younger members of the population. (p. 401)

Although it is reasonable for all individuals to expect age-related changes in health and physical functioning as they grow older, individual differences are the rule. For the most part, we control our own health, and how we grow older. Table 3.1 lists some of the structural changes that are associated with aging, the functional effects of these structural changes, and the beneficial or compensatory effects of exercise with regard to these changes.

The body's capacity for exercise in late adulthood is influenced by the extent to which the individual has kept his or her body physically fit at earlier points in the life cycle. It is not uncommon to find that older individuals who continue to be physically active, such as those who participate in the Senior Olympics, are healthier than many individuals who are much younger (see Research Focus 3.3).

*Table 3.1*

### Physiological Decline Associated with Aging and the Possible Benefit of Regular Strength and Endurance Exercise

| Structural Changes | Functional Effects | Effects of Exercise |
|---|---|---|
| | **Musculoskeletal System** | |
| 1. Muscular atrophy with decrease in both number and size of muscle fibers<br>2. Neuromuscular weakness<br>3. Demineralization of bones<br>4. Decline in joint function—loss of elasticity in ligaments and cartilage<br>5. Degeneration and calcification on articulating surface of joint | 1. Loss of muscle size<br>2. Decline of strength<br>3. Reduced range of motion<br>4. Reduced speed of movement<br>5. Joint stiffness<br>6. Declining neuromotor performance<br>7. Changes in posture<br>8. Frequent cramping<br>9. Gait characteristics affected:<br>a. Center of gravity<br>b. Span (height/arm length)<br>c. Stride length, speed<br>d. Width of stance<br>10. Shrinkage in height<br>11. Increased flexion at joints due to connective tissue change | 1. Increased strength of bone<br>2. Increased thickness of articular cartilage<br>3. Muscle hypertrophy<br>4. Increased muscle strength<br>5. Increased muscle capillary density<br>6. Increased strength of ligaments and tendons |
| | **Respiratory System** | |
| 1. Hardening of airways and support tissue<br>2. Degeneration of bronchi<br>3. Reduced elasticity and mobility of the intercostal cartilage | 1. Reduced vital capacity with increased residual volume<br>2. Reduced $O_2$ diffusing capacity<br>3. Spinal changes lead to increased rigidity of the chest wall<br>4. Declining functional reserve capacity | 1. Exercise has no chronic effect on lung volumes but may improve maximal ventilation during exercise and breathing mechanics |
| | **Cardiovascular System** | |
| 1. Elastic changes in aorta and heart<br>2. Valvular degeneration and calcification<br>3. Changes in myocardium<br>a. Delayed contractility and irritability<br>b. Decline in oxygen consumption<br>c. Increased fibrosis<br>d. Appearance of lipofuscin<br>4. Increase in vagal control | 1. A diminished cardiac reserve<br>2. Increased peripheral resistance<br>3. Reduced exercise capacity<br>4. Decrease in maximum coronary blood flow<br>5. Elevated blood pressure<br>6. Decreased maximal heart rate | 1. Increased heart volume and heart weight<br>2. Increased blood volume<br>3. Increase in maximal stroke volume and cardiac output<br>4. Decreased arterial blood pressure<br>5. Increase in maximal oxygen consumption<br>6. Myocardial effects increased:<br>a. Mitochondrial size<br>b. Nuclei<br>c. Protein synthesis<br>d. Myosin synthesis<br>e. Capillary density<br>7. Decreased resting heart rate |

*From Robert A. Wiswell, "Relaxation, Exercise, and Aging" in* Handbook of Mental Health and Aging, *edited by Birren/Sloane, ©1980, p. 945. Reprinted by permission of Prentice-Hall, Inc., Englewood Cliffs, NJ.*

# Aging and Peak Athletic Performance

Although peak levels of performance in running, swimming, and other athletic events is usually attained in young adulthood, age-related changes in athletic performance are much smaller than most individuals imagine. Furthermore, continued training by older athletes may help them display high levels of athletic competence in the face of age-related declines in physiological functioning (Schulz, Musa, Staszewski, & Siegler, 1994).

K. Anders Ericsson and Crutcher (1990) reviewed a great deal of the research regarding age changes in swimming and running performance. These sports were chosen for analysis because (1) the distances of specific races within these sports have been fixed for approximately the last century, and (2) performance within these sports is measured objectively by specific units of time (minutes, seconds, and so on)—there is no subjective element in measuring performance in these sports, as there is in boxing or gymnastics. These attributes allowed researchers to make valid comparisons of changes in swimming and running performance from one historical era (the 1920s) to another (the 1980s).

Examination of the world records and Olympic gold medal performances in these sports from 1896 (the year of the first modern-day Olympic games) to the present revealed four major findings. First, over this time span, gold medalists and world record holders have generally achieved their feats during young adulthood, usually between 20 and 30 years of age. Second, world record and gold medal times have steadily and significantly decreased. Third, the shorter the distance of the race, the younger the age of the gold medalists and/or world record holders. Fourth, winners of shorter swimming events are becoming younger (in their early twenties); while the winners of longer running events such as the marathon are becoming older (in their late twenties to midthirties). For example, Carlos Lopes won the 1984 Olympic marathon at the age of 37.

Ericsson also examined age-related changes in maximum performance of well-trained athletes. Figures 3.C & 3.D show the *best* times as well as the *average* times achieved by

**Box Figure 3.C** Changes in the *best* race times for expert swimmers 25 to 70 years of age. *Source: Data from M. Letzelter, et al., "Swimming Performance in Old Age" in* Zeitschrift für Gerontologie, *19: 389–395, 1986.*

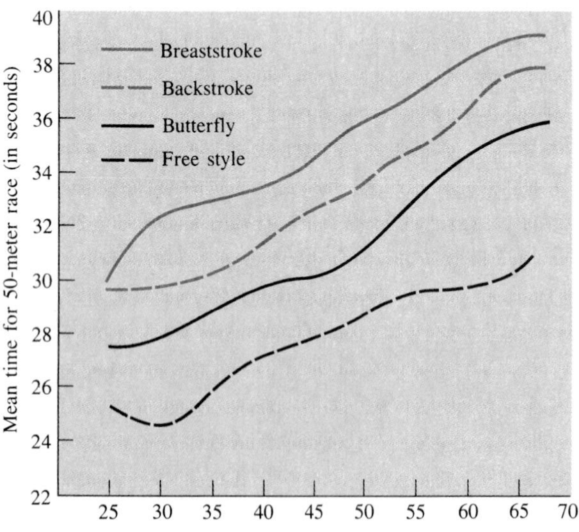


**Box Figure 3.D** Changes in the *average* race times for expert swimmers 25 to 70 years of age. *Source: Data from M. Letzelter, et al., "Swimming Performance in Old Age," in* Zeitschrift für Gerontologie, *19: 389–395, 1986.*

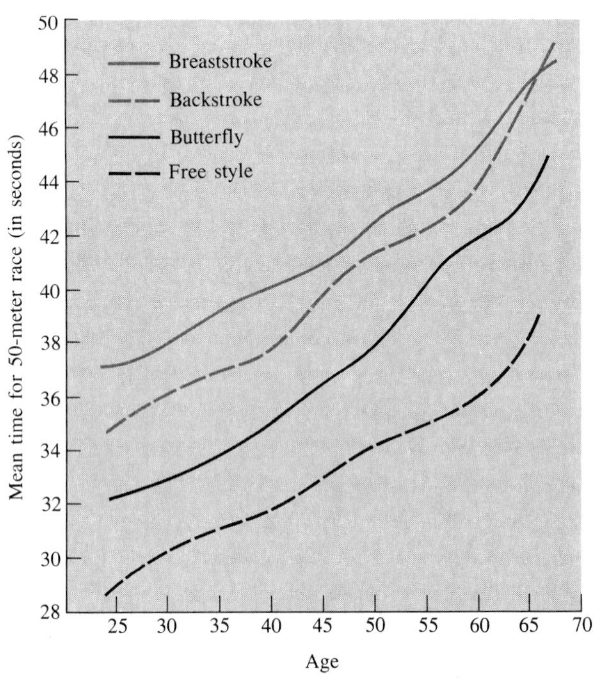

swimmers between 25 and 75 years of age. Both of these figures show a decrease in performance with age. This decrease becomes more rapid, however, when the average performance of swimmers over 60 years of age is examined. Also of interest was the finding that the best performance of the over-65-year-old group equalled the average performance of swimmers about 40 years of age.

The findings of longitudinal studies by Letzelter, Jungeman, and Freitag (1986), and others suggest that athletes can maintain (and sometimes improve) their performance through middle adulthood and late adulthood. This occurs only if adults maintain (or increase) their levels of practice and training. Hagberg (1987) has argued that continued exercise is an important factor in minimizing the losses in *aerobic power* that are usually observed during adulthood. Aerobic power, which refers to the body's maximal ability to take in oxygen, is arguably the best predictor of performance in endurance events (long-distance running, for example).

Changes in training methods are in part responsible for the steady decrease in world record times in running and swimming events over the last hundred years. Table 3.A compares the winning times for several running events in the 1896 Olympics and the best performances of "master" athletes in 1979. As can be seen in table 3.A there are a number of performances by master athletes that surpass the performance of these earlier (and younger) gold medalists—even in the marathon, a distance of twenty-six miles and 385 yards!!

***Table 3.A***

***Winning Times for Olympic Gold Medalists in 1896 and Best Times for Master Athletes in 1979***

| *Event* | *Olympic Gold Medalists in 1896* | *Master Athletes in Different Age Groups in 1979* | | | |
|---|---|---|---|---|---|
| | | *50–54* | *55–59* | *60–64* | *65–69* |
| 100 m * | 12.0 | 11.4 | 11.6 | 12.0 | 13.2 |
| 200 m * | 22.2 | 23.6 | 23.6 | 24.9 | 27.9 |
| 400 m * | 54.2 | 52.9 | 54.6 | 59.1 | 65.1 |
| 800 m ** | 2:11 | 2:01 | 2:11 | 2:20 | 2:27 |
| 1,500 m ** | 4:33 | 4:14 | 4:20 | 4:53 | 4:59 |
| Marathon *** | 2:59 | 2:25 | 2:26 | 2:47 | 2:53 |

* *event timed in seconds*

** *event timed in minutes and seconds*

*** *event timed in hours and minutes*

*Source: Data from K. A. Ericsson, "Peak Performance and Age. An Examination of Peak Performance in Sports" in* Successful Aging: Perspectives from the Behavioral Sciences, *P. B. Baltes and M. M. Baltes (eds), Cambridge University Press, New York, NY.*

## Summary

A number of biological theories of aging have been proposed, several of which stress the role of genetic mechanisms. There is considerable controversy about the biological causes of aging. Scientists argue as to whether the processes that control aging reside in the cells of our body, in the biochemical nature of genes, or at a more macrobiological level.

Most people reach their peak health in early adulthood. However, because young adults can bounce back readily from physical abuse of their bodies, it is easy for them to ignore bad health habits. Health becomes a major concern in middle adulthood. Heart disease, cancer, and obesity are the greatest health concerns of middle-aged adults. A pattern of emotional stability and controlled response to stress is associated with good health at midlife. Coronary disease is influenced by many factors, including diet, smoking, obesity, and genetic predisposition. There is reason to believe that individuals who display Type A behavioral styles are more likely to develop coronary problems than those without these behavioral tendencies. At some point in late adulthood, biological deterioration is inevitable. The age and rate of decline varies considerably from one individual to another. There are large individual differences in how adults cope with disease. Effective coping strategies involve optimism, mastery, and self-enhancement.

The human brain has three major components: the brain stem (including the cerebellum), the limbic system, and the cerebrum. The hippocampus, a structure within the limbic system, seems to be involved in the process of remembering and storing information. The cortex, the top covering of the cerebrum, is responsible for all higher-order psychological functioning. The cortex may undergo widespread or localized damage in aged individuals.

The brain is composed of specialized cells called neurons. Neurons communicate by releasing special chemical substances called neurotransmitters. It is generally agreed that we lose a large number of neurons as we grow old, but there are few precise conclusions about the psychological effects of neuronal loss. With increasing age comes an increase in the amount of lipofuscin, the number of granular particles, and the number of neurofibrillary tangles inside the neurons. Senile plaques have also been found to increase in the synaptic area between neurons.

It is possible to observe the brain in a noninvasive manner by the use of the CT scan, PET scan, or MRI. The electroencephalogram (EEG) has been used to measure the electrical output of the brain in general, and the cortex in particular. The alpha rhythm, as measured by the EEG, begins to slow as we approach older adulthood. Some psychologists have linked the slowing of alpha activity to the generalized pattern of psychomotor slowing. The delta rhythm also changes with age. Alterations in delta activity have been linked to changes in sleep patterns and sleep satisfaction among the elderly. Age-related changes in evoked brain potentials are also of interest to gerontologists. Of particular importance is the latency of the P300 brain wave.

The term **sensorimotor development** refers to the sensory systems that input information from the environment and the motor systems that enable us to perform physical actions in the environment. Vision and hearing are the two most important sensory systems in adulthood. Visual decline in late adulthood is characteristic of most individuals and can be traced to physiological changes in the visual system, including changes that limit the quality and intensity of light reaching the retina. It is important to make a distinction between visual acuity and contrast sensitivity. With increasing age, important changes take place in both contrast sensitivity and visual acuity.

Hearing usually reaches its peak in adolescence and remains reasonably stable during early adulthood, but in middle adulthood it may start to decline. Less than 20 percent of individuals between 45 and 54 years of age have a hearing problem, but for those between 75 and 79, the figure rises to 75 percent. We also become less sensitive to taste, smell, and pain as we grow older.

Motor skills usually peak during young adulthood. One of the most common measures of motor performance is reaction time. Many studies have shown that reaction time becomes gradually slower as we approach older adulthood. Decrements in reaction time may have potentially significant effects on the ability of older adults to function effectively in our complex, modern society. Experts disagree over the extent to which age-related psychomotor slowing is due to the deterioration of central rather than peripheral processes. With practice and exercise, physical abilities—even demanding physical sports—may be maintained at high levels throughout adulthood.

## Review Questions

1. Discuss the different biological theories of aging. Why is the wear-and-tear theory of aging the least acceptable? What does biological aging have to do with "senescence"?
2. Explain the differences between the following pairs of terms: "normal aging and successful aging"; "primary aging and secondary aging."
3. Describe some of the changes in physical appearance that accompany the aging process.
4. What is the biggest threat to good health in early, middle, and late adulthood?
5. How do lifestyle and coping style influence the incidence and progression of physical illness?
6. Discuss the development of sensory systems during the adult years, focusing especially on vision and hearing.
7. Explain the difference between visual acuity and contrast sensitivity.
8. Describe the changes that take place in motor performance during adulthood. What is the significance of these changes? Are these changes more likely to be related to central or peripheral processes?
9. What are the major changes that take place at the neuronal level as we age?
10. Describe the age-related changes in the electrical activity of the brain. How do these changes in brain activity influence the behavioral abilities and sleep patterns of older adults?
11. Discuss the factors that are responsible for peak athletic performance during adulthood.

## For Further Reading


Finch, C. E. (1990). *Longevity, senescence, and genome.* Chicago: University of Chicago Press.

Fries, J. F., & Crapo, L. M. (1981). *Vitality and aging.* San Francisco: Freeman.

Rose, M. R. (1990). *Evolutionary biology of aging.* New York: Oxford University Press.

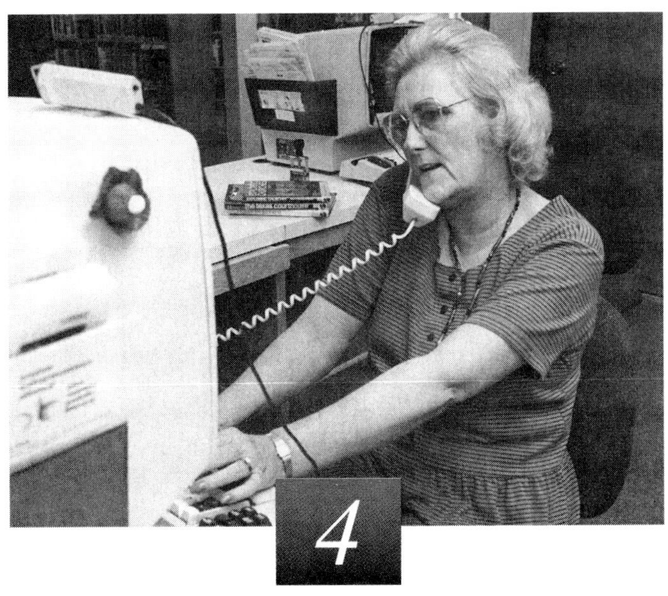

4

# Information Processing
## Perception, Attention, and Memory

*The questions which belong to different domains of thought, differ very often not only in the kinds of subject matter that they are about, but in the kinds of thinking that they require.*
—G. Ryle, *Dilemmas*

## *Introduction*

In chapter 3, we learned that there are age-related declines in the sensory processes that are responsible for the reception of information in the environment. Aging of the sensory mechanisms that respond to light, sound, vibration, and other types of stimulus energy in the environment produces *signal limitations* that affect our ability to understand a conversation, to recognize a friend in a crowd, or to remember an event that we experienced. In this chapter, we focus on age-related limitations in perception, attention, and memory. We describe what is known about age-related changes in the ability to perceive, select, and remember information.

## *The Study of Cognitive Aging*

*Cognition* refers to the collection of processes that serves to transform, organize, select, retain, and interpret information. The study of normal age-related changes in cognition is one of the most active areas of research in the psychology of adult development and aging.

In everyday situations, adults, especially older adults, may experience some difficulties with some aspects of cognition, such as memory retrieval problems, whereas other aspects of remembering may be entirely unaffected by aging. Probably the most important point to keep in mind as you read this chapter is that some aspects of cognition are unaffected by aging while other aspects of cognition show decline with aging.

### What Is Information Processing?

In this chapter, we consider the effects of aging on various aspects of information processing, from pickup to knowledge use. Many cognitive-aging researchers use an **information-processing approach** as a way to investigate the aspects of cognitive functioning that are age-sensitive, and to identify aspects of cognition that are unaffected by aging. From an information-processing perspective, researchers are interested in the extent to which there are individual differences and age-related intraindividual changes on tasks that are presumed to be components of complex cognition. Some of the kinds of information-processing tasks that reveal age

*Have you ever had difficulty remembering where you parked your car at the mall? As we get older, we pay more attention to* encoding *such things as where we park as a way of avoiding memory failures.*

differences, and some that reveal no differences, are shown in figure 4.1. Older adults are slower at perceptual identification and at finding or localizing information in complex visual tasks (e.g., Plude & Hoyer, 1985), and at mental rotation (Berg, Hertzog, & Hunt, 1982; Cerella, Poon, & Fozard, 1981; Salthouse, Mitchell, & Palmon, 1989). In contrast, young adults and older adults frequently do not perform differently on measures of simple numerical calculation and verbal fluency or vocabulary (e.g., Schaie & Willis, 1993).

## *Perception and Aging*

**Perception** refers to the ability to detect structures and events in the environment. In contrast to the sensory processes that are associated with the reception and transmission of information, perception involves the organization and interpretation of information. Many aspects of perception undergo decline as people grow older. For example, with aging, there are declines in the ability to detect figures or forms embedded in complex patterns (Capitani, Della Sala, Lucchelli, Soave, & Spinnler, 1988), and there are declines in the ability to recognize objects that are fragmented or incomplete (Frazier & Hoyer, 1992; Salthouse & Prill, 1988). It has also been reported that older adults are less able to change perceptual set when shown ambiguous figures (Korchin & Basowitz, 1956), and that older adults detect fewer reversals

**Figure 4.1**
Frequently, younger and older adults perform differently on the kinds of information processing tasks shown here. Research suggests that these relatively simple tasks represent basic components of cognitive function. Individuals who perform well on particular measures usually perform well on complex cognitive tasks that involve those basic components (Hoyer, 1985). In studies of adult age differences in cognitive performance, differences between groups are tested. Keep in mind that there is overlap in the distributions of the scores for different age groups. In other words, although studies report that there are group differences between younger and older adults, there are large individual differences in the patterns of performance within the age groups.

1. Younger adults perform better than older adults on tasks that require the rapid **identification** of visual information or that require simple matching or **perceptual comparison** of visual items. One measure of perceptual speed used in research studies requires subjects to match the item shown on the far left with its exact twin, as shown below:

2. Younger adults perform better than older adults on tasks that require **localization** of an object in an array (Plude & Hoyer, 1986). An example is shown below:

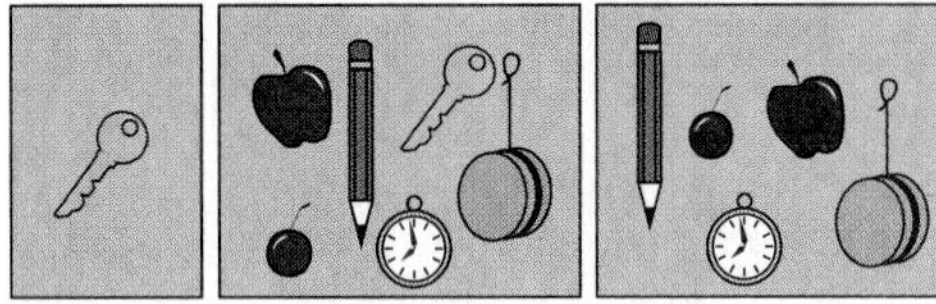

3. Younger adults outperform older adults on tasks that require finding a simple shape that is hidden within a complex display (Capitani, Della Sala, Lucchelli, Soave, & Spinnler, 1990). An example of a hidden figure problem is shown below:

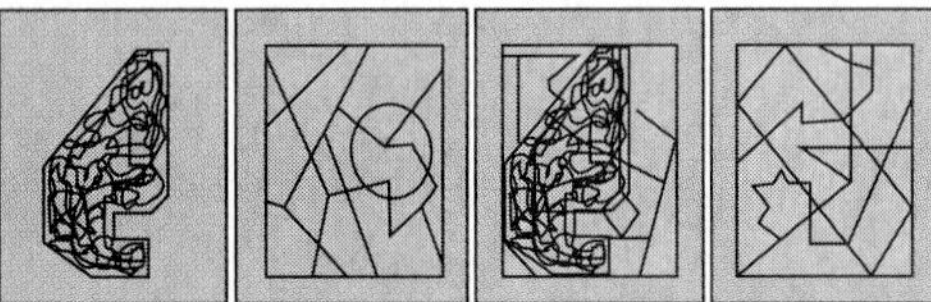

4. Age differences are small or non-existent on measures of **ideational fluency** and **verbal fluency** (Horn, 1970). Ideational fluency is measured by asking individuals to list objects that are the same color, or that have the same purpose or function (e.g., tools, modes of transportation). Verbal fluency is measured by asking individuals to list words that begin with the same letter (e.g., say as many words as you can that begin with the letter, B).

B_ _ _ Bait, Boat, Bake, Bark, Buck, Bent, . . .

5. Although there are large differences between young and older adults on complex computational tasks (Allen, 1992; Charness & Campbell, 1988), frequently it is reported that age differences are small or nonexistent on simple mathematical calculation tasks (e.g., Schaie, 1993). Examples of relatively complex computational problems that would probably yield an age difference favoring young adults in terms of speed of performance are shown below:

77 $14 \times 4 - 16 + 37 = ?$
219 $3(13 + 5) + 28 - 4 = ?$

6. Young adults tend to perform better than older adults on spatial tasks that require mental rotation of an object in space. An example of a mental rotation task is illustrated below:

(a)

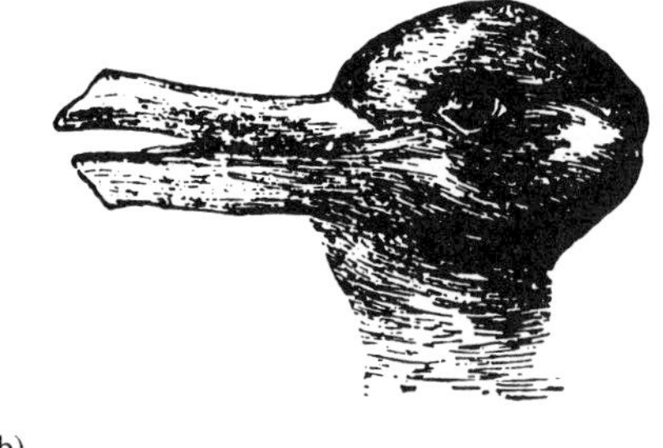

(b)

(c)

(d)

**Figure 4.2**
Ambiguous or "reversible" figures and incomplete figures. In (a)–(d), at least two scenes can arise from the same sensory pattern.
(a) This person can either be seen as a beautiful young woman or an unattractive old one.
(b) Is this figure a rabbit or a duck?
(c) The Necker Cube. Stare at the interior corner that you think is nearest to you, and you will suddenly discover that it has become the farthest corner. The cube spontaneously reverses in depth.
(d) Viewed up close, this scene reveals to most people a woman examining herself in the mirror; at a distance, the same scene reveals a skull.

while looking at a Necker cube (Heath & Orbach, 1963). Examples of these kinds of perceptual tasks are shown in the panels of figure 4.2.

That there are differences between young and elderly adults on a variety of perceptual tasks is not surprising (Fozard, 1990). Cognitive-aging researchers are mainly interested in trying to understand the mechanisms that account for age-related changes in perception. Specifically, there is considerable interest in determining the extent to which perceptual aging is due to biological and experiential phenomena. Researchers are also very interested in the computational aspects of perceptual aging, and in the effects of age-related slowing of the rate of information processing on complex cognitive performance. We now consider these topics.

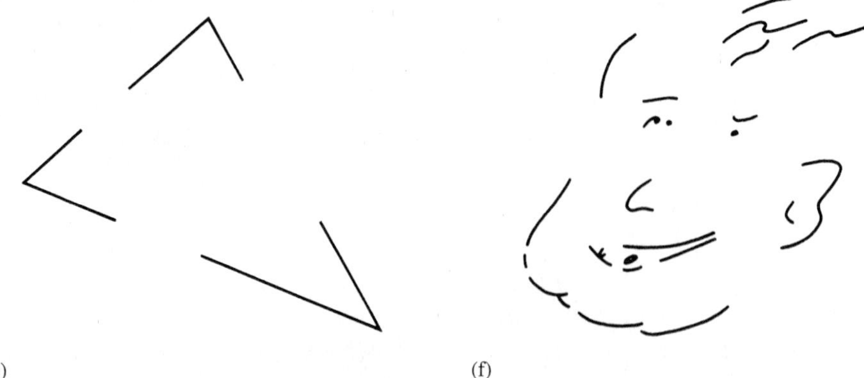

**Figure 4.2**
Continued
(e) & (f) Incomplete figures. Older adults find it more difficult to identify the content of such drawings. They also have difficulty reversing ambiguous figures once they have formed a perception.

(e) (f)

## Perception and Experience

One way of examining the causes of age-related changes in perception is to investigate the effects of practice and experience on age differences in perceptual performance. If the age differences that are observed in perception are due to irreversible deficits in the neural mechanisms responsible for information processing, then it would be unlikely or impossible that age differences in performance could be eliminated through practice. Baltes (1993) has suggested that much can be learned by "testing the limits" of performance by exposing individuals to training and other conditions that are likely to optimize performance. Baltes and his colleagues have demonstrated that training is effective in reducing age-related deficits in memory and intelligence. Salthouse and Somberg (1982) examined the effects of extensive practice on adult age differences in visual-detection performance. In the Salthouse and Somberg study, young and older adults were required to detect movement in patterns of dots that were presented for 250 milliseconds. As can be seen in figure 4.3, Salthouse and Somberg found that the performance of both age groups improved with practice. With training, older adults performed better than untrained younger adults, but the performance difference between young and elderly adults did not disappear with practice. Salthouse and Somberg concluded that older adults go through essentially the same processing operations as young adults but at a slower rate. They attributed this reduced rate of processing to physiological changes in the nervous system.

## Perception as Computation

Generally, age differences in perceptual processing increase as the task becomes more complex in terms of *computational demands* (Mayr & Kliegl, 1993). For example, age differences are typically found on mental arithmetic tasks and other tasks that require individuals to carry out mental calculations of some sort (Charness & Campbell, 1988). In the Charness and Campbell study, young, middle-aged, and

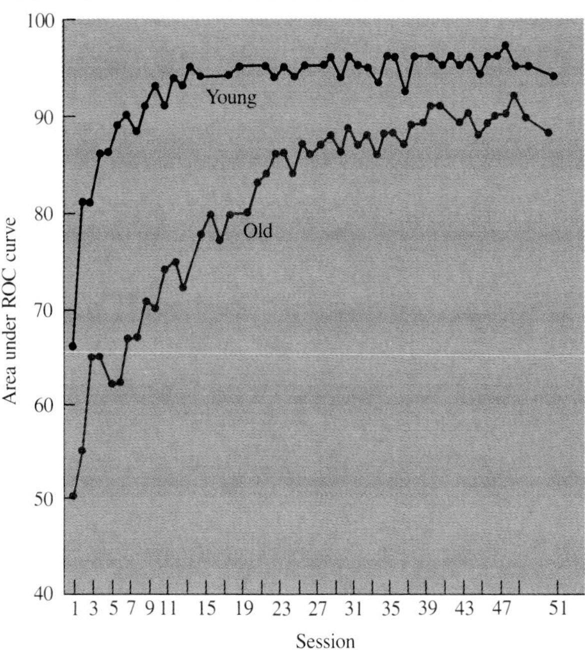


**Figure 4.3** Mean signal-detection performance for young and old adults as a function of extended practice
*From: Salthouse & Somberg, 1982.*

older adults practiced an instructed algorithm for squaring two-digit numbers. After training, older adults performed as accurately as younger adults, but slower. The performance of the middle-aged participants resembled that of the old group initially, but resembled the performance of the young group after practice.

One of the newest ways to investigate aging of the computational aspects of perception and information processing has to do with application of neural network models (Cerella, 1990; Hannon & Hoyer, 1994; Salthouse, 1988). Computer models can be designed to emulate brain networks and to represent alterations in brain networks brought about by aging.

## Rate of Information Processing

It is well established that the rate of visual information processing slows with age (Birren, 1965; Cerella, 1990; Salthouse, 1985). Many kinds of information-processing deficits that occur with aging can be simply attributed to reductions in the speed of processing, and some researchers have gone so far as to attribute practically all of the differences in cognitive performance to age-related slowing of the rate of information processing. If each step in an information-processing task is slower with aging by some constant amount, then overall performance on a complex task can be described in terms of general age-related slowing. However, researchers still need to determine more precisely the mechanisms and locus of perceptual differences between young and elderly adults (Hoyer & Hannon, 1993; Johnson & Rybash, 1993). Is age-related cognitive slowing caused by slowing of neural mechanisms?

## *Attention and Aging*

**Attention** has been defined as the capacity or energy to support cognitive processing (Plude & Hoyer, 1985). This definition suggests that there is a limited amount of capacity to support information processing, and that there are age-related changes in the amount or availability of attentional resources (e.g., Hartley, 1992). In general usage, the term attention refers to a variety of processes, including arousal and alertness, the processes associated with information selection, and the ability to handle multiple sources of information.

### Selective Attention

The two aspects of attention that seem most affected by aging are selective attention and divided attention (Madden & Plude, 1993; McDowd & Birren, 1990). **Selective attention** refers to the ability to distinguish relevant from irrelevant information. For example, selective attention abilities are used when we are trying to concentrate on something we are reading while at the same time trying to ignore information that is irrelevant or interfering such as loud or unpleasant music. In many studies, it has been found that there are age-related declines in the ability to attend to relevant information while trying to ignore distracting information (Connelly & Hasher, 1993; Hasher, Stoltzfus, Zacks, & Rypma, 1991; Kotary & Hoyer, 1995; Plude & Hoyer, 1986; Tipper, 1991).

Our ability to ignore or inhibit irrelevant information affects our performance in many kinds of tasks. One of the primary hypotheses in cognitive aging is that age decrements in inhibitory processes can account for many aspects of aging and cognitive functioning (e.g., Hartley, 1992; Hasher & Zacks, 1988; McDowd, Oseas-Kreger, & Filion, 1994).

It has also been reported that there are age-related declines in divided attention (Madden & Plude, 1993; McDowd & Birren, 1990). **Divided attention** deficits are evident when there are problems in processing all of the important information that is available in a situation. Generally, when we have to do two or more tasks at once, our performance on each of the tasks suffers; for example, when it might be difficult to track two conversations at the same time, or to concentrate on what we are reading while also listening to an interesting conversation.

In the laboratory, researchers frequently use *visual search* tasks to study age-related differences in the factors that affect selective attention. In a visual search task, the subject decides if the target item is present in displays containing different numbers of distractor items. Typically, older adults are more affected by distractor information than are younger adults (Madden & Plude, 1993). It has also been reported that older adults are at a disadvantage when the target can appear anywhere in the display to be searched, and the task is to find or localize the target (Plude & Hoyer, 1986). Age differences are smaller or nonexistent in *filtering* tasks, in which the target item is always in the same location, and the subject's task is to identify the item in the presence or absence of distractor information (Farkas & Hoyer, 1980; Wright & Elias, 1979).

*Complex everyday tasks require divided attention. Age-related declines in divided attention performance have been attributed to a number of factors, including limited processing resources, an additive increase in task complexity, and the costs of having to switch attention from one task to another.*

## Divided Attention

Divided-attention tasks require simultaneous processing of two or more sources of information. For example, driving a car in heavy traffic while looking for a specific road sign is an example of a real-life divided-attention task (Ponds, Brouwer, & Van Wolffelaar, 1988). Although it is frequently reported that there are age-related deficits in divided attention (e.g., Hartley, 1992; McDowd & Craik, 1988), older adults are not any worse than younger adults in relatively simple divided-attention situations (McDowd & Birren, 1990) or when initial age differences in nondivided attention are taken into account (Salthouse & Somberg, 1982). One way of assessing possible age differences in divided attention is to measure performance differences under single-task and **dual-task** conditions. Somberg and Salthouse devised a dual-task experiment in which **single-task performance** was controlled. In this experiment, participants were asked to view a computer monitor. On each trial, a pattern consisting of four *X* symbols (forming a rectangle) and four + symbols (forming a smaller rectangle) were presented for less than a second. The participants' task was to judge whether one of the four *X*s contained a target (a small vertical or horizontal line extending from one of the *X*s) and also to judge whether one of the four + signs contained a target (a small diagonal line extending from one of them). Since the *X*s and + signs were presented simultaneously, the participants' task was one of divided attention.

Somberg and Salthouse controlled for initial differences in single-task performance by using a measure of performance under single-task conditions (with *X*s only and with + signs only) to adjust the duration of the displays for each participant. Specifically, the duration of the displays was matched to the exposure time under which each participant responded correctly between 80 and 90 percent of the time under single-task conditions. Second, the investigators systematically varied the resource allocation strategies by providing financial rewards for accurate performance and by giving varying rewards in different conditions (e.g., rewarding more for the *X* task than for the + task or vice versa, or by making rewards equal for the *X* and the + tasks).

The results of the experiment were straightforward. Both age groups showed lower performance under dual-task (divided-attention) conditions than under single-task conditions. Of greater importance, however, was that the authors found *no* evidence that elderly participants performed disproportionally poorer in the dual-task condition than younger individuals. Further, both age groups were able to allocate attention in accordance with task rewards.

Wickens, Braune, and Stokes (1987) also reported that there were no age differences in divided-attention performance. Participants ranging from 20 to 65 years of age performed a perceptual motor task either alone or concurrently with a memory-search task. In memory search, subjects are asked to decide if a visual display contains a previously presented item. When both types of tasks were performed separately, results indicated that older participants took longer to perform the memory-search task, and they made more errors on the perceptual-motor task. When both tasks were performed concurrently (a divided-attention task), older participants displayed a greater decrement in performance on both tasks than the younger participants. Following Somberg and Salthouse, when Wickens et al. (1987) took into account age-related differences in single-task performance, older participants did not perform any more poorly than when performing the tasks concurrently. Wickens et al. (1987) concluded that although information-processing speed significantly decreases with age, the ability to divide attention does not change with age.

Other researchers (Madden, 1986; McDowd & Craik, 1988), using methodologies different from both Somberg and Salthouse (1982) and Wickens et al. (1987), have obtained evidence suggesting an age-related decrease in divided attention. Specifically, McDowd and Craik (1988) found that age-related differences in divided attention emerge when complex tasks are given to participants, but age-related decrements are negligible when simple and relatively automatic tasks (such as those employed by Somberg and Salthouse) are used. In fact, McDowd and Craik suggested that overall task complexity, rather than the requirement to divide attention per se, may account for age-related performance decrements on divided-attention tasks.

## Limited Attentional Resources

Age-related differences in attention have been described in terms of limitations in *general-purpose processing resources.* Although several kinds of evidence suggest that there are age-related limitations in processing resources, researchers must be careful to avoid circular explanations of aging phenomena. That is, age differences should *not* be attributed to a decline in some resource or capacity that cannot be measured. Perhaps the strongest evidence to suggest an age-related decline in processing resources comes from comparisons between **effortful information processing,** which is thought to draw on limited attentional capacity, and **automatic information processing,** which presumably does not draw on limited attentional capacity. In a study by Plude and Hoyer (1981), young and elderly women searched for two or four target letters in computer displays composed of one-, four-, or nine-letter arrays. Half of the women in each age group were placed in a *varied-mapping condition;* they looked for different target letters on different trials. The remaining women were included in a *consistent-mapping condition;* they looked for the same letters on all trials. There is good evidence that practice on the consistent-mapping procedure results in automatic processing, or processing that is independent of other demands on limited attentional capacity. Interestingly, Plude and Hoyer found only very small age-related differences in the consistent-mapping condition. In contrast, the varied-mapping condition, which demanded effortful processing, produced a large deficit in the elderly participants. The results support the contention that there are age-related differences in effortful processing, but not in automatic processing (see also Fisk & Rogers, 1991; Plude, Kaye, Hoyer, Post, Saynisch, & Hahn, 1983).

## *Memory and Aging*

The clearest observation to make about memory aging is that there are age-related declines on some kinds of memory tasks and no age-related declines on other kinds of memory tasks. Many different kinds of tests are used to assess memory, and the extent to which age-related changes in memory are observed depends on the type of memory task, and the type of materials contained in the task (Bowles, 1993; Craik & Jennings, 1992; Hultsch & Dixon, 1990; Light, 1991). Some researchers have interpreted these patterns of intraindividual differences across tasks as evidence that there are several distinct types of memory (Mitchell, 1989; Schacter, Kihlstrom, Kaszniak, & Valdiserri, 1993; Tulving, 1993). Other researchers maintain that there is really only one memory system, and that intraindividual differences in performance across tasks are attributable to differences in task demands and processing strategies (e.g., Roediger, Weldon, & Challis, 1989). We have organized our discussion of memory aging in terms of what is known about the effects of aging on different types of memory.

## *Age Differences in Functional Memory Systems*

### Semantic Memory and Episodic Memory

Memory researchers are interested in investigating memory performance on different kinds of memory tasks as a way of understanding the operations and functions of memory. For example, Tulving (1993) and others have suggested that different types of memory are involved when we are trying to remember knowledge in the broadest sense and when we are trying to remember the specific details of a particular event or episode that we experienced. **Semantic memory** refers to acquired knowledge about the world. We use semantic memory when we think about the meanings of concepts without reference to when or how we acquired such knowledge (Chiarello, 1994). **Episodic memory** refers to memory for the details of personally experienced events. For example, we might have retained an understanding of how to play a card game that we learned in childhood, even though we have no episodic recollection of when or how we learned the game. Generally, older adults exhibit preserved semantic memory, even though there are substantial age-related declines in episodic memory (Bächman, Mantyla, & Herlitz, 1990).

Tulving and his colleagues (Tulving & Schacter, 1990) have also suggested that there are functionally distinct systems for *procedural memory, perceptual representation,* and *short-term memory.* Even though these systems might interact when we are carrying out memory tasks in everyday life, there is good evidence to suggest that these types of memory serve particular functions. Procedural memory refers to knowing how to do something and is measured by observing a person carry out the procedures of a task. Individuals (e.g., amnesiacs) can show procedural memory, even in the absence of *declarative* memory regarding the procedure. Generally, there are no age differences in procedural memory, and there are age-related differences in the declarative aspects of the memory (Hultsch & Dixon, 1990). The perceptual representation system, which refers to knowledge of the perceptual structure and characteristics of objects in the world, is probably unaffected by aging (Schacter et al., 1993). Finally, short-term memory span, or the ability to hold a number of items in consciousness for a brief period of time, is also unaffected by aging, as discussed in the next section.

Thus, some types of memory or memory systems are more affected by aging than others. There are different age trends depending on whether we are measuring episodic or semantic memory, and there are negligible declines or no age differences in procedural memory, perceptual representation, and simple short-term memory.

### Short-Term Memory Span and Working Memory

Although age-related differences seldom appear on simple measures of short-term memory such as digit-span (Craik, 1977), it is frequently reported that there are age-related declines in short-term working memory and when individuals are required to actively search through the contents of short-term memory (Craik & Jennings, 1992).

*TABLE 4.1*

| *Memory Span for Letters Presented Auditorily* | | | | | | |
|---|---|---|---|---|---|---|
| | *Age (Years)* | | | | | |
| | *20s* | *30s* | *40s* | *50s* | *60s* | *70s* |
| *Span* | *6.7* | *6.2* | *6.5* | *6.5* | *5.5* | *5.4* |

*From Jack Botwinick and Martha Storandt,* Memory-Related Functions and Age, *1974. Courtesy of Charles C. Thomas, Publisher, Springfield, Illinois.*

Consider the findings of Botwinick and Storandt's (1974) study of age differences in memory span for letters. These results are shown in table 4.1. The measure of short-term memory span was the number of items a person could repeat in order without error. Note that memory span was only about one letter shorter for 70-year-olds than for 20-year-olds.

In contrast to the results of simple tests of memory span, it should be noted that age differences are evident on other more complicated span measures, such as backward span, which requires the person to recall the items that were presented in the reverse order (Craik, 1977).

***Age Differences in Working Memory*** **Working memory** refers to the processes and structures involved in simultaneously holding information and using that information. Frequently, working memory tasks involve manipulating the contents of short-term memory or combining information held in mind with new or incoming information. Complex mental multiplication is an example of working memory. Working-memory tasks generally require the individual to mentally carry out some operation while also keeping in mind or storing other information.

Dobbs and Rule (1990) presented individuals in five age groups (in their thirties, forties, fifties, sixties, and over seventy) with a standard memory-span task and a working-memory task. In the latter, participants heard a list of randomly ordered digits at a rate of one digit every 1.8 seconds. After the presentation of each digit, participants were required to repeat (1) the digit they just heard, (2) the digit prior to the one they just heard, or (3) the digit two prior to the one they just heard. Results showed that performance on the standard memory-span task was related to the participant's education level but *not* to age level. Importantly, the age of the participant was related to performance on the working-memory task. Specifically, subjects over 60 years of age performed poorly on this task. Dobbs and Rule concluded that aging has a pronounced effect on the ability to manipulate processing and a lesser or negligible effect on the passive (storage) aspects of memory.

***Age Differences in Memory Search*** Compared with young adults, older adults are slower in searching or scanning short-term memory (e.g., Fisk & Rogers, 1991). Saul Sternberg (1969) developed an ingenious procedure for measuring search speed, which has been used to test elderly individuals. In this procedure, people are

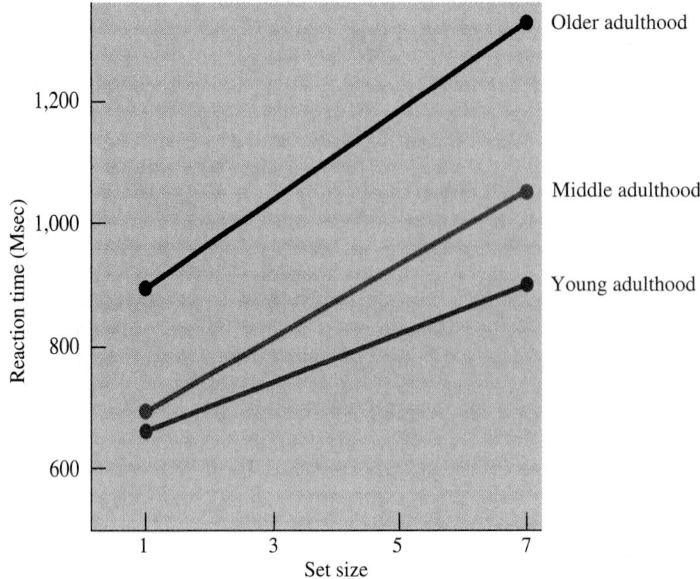


**Figure 4.4** Mean reaction times as a function of age and set size.

presented with a set of items (usually digits, such as 6, 3, and 9) to hold in memory. Then they are presented another digit (e.g., 9). The subject's task is to decide whether the digit matches one of the digits in the memory set. Memory sets of varying lengths are used, and as might be expected, reaction times increase (answers are given more slowly) as the length of the memory set increases. Figure 4.4 shows the results from one study (Anders, Fozard, & Lillyquist, 1972) that compared the speed of short-term memory search for individuals in early, middle, and late adulthood. Note that longer memory sets produced longer reaction times. Note also that the slope (i.e., the steepness or the angle) of the reaction-time curve is greater for individuals in middle and late adulthood than for those in early adulthood. This difference in slope indicates that the two older adult groups scan through lists of items in short-term memory at a slower pace than younger adults.

***Age Differences in Spatial Processing*** *Visual-spatial processing* in short-term memory also slows in older people (Cerella, 1985; Cerella, Poon, & Fozard, 1981; Hoyer & Rybash, 1992b). In Cerella's studies, younger and older adults were shown a capital letter at different degrees of tilt. Sometimes the letter was in the normal plane and sometimes the letter was reversed from left to right (reflected). The task was to decide as quickly as possible whether each letter was normal or reflected. Judgments were made by pressing one of two response keys. The latencies, or how long it takes to make these responses, were longer as the degree of tilt increased. This effect of tilt on latency indicated that adults must mentally rotate the tilted letters to upright before making their judgment (see figure 4.5).

Cerella et al. (1981) examined age-related differences in the speed of **mental rotation.** The results of this study are shown in figure 4.6. Note that the latencies

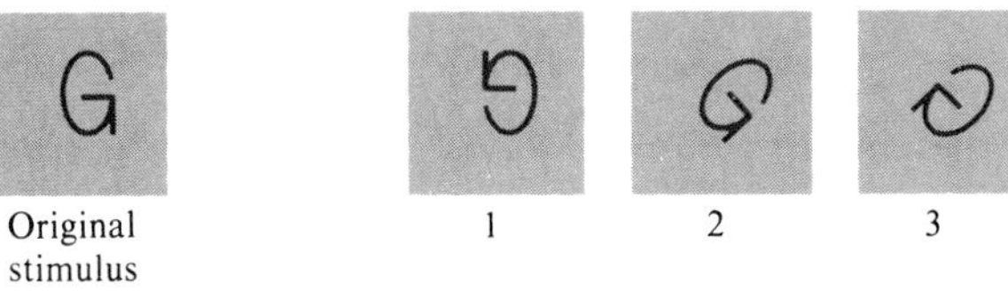


**Figure 4.5** Examples of the stimuli employed in an imagery task examining mental rotation.

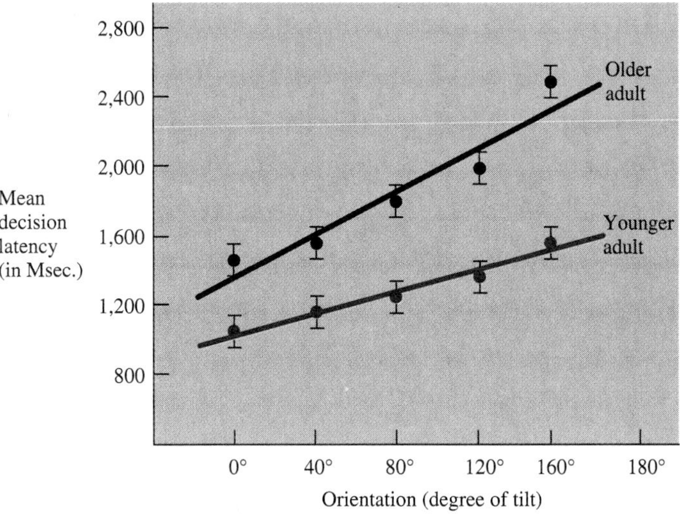


**Figure 4.6** Mean decision latency for young and old adults as a function of stimulus orientation.

grow longer with greater departures from vertical orientation; this supports the idea that response time is a measure of the amount of mental rotation required. Note also that the slope or steepness of the line relating orientation to latency was greater for older adults. This pattern suggests that the process of mental rotation is slower in older adults than younger adults. A more recent study conducted by Sharps and Gollin (1987) also found that the speed of mental rotation declined with age.

Part of the age difference in memory search can be eliminated with practice. The study by Salthouse and Somberg (1982), discussed earlier, examined a memory-search performance over fifty sessions. After forty sessions, the slope of the function relating reaction time and memory-set size was comparable for young and elderly adults.

## Long-term Memory

Tests that require **long-term memory** (typically more than 60 seconds) or the remembrance of events that have left consciousness often show age-related declines. (See Research Focus 4.1.) Long-term memory can be assessed using a variety of measures, including **free recall,** *cued recall,* or *recognition.* In a free-recall task, a list of items—usually common words—is presented to adults, who then attempt to

## Differences Between Short-Term and Long-Term Memory

Many years ago, the famous psychologist William James (1890) distinguished between *primary memory* and *secondary memory.* James identified primary memory with conscious awareness of recently perceived events and secondary memory with the recall of events that have left consciousness. James's distinction was based primarily on his own introspections, but a similar distinction is supported by a great deal of experimental evidence. Today a host of information-processing models incorporate a distinction between primary or **short-term memory,** and secondary or **long-term memory.**

A generalized three-stage model of memory is presented in figure 4.A. The model includes a system of sensory stores in addition to short-term and long-term stores. Note that figure 4.A indicates processes that transfer information from one store to another: transfer from sensory to short-term memory entails attention, and transfer from short-term to **long-term memory** requires rehearsal. Finally, the model hypothesizes different laws of forgetting for the three memory stores. Forgetting from sensory stores is thought to result from the process of simple *decay;* information is lost (within less than a second) simply as a function of time. Forgetting from short-term memory generally results from *displacement;* new information bumps out old information. Finally, forgetting from long-term memory results from *interference* that occurs between memory for one piece of information and other information learned previously or subsequently. Indeed, many investigators believe that interference does not destroy information in long-term memory but simply impairs the *retrievability* of information from long-term memory.

**Box Figure 4.A** A generalized three-stage model of memory.

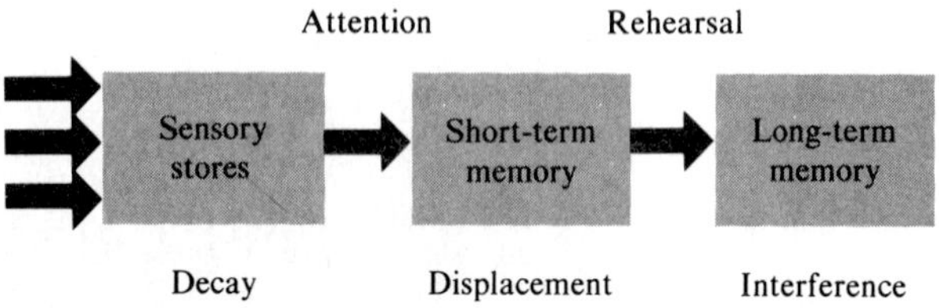

Several psychologists are examining the manner by which information is transferred from short- to long-term memory. Today it is recognized that simple rote rehearsal is not the only path, or even a very efficient path, to learning and remembering. Processes of organization, semantic elaboration, and imagery can be highly effective for enhancing long-term memory.

remember as many items as possible in any order. Results of an experiment by Schonfield and Robertson (1966) are shown in figure 4.7. The lower line shows that there is an age-related decline for long-term free recall, but the recall span or capacity of short-term memory is relatively unimpaired by aging.

Although age-related differences are common in long-term memory, the magnitude of these differences—indeed, their very existence—depends on the nature of the information-processing strategies individuals use. Three types of encoding processes appear especially important: organization, semantic elaboration, and mental imagery. Research suggests that all three processes—the characteristics of which are summarized in table 4.2—might be less efficient or less likely to occur in old age. This research also suggests that with appropriate techniques, older adults can overcome or at least reduce this deficiency.

Effective **organization** of information to be remembered is an aid to memory, especially for older adults (Bäckman et al., 1990; Hultsch, 1971). Hultsch compared the recall performance of young adults, middle-aged adults, and older adults. Subjects were given instructions to sort or organize the material by categories, or were not told to do so. Older adults who were not told to organize the material tended to not do so on their own, and performed worse than the other age groups.

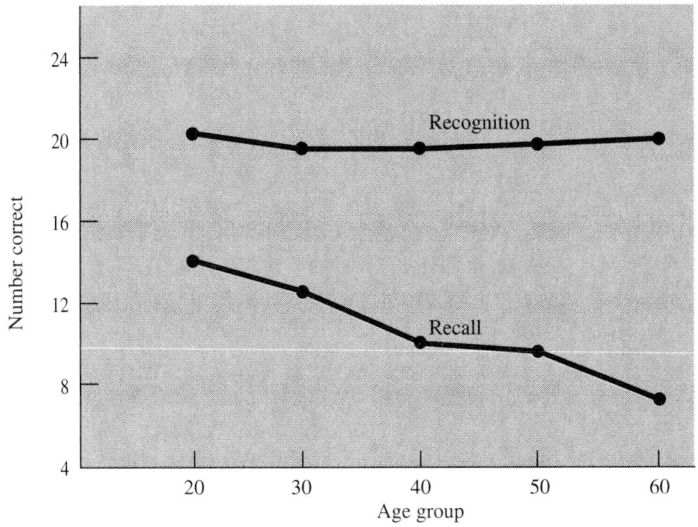

Figure 4.7
Recognition and recall scores as a function of age.

TABLE 4.2

*Characteristics of the Processing Strategies*

| *Process* | *Time of Occurrence in Memory Task* | *Description of Process* |
|---|---|---|
| Organization | Learning the material | The learner actively groups input items together into higher-order units or chunks. For example, in a long list of words, the learner might group together *raisin, apple,* and *pear* and treat them as a single unit (*fruits*). |
| Semantic elaboration | Learning the material | The learner associates presented items with long-term memory representations that give access to the meaning of the items. Semantic elaboration is usually involved in organization as well as imagery, though it might occur without these processes. |
| Imagery | Learning the material | The learner generates a "picture in the head," "tape recording in the head," or other mental image. |

***Note:*** *While there are many different theories of how memory operates, the importance of these and other information-processing activities is widely acknowledged. Thus age-related differences in one or more of these processes would be expected to produce age-related differences in memory. Improving the utilization of these processes in individuals in middle or late adulthood may markedly improve the memory performance of older people. Note also that these processes have been explored primarily in the domain of verbal memory; much less is known about their nature and importance for nonverbal memory (memory for faces, songs, and so forth).*

Hilary Ratner and her colleagues (1987) examined age-related differences in organizational strategies in three groups of women: (1) young adult female college students, (2) young adult female high school graduates not enrolled in college, and (3) retired elderly females not enrolled in college. All of the women were required to learn different types of stories. Half of the women in each of the three groups were told simply to learn the stories; the other half were told to memorize the stories *verbatim.* In a memory test on the stories, the college students performed the best. It was discovered that they studied longer than the other groups and were more likely to use a variety of organizational strategies to help them remember the stories. The researchers did not observe the use of complex organizational strategies in either the young nonstudents or the older adults. Without such spontaneously constructed organizational strategies, memory deficits were likely to occur in both of these groups of women.

Ratner and her associates suggest that the older women (as well as younger women who did not attend college) generally found themselves in nondemanding social environments. These environments did not require them to develop sophisticated strategies to help them organize information. This suggests that memory deficits in older adults may be attributed to environmental circumstances, not age per se. New research by Stine (1990) and Zabrucky and Moore (1994) shows that there are both quantitative and qualitative age differences in reading and comprehending text materials.

**Semantic elaboration** of information has also been found to improve older adults' memories. Smith (1977) required adults to study a list of words under three different conditions. Adults in the *no-cue* condition were shown a list of words (e.g., *apple, yellow, horse, etc.*) and instructed to learn it. Those in the *structural-cue* condition saw each word on the list along with its first letter (*apple—A*). In the *semantic-cue* condition, the participants saw each word on the list along with a category the word belonged to (*apple—fruit*).

In the first two conditions, age-related differences in free recall appeared. The young group (aged 20 to 39) had the best recall, the late adulthood group (aged 60 to 80) showed the poorest recall, and the middle-aged group (aged 40 to 59) was intermediate. However, in the third condition, which involved semantic-category cues, recall was approximately equal in all age groups! These findings suggest that an age-related decline occurs in recall memory, a decline that begins by middle age. But it also appears that this decline can be eliminated by incorporating semantic elaboration of the words to be recalled at the time of study.

Another process that is known to affect long-term memory performance is **imagery.** One study (Mason & Smith, 1977) focused on the recall of individuals in early, middle, and late adulthood. Those in the imagery condition were instructed to form mental images for each word on a list, but those in the control condition were given no instructions to aid recall. Imagery instructions did not affect recall in the early and late adulthood groups but did improve recall in the middle adulthood groups. Indeed, middle-aged adults in the imagery condition performed as well as young adults, though in the control condition they fell below young adults. Again, these results indicate an age-related deficiency in recall memory that can be eliminated through appropriate learning procedures. In this case, however, the learning procedure effective with middle-aged adults was *not* effective with elderly adults.

***Recall versus Recognition*** We previously discussed age-related differences in free recall observed by Schonfield and Robertson (1966; see figure 4.7). Their experiment also included a **recognition test.** The test included previously studied words along with new words; the participants attempted to recognize the former. Performance on this recognition test is shown by the top line in figure 4.7. As the figure shows, there was no evidence of an age-related deficit in recognition. Why are age-related memory deficits attenuated when recognition tests are employed in research? One possibility is that recall tests place a great demand upon effortful search or retrieval from memory. In a recognition test, previously studied items are actually presented to the participant; he or she only has to distinguish these items from distractors that have not been previously studied. This procedure may lessen the need to initiate effortful or controlled search processes. This argument makes sense given the information we have about the dwindling attentional resources available to the elderly.

The interplay among the factors of age, processing requirements at input (encoding), and type of test is complex. When adults receive instructions for processing stimulus materials (e.g., "learn the words"), age-related deficits often appear, regardless of recall versus recognition testing. In contrast, when elderly adults are instructed to process materials in a semantically elaborate manner, age-related differences in memory are less likely to occur—especially when memory is assessed using recognition tests. Perlmutter and Mitchell (1982) concluded that when retrieval support was provided, and encoding operations were directed, age differences seemed to vanish. Their conclusion suggests that the encoding abilities of younger and older adults do not differ. What differs is their *spontaneous* use of complex encoding strategies (Perlmutter & Mitchell, 1982).

***Implicit and Explicit Memory*** A recall task is quite different from a recognition task, but both require *conscious* recollection of previous experiences. In both of these tasks, a person is deliberately trying to remember something experienced in the past. A memory task in which a person is instructed to consciously recollect a previous experience taps **explicit memory** (Schacter, 1987). Tasks that do not require an individual to consciously recollect a past event tap **implicit memory.** On implicit memory tasks, a person is not aware that he or she is remembering something (Schacter, 1987). Recently, there has been considerable interest in the study of developmental changes in forms of memory that do not seem to involve conscious recall or recognition. The findings of these studies suggest a relative preservation of certain types of implicit (or unconscious) memory in old age (Howard, 1991; Light & LaVoie, 1993; Rybash, 1994). Specifically, age deficits are found on measures that directly or explicitly assess recall or recognition of previous information, but not on measures that assess the nonconscious, implicit, or indirect effects of experience on subsequent performance. It should be pointed out that some investigators have found age-related declines using implicit measures (Chiarello & Hoyer, 1988; Davis, Cohen, Gandy, Colombo, VanDusseldorp, Simolke, & Romano, 1990; Hultsch, Masson, & Small, 1991), but the magnitude of the age deficit was less compared with that obtained using explicit measures of memory (see Research Focus 4.2).

### *Research Focus 4.2*

## *Age-Related Differences in Implicit and Explicit Memory*

Age-related differences in long-term memory are more likely to be revealed if memory is measured by a *recall* rather than a *recognition* task. A recall task is quite different from a recognition task but they do share one important characteristic—they both require *conscious* recollection of previous experiences. In both of these tasks, a person is *aware* of the fact that he or she is to remember something experienced in the past. Any memory task in which a person is instructed to consciously recollect (or become aware of) a previous experience is called an explicit memory task (Schacter, 1987).

By contrast, an implicit memory task is one that does not require an individual to consciously recollect a past event. Implicit memory has been referred to as memory without awareness. A person is not aware of the fact that he or she is remembering something while performing an implicit memory task (Schacter, 1987).

The distinction between implicit and explicit memory was first drawn by studying patients suffering from amnesia. In these experiments, participants were given an orienting task in which they were required to make judgments about the words in a list. For example, amnesiacs might see the word *sharp* and then be asked a letter-identification question (Is there an *e* in this word?) or a semantic question (Is this word the opposite of *dull?*). Next, they are given an explicit memory task (involving recognition or recall) as well as an implicit memory task. Implicit memory is typically measured by a *word-stem completion task.* In such a task, an amnesiac is shown a word fragment (that is, they see only some of the letters of a previously encountered word arranged in their correct locations). The participant is then asked to complete the stem with any letters that pop into mind. If the word *sharp* appeared in the first part of the experiment, for example, the participant might later be asked to complete the stem *sha* __ __. The stem-completion task may be given at different time intervals following the initial presentation of the word list (one hour later, one week later, and so on). Results show that profoundly amnesiac patients can remember a substantial number of words on a word-completion (implicit memory) task, yet be incapable of recalling or recognizing any of the words on the original (explicit memory) list. Thus, researchers conclude (e.g., Schacter, 1987), that in amnesia explicit memory is impaired, but implicit memory is spared.

In the late 1980s, two teams of researchers, Christine Chiarello and William Hoyer (1988), and Leah Light and Andrea Singh (1987), examined age-related differences in implicit and explicit memory in healthy, community-dwelling adults. As would be expected, these researchers found that older adults performed significantly more poorly than younger adults on tasks of explicit memory (recall and recognition). Furthermore, they reported that older adults scored lower than young adults on tasks of implicit memory (for example, word-stem completion) than young adults. However, age differences were smaller or nonexistent on the implicit memory task.

---

The evidence for a dissociation between direct and indirect memory measures with healthy adults as well as with amnesic patients has led some researchers to suggest that there are two structurally distinct memory systems (e.g., Moscovitch & Winocur, 1992; Schacter, 1994). From a developmental perspective, one implication of the growing body of research suggesting that memory systems can be experimentally dissociated in normal and neuro-pathological samples is that such measures might help us to understand the mechanisms that underlie observed patterns of age-related gains and losses in memory processes.

***Priming as a Measure of Memory Aging*** Implicit memory is typically measured by *priming tasks* in which subjects are asked to identify, make judgments about, or perform actions upon previously presented stimuli relative to control stimuli. Priming is demonstrated if exposure to stimuli during a study phase results in enhanced performance (e.g., reduced latency of response, or increased accuracy of response) relative to control items during a test phase.

Rybash (1994) identified several types or categories of priming tasks. Tasks of *retrieval-free priming* are those in which a subject must make a simple response to a test stimulus that is exactly the same as the item that was presented in the study phase. For example, during the test phase of a priming experiment, a subject may be shown the word MOTEL and may be instructed to read the stimulus, name the stimulus, or decide if the stimulus represents a valid word. Priming is measured by comparing the speed at which the subject responds to items that appeared on a study list relative to those that did not. Performance on tasks of retrieval-free priming seems to depend on presemantic representations of words and objects that are processed by posterior brain sites.

Tasks of *retrieval-dependent priming* are those in which a subject must use a portion of a stimulus as a retrieval cue to re-create the holistic form of that stimulus. Tasks of retrieval-dependent priming, such as "word stem completion," make pronounced retrieval demands upon a subject. For example, a subject must make a deliberate attempt to retrieve items from semantic memory (MOT*EL,* MOT*OR,* MOT*ION,* etc.) to complete a word stem (MOT _____ ). Priming, on this task, is measured by comparing the number of correctly completed word stems for items that appeared on a study list relative to those that did not. Tasks of retrieval-dependent priming seem to draw on a complex blend of semantic and presemantic representations as well as anterior and posterior neural structures.

Tasks of *motoric priming* do not employ words or pictures as stimuli. Motoric priming tasks may be measured by the serial reaction time (RT) task developed by Nissen and Bullemer (1987) in which a subject must learn (and retain) a specific sequence of finger movements. Performance on tasks of motoric priming seems to depend on a representation of a specific sequence of body movements that is processed by subcortical neural mechanisms.

Rybash (1994) argued that older adults exhibit impaired performance on tasks of retrieval-dependent priming, but not on tasks of retrieval-free or motoric priming. Furthermore, he suggested that the performance of older adults on various priming tasks is more similar to the performance of Alzheimer's Disease patients than patients with either amnesia or Huntington's Disease. The crucial finding is that Alzheimer's Disease patients and healthy older adults display impaired performance on tasks of retrieval-dependent, but not on tasks of retrieval-free and motoric priming. (It should be emphasized that the deficits displayed by Alzheimer's Disease patients on these priming tasks are much more pronounced than the deficits displayed by healthy older adults.) Amnesics exhibit intact performance on all three of these categories of priming, whereas Huntington's Disease patients display impaired performance on tasks of motoric priming but not retrieval-free or retrieval-dependent priming. Collectively, these findings suggest that neither amnesia or Huntington's Disease serves as an adequate model for understanding age-related changes in human memory, and that the memory changes associated with Alzheimer's Disease and normative aging are united by a common thread. These conclusions do not necessarily mean, of course, that Alzheimer's

Disease represents an acceleration of the normal aging process, or that normal aging is inherently pathological.

***Source Memory*** **Source memory** is the ability to remember the context in which a particular piece of information has been learned. For example, knowing who told you where to get the best pizza on campus or knowing where you read about the results of a study require source memory. Traditionally, memory for source has been measured by presenting subjects with fictitious facts (*Bob Hope's father was a fireman*) or obscure facts (*Bingo is the name of the dog on the Cracker Jack box*). If, at a later date, individuals are unable to remember when and/or where they first learned a recalled/recognized fact, they have made a source error. Using this methodology, it has been shown (Janowsky, Shimamura, & Squire, 1989; Shimamura & Squire, 1991) that source memory and fact memory may be entirely different types of memory.

Since the frontal lobes are for placing newly acquired information within a spatial-temporal context (Squire, 1992), it has been hypothesized that source memory may have its neurological locus in this brain region. Consistent with this position, researchers (Janowsky et al., 1989) have found that neurological patients with prefrontal damage display pronounced source memory deficits. Furthermore, it has also been shown (Craik, Morris, Morris, & Loewen, 1990; McIntyre & Craik, 1987; Schacter, Kasniak, Kihlstrom, & Valdiserri, 1991) that elderly adults are more likely to commit more source errors than younger adults and that the magnitude of their source error rate is related to their performance on neuropsychological measures of frontal lobe function. This means that an older adult may remember a particular piece of information such as "Eating brussel sprouts reduces hypertension" but may be uncertain as to whether he or she learned this from watching the evening news or reading the front cover of a tabloid in the supermarket checkout line. Or, an older person might not remember when he last took his hypertension medication.

Usually, it is not commonplace to directly ask an individual to recall the source of a particular piece of information. Thus, assessing source memory via the previously described methodology may yield an overly liberal estimate of an individual's ability to monitor source within real-life contexts. Source monitoring usually takes place on an implicit basis as a component of some ongoing cognitive activity. This indirect and unintentional form of source memory may have the greatest impact on everyday behavior and decision making.

Because tests of source monitoring may not generalize to situations outside of the laboratory, Larry Jacoby and his colleagues (Jacoby, Kelley, Brown, & Jasechko, 1989) developed an alternative methodology—the *Fame Judgment Task*. In this paradigm, subjects are required to read a series of nonfamous names such as Bruce Hudson. Then, they are shown a list of names and are asked to indicate which of the names are famous. Items consist of previously presented nonfamous names (e.g., Bruce Hudson), nonfamous names that subjects were not previously exposed to (e.g., Shawn Johnson), and famous names (e.g., John Milton). Subjects are reminded that all of the names they previously read were nonfamous and that some of these names may appear on the current list. If a subject consciously recollects that a name on the list was previously read, the name should be judged "nonfamous" without hesitation. Alternatively, if a subject fails to remember that a name appeared on the reading task, but is nevertheless familiar with the name due to its prior exposure, the name might mistakenly be judged "famous." A misattribution of fame to a previously presented nonfamous name is defined as a source error. Thus, the *Fame Judgment Task* allows an experimenter to determine if, in the absence of conscious recollection, a subject can monitor the source of the familiarity that accompanies a test item.

Dywan and Jacoby (1990) have found that elderly adults are much more likely than younger adults to display heightened source error rates on the *Fame Judgment Task.* Dywan and Jacoby (1990) offer several instances of how an inability to monitor source on an implicit basis might affect an older adult's ability to function in everyday life. For example, sitting down to play cards with a group of friends may serve as a cue for an older adult to remember a funny story from her distant past. Telling the story the first time at the card table might have the unconscious influence of making the story pop into her mind during future card games with her friends. If her conscious memory for telling the story does not oppose her unconscious tendency to repeat it, she may retell the story countless times to her card-playing companions.

## Metamemory

Middle-aged and older adults frequently notice changes in some aspects of their own memory, but frequently they overestimate the degree and type of changes that occur. **Metamemory** refers to self-appraisal or self-monitoring of memory. This is an important area of research, since older adults may remember less well because they have incorrect beliefs about their own performance and what strategies to use in particular situations. Older adults are generally less accurate in their self-assessments of memory than are younger adults (Hultsch, Hertzog, & Dixon, 1987). Relatives and health-care professionals, as well as the elderly themselves, tend to *overestimate* the degree of memory problems. Zarit, Cole, and Guider (1981) found that older adults not only report more memory failures than younger adults, but they are more likely to become upset and frustrated when they experience a memory failure.

## Very Long-Term Memories

*Memory is the thread of personal identity.*
—Richard Hofstadter

***Autobiographical Memory*** When people are asked to remember a real-life experience, they are engaging in an **autobiographical memory task.** For example, can you remember your first day of college or your first day of kindergarten? One

*Did I take my pills today? Older adults frequently rely on a mnemonic aid of some sort, such as a time-coded pill box, to help them keep track of complicated medical regimens.*

of the most important functions of autobiographical memory is to allow each of us to become our own personal historian. We are continually engaged in the process of writing, editing, and updating the story of our own life.

One characteristic of human memory is the reconstruction of previous experience. An individual actively reconstructs (or reinterprets) past experiences from the point of view of the present. Labouvie-Vief and Schell (1982) argued that older

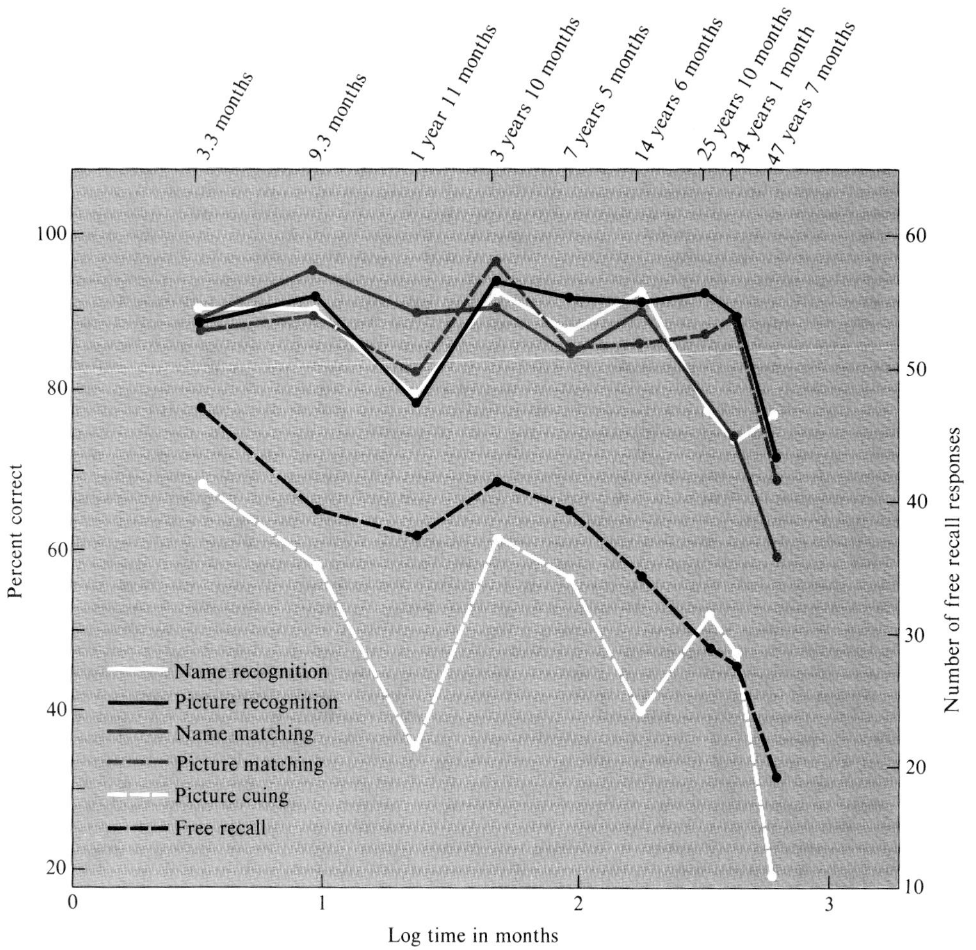

**Figure 4.8**
Recognition and recall of names and faces of high school colleagues.

adults reconstruct the past by developing new processing styles to replace ones that have become less effective. For example, when comprehending story information, older adults are more likely to remember the gist of the information, whereas younger adults are more likely to remember the details. Thus there may be different types of information-processing styles that are adaptive at particular times in adult development.

Not all remote memories are autobiographical. Bahrick, Bahrick, and Wittlinger (1975) investigated memory for one's high school classmates over a long interval. The research assessed face recognition, name recognition, and name-face matching. Free recall of names and cued recall of names in response to faces were also evaluated. The participants differed in the number of years that had elapsed since their high school graduation (from three months to forty-seven years since graduation). It is clear from figure 4.8 that recognition and matching performance remained virtually constant (and nearly perfect) up to a retention interval of thirty-four

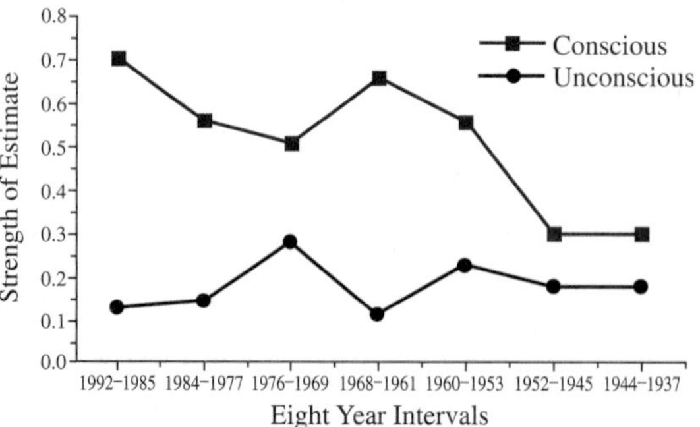


**Figure 4.9** The degree to which conscious and unconscious factors influence adults' ability to recognize actors and actresses who won Academy Awards for their performances in specific motion pictures between 1937 and 1992.

years. This means that adults in their midfifties were performing about as well as 18-year-olds. In contrast, the recall measures, particularly free recall, showed clear evidence of age-related decline that began shortly after graduation. Note especially the steady drop in free recall from the three-year interval (adults about 21 years old) to the forty-seven-year interval (adults about 65 years old).

In a more recent study of remote semantic memory, John Rybash, Kelli Deluca, and Lauren Rubenstein (1994) measured older adults' ability to recognize the names of famous actors and actresses who won Academy Awards for their performances in certain motion pictures between 1937 and 1992. For example, "Did Cher win an Oscar for her performance in *One Flew over the Cuckoo's Nest?*" "Was Burt Lancaster the star of *From Here to Eternity?*" As would be expected, older subjects' conscious recognition of Oscar winners was more accurate for movies from the recent than the distant past. However, it was also discovered that the unconscious component of recognition memory was just as strong for subjects' knowledge of Oscar-winning performances at all points across the entire fifty-six year period sampled in this experiment (see figure 4.9). This research provides evidence that conscious and unconscious memory processes may be disassociated from each other for real-life information, and that unconscious contributions to memory are relatively unaffected by age.

***Vivid Memories*** Joseph Fitzgerald has examined age differences in different aspects of autobiographical memory. Fitzgerald and Lawrence (1984) presented older adults with a series of forty common words. Each participant was required to think of a specific autobiographical memory that would trigger each word. The results of this study displayed a typical *retention function.* This means that the participants were most likely to remember events that had just occurred rather than those that had occurred years ago. In fact, most of the autobiographical memories reported by the subjects happened within the last few years prior to the study. In a more recent study, Fitzgerald (1988) asked a group of older adults (approximately 70 years of age) to write a paragraph describing three different *vivid* or **flashbulb memories.** Specifically, the participants were told that a flashbulb memory occurs when an individual's mind takes an exceptionally vivid, detailed, and long-lasting picture of a personally experienced event. The participants were given the freedom to write about vivid memories that occurred at any time over the course of their lives. Finally, Fitzgerald asked the older adults to rate each vivid memory on a number of different dimensions. These dimensions included personal importance, national importance, frequency of rehearsal, and intensity of emotional reaction.

Unlike the data collected in the Fitzgerald and Lawrence (1984) study, Fitzgerald's (1988) study showed that vivid memories do *not* exhibit a normal retention function. Participants were very unlikely to recall vivid memories from middle adulthood or old age. Instead, these older adults were most likely to recall vivid memories from their late adolescence and early adulthood. More specifically, the vivid memories reported by the participants were based on personal experiences that occurred, on average, forty years earlier. Also, the data for the study were collected shortly after the Challenger explosion; yet, none of the participants included this event in their list of vivid memories. Some of the older adults' vivid memories possessed a great deal of personal importance and were steeped in emotion (e.g., a soldier remembering his friends dying in combat, and a mother remembering the birth of her child). However, most of these vivid memories were not of great personal or national importance, nor were they highly emotional (e.g., remembering baking a cake or walking to school).

Why doesn't the age distribution of vivid memories show a normal retention function? Why are older adults most likely to recall vivid memories of events that occurred in their youth? Fitzgerald (1988) notes that adolescence and young adulthood may represent that period of the life span when we are in the process of forming unique personal identities. We may use this period as a marker or anchor point from which to begin the story of our adult psychological selves. Thus, because of the special status we attach to youth, we may be likely to have vivid memories from this period of our lives. Fitzgerald (1988) also suggests that because we live in a youth-oriented society, a rich storehouse of vivid memories from youth would allow older adults to maintain contact with a point in the life span when they were young, healthy, and had their lives in front of them.

## *Explanations of Memory Aging*

Age-related differences in memory can be caused by neural changes in the brain, by processing differences, or both. With increasing age, there are a number of changes in the neurons of the brain (senile plaques, neurofibrillary tangles) and in the efficiency of the neurotransmitters such as acetylcholine that affect the transmission of information across neurons. These changes, which occur to varying degrees throughout the brain but especially within the hippocampus, may be responsible for some kinds of memory impairments.

Parasuraman, Greenwood, Haxby, and Grady (1992) suggested that age-related damage to the cortex may result in attentional deficits that, in turn, cause memory deficits. Older people may have poor memories because they are more distracted by irrelevant task information (Hoyer, Rebok, & Sved, 1979). Attentional and memory deficits in the elderly may be caused by damage to the frontal lobes of the cortex. Healthy older adults often make the same types of errors on neuropsychological tests as patients who suffer from frontal lobe damage. Craik et al. (1990) suggested that damage to the frontal lobes leads to memory problems because the ability to plan and execute sophisticated encoding and retrieval processes is located in this part of the brain, but some investigators have questioned whether changes in the frontal lobes can account for memory aging (Spencer & Raz, 1994).

Another kind of explanation of memory aging puts emphasis on the specification of the kinds of processes involved in performing different kinds of memory tasks. That is, some researchers have focused on the nature of age differences in the encoding, storage, and retrieval aspects of memory. *Encoding* refers to the registration or pickup of information. *Storage* refers to the retention of information in memory. *Retrieval* refers to finding or using information in memory. From a memory processing perspective, researchers are trying to understand the factors that are associated with age differences in the efficiency of encoding, storage and retrieval. Interestingly, there is a large amount of evidence to suggest an age-related **encoding deficit,** and an equally large amount of evidence to suggest an age-related **retrieval deficit.** An encoding deficit suggests that elderly persons are less capable of engaging in the organizational, elaborative, and imagery processes that are helpful in memory tasks. Encoding deficits could be related to age-related declines in attentional capacity (Craik & Jennings, 1992). That is, elderly people may show memory deficits because they have less attentional capacity needed for encoding.

Other psychologists have shown that there is an age-related retrieval deficit, even under conditions that equate younger and older adults for the amount of encoding. It is well established that older adults are at a disadvantage compared with younger adults in naming tasks and word-finding. The notion of an age-associated retrieval deficit is also consistent with the fact that older adults generally perform better on recognition than recall tests. Of course, the ability to retrieve information generally depends on how well the material was encoded. Age differences are minimized when there is similarity between the contexts of encoding and retrieval.

## *Individual Differences in Memory Performance*

The unique abilities and experiences of individuals affect memory performance. On the one hand, for example, some people may experience health problems such as depression or dementia that have a negative effect on memory function. On the other hand, some people may enjoy an unusually enriched life or have worked many years in a situation that enabled them to develop and maintain particular kinds of memory skills.

Many characteristics of the person apart from age can determine performance in memory tasks. These characteristics include attitudes, interests, health-related factors, intellectual abilities, and styles of learning. In one experiment, Craik, Byrd, and Swanson (1987) studied memory ability in three groups of elderly people who ranged from 64 to 88 years of age. Group 1 consisted of highly intelligent and relatively affluent individuals. Group 2 was composed of individuals somewhat lower in intelligence and socioeconomic status who were actively involved in the community.

| Condition | Old 3 | Old 2 | Old 1 | Young |
|---|---|---|---|---|
| Cued—Cued | 5.5 | 7.3 | 8.1 | 7.8 |
| Cued—Free | 2.2 | 5.4 | 5.8 | 5.6 |
| Free—Cued | 2.2 | 4.5 | 5.3 | 5.8 |
| Free—Free | 2.4 | 4.6 | 4.7 | 6.0 |

**Figure 4.10** Word recall scores grouped into four levels of performance.

Group 3 consisted of individuals of lower intelligence and socioeconomic status who were not involved in community or social affairs. Furthermore, Craik, Byrd, and Swanson studied a group of college students matched on verbal intelligence with the first group of elderly participants. All participants received lists of words to remember. The participants differed, however, in the number of cues (i.e., contextual support) they were given at encoding and/or retrieval. Some participants were provided cues when they were initially presented with each word on a list (e.g., "a type of bird—LARK") but not during recall. Other participants were given this cue during recall but not during presentation; others were cued during both presentation and recall; and still others were not cued during either presentation or recall. The extent of age-related differences in memory was found to depend on the amount of support offered in the task and the characteristics of the persons performing the task. Among the participants who received the greatest degree of support (cued presentation and cued recall), all of the elderly groups with the exception of group 3 (low IQ, low socioeconomic class) performed just as well as the college students. Among the participants who received an intermediate amount of support (noncued presentation and cued recall), only the first elderly group performed as well as the college students. When participants were not provided with any support (noncued presentation and noncued recall), the college students performed better than all of the elderly groups. Figure 4.10 illustrates the different levels of performance for the participants.

Probably the most important source of individual differences in memory has to do with differences in acquired knowledge and skills. Almost everyone has a rich foundation of knowledge in several areas of work, sports, hobbies, or entertainment. For healthy individuals, access to such knowledge is unaffected by aging. Mr. Stephen Powelson, a 76-year-old retired accountant, for example, has almost finished memorizing all 15,693 lines of Homer's *Iliad* in ancient Greek. Mr. Powelson has visited a number of college campuses to recite the lines of the *Iliad* before audiences of classics professors and their students (*Chronicle of Higher Education,* 1994). Many of the young adult students who hear Mr. Powelson have to change their stereotypically held view about memory aging. Individuals maintain their ability to use well-learned knowledge, strategies, and skills throughout middle age and into old age (Clancy & Hoyer, 1994; Rybash, Hoyer, & Roodin, 1986). Tests of factual knowledge (e.g., vocabulary or events of the news) typically show no decline from young adulthood to old age (Perlmutter, 1980).

Perlmutter (1980) made a distinction between *memory processing* and *memory knowledge.* Aging is associated with a decline in the speed and efficiency of the processes responsible for establishing new memories. This decline, however, does not affect the amount of knowledge *already stored* within memory, which is available for use in many different tasks. Thus, age-related declines may be restricted to tasks in which a person's prior knowledge is not accessed. Tasks that capitalize on previously learned information may show no age-related declines; indeed, on such tasks older people may even outperform young adults. The distinction between memory processing and knowledge is similar to Rybash, Hoyer, and Roodin's (1986) theory of encapsulation, and Horn and Donaldson's (1976) distinction between fluid and crystallized intelligence (discussed in chapter 5).

## Normal versus Pathological Memory Loss

Until now we have focused mainly on the description of age differences in cognition in healthy older adults. Older adults who are in good health and who do not have any debilitating disease usually exhibit only minor declines in their everyday cognitive functions. As individuals age, however, some diseases that produce memory loss and deficits in other aspects of cognitive function are more likely to occur. For example, Alzheimer's disease, which produces progressive and severe memory and attentional losses is more likely to occur in late life than in midlife.

It is important to differentiate normal memory loss from memory loss due to Alzheimer's disease and other kinds of dementia. The nonpathological loss of memory in the normal elderly has been labeled as **benign senescent forgetfulness.** This type of memory impairment is benign because it does not interfere with a person's ability to function in everyday life. Some adults notice a decrease in memory ability as early as 50 to 60 years of age, although it is more common to become aware of memory problems after 60 years of age. In many instances, the elderly become very concerned about their self-recognized memory loss. They want to know if their failing memory is normal for their age or a sign of an abnormal disease process (Grobert & Buschke, 1987).

Read (1987) identified *at what points* memory problems can occur in information processing. First, Read suggested that the ability to recall events from the recent past can be negatively affected by (1) lack of attention to or a difficulty in understanding what has happened (an encoding deficit), (2) a failure to store the event, or (3) difficulty retrieving events already stored in memory. Second, Read argued that the benign memory loss observed in normal elderly adults is caused by a combination of mild deficits in encoding and retrieval, *not* by an inability to store information. Third, he suggested that among elderly adults with depression, poor memory performance stems from both encoding and retrieval deficits that are more severe than those found in the normal elderly. Depressed individuals, for example, may be so preoccupied that they do not expend the effort to encode new information in a meaningful way; and even if they encode and store information, they make little effort to retrieve it. Fourth, Read argued that in Alzheimer's disease the major cause of memory loss is the brain's inability to *store* information. Memory loss in Alzheimer's disease patients should persist, therefore, even if they engage in meaningful encoding processes and are given the utmost support during retrieval. Note that Read does not deny that adults with Alzheimer's disease experience severe deficits in both encoding and retrieval (see Hart, Kwentus, Hamer, & Taylor, 1987). Rather, the thrust of Read's argument is that storage deficits are unique to patients suffering from AD.

A distinction can be made between apparent memory deficits and genuine memory deficits (Grober & Buschke, 1987). **Apparent memory deficits** are memory problems resulting from the use of ineffective encoding and retrieval strategies. Apparent memory deficits can be overcome by inducing individuals to process information in an effective way or by providing individuals with effective retrieval aids. **Genuine memory deficits** are memory problems that persist even after individuals have carried out effective encoding and retrieval activities. In other words, genuine memory deficits are largely irreversible (Grober & Buschke, 1987). In contrast, nondemented individuals (both normal elderly and depressives) would be more likely to experience apparent memory deficits than genuine memory deficits.

Grober and Buschke (1987) performed an experiment in which normal older adults and Alzheimer's disease patients engaged in a special set of controlled-learning activities. These activities allowed them to effectively encode and retrieve a list of sixteen common words. Grober and Buschke (1987) hypothesized that the controlled-learning activities should compensate for the apparent memory deficits of the normal elderly adults and have no effect on the genuine memory deficits experienced by the demented patients. The patients, in other words, should have had extremely poor memories even when they were given a great deal of help during encoding and retrieval. Their results were supportive of the distinction between genuine and apparent memory deficits (see Research Focus 4.3).

Hart et al. (1987) reported that depressed elderly patients, but not Alzheimer's disease patients, displayed better memory scores when they were given support in encoding and retrieving information. This finding is consistent with the idea that memory loss in depressed individuals is more apparent than genuine, and that depressives are more likely to display better memory when they are placed in a supportive context. Even with the extra help, however, depressed patients were found, on the whole, to remember less than the normal elderly.

Another important distinction between normal elderly and depressed elderly centers around the different response bias displayed by both of these groups (Neiderehe, 1986). Depressed elderly people have been found to display a conservative response bias on memory-recognition tasks. When they are unsure about a test item, the depressed elderly are likely to respond, "I can't remember," whereas normal elderly individuals are more likely to take chances and guess. In fact, Neiderehe (1986) has argued that differences in response bias may be the single most important characteristic in differentiating normal from depressed elderly. More information about the differences between dementia and depression is presented later in the text.

## Research Focus 4.3

# *Memory Abilities in Normal and Demented Elderly*

Ellen Grober and Herman Buschke (1987) have developed a methodology that distinguishes between genuine memory deficits and apparent memory deficits. This methodology combines both *controlled learning* and *cued recall.* Controlled-learning procedures ensure that an individual encodes information as effectively as possible. Cued recall ensures that an individual retrieves information as effectively as possible.

In the controlled-learning component of their experiment, Grober and Buschke presented groups of normal and demented elderly with a list of sixteen common items drawn from different conceptual categories. The items were presented four at a time on four different sheets of paper. Each item was presented as a picture (e.g., a picture of a bunch of grapes) with the name of the item boldly printed above the picture (e.g., GRAPES). The participants were given the name of a conceptual category (in this case, "fruit") and were told to point to and name the picture on the card that corresponded to the category (grapes). After identifying all four items on a sheet of paper, the participants were given an immediate recall task. In this task, the participants had to recall the names of the specific items they had just identified. If a participant could not recall the items, the sheet of paper was represented, the identification procedure was repeated, and the participant was given another chance to recall the item. This entire procedure was repeated again if necessary. Then, the remaining twelve items (four items drawn and labeled on three different sheets of paper) were presented, identified, and recalled in the same manner. All of these controlled-learning procedures ensured that the participants attended to all of the items, briefly stored the items, and could immediately recall the items.

**Box Figure 4.B** Free recall (open circles) and total recall (closed circles) of sixteen unrelated pictures by normal elderly adults and by elderly patients with dementia. Total recall is obtained by adding items from cued recall to the number remembered from free recall. *Source: Data from E. Grober and H. Buschke, "Genuine Memory Deficits in Dementia" in* Developmental Neuropsychology *3:13–36, 1987.*

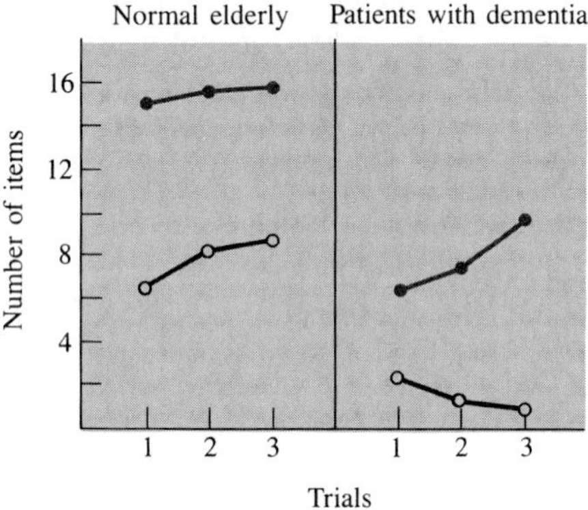


Twenty seconds after the controlled-learning phase was over, the participants were given three separate recall trials for the entire sixteen items. Each recall trial consisted of two distinct tasks: a *free recall task* and a *cued recall task.* During the free recall task, participants were allowed two minutes to remember as many of the sixteen items as possible. In the cued recall task, participants were provided with conceptual cues for the items they did not remember in the free recall task.

## Summary

In this chapter, we have described age-related changes in perception, attention, and memory from an information-processing perspective. Several aspects of perception appear to show deficits as people age. The evidence for age-related differences in speed of perceptual processing is especially strong. It has been shown that age-related perceptual slowing can be attenuated (but not totally eliminated) by extensive practice.

Our discussion of attention began with an examination of the topics of selective attention (the ability to discriminate relevant from irrelevant information), and divided attention (the ability to perform two tasks simultaneously). Overall, the research suggests that there are age-related differences in divided attention and in selective attention.

Some researchers have suggested that there is an age-related decrement in attentional capacity (i.e., a decrease in the amount of psychological energy available to perform mental work). Some of this research has compared age-related differences in

(For example, a researcher might ask, "What was the type of fruit pictured on the card?") Two different types of recall scores were obtained for each participant: a *free recall score* and a *total recall score.* The free recall score represented the number of items retrieved without cues on each trial. The total recall score consisted of the total number of items recalled on each trial by both free recall and cued recall.

Grober and Buschke (1987) reasoned that the total recall score should provide a valid estimate of the total number of items stored in memory and potentially available for recall. Thus, a participant's total recall score, rather than free recall score, should be a better predictor of whether he or she belonged to the normal or demented group.

The results of the study were straightforward. First, as can be seen in figure 4.B, free recall dramatically underrepresents the amount of learning and memory that has taken place in both the normal and demented groups. Figure 4.B also shows that the normal group, because they had near-perfect total memory scores, had stored all sixteen test items. The demented group, on the other hand, stored only about one-half of the sixteen items.

From the evidence illustrated in figure 4.B, it appears that knowledge of either a participant's free or total recall score should be equally useful in predicting if he is demented. The data portrayed in figure 4.C, however, indicates this is not the case—total recall is better than free recall at distinguishing normal from demented elderly. More specifically, figure 4.C shows the free and total recall scores of three participants. Graph A represents the scores of an 89-year-old normal participant who had exceptionally good free recall. Graph B represents the scores of an 87-year-old normal participant who had an average range of free recall scores. Graph C represents the scores on an 86-year-old patient suffering from Alzheimer's disease whose free recall scores are almost identical to those shown in graph B. The normal participants (A and B) had perfect total recall scores, while person B and the demented person (C) had identical free recall scores but differed in total recall. In other words, total recall proved to be a better indicator of dementia because normal elderly, but not demented patients, displayed near-perfect performance on the total recall score regardless of their free recall scores.

**Box Figure 4.C** Free recall (open circles) and total recall (closed circles) by (A) a normal 89-year-old man, (B) a normal 87-year-old woman, and (C) an 86-year-old woman with Alzheimer's disease. *Source: Data from E. Grober and H. Buschke, "Genuine Memory Deficits in Dementia" in* Developmental Neuropsychology *3:13–36, 1987.*

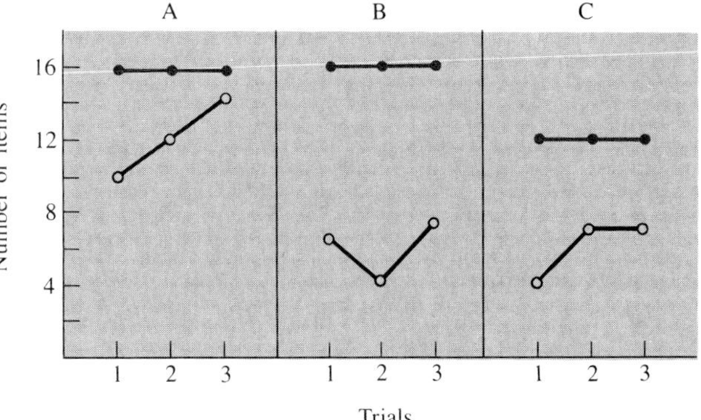


automatic processing versus effortful processing and suggests that age-related differences in the latter are stronger. Several investigators have found little, if any, age-related changes in attention (or perception) for highly automatic tasks. As a general rule, older adults perform most poorly when confronted with highly unfamiliar tasks that demand a great deal of effortful processing.

The capacity of short-term memory does not undergo significant change with age. However, age-related deficits in active short-term memory (working-memory) tasks and in the speed of short-term memory search have been reported. Older adults perform more poorly than young adults on tasks of long-term memory, especially when recall rather than recognition is tested. Memory in the elderly is more robust when it is measured by implicit rather than explicit memory tasks.

When older adults are instructed to use efficient encoding strategies, older adults show an improvement in their ability to remember. Age-related differences in memory are unlikely to occur when older adults draw upon previous knowledge to help them remember. Researchers try to explain age-related changes in memory using two perspectives. The biological perspective suggests that the age-related deterioration of the brain causes decrements in memory. The processing perspective suggests that age-related changes in memory are the result of strategy differences for encoding and retrieving information.

Some researchers are interested in memory as a reconstructive autobiographical process. With aging, there may be a normal decline in the ability to remember information. This type of benign senescent forgetfulness does not seriously affect an older adult's ability to function in everyday life. Older adults tend to overestimate the magnitude and the significance of the memory problems experienced by the normal elderly.

## Review Questions

1. Discuss the research on perceptual change in adulthood. How does practice affect the perceptual abilities of older adults?
2. What is the difference between selective attention and divided attention? Discuss the research that has been conducted in this area.
3. What is meant by the term *attentional capacity?* Do older adults display poorer performance than younger adults on tasks that demand effortful processing or automatic processing?
4. Discuss the nature of short-term and long-term memory and their development during adulthood.
5. Explain the differences between explicit and implicit memory.
6. Discuss the differences between the biological and processing perspectives. Is one of these perspectives more useful or valid than the others?
7. What is benign senescent forgetfulness?
8. Explain the differences between the memory impairments that occur in the normal elderly versus those that occur in someone who suffers from a dementia such as Alzheimer's disease.

## For Further Reading


Cerella, J., Rybash, J. M., Hoyer, W. J., & Commons, M. A. (Eds.). (1993). *Adult information processing: Limits on loss.* San Diego: Academic Press.

Craik, F. I. M., & Salthouse, T. A. (Eds.). (1992). *Handbook of aging and cognition.* Hillsdale, NJ: Erlbaum.

Fozard, J. L. (1990). Vision and hearing and aging. In J. E. Birren & K. W. Schaie (Eds.), *Handbook of the psychology of aging* (3rd ed., pp. 150–171). San Diego: Academic Press.

Hultsch, D. F., & Dixon, R. A. (1990). Learning and memory and aging. In J. E. Birren & K. W. Schaie (Eds.), *Handbook of the psychology of aging* (3rd ed., pp. 258–274). San Diego, CA: Academic Press.

# 5

# INTELLIGENCE AND CREATIVITY

*I have always maintained that excepting fools, men do not differ much in intellect, only in zeal and hard work.*
—Charles Darwin

*Give me a young man in whom there is something old, and an old man in whom there is something young: guided so, a man will grow older in body but never in mind.*
—Cicero

## *Introduction*

This is the second of the three chapters that focus on adult cognitive development. Cognitive change is one of the key features of adult development. More research has been conducted on cognitive functioning than any other aspect of adult development (Baltes, 1987). There are several different perspectives from which to study adult cognition. In this chapter we center our attention on the psychometric approach, a measurement-based view that has sparked considerable debate on the very nature of intelligence, the way it is assessed, and its development (and possible decline) during adulthood. We examine the roles of physical health and generational (or cohort) influences in adult intellectual change. Furthermore, we discuss the relationship between adult scores on psychometric intelligence tests and the ability of those adults to solve real-life problems. Next, we examine the issue of creativity. We'll distinguish between creativity and intelligence and chart the developmental course of creativity over the adult years. Finally, we examine the relationship between aging, intelligence, education, and work, specifically, how age-related changes in intelligence impact on education and occupational productivity over the adult years.

## *The Psychometric Approach to the Study of Intelligence*

The term **psychometric** literally means "the measurement of the mind." More specifically, psychometricians construct and validate various tests that measure a number of relatively enduring characteristics of the individual. It seems safe to say that the greatest emphasis in psychometric research has been placed on the measurement of human intelligence. In this chapter, we'll present information about age-related changes in psychometrically measured intelligence. But before we can determine the changes that take place in intelligence during adulthood, we need to determine what, exactly, intelligence *is.*

### The Nature of Intelligence

*The voice of intellect is a soft one, but it will not rest till it has gained a hearing.*
—Sigmund Freud

Intelligence is a concept that is easy to understand but hard to define. The word *intelligence* is derived from the Latin words that mean "to choose between" and "to make wise choices" (Rebok, 1987; Schaie & Willis, 1986). These literal meanings of intelligence are, at best, vague. How can we determine if an individual has made a truly wise choice? Are psychologists capable of developing a precise, meaningful definition of intelligence? In a well-known symposium sponsored by the *Journal of Educational Psychology* in 1921, a number of expert psychologists gave the following definitions of intelligence:

> The ability to carry on abstract thinking. (Louis Terman)
> The ability to give true or factual responses. (Edward Thorndike)
> The ability to learn to adjust oneself to the environment. (S. S. Colvin)
> The ability to adapt to new situations, which reflects the general modifiability of the nervous system. (Rudolf Pinter)
> The capacity to acquire new abilities. (Herbert Woodrow)
> A group of complex mental processes traditionally defined as sensation, perception, association, memory, imagination, discrimination, judgment, and reasoning. (M. E. Haggerty)

These definitions seem to possess as much generality and tenuousness as you would expect from the proverbial man on the street! If we analyze each of the definitions, however, an important issue emerges: is intelligence a general, single, or unitary process? Or does intelligence consist of a number of different, independent, or separate mental abilities? Charles Spearman (1927), a well-known English psychologist in the earlier part of this century, argued that intelligence consisted primarily of a single ability that an individual could apply to any task. Spearman called this unitary ability the **g factor**—"g" for "general capacity." Spearman assumed that because of the g factor, an individual should perform at the same level of proficiency regardless of the type of task he or she had to solve. The notion that intelligence is best conceptualized as a single, general ability was also held by Alfred Binet. Binet was the French psychologist who developed the first intelligence assessment in 1906. Today, Spearman and Binet would be likely to conceptualize intelligence as a very general and abstract computer program. This program would be so general that it could be applied, with the same degree of success, to any problem it was called upon to solve.

Several other psychologists have suggested that intelligence consists of a number of separate, independent mental abilities. This position was originally advocated by Thurstone (1938), who proposed that there are a small number of **primary mental abilities.** These primary mental abilities include verbal comprehension, word fluency, number, space, associative memory, perceptual speed, and induction. Table 5.1 contains a description of each of these abilities. K. Warner Schaie, a well-known advocate of the psychometric approach, has recently developed an adult intelligence test based on Thurstone's research. This test is called the **Schaie-Thurstone Adult Mental Abilities Test** (Schaie, 1985). To use a computer analogy, Thurstone, Schaie, and their associates would likely argue that intelligence consists of a number of separate, specialized computer programs. Each program would be designed to solve a particular type of task.

Some psychometricians have even gone a step further than Thurstone and Schaie. They believe there are more basic components of intelligence than these psychologists originally envisioned. Ekstrom, French, and Harman (1979), for example,

*TABLE 5.1*

| ***The Primary Mental Abilities*** |
|---|
| *Verbal comprehension:* The principal factor in such tests as reading comprehension, verbal analogies, disarranged sentences, verbal reasoning, and proverb matching. It is most adequately measured by vocabulary tests. |
| *Word fluency:* Found in such tests as anagrams, rhyming, or naming words in a given category (e.g., boys' names or words beginning with the letter *T*). |
| *Number:* Most closely identified with speed and accuracy of simple arithmetic computation. |
| *Space (or spatial orientation):* May represent two distinct factors, one covering perception of fixed spatial or geometric relations, the other manipulatory visualizations in which changed positions or transformations must be visualized. |
| *Associative memory:* Found principally in tests demanding rote memory for paired associates. There is some evidence to suggest that this factor may reflect the extent to which memory crutches are utilized. The evidence is against the presence of a broader factor through all memory tests. Other restricted memory factors, such as memory for temporal sequences and for spatial position, have been suggested by some investigations. |
| *Perceptual speed:* Quick and accurate grasping of visual details, similarities, and differences. |
| *Induction (or general reasoning):* Early researchers proposed an inductive and a deductive factor. The latter was best measured by tests of syllogistic reasoning and the former by tests requiring the subject to find a rule, as in a number series completion test. Evidence for the deductive factor, however, was much weaker than for the inductive. Moreover, other investigators suggested a general reasoning factor, best measured by arithmetic reasoning tests. |

*From Macmillan Publishing Company,* Psychological Testing, *6th ed., by Anne Anastasi. Copyright © 1988 by Anne Anastasi.*

have isolated 29 separate mental abilities. And Guilford (1959a, 1959b, 1967) has argued for the existence of an astonishing 120 independent components of intelligence!

Cattell (1971) and Horn (1970, 1982a, 1982b) have pointed out that a model based on a large number of mental abilities (e.g., 29 or 120) is too unwieldy. They suggested that it is difficult, if not impossible, to represent a large number of mental abilities in an internally consistent, parsimonious, coherent, and empirically sound fashion. For this reason, Horn (1970) has argued for the existence of two highly abstract components of intelligence that subsume the various primary mental abilities. These two abstract components are crystallized intelligence and fluid intelligence. **Crystallized intelligence** roughly represents the extent to which individuals have incorporated the valued knowledge of their culture. It is measured by a large inventory of behaviors that reflect the breadth of culturally valued knowledge and experience, the comprehension of communications, and the development of judgment, understanding, and reasonable thinking in everyday affairs. Some of the primary mental abilities associated with crystallized intelligence are verbal comprehension, concept formation, logical reasoning, and induction. Tests used to measure the crystallized factor include vocabulary, simple analogies, remote associations, and social judgment.

**Fluid intelligence** represents an individual's "pure" ability to perceive, remember, and think about a wide variety of basic information. In other words, fluid intelligence involves mental abilities that are *not* imparted by one's culture. Abilities included under the heading of fluid intelligence are seeing relationships among patterns, drawing inferences from relationships, and comprehending implications. Some of the primary mental abilities that best reflect this factor are number, space, and perceptual speed. Tasks measuring fluid intelligence include letter series, matrices, and

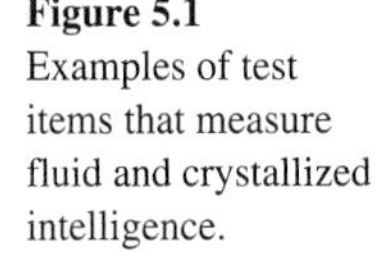

**Figure 5.1**
Examples of test items that measure fluid and crystallized intelligence.

Fluid intelligence

*Matrices* Indicate the figure that completes the matrix.

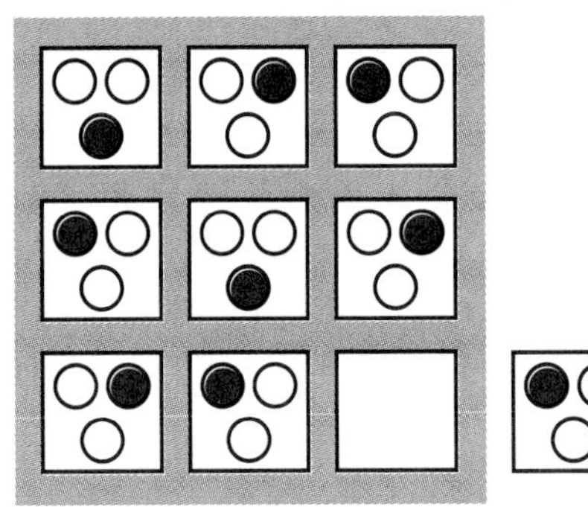

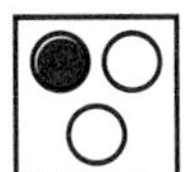

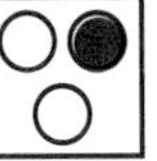

*Letter series* Decide which letter comes next in the series.
A D G J M P ?

*Topology* Find the figure on the right where the dot can be placed in the same relation to the triangle, square, and circle as in the example on the left.

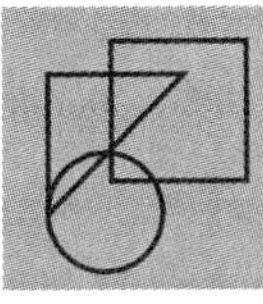

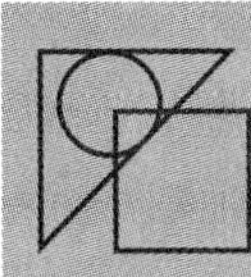

Crystallized intelligence

*Analogies* Fill in the blank.
Atom is to ________ as cell is to organism.

*Remote associations* What one word is well associated with the words *bathtub, prizefighting,* and *wedding*?

*Judgment* You notice that a fire has just started in a crowded cafe.
What should one do to prevent death and injury?

spatial orientation. It has been suggested that fluid intelligence represents the integrity of the central nervous system (Horn, 1982b). See figure 5.1 to gain a better understanding of the differences between crystallized and fluid intelligence. This figure contains a number of sample tasks that measure both of these types of intelligence.

## The Measurement of Intelligence

It is one thing to develop a theory of intelligence and another thing to develop a valid and reliable test or measure of intelligence. A psychometrician must take a number of factors into account in developing an intelligence test. First, it is important to realize that intelligence does not really exist! Intelligence is a **hypothetical construct** rather than a real entity. It is not possible, for example, to look inside the brain of an individual and see the amount of intelligence she possesses in the same way that one can look inside a refrigerator to see the amount of food stored there. This means that psychometric tests must measure intelligence *indirectly* by examining performance on tasks that depend on the generation and application of intelligent behavior.

A second factor psychometricians must consider, since intelligence cannot be directly measured by any psychometric test, is that intelligence test performance is influenced by many factors other than intelligence. These factors include personality characteristics, motivation, educational background, anxiety, fatigue, and so on. Despite the influence of these extraneous factors, however, psychometricians still assume that intelligence tests primarily measure intelligence.

A third consideration for psychometricians to remember in developing an intelligence test is that it is necessary to present individuals with a wide variety of tasks to evaluate whether intelligence is a single ability such as a g factor or a number of independent abilities. This is why contemporary intelligence tests consist of a number of different *scales* or minitests or subtests. One of the most commonly used tests to measure adult intelligence is the **Wechsler Adult Intelligence Scale (WAIS).** This test consists of eleven subtests. Six of the subtests compose a *verbal scale.* These subtests include general information, digit span, vocabulary, arithmetic, comprehension, and similarities. The items on this scale require a strong language component. The remaining five subtests make up a *performance scale.* The subtests on this scale include picture completion, picture arrangement, block design, object assembly, and digit symbol substitution. On this scale, a person is required to make a nonverbal response (e.g., arranging a number of pictures in a logical sequence so as to tell a story) after a careful appraisal of each problem. Table 5.2 contains a brief description of all of the subtests on both the verbal and performance scales of the WAIS.

Another thing to consider in developing intelligence tests is that although we can construct tests that possess a large number of subtests, this does not necessarily mean that each subtest measures a different aspect of intelligence. Each subtest might measure the same mental ability, the *g factor* for example, but in a different way. To determine whether the various subtests of an intelligence test are measuring a single ability or a number of special abilities, researchers developed the technique of **factor analysis.** Factor analysis (discussed later) is a statistical procedure used to determine how scores on a large number of tasks intercorrelate (or fail to intercorrelate) with one another. Using the method of factor analysis, Thurstone discovered the different primary mental abilities. Cattell and Horn also used factor analytic procedures to discern the difference between crystallized and fluid intelligence.

Finally, it is important to understand how a person's IQ score is calculated. The first intelligence tests were constructed solely for children and young adolescents. On these tests, IQ was computed by multiplying the ratio of mental age to chronological age by 100 ($IQ = MA/CA \times 100$). A child's mental age was measured by the items passed on the IQ test. For example, if a child passed all of the items that a typical 6-year-old could pass but could not pass any of the items solved by children 7 years of age and above, a mental age of 6 years was assigned to that child. Then the child's IQ could be computed by determining the ratio between mental age and chronological

*TABLE 5.2*

| ***Subtests of the WAIS*** |
|---|
| ***Verbal Scale*** |
| *Information:* Twenty-nine questions covering a wide variety of information that adults have presumably had an opportunity to acquire in our culture. An effort was made to avoid specialized or academic knowledge. |
| *Comprehension:* Fourteen items, in each of which the examinee explains what should be done under certain circumstances, why certain practices are followed, the meaning of proverbs, and so forth. Designed to measure practical judgment and common sense. |
| *Arithmetic:* Fourteen problems similar to those encountered in elementary school arithmetic. Each problem is orally presented and is to be solved without the use of paper and pencil. |
| *Similarities:* Thirteen items requiring the subject to say in what way two things are alike. |
| *Digit span:* Orally presented lists of three to nine digits to be orally reproduced. In the second part, the examinee must reproduce lists of two to eight digits backwards. |
| *Vocabulary:* Forty words of increasing difficulty presented both orally and visually. The examinee is asked what each word means. |
| ***Performance Scale*** |
| *Digit symbol:* A version of the familiar code-substitution test, which has often been included in nonlanguage intelligence scales. The key contains nine symbols paired with the nine digits. With this key before him, the examinee has one and a half minutes to fill in as many symbols as he can under the numbers on the answer sheet. |
| *Picture completion:* Twenty-one cards, each containing a picture from which some part is missing. Examinee must tell what is missing from each picture. |
| *Block design:* A set of cards containing designs in red and white and a set of identical one-inch blocks whose sides are painted red, white, and half red and half white. The examinee is shown one design at a time, which he or she must reproduce by choosing and assembling the proper blocks. |
| *Picture arrangement:* Each item consists of a set of cards containing pictures to be rearranged in the proper sequence so as to tell a story. |
| *Object assembly:* In each of the four parts of this subtest, cutouts are to be assembled to make a flat picture of a familiar object. |

*From Macmillan Publishing Company,* Psychological Testing, *6th ed., by Anne Anastasi. Copyright 1988 by Anne Anastasi.*

age and multiplying by 100. For example, if the child with a mental age of 6 is 6 years old chronologically, the child's IQ is 100 (IQ = 6/6 × 100). Thus, an average IQ, regardless of the age of the person tested, is always 100.

Psychometricians discovered that it was very easy to classify the mental ages of children. However, the concept of mental age broke down when applied to adults. It is relatively easy to develop questions that distinguish between children with mental ages of 6 and 7; but it is impossible to develop questions that distinguish between adults with mental ages of 66 and 67. The IQ formula used for children could thus not be used to determine adult intelligence. To resolve this problem two approaches were taken. The first approach, which is no longer used today, was to assign a mental age of no greater than 16 to adults' IQ test items. This approach wrongly assumed that little, if any, development in intelligence occurs beyond midadolescence. The second approach, the one adopted by contemporary psychologists, is to determine an adult's IQ by comparing the number of correct answers a person achieves on the whole test to people of the same chronological age. A score of 100 is arbitrarily assigned to those performing at the average for their age group, while IQs greater or lesser than 100 are assigned according to the degree of statistical deviation from this average.

Using this scoring system, it is possible for different-aged adults to perform in a manner identical to one another yet receive radically different IQ scores. To take a simple example, suppose that the average 25-year-old can pass sixty-five questions on an IQ test while the average 75-year-old can pass forty-five questions on the same test. Thus, a 25-year-old who passed fifty-five questions would be assessed to have a below-average IQ, while a 75-year-old who passed fifty-five questions would be assessed as having an above-average IQ. This discovery leads to an interesting question. What should we pay closest attention to when we conduct research on developmental changes in adult intelligence? Should we focus on the raw scores (the total number of questions correctly answered) obtained by different-aged adults or on the adjusted IQ scores (the comparison of the raw score to the average score for a particular age group) for different-aged adults? It seems that examining raw scores would provide more valuable information about developmental changes in test performance than examining the adjusted scores (the IQ scores). Significant changes in test performance would most certainly be obscured if we focused attention on the IQ scores alone.

## *Developmental Changes in Intelligence*

There is no doubt that the raw scores that adults obtain on intelligence tests decline with age. However, the age at which decrements in IQ test performance first begin, as well as the magnitude of the decline, depends on the research design employed to measure developmental change. In this section we'll compare the results of various cross-sectional and longitudinal studies of adult intellectual development. Overall, we will see that declines in intelligence (1) occur much later than was earlier thought, (2) affect a smaller number of individuals than was earlier thought, and (3) affect a smaller number of intellectual abilities than was earlier thought.

### Cross-Sectional Studies

Initially, a number of cross-sectional studies (Garret, 1957; Jones & Conrad, 1933; Wechsler, 1939) showed that raw or unadjusted scores on intelligence tests decreased with age. Decrements in test scores began in late adolescence and early adulthood (at about 20 years of age) and steadily continued over the remainder of the life span. These results suggested that intelligence peaked in early life, and this conclusion was not at all surprising to the psychologists of this era. At this point in time, you will remember, psychologists held a child-focused perspective on developmental change. A child-focused approach assumes that adulthood can only be characterized by the decline of intellectual abilities.

A few researchers began to notice that adults displayed a steeper rate of decline on some types of intellectual tasks in comparison to others. For example, Wechsler (1958, 1972) and Siegler (1983) reported that with increasing age, the scores on performance subtests of the WAIS declined more rapidly than the scores on the verbal subtests. It should be noted, however, that performance subtests are speeded while

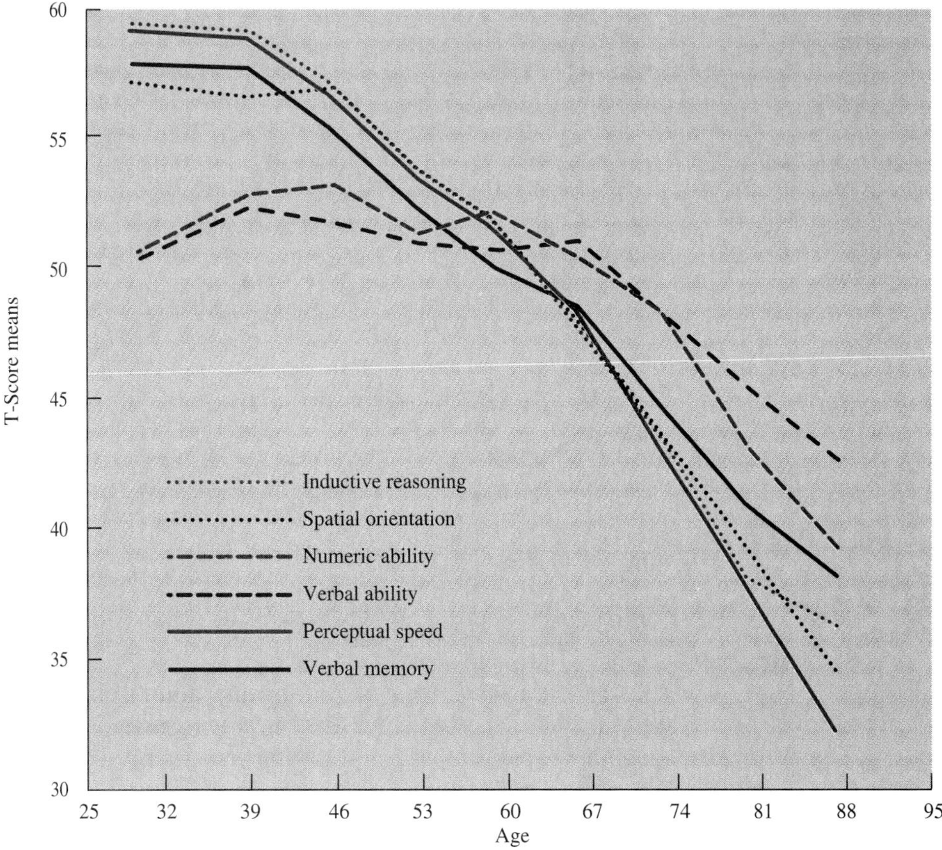


**Figure 5.2** Cross-sectional age differences in several primary mental abilities.

verbal subtests are nonspeeded. A speeded subtest is one in which individuals must make their responses as quickly as possible, while in a nonspeeded test, individuals are allowed to take their time answering items. These data suggest that speed of responding may underlie the poor performance of the elderly on nonverbal tasks. However, many older adults continue to perform poorly on the performance subtests of the WAIS even if given unlimited time to respond (Botwinick, 1977).

The conclusion that various components of intelligence decline at different rates has been illustrated, rather nicely, by a recent study conducted by Schaie and Willis (1993). These researchers administered a battery of tasks that measured the primary mental abilities of inductive reasoning, space, number, verbal comprehension, speed perception, and associative memory to 1,628 community dwelling adults between 20 to 90 years of age. The results of this study are depicted in figure 5.2. Three findings are noteworthy. First, there are age-related decrements in all of the primary mental abilities. Second, verbal comprehension is least affected by age, whereas perceptual speed is the most affected by age. Third, after midlife, performance on the different mental abilities becomes more variable.

Similarly, when the developmental changes in crystallized and fluid intelligence are analyzed in a cross-sectional manner, an interesting pattern emerges. With advancing

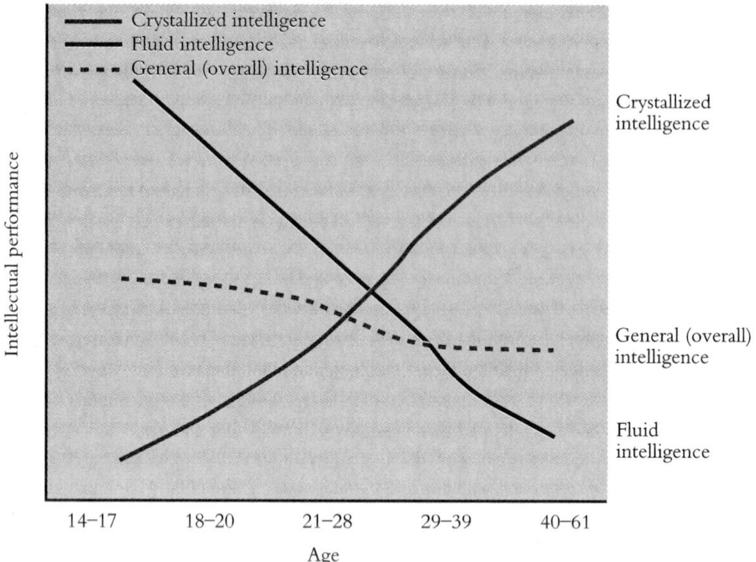


**Figure 5.3** Age-related changes in crystallized intelligence, fluid intelligence, and general intelligence from adolescence to older adulthood.

age, crystallized intelligence shows increases up until the sixth decade of life (Horn, 1970, 1982a, 1982b; Horn & Donaldson, 1976). On the other hand, fluid intelligence exhibits a steady decline beginning in early adulthood. The net effect is that the increases in crystallized intelligence tend to cancel out the decreases in fluid intelligence. Therefore, if one did not make a distinction between crystallized and fluid abilities, one would conclude that intelligence, as a general ability, remains relatively stable until the onset of late adulthood. Figure 5.3 contains a schematic representation of the relationship between crystallized intelligence, fluid intelligence, and general intelligence.

In summary, cross-sectional research seems to indicate that intellectual and physical development followed the same pattern of steady decline—a pattern of irreversible decrement. Furthermore, it has been consistently shown that scores on nonverbal or fluid abilities display an earlier, steeper decline than scores on verbal or crystallized abilities. The tendency for nonverbal abilities to deteriorate more rapidly than verbal abilities has been referred to as the *classic aging pattern* (Botwinick, 1977). How can we understand this phenomenon? John Horn and colleagues (Horn, 1982a; Horn & Donaldson, 1976) have proposed that crystallized intelligence is spared by age because it reflects the cumulative effects of experience, education, and acculturation; whereas fluid intelligence is impaired by age because of a gradual age-related deterioration of the physiological and neurological mechanisms necessary for basic intellectual functioning.

## Longitudinal Studies

Longitudinal studies offer a very different impression of adult intellectual development than cross-sectional studies. Schaie and Willis (1986) have observed that a number of longitudinal studies were initiated during the early 1920s. It was at this time that incoming groups of college freshmen in the United States were administered intelligence tests on a routine basis. Psychologists kept track of these individuals as they grew older, retesting them at different intervals during adulthood. To the amazement of many developmentalists, the participants in these longitudinal studies showed an increase in IQ test performance up to approximately age 50 (Owens, 1966). After age 50, these gains were usually maintained or sometimes evidenced a small decline (Cunningham & Owens, 1983).

In one longitudinal study, Schwartzman, Gold, Andres, Arbuckle, and Chiakelson (1987) analyzed the intelligence test scores of a group of 260 men. These men were first administered intelligence tests when they were army recruits during World War II. Forty years later, the men were retested. At the second testing, the participants were approximately 65 years of age. They had completed, on average, nine years of formal education. One of the interesting twists of this study was that at the forty-year retesting, the men were given the intelligence test under two different conditions: a normal-time condition in which participants were given the standard amount of time to answer the test questions, and a double-time condition in which participants were given twice as much time to answer the test questions. Overall results showed a slight decline in test scores under the normal-time condition but a reliable and significant improvement in scores in the double-time condition! IQ gains were most likely to occur in those portions of the test that measured verbal abilities (e.g., vocabulary), while losses in IQ appeared in essentially nonverbal abilities (e.g., spatial problem solving). Three other findings are especially noteworthy. First, individual differences in IQ scores remained very stable over the forty-year time span. Second, gains in IQ were more highly associated with the number of years of formal education the men had attained than with their ages at the retesting. Third, self-reported activity levels and personal lifestyle differences were related to IQ scores at both times of testing.

One way to compare the results of cross-sectional and longitudinal studies of adult intellectual change is to examine the information illustrated in figure 5.4. The cross-sectional data indicate that adults show a peak in verbal ability at 35 years of age, followed by a significant decline thereafter. The longitudinal data, on the other hand, show that verbal ability peaks at about age 55. In addition, the longitudinal data exhibit only a very small decline up until 70 years of age, while the cross-sectional data show a more dramatic and earlier rate of decline.

One of the most informative investigations of adult intelligence is the Seattle Longitudinal Study (SLS) of K. Warner Schaie and his associates. This investigation employed a sequential research design (i.e., a combination of both cross-sectional and longitudinal methods of data collection). The study began in 1956 when 500 participants between 22 and 70 years of age were administered the Primary Mental Abilities Test. These subjects were retested at seven-year intervals in 1963, 1970, 1977, and 1984. Thus, this research project consisted of five cross-sectional studies and one longitudinal study covering a twenty-one-year period.

A large number of published reports have summarized the outcomes of the SLS (Schaie, 1979, 1983; Schaie & Hertzog, 1983, 1985; Schaie & Labouvie-Vief, 1974). Generally, the cross-sectional comparison exhibited the typical pattern of decline across all of the different primary mental abilities. These comparisons support the irreversible decrement model of intellectual aging. The longitudinal findings, however, tell a different story. They indicate that intelligence test scores either increase or remain stable until

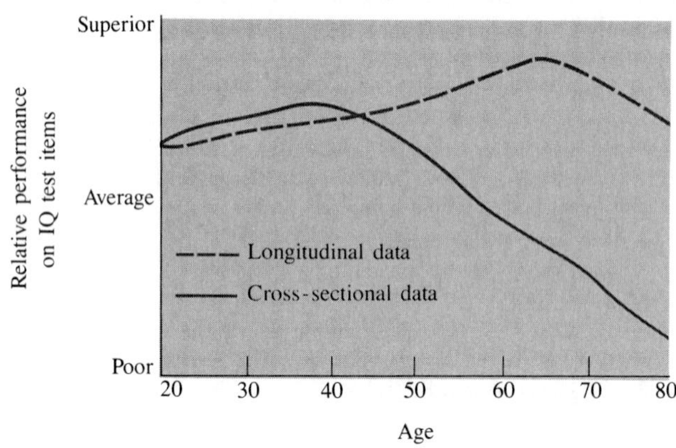


**Figure 5.4** A comparison of the results of cross-sectional and longitudinal studies investigating the relationship between age and verbal intelligence. *Source: Data from K. W. Schaie and S. L. Willis, 1986.*

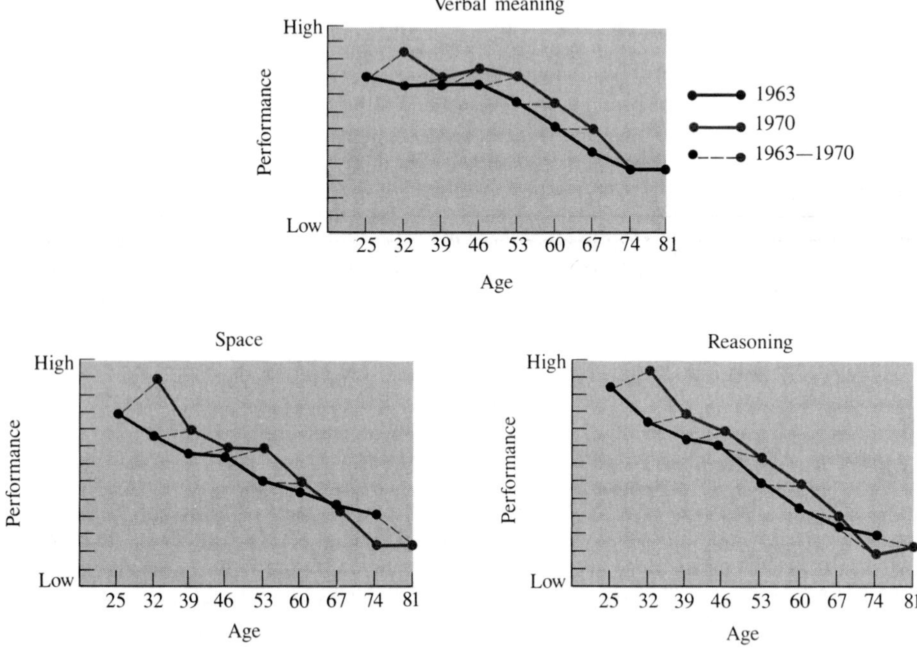


**Figure 5.5** A comparison of cross-sectional and longitudinal findings concerning the relationship between age and intelligence based on the data obtained by Schaie and Labouvie-Vief (1974). *Source: Data from K. W. Schaie and G. Labouvie-Vief, "Generational Versus Ontogenetic Components of Change in Adult Cognitive Behavior: A Fourteen-Year Cross-Sequential Study" in* Developmental Psychology, *10:305–320, 1974.*

approximately age 60, when a small decline becomes evident. The results from one of the first reports of this investigation are illustrated in figure 5.5. This figure, based on the findings of Schaie and Labouvie-Vief (1974), compares the cross-sectional data collected in 1963 (black lines) with the cross-sectional data collected in 1970 (colored lines). The longitudinal data is signified by the dashed lines connecting the black and colored lines.

Two of the more recent reports (Hertzog & Schaie, 1988; Schaie, 1990) based on the SLS are especially important. Hertzog and Schaie (1988) examined the relationship between the *mean stability* of intelligence (e.g., the extent to which the average intellectual performance of a group of 70-year-olds differs from the average performance of a

*TABLE 5.3*

| Proportion of Individuals Showing a Decline in Specific Intellectual Abilities | | | | |
|---|---|---|---|---|
| *Intellectual Ability* | *Age 53 to Age 60* | *Age 60 to Age 67* | *Age 67 to Age 74* | *Age 74 to Age 81* |
| *Verbal Meaning* | 15.2 | 24.8 | 26.8 | 35.7 |
| *Spatial Orientation* | 21.1 | 27.0 | 29.6 | 32.6 |
| *Inductive Reasoning* | 14.0 | 26.5 | 23.6 | 27.9 |
| *Number* | 17.2 | 26.2 | 26.2 | 31.8 |
| *Word Fluency* | 23.6 | 28.4 | 27.5 | 37.2 |

*Source: Data from K. W. Schaie, "The Optimization of Cognitive Functioning in Old Age: Prediction Based on Cohort-Sequential and Longitudinal Data" in P. B. Baltes and M. Baltes (Eds.),* Longitudinal Research and the Study of Successful (Optimal) Aging, *Cambridge University Press, Cambridge, England, 1990, pp. 94–117.*

*TABLE 5.4*

| Proportion of Individuals Showing Decline in Intellectual Abilities | | | | |
|---|---|---|---|---|
| *Number of Abilities* | *Age 53 to Age 60* | *Age 60 to Age 67* | *Age 67 to Age 74* | *Age 74 to Age 81* |
| *None* | 41.3 | 26.7 | 24.3 | 15.5 |
| *One* | 35.3 | 35.1 | 37.7 | 37.2 |
| *Two* | 17.0 | 22.0 | 21.8 | 24.8 |
| *Three* | 4.8 | 10.3 | 11.3 | 14.0 |
| *Four* | 1.2 | 5.0 | 3.9 | 6.2 |
| *All Five* | 0.5 | 0.8 | 1.1 | 2.3 |

*Source: Data from K. W. Schaie, "The Optimization of Cognitive Functioning in Old Age: Prediction Based on Cohort-Sequential and Longitudinal Data" in P. B. Baltes and M. Baltes (Eds.),* Longitudinal Research and the Study of Successful (Optimal) Aging, *Cambridge University Press, Cambridge, England, 1990, pp. 94–117.*

group of 50-year-olds) and the *covariance stability* in intelligence (e.g., how individuals perform compared to their agemates at 50 versus 70 years of age). Participants were between 22 and 70 years of age at the beginning of the study. They were tested three times over a fourteen-year period on five different primary mental abilities. Results showed that the mean stability of the participants' performance was affected by age. The youngest participants displayed progressively higher levels of performance, middle-aged adults showed stability of performance, and older adults displayed a significant linear decline in performance—a decline that seems to take place for the majority of individuals somewhere between 55 and 70 years of age. On the other hand, all of the participants displayed exceptionally high levels of covariance stability across the fourteen-year period during which they were tested. These data provide substantial evidence for normative age-related changes in the mean stability of intelligence and the maintenance of individual differences in intellectual performance throughout the adult years.

Schaie (1990) examined the effects of age on the mental abilities of verbal meaning, spatial orientation, inductive reasoning, number, and word fluency. Longitudinal data were collected on subjects from ages 53 to 60, 60 to 67, 67 to 74, and 74 to 81. Table 5.3 reveals that, as age increased, participants were more likely to display a decline on any specific mental ability. More importantly, only about one-third of the participants showed a significant decline on any ability between 74 to 81 years of age. Likewise, table 5.4 shows that very few individuals

## *Research Focus 5.1*

### *Self-Conceptions of Intelligence Across the Adult Life Span*

Much has been learned about the aging of intelligence via the traditional psychometric approach. What seems to be lacking in the psychological literature, however, is a thorough examination of peoples' intuitive beliefs about intelligence and how different facets of intelligence change across the adult years. One of the first empirical studies to address this topic was conducted by Heckhausen, Dixon, and Baltes (1989). These researchers presented 102 adults between the ages of 20 to 85 with a list of 358 adjectives that characterized a broad range of intellectual (intelligent), personality (skeptical), and social (friendly) attributes. With each of these three categories there were approximately equal numbers of desirable (wise) and undesirable (forgetful) traits. Participants were asked to rate (1) the extent to which each attribute is expected to increase at any period from 20 to 90 years of age; (2) the extent to which an increase in an attribute is desirable; and (3) the age at which the increase in a specific attribute begins and ends. Increases in desirable and undesirable traits were characterized as developmental gains and losses, respectively. Results (see figure 5.A) reflected the common theme that gains outweighed losses except for the oldest-old. Contrary to the negative aging stereotype, these data reflect a fair amount of optimism about the nature of adult developmental change. More interestingly, the oldest participants in this study (aged 60–85) were most likely to perceive psychological attributes as subject to developmental change and had more specific views about the exact timing of these changes. Thus, these participants were more likely than younger and middle-aged adults to view adult development as a complex multifaceted process—which, in itself, is an indicator of cognitive sophistication.

Somewhat similar findings have been reported by Berg and Sternberg (1992). They required groups of young (aged 22 to 40), middle-aged (aged 41 to 59), and older adults (aged 60 to 85) to rate a list of 55 behaviors (is inquisitive, acts responsibly, displays good vocabulary, etc.) in terms of which each behavior was representative of an individual of either 30, 50, or 70 years of age who possesses exceptional intelligence. Factor analysis of the data showed that participants in all three age groups perceived intelligence as characterized by three independent dimensions: *ability to deal with novelty, everyday competence,* and *verbal competence.* Furthermore, all participants rated behaviors indicative of *everyday competence* and *verbal competence* to be more representative of 50- and 70-year-olds than 30-year-olds, whereas behaviors reflective of *ability to deal with novelty* showed the opposite developmental trend. Finally, participants from all three age groups believed that across the entire adult life span individuals can become more intelligent because of experience, training, and practice and less intelligent because of lack of stimulation and illness.

Overall, the findings of Heckhausen et al. (1989) along with Berg and Sternberg (1992) suggest that adults have a rather multidimensional and optimistic conceptualization of intellectual change. It would seem as if psychometricians would be wise to develop standardized instruments that capture the intellectual gains, especially those involving everyday competence in interpersonal affairs, as well as the losses that accompany the aging process.

---

showed global intellectual decline. For example, at age 60, about 75 percent of the participants maintained their performance on at least four out of five primary mental abilities. This level of maintenance was also found for slightly more than half of the 81-year-olds in the sample. Also, only 2 percent of the participants showed a decline on all five abilities between 74 to 81 years of age. Finally, it was discovered that no participants displayed constant intellectual decline on all five primary mental abilities over the twenty-eight years during which data were collected! Overall, these results suggest that constant, linear, and all-pervasive intellectual decline is more mythical than real. More positively stated, these data show that a significant percentage of individuals maintain most of their intellectual abilities well into old age.

The idea that the aging of intelligence is associated with both gains and losses is supported by more than just psychometric research. See Research Focus Box 5.1 for more details.

**Box Figure 5.A** Age-related pattern involving 163 psychological attributes: expected gains (increase in desirable attributes) and losses (increase in undesirable attributes) across the adult life span.
*Source: Data from Heckhausen, Dixon, & P. Baltes, 1989.*

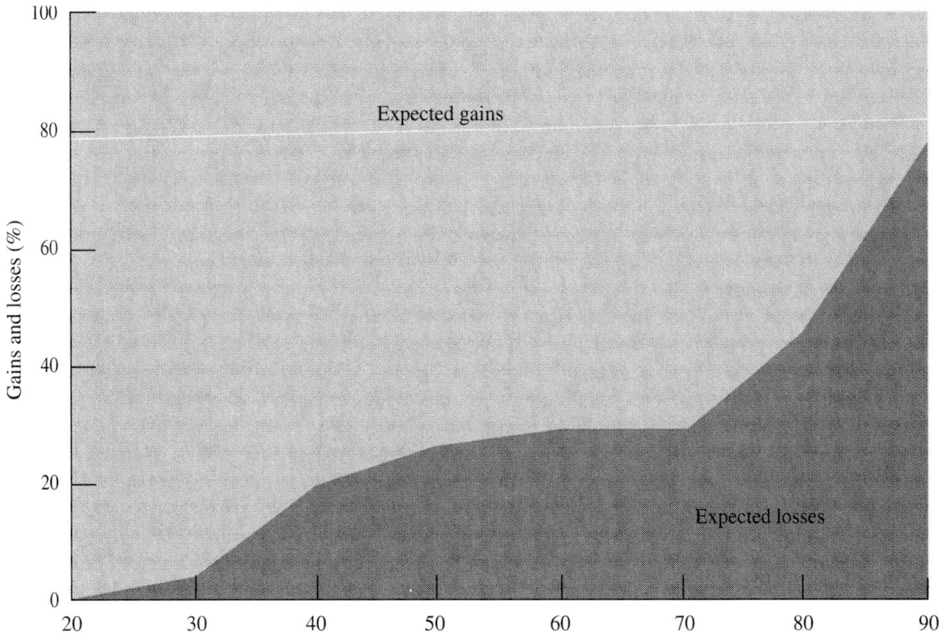


## *Factors Responsible for Developmental Changes in Intelligence*

Several investigators (e.g., Horn, 1982b) have suggested that intellectual decline results from the deterioration of the central nervous system. Without doubt, age-related changes in the brain have a significant impact on adult intellectual functioning. However, these changes alone cannot account for the pattern of results researchers found, nor can they adequately explain the individual differences that dispute the claim of universal biologically based loss. In this section, we'll discuss a variety of factors that may have a profound impact on intellectual performance during adulthood.

### Cohort Effects

Why do cross-sectional studies paint a more pessimistic picture of adult intellectual change than longitudinal studies? The answer may be that in cross-sectional

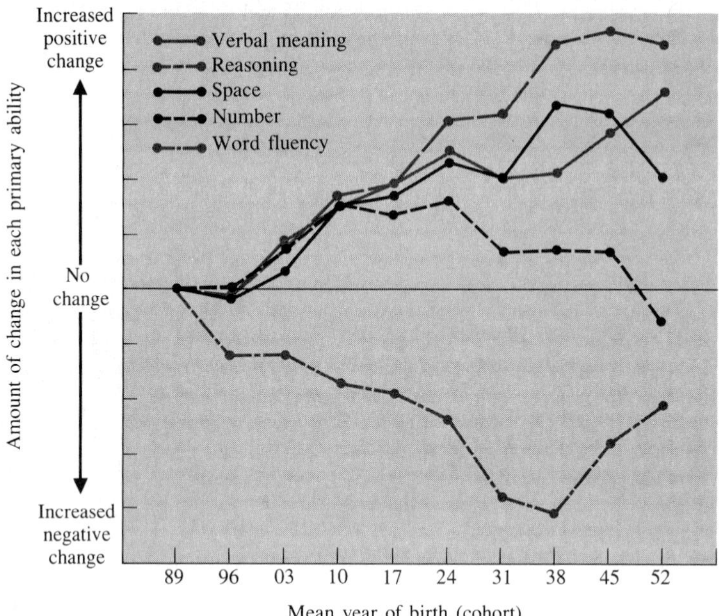


**Figure 5.6** Cohort changes in the primary mental abilities.

studies age-related differences are confounded with cohort differences. **Cohort** means the generation one is born into, or the year of one's birth.

In a cohort-sequential analysis of the data from the Seattle Longitudinal Study, Schaie (1979, 1983) discovered that adults' intellectual performance changed as a function of both age and cohort. Figure 5.6, adapted from Schaie's (1979) data, illustrates the profound influence of cohort effects on five different primary mental abilities. This graph represents the IQ test performance of individuals from ten successive birth cohorts (1889 to 1952). Notice the multidirectional manner in which the abilities change. The graph shows that space and reasoning abilities increased until the 1938 birth cohort, at which time the abilities either declined or leveled off. Verbal meaning displays a progressive increase over all cohorts measured. Number ability seems to have peaked with the 1924 cohort and declined since then. Finally, word fluency declined steadily until the 1938 cohort; since then it has displayed upward movement.

Gisela Labouvie-Vief (1985) has called attention to the fact that performance on tasks of fluid intelligence (e.g., space) is not immune to cohort effects. Even measures of fluid intelligence do not assess the pure information-processing abilities of the human mind; they are influenced by socioenvironmental forces such as cohort.

Cohort effects do not necessarily affect intellectual development negatively. Paul Baltes (1987) has described three different ways in which cohort differences can boost intellectual performance: in terms of education, health, and work. First, successive generations have received increasingly more formal education. Educational experience has been positively correlated with IQ scores. Second, each succeeding generation has been treated more effectively for a variety of illnesses (e.g., hypertension) that are known to have a negative impact on intellectual performance. Third, changes in the work life of more recent generations have placed a much stronger focus on cognitively oriented labor. Many of our grandfathers or great-grandfathers may have been farmers or manual laborers. Today, we are more likely to find jobs in service fields, such as emergency medical assistants, paralegal aides, or computer operators. This increased emphasis on cognitively oriented occupations most assuredly modifies and enhances intellectual abilities.

## Selective Dropout

The **selective dropout** of participants may mean that longitudinal studies provide an overly optimistic view of adult intellectual change. The concept of selective dropout is based on the idea that as information is gathered during a longitudinal study it becomes harder and harder to keep one's original sample of participants intact. Specifically, participants who are unhealthy, unmotivated, or who consider themselves to be performing poorly on an intelligence test are not likely to return for repeated testing. As a longitudinal study progresses, a positively biased sample of participants is thus likely to evolve. This biased sample consists of adults who tend to do well on measures of intellectual functioning—that is, those who are highly educated, successful, motivated, and healthy.

## Health

It seems obvious that individuals who are in good physical health can think, reason, and remember better than those in ill health. Even 20-year-old college students may find it difficult to concentrate during an exam if they are ill with the flu or some other illness. The problem for developmental researchers, of course, is that older adults are much more likely to suffer from chronic illness than younger people are. The relatively poor health of the elderly population can bias both cross-sectional and longitudinal studies. The older the population studied, the greater the number of persons with limiting health problems (Siegler & Costa, 1985).

Developmental psychologists must concern themselves with two interrelated issues. First, they must recognize that health may become much more of a determinant of intellectual functioning as individuals move through the life span (Siegler & Costa, 1985). Second, they must try to develop methodologies that separate the effects of aging from the effects of disease on psychological abilities.

Research has shown that the incidence of hypertension (high blood pressure) is related to a decline in intellectual abilities. Wilkie and Eisdorfer (1971) discovered in a longitudinal study that hypertension was linked to decreases on the WAIS for adults over age 60. Schaie (1990) found that hypertension was a better predictor of the intellectual performance of older adults than was a measure of overall health status. Schultz, Elias, Robbins, Streeten, and Blakeman (1986), in a longitudinal study of middle-aged adults, reported that nonhypertensive subjects displayed increases in performance on the WAIS, whereas hypertensives showed no significant change in performance on the WAIS. Another longitudinal study

*Health and physical fitness become increasingly important predictors of intellectual functioning as adults move through the life span.*

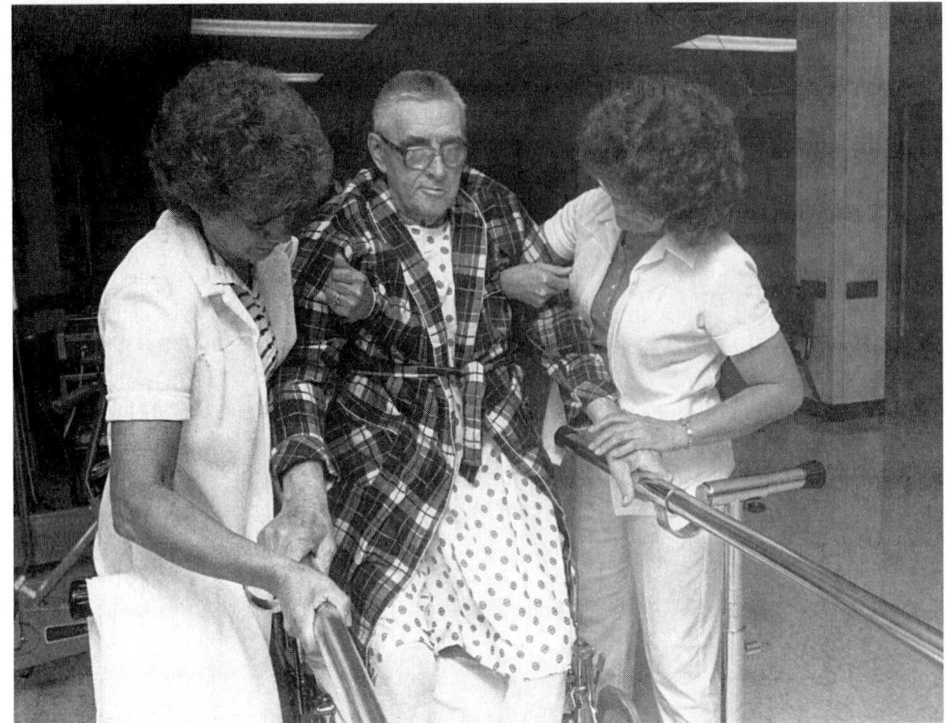

conducted by Sands and Meredith (1992) showed that hypertension predicts performance on certain aspects of intelligence independent of the contributions of age, education, and gender.

At a more general level, recent studies have investigated the degree to which a healthy lifestyle influences intellectual abilities. Hultsch, Hammer, and Small (1993) found that, for a sample of adults between 55 and 86 years of age, self-reported health status, alcohol and tobacco use, and level of participation in daily activities predicted performance on a wide range of mental abilities. More specifically, Hultsch et al. (1993) discovered that these measures were better predictors of fluid rather than crystallized measures of intellectual function, especially for older participants. In a related study, Hill, Storandt, and Malley (1993) charted the effects of a year-long aerobic exercise program on a group of eighty-seven sedentary older adults. They reported that long-term exercise increased cardiovascular fitness and morale, and prevented an age-related decline in verbal memory, for the participants in their study.

## Terminal Drop

Closely associated with selective dropout and health status is the notion of **terminal drop.** Terminal drop refers to the tendency for an individual's psychological and biological abilities to exhibit a dramatic decrease in the last few years prior to death. Terminal drop occurs when individuals die of chronic illnesses that drain them of their strength, energy, and motivation. Most older people die of chronic diseases rather than accidents or injuries. Chronic diseases reduce older adults' capacities for clear thinking, undivided attention, and mental effort. As a result, their scores on cognitive tasks drop off dramatically (Kleemeier, 1972; Riegel & Riegel, 1972). Given the greater number of older versus younger adults being tested near their deaths, the intelligence test scores of older adults are much more likely to reflect terminal drop than the test scores of younger adults. Thus, the declines in intelligence revealed in cross-sectional and longitudinal studies may be, at least in part, a statistical artifact caused by terminal drop.

More recently, White and Cunningham (1988) have examined the relationship between distance from death and adults' scores on tests of vocabulary, numerical facility, and perceptual speed. They found that vocabulary scores were most likely to decline in the years just prior to a person's death. Thus, terminal drop may be limited to those abilities (such as vocabulary and other verbal abilities) that are usually the least affected by age.

## Processing Speed

As mentioned previously, one of the most ubiquitous findings in developmental psychology is an age-related slowing of behavior and information processing. If the slowing of cognitive processing is one of the major hallmarks of aging, could it be the case that a decrement in processing speed is the primary determinant of intellectual decline in older adulthood? This hypothesis was examined in a recent study by

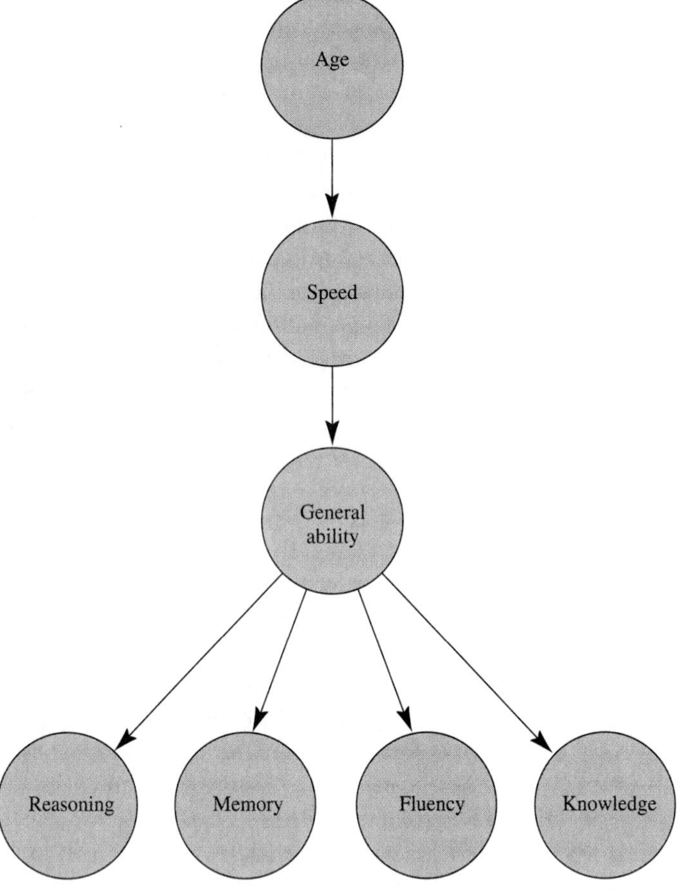


**Figure 5.7** Schematic relationship between age, speed of processing, intelligence, and the primary mental abilities in old age.

Lindenberger, Mayr, and Kliegl (1993). They administered measures of processing speed (e.g., the digit symbol substitution task) as well as tasks of fluid (reasoning and associative memory) and crystallized intelligence (knowledge and verbal fluency) to 146 individuals between 70 to 103 years of age. Results showed that negative age differences on all of the measures of crystallized *and* fluid intelligence were mediated through age differences in speed of processing. In other words, the amount of variability in subjects' performance due to age per se was exceptionally small, whereas the variability in performance due to speed by itself, and speed in combination with age, was exceptionally high. It is interesting to note that speed of processing was highly related to performance on the knowledge tasks even though these measures were untimed! Lindenberger et al. (1993) suggested (see figure 5.7) that age affects speed of processing, which negatively affects general intellectual ability, which, in turn, affects performance on individual tasks. Finally, the absence of a differential relationship between speed of processing and performance on crystallized versus fluid tasks suggests that age differences in speed may be responsible for a dedifferentiation or convergence of intellectual ability in advanced old age.

*Individuals such as Georgia O'Keeffe may well maintain their creativity in older adulthood.*

## Mental Exercise and Training

The idea that mental abilities can be improved by training, experience, or exercise has intrigued psychologists for many years. The enhancement of mental abilities via training is consistent with Baltes's (1987) notion of the *plasticity* of adult intellectual development. The concept of plasticity suggests that older adults have substantial cognitive reserve capacity and that training makes use of untapped reserve (Baltes, Sowarka, & Kliegel, 1989; Kliegel, 1990). Baltes and Kliegel (1986) and Willis (1985) hypothesized, for example, that older adults have little everyday experience with test items that measure fluid intelligence. But they also assumed that older adults possess the reserve capacity to raise their levels of performance on fluid-intelligence tasks. These researchers found that older adults between 60 and 80 years old who were exposed to a program of cognitive training exhibited performance levels on fluid tasks that were comparable to the performance levels of a group of untreated younger adults. Baltes et al. (1989) have even shown that older adults can train themselves to become more proficient in tasks of fluid intelligence.

*Older adults, unlike college students, are often unfamiliar with standardized tests and testing situations.*

However, Dittmann-Kohli, Lachman, Kliegl, and Baltes (1991) discovered that boosting the fluid intellectual abilities of older adults did not increase their perceived intellectual self-efficacy in real-life situations.

Nancy Denney (1984) suggested a distinction between *unexercised* ability (the level of performance that can be expected if the individual has had no exercise and/or training on a specific ability) and *optimally exercised* ability (the level of performance expected if the individual has received optimal exercise and/or training). The region between the two abilities in figure 5.8 represents the degree to which mental exercise and/or training can affect abilities. Of course, exercise or training can accumulate over a long period of time, even years or decades. Thus some types of ability might be essentially unexercised for many young adults but optimally exercised for middle-aged adults. Such abilities should not decline from young adulthood to middle adulthood. Indeed, they might even improve.

Willis and Schaie (1986), along with Schaie, Willis, Hertzog, and Schulenberg (1987), have found that older adults can, with training, show significant gains on different primary mental abilities. Moreover, gains in specific primary abilities derived from the training programs were found to generalize to other tasks measuring the same mental ability. These researchers discovered, therefore, that increases in intellectual ability associated with training studies go beyond merely teaching the test or changing the ability that is trained.

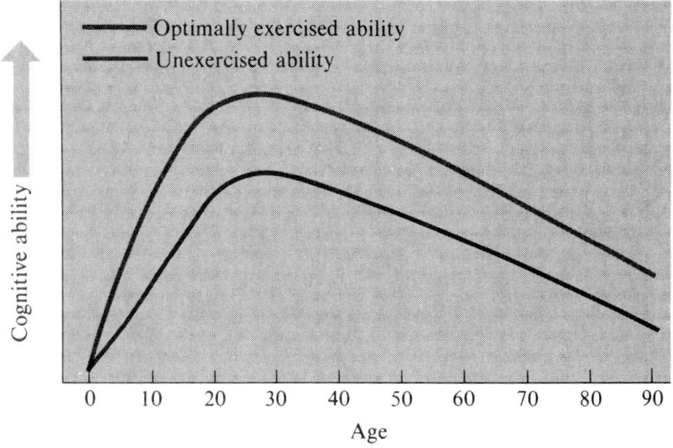


**Figure 5.8** The hypothesized relationship between age and both unexercised ability and optimally exercised ability.
*From: Nancy Wadsworth Denney, "Aging and Cognitive Changes" in* Handbook of Developmental Psychology, *edited by B. J. Wolman, © 1982, p. 819. Prentice-Hall, Inc., Englewood Cliffs, N.J.*

*TABLE 5.5*

| *Factors That Reduce the Risk of Intellectual Decline During Older Adulthood* |
|---|
| Absence of cardiovascular and other chronic diseases |
| Favorable environment mediated by high socioeconomic status |
| Involvement in complex and intellectually stimulating environment |
| Flexible personality style at midlife |
| High cognitive status of spouse |
| Maintenance of high levels of perceptual processing speed |

*From K. W. Schaie. (1993). The Seattle longitudinal studies of adult intelligence.* Current Directions in Psychological Science, *2, 171–174.*

These results are especially significant in light of the criticisms leveled at training studies by Donaldson (1981). He suggested that training programs designed to improve fluid intelligence may provide misleading results. More specifically, he argued that fluid abilities themselves become "crystallized" with extensive training. Thus, successful intervention programs transform a fluid ability into a crystallized ability. This speculation seems less credible given the results obtained by Baltes and Schaie and their associates.

Finally, even though the fluid abilities of older adults may be significantly boosted by training programs, it is important to realize that training has a much *more beneficial* effect for younger than older adults. It is certainly possible to teach older adults to display better performance on some components of intelligence in comparison to *untrained* younger adults. But, all things being equal, younger adults show greater gains from training than do their older counterparts. See table 5.5 for a general summary of the factors that K. Warner Schaie believes reduce the risk of intellectual decline during later adulthood.

## INTELLIGENCE AND EVERYDAY LIFE

At first glance, there seem to be a number of reasons why IQ test scores are poor indicators of everyday problem-solving abilities. First, several of the items in IQ tests—such as defining unusual words, solving arithmetic problems, arranging pictures in a particular sequence, and so on—seem to have little in common with the problems adults face in real life. Second, many of the performance items on IQ tests are speeded in nature. This puts older adults at a disadvantage given the phenomenon of psychomotor slowing. Their responses are slower than those of the typical younger adult. Third, older adults are not as accustomed as younger adults to taking tests and as a result may be more anxious and/or cautious. Fourth, older adults seem to be less motivated than younger adults to take IQ tests seriously and to perform at their optimal levels. Fifth, the original goal of IQ tests was to predict school success or failure among groups of children and adolescents. This goal seems to possess little meaning when applied to older individuals.

Despite the above-mentioned factors, many psychologists have found that scores on various psychometric intelligence tests are somewhat predictive to real-life problem solving. Willis and Schaie (1985), for example, administered a test of the seven primary mental abilities to a group of 80-year-olds along with a variety of everyday intellectual tasks: reading street maps, interpreting the information found on medicine bottles, filling out forms, comprehending Yellow Page advertisements, and so forth. Willis and Schaie found that performance across all of the everyday tasks was related to several of the primary abilities, especially reasoning.

Cornelius and Capsi (1987) investigated the relationship between aging and the *implicit* and *explicit* dimensions of intelligence. Implicit theories of intelligence (Sternberg, 1985) refer to people's commonsense beliefs about intelligence and how it develops. Explicit theories, in contrast, are concerned with formalized psychometric notions about what intelligence is and how it is best measured. It has been found that implicit views place a heavy emphasis on the practical or social aspect of intelligence. Practical or social intelligence involves sizing up situations, admitting mistakes, determining how to achieve goals, and so on. These types of abilities are *not* measured by the items found on traditional IQ tests.

Cornelius and Capsi's (1987) study assessed the relationship between practical intelligence and measures of crystallized and fluid intelligence. Their study consisted of two phases. In phase 1, these researchers developed a measure of practical intelligence called the *Everyday Problem-Solving Inventory.* This test consisted of forty-eight problems within six different social areas such as managing domestic issues and resolving interpersonal conflicts between family members, friends, and coworkers. Phase 2 involved the administration of the *Everyday Problem-Solving Inventory* along with measures of crystallized intelligence (the *Verbal Meaning Test*) and fluid intelligence (the *Letter Series Test*) to groups of young, middle-aged, and older adults. The results of this study, illustrated in figure 5.9, indicate that performance on the *Everyday Problem-Solving Inventory* and the *Verbal Meaning Test* increased with age, while performance on the *Letter Series Test* decreased with age. Furthermore, a modest correlation was found between scores on the *Problem-Solving Inventory* and both the *Verbal Meaning Test* and the *Letter Series Test.* Finally, it was discovered that familiarity with problems on the *Everyday Problem-Solving Inventory* was not related to scores on this measure.

These results suggest that practical problem solving, an important component of people's implicit view of intelligence, may be somewhat distinct from traditional

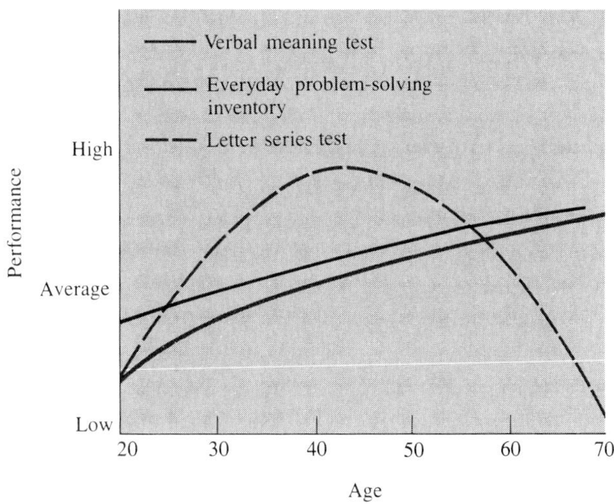


**Figure 5.9** An illustration of age-related changes on the Everyday problem-solving inventory, the Verbal meaning test, and the Letter series test. *Source: Data from S. W. Cornelius and A. Capsi, "Everyday Problem Solving in Adulthood and Old Age" in* Psychology and Aging, *2:144–153, American Psychological Association, Washington DC, 1987.*

measures of fluid and crystallized intelligence. The results also seem contrary to Denney's (1984) position that older adults perform better on measures of practical intelligence because they have much more experience in solving these problems. More positively, the results of this study support the viewpoint advocated by Paul Baltes and his associates (Dittmann-Kohli & Baltes, 1988; Dixon & Baltes, 1986). These investigators suggested that practical or social intelligence increases with age and has little in common with traditional psychometric measures of intelligence.

## *Conclusions About Adult Intellectual Change*

*When I was fourteen, my father was so ignorant I could hardly stand to have him around. But when I got to be twenty-one, I was astonished at how much he had learned in seven years.*
—Mark Twain

One of the major goals of this chapter was to answer what seems to be a relatively simple question: What happens to intelligence as one ages? As we have seen, however, there is not a simple answer to this question. Cross-sectional studies show a more dramatic and steeper rate of intellectual decline than longitudinal studies. Cross-sectional studies, because they are likely to be contaminated by cohort effects and terminal drop, are likely to paint an overly pessimistic picture of adult intellectual change. Longitudinal and sequential studies indicate that intelligence remains stable (or actually increases) until approximately 60 years of age, after which a slight decline may be observed. This conclusion seems most valid, however, for healthy, well-educated adults. Furthermore, the findings of longitudinal studies may be contaminated by selective dropout.

We have also seen that different types of intelligence show different patterns of change over age. Crystallized and verbal components of intelligence seem to increase with age, while fluid intelligence as well as performance measures of intelligence decline with age. Despite these predictable patterns of age-related change, there is a

## Research Focus 5.2

# Multiple Intelligences and Aging

Howard Gardner has developed a unique theory that challenges the traditional psychometric views concerning the measurement and meaning of intelligence. In a controversial book entitled *Frames of Mind,* he proposed a theory of multiple intelligences. This theory suggests that there are seven different human intelligences, each of which is localized in a different area in the brain. The different intelligences identified by Gardner are *linguistic intelligence, logical-mathematical intelligence, spatial intelligence, musical intelligence, bodily-kinesthetic intelligence, interpersonal intelligence,* and *intrapersonal intelligence.* Each of these different intelligences makes use of a different symbol system through which individuals represent or structure experience. For example, experience can be symbolized through words; logical-numerical relationships; visual images; tones, pitches, or rhythms; body movements; and so forth. Furthermore, Gardner maintains that only the first three of the above-mentioned intelligences are measured on traditional IQ tests.

Gardner's criteria for identifying specific types of intelligences include: (1) each intelligence can be independently represented in the brain and destroyed by damage or injury to a localized brain site; (2) exceptional individuals, child prodigies, and idiot savants may exhibit extraordinary performance in one form of intelligence but moderate or poor performance in other forms of intelligence; (3) each intelligence has a unique developmental history; (4) each intelligence consists of a core set of operations that are automatically triggered by particular types of experiences or information; (5) each intelligence has an evolutionary history; (6) the existence of each intelligence can be demonstrated by laboratory experiments and psychometric research; and (7) each intelligence possesses its own unique symbol system.

Gardner's theory is new enough that it has not been assessed fully in adult and/or aged populations. It would certainly be interesting, however, to determine what types of intelligence are likely to remain stable, decline, or increase with age.

great deal of plasticity in adult intelligence. It is possible to train adults to increase their scores on intelligence tests, even on tasks that measure fluid abilities. But, training effects are larger for younger than older adults.

Finally, we reported that traditional measures of intelligence are modestly related to measures of practical or social intelligence during adulthood. This finding does *not* mean that traditional tests are invalid measures of intelligence. Rather it suggests that psychometricians need to develop a more differentiated theory (and tests) of intelligence—a theory that does full justice to the broad array of intellectual abilities manifested by adults as they age. Research Focus 5.2 presents the basic ideas that underlie such a theory.

## Creativity

*This world is but a canvas to our imaginations.*
—Henry David Thoreau

Psychologists have assigned an important role to the study of creativity. David Wechsler suggested that, "Wisdom and experience are necessary to make the world go round; creative ability to make it go forward" (1958, p. 143).

What is it about someone like Thomas Edison that made him able to create so many inventions? Was he simply more intelligent than most people? Did he spend long hours toiling away in private? Surprisingly, when Edison was a young boy, his teacher told him he was too dumb to learn anything! There are other examples of famous individuals whose creative genius went unnoticed when they were younger

(Larsen, 1973): Walt Disney was fired from a newspaper job because he didn't have any good ideas; Enrico Caruso's music teacher informed him that he could not sing and that his voice was terrible; Winston Churchill failed one year of secondary school. Finally, consider the following comments made by John Lennon: "People like me are aware of their so-called genius at ten, eight, nine . . . I always wondered, 'Why has nobody discovered me? In school, didn't they see that I'm more clever than anybody in this school? That the teachers were stupid, too? That all they had was information that I didn't need.' It was obvious to me. Why didn't they put me in art school? Why didn't they train me? I was different, I was always different. Why didn't anybody notice me?" (quoted in Gardner, 1983, p. 115).

One of the reasons that creative ability is overlooked is because we have such difficulty in defining and measuring creativity.

## Definition and Measurement of Creativity

The prevailing belief of experts who study creativity is that intelligence and creativity are not the same. Just think about it: if intelligence and creativity were identical, there would be no reason to make a distinction between them! We could choose one of these terms—intelligence or creativity—to describe the same phenomenon.

Distinguishing between creativity and intelligence is a difficult task. David Ausubel (1968) has emphasized that creativity is one of the most ambiguous and confusing terms in psychology. He believes the term *creative* should be reserved for people who make unique and original contributions to society. Surely a list of creative individuals, from this point of view, would include Marie Curie, Charles Darwin, Thomas Edison, Georgia O'Keeffe, Pablo Picasso, and William Shakespeare—they possessed creative genius, or **exceptional creativity.** The world we live in has been shaped and influenced by the creative acts of these individuals. Several other researchers (e.g., Mumford & Gustafson, 1988; Simonton, 1988, 1990) have also agreed that psychologists should focus their attention on the study of exceptional creativity.

Robert Weisberg (1986) has argued for the existence of what may be called **ordinary creativity.** Ordinary creativity is exhibited in the behavior of "ordinary" adults who find themselves in "ordinary" real-life situations. George Rebok (1987) also described a kind of ordinary or everyday creativity in which we respond in give-and-take banter with friends, add new spices as we cook old family recipes, or create new outfits from old wardrobes.

J. P. Guilford's model of intelligence (1967) has important implications for creative thinking. The aspect of his model most closely related to creativity is what he calls **divergent thinking,** a type of thinking that produces many different answers to a single question. Divergent thinking is distinguished from **convergent thinking,** a type of thinking that moves toward one correct answer. For example, there is one correct answer to the question, How many quarters can you trade for sixty dimes? This question calls for convergent thinking. But there are many possible answers to the question, What are some uses for a coat hanger? This question requires divergent thinking.

Rebok (1987), while in general agreement with the position advocated by Guilford (1967), has suggested that the generation of novel ideas (divergent thinking) should be viewed as a necessary but not sufficient condition for creativity. Rebok points out that creativity depends on possessing a critical amount of knowledge within a particular area of interest. For example, it would be very difficult to be a creative composer if one did not know much about musical composition. Researchers interested in creativity should simultaneously assess an individual's thinking style and the degree of knowledge he or she possesses within a particular domain. This suggestion may be especially important when we examine creativity in older adults. As individuals age, they may be more likely to develop a sophisticated knowledge base within a particular area.

## Developmental Changes in Creativity

Because of the different conceptualizations of creativity, we'll divide this section into two parts. First, we'll discuss age-related trends in exceptional creativity—the important, creative accomplishments of well-known people within various fields of specialization. Second, we'll discuss age-related differences in ordinary creativity. This form of creativity has been measured by administering psychometric tests of creativity to typical as opposed to exceptional individuals.

***Exceptional Creativity*** Beyond any doubt, older adults have produced an impressive number of exceptionally creative accomplishments (see table 5.6). Lehman (1953, 1960) and Dennis (1966, 1968) conducted some of the earliest and most influential research on age-related changes in exceptional creativity in adulthood. Lehman (1953) charted the ages at which adults produced highly creative works that had a significant impact on their fields. As shown in figure 5.10a, the quality of productivity was highest when such individuals were in their thirties and then gradually declined. Lehman argued that approximately 80 percent of the most important creative contributions are completed by age 50. Lehman concluded that ". . . genius does not function equally throughout the years of adulthood. Superior creativity rises rapidly to a maximum which occurs usually in the thirties and then falls off slowly" (Lehman, 1953, pp. 330–331).

Unlike Lehman (1953), Wayne Dennis (1966) studied the *total productivity,* not just the superior works, of creative people in the arts, sciences, and humanities who lived long lives. He discovered (see figure 5.10b) that the point at which creative production peaked in adult life varied from one discipline to another. For example, in the humanities, people in their seventies appeared equally creative as people in their forties. Artists and scientists, however, began to show a decline in creative productivity in their fifties. In all instances, the twenties was the least productive age period in terms of creativity.

*Table 5.6*

| Some Creative Accomplishments of Older Adults | |
|---|---|
| ***Accomplishment*** | ***Age*** |
| George Bernard Shaw writes his first play | 48 |
| Sophocles writes *Oedipus Rex* | 75 |
| Sigmund Freud writes last book | 83 |
| Benjamin Franklin invents the bifocal lens | 78 |
| Claude Monet begins the Water Lily series | 73 |
| Michelangelo creates St. Peter's and frescoes the Pauline Chapel | 71–89 |
| Mahatma Gandhi launches the Indian Independence Movement | 72 |
| DeGaulle returns to power in France | 68 |
| Frank Lloyd Wright completes the Guggenheim Museum | 91 |

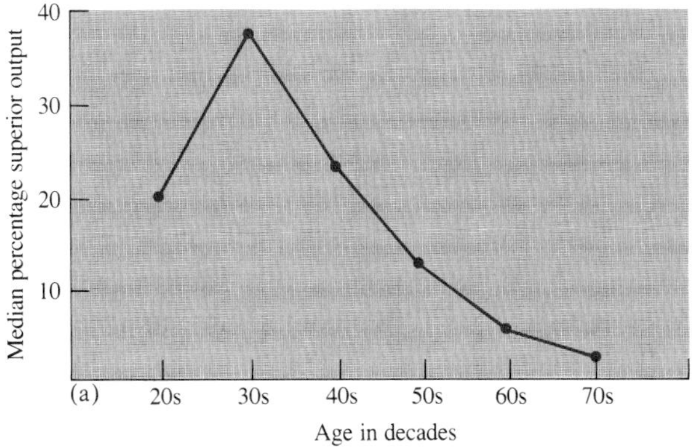


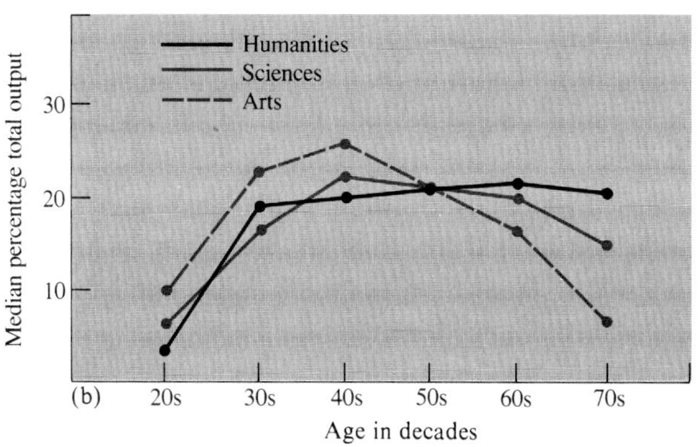


**Figure 5.10** (a) The percentage of superior output as a function of age. This generalized curve represents a combination of various fields of endeavor and various estimates of quality. *Source: Data from Lehman, table 34,1953.* (b) The percentage of total output as a function of age. The humanities, sciences, and arts are represented by the means of several specific disciplines. *Source: Data from Dennis, table 1, 1966.*

Dennis (1968) also examined the creative output of famous scholars, scientists, and artists who lived until at least 80 years of age. Dennis discovered that, on the average, the sixties was the most creative decade in the lives of these individuals! Thirty-five percent of the total output of scientists was produced after age 60—20 percent while they were in their sixties and 15 percent while they were in their seventies. Famous inventors produced more than half of their lives' work after age 60. Approximately 20 percent of the total output of artists was achieved after age 60. In a study of Nobel laureates in science, it was found that the average age at which they published their first major paper was 25. Furthermore, all of the laureates in this study who were past 70 continued to publish scholarly papers in scientific journals. Therefore, by relaxing the criteria for defining exceptional creativity (i.e., by examining the total creative output of individuals, not just their best work), we see that creativity may not decline as early as Lehman (1953) suggested. It seems as if individuals who are bright and productive in early and middle adulthood have a good chance of maintaining their creativity in older adulthood. This conclusion is consistent with Simonton's statement that the most creative individuals "tend to start early, end late, and produce at above-average rates . . ." (1988, p. 253).

Raymond Over (1989) examined the relationship between age and exceptional creativity by analyzing the percentage of both high- and low-impact articles published by scientists at different ages. He discovered that young scientists published more high-impact *and* low-impact works than older scientists. This finding is consistent with Simonton's (1990) conclusion that the "periods in a creator's life that see the most masterpieces also witness the most easily forgotten productions . . . the 'quality ratio,' or the proportion of major products to total output per age unit, tends to fluctuate randomly over the course of any career. The quality ratio neither increases or decreases with age . . ." (p. 323).

***Ordinary Creativity*** What happens when we administer psychometric tests of creativity to "typical" as opposed to "exceptional" groups of aging individuals? Does ordinary creativity show a pattern of age-related change? One of the first scientific studies on this topic was conducted by Alpaugh and Birren (1977). Their cross-sectional sample consisted of 111 teachers between 20 and 84 years of age. These subjects were administered the WAIS as well as a battery of psychometric tasks that measure creativity. Within this well-educated sample, scores on the WAIS remained stable across adulthood. However, scores on the measures of creativity were found to peak at 30 and decline thereafter.

In another study, Ruth and Birren (1985) tested 150 persons enrolled in adult education classes in Finland with several psychometric tests of creativity as well as measures of crystallized and fluid intelligence. The adults ranged from 25 to 75 years old. Results indicated that performance on the creativity measures declined with age. The great majority of this decline, however, was found to occur between young and middle adulthood. No age-related differences were found on the measure of crystallized intelligence; but scores on the fluid tasks were found to decline with age.

One of the major problems associated with the Alpaugh and Birren (1977) and Ruth and Birren (1985) studies is the use of a cross-sectional methodology. In comparison, Schaie and Hertzog (1983), in a longitudinal study on aging and creativity, discovered that only one aspect of divergent thinking (word fluency) declined with age. Unfortunately, the results of this study are clouded by the fact that the word fluency task was highly speeded. This may have placed the older adults at a greater disadvantage than the younger adults.

In one of the most comprehensive studies of aging and creativity, McCrae, Arenberg, and Costa (1987) combined cross-sectional, longitudinal, and cross-sequential methods of data collection. Their research, a component of the Baltimore Longitudinal Study of Aging, involved testing 825 well-educated men at regular intervals between 1959 and 1972. The men ranged from 17 to 101 years old. All of the participants were administered several different divergent-thinking tasks. These tasks involved (1) *associational fluency*—the ability to provide synonyms for specific words; (2) *expressional fluency*—the ability to write sentences with words beginning with certain letters; (3) *ideational fluency*—the ability to name objects in specific classes; (4) *word fluency*—the ability to write words containing a designated letter; and (5) *consequences*—the ability to imagine unusual, novel outcomes for particular situations. The participants were also administered the vocabulary test from the WAIS.

Results indicated that scores on the measures of creativity and the WAIS were distinct from each other. This is surprising, given the fact that the vocabulary test and all of the measures of creativity were verbal in nature. Furthermore, all the different methods of data collection and analysis (cross-sectional, longitudinal, and cross-sequential) revealed that scores on the measures of creativity declined with age. Based on these results, McCrae et al. (1987) concluded that creativity, like fluid intelligence, declines with age. However, the correlations between age and performance on the measures of creativity, although statistically significant, were in the modest range (–.10 to –.30). Also, McCrae and his colleagues administered the tests of creativity under standardized conditions with strict time limits, a procedure that may be especially disadvantageous to older participants.

Perhaps the complex and somewhat confusing nature of developmental changes in creativity may be best understood by approaching creativity from a **contextual perspective.** A contextual view suggests that a number of psychological and social changes may influence creativity during adulthood. In a discussion of life-span creativity, Jean and Michael Romaniuk (1981) provide an example from the academic world of how incentives for productivity may influence an individual's creativity. Tenure and the pressure to publish may affect creative accomplishment. Shifts in career interests and activities, such as transferring from research to administrative activity, individual shifts in priorities concerning career goals and job security, and attention to refining earlier creative accomplishments may influence creativity. And the opening of new research fields, along with the saturation of existing fields, may also influence creative accomplishments.

At a more general level, it would seem that as people age they may become less interested (due to internal as well as external pressures) in the creation of new ideas. Alternatively, they may become more interested in reflecting on the meaning of the knowledge that has already been created and on using that knowledge to help them come to grips with the meaning of their own lives and to help their culture evolve in an adaptive manner. Thus, as Simonton (1990) has suggested, with age, the desire to be creative may be replaced with the need to be wise. This viewpoint is consistent with Simonton's (1988) observation that older individuals occupy positions of power and leadership within a number of social, political, and religious institutions, while younger adults are more likely to create new institutions and to revolutionize existing ones. For example, a typical pope of the Roman Catholic Church assumes his position at approximately double the age at which Jesus of Nazareth ended his ministry. This seems to support Hall's (1922) position that ". . . men in their prime conceived the great religions, the old made them prevail" (p. 420).

In summary, we have seen that creativity is an elusive concept, one that is difficult to define, measure, and chart. It seems that exceptionally creative individuals may continue to function in a creative manner well into middle and late adulthood. In fact, many creative people do some of their best work late in life. The need to be creative, however, may decline with advancing age for a variety of psychosocial as well as intrapersonal reasons.

## *Genius*

*To believe your own thought, to believe that what is true for you in your private heart is true for all men—that is genius.*
—Ralph Waldo Emerson

In today's world, there are large numbers of exceptionally creative and highly intelligent adults. However, there seems to be something above and beyond creativity and intelligence—*genius.* What factors are responsible for the development of genius? At what age can genius first be identified? Until what age can genius be maintained? At present, many developmental psychologists are attempting to answer questions such as these. For example, in a recent book entitled *Creating Minds* (1993), Howard Gardner has analyzed the lives of seven geniuses of the modern era: Einstein, Freud, Picasso, Stravinsky, T. S. Eliot, Mahatma Ghandi, and Martha Graham. What can we learn about "genius" by studying these individuals?

First, it should be recognized that intelligence and creativity are a necessary but not sufficient condition for the development of genius. Second, geniuses are not content with solving problems. They relish the enterprise of **problem finding.** As Begley (1993) has observed, it isn't necessary to be a genius to interpret a dream; but it was Freud's genius that made him question the significance of dreams in human affairs. Third, geniuses seem to approach their work with a combined sense of childlike enthusiasm and obsessiveness. Geniuses work hard and they gain their fundamental insights by asking questions that are childlike in nature. For example, Einstein wondered about space and time (things that the average adult may have thought about as a child) from the point of view of a scientist. Fourth, geniuses seem to synthesize different modes of thought to produce their work. Composers, for example, often maintain they can see music, whereas painters often remark that they experience sounds as visual symbols. Fifth, there seems to be a critical amount of knowledge that a person must possess about a certain domain in order to make a geniuslike contribution. Too much knowledge and too much time spent thinking about the same problem may be just as antagonistic to genius as too little knowledge and too little thought. This may account for the fact that genius is a phenomenon of young and middle adulthood. The child may be prodigious. The older adult may be wise. But the individual who creates a major revolution in art, science, or literature is likely to be in her twenties or thirties.

## *Intelligence, Education, and Work*

In recent years, there has been a tremendous increase in adult education—both formal and informal. Adults today constitute more than half of all full- and part-time college students. Millions of adults are learning at their places of employment as American industries mandate skill enhancement and retraining programs.

In the past, most of our society's educational efforts were focused on children and adolescents. As Sherry Willis (1985) has commented, in today's complex, fast-paced, and changing world, the education children receive will simply not last a lifetime. Our society needs to reeducate and resocialize adults into roles they were not prepared for in their youths. We must view education as a process that helps maximize the development of individuals across the entire human life span. Willis (1985) identified five possible goals of adult education:

1. *Education as a means of comprehending sociocultural change.* Older adults need to understand the social and technological changes that have produced dramatic changes in their personal behavior.
2. *Education as a means of combatting technological and sociocultural obsolescence.* The education most older adults obtained in their youth does not allow them to cope with societal and career demands many decades later. Education becomes a means, therefore, of overcoming generational differences in both relevant knowledge and relevant skills.
3. *Second-career education.* Middle-aged to older workers who seek to remain competitive in the work force may have to undergo routine boosts or changes in their education. In the past, individuals made career choices in adolescence and young adulthood and stuck with those choices throughout life. Today, this pattern has dramatically changed. Because of technological change, several occupations that existed fifteen years ago no longer exist today. Conversely, several of today's occupations were not even identifiable fifteen years ago.
4. *Education as a source of satisfactory retirement roles.* Much of our adult work life does not provide us with the skills we need to adapt to retirement. Educational programs focusing on self-discovery and leisure-time activities may aid individuals making the transition into retirement.

5. *Education as a means of comprehending one's own aging.* As individuals grow older, they feel a greater need to seek information about the direction and meaning of the aging process.

Does the information we have explored about age-related changes in intelligence and creativity have a bearing on adult education? Most certainly it does! If you remember, most of the longitudinal studies of intelligence revealed that mental abilities actually increase until midadulthood, after which they either remain stable or show a small decline. Findings such as these have led Willis (1985) to suggest that individuals in their thirties, forties, and fifties may be particularly suited for higher educational pursuits—rather than people in their twenties, as we have come to expect. Furthermore, longitudinal studies suggest that adult education may have different functions at different times in the adult life span. The acquisition of new information and the sharpening of basic abilities may be the wisest goal of education until individuals reach their fifties. During the sixties and beyond, because of the declines seen in some intellectual abilities, the basic goal of education should probably be to maintain and support established abilities.

The importance attached to cohort effects in the study of intellectual aging has important implications for adult education programs. The goals of an education program aimed at older adults should be the remediation of intellectual deficits due to cohort and/or age. Older adults, in other words, may have two strikes against them when entering an educational program. First, coming from an earlier birth cohort, they may lack a number of the basic skills and areas of knowledge possessed by younger persons. Second, older adults may experience a decline in some (but not all) of their basic intellectual abilities.

Earl Hunt (1993) has reached a similar set of conclusions while commenting on the impact of computerization on the American work force. For example, he noted that older people are not adept in performing jobs in which they must make quick decisions, recognize stimuli embedded in a noisy background, and keep track of several pieces of information at once. However, these are the kinds of tasks that computers excel at. Thus, older (as well as younger) workers who possess the skills necessary to perform highly speeded perceptual-motor tasks run the risk of being replaced by machines. On the other hand, machines are not capable of dealing with the "novel" problems that arise in any industry or occupation. Hunt maintained that fluid intellectual abilities are needed to solve these types of problems. He also suggested that understanding why fluid intelligence declines during middle adulthood and how this decrement may be prevented and ameliorated will be of major economic necessity. Hunt's message to the employers (and employees) of the twenty-first century is rather straightforward, "The simple fact is that fluid intelligence will be in demand. Crystallized intelligence is only of use in a crystallized society" (Hunt, 1993, p. 597).

## Summary

The psychometric approach emphasizes a measurement-based orientation to the study of adult intellectual change. Psychometricians differ on the issue of whether intelligence is a general ability or a constellation of separate abilities. Intelligence, from the psychometric perspective, is assessed by the use of standardized tests. One of the most widely used tests to assess adult intelligence is the *Wechsler Adult Intelligence Scale* (*WAIS*). This test contains both verbal and performance scales.

Different types of developmental studies have reflected different patterns of age-related changes in intelligence. Cross-sectional studies show that intelligence declines sharply from early adulthood onward. Longitudinal studies, on the other hand, indicate that intelligence remains stable until late adulthood, when it may undergo a slight decline. Verbal intelligence is likely to improve with age, while nonverbal or performance components of intelligence are likely to decline with age. Put somewhat differently, crystallized intelligence has been found to increase with age, but fluid intelligence seems to decrease with age. Several factors appear to contribute to the observed age-related changes in intelligence. These factors include cohort effects, selective dropout, health status, reduced processing speed, and terminal drop. It has been shown that adults who actively exercise specific mental abilities, or who receive special training in specific abilities, do not display significant age-related decrements in those abilities.

Research on developmental changes in exceptional creativity suggests that in the arts and sciences, creative thought may peak in the forties, whereas in the humanities, creativity maintains itself well into the early part of late adulthood. Regardless of when creativity reaches its peak, research shows that for the majority of individuals creative output continues throughout midadulthood to later life. Research designed to study everyday creativity in typical individuals has shown a modest, but statistically significant, decline in divergent thinking over the adult life span. This research, however, may be marred by various methodological problems (including the speeded nature of standardized tests of creativity).

## Review Questions

1. What does the term *psychometric* mean?
2. Explain how psychometricians determine the IQs of different-aged adults.
3. What does it mean to say that intelligence reflects the operation of a single g factor? Have researchers obtained data supporting the g factor theory?
4. Explain the difference between crystallized and fluid intelligence. How do these different forms of intelligence change over time?
5. Explain the different results obtained by cross-sectional versus longitudinal studies of adult intellectual change.
6. Explain how cohort effects, selective dropout, health status, and terminal drop influence IQ test scores.
7. Discuss the concepts of mental exercise, plasticity, and cognitive intervention in late adulthood.
8. Describe two different approaches to the study of creativity and explain what you think is the best way to measure it.
9. Trace the developmental course of creativity during adulthood. How do developmental changes in "exceptional" creativity differ from those in "ordinary" creativity?

## FOR FURTHER READING

Baltes, P. B., & Baltes, M. (Eds.). (1990). *Longitudinal research and the study of successful (optimal) aging.* Cambridge, England: Cambridge University Press.

Gardner, H. (1983). *Frames of mind: The theory of multiple intelligences.* New York: Basic Books.

Gardner, H. (1993). *Creating minds.* New York: Basic Books.

Schaie, K. W. (1993). The Seattle longitudinal studies of adult intelligence. *Current Directions in Psychological Science, 2,* 171–174.

Simonton, D. K. (1990). Creativity and wisdom in aging. In J. E. Birren and K. W. Schaie (Eds.), *Handbook of the psychology of aging*, 3rd ed. (pp. 320–329). San Diego, CA: Academic Press.

Sternberg, R. J. & Berg, C. (Eds.), (1992). *Intellectual development.* New York: Cambridge University Press.

6

# COGNITIVE STAGES, WISDOM, AND EXPERTISE

*He who knows others is wise; he who knows himself is enlightened.*
—Lao Tzu

*It is on knowledge of the heart and of the instincts that reason must establish itself and create the foundation for all of its discourse.*
—Pascal

## *Introduction*

The information presented in the preceding chapters indicates that some degree of cognitive decline is an inevitable aspect of the aging process. Developmentalists have been unable to discover any measures of intelligence, attention, or memory on which older adults significantly outperform younger adults. Research stemming from the information-processing and psychometric perspectives seems to reinforce one of the most common images of adult cognitive development—as you age, you become less intelligent, less attentive, and less able to remember.

But another image many of us possess about the older adult's mental abilities is that with advancing age, some older people acquire wisdom. **Wisdom** is a particular mental quality associated with the cognitive abilities of some aged individuals but *not* with younger individuals. With the attainment of wisdom, older people are able to blend personal history and important information from the past to resolve a current problem (Clayton & Birren, 1980; Dittmann-Kohli & Baltes, 1988). Those considered to possess wisdom combine reflective abilities such as self-analysis and introspection along with affective components such as "empathy, gentleness, and peacefulness" (Huyck & Hoyer, 1982, p. 184). Wisdom is more than the sum total of an elderly person's cognitive abilities; it is composed of reflection, affect, and knowledge. Certainly, traditional psychometric and information-processing approaches have little, if anything, to say about the development of wisdom during older adulthood.

Which is the more valid image to hold of the cognitive abilities of the older adult? Are the elderly forgetful, inattentive, unintelligent, and foolish; or wise, knowledgeable, and sage? To help you make a meaningful choice between these two contrasting images, this chapter focuses on the application of *stage theory* to adult cognitive development. Stage theories stress the idea that new, more sophisticated ways of thinking emerge during adulthood.

We begin this chapter with a description of Piaget's theory of cognitive development, paying special attention to Piaget's description of *formal operations.* This stage was originally thought to be the final, most advanced stage of cognitive development. Next, we consider newer research that has sought to identify a stage of cognitive development beyond formal operations. This stage, which only emerges during the adult years, has been referred to as *postformal* operations. We review the basic characteristics of postformal thinking and summarize some of the research studies that have investigated the differences between formal and postformal thought, especially those that have focused on *social cognition*—the manner in which people understand and resolve the interpersonal problems characteristic of everyday life.

Then, we discuss the *encapsulation model* of adult cognitive development. This model, developed by John Rybash, William Hoyer, and Paul Roodin integrates and extends the different theoretical perspectives (the psychometric, information-processing, and developmental stage theories) that bear on the topic of adult cognition. We illustrate the basic tenets of the encapsulation model by describing recent research dealing with aging and cognitive expertise, and the growth of wisdom during the adult years.

## *Stage Theories of Adult Cognitive Development*

The concept of "stage" is probably one of the most overused and misunderstood terms used by nonpsychologists. It seems as if people often say, "He's in a stage," or "She's going through a stage," in speaking of development. Unlike laypersons, developmental psychologists use a set of very strict criteria to identify a *stage* of development.

### Characteristics of Cognitive Stages

Traditionally, psychologists have argued that a true set of cognitive stages must satisfy five different criteria: invariant movement, qualitative change, hierarchical integration, universal progression, and structured wholeness.

The notion of **invariant movement** suggests that there is a single, unchangeable sequence of stages that individuals must pass through during development. For example, if a stage theorist maintains that cognitive development consists of a four-stage sequence, then individuals must move through the stages in order: stage 1 → stage 2; stage 2 → stage 3; stage 3 → stage 4. It would be impossible to skip stages (e.g., to go directly from stage 2 to stage 4 by skipping stage 3), or to regress through the stages (e.g., to go backwards, from stage 3 to stage 2).

The concept of **qualitative change** suggests that at each different stage an individual actively constructs a completely different set of cognitive structures. Cognitive structures refer to a set of highly abstract, internal, and generalizable rules that are used to represent and understand reality. These thought structures are assumed to be as different from one another as apples are from oranges. Thus, stage theorists assume that mental development involves the growth of *qualitatively* different ways of thinking about the world. In other words, a stage theorist would argue that a person's intellectual functioning is determined by the manner in which the individual understands reality, not by the quantity of information the individual possesses.

**Hierarchical integration** implies that each stage in a developmental sequence should be viewed as an incorporation as well as an extension of the stage that preceded it. This means, for example, that stage 3 in a cognitive sequence has its basis in the thought structures laid down in stage 2. It also means that stage 3 extends the structures laid down in stage 2.

The idea of **universal progression** suggests that all individuals in all cultures progress through a set of stages in the same invariant sequence. This means that stage theories do not just apply to certain groups of individuals who live in certain social environments (e.g., middle-class, well-educated individuals from an industrialized society). A valid stage theory must apply to all individuals, regardless of social class, race, ethnicity, educational level, or culture.

The criterion of **structured wholeness,** which may be the most controversial aspect of stage theories, implies that individuals can only understand reality one stage at a time. This means, for example, that if an individual is at stage 2 within a particular cognitive developmental sequence, she will find herself thinking about every issue or problem she might potentially confront from the perspective of that stage. In other words, a person would not be expected to reason about mathematical problems from the perspective of stage 4 and interpersonal problems from the perspective of stage 2—such an inconsistency would violate the concept of structured wholeness.

## *Piaget's Stage Theory*

Beyond any doubt, Jean Piaget (see Piaget, 1970; Piaget & Inhelder, 1969) has formulated the most important and far-reaching stage theory of cognitive development. Although Piaget died in 1980, his theory continues to serve as a basis for a great deal of contemporary research in life-span developmental psychology.

### Overview of the Piagetian Stages

Piaget identified four stages of intellectual development: the sensorimotor stage, the preoperational stage, the concrete-operational stage, and the formal-operational stage. The **sensorimotor stage** lasts from birth to about 2 years of age and is thus synonymous with the period most people refer to as infancy. Piaget (1954) argued that infants cannot think about the world by means of internal mental symbols (such as words, visual images, and so on). Instead, infants can only represent objects or events by external body movements.

During the **preoperational stage,** which begins at about 2 years of age and lasts until 7 years of age, children can form internal mental symbols. At this stage, however, children have a great deal of difficulty in distinguishing between internal mental symbols and their referents. A referent is the object or event a mental symbol stands for. Mental symbols can represent concrete or imaginary events and objects. Thus, preoperational children have a great deal of difficulty distinguishing the real from the imaginary. For example, young children find it difficult to understand that dreams are mental rather than real-life events. In the preoperational stage, children's thinking may also be *irreversible.* This means that preoperational children do not understand that every action has an opposite action that is the reverse of the original. For example, preoperational thinkers have difficulty grasping the idea that addition is the reverse of subtraction. Thus, they do not understand that the best way to solve the following subtraction problem: ? – 7 = 1 is to transform it into an addition problem: 7 + 1 = ?.

In the **concrete operational stage,** which lasts from approximately 7 to 12 years of age, children and young adolescents can distinguish between mental symbols and real-life events or objects. Thus, children at this stage understand that Santa Claus is not a real person. Also, individuals begin to think in a *reversible* manner. Not only can concrete thinkers understand the complementary relationship between addition and subtraction, they can understand a relationship from different or reversible points of view. For example, when shown two pairs of sticks, the concrete thinker can understand that (1) if the red stick is taller than the blue stick (R > B), and (2) the blue stick is taller than the green stick (B > G), then the red stick must be taller than the green stick (R > G). Put another way, the concrete thinker is able to reason that "If the blue stick is shorter than the red stick but taller than the green stick, then the red stick must be taller than the green stick."

Concrete thinking is best suited for the solution of problems that involve concrete stimuli—stimuli that can be seen, heard, touched, smelled, and so on. For example, a concrete thinker could easily solve the previously mentioned problem involving the three different-sized sticks, but not the following verbal problem: "Imagine there are three girls walking down the street. Of these three girls, Mary is taller than Jane but shorter than Susan. Who is the tallest of the three?" This problem is very similar to the stick problem, but the stimuli in the former problem were concrete (they were actually seen and touched) while the stimuli in the latter task were hypothetical (they had to be imagined). Piaget maintained that it is only during the fourth and last stage of cognitive development, the stage he termed formal operations, that individuals can reason about hypothetical, abstract relationships.

## *Formal Operations*

*If Piaget's assertion that formal thought constitutes the crowning achievement of human ontogeny is accepted . . . a pessimistic view of adulthood becomes a logical necessity.*
—Gisela Labouvie-Vief

The stage of **formal operations,** which according to Piaget emerges somewhere around early- to mid-adolescence, has occupied an important place in the study of adult cognition. The importance of formal operations lies in the fact that since it is the last stage in Piaget's developmental stage theory, it represents Piaget's view of mature adult cognition, the most powerful and sophisticated form of thinking available to adults.

### Characteristics of Formal Operations

Piaget and his associates (Inhelder & Piaget, 1958; Piaget and Inhelder, 1969) have discovered three important characteristics of formal thinking:

1. A reversal in the relationship between reality and possibility.
2. An ability to think in a hypothetical-deductive manner.
3. A capacity to think about the nature of thinking.

With regard to the first of these characteristics, Piaget suggested that a concrete thinker's understanding of reality consists of a series of generalizations based on specific, real-life experiences. At the level of concrete operations, therefore, real experiences are more important than possible (or hypothetical or abstract) experiences. Formal thinkers, however, are capable of creating a reversal in the relative importance they attach to real versus possible experiences. This reversal allows formal thinkers to think logically about *verbal propositions.* Verbal propositions may be regarded as pure ideas. The truth value of a verbal proposition depends on its logical relationship to other propositions, not on its relationship to concrete, real-life events. Thus, formal thinkers can reason about contrary-to-fact ideas and experiences. For example, think about the following problems: (1) Would the weather be any different if snow was black, not white? (2) If it was so cold in a freezer that a frozen steak burst into flames, what would happen if this burning steak was placed in a very hot oven? A concrete thinker would probably argue that both of these problems are silly because in real life, snow is not black, and intense cold cannot make things burn. Formal thinkers, on the other hand, can rise above the constraints of reality. They understand that even though snow is not black and cold cannot burn, it is nevertheless logical to conclude that *if* snow was black the weather would change because the temperature would change (if large portions of the earth's surface were covered by a black substance, the earth would become hotter because the dark surface would absorb heat) and, *if* cold could make things burn, then putting the flaming steak into the hot oven should make it freeze.

The concept of *hypothetical-deductive thinking* means that formal thinkers are capable of reasoning like scientists. They can create abstract hypotheses or theories and then test the validity of these hypotheses by observing the results of well-controlled experiments. Thus, scientific thinking is deductive in that it proceeds from the general (the abstract hypothesis) to the specific (creating a single experiment designed to test the theory).

The notion of *thinking about thinking* means that formal thinkers can ponder the meaning and significance of their mental experiences from multiple points of view. For example, an individual at the formal operational stage can think, "I want to be married," and can then generate a number of hypothetical explanations of the meaning and significance of that thought from his point of view as well as the point of view of others (parents, for example). The ability to think about thinking accounts for the fact that adolescents and adults become very introspective. They often become armchair psychologists who find it intriguing to analyze their own mental activity as well as the thoughts and feelings of others.

## Measurement of Formal Operations

Piaget and his colleagues (Inhelder & Piaget, 1958) invented several different types of tasks to determine if an individual has reached the stage of formal operations. In this section we discuss two of these tasks: the proportional-thinking task, and the isolation-of-variables task.

A *proportional-thinking task* refers to a type of problem that can only be solved if an individual thinks about mathematical relationships in an abstract, relational, or proportional manner, rather than a concrete, absolute manner. More specifically, this type of task determines if a person approaches a mathematical problem by using simple arithmetic (a concrete operational strategy) or by using algebraic reasoning (a formal operational strategy). For example, consider the following:

> Your task is to estimate the number of beans in a large bowl. To help you make a reasonable estimate, a psychologist performs the following experiment. She takes a cup, dips it into the bowl, and pulls out eighty beans. Next, the psychologist takes a felt-tipped pen and places a large *X* on each of the eighty beans. The psychologist puts the marked beans back into the bowl and randomly mixes the beans. Then she dips the cup back into the bowl and extracts another sample. She discovers that there are seventy-five beans in the cup and that fifteen of the seventy-five beans have an *X* on them. What would you estimate the total number of beans in the bowl to be?

A concrete thinker, using simple arithmetic, might answer 140 (adding the 60 unmarked beans in the second sample to the 80 marked beans in the first sample). A formal thinker, using algebraic reasoning, would say 400 (if one-fifth of the beans from the second sample were marked, it is logical to assume that one-fifth of the total number of beans were obtained on the first sample. Therefore, if 80 is one-fifth of the total number of beans, there are 400 beans because $5 \times 80 = 400$).

In the *isolation-of-variables problem,* a person must determine which of a large number of variables produces a specific outcome. One of the most widely used problems of this type is the *pendulum task* in which a participant is asked to determine the factor(s) influencing the speed at which a pendulum swings back and forth. These factors include the length of the pendulum string, the weight of the object placed at the end of the string, the height at which the pendulum is released, and the force with which the pendulum is pushed. Participants are given a pendulum apparatus that comes with two different strings (a long string and a short string) and two objects of different weights that can be placed on the ends of the strings (a heavy weight and a lighter weight). Given the materials at their disposal, the participants are told to do as many experiments as they need to solve the problem. This task measures formal operational thinking because it requires participants to behave like scientists. They must develop a theory about what controls the oscillation of the pendulum and then perform the crucial experiments to test the theory. Only at the stage of formal operations do individuals approach this problem in a scientific and systematic manner; that is, they evaluate each of the potential factors one at a time (keeping all of the other factors constant). Using this approach, they discover that the length of the string, not any of the other factors, determines the speed of oscillation.

## Research on Formal Operations

Piaget (1972) assumed that individuals begin to develop formal operational thinking skills at about 11 years of age and that they fully complete the transition from concrete to formal operations at no later than 15 to 20 years of age. A great deal of

*Complex logical problem solving remains a salient feature of adult thinking.*

research (see Flavell, 1985; Neimark, 1975, 1982; Papalia & Bielby, 1974; Tomlinson-Keasey, 1972) has examined Piaget's assertions about the age at which individuals attain formal reasoning. Surprisingly, it has been discovered that a significant percentage of young adults, middle-aged adults, and older adults do *not* attain the stage of formal operations. Furthermore, it has been shown that being able to solve one type of formal-thinking task does not guarantee that a person will be able to solve another type of formal-thinking task (Bart, 1971; Berzonsky, 1978; Brainerd, 1978). For example, adults who are able to solve an isolation-of-variables task are not necessarily capable of solving a proportional-thinking task, and vice versa.

Overall, the available research seems to indicate that the earliest point in development during which formal operational thinking may appear is early adolescence to midadolescence. But this does not mean that all individuals begin thinking in a formal manner at this time; nor does it mean that all individuals will ultimately reach formal operations. These results are both important and somewhat startling. In fact, these findings have forced psychologists to reconsider Piaget's conception of formal operations.

## Reconceptualizing Formal Operations

One of the reasons why not all adults attain formal operations concerns the nature of the tasks used to measure formal thinking. As you may have recognized, the tasks Piaget constructed for assessing formal thought focus on problems from the fields of mathematics and physics. Without the prerequisite educational background and cultural experience, many adolescents and adults are at a distinct disadvantage when given these tasks.

In an important paper published in 1972, Piaget modified his view on formal operations. Piaget argued that the stage criteria of structured wholeness may not apply to formal operations. He maintained that based on aptitude, educational

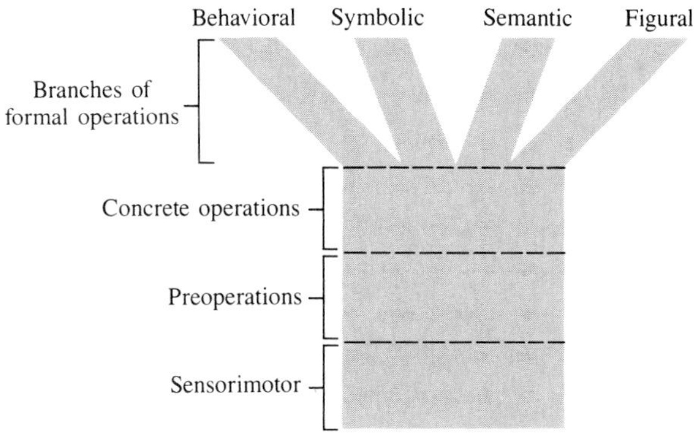


The behavioral branch involves an understanding of interpersonal and intrapersonal psychological processes.

The symbolic branch involves the ability to represent and manipulate arithematic and algebraic symbols.

The semantic branch involves the representation and manipulation of ideas within a verbal medium.

The figural branch involves the representation and manipulation of ideas and concrete objects within a visual medium.

**Figure 6.1** An illustration of Berzonsky's branching model of formal operations.

experience, motivation, professional specialization, and other factors, adults may develop formal thinking in some, but *not* all, areas. For example, an experienced garage mechanic may use formal reasoning to diagnose (and correct) the problem with a faulty automobile engine; but the same mechanic may have a concrete understanding of a critically ill patient's right to refuse medical treatment. On the other hand, a physician may reason at the formal level when thinking about problems involving medical ethics; but the same physician may continue to use concrete thinking to figure out why the family car keeps stalling.

One of the more interesting extensions of Piaget's (1972) modified view of formal operations has been articulated by Michael Berzonsky (1978). He proposed that Piaget's theory can be conceptualized as a tree (see figure 6.1). The first three stages of the theory make up the trunk of the tree. The formal operational stage represents the branches. These branches, which are based on Guilford's (1967) ideas about the different dimensions of intelligence, represent the areas within which an adult could develop formal-thinking skills. As you can see, it is possible to develop formal reasoning in any of a number of different domains (e.g., reasoning about interpersonal relations; reasoning about art, music, and literature; reasoning about mathematical or scientific issues; and so forth).

## Critique of Formal Operations

Formal operational thinking provides a powerful, but somewhat limited, mode of thought. In this section, we discuss six limitations of formal thinking as identified by Rybash, Hoyer, and Roodin (1986).

1. *Formal operations overemphasizes the power of pure logic in problem solving.* This limitation is expressed in the following passage: "Reason reveals relations within any given context. . . . But there is a limit. In the end, reason itself remains reflexively relativistic, a property which turns reason back upon reason's own findings. In even its farthest reaches, then, reason will leave the thinker with several legitimate contexts and no way of choosing among them—no way, at least, that can be justified through reason alone. If he still is to honor reason he must now also transcend it; he must affirm his own position from within himself in full awareness that reason can never completely justify him or assure him" (Perry, 1968, pp. 135–136).

2. *Formal operations underemphasizes the pragmatic qualities of real-life cognitive activity.* Labouvie-Vief (1984) reinforced this point when she noted that upon entry into adulthood, ". . . there is a concern with the concrete constraints of real life or the refusal to sever cognition from its affective, social, and pragmatic ties" (p. 159).

3. *Formal thinking is only suited for the problems that call for scientific thinking and logical mathematical analysis.* Piaget assumed that the goal of the cognitively mature adult was to reason like a scientist or a mathematician. Consequently, he did not examine how cognition is applied to real-life social or interpersonal problems. In connection with this point, Flavell (1977) maintained that "Real problems with meaningful content are obviously more important in everyday human adaptation (than abstract, wholly logical problems), and it is possible that these are the kinds of problems our cognitive apparatus has evolved to solve" (p. 117).

4. *Formal operations is geared for the solution of closed-system, well-defined problems.* A closed-system problem is one in which a person determines how a limited number of controllable and specific variables produce a specific and reliable outcome. For example, in the pendulum task, a series of miniexperiments help to determine how a limited number of controllable and specific variables influence the oscillation of a pendulum. Closed-system problems are also well defined in that they have a single, correct solution (it *is* the length of the string that controls the oscillation of the pendulum). Real-life problems, in contrast, are open to the extent that they are characterized by an unlimited number of uncontrollable, fuzzy variables (see Basseches, 1984; Koplowitz, 1984). For example, a woman must consider an infinite number of constantly changing variables when deciding whether to pursue a business career or take time off from business when having a child. Furthermore, open-system problems are ill-defined because they emerge from changeable and uncontrollable variables and do not have a single correct solution (there is no one correct solution, for example, to the woman's problem about whether to pursue her career or take time off when she becomes a mother).

5. *Formal operations does not recognize the relative nature of knowledge and the need to adopt multiple frames of reference.* Thinking from a relativistic standpoint has been referred to as "intersystemic thinking" by Gisela Labouvie-Vief (1982). She argued that intersystemic thinking" . . . reveals the basic duality of logical truth. This realization initiates a movement from logical absolutism to logical relativism. . . . Much as truth now is relativistic, one's actions must be singular and particularized. The erosion of logical certainty throws the self explicitly back on its own resources" (Labouvie-Vief, 1982, p. 182).
6. *Formal thinking places a greater emphasis on problem solving than on problem finding.* This means that formal thought is best suited for generating and testing hypotheses that aid in the solution of closed-system, well-defined problems. *Problem finding,* in contrast, represents the ability to generate new questions that arise from ill-defined problems (Arlin, 1975, 1984; Mackworth, 1965). It reflects the ability of adults to ask novel questions about themselves, their work, and the events that surround them. Arlin (1984) observed that the essence of problem finding was described by Wertheimer (1945). Wertheimer suggested that "the function of thinking is not just solving an actual problem but discovering, envisaging, and going into deeper questions. Often in great discovery the most important thing is that a certain question is found" (p. 46). Problem finding may be evident in periods of scientific revolution during which insightful adults (such as Darwin, Freud, and Einstein) address old facts from the perspective of new questions and worldviews.

## *Postformal Cognitive Development*

*There is no absolute knowledge. And those who claim it, whether they be scientists or dogmatists, open the door to tragedy.*
—Jacob Bronowski

The problems and shortcomings of formal thinking have set the stage for a major conceptual revision of Piagetian theory. It is now assumed that a type of thinking that is qualitatively different from formal operations emerges during the adult years. This type of thinking has been labeled **postformal operations** (Commons, Richards, & Armon, 1984; Commons, Sinnott, Richards, & Armon, 1989). In this section, we review current theory and research on the growth of postformal thinking during adulthood.

### Characteristics of Postformal Thinking

Diedre Kramer (1983) identified three basic features of postformal reasoners. First, postformal thinkers *possess an understanding of the relative, nonabsolute nature of knowledge.* Second, postformal thinkers *accept contradiction as a basic aspect of reality.* For example, a physicist might come to understand light as being both waves and particles, or an individual might realize that his feelings about another person cannot be described in terms of love *or* hate alone, but by the simultaneous existence of these

## RESEARCH FOCUS 6.1

# Basseches's View of Dialectic Thinking

Michael Basseches's (1984) view of postformal thought focuses on the means by which the adult thinker envisions reality as a multitude of relationships or systems that continuously change over time. Furthermore, Basseches proposed that the adult thinker comprehends these constantly changing systems in a constantly changing world through the principle of the dialectic. The term *dialectic* refers to an understanding of how transformations occur through constitutive and interactive relationships.

Relationships are *constitutive* in that the elements of a relationship are created by the whole relationship they make up. The whole relationship could not exist, however, without its component parts. Therefore, it is both the relationship that creates the elements and the elements that create the relationship.

Relationships are also *interactive:* they are characterized by mutual (or reciprocal) influence. In other words, the components of a relationship are changed *by* one another to the same extent that they change one another.

Let's look at an illustration that contrasts formal thinking with dialectic or postformal thinking. This example, which is drawn from Basseches (1984, pp. 26–27), deals with the topic of marriage and the problems that could arise between husband and wife.

A formal thinker would probably view the partners of a marriage as two individuals, each of whom possesses a number of fixed and stable traits. The traits that characterize the husband's personality exist independently of those that characterize the wife's personality, and vice versa. Therefore, the marriage of these individuals represents a connection between two elements (husband and wife) that have a separate existence outside of the relationship they are entering. These two sets of fixed traits should give rise to a relationship that remains fixed and stable over time. Marital problems from a formal perspective might develop for two reasons. First, they could result from a permanent flaw or shortcoming in either the husband's or wife's personality (e.g., one of the marriage partners made a bad choice—he or she picked a mate with a totally incompatible personality). Second, it could be that neither of the partners was intrinsically flawed; their marriage developed problems because in some cases the interaction of the personalities of two good people proves to be problematic (they were two nice people who weren't meant for each other).

A dialectic thinker would view the elements of any relationship as being in a state of constant flux. Therefore, the traits of the man and the woman who enter the marriage are not regarded as stable and permanent over time. More importantly, it is assumed that the traits of both husband and wife could not exist independently of one another. The traits of the man as a husband are influenced by his relationship with his wife, and vice versa. In other words, marriage is a constitutive relationship in which the elements of the relationship are totally interdependent on each other. Furthermore, dialectic thinkers view marriage as an interactive relationship, a relationship in which the elements of the relationship (husband and wife) mutually change and are changed by each other. Finally, a dialectic thinker would regard marital problems as the results of a relationship that has evolved in an increasingly maladaptive manner. The maladaptivity affects the whole of the relationship—the marriage—to the same extent that it interferes with the growth of the parties of the relationship (the husband and wife who create and are created by the relationship). Viewing a problematic relationship from this perspective allows husband and wife to avoid blaming each other as the cause of the problems. It also allows them to value their relationship as something that was meaningful at some point in its growth and evolution. The crucial question the dialectic thinker asks is, "How does our marriage need to change in response to the changes it has brought about in both of us?"

apparently contrasting emotions. Third, postformal thinkers are *capable of dialectic reasoning.* They possess an ability to synthesize contradictory thoughts, emotions, and experiences. Instead of viewing a contradictory situation as a choice between alternatives, the postformal reasoner views it as a call to integrate alternatives. See Research Focus 6.1 for Michael Basseches's (1984) conception of dialectic thinking.

In addition to the insights offered by Kramer (1983), we suggest that postformal thinkers adopt a *contextual approach* to problem solving. That is, they solve problems by continuously creating new principles based on the changing circumstances of their lives—rather than by applying a set of absolute principles or standards across all contexts and circumstances. This may be especially true

*Advanced intellectual skills remain functional in highly-specific domains throughout adult life.*

when adults reason about the ill-defined problems characteristic of everyday social life. Furthermore, postformal thinking seems to be *domain-specific* in nature. This means that adults develop postformal thinking within some, but not all, areas of knowledge. Finally, postformal thinking may be more directed toward *problem finding* than problem solving.

## Research on Postformal Thinking

In this section, we examine research studies focusing on two aspects of postformal thinking: (1) the relativistic nature of knowledge; and (2) the change in emphasis from problem solving to problem finding.

***Relativistic Thinking*** William Perry (1968) was one of the first researchers to address the topic of postformal thought. He conducted a longitudinal study in which he questioned university students about their educational and personal experiences. Perry found that freshman students approached various intellectual and ethical problems from a dualistic (formal) perspective. These students assumed that any problem or ethical dilemma could have only one correct answer, and that it was the task of authority figures (in their case, perhaps, professors) to teach them the correct answer. In time, the students began to realize the inherent subjectivity of experience. This led

*TABLE 6.1*

| Stages in Kitchener and King's Reflective Judgment Model |
|---|
| *Stage 1:* Belief in the absolute correspondence between reality and perception. Therefore, beliefs require no justification because to observe reality means to know reality. |
| *Stage 2:* Belief in the existence of an objective reality and absolute knowledge of this reality. It is the role of authority figures (e.g., professors) to know and transmit objective knowledge. Therefore, personal beliefs are justified by their correspondence to the beliefs of authorities. |
| *Stage 3:* Belief that authorities may be temporarily unaware of particular types of absolute knowledge. It is also assumed that while such missing knowledge will ultimately be obtained, it is permissible to believe in what "feels right" to the self. |
| *Stage 4:* Belief that there is an objective reality that can never be known with certainty. Therefore, all knowledge, even knowledge possessed by authorities, must be conceptualized as relative to the individual's point of view. |
| *Stage 5:* Belief that not only is knowledge subjective or relative, but that all of reality is subjective or relative as well. Since reality and knowledge of reality can only be understood through subjective interpretation, understanding is contextual and cannot be generalized. |
| *Stage 6:* Characterized by the belief that even though all knowledge is subjective, some forms of knowledge may be more valid than others. This claim is based on the premise that there are principles of inquiry which generalize across contexts. |
| *Stage 7:* Characterized by the belief that knowledge is the result of critical inquiry. Valid knowledge claims may be made by evaluating the work of many individuals over a long period of time. The process of critical inquiry, however, may give rise to fallible knowledge. Therefore, all knowledge claims must remain open to reevaluation vis-à-vis the formulation of new theoretical paradigms and the accumulation of new data. |

*From K. S. Kitchener and P. M. King, "Reflective Judgment: Concepts of Justification and Their Relationship to Age and Education" in* Journal of Applied Developmental Psychology, *2: 89–111. Copyright © 1981 Ablex Publishing Corporation, Norwood, NJ. Reprinted with the permission of Ablex Publishing Corporation.*

the students to conceptualize all knowledge and value systems—even those espoused by authorities—as relative and nonabsolute. At this level, the students felt as if they were adrift in an ocean of uncertainty. They thought that any problem could be approached from a variety of viewpoints, each of which seemed to possess equal merit and validity. Finally, some students reached a developmental level indicating postformal thinking termed *contextual relativism.* They still understood the relativity of knowledge, but they were no longer overwhelmed by it. In addition to accepting the contextual and subjective nature of knowledge and values, these students became committed to a self-constructed intellectual and ethical point of view. These students, in other words, were capable of both accepting and transcending relativity.

Karen Kitchener and Patricia King (1981) have investigated the relativistic nature of adult thinking with their *reflective judgment model.* This model postulates the existence of a series of seven stages, each characterized by a set of assumptions upon which individuals justify their beliefs about reality and knowledge. Table 6.1 contains a brief description of each of these stages. Several researchers (King, Kitchener, Davison, Parker, & Wood, 1983; Kitchener & Wood, 1987) using interview data have discovered that individuals systematically pass through these different stages from adolescence to middle adulthood. To date, this model has not been extended to research involving the elderly.

Jan Sinnott (1981, 1984, 1989) maintained that relativistic thinking can be directed at several different intellectual domains (e.g., the physical sciences or mathematics). But Sinnott also contended that it is easiest to understand the relativistic nature of postformal reasoning within the area of interpersonal reality. Specifically, she applied the term *necessary subjectivity* to describe relativistic thinking within the area of interpersonal relations. Necessary subjectivity means that when adults solve interpersonal problems, they are guided by the premise that subjectivity, or mutually contradictory frames of reference, is a basic characteristic of interpersonal reality. This contrasts with the typical view of physical reality, in which subjectivity is considered to be faulty thinking and eliminated from problem analysis. To examine the relativistic nature of adult cognition, Sinnott (1984) presented a group of adults between 26 and 89 years of age with a variety of problems designed to detect the presence of formal thinking and relativistic thinking. The results showed that older adults were more likely to use relativistic, postformal thinking styles to deal with real-life rather than abstract problems. Younger participants were more likely to solve all types of problems by adopting a nonrelativistic, formal mode of thinking.

Rakfeldt, Rybash, and Roodin (in press) examined the relationship between postformal thinking and the ability to profit from psychotherapy. The participants in this study were adult, first-admission patients in a psychiatric hospital who were given a series of open-ended interviews. These interviews assessed the manner, formal or postformal, by which the patients conceptualized themselves, their relationships with others, and their psychiatric disorders. The participants also took a large battery of standardized tests that measured their premorbid levels of social adjustment and the degree to which they were benefiting from psychotherapy. When social adjustment prior to institutionalization was controlled, it was discovered that patients who displayed relativistic thinking tended to have a more efficacious understanding of themselves, their disorders, and their relationships with others. These patients also seemed to take an active role in their healing. In contrast, patients who adopted an absolute (that is, formal) perspective seemed to make less significant therapeutic gains. Formal thinkers believed it was the duty of authority figures—their psychiatrists—to discover the "true" disorder they suffered from, and treat the disorder while the patients adopted a passive stance. Rakfeldt et al. concluded that relativistic thinking allows patients to better understand the complexities and paradoxes of their psychiatric disturbances as well as the choices and options open to them within the therapeutic encounter.

Kramer, Kahlbaugh, and Goldston (1992) developed an objective measure of postformal reasoning called the *Social Paradigm Belief Inventory (SPBI).* This test consisted of twenty-seven statements about social, interpersonal, and intrapersonal issues, each of which was written in absolute, relativistic, and dialectic versions. Participants were required to choose the one version that best captured their viewpoint on a particular issue (see table 6.2 for an example of a test item, and table 6.3 for some of the basic assumptions that underlie absolute, relativistic, and dialectic thinking). Kramer et al. (1992) administered the SPBI to subjects within five age groups: college students (aged 17 to 20) to older adults (aged 60 to 83). Results, which are illustrated in figure 6.2, indicated that statements which espoused a simplistic, absolute orientation were uniformly rejected by participants within each of the five groups. Importantly, it was discovered that as age increased, participants were more likely to endorse dialectic

*TABLE 6.2*

| ***Examples of Absolute, Relativistic, and Dialectic Statements on the Social Paradigm Belief Inventory*** |
|---|
| *Absolute Statement:* Change comes from the outside. It is for the most part forced on us by job changes, financial circumstances, and the like. |
| *Relativistic Statement:* Change comes from the inside. It comes from a change in outlook on things; no matter what happens on the outside you can always alter your view of things and you will be different. |
| *Dialectic Statement:* Change comes neither from the inside or the outside. It comes from an interaction of natural changes the person goes through with changes in the environment and how these changes are seen by the person. |

*From D. A. Kramer, P. E. Kahlbaugh, & R. B. Goldston, "A Measure of Paradigm Beliefs about the Social World"* in Journal of Gerontology: Psychological Sciences, *47: 189. Copyright © 1992 The Gerontological Society of America.*

*TABLE 6.3*

***Basic Assumptions of Absolute, Relativistic, and Dialectical Perspectives on Personal and Social Issues***

| *Perspective* | *Basic Assumptions* |
|---|---|
| ***Absolute*** | Belief in the inherent stability of all things.<br>Individual seen as passive in environmental influence of behavior.<br>Causality is seen as linear, deterministic, and universal.<br>Belief in absolute, universal principles and ideals.<br>Belief in validity of one-sided solutions.<br>All phenomena and knowledge are seen as inherently noncontradictory. |
| ***Relativistic*** | Decision making on pragmatic, rather than absolute criteria.<br>Change is basic to reality.<br>Every person, relationship, system, or situation is unique.<br>Unpredictability and indeterminism are central to reality.<br>Contradiction is seen as a primary feature of reality. |
| ***Dialectical*** | All phenomena imply their opposites.<br>Emergence characterizes systems, whereby the whole defines the parts; all life is systemic.<br>Development occurs via increasingly adapted forms.<br>All change is characterized by reciprocity, where a change in any one part affects the whole system. |

*From D. A. Kramer, P. E. Kahlbaugh, & R. B. Goldston, "A Measure of Paradigm Beliefs about the Social World"* in Journal of Gerontology: Psychological Sciences, *47: 189. Copyright © 1992 The Gerontological Society of America.*

statements and less likely to choose relativistic ones. Furthermore, participants' responses on the SPBI were found to be unrelated to verbal intelligence and several personality variables such as dogmatism, tolerance of ambiguity, and social desirability. These findings suggest that relativistic thinking may be the first component of postformal thought to emerge during late adolescence/early adulthood; and,with age and experience, dialecticism replaces relativism as the main characteristic of mature thought.

***Problem Finding*** Patricia Arlin (1975) conducted the first research that suggested that postformal thinking is primarily geared to the task of problem finding—generating new problems by examining situations from a novel and creative point of view. Arlin presented college freshmen and seniors with measures

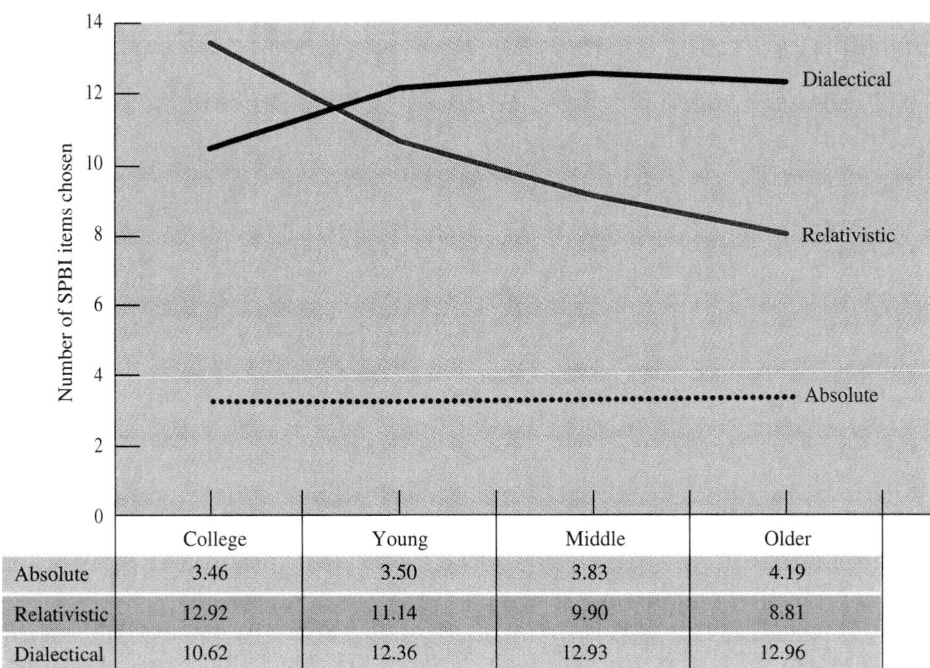


| | College | Young | Middle | Older |
|---|---|---|---|---|
| Absolute | 3.46 | 3.50 | 3.83 | 4.19 |
| Relativistic | 12.92 | 11.14 | 9.90 | 8.81 |
| Dialectical | 10.62 | 12.36 | 12.93 | 12.96 |

**Figure 6.2** The number of absolute, relativistic, and dialectical items chosen as a function of age.

of both problem-solving and problem-finding skills. The problem-finding task invited participants to raise questions about the arrangement of a number of disparate objects (e.g., a C-clamp, a quarter, three candles, a boxtop, and ten thumb tacks). Very generalized and abstract questions were assumed to reflect a problem-finding orientation, whereas very specific and concrete questions were assumed to reflect a preoccupation with problem solving. Results showed that success on the Piagetian measures of formal operations was a necessary but not sufficient condition to produce high levels of performance on the problem-finding task.

Arlin (1984, 1989) also studied problem finding in a group of young adult artists, all of whom performed equally well on measures of formal thought. These artists were given a problem-finding test similar to that employed by Arlin in her earlier research (Arlin, 1975). Artists who were judged to produce highly creative and original works scored higher on the problem-finding measure than the artists whose work was rated noncreative. Differences between artists who were classified as either formal or postformal in their cognitive orientation were related to their answers to questions such as, "Could any of the elements in your drawing be eliminated or altered without destroying its characteristics?" The formal-thinking artists viewed their works as fixed, unalterable, and finished, while the postformal artists viewed their works as changeable and unfinished. Arlin suggested that the more creative artists were postformal thinkers who (1) did not adopt a single, fixed, and absolute view of their work, (2) accepted the idea that their work could evolve and change over time, and (3) actively tried to find new perspectives from which to view their work.

## Conclusions about Postformal Cognitive Development

Clearly, some adults are capable of conceptualizing reality in a postformal manner. Furthermore, the postformal cognitive orientation displayed by these adults is very different from the formal orientation displayed by adolescents. Postformal thinking seems to be a necessity if adults are to truly appreciate the complexities of both physical and social reality. It would be a mistake, however, to believe that *all* adults display *all* of the characteristics of postformal development.

Reasoning about social matters clearly occupies a central role in post-Piagetian attempts to identify the levels or stages of postformal cognitive development. Indeed, one characteristic of all of the Piagetian revisionists described in this chapter is the dominant theme that adult cognition involves the interchange of the individual with his or her social world. Reasoning about the social and interpersonal world is termed **social cognition.** Our social cognitions are a pervasive aspect of our lives (Flavell, 1985). We may weigh the pitfalls of giving up our independence versus the benefits of romance and marriage; we may make decisions about whether to have children and if so, how many; we may have to decide whether to tell a parent that she suffers from a terminal illness. Quite clearly, considerable cognitive activity is enmeshed in our interpersonal and social lives.

There continues to be a great deal of controversy concerning the stagelike characteristics of postformal reasoning. Some psychologists believe that postformal thinking reflects a genuine stage of cognitive development well beyond formal operations (Commons, Sinnott, Richards, & Armon, 1989). With regard to the stage issue, Lamberson and Fischer (1988) have made a distinction between *optimal level* and *functional level.* Optimal level refers to the best or highest level of stagelike performance a person can achieve under ideal conditions. Functional level refers to a person's stagelike performance under normal, nonoptimal conditions where the individual is offered little environmental support. Lamberson and Fischer argue that it is only possible to observe genuine stages of development if we measure an individual's optimal level, not his or her functional level. They also suggest that we focus our attention on an individual's *developmental range*—the gap between the person's optimal and functional levels. Other psychologists have suggested that developmental changes in thought beyond formal operations, even when measured under optimal conditions, may not meet the criteria that define genuine cognitive stages. Rybash et al. (1986), for example, argued that postformal development may be best understood as a set of styles of thinking (relativistic thinking, dialectic thinking, problem finding, and so forth) that emerge during adulthood rather than a true stage.

Finally, several developmental psychologists have expressed reservations about the need for the stage concept itself. For example, Brainerd (1978), Gelman (1979), and Gardner (1983) have commented that the cognitive performance of children and adolescents is so inconsistent and variable that it is difficult to embrace the existence of a set of stages that comprise cognitive development. Certainly, adult cognitive performance may reflect even greater individual variability and inconsistency due to the accumulation of different experiences.

## *Adult Cognition: An Integration*

In the last three chapters of this text, we have reviewed theory and research that bears on the different approaches to the study of adult cognition: the psychometric approach, the information-processing approach, and the stage approach. Each of these different approaches provides valuable information and perspective about the nature of adult cognitive development. However, each of these different theoretical views focuses on a different aspect of cognition, and each has a number of major limitations. In this section, we describe a perspective on adult cognitive development proposed by John Rybash, William Hoyer, and Paul Roodin (1986). This approach, referred to as the **encapsulation model,** integrates and extends the basic features of the traditional approaches to the study of adult cognition.

### The Encapsulation Model

The encapsulation model makes the fundamental assumption that cognition consists of three interrelated dimensions: processing, knowing, and thinking. *Processing* refers to the way in which various mental abilities and/or capacities are used to process (encode, store, and retrieve) information. *Knowing* refers to the way in which extant knowledge aids in information processing and problem solving. *Thinking* refers to an individual's understanding or perspective on the knowledge that she has accumulated during her development. Unfortunately, these three facets of cognition have been examined in relative isolation from each other by psychologists interested in the study of adult cognitive development.

Processing has been explored by adherents of the information-processing and psychometric approaches. In general, researchers working within these traditions have viewed adulthood as a period of negative developmental change. They have concluded that adults become less adept at general problem solving because they process reduced amounts of information in a progressively slower and less efficient manner.

Knowing has been the primary focus of the cognitive-science perspective on cognition. The dominant concern within this tradition has been with the growth and representation of knowledge and with the development of artificial intelligence software systems (see Gardner, 1985; Hillman, 1985; Waldrop, 1984). Cognitive scientists assume that intelligent problem solving has its source in the size and breadth of the individual's knowledge base rather than in the power of the individual's generalized mental abilities (fluid intelligence), mental capacities (attention, memory), or internalized thought structures (postformal thinking). Research conducted within the context of this approach is essentially nondevelopmental. It has been suggested (Charness, 1988), however, that research within the cognitive-science tradition has important implications for the study of adult cognitive development. Adulthood is the portion of the life span during which individuals develop domain-specific cognitive expertise. Thus, older adults are likely to display sophisticated cognitive performance in the areas of specialization within which they have developed an expertlike knowledge base. Read Research Focus 6.2 to gain a better understanding of the cognitive-science approach to the study of cognition.

## *The Cognitive Science Approach*

Rybash, Hoyer, and Roodin (1986) noted that psychologists studying cognitive development during adulthood are faced with an apparent paradox. Research based on psychometric and information-processing theory indicates a deterioration of generalized cognitive ability with age, while everyday observation of adults within their occupational roles, social interactions, and hobbies indicates that with increasing age comes stability (and sometimes even enhancement) of cognitive performance.

An important line of research that bears on the resolution of this paradox is represented by the *cognitive-science approach* to the study of cognition. This approach suggests that intelligent problem solving lies in the possession and utilization of a great deal of specific *knowledge* about the world. Waldrop (1984), in tracing the influence of the cognitive-science approach on the study of artificial intelligence (AI), comments that "The essence of intelligence was no longer seen to be reasoning ability alone. More important was having lots of highly specific knowledge about lots of things—a notion inevitably stated as, 'Knowledge is power' " (p. 1280).

Thus, in contrast to the earlier approaches (such as the psychometric and information-processing perspectives) that represented human problem solving as a generalized mental process, capacity, and/or ability, contemporary cognitive scientists suggest that problem solving in adulthood requires *expert knowledge.*

Importantly, expert performance has been found to be *domain-specific*, independent of generalized mental abilities, and the end-result of many years (and thousands of hours) of deliberate practice and hard work (Ericsson & Charness, 1994). For example, Chase and Simon (1973) and de Groot (1965) carried out a number of ground-breaking studies on chess experts and novices. These researchers found that chess experts (i.e., grand masters) could reconstruct the positions of approximately twenty-five chess pieces arranged in a gamelike configuration on a chessboard after having seen the display for only five seconds; novice players, on the other hand, could only remember the positions of about six or seven pieces. When the same twenty-five pieces were arranged in a random configuration on a chessboard, both the experts and the novices remembered the positions of the same number of pieces—approximately seven. Furthermore, experts and novices were not found to differ from each other with regard to generalized measures of memory span and short-term memory. And expert players did not evidence a superiority in general intellectual ability as measured by IQ test performance. It seems safe to conclude that chess experts have exceptionally good memories for gamelike positions on a chessboard because of the vast amount of specific knowledge they possess about gamelike configurations of chess pieces. In fact, it has been estimated that chess experts have stored, in long-term memory, approximately 40,000 different gamelike configurations!

Ceci and Liker (1986) investigated the ability of gamblers to handicap horse races. The individuals in the study were avid horse-racing enthusiasts who went to the racetrack nearly every day. Ceci and Liker gave all these participants an early form of a racing sheet. This allowed the gamblers to study the past performances of the horses that would be competing in all ten races the next day at a real racetrack. The researchers asked the men to pick (1) the favorite in each of the ten races, and (2) the top three finishers in each of the ten races in the correct order. The men's selections were compared to the posttime odds for the horses in each race as well as to the actual order of finish for each race. Based on their analysis, Ceci and Liker identified fourteen "experts" and sixteen "nonexperts." The experts selected the horse with the best posttime odds in nine out of the ten races and the top three horses in at least one-half of the races. The nonexperts performed much more poorly. The experts were found to use very complex mental models to make their selections. These models took into account the interaction of about seven different variables: the horse's times during the first and last quarter-miles of a race, the quality of the horses it had competed against in the past, the jockey riding it, and so on. In comparison, the nonexperts used very simplistic models to make their picks.

Most surprisingly, Ceci and Liker found that the experts and nonexperts did *not* differ on a number of variables that would seem to be good predictors of their handicapping skill. For example, these two groups did not differ in IQ score, years of education, occupational status, or number of years of handicapping experience—both groups had been going to the track for about sixteen years! Ceci and Liker concluded that expertise in handicapping is not purely dependent on past experience or general intelligence.

Developmental changes in thinking have been the focus of theory and research inspired by traditional Piagetian theory. Neo-Piagetian theorists have viewed adulthood as a period of positive developmental change marked by the transition from formal to postformal styles of thinking. Postformal thinking permits adults to view reality in relativistic and dialectic terms. Such thinking styles provide the necessary basis for the solution of both well- and ill-defined problems and

*World-renowned British astrophysicist Stephen Hawking, at age 47, held the Newton Rostrum at Cambridge University. Hawking, who authored the book* A Brief History of Time, *suffers from motor neurone disease, cannot walk or talk, and communicates with the help of a voice-equipped computer.*

the discovery of new perspectives from which new problems may be identified. The postformal approach certainly has its merits. Postformal theorists, however, appear to paint an overly optimistic picture of aging. They fail to acknowledge the cognitive losses and declines that play a salient role in development during the middle and later years of adulthood.

The encapsulation model suggests that basic mental capacities and fluid mental abilities become increasingly dedicated to and encapsulated within specific domains of knowledge during the course of adult development. As general processes and abilities become encapsulated within domains, adults' knowledge becomes more differentiated, accessible, usable, and "expert" in nature.

The encapsulation model also suggests that the acquisition of new knowledge (knowledge *unrelated* to that already encapsulated in specific domains) becomes increasingly less efficient with advances in age. Mastery of new domains is somewhat uncharacteristic of older adults, who are not ideal "learning machines." Childhood and adolescence are periods of the life span characterized by the acquisition of new knowledge in a variety of ever-expanding domains. Adulthood may be a time during which individuals refine and develop a perspective on their knowledge.

The reduced capacity to acquire new knowledge during adulthood may be compensated for by the development of expert knowledge within existing domains and by the development of a postformal perspective on that knowledge. Once adults conceptualize their domain-specific knowledge in a relativistic, dialectic, and open-ended manner, they become capable of solving the ill-defined problems

*TABLE 6.4*

| Basic Assumptions of the Encapsulation Model |
|---|
| 1. Processing, knowing, and thinking are the three dimensions of cognition that must be addressed in any comprehensive theory of adult cognitive development. |
| 2. The processes associated with the acquisition, utilization, and representation of knowledge become encapsulated within particular domains as one grows older. |
| 3. Mental capacities appear to decline with age when assessed as general abilities, but show minimal age-related decline when assessed within encapsulated domains. |
| 4. Adult cognitive development is characterized by the growth of expert knowledge and the emergence of postformal styles of thought. Adult styles of thinking and forms of knowing are the result of the process of encapsulation. |

*Source: Data from J. M. Rybash, W. J. Hoyer, and P. A. Roodin,* Adult Cognition and Aging: Developmental Changes in Processing, Knowing, and Thinking, *Pergamon Press, Inc., Elmsford, New York, 1986.*

characteristic of real life, finding new problems and new perspectives from which these problems may be solved, and producing creative and sophisticated works within defined areas of expertise.

The encapsulation of thinking and knowing within specific domains seems to represent a necessary and adaptive feature of adult cognitive development. Thus, the age-related loss of general intellectual abilities as reported in psychometric and information-processing research may have little functional significance for most adults in most situations. Although age-related declines in fluid abilities and mental capacities are indeed documented, these findings seem to result from the practice of assessing mental processes apart from the domains in which they have become encapsulated. Age-related differences in the component processes of cognition (memory, attention, and so forth) cannot be meaningfully assessed apart from the domain in which these processes are encapsulated. A summary of the encapsulation model is provided in table 6.4.

We can illustrate the basic claims of the encapsulation model by examining two different lines of research. First, we present the results of several studies that have examined the relationship between aging, information processing, and cognitive expertise. Second, we review studies on the growth of wisdom during adulthood.

## *AGING, INFORMATION PROCESSING, AND COGNITIVE EXPERTISE*

*Experts are ordinary fellers who live far away.*
—O. A. "Bum" Phillips

The encapsulation model suggests that adults continue to accumulate knowledge, which becomes increasingly refined with age and experience. Accumulated domain-specific knowledge can take on a compensatory function for older adults. This means that older adults can continue to function effectively when given tasks that allow them to draw upon their expert knowledge (Hoyer & Rybash, 1992a, 1994; Hoyer, Ingolfsdottir, & Clancy-Dollinger, 1994; Morrow, Leirer, Alteri, & Fitzsimmons, 1992). This occurs in spite of the significant reduction in the generalized information-processing skills and/or fluid intellectual abilities that accompany the aging process. Evidence for this point of view comes from several sources. Timothy Salthouse (1984, 1990), Neil Charness (1981, 1985, 1988), and Stephanie Clancy and William Hoyer (1988, 1994) have all shown that expert knowledge can compensate for general losses in processing speed and working memory in older adults.

## Typing

Salthouse (1984) conducted an experiment with typists who differed in age (young adults versus older adults) and skill level (novices versus experts). As might be expected, Salthouse discovered that the older typists performed more poorly than younger typists on tasks assessing (1) simple reaction time, (2) the fastest speed at which they could tap their fingers, and (3) digit-symbol substitution. (Remember that the digit-symbol substitution task is a component of the WAIS. In this task, a person is asked to match, as quickly as possible, a series of numbers with a series of abstract geometric patterns.) More importantly, Salthouse also discovered that the participants' typing speed was uncorrelated with age but *was* significantly related to the participants' skill level. The expert typists (both young and old) were significantly quicker than the novice typists (both young and old). Through a set of ingenious experiments, Salthouse was able to determine that older expert typists compensated for age-related declines in speed and reaction time by looking farther ahead at printed text, thereby giving themselves more time to plan what their next keystroke should be. Finally, Salthouse's findings illustrate the domain-specific nature of older adults' compensatory mechanisms. Older expert typists did not employ the same look-ahead strategy on any of the other tasks Salthouse administered (e.g., digit-symbol substitution), although the implementation of this strategy would have improved their performance.

## Chess

Charness (1981, 1985) reported that older chess experts were found to be as competent as younger chess experts in choosing the best chess move from four possible alternatives. More specifically, older experts were found to search just as many moves ahead as younger experts. But they were also found to entertain fewer possible moves than their younger counterparts, showing even greater efficiency. Charness concluded that older chess experts compensate for general processing and memory deficits by using an elaborate knowledge base acquired over years of practice. The growth of this vast and highly organized knowledge base allows older experts to search for appropriate moves as quickly as (and perhaps even more efficiently than) younger experts.

## Medical Diagnostics

Clancy and Hoyer (1988) conducted an experiment with medical laboratory technologists who differed in both age (young adults versus older adults) and skill level (novices versus experts). Keep in mind that a medical laboratory technologist, as an integral part of his or her job, performs a number of complex visual identification tasks such as looking at slides of tissue or blood under a microscope to identify certain diseases. This experiment consisted of two parts. In the first part, the participants had to identify several unfamiliar visual stimuli (e.g., abstract geometric figures) that were flashed on a video screen for less than a second. As expected, results showed that younger participants scored better on this domain-general task than older participants. Also, the participants' success on this task was unrelated to their skill level within the field of medical laboratory technology.

In the second part of the study, the technologists were briefly shown pictures of complex microscopic slides of actual laboratory specimens. Each slide contained a number of clinically significant and clinically insignificant pieces of information. Clinically significant information was defined as a piece of visual information crucial to the diagnosis of a particular disease. On the other hand, clinically insignificant information was defined as visual information that does not serve as an effective diagnostic aid. The participants were shown a single piece of visual information and asked if it was present in the original complex slide. Results indicated that both the younger and older experts were equally quick and accurate in determining if a clinically significant piece of information was present in a previously seen complex slide. Furthermore, the performance of both expert groups on this task was unaffected by having to perform another task concurrently—pressing a button whenever a tone sounded. In contrast, both younger and older novices performed poorly on this microscopic identification task, especially under dual-task conditions (when they were also required to perform the button-pressing task).

Clancy and Hoyer (1994) performed another experiment that examined the effects of age and experience on information processing. They administered domain-general and domain-specific visual search tasks to medical laboratory technologists and control subjects at two age levels (young adulthood and middle adulthood). The domain-general task involved finding a letter of the alphabet in a briefly presented visual display. In the skilled task, subjects searched a visual display for a specific type of bacteria specimen. Also, prior to the presentation of the bacteria samples, participants were shown word cues that were informative, noninformative, or neutral with regard to the target they had to search for. Results indicated that middle-aged control subjects performed more poorly than younger control subjects on the domain-general and domain-specific tasks. When the data from the experts were analyzed, a different pattern emerged. Middle-aged experts performed worse than younger experts on the domain-general task but *not* the domain-specific task. And, both expert groups benefited to the *same* extent when informative cue words were presented prior to the domain-specific search task.

## Limits of Expertise

Finally, note that cognitive expertise is not powerful enough to compensate for the reductions in the mental capacities and physical abilities that underlie performance in all domains. For example, performance in such sports as golf, tennis, basketball, and football declines with age even among individuals who possess a great deal of expert knowledge about these sports. On the other hand, performance within domains that allow more time for planning and reflection, that demand fewer snap decisions and less physical exertion (e.g., musical composition or visual art), may actually improve because of the cumulative effects of age and experience. In connection with this point, Charness (1985) has commented that ". . . when people can draw upon domain-specific knowledge and when they have developed appropriate compensatory mechanisms, they can treat us to a memorable performance, whether on the keyboard of a typewriter, a piano, or on the podium of an orchestral stage. When the task environment does not afford the same predictability or opportunity to plan ahead, however, as is the case in fast-moving sports environments, degradation in hardware cannot be compensated for by more efficient software" (p. 23).

Furthermore, for expertise to aid problem solving there needs to be an exact match between the older person's knowledge and the task that he or she is given to solve. In other words, expertise does not enhance (or even maintain) the domain-general abilities upon which the expertise seems to be based. The conclusion is based on the work of Lindenberger, Kliegl, and Baltes (1992) and Salthouse, Babcock, Skovronek, Mitchell, and Palmon (1990). Both of the research groups discovered that older adult experts in architecture and graphic design—occupations that place a premium in visual cognition—displayed significant declines in domain-general visual thinking and mental imagery.

## *Wisdom*

*When it comes to understanding life, experiential learning is the only worthwhile kind; everything else is hearsay.*
—Joan Erikson

*The fool doth think he is wise;*
*But the wise man knows himself to be a fool.*
—William Shakespeare

Wisdom is a mental characteristic or ability that has long been associated with aging within both Eastern and Western cultural traditions (Clayton & Birren, 1980). Beyond any doubt, the most exciting and provocative work on the topic of wisdom has been conducted by Paul Baltes and his colleagues at the Max Planck Institute in Berlin, Germany. Dittmann-Kohli and Baltes (1988) distinguished between philosophical wisdom and practical wisdom. **Philosophical wisdom** refers to an understanding of the abstract relationship between one's self and the rest of humanity. Alternatively, **practical wisdom** refers to the ability to display superior judgment with regard to important matters of real life. Recently, Baltes and Staudinger (1993) defined this latter form of *wisdom* as ". . . an expert knowledge system in the fundamental pragmatics of life permitting exceptional insight, judgment, and advice involving complex and uncertain matters of the human condition" (p. 76). And, they suggested (see figure 6.3) that wisdom may be characterized by

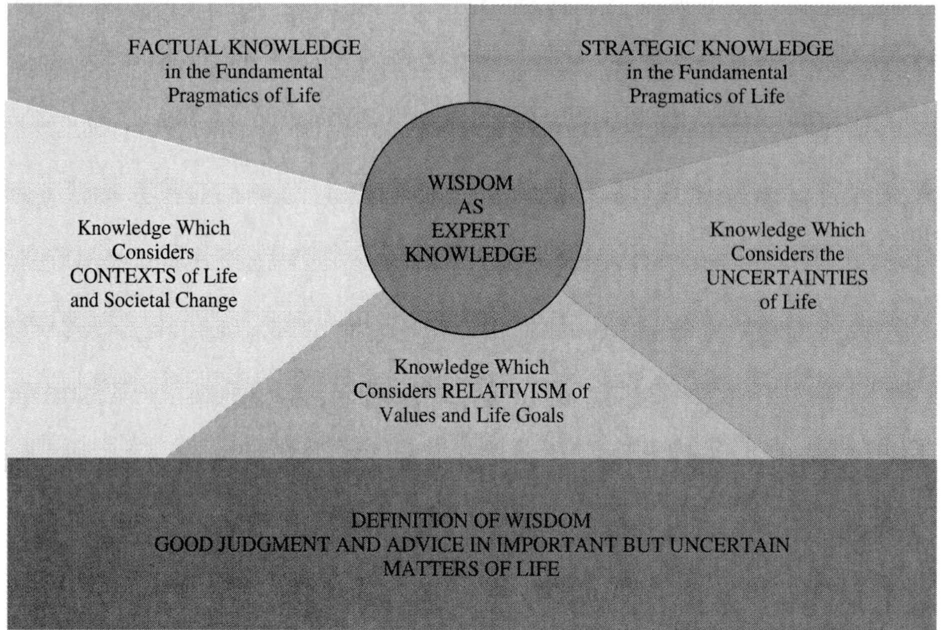


**Figure 6.3** The Berlin model of wisdom as an expert knowledge and behavior system in the fundamental pragmatics of life.

a family of dimensions that, over the course of human history, has been identified as important by many diverse cultures. Note that these characteristics reflect the essential features of knowledge encapsulation and postformal thinking.

## Fluid Mechanics and Crystallized Pragmatics

Baltes's research on age-related changes in wisdom is a component of his overarching viewpoint that the human mind possesses two fundamental dimensions (Baltes, 1987). First, the **mechanics of mind** involves the raw, basic operations of our human information-processing system. It represents elementary "mental hardware" such as sensation, perception, and memory. These processes are typically measured by the speed and accuracy with which people can perform simple tasks. In general, these tasks measure what psychometricians refer to as fluid intellectual abilities and reflect the operation of neurologically based processes. With age, there seems to be a gradual, progressive, and irreversible decrement in the mechanics of the mind. Like it or not, we cannot seem to overcome the effects of age-related biological decline on fluid ability and general information-processing ability.

Second, the **pragmatics of mind** refers to the "mental software" that encompasses the general system of factual and strategic knowledge accessible to members of a particular culture, the specialized systems of knowledge available to individuals within particular occupations and avocations, and an understanding of how to effectively activate these different types of knowledge within particular contexts to aid problem solving. Most importantly, the pragmatic quality of mind

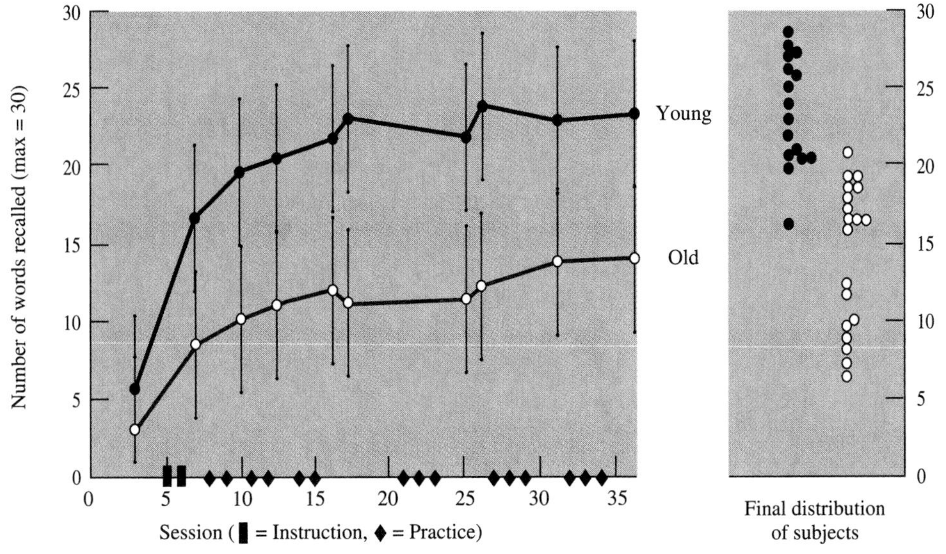


**Figure 6.4** Performance by young and old adults in serial recall of lists of words as function of training in the method of loci (left panel). (The bars indicate standard deviations. In the right panel, individual scores are given for the last assessment sessions [36/37]. Max = maximum.)

allows us to develop a strategy—wisdom—for negotiating the major and minor obstacles of everyday life. Furthermore, since cultural (not biological) factors influence mental pragmatics, it may be the case that aging is accompanied by cognitive growth—a growth in wisdom—not decline or stagnation.

## Testing the Limits of Cognitive Reserve

To evaluate his ideas about the mechanics of mind, Baltes and his coworkers (Baltes & Kliegl, 1992; Kliegl, Smith, & Baltes, 1989) have used the technique of **testing-the-limits** of maximum cognitive reserve. In this methodology, groups of younger adults and older adults are required to recall a list of thirty familiar nouns (plane, chair, etc.) in the order in which they were presented. Then they are taught a mnemonic strategy—*the method of loci*—to increase their recall. In this memory enhancement procedure, individuals are instructed to create mental images that allow them to associate list items with familiar landmarks. For example, a person may think about driving to work in the morning while visualizing list items. One might imagine an airplane at the end of one's driveway, a chair perched upon the top of the stop sign at the end of one's street, and so on. When given a memory test, the person re-creates these images one location after another.

Using this technique, Baltes and Kliegl (1992) gave groups of younger (20-year-olds) and older (70-year-olds) participants thirty-five training and testing sessions over a period of one year and four months. Across all sessions, each participant performed 4,380 trials of trying to generate a mental image that linked a familiar location to a list item. The results of this research are displayed in figure 6.4. In the initial testing session, participants remembered about six words and younger adults performed slightly better than older adults. With extended practice, the memory of both younger and older participants increased in a spectacular fashion. Now, a large proportion of the participants could remember between twenty to thirty words in the correct order. However, the training increased (rather than decreased) the difference in memory performance between the two age groups. In fact, the older adults who displayed the best performance at the end of the experiment seemed to be on a par with the younger adults who displayed the worst performance! And, after all of the training sessions, the older adults did not achieve a level of performance that the younger adults exhibited after just a few sessions. Baltes and Kliegl suggested that older adults do not benefit from practice as much as younger adults because of an age-related deterioration in mental reserve capacity that is similar to the loss of reserve capacity in biological domains such as cardiovascular or respiratory potential.

## Wisdom, Age, and Professional Specialization

Are the inevitable declines in the mechanics of mind offset by positive changes in the pragmatics of mind—in wisdom? This is a rather complex question, because living a long life would seem to be a sufficient condition to produce a decline in basic mental abilities; but, a long life, by itself, does not seem to be a sufficient condition for the growth of wisdom. Consequently, Baltes and his colleagues (Baltes & Staudinger, 1993; Smith & Baltes, 1990; Staudinger, Smith, & Baltes, 1992) hypothesized that wisdom is the end-result of a coalition of three factors: advanced chronological age, favorable personality traits such as openness to experience, and specific experiences in matters relating to life planning and the resolution of personal, ethical dilemmas.

Given this orientation, Staudinger et al. (1992) investigated the growth of wisdom via the **age by experience paradigm,** a method that possesses a great deal of commonality with the strategy that researchers such as Clancy and Hoyer (1994) have used to assess the role of age and expertise on information processing. Specifically, Staudinger et al. (1992) tried to find groups of individuals who differed in age as well as exposure to life experiences that would be considered facilitative to the development of wisdom. For example, they argued that certain professions such as clinical psychology might give rise to a series of life experiences that are more conducive to wisdom than the life experiences associated with a career in a nonhuman services field such as accounting. This research strategy enabled Staudinger et al. (1992) to assess the separate, and interactive, effects of age *and* experience on wisdom.

Staudinger et al. (1992) selected a subject sample that consisted of younger (average age 32 years) and older (average age 71 years) women who were either clinical psychologists or professionals from outside the area of psychology (e.g., architects, journalists, and natural scientists). All of the participants, regardless of age and professional specialization, were similar in terms of formal education and socioeconomic status and displayed identical scores on a measure of crystallized intelligence. As would be expected, however, younger adults performed better than older adults on a measure of fluid intelligence.

*Wisdom-related skills and personal intelligence are characteristics that help determine a successful psychotherapist or counselor.*

*TABLE 6.5*

**Two Life Review Problems**

| ***Young Version*** |
|---|
| Martha, a young woman, had decided to have a family and not to have a career. She is married and has children. One day Martha meets a woman friend whom she has not seen for a long time. The friend had decided to have a career and no family. She is about to establish herself in her career. |
| ***Old Version*** |
| Martha, an elderly woman, had once decided to have a family and not to have a career. Her children left home some years ago. One day Martha meets a woman friend whom she has not seen for a long time. The friend had decided to have a career and no family. She had retired some years ago. |
| ***Standard Probe Questions for Both Versions of the Life Review Problem*** |
| This meeting causes Martha to think back over her life.<br>1. What might her life review look like?<br>2. Which aspects of her life might she remember?<br>3. How might she explain her life?<br>4. How might she evaluate her life retrospectively? |

*From U. M. Staudinger, J. Smith, and P. B. Baltes, "Wisdom-Related Knowledge in a Life Review Task: Age Differences and the Role of Professional Specialization" in* Psychology and Aging, *7: 271–281. Copyright 1992 by the American Psychological Association. Reprinted by permission.*

In the main part of the experiment, Staudinger et al. presented the participants with a "life review problem" in which the main character was either a young or an elderly woman who had to reflect on her decision to have a career rather than a family (see table 6.5 for the actual problems and a list of the standard probe questions). Participants' responses to the life review problems were scored on the five different dimensions of wisdom as identified by Baltes and his colleagues.

***Table 6.6***

| Illustration of the Characteristics of a Wise Response to the Life Review Tasks | |
|---|---|
| ***Dimension of Wisdom*** | ***Characteristics of an Ideal Wise Response*** |
| ***Factual Knowledge*** | Knowledge about the human condition as it relates to the life review situation (e.g., achievement motivation, emotions, vulnerability, and societal norms). |
| | Knowledge about life events relevant to a mother's versus a professional woman's life. |
| ***Strategic Knowledge*** | Cost-benefit analysis: developing various scenarios of life interpretation. |
| | Means-goals analysis: what did/does the woman want and how can she/did she try to achieve it. |
| ***Contextualism*** | Discussion of the life review tasks in age-graded (e.g., timing of childrearing and professional training), culturally graded (e.g., change in woman's roles), and idiosyncratic (e.g., no money for education) contexts. |
| | The three contexts are discussed across different domains of life (e.g., family, profession, and leisure) and across time (past, present, future). |
| | The contexts are not independent; sometimes their combination creates conflict and tension that can be solved. |
| ***Relativism*** | Life goals differ depending on the individual and the culture. |
| | The origins of these differences is understood and the differences are respected. |
| | No absolute relativism but a set of "universal" values is acknowledged. |
| ***Uncertainty*** | Plans can be disrupted; decisions have to be taken with uncertainty; the past cannot be perfectly explained nor the future fully predicted (e.g., marriage does not work out, children handicapped, or professional failure). |
| | One can work, however, from experience and knowledge-based assumptions and continuously modify those as new information becomes available. |

*From U. M. Staudinger, J. Smith, & P. B. Baltes, "Wisdom-Related Knowledge in a Life Review Task: Age Differences and the Role of Professional Specialization"* in Psychology and Aging, *7: 271–281. Copyright 1992 by the American Psychological Association. Reprinted by permission.*

Table 6.6 contains examples of wise responses to the life review problems from the perspective of each of these dimensions. Results of the Staudinger et al. study were straightforward (see figure 6.5). First, younger and older women did not differ in their overall level of performance. Second, clinical psychologists exhibited a greater amount of wisdom-based responses than the nonclinicians. Third, older adults displayed better performance than younger adults when the life review dilemma involved an elderly woman; but younger and older adults displayed identical performance when the life review problem focused on a young woman. Fourth, when the top 25 percent of the responses to the life review problems were examined, it was found that the older clinicians were the group most likely to generate wise responses. Fifth, participants' performance on standardized measures of fluid and crystallized intelligence accounted for very little of their performance on the life review tasks.

Overall, these findings are important for several reasons. First, unlike fluid mechanics, age differences are eliminated on wisdom-related tasks, and older adults seem to display the "best" levels of performance. Second, life experience

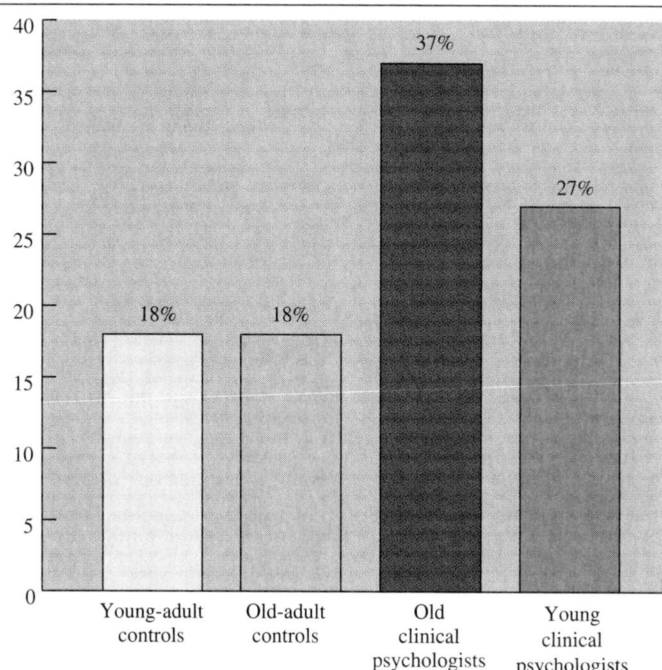


**Figure 6.5**
Distribution of the top 25% of responses in a wisdom-related task of life review. Clinical psychologists (a sample case of professionals with exposure to structured tutoring and practice in the meaning and conduct of life) outperformed matched control subjects. In addition, older clinical psychologists contributed a major share to the top performances.
*Source: Data from Baltes and Staudinger, 1993.*

and professional specialization seem to interact. The highest level of performance was displayed by older adults who responded to a dilemma involving an older person. Younger adults, on the other hand, were not capable of using knowledge about their own life stage when responding to the dilemma involving a younger person.

## Selective Optimization and Compensation

Given the results of the research studies that have investigated age-related changes in the mechanics and pragmatics of mind, psychologists should realize that cognitive aging is a dynamic process that involves a changing gain/loss ratio in which decrements in reserve capacity may be offset by the accumulation of expertise. Baltes and Baltes (1990) have developed a strategy for successful aging, termed **selective optimization with compensation,** based on the insights gained from this research. The notion of *selection* means that individuals should restrict their life work to fewer intellectual domains because of an age-related loss in adaptive ability and reserve potential. These domains should be selected because of their personal (and societal) importance and relevance. *Optimization* refers to the idea that adults engage in activities that maintain their mental reserves and increase their domain-specific knowledge to maximize their chosen life path. The term *compensation* involves the use of a new strategy or technique to adapt to a life task when a long-used psychological (or physical) skill or ability is lost or falls below a critical level. This model, which was originally developed to foster successful "intellectual aging," also offers valuable advice about how nonintellectual facets of development may be maximized across the adult

*Table 6.7*

**Illustration of the Principles of Selection, Optimization, and Compensation**

| *Type of Individual* | *Principle* |
|---|---|
| ***Nursing Home Resident*** | Selection—teach resident to become responsible for a few, but important, aspects of his daily life |
| | Optimization—offer resident extensive practice in those domains which were selected as important |
| | Compensation—give resident access to technological aids and medical interventions that support functions with diminished reserve capacities |
| ***Marathon Runner*** | Selection—instruct the person to give up those activities that take away from running |
| | Optimization—have the person increase the quality and quantity of her training and develop better dietary habits |
| | Compensation—have the person pay more attention to the running shoes she buys, and new techniques for healing injuries |
| ***Musician**** ***(*comments made by the pianist A. Rubenstein during a TV interview)*** | Selection—reduce your repertoire, play fewer pieces |
| | Optimization—practice more |
| | Compensation—slow down playing speed prior to fast movements, thereby producing a contrast that gives the impression of "speed" in the fast movement |

*Source: From P. B. Baltes & M. Baltes, "Psychological Perspectives on Successful Aging: The Model of Selective Optimization with Compensation." In P. B. Baltes and M. Baltes (eds.),* Longitudinal Research and the Study of Successful (Optimal) Aging, *Cambridge University Press, Cambridge, England, 1990, pp. 1–49.*

years. For example, table 6.7 provides insights about how nursing home residents, athletes, and musicians might use the principles of selection, optimization, and compensation to maintain (or enhance) their performance upon entry into older adulthood.

At the most general level, the work of Baltes and his associates may be viewed as an attempt to understand the relationship between biology, society, and the aging individual. Baltes and Staudinger (1993) have made this point in a very elegant way:

> . . . because of the enriching and compensatory power of culture and knowledge-based factors, we have come to believe that the potential for future enhancement of the aging mind is considerable despite biological limits. Why? From the point of view of civilization, old age is young; it is only during the last century that many people have reached old age. Therefore, there has not been much of an opportunity for the development and refinement of a culture for and of old age. Culture, however, has the power not only to "activate" whatever biological potential is available, but also, within certain limits, to outwit the constraints (losses) of biology.
>
> Our concluding kernel of truth is this: The complete story of old age cannot be told based on the current reality about old age. . . . What also must be considered are the special strengths of *Homo sapiens:* the unrivaled ability to produce a powerful stream of cultural inheritance and cultural innovation and to compensate for biological vulnerability. Searching for a better culture of old age is not only a challenge for the future. It is the future, because the future is not something people enter, it is something people help create. In this sense research on wisdom offers a challenge to look beyond (p. 80).

## Summary

The stage approach to the study of adult cognition offers an important alternative to the psychometric and information-processing perspectives. Genuine cognitive stages must meet a strict set of criteria. These criteria include (1) invariant movement, (2) qualitative restructuring, (3) hierarchical integration, (4) structured wholeness, and (5) universal progression. Jean Piaget developed the most significant stage theory of cognitive development. Originally, Piaget argued for the existence of four different cognitive stages. The fourth stage, formal operations, which Piaget thought emerged during adolescence, was thought to be representative of mature adult cognition. Piaget viewed formal operational thought as a form of scientific thinking, described as hypothetico-deductive, logical, and abstract. Formal thought seems best suited for the solution of well-defined, closed-system problems. In the mid- to late-1970s, it became clear that Piaget's stage of formal operations did not capture the essential features of mature adult thought. Thus, psychologists began to search for a fifth, postformal stage of cognitive development. Postformal thought allows adults to solve ill-defined, open-system problems as well as to focus on problem finding, not just problem solving. Several research studies examined two essential features of postformal cognitive development: relativistic thinking and problem finding. We concluded that postformal development may be best understood as a number of unique styles of thinking that emerge during adulthood, not as a genuine stage of cognitive development. We also concluded that postformal accounts of adult cognition place an emphasis on social cognition. Social cognition refers to reasoning about the social, interpersonal, and ethical problems characteristic of everyday living.

We briefly described the encapsulation model of adult cognition. This model integrates the theory and research stemming from the psychometric, information-processing, cognitive-science, and cognitive-stage perspectives. It suggests that the salient dimensions of cognition are processing, knowing, and thinking. It also suggests that the most important characteristics of adult cognition (the development of domain-specific expert knowledge and postformal thinking) result from the encapsulation of basic cognitive processes and abilities. We illustrated the encapsulation model through a discussion of the relationships between aging, cognitive expertise, and information processing; and by a discussion of the growth of wisdom during the adult years.

## Review Questions

1. Describe each of the different criteria that define genuine cognitive stages.
2. Discuss the essential features of formal operations. Describe some of the different problems that may be used to test for the presence of formal thinking.
3. Why did psychologists become disenchanted with Piaget's contention that formal operational thinking was the final stage of cognitive development?
4. Describe the essential features of postformal cognitive development. What aspect of postformal thinking (relativistic thinking, dialectic thinking, or problem finding) do you think has generated the most meaningful and important research? Why?
5. What is social cognition? Is the research regarding formal or postformal thinking more focused on the topic of social cognition? Why?

6. Compare and contrast the psychometric, information-processing, and cognitive-stage approaches to the study of adult cognition. Indicate the focal point as well as the strengths and weaknesses of each approach.
7. Explain the basic tenets of the cognitive-science approach to the study of cognition. What are the implications of the cognitive-science approach for psychologists interested in the study of adult cognition?
8. Explain the basic features of the encapsulation model. Explain the differences between processing, knowing, and thinking.
9. Discuss the research studies that suggest that adults continue to function effectively on tasks within which they have developed cognitive expertise.
10. Explain how psychologists have attempted to examine the concept of wisdom. What insights have psychologists gained about the relationship between the biological and cultural dimensions of aging by studying wisdom?
11. Explain how Baltes's distinction between the mechanics and pragmatics of mind relate to the basic features of the encapsulation model.

## For Further Reading


Baltes, P. B., Smith, J., & Staudinger, U. M. (1992). Wisdom and successful aging. In M. T. Sonderegger (Ed.), *The Nebraska symposium on motivation: Volume 19. The psychology of aging.* Lincoln, NE: University of Nebraska Press.

Commons, M. L., Sinnott, J. D., Richards, F. A., & Armon, C. (Eds.). (1989). *Adult development: Vol. 1. Comparisons and applications of developmental models.* New York: Praeger.

Ericsson, K. A., & Charness, N. (1994). Expert performance: Its structure and acquisition. *American Psychologist, 49,* 725–747.

Rybash, J. M., Hoyer, W. J., & Roodin, P. A. (1986). *Adult cognition and aging: Developmental changes in processing, knowing, and thinking.* New York: Pergamon Press.

Sternberg, R. J. (Ed.). (1990). *Wisdom: Its nature, origins, and development.* New York: Cambridge University Press.

7

# RELATIONSHIPS AND SEXUALITY

*Seems like by now*
*I'd find a love, a love who'd care, care just for me*
*Then we'd go runnin' on faith*
*All of our dreams would come true*
*And our world would be right*
*If love comes over me and you*
—Eric Clapton

*Love is an irresistible desire to be irresistibly desired.*
—Robert Frost

## *Introduction*

In this chapter we explore the personal relationships of adults. We begin with an analysis of the building blocks of adult relationships: love, intimacy, and friendship. Then we discuss a particularly significant relationship of the adult years—marriage. We also highlight the parent and grandparent roles. And, we discuss some of the lifestyles of those adults who choose not to marry. Finally, we discuss the sexual dimension of adult interpersonal relationships from young adulthood to old age.

## *Building Relationships: Love, Intimacy, and Friendship*

*Age does not protect you from love. But love,*
*to some extent, protects you from age.*
—Jeanne Moreau

Adults usually seek two kinds of relationships with others—one an emotional, intimate attachment to one other person (usually a lover or spouse), the other social ties to a number of friends. The two sets of relationships, as we shall see, serve different needs.

### Attachment and Love

Though not easily defined and measured, love is, nevertheless, a pervasive aspect of interpersonal relationships in adulthood. Many adults spend hour after hour thinking about love, anticipating a romantic love relationship, watching love relationships on soap operas, reading about love in magazines or books, and listening to music filled with references to love. Psychologist Zick Rubin (1970, 1973) has made a distinction between liking and loving. *Liking* refers to the cognitive belief that someone is similar to us and involves our positive evaluation of that person. *Loving,* on the other

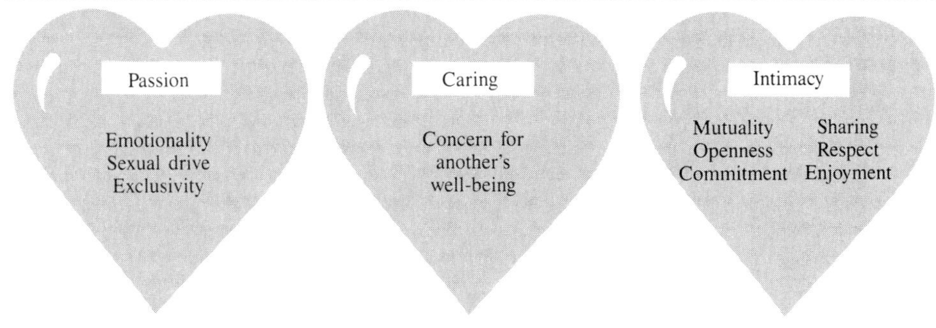


**Figure 7.1** Davis's conceptualization of the components of love.

hand, involves more selfless orientation to another. It is embodied by the qualities of exclusiveness and absorption. In other words, love triggers a preoccupation with another person, including feelings of possessiveness.

Allan Bloom (1993) maintains that our culture has trivialized the concept of love and blurred the distinction between love and sex. He comments that

> The word "love" now applies to almost everything except the overwhelming attraction of one individual for another. And sex is a timid pseudoscientific word which tells us only that individuals have certain bodily needs. . . . Isolation, a sense of profound lack of contact with other human beings seems to be the disease of our time. . . . The most insistent demand nowadays of people in general and young people in particular remains human connection, a connection that transcends the isolation of personal selfishness, and in which *the thought of oneself is inextricably bound up with the thought of another.* (p. 27, italics added)

Rubin's and Bloom's ideas seem to correspond to the "theories" of love developed by Berscheid (1988), Davis (1985), and Sternberg (1986). They suggested that love involves a relationship marked, in part, by three underlying themes: (1) emotionality or passion, (2) a sense of commitment or loyalty, and (3) a degree of sharing, openness, or mutual expression of personal identity. These three themes appear in different proportions in each theory. For example, Davis (1985) views loving as composed of intense emotion, a sense of genuine regard and sincere concern for the one who is loved, and also a degree of intimacy unmatched in other relationships (see figure 7.1). Berscheid (1988) suggests that the intensely arousing passions we call "being in love" cannot be sustained. Sternberg (1986) agrees, describing this early phase as predominant in the initial establishment of a love relationship.

Margaret Reedy, James Birren, and K. Warner Schaie (1981) suggested that the passionate fires of youthful love are somehow transformed into the deeper, more serene and tender love of advanced age. From their perspective, physical attraction, perceived similarity of the loved one, self-disclosure, romance, and passion are important in emerging relationships, whereas security, loyalty, and mutual emotional interest in the relationship sustain love relationships over long periods of time.

To test these hypotheses, Reedy et al. (1981) studied 102 happily married couples in early (average age 28), middle (average age 45), and late adulthood (average age 65). As figure 7.2 shows, the researchers found age-related differences in the

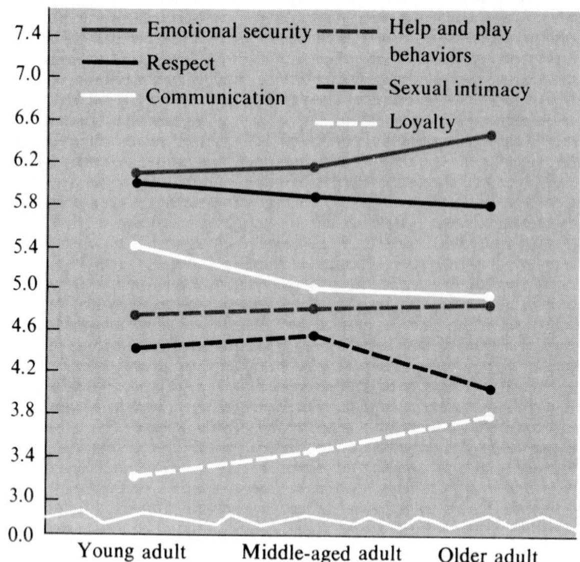


**Figure 7.2** Changes in the components of satisfying love relationships across the life span.

nature of satisfying love relationships. Passion and sexual intimacy were more important in early adulthood than late adulthood, whereas tender feelings of affection and loyalty were most predominated in later-life love relationships.

Aside from the age-related differences, however, there were some striking similarities in the nature of satisfying love relationships in the Reedy et al. study. At all ages, emotional security was ranked as the most important factor in love, followed by respect, communication, help and play behaviors, sexual intimacy, and loyalty. These findings indicate that a new historical trend in the quality of relationships may be emerging. Earlier there was extensive interest in individual freedom and independence in love relationships, but the data suggest a shift toward security, fidelity, trust, and commitment in relationships (Hendricks & Hendricks, 1983). This shift occurs at a time when worldwide concern is focused on acquired immune deficiency syndrome (AIDS), which can be transmitted in several ways, including heterosexual contact with infected carriers (Sande, 1986).

## Intimacy

Although research suggests that intimacy is a more central factor in a satisfying love relationship as marriages age, life-span theorist Erik Erikson believed that early adulthood is the period in which the development of intimacy attains paramount status. Importantly, Erikson (1968) suggested that intimacy and self-identity have a special relationship with one another. It may be the case that intimacy is only possible after individuals are well on their way to achieving a stable personal identity. Erikson has commented:

> As the young individual seeks at least tentative forms of playful intimacy in friendship and competition, in sex play and love, in argument and gossip, he is apt to experience a peculiar strain, as if such tentative engagement might turn into an interpersonal fusion

> amounting to a loss of identity. . . . Where a youth does not resolve such a commitment, he may isolate himself and enter, at best, only stereotyped and formalized interpersonal relations; or he may, in repeated hectic attempts and dismal failures, seek intimacy with the most improbable of partners. (p. 167)

An inability to develop meaningful relationships with others during young adulthood can be harmful to an individual's personality. It may lead a person to repudiate, ignore, or attack others. Erikson (1968) asserts that this inability to form a relationship can account for the shallow, almost pathetic attempts of youth to merge themselves with a leader or cult figure. Many youths want to be apprentices or disciples of leaders who will shelter them from the harm of an "out-group" world. If this fails, and Erikson believes that it must, then sooner or later the individual will recoil into a self-search to discover where he or she went wrong. Such introspection sometimes leads to painful feelings of isolation and depression. It also may contribute to mistrust of others and restrict the individual's willingness to act on his or her own initiative.

## Friendships

Friendship involves *enjoyment* (spending time with our friends); *acceptance* (valuing our friends as they are without trying to change them); *trust* (believing that our friends act on our behalf); *respect* (thinking our friends have the right to make their own judgments); *mutual assistance* (helping and supporting our friends and allowing them to do so for us); *confiding* (sharing experiences and confidential matters with our friends); *understanding* (feeling that our friends know us well and understand what we are like); and *spontaneity* (doing and saying as we like with a friend) (Davis, 1985; Tesch, Whitbourne, & Nehrke, 1981).

Marjorie Lowenthal and her colleagues suggested that the presence of a *confidant*—an extremely close friend—is a critical aspect of psychological adaptation to aging as measured by morale, avoidance of psychosomatic symptoms, and the ability to cope with stress (Lowenthal, Turnher, & Chiriboga, 1975). The presence of a close confidant or mentor helps adult males in their twenties and early thirties to become successful in their careers (Levinson, 1986). The mentor serves as coach to those beginning their careers, providing a supervised internship as well as support, nurturance, and encouragement. By contrast, extreme social isolation is associated with psychiatric illness, poor achievement, failure to thrive, and limited job success. Indeed, being embedded in a network of close interpersonal ties is related to general life satisfaction and a sense of belonging, competence, and self-worth (Sarason, Sarason, & Pierce, 1989).

Connidis and Davies (1990b) have found that adults are likely to reveal confidences to their relatives, but are more likely to seek out spouses and friends as companions. That is, people usually tell their personal secrets and problems to their relatives (e.g., complain about poor health or finances), but do things (e.g., go out to dinner) with their friends. It may come as no surprise, therefore, that Crohan and Antonucci (1989) have reported that relationships with friends are more strongly related to psychological well-being than relationships with family.

It has been suggested that female friendships are characterized by more intimacy than male friendships (Antonucci, 1990; Berndt, 1982). Indeed, females are much more likely to disclose themselves to males than vice versa and are much more prone to share their private inner lives than males. Females bring the capacity for intimacy to courtship and then train males to be intimate. The importance of friendship among older women in our society continues to emerge in more recent investigations. In one study, both friendships and family supports were found to be equally effective among married and never-married women in combatting loneliness and isolation (Essex & Nam, 1987).

Friendships are marked by many of the same characteristics as relationships between spouses or lovers (Davis, 1985). Both share the characteristics of acceptance, trust, respect, confiding, understanding, spontaneity, mutual assistance, and happiness. However, relationships with spouses and lovers, unlike friendships, are marked by strong emotion (passionate love) and strong caring. Interestingly, relationships with friends are perceived to be more stable than relationships among spouses or lovers.

## Friendships across the Adult Years

One life-span developmental study of friendships found that newly married young adults have more friends than adolescents, middle-aged adults, or the elderly (Weiss & Lowenthal, 1975). Also, young married couples report that friendships established in their single days are likely to dissipate. Often friendships among young married adults are based on a four-party relationship (two couples) rather than a two-party relationship (one couple); the two couples may go out to the movies or have dinner together, and so forth.

By middle adulthood many friends are "old friends." Closeness and convenience seem less salient in establishing friendships during midlife than in early adulthood. In one investigation of 150 middle-aged adults who had moved within the last five years, a majority of the individuals named someone from their former locale as their best friend (Hess, 1971). This indicates that the friendship role does not need to be filled by someone who is physically present. In other words, what seems to matter to people is the perception that "there is someone out there who really cares about me."

Antonucci (1990) uses the term **social convoy** to describe the network of close relationships that accompany an individual throughout life. The size of the social convoy—most people have somewhere between two to five close relationships—does not seem to change much during adulthood. Of course, the actual members of the convoy may change due to many factors such as death, change of residence, etcetera. Interestingly, younger and middle-aged adults are more likely to perceive the size and emotional intensity of their convoys as inadequate relative to elderly adults.

Throughout the adult years, women seem to have larger social convoys than men and they maintain their friendships longer than men do (Antonucci, 1990; Essex & Nam, 1987). Women in old age expect friendships to be as reciprocal as they were in middle adulthood, even though they expect their children to provide more for them than previously (Ingersoll-Dayton & Antonucci, 1988; Rook, 1987). Recently, O'Connor (1993) has shown that older women tend to have especially meaningful cross-gender friendships with men. These are typically platonic relationships in which men provide a range of domestic services (e.g., grocery shopping and window washing) as well as psychological closeness and support.

Because women have larger social convoys than men, they are more likely to suffer psychologically because of the negative life experiences that befall their friends, confidants, and spouses. Furthermore, due to sex differences in longevity, women are more often called upon to adjust to one of life's most significant stressors, the death of a spouse.

## Loneliness

Robert Weiss (1973) believes that there are two kinds of loneliness: *emotional isolation,* which results from the loss or absence of an emotional attachment, and *social isolation,* which occurs through the loss or absence of social ties. Either type of loneliness is likely to make an individual feel empty and sad. Weiss suggested that one type of relationship cannot easily substitute for another to diminish the loneliness. Consequently, an adult grieving over the loss of a love relationship is likely to still feel very lonely even in the company of friends.

Similarly, people who have close emotional attachments may still feel a great deal of loneliness if they do not also have friends. Weiss described one woman who had a happy marriage but whose husband had to take a job in another state where they knew no one. In their new location she listened to her husband describe all the new friends he was developing on his new job while she was home taking care of the kids. She was bored and miserable. Finally the family moved to a neighborhood where each was able to develop friendships.

Being alone is different from being lonely. Most of us cherish moments when we can be alone for a while, away from the hectic pace of our lives. Rubin (1979) has commented that for people in high-pressure jobs, aloneness may heal, while loneliness can hurt. In our society we are conditioned to believe that aloneness is to be dreaded, so we develop the expectation that solitude may bring sadness. However, research has revealed that people who choose to live alone are no more lonely than people who live with others (Rubenstein & Shaver, 1981).

As would be expected, an older person's health has a great deal to do with the amount of contact he receives from his family and friends, and the subsequent amount of closeness (or loneliness) he experiences. Field, Minkler, Falk, and Leino (1993) have shown that elderly adults who were in very good health had *more* contacts with relatives and friends than those elderly individuals who were in poor health. Thus the participants who experienced the most loneliness, in reality, should have received the most social support. These results strongly suggest that to maintain closeness with family members and friends, older adults need to possess a certain threshold level of physical vitality. Without health and vitality, it may be difficult, if not impossible, to maintain reciprocal interpersonal relations.

## *Development of Marital Relationships*

*Ideally, couples need three lives: one for him, one for her, and one for them together.*
—Jacqueline Bisset

For the vast majority of individuals, the most intense and important relationship they enter during adulthood is the marital relationship. In this section, we discuss different aspects of marital relationships.

From the time two people marry, an average of two years pass before they have their first child, and the next twenty-five to thirty-five years are devoted to childrearing and launching. Although this represents a sizable segment of the life span, the typical married couple experiences more than one-half of their total years together *after* their last child leaves home. This extended period of shared time is a recent occurrence. Since the turn of the century, as people have married earlier and stayed married longer, an average of ten years has been added to the average length of married life (assuming that divorce has not occurred). In the average family of 1900, the last child left home about two years after the death of one parent. Today, both parents are usually alive when the youngest child departs. Often both marital partners now live long enough to go from early old age (55 to 74) to late old age (75 plus) in the life cycle.

### Courtship

How do we choose our marriage partners? Initially, physical appearance is often an important factor. Some psychologists believe that the choice of a mate entails a selection process based on mutual qualities and interests (Murstein, 1982). Alternatively, some have argued that complementary needs play an important part in the mate-selection process (Winch, 1974). For example, if one person tends to be introverted, a socially outgoing spouse may complement him or her. Not all marital choices, of course, are made on the basis of such complementary qualities. Most of us choose a mate who shares some characteristics that are similar to our own and some that are not.

### The Early Years of Marriage

The first few months of marriage are filled with exploration and evaluation. Gradually, a couple begins to adjust their expectations and fantasies about marriage to correspond with reality. For couples who have lived together before marriage, many adjustments need to be made. Couples who live together prior to marriage face exactly the same challenges as other couples in their early years of marriage. In fact, cohabitation and marital satisfaction were reported to be inversely related for couples in first-time marriages (Demaris, 1984)! Certainly every couple has had the experience of realizing that their "perfect" mate has faults, defects, and flaws which they previously overlooked. Cohabitation does not eliminate these early phases of marital adjustment.

Since most marriages begin when people are in their twenties, young married couples are not only involved in their marriage roles but also in becoming established in occupations. As more women become involved in meaningful careers, they must make decisions about when and if they will interrupt their careers to bear children. The process of fitting varied role expectations to each spouse and working through compromises and negotiated settlements is described by Murstein (1982) as *role compatibility.* More importantly, developing role compatibility is a lengthy process as each marriage partner discards old roles and adopts new ones.

## The Childbearing and Childrearing Years

Historically, childbearing and childrearing have been associated with the very beginning of the adult portion of the life span. David Gutmann (1975, 1977) describes this as a biological period in which adults respond to a *parental imperative* designed to make maximal use of the division of labor between the sexes and to ensure the continuity of the social community. In more recent times, couples are delaying childbearing until early middle age, and some are deciding not to have any children. Childlessness has become an acceptable option as more couples choose a personal lifestyle of freedom and independence or respond to worldwide problems of overpopulation.

## Childlessness

Not all married couples want or plan to have children. At present, these couples are highly educated and strongly career-oriented. Approximately 5 to 10 percent of married couples who remain childless do not make the final decision until their late thirties or early forties (Hoffman, 1982). In one investigation, Veevers (1980) questioned married couples who did not want to have children. Some couples recognized that from as far back as their own childhood or adolescence they knew they did not want to have children. Veevers calls these individuals (usually the wife) *early articulators.* Early articulators clearly conveyed their decisions to their prospective spouses during serious discussions well before marriage. Another group, called *postponers,* simply continued to delay the decision to have children until it became obvious to the couple that children were not going to be a part of their marriage. These couples seemed to let the decision to remain child-free emerge by placing other priorities (e.g., their relationships, careers, personal freedom, travel, or other priorities) ahead of childbearing. Early articulators have been found to be more expressive of affection toward each other than postponers (Callan, 1984, 1987), and early articulators appear slightly more satisfied with their marriages than postponers (Bram, 1985–1987).

Childless couples spend more time together than couples with children as they share plans, discuss activities, and evolve a compatible lifestyle (Callan, 1984). Overall, being childless has not been found to diminish the quality or satisfaction of marriage (Callan, 1984, 1987; Hoffman, 1982). Perhaps the childless couple invests greater emotional commitment and more time and energy into the marital relationship (Bram, 1985–1987).

*The joys of child rearing may be juxtaposed against the unanticipated restrictions couples sometimes experience in their own relationship and personal freedom.*

## Having Children

For the majority of couples who desire children and who are fertile or willing to adopt, a number of potential problems exist. For example, it is during the early years of the child's life that parents report a high degree of dissatisfaction and frustration with marriage (Rollins & Feldman, 1970; Rollins & Gallagher, 1978). Belsky (1981) reports that childrearing contains many stresses as well as immense pleasures. With the birth of a child, couples no longer have as much individual freedom, and their own relationship diminishes in importance and satisfaction.

The increasing financial responsibilities of childrearing also play an important role. Most couples feel the child dominates their lives, restricting their outside friendships, hobbies, and community involvement. The financial costs of raising children are considerable. This causes more and more mothers to seek employment. For example, although married women historically have tended to drop out of the labor market, in the 1980s nearly 50 percent of women with preschoolers were employed (U.S. Dept. of Labor, 1987).

## Postchildrearing Years: The Empty Nest

A time comes in a couple's life when their children become independent and begin to provide for themselves and form friendships outside the family unit. Instead of maintaining a parent-child relationship at this time, parents and offspring gradually begin interacting with each other as one adult to another. The growing realization of adult children that a parent is an adult like themselves, with strengths and weaknesses, is called **filial maturity.**

This period is a time of reorganization, especially for parents. Couples who have learned to relate to each other through their children no longer have their children to buffer their relationship. They must now rely more on their relationship with each other (Rhodes, 1977). It is not surprising to find that this is another point in life when the incidence of divorce rises.

When adolescents or young adult offspring leave home, *some* parents experience a deep sense of loss called the **empty nest syndrome.** Researchers have identified a relationship between strict role division and the empty nest syndrome through lengthy interviews with middle-aged women suffering from acute depression after their children left home (Bart, 1973). The greater a mother's involvement with her children, the greater her difficulty in seeing them leave home. Women who defined themselves primarily in terms of the maternal role and whose lives had been focused exclusively on their children felt as though they had nothing to live for when their offspring left the nest. They had dedicated themselves to living selfless, nurturing lives on behalf of their spouses and children and anticipated some reward for this self-denial at the end of their childrearing years. All of these "supermothers," when asked what they were most proud of, said, "my children." None mentioned an accomplishment of their own.

Some research suggests that the empty nest may be welcomed by another group of mothers—those who have maintained a career, hobby, or a work-defined self-concept to which they can return after the nest is empty. For these women, the empty nest means a welcome role loss and the easing of role conflict and stress (Coleman & Antonucci, 1983). As evidence that some couples adjust relatively quickly to the empty nest, consider the oft-cited data showing marital satisfaction and the **upswing hypothesis** (see figure 7.3). The upswing hypothesis suggests that marital satisfaction is highest before childrearing begins, declines during childrearing, and increases when children have left the nest (Anderson, Russell, & Schumm, 1983). Thus, some couples seem to find renewal in their relationships when the nest is empty. They appreciate the increased free time for individual self-enhancement, greater involvement with a spouse, hobbies, and community involvement. Some couples have empty nest parties to celebrate the new opportunities this transition creates!

*An "empty nest" may increase (or decrease) stress levels, role conflict, and marital satisfaction.*

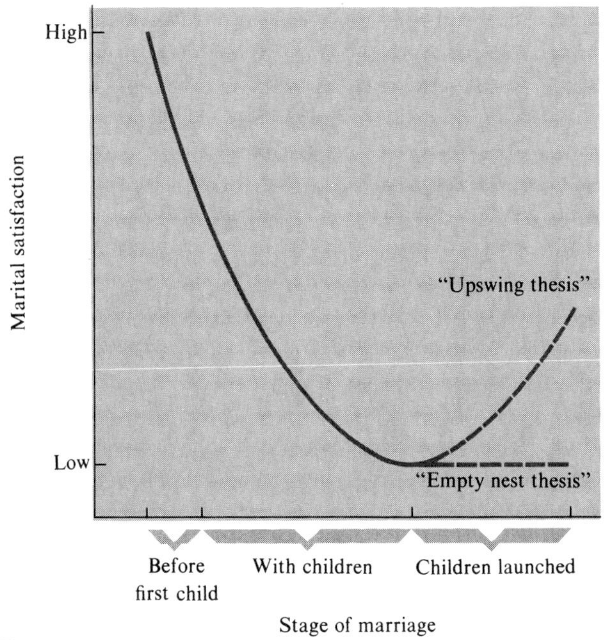

Marital satisfaction

High

Low

"Upswing thesis"

"Empty nest thesis"

Before first child

With children

Children launched

Stage of marriage

**Figure 7.3** The relationship between marital satisfaction and stage of marriage.

David Gutmann (1977) has offered another perspective on the upswing hypothesis. He suggests that since the divorce rate has increased, couples who earlier in history were likely to be categorized as dissatisfied are no longer in the middle-aged marital grouping. This selective dropout of unhappily married individuals may account, in part, for the upswing.

## The Aging Couple

*The morning sun when it's in your face really shows your age*
*But that don't worry me none in my eyes you're everything.*
—Rod Stewart

The time from retirement until the death of a spouse signals the final stage of the marriage process. Retirement undoubtedly alters a couple's lifestyle and requires some adaptation in their relationship. The greatest changes may occur in families in which the husband works and the wife is a homemaker. The husband may not know what to do with himself, and the wife may feel uneasy having him around the house all the time. In such families, both spouses may need to move toward more expressive roles (Troll, 1971).

Marriages in which both husband and wife have worked take on a somewhat different pattern of adjustment to retirement, one marked by a simpler transition. In retirement, these couples display more egalitarian and far more cooperative

## Sources of Conflict and Pleasure in Middle-Aged and Elderly Couples

Levenson, Carstensen, and Gottman (1993) noted an interesting paradox. Marriage has the potential to be the most long-lasting and intimate of all of the close relationships that we will encounter during our lives. But, the vast majority of psychological research on the topic of marriage has focused on young and middle-aged couples, especially those whose marriages end in divorce. Why don't psychologists study long-term marriages that have survived for three or more decades? Do the members of an older marriage experience greater levels of satisfaction and pleasure than the members of a middle-aged marriage? Or, do older married people feel "stuck" and dissatisfied with each other more than middle-aged married people do? These are important issues because as life expectancy increases, the potential for a long-term marriage increases as well.

To examine these issues, Levenson et al. (1993) studied groups of *middle-aged* and *older* married couples. The middle-aged and older couples were between 40 and 50 or 60 and 70 years of age and had been married for at least fifteen or thirty-five years, respectively. Overall, couples within these two age groups did not differ in terms of educational background, physical and psychological health status, alcohol consumption, and income. The vast majority of all of the couples had children. And, as would be expected, the children of the older couples (on average, 36 years of age) were older than the children of the middle-aged couples (on average, 17 years of age).

Each spouse, within the 156 pairs of couples in this study, was asked to rate the potential sources of conflict and pleasure he/she perceived in marriage. This was accomplished by presenting the participants with ten potential conflict domains (e.g., money, communication, sex, children, etc.) and sixteen potential areas of pleasure (e.g., vacations, children, watching TV, etc.). Participants rated each of these twenty-six items on a scale of 0 to 100. The higher the rating, the greater the perceived conflict or pleasure.

The major results of the Levenson et al. research are illustrated in table 7.A. In a very general sense, it seems that older marriages contain lower levels of conflict and higher levels of pleasure than middle-aged marriages, and older and middle-aged couples rank-order sources of conflict and pleasures in a similar way. More specifically, older couples attributed less conflict than middle-aged couples to money, religion, recreation, and children; they attributed more pleasure than middle-aged couples to children, things done together, dreams, and vacations. With regard to the ranking data, it seems as if children become a greater source of pleasure and lesser source of conflict as marriages grow older.

Overall, these results paint a very encouraging picture of long-term marital relationships. The positive state of these marriages could provide a very firm foundation for the increased interdependencies that marriage partners will probably experience in their later years. On another level, the findings obtained by Levenson et al. (1993) are consistent with a concept—selective optimization with compensation as developed by Baltes and Baltes (1990)—that was already discussed in chapter 6. Namely, as couples age, they may actively seek to narrow their social networks and maximize the amount of satisfaction they experience with one another.

---

relationships (Tryban, 1985). Among the retired working-class couples interviewed in one study, the dual-career couples derived increased happiness, satisfaction, and involvement in retirement when compared to single-wage-earner families (Tryban, 1985).

Married older adults appear to be happier than those who are single (Lee, 1978). Such satisfaction seems to be greater for women than for men, possibly because women place more emphasis on attaining satisfaction through marriage than men do. However, as more women develop careers, this relationship between satisfaction

*TABLE 7.A*

**Ranks and Mean Levels of Sources of Conflict and Pleasure for Middle-Aged and Older Couples**

| | Middle-aged couples | | Older couples | |
|---|---|---|---|---|
| Rank | Topic | Mean | Topic | Mean |
| | | *Sources of conflict* | | |
| 1 | Children | 25.7 | Communication | 19.3 |
| 2 | Money | 25.6 | Recreation | 16.3 |
| 3 | Communication | 25.4 | Money | 15.9 |
| 4 | Recreation | 24.8 | Children | 13.7 |
| 5 | Sex | 19.8 | Sex | 13.1 |
| 6 | In-laws | 18.1 | In-laws | 11.8 |
| 7 | Friends | 14.6 | Friends | 10.9 |
| 8 | Religion | 13.8 | Religion | 6.6 |
| 9 | Alcohol and drugs | 9.6 | Jealousy | 6.4 |
| 10 | Jealousy | 8.3 | Alcohol and drugs | 5.4 |
| | | *Sources of pleasure* | | |
| 1 | Good times in the past | 75.5 | Children or granchildren | 83.0 |
| 2 | Other people | 73.6 | Good times in the past | 79.9 |
| 3 | Children or grandchildren | 72.9 | Vacations taken | 79.3 |
| 4 | Vacations taken | 70.6 | Things done together recently | 78.5 |
| 5 | Things done together recently | 70.0 | Other people | 76.4 |
| 6 | Silly and fun things | 69.3 | Plans for the future | 74.8 |
| 7 | Plans for the future | 67.9 | Television, radio, and reading | 73.9 |
| 8 | Television, radio, and reading | 67.6 | Casual and informal things | 68.2 |
| 9 | Casual and informal things | 66.4 | Silly and fun things | 67.4 |
| 10 | Accomplishments | 60.4 | Accomplishments | 64.1 |
| 11 | Views on issues | 59.5 | Politics and current events | 63.2 |
| 12 | Politics and current events | 57.7 | Views on issues | 60.5 |
| 13 | Things happening in town | 46.0 | Things happening in town | 51.3 |
| 14 | Family pets | 45.3 | Family pets | 48.0 |
| 15 | Things to do around the house | 40.2 | Things to do around the house | 46.1 |
| 16 | Dreams | 36.6 | Dreams | 45.6 |

*From: R. W. Levenson, L. L. Carstenson, and J. M. Gottman. "Long-Term Marriage: Age, Gender and Satisfaction." in* Psychology and Aging, *8: 301–313. Copyright © 1993 by the American Psychological Association. Reprinted by permission.*

and marriage may not hold. (See Research Focus 7.1 for a discussion of other research on the sources of conflict and pleasure for middle-aged and elderly couples.)

Of course, not all individuals in late adulthood are married. At least 8 percent of people who reach the age of 65 have never been married. Contrary to the popular stereotypes, those older people seem to have the least difficulty coping with loneliness in old age. Many of them learned long ago to live autonomously, sustain friendships, and maintain self-reliance (Essex & Nam, 1987; Gubrium, 1975).

**Figure 7.4** Marital status of persons 65 plus. *Source: Data from U.S. Bureau of the Census, 1990.*

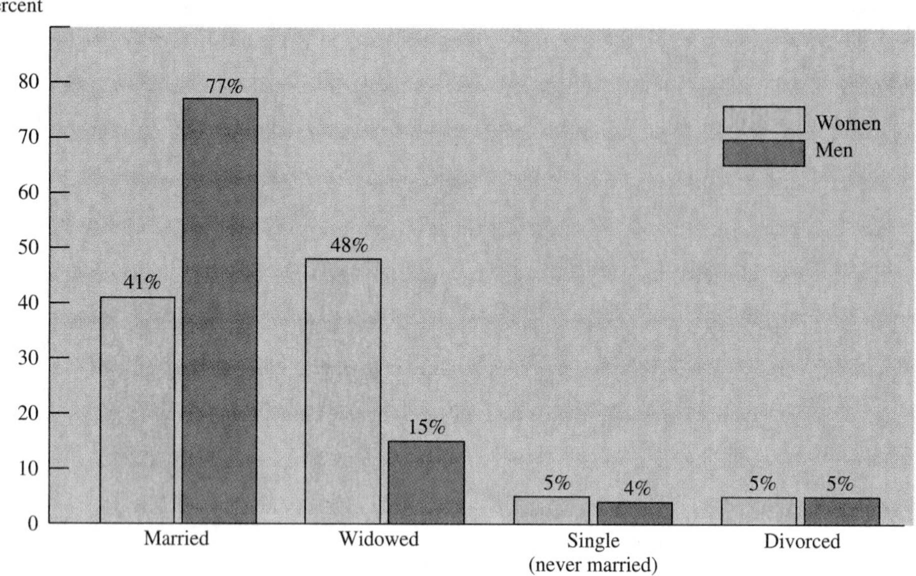


## Widowhood

As can be seen in figure 7.4, a substantial percentage of the older population of the United States is widowed. Not surprisingly, women are much more likely than men to experience the death of a spouse. In fact, widows outnumber widowers nearly six to one (U.S. Bureau of the Census, 1990).

When a spouse dies, the surviving marital partner goes through a period of grieving. Some researchers call the bereavement process (discussed later in the text) of widows or widowers in the year after the death of a spouse **grief work** (Parkes, 1972). The individual's structure or model of the world is disrupted because of the loss of a strong attachment bond (Bowlby, 1980). Grief work may lead to a new identity for the individual, an identity that can be healthy or unhealthy.

Over the course of a year, most individuals come to accept the loss of a spouse and seem to adapt reasonably well. Women seem to adjust better than men to the death of a spouse, and older people seem to adjust better than younger people (Carey, 1977). Women are perhaps better able to cope because they are used to managing most of the day-to-day tasks required in the home and have a greater number of intimate friendships to draw upon for support. At the same time, today's older widow faces difficulties if she cannot drive, manage the complex world of banking, stocks, and insurance, and establish an independent credit rating. Surely such data are, in part, the result of cohort effects. With dual-career marriages, divorce, and separation so common today, we will likely find both men and women now in midlife to be far more independent, self-sufficient, and capable in facing life alone following the death of their spouse.

The death of a husband may be especially difficult for a wife who has not developed a separate identity of her own (e.g., through a career). But even for women who have roles and interests outside of their husband's identities, the death of a spouse is a traumatic experience. With no husband to provide for her, the older widow may have to live on public support or find a job. Reduced income and subsistence near poverty level make coping with the death of a husband especially difficult. Elderly women reported a median annual income of $8,188 per year, in comparison to $14,548 among comparably aged men (U.S. Bureau of the Census, 1993). Furthermore, the older a woman is, the poorer she becomes. Among women 85 years of age or older, one in four was living at or below the level of poverty in the mid-1980s (Bould, Sanborn, & Rief, 1989). Widows may be criticized by family and friends for developing a relationship with another man too soon after the death of her husband. Families rarely recognize that widows have attachment or intimacy needs that are often unfulfilled. This may account, in part, for the finding that most widowers remarry whereas most widows do not.

Men are not isolated from the trauma of a spouse's death, either. They have typically relied on their wives for emotional support, intimacy, and sexual satisfaction. The loss of their mates usually triggers a great deal of grief and stress. Support systems, such as a circle of friends, are usually more available to the wife whose husband has died than vice versa, particularly because there are many more older women than older men in our society. One advantage the widower has over the widow in late adulthood is that if he decides to date and/or remarry, the available pool of women is large.

Even though widowed older people report a fairly high degree of loneliness, the marriage rate for those in late adulthood is not very high. Furthermore, the older a surviving spouse is at the time of the death of a husband or wife, the less the likelihood of remarriage (Bould et al., 1989). Approximately 20 percent of widowers over 65 and less than 5 percent of widows over 55 years of age will remarry (George, 1980). Among some older people (and their adult children), remarriage may be viewed as a betrayal of the deceased spouse.

## *Parenting and Grandparenting*

### Parenting

In earlier times, women considered motherhood a full-time occupation. Currently, couples tend to have fewer children, and as birth control has become common practice, many people choose the time for children and the number of children they will raise. The number of one-child families is increasing. Giving birth to fewer children and reducing the demands of child care free up a significant portion of a parent's life span for other endeavors.

Over the last two decades we have observed three important changes in parenting: (1) women may invest less time in maternal practices than in the past; (2) men are apt to invest a greater amount of time in fathering; and (3) parental care in the home is often supplemented by institutional care (e.g., day-care centers). As a result of these changes, questions of how to integrate child care with other roles has become an increasingly important issue (Rossi, 1977).

*Table 7.1*

| Myths about Parenting |
|---|
| 1. The birth of a child will save a failing marriage. |
| 2. Because the child is a possession or extension of the parent, the child will think, feel, and behave as the parents did in their childhoods. |
| 3. Children will always take care of parents in old age. |
| 4. Parents can expect respect and obedience from their children. |
| 5. Having a child means that the parents will always have someone who loves them and who will be their best friend. |
| 6. Having a child gives the parents a second chance to achieve what they should have achieved. |
| 7. If parents learn the right techniques, they can mold their children to be what they want. |
| 8. It's the parents' fault when children fail. |
| 9. Mothers are naturally better parents than fathers. |
| 10. Parenting is an instinct and requires no training. |

In American culture, the term "mothering" is often confused with the term "parenting." In fact, the attachment bond between the mother and the infant is viewed as the basis for the development of a healthy personality later in life. Jerome Kagan (1979) believes this idea is one of the few sacred, transcendental themes in American culture. Emotions are aroused when discussion of surrogate care outside the home begins. Today more infants and children than ever before in the United States are spending less time with their mothers. Approximately two-thirds of mothers with a child under the age of 6 is employed. And about 80 percent of the mothers of children aged 6 to 17 work outside the home (Wall Street Journal, 1993). Although opinion polls indicate that a majority of the public believes that maternal employment harms the family and that day care itself has a negative influence on children (Belsky, 1987), much of the research evidence suggests a more positive conclusion (Hoffman, 1979, 1986; Phillips, McCartney, & Scarr, 1987).

The parenting role carries another important distinction. Unlike most adult responsibilities, the parenting role cannot be acceptably changed or discarded. We can quit one job and take another, or we can undergo retraining for an entirely different job. We can also divorce and remarry. However, once children are born, they require a commitment over a period of time; we cannot acceptably revert to nonparent status. Ideally, potential parents must realistically assess whether they are willing to make the extensive investment in time, physical energy, and emotional involvement required to rear competent children.

Unfortunately, we seem to have a number of unrealistic expectations about parenting. Table 7.1 presents several of these mythical expectations as identified by Okun and Rappaport (1980).

To be sure, parents have a significant impact on the psychological health and well-being of their children. However, some current evidence suggests that the effects of parental practices may be more pronounced during adulthood than childhood! See Research Focus 7.2 for more details.

## *Parental Favoritism and the Quality of Parent-Child Relations in Adulthood*

How do children who are disfavored by their parents during childhood relate to their parents during adulthood? This question, which seems relatively straightforward, is much more complex than one would assume. For example, Victoria Bedford (1992) has suggested that a child's self-esteem is threatened if she believes that she is not liked by her parents. To dissipate this threat and reduce feelings of inferiority, a child could develop a profound hatred for her parents. Such a strategy, however, could prove to be very counterproductive, because parents are the primary source of a child's need fulfillment, and it would be unwise to alienate them with signals of resentment. From the perspective of psychoanalytic theory, children might resolve this dilemma by unconsciously displacing feelings of animosity from their parents to their siblings. This would yield two significant accomplishments. First, parents would no longer be perceived as cruel, unfair, or unloving. Second, the child's self-esteem could be maintained. Bedford (1992) has noted that there are several examples of such displacements throughout Western literature, especially in the Bible. For example, "Due to Jacob's preference for Joseph, Joseph's brothers left him to die; because God, the supreme parent figure, preferred Abel's sacrifice to Cain's, Cain murdered Abel . . ." (Bedford, 1992, p. 150).

What happens when these "least favored children" grow older and enter adulthood? Adults are much less dependent on their parents for support than are children. Therefore, given the reasoning described in the previous paragraph, it may be that adults display more resentment toward their parents and less resentment toward their siblings as they age! Bedford (1992) has provided two pieces of evidence in support of this hypothesis. First, she discovered that young and middle-aged adults who felt they had been treated worse than their siblings during childhood experienced less affection for and more conflict with their parents than similarly aged adults who had memories of being favored by their parents. Interestingly, she also reported that the psychological consequences of being a "least favored child" were more pronounced from the perspective of adults who were least favored during adulthood than from the perspective of their parents. Second, Bedford (1992) as well as other researchers found that as siblings age they tend to become much more congenial toward each other.

Bedford (1992) concludes that her psychodynamically inspired research findings have ". . . demonstrated rather convincingly that childhood memories contribute consistently to the perceived quality of the intergenerational bond" (p. 154). She also reminds us that adult children's memories of early parental favoritism may have a significant effect on the degree to which they offer care and support to their elderly parents and siblings during times of crisis.

## Grandparenting

Although the grandparenting role is prevalent in our society, it still is not well understood or well researched. We generally think of grandparents as old people, but there are many middle-aged grandparents in their forties and fifties as well (Nahemow, 1984). The average ages for first-time grandmothers and grandfathers are 50 and 52 years old, respectively (Tinsley & Parke, 1987). With increased life expectancy and modifications in fertility patterns, the duration and experience of grandparenting has significantly changed in the following ways:

1. More people become grandparents than ever before.
2. The entry into grandparent status typically occurs at midlife, and many people spend four or more decades as grandparents.
3. Multigenerational families are common, and many grandparents also become great- and great-great-grandparents.
4. Parenthood and grandparenthood have become distinct from each other, both as individual life experiences and as two kinds of family status (Hagestad, 1985).

It appears that the way in which grandparents and grandchildren interact is partially a function of the age of the grandparents. Nahemow (1985) suggests that today's younger grandparents are nontraditional in their interactions with their grandchildren. She believes that our societal definition of the traditional grandparent role is far more likely to be seen among great-grandparents or great-great-grandparents than among grandparents. Thomas (1986a) reports that younger grandparents feel far more responsibility for their grandchildren in terms of discipline, caretaking, and childrearing advice than older grandparents. Thomas (1986b) also observes that most grandparents, by age 70, seek less direct physical intervention and day-to-day care of their grandchildren. "One of the nicest things about being a 72-year-old grandmother," said one woman, "is that you can say good-bye to your grandchildren when they come for a visit."

Regardless of age, grandparenting is a role that has few norms in our society. In one investigation (Neugarten & Weinstein, 1984), seventy pairs of grandparents were interviewed about their relationships with their grandchildren. At least one-third of the grandparents said they had some difficulties with the grandparent role, in terms of thinking of themselves as grandparents, in how they should act as grandparents, and in terms of conflicts with their own children over how to rear the grandchildren.

Kivnick (1983) has separated grandparenting into three components: (1) the meaning of the grandparenting role—*role meaning*; (2) the behavior a grandparent adopts—*role behavior*; and (3) the enjoyment of being a grandparent—*role satisfaction.* For some individuals, the role meaning in being a grandparent was a source of biological renewal and/or continuity. In such cases, feelings of renewal (youth) or extensions of the self and family into the future (continuity) appeared. For others, being a grandparent meant emotional self-fulfillment, generating feelings of companionship, and finding satisfaction from the development of a relationship between adult and grandchild that was often missing in earlier parent-child relationships. For still others, the grandparent role was seen as remote, indicating that the role had little importance in their lives.

In addition to evaluating the meaning of grandparenting, researchers have assessed the behavioral roles exhibited by grandparents in interacting with their grandchildren. In fact, this dimension of grandparent-role behavior is the most frequently studied aspect of grandparenting (Hess, 1988). Kivnick (1983), for example, noted three behavioral roles: formal, fun-seeking, and distant-figure. The *formal role* involved performing what was considered a proper and prescribed role. The *fun-seeking role* was typified by informality and playfulness. Grandchildren were viewed as a source of leisure activity, and mutual satisfaction was emphasized. The *distant-figure role* was characterized by benevolent but infrequent contact between grandparent and grandchild. Two new roles adopted by modern grandparents are that of *surrogate caretaker* (Cherlin & Furstenberg, 1985, 1986) and *family watchdog* (Troll, 1983).

Grandparents often play a significant role in the lives of their grandchildren. In one investigation (Robertson, 1976), 92 percent of young-adult grandchildren

*Grandparents communicate with their grandchildren at many levels, such as direct teaching of skills and cultural traditions.*

indicated that they would have missed some important things in life if there had been no grandparents present when they were growing up; 70 percent said that teenagers do not see grandparents as boring. Such information suggests that the grandparent-grandchild relationship is reciprocal.

Despite the tendency of research investigators to view grandparenting as a generic term, there are real and significant differences between the roles of grandmother and grandfather. Grandmothers, for example, tend to outlive grandfathers, thus occupying their role for a longer period of time and potentially having a different impact on their grandchildren (Hess, 1988). Grandmothers typically have closer ties to grandchildren of both sexes than grandfathers do (Hagestad, 1982), whereas grandfathers appear to establish closer ties with their grandsons than with their granddaughters (Bengtson, Mangen, & Landry, 1984). Generally, maternal grandparents have more contact with grandchildren than paternal grandparents (Kahana & Kahana, 1970). In times of family crisis, the maternal grandparents are more frequently sought for help and more frequently provide assistance (Cherlin & Furstenberg, 1986).

In a survey of 177 grandmothers and 102 grandfathers, Thomas (1986a) found that grandmothers derived greater satisfaction from their roles than grandfathers. Interestingly, grandmothers are more likely than grandfathers to consider grandparenting a second chance at parenting. And grandmothers appear more willing than grandfathers to accept the role of passing along to grandchildren family traditions,

## *Research Focus 7.3*

# *Grandparents' Visitation Rights*

During the last ten to fifteen years, most states have passed laws granting grandparents the right to petition a court to legally obtain visitation privileges with their grandchildren. Ross Thompson, Barbara Tinsley, Mario Scalora, and Ross Parke (1989) have noted that this is a significant change from traditional laws that gave grandparents visitation rights only if the child's parents consented to such visitation. Now grandparents may be allowed visitation privileges even if parents object.

What made legislators change their minds about grandparents' visitation rights? One of the most important factors is the emerging political influence of older adults. Also, lawmakers seem to believe that grandparent visitation is a way of preserving intergenerational ties within a family, and that grandparents provide their grandchildren with a powerful source of psychological support above and beyond that offered by parents.

Thompson et al. (1989) question whether there is sufficient psychological research to substantiate these beliefs. One of the things psychologists know, however, is that the benefits that children derive from interacting with their grandparents are directly related to the quality of the relationship that exists between the grandparents and the child's parents (Johnson, 1988). For example, if this relationship is typified by ill-will and hostility, little, if any, benefits may be derived from grandparent visitation. In fact, children may even suffer from extended contact with their grandparents if significant intergenerational conflict exists. With regard to this issue, Thompson et al. (1989) have commented that

> Grandparents are likely to turn to the courts only if they cannot come to an agreement with the child's parents about visitation with grandchildren. Children are likely to encounter loyalty conflicts during the judicial proceedings, and if a visitation is granted, loyalty conflicts are likely to be maintained as the child remains the focus of intergenerational conflict. Because a child already experiences distress owing to the triggering conditions linked to a visitation petition (for example, parental divorce or death), it is hard to see how further legal conflict between the family members can assist the child in coping. (p. 1220)

A similar problem may arise, of course, when a child visits a noncustodial parent after a divorce. But Thompson et al. (1989) maintain that the relationship a child shares with a noncustodial parent may be more salient than the relationship he or she shares with grandparents. In fact, it has been shown that children benefit from visiting a noncustodial parent even when there is friction between the custodial and noncustodial parents.

By granting visitation privileges to grandparents, the courts have broadened the degree of "extraparental" parenting to which the child is exposed. This has eroded the traditional notion that parents have virtual autonomy in childrearing matters. Also, grandparent visitation privileges may inadvertently foster changes in how family disputes are resolved. Bargaining between parents and grandparents over visitation privileges now takes place within the shadow of the law. Thompson et al. (1989) suggest that parents could be at a disadvantage in such circumstances because the conditions that allow grandparents to petition for visitation (e.g., divorce or the death of a parent) often render a parent less prepared, both psychologically and financially, for a court battle than the child's grandparents.

Should grandparents have visitation privileges over the objections of a parent? Is court-enforced grandparental visitation really in a child's best interests? Thompson et al. (1989) argue that we do not know enough about grandparenthood to answer these questions. Our ideas about grandparenthood are probably too naive and idealized. We may overestimate the benefits of grandparental visitation and underestimate its costs. Clearly, this is one area where research is needed to help address these basic issues.

---

history, and customs. Grandfathers appear more as "secretaries of state" (Troll, 1983) or heads of the family, whereas grandmothers are more "kinkeepers" (Cohler & Grunebaum, 1981), making sure the family stays together and maintains family protocol. Perhaps these factors are responsible for the loss grandparents feel when they witness a divorce (see Research Focus 7.3).

In addition to gender, both cultural and ethnic diversity lead to differences in grandparenting. Black grandmothers, for example, tend to adopt roles that allow them considerable control and authority over their grandchildren. White, Asian,

*TABLE 7.2*

| Forms of Elder Abuse |
|---|
| *Physical Abuse*: Lack of personal care, lack of supervision, visible bruises and welts, repeated beatings, and lack of food |
| *Psychological Abuse*: Verbal assaults, isolation, fear and threats |
| *Financial or Material Abuse*: Misuse or theft of money or property |
| *Extremely Unsatisfactory Individual Environment*: Dirty and unclean home, urine odor in the home, hazardous living environment |
| *Violation of Constitutional Rights*: Reduction of personal freedom, autonomy, involuntary commitment, guardianship, protection, psychiatric "incompetence," false imprisonment |

and Hispanic cultures tend to be far more varied in their grandparenting styles (Cherlin and Furstenberg, 1985). In one investigation, Bengtson (1985) reported that Mexican-American grandparenting was marked by many more intergenerational relationships (more children, grandchildren, and great-grandchildren) than black or white families.

The role of *great-grandparent* has emerged with increasing frequency among the elderly. Families composed of four living generations represent a fairly new area for study. There is evidence that younger individuals with living grandparents and great-grandparents maintain very positive attitudes toward the elderly as well as great love and affection for these relatives (Bekker, DeMoyne, & Taylor, 1966; Boyd, 1969). These feelings seem to be reciprocal, in that, in a study of forty great-grandparents (thirty-five women and five men), 93 percent indicated very favorable attitudes toward and emotional significance in their new role (Doka & Mertz, 1988). Most viewed the acquisition of great-grandparenthood as a positive mark of successful aging or longevity.

## *PARENTAL ABUSE*

The phenomenon of parental abuse has become an increasingly visible part of American life. Pillemer and Wolf (1986) believe that elder abuse, like other forms of family violence such as child abuse and spouse abuse, is a reflection of our violent society. Because of varying definitions and state reporting standards, the incidence of elder abuse nationwide is estimated to be in the range of 1 to 10 percent (Pillemer & Wolf, 1986). In a large metropolitan city, a random sampling of incidents of physical violence, verbal aggression, and neglect revealed rates of 32 per 1,000 among older adults (Pillemer & Finkelhor, 1988). Estimates put the incidence of elder abuse at between 700,000 to 1.1 million cases per year nationwide (Pillemer & Finkelhor, 1988). A comprehensive definition of elder abuse includes physical, psychological, and financial dimensions (see table 7.2).

Passive forms of neglect are more prevalent than active forms of physical violence. The House Select Committee on Aging estimated that four of every five cases of elder abuse goes unreported and uninvestigated (Church et al., 1988). Furthermore, elder abuse is a repetitive pattern of behavior, not an isolated or single occurrence.

The elderly are most often abused by their own spouses (Pillemer & Finkelhor, 1988). Previous research (Yin, 1985) suggested that women were more likely to be abused than men; however, more recent evidence has revealed nearly equal rates of abuse among older men and women (Pillemer & Finkelhor, 1988). It is clear that abusers of the elderly are typically relatives who act as caregivers (Pillemer & Wolf, 1986). And it appears that abuse is far more likely among the elderly who live with a spouse, child, or another relative than among the elderly who live alone (Quinn & Tomita, 1986).

The causes of elder abuse are varied. Investigators have focused their attention on a recurrent stress pattern found among both abused and abuser (Pillemer & Wolf, 1986). The constant responsibility for the care of an older, frail adult often falls on those who neither choose this relationship nor are able to cope with the financial, interpersonal, and time demands placed upon them (Lau & Kosberg, 1979). Abusers are frequently those who have experienced marital problems, financial hardships, drug abuse, alcoholism, and child abuse (Church et al., 1988). Pillemer (1986) observed that dependency is commonly a factor in the background of the abused elderly. Initially, researchers focused on the abused's dependency on the perpetrator of abuse (Quinn & Tomita, 1986). However, other data (Pillemer, 1986) suggest that caretakers who abuse the elderly are dependent on those whom they target for abuse. The abuser may be dependent on the elderly victim for housing, for assistance with routine household tasks, or for financial support.

Research also supports the notion that through abuse, the caretaker is able to continue a cycle of abuse that characterized the relationship at earlier periods of development (Steinmetz, 1978, 1981). Resentment over the lack of freedom and free time are also implicated in the development of abusive patterns by those who care for the elderly. The commitment caregivers must make to the elderly person for whom they care is often not recognized by anyone, neither the elderly person nor others in the immediate family. The individual sacrifice and effort required of caretakers is not sufficiently rewarded socially or economically, and the absence of reward and recognition leads to further cycles of abuse (Myers & Shelton, 1987). In providing care for an elderly parent, for example, adult children in their late thirties and forties are forced to make difficult choices: (1) limiting their career to provide routine elder care; (2) postponing vacations or forgoing evenings out with spouse or friends; (3) providing financial assistance (nursing care or a special diet) at a time when most families face the burgeoning costs of their growing children; and (4) giving retirement planning and financial savings secondary concern (Church et al., 1988). Finally, it should be noted that elderly victims of neglect are generally old, frail, and cognitively and/or physically impaired; they view themselves as helpless and dependent (Myers & Shelton, 1987; Pillemer & Wolf, 1986).

## *Nonmarriage*

In the previous sections, we described developmental changes in what many individuals would consider to be the prototypical lifestyle adopted by adults in our society: a partner within a marriage. In this next section, we turn our attention to adults who are

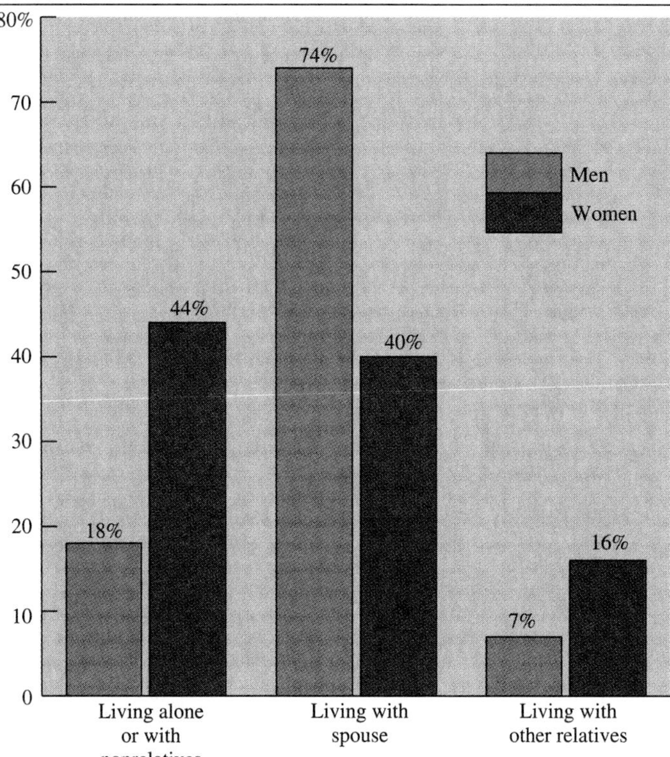


**Figure 7.5** Living arrangements of persons 65+: 1990. *Source: Data from U.S. Bureau of Census, 1990 Census of Population and Housing.*

single rather than married. Specifically, we discuss the different reasons why adults adopt the single lifestyle, and we point out some of the special problems encountered by single adults.

## Single Adults

A greater proportion of the adult population is single now than in the past. In the 1970s, for example, the number of men living by themselves increased 97 percent, while the number of women living alone increased 55 percent. In the 1980s, this growth has slowed somewhat, but it is expected to continue through 1995. In 1985, 20.6 million individuals lived alone in the United States, accounting for 11 percent of adults and 25 percent of all households (U.S. Bureau of the Census, 1986). In 1990, approximately 44 percent and 18 percent of the women and men in the United States lived alone or with nonrelatives (see figure 7.5).

Some people choose to be single as a preferred lifestyle. For others, however, singleness occurs by circumstances such as the death of a spouse or divorce, or other situations that hinder a person's selection of a mate. At any given time, about 30 percent of all adult males and 37 percent of adult females are unmarried (Macklin, 1980). Kasper (1988) reports that nearly one of every three elderly persons lives alone without a spouse, child, sibling, or friends. Among men 65 to 74 years of age, 79 percent live with their wives as compared to 67 percent over age 75 (Church et al.,

1988). Comparable data for women, however, suggest that only 50 percent of those 65 to 74 years of age and less than 25 percent of those over 75 years of age live with a husband. Thus, aging is a different phenomenon depending on one's sex; men typically age with a spouse, whereas many women age alone.

In the 1970s the number of never-married people under age 30 living by themselves more than tripled. One circumstance that has caused increasing numbers of women to remain single is called the "marriage squeeze" (Glick & Carter, 1976). In the 1940s and 1950s, the postwar baby boom occurred. Because females often marry males who are older, a shortage of males of desirable age developed in the 1970s and 1980s. In the 1990s there will continue to be a steadily increasing number of women who have difficulty finding a desirable mate.

Many myths and stereotypes are associated with being single (Van Hoose & Worth, 1982). These stereotypes range from the swinging-singles lifestyle to the desperately lonely, suicidal adult. Most single adults, of course, are somewhere between these somewhat illusory extremes. Quite commonly, single adults' concerns center around issues of intimate relationships with other adults, confronting loneliness, and finding a place in a marriage-oriented society. Singles are often challenged by others to get married (Edwards, 1977). Clearly, though, there are advantages to being single. These include time to make decisions about the course of life one wants to follow; time to develop the personal resources to meet goals; freedom to make autonomous decisions and pursue one's own schedule and interests; opportunity to explore new places and try out new things; and availability of privacy (Edwards, 1977).

Choosing a single lifestyle offers flexibility. This freedom partially explains why some adults choose to marry later in life and why the number of single people aged 35 and under is rapidly growing. Another factor in this choice is the change in attitude of many women toward careers and personal fulfillment. Many women (and men) choose to develop their careers before assuming marriage responsibilities. Birth control devices and changing attitudes about premarital sex also make it possible for single adults to explore their sexuality outside the bounds of marriage. However, some psychologists think that adults will limit the range of their sexual partners (as well as the range of their sexual practices) because they fear contracting AIDS.

One of the potential drawbacks associated with a single lifestyle is a lost sense of immortality. In a probing study, Rubenstein, Alexander, Goodman, and Luborsky (1991) found that never-married, childless, elderly women developed close, enduring ties with family members and friends during late life and had led successful generative lives. Yet many of these women felt that something was missing. Specifically, they did not experience the sense of "cultural validation" that is afforded to the members of our society who have children. They saw more than their individual lives ending upon their death. As one of the informants in the Rubenstein et al. study said, "It's hard to think there'll be nothing of you left when you are gone" (p. 276).

## Homosexual Adults

The recognition that one is homosexual is a challenge that must be confronted throughout the adolescent and early adult years (Remafedi, 1987a, 1987b). Self-acceptance of

*Gay and lesbian couples experience the positive benefits of long-lasting personal relationships throughout adult life and old age.*

sexual preferences by gay men and lesbian women is initially difficult as social forces provide painful comparisons that indicate that something is "wrong." In one investigation, males in late adolescence continued to question their sexual orientations despite clear evidence that they were homosexual (Remafedi, 1987a). Young homosexual adults, fearful of the censure of parents, straight peers, and coworkers, continue to feel pressure to protect themselves from disclosure of their sexual preferences. Despite legal mandates, homosexuality carries a threat of discrimination in terms of hiring and career advancement. Gay rights activists have helped many young adults to face their sexual preferences—to come out of the closet willingly, rather than to be dragged out with the threat of lowered self-esteem and anxiety over public disclosure.

Within the homosexual lifestyle, short-term relationships seem to be the norm in young adulthood, particularly for gay men up to their mid- to late thirties (Corby & Solnick, 1980). It has been estimated that 72 percent of homosexual men had no long-term commitment to a partner, while the percentage of lesbian women who were uncommitted to a partner was less than 55 percent (Bell & Weinberg, 1978; Bell, Weinberg, & Mannersmith, 1981). For those able to establish emotional intimacy and commitment, a long-term relationship may evolve.

Studies of long-term homosexual relationships suggest that such couples emerge after an extended period of time as single dating partners. The period in adulthood in which such commitments are made is often just prior to middle age (in the mid- to late thirties for males). Homosexual couples committed to each other may elect to maintain

*TABLE 7.3*

***Percent of Aging Gay Men and Lesbians Indicating Different Levels of Life Satisfaction, Loneliness, and Acceptance of Aging***

| | *n = 80* *Total* | *n = 49* *<60* | *n = 31* *>60* | *n = 41* *Women* | *n = 39* *Men* |
|---|---|---|---|---|---|
| | | | *Age* | | |
| 50–59 | 61.3 | | | 74.4 | 48.8 |
| 60+ | 38.8 | | | 25.6 | 51.2 |
| | | | *Gender* | | |
| Male | 51.3 | 40.8 | 67.7 | | |
| Female | 48.8 | 59.2 | 32.3 | | |
| | | | *Acceptance of aging process* | | |
| Very accepting | 35.0 | 27.1 | 48.4 | 26.3 | 43.9 |
| Somewhat accepting | 42.5 | 43.8 | 41.9 | 55.3 | 31.7 |
| Neutral | 3.8 | 6.3 | 0.0 | 5.3 | 2.4 |
| Somewhat unaccepting | 16.3 | 20.8 | 9.7 | 10.5 | 22.0 |
| Very unaccepting | 1.3 | 2.1 | 0.0 | 2.6 | 0.0 |
| | | | *Life satisfaction* | | |
| First quartile | 6.3 | 6.7 | 6.1 | 5.1 | 7.5 |
| Second quartile | 11.4 | 6.6 | 14.3 | 5.2 | 17.5 |
| Third quartile | 31.6 | 30.0 | 32.7 | 25.7 | 37.5 |
| Fourth quartile | 50.6 | 56.7 | 46.9 | 64.0 | 37.5 |
| | | | *Loneliness a problem* | | |
| Yes | 20.0 | 20.4 | 19.4 | 10.3 | 29.3 |
| Sometimes | 47.5 | 49.0 | 45.2 | 56.4 | 39.0 |
| No | 31.3 | 28.6 | 35.5 | 30.3 | 31.7 |

*From J. K. Quam, and G. S. Whitford. "Adaptation and Age-Related Expectations of Older Gay and Lesbian Adults" in* The Gerontologist, *32: 367–374. Copyright © 1992 The Gerontological Society of America.*

closed, monogamous relationships or open, nonmonogamous relationships. Closed relationships have been found to be associated with greater levels of social support, positive attitudes, and lower anxiety levels than open relationships (Kurdek & Schmitt, 1985-86).

Concern about the increase in AIDS among the elderly population forces us to focus our attention on aging homosexual and bisexual males. In 1987, these men represented 65.8 percent of all older persons with AIDS (Stall, Catania, & Pollack, 1988). Recent evidence shows that unprotected sexual activity places older homosexual males at risk (Curran et al., 1988; Lifson, 1988). Yet this group is more knowledgeable about safe sex than comparably aged heterosexual males (Catania et al., 1989). Despite the risks, most older homosexual males remain sexually active, although they less frequently engage in one-night encounters (Catania et al., 1989). The question is whether the aging homosexual community will practice what it clearly knows about safe sex.

In a recent study, Quam and Whitford (1992) sought to measure how older gay and lesbian women adapted to the aging process. They discovered (see table 7.3) that the majority of older homosexual adults has very positive expectations about aging and displayed high levels of life satisfaction. Most of the respondents indicated that being a lesbian woman or gay man helped them adjust to aging. One man commented, "I've been aware of an enhanced psychological and spiritual scope because of the stresses of being in a sexual and a social minority." Similarly, a woman maintained, "My lesbian 'family'—in which I am the oldest—has been a constant source of support. We are learning about aging as a group" (Quam & Whitford, 1992, p. 373). The major areas of concern for these aging gay men and lesbian woman are the same as those experienced by most heterosexual adults—loneliness, health, and finances.

## Divorced Adults

In many respects, divorced and widowed adults experience many of the same emotions. In both instances, the individuals experience the death of a relationship. Next to a death of a spouse, a divorce causes the most trauma in the lives of individuals (Pearlin, 1985). Until recently, divorce was increasing annually by 10 percent, although the rate of increase slowed as we entered the 1990s. Though divorce has increased in all socioeconomic groups, people from lower social classes have the highest divorce rates. Among lower socioeconomic classes, factors associated with divorce include marriage at an early age, low levels of education, and low income (Spanier & Glick, 1981; U.S. Bureau of the Census, 1985). Premarital pregnancy is another critical factor. In one investigation, half of the women who were pregnant before marriage failed to live with their husbands for more than five years (Sauber & Corrigan, 1970). Because the median age for divorce is thirty-eight, many divorced people must rear dependent children (Hetherington, Stanley-Hagan, & Anderson, 1989; Kaslow & Schwartz, 1987).

Weiss (1975) suggested that although divorce is a marker event in the relationship between spouses, it often does not signal the end of the relationship. Mavis Hetherington (Hetherington, Cox, & Cox, 1978) reported that of forty-eight divorced couples observed, six of these couples had sexual intercourse during the first two months after separation. Weiss believes that the attachment to each other endures regardless of whether the former couple respects or likes one another or are satisfied with the present relationship. Kelley (1982), however, reported that this attachment bond is more characteristic of one of the partners, not both.

Former spouses often alternate between feelings of seductiveness and hostility (Hunt & Hunt, 1977). And though at times they may express love toward their former mate, the majority of their feelings are negative and include anger and hate. Certainly, couples find the few months just prior to divorce among the most unpleasant and difficult to endure (Thompson & Spanier, 1983).

## Sex Differences in Divorce

Divorce may have different effects on a woman than on a man. For example, one investigation found that divorce is more traumatic for women than for men (Hetherington, Stanley-Hagan, & Anderson, 1989). Women who have gained much of their identity through the roles of wife and mother are particularly vulnerable after divorce. The term *displaced homemaker* describes the dilemma of many divorced or widowed women. These women always assumed that their work would be in the home. Although they may have considerable expertise at managing a home, prospective employers do not recognize this as work experience. Creating a positive identity as an independent person is essential for many divorced women. Following divorce, these women need to overcome loneliness, lack of autonomy, and financial hardship (Ahrons & Rodgers, 1987; Kaslow & Schwartz, 1987).

Men, it should be emphasized, do not go through a divorce unscathed. They usually have fewer rights to their children, experience a decline in income, and receive little emotional support (Hetherington et al., 1989).

## Parenting by Divorced Men and Women

During the first year after the divorce, the quality of parenting that the child experiences is often very poor; parents seem to be preoccupied with their own needs and adjustment. This has a negative impact on parents' ability to respond sensitively to the child's needs. During this period, parents tend to discipline the child inconsistently, are less affectionate, and are somewhat ineffective in controlling the child. But during the second year after the divorce, parents are more effective at these important childrearing duties (Hetherington et al., 1989; Kaslow & Schwartz, 1987).

The psychological well-being and childrearing capabilities of the custodial father or mother are central to the child's ability to cope with the stress of divorce. It appears that divorced mothers have more difficulty with sons than daughters. Hetherington (1979) believes that divorced mothers and their sons often get involved in what she calls a cycle of coercive interaction. But what about boys growing up in homes in which the father has custody—does the same coercive cycle occur? In one investigation, sons showed more competent social behavior when their fathers had custody, whereas girls were better adjusted when their mothers had custody (Santrock & Warshak, 1979).

## Support Systems

Most information we have about divorced families emphasizes the absent father or the relationship between the custodial parent and the child, but mental health experts have become increasingly interested in the role of support systems available to the child and the family (Hetherington et al., 1989). Support systems such as the extended family and community-based agencies are particularly important for low-income families following divorce (Colletta, 1978; Kurdek, 1981; Spicer & Hampe, 1975). Competent support systems may be particularly needed by divorced parents with infant and preschool children, because the majority of these parents must work full-time to make ends meet. Networks to assist newly divorced women, in particular, provide emotional support, legal counseling, and career advice at a crucial time of crisis. With such networking, women may more easily provide continuity and consistency in parenting.

## Divorce in Later Life

Although research on divorce has increased tremendously in recent years, little attention has been paid to how this critical life event may influence those who have been married a long time (Chiriboga, 1982a; Kaslow & Schwartz, 1987). One view suggests that since middle-aged adults have more maturity and greater resources, divorce in middle age allows the simplification of life patterns and ends an incompatible relationship (Golan, 1986). However, the emotional commitment to a long-term marriage is not easily cast aside. Many middle-aged individuals perceive the divorce as the failure or repudiation of the best years of their lives. The partner initiating the divorce may view it as an escape from an untenable relationship; the divorced partner, however, usually feels betrayal, sadness over the end of a long-standing relationship, and emotional grief over the loss of trust and commitment (Golan, 1986).

David Chiriboga (1982a) evaluated the psychosocial functioning of 310 recently separated men and women ranging in age from twenty to the mid-seventies. Included in the analyses were measures of morale, psychiatric symptoms, time perspective, self-reported physical health, social disruption, and divorce-induced upset. People in their fifties stood out as being the most maladapted in the face of divorce. With late-age divorce, both men and women feel they lack resources and choices when they compare themselves to the younger population playing the dating game or when they search for an available social group. Thus, older adults seem to have fewer options and a general uncertainty about what to do following divorce. In fact, Uhlenberg, Cooney, and Boyd (1990) found that divorced men over 50 were unable to anticipate what their lives would be like one year into the future.

## Remarriage

Remarriage is somewhat less prevalent in our society than was the case nearly two decades ago (Glick & Ling-Lin, 1986). Various authorities have explained this by referring to the greater mobility of our population and the higher rate of cohabitation (Glick, 1984). Statistics suggest that remarriage is still a popular choice among those couples who have experienced divorce for the first time (Glick & Ling-Lin, 1986). Approximately 80 percent of all divorced people decide to remarry; yet, of these remarriages, 60 percent will end in divorce (versus a 50 percent rate of divorce for first marriages). In connection with this point, Wallerstein and Blakeslee (1988) remind us that second marriages are highly complex "second chances," with excess baggage such as "his and her small children, lowered income due to alimony, and the ghost of a failed marriage."

The number of remarriages in which children are involved has been steadily growing. Remarried families are usually referred to as stepfamilies, blended families, or reconstituted families. About 10 to 15 percent of all households in the United States are composed of stepfamilies, which represents more than 500,000 families (Prosen & Farmer, 1982). Projections into the 1990s estimate that approximately 25 to 30 percent of all children will be part of a stepfamily before their 18th birthday (Glick, 1984). For better or worse, divorced people seem firmly committed to the institution of marriage.

## *Sexuality*

*If you can't be with the one you love, honey, love the one you're with.*
—Crosby, Stills, Nash, & Young

One of the most important elements of adult relationships is sexuality. In this section we discuss several aspects of adult sexuality and focus on various age-related changes in sexual functioning. Finally, we pay special attention to menopause and the male climacteric.

### Sexual Attitudes and Behavior

Several aspects of our sexuality are a consequence of the way we are socialized. Many of us were brought up to believe that premarital sex is acceptable for males but not females. Often males are reared to associate the sexual act with power and masculine worth, and they distance themselves from a caring commitment to the other person. Males also are believed to have more sexual knowledge than females. Men, then, often enter long-term sexual relationships and/or marriage with the belief that they are responsible for the satisfaction of the couple's sexual needs. In a sexual relationship, if either one or both of the partners do not climax, the blame usually rests with the male (Masters & Johnson, 1970). Such a perspective leads the male to think that his most important function is to get the job done rather than to spend time relating to his partner's sensual and emotional needs.

Females who adopt a passive role in sexual relationships and who remain naive about sexual techniques may contribute to the difficulties many couples experience. In recent decades, it has become more culturally acceptable for females to express their sexuality, to be knowledgeable about sexual matters and techniques, and to share responsibility for the success of a sexual relationship. For sexual fulfillment, it is best that both partners be informed and active in exploring their sexuality and in communicating their needs to each other (Sarrell & Sarrell, 1974).

### Premarital Sex

Our cultural standards concerning *premarital sex* have changed substantially during the course of this century. For example, consider the data that have been collected on 19-year-old unmarried men and women. During the 1930s and 1940s, 20 percent of females and 45 percent of males within this age group reported having sexual intercourse (Kinsey, Pomeroy, & Martin, 1948). By the mid-1970s, the incidence rate increased to about 55 percent for females and 60 percent of males (Zelnick & Kanter, 1977). At present, it is estimated that 75 percent of both females and males within this age group have had intercourse (Centers for Disease Control, 1992).

As students progress from the freshman to the senior year of college in the United States, the incidence of premarital sex typically increases. The statistics for men engaging in premarital sex jump from 28 percent at the beginning of college to 82 percent during the senior year; for women, the corresponding figures are 29 and

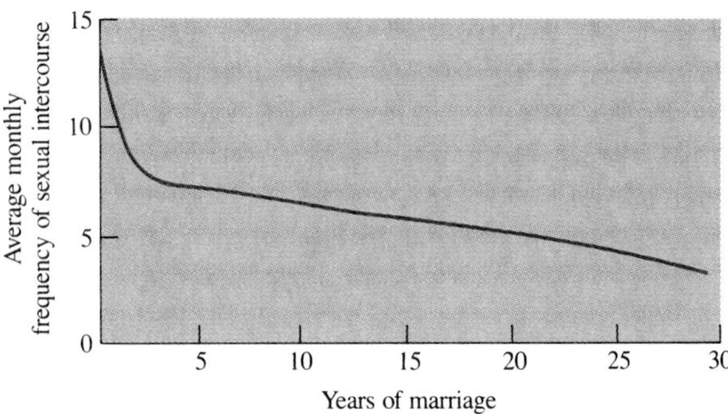


**Figure 7.6** Average monthly frequency of sexual intercourse over thirty years of marriage. *Source: Data from* From Now to Zero: Fertility, Contraception, and Abortion in America. *Copyright © 1968, 1971 Charles F. Westoff and Leslie Aldridge Westoff. Little, Brown and Company, Boston, MA.*

86 percent, not much different from the statistics for men. It is important to realize, however, that men and woman may perceive premarital sexual activity in different ways. Hunt (1974), for example, has shown that women limit their relationships to one or two partners whom they are emotionally involved with. Men, in contrast, tend to have more partners to whom they feel less emotionally attached.

## Sexual Intercourse in Marriage

Evidence that sexual intercourse in marriage is a highly satisfying physical experience, particularly for wives, comes from data reported by more than 2,000 middle-class American married women (Bell & Lobsenz, 1979). Married women in their twenties reported that they enjoyed the physical aspects of sexual intercourse more than their counterparts in their thirties, who were more inclined to enjoy its emotional aspects. Most of the women reported that they experienced orgasms, and those who had orgasms more frequently were also more likely to indicate they were happy. Women who had never had an orgasm typically were brought up in restrictive homes and were somewhat religious (Geer, O'Donohue, & Schorman, 1986). Less than 10 percent of women have never had an orgasm (Hunt, 1974), and such women appear clinically to be rather sensitive to criticism and marginally depressive (Derogatis, Meyer, & King, 1981). Married women in their twenties and thirties said that they practiced oral-genital sex more than older groups of married women. The young women also indicated that their husbands, rather than they, were more likely to initiate love-making sessions.

It appears that sexual relations follow a predictable pattern depending on how long a couple has been married. For example, intercourse is practiced frequently in the early months of marriage and then decreases over the length of the marriage. Doddridge, Schumm, and Bergen (1987) noted that when married couples reported the preferred frequency of sexual intercourse, the older the couple and the longer the marriage, the lower the preferred frequency. Mirroring these data, figure 7.6 traces the average monthly incidence of intercourse through thirty years of marriage. The information in this figure is consistent with data gathered by Masters, Johnson, and Kolodny (1991). They suggested that the average American couple has intercourse about two or three times a week during young adulthood, and about once a week after age 50.

The link between frequency of intercourse and marital satisfaction is not the same in every marriage and may not be the same for partners in the same marriage. Nonetheless, there is a substantial association between marital satisfaction and the incidence of intercourse when large numbers of couples are surveyed (Bell & Bell, 1972; Levinger, 1970). The most common reason given for sexual abstinence among married couples is marital conflict. Other reasons include physical illness, loss of interest, and emotional stress (Edwards & Booth, 1976; Gambert, 1987). The greatest obstacle to sexual happiness among couples is the level of tension or anxiety in the marriage. In virtually every case of sexual dysfunction, significant psychological depression, anxiety, and anger are present (Gambert, 1987).

Extramarital sex, though considered acceptable to some individuals, still is not condoned as morally appropriate conduct by the majority of our society. Yankelovich (1982) found that 76 percent of adult Americans disapprove of men having extramarital affairs. One estimate reported that nearly 50 percent of married men and 20 to 40 percent of married women have had an extramarital affair (Knox, 1985). Spanier and Margolis (1983) note that reported affairs may often be for only one night.

Men report an interest in extramarital relationships primarily for sex or variety, while women most often seek extramarital relationships for emotional reasons (Glass & Wright, 1985). Women involved in extramarital relationships report more marital dissatisfaction than their male counterparts. After marital dissatisfaction, extramarital affairs appear most often to be based on proximity, availability, and common interests (e.g., among coworkers); enhancing self-esteem and excitement are less frequently identified factors (Wiggins & Lederer, 1984).

Some extramarital affairs are long-lasting, intense relationships. Others take on the status of a *one-night stand.* Masters et al. (1991) believe the latter relationship is much more common than the former. As is the case with longer affairs, there is a great deal of variability in both the motivations and emotional reactions that accompany a *one-night stand.* Consider the following comments made by a 31-year-old woman: ". . . it was beautiful sex . . . just like a novel. . . . It just felt good to know that I had the experience. I never told my husband and I don't plan to" (Masters et al., 1991, p. 308); and a 36-year-old man: ". . . it was a stupid thing to do—not much fun, and lots of guilt afterwards—and I don't think I'll ever do it again" (Masters et al., 1991, p. 308).

## Sexual Attitudes and Behavior at Midlife

Although there is usually little biological decline in a man or woman's ability to function sexually in middle adulthood, middle-aged adults usually engage in sexual activity less frequently than people in early adulthood. Career interests, family concerns, and energy levels may contribute to a decline in sexual activity.

Still, a large percentage of individuals in middle adulthood continue to show moderate or strong sexual interest and continue to engage in sexual activity on a reasonably frequent basis. For example, in one national survey of 502 men and women, approximately 52 percent said they had sexual intercourse once a week or more (Pfeiffer, Verwoerdt, & Davis, 1974).

Typically, surveys note sex differences in sexual interest and activity in middle adulthood. Men consistently report greater interest in sex and indicate that they engage in sexual activity more than women. For example, in the survey mentioned in the previous paragraph, 81 percent of the men but only 56 percent of the women between the ages of 51 and 55 said that they had a moderate or strong interest in sex; 66 percent of the men but only 39 percent of the women said they had sexual intercourse one or more times per week (Pfeiffer et al., 1974). Often postmenopausal women actually show an increase in sexual interest as the fear of pregnancy is removed and family concerns are replaced by healthy self-interests and individual assertiveness.

One of the problems that women face adjusting to midlife is the double standard that contemporary society attaches to the physical attractiveness of men versus women. Many people seem to have the opinion that entry into middle-age makes men more attractive, but women less attractive. With regard to this matter, the noted sociologist, Alice Rossi, has stated: "It's the physical manifestation of aging—and a woman's reaction to it—that's critical in predicting whether the years from 45 to 55 will be difficult or not. Society's image of an attractive woman is ten years younger than that of an attractive man. Graying at the temples and filling out a bit can be attractive in a man—look at Clinton and Gore. But their wives are still trying to look 28" (quoted in Gallagher, 1993, p. 58).

This double standard becomes even more perplexing when one considers that Masters et al. (1991) have found that young women do not place much importance on the physical features of the middle-aged men they are attracted to. But, young men attach a great deal of importance to the physical attractiveness of the middle-aged women they become involved with!

## Menopause

Perhaps the subject of strongest interest to researchers studying sexuality in middle adulthood is the range of changes that accompanies menopause. Most of us know something about menopause (Sheehy, 1993). But is what we know accurate? Here are some comments made by two women who have experienced menopause.

> "My first sign of menopause was the night sweat. . . . It was a little frightening to wake up in the middle of the night with my sheets all drenched. It was hard not to feel that something was very wrong with me."
>
> "I am constantly amazed and delighted to discover new things about my body, something menstruation did not allow me to do. I have new responses, desires, sensations, freed and apart from the distraction of menses [periods] . . ." (Boston Women's Health Book Collective, 1976, pp. 327, 328).

These comments suggest both negative and positive reactions to menopause. They help dispel popular stereotypes of the menopausal woman: exhausted, irritable, unsexy, hard to live with, and irrationally depressed.

Biologically, **menopause** is defined as the end of menstruation, a marker that signals the cessation of childbearing capacity. Menopause is accompanied by a reduction of **estrogen,** the primary female sex hormone, to one-tenth of earlier levels.

*Table 7.4*

| Clinical Findings Associated with Menopause |
|---|
| ***Physical Effects*** |
| 1. Blood pressure disturbances ("hot flashes") |
| 2. Osteoporosis (thinning of the bones, calcium absorption deficiency) |
| 3. Atrophy of the vaginal walls, vaginal shortening, and reduced lubricity |
| 4. Increase in incidence of cardiovascular disease |
| ***Psychological Effects (Wide Ranging, Great Degree of Interindividual Variability)*** |
| 5. Insomnia |
| 6. Anxiety |
| 7. Depression |

Menopause is considered to have occurred when twelve consecutive months have passed without a menstrual period (Block, Davidson, & Grambs, 1981); the average age at menopause in the United States is fifty (Masters et al., 1991). Despite the number of symptoms reported to accompany menopause, only two—hot flashes and the atrophy of the vagina—are believed to be directly related to decreased estrogen levels (Katchadourian, 1987).

The *hot flash,* a feeling of extreme heat that is usually confined to the upper part of the body and often is accompanied by a drenching sweat, is the most commonly experienced symptom of menopause. Hot flashes gradually diminish in frequency and generally disappear completely within a year or two. *Atrophy of the cells of the vaginal walls* means that the vagina becomes drier, the layer of cell walls thinner, and the amount of lubricants secreted during sexual arousal is reduced. These conditions can make sexual intercourse painful for some women. They may require the use of artificial lubrications during intercourse (Gambert, 1987; Masters et al., 1991).

Gambert (1987) has identified a large number of physical and psychological effects that may be directly or indirectly associated with menopause (see table 7.4). As previously mentioned, hot flashes and atrophy of the vaginal walls are the direct results of menopause. On the other hand, *osteoporosis* (thinning of the bones) is directly caused by a woman's inability to uptake calcium to strengthen her bones; this, in turn, is caused by a reduction in available estrogen. Osteoporosis is a common cause of the postural stoop in older people and a contributor to the brittleness of bones, which break easily in old age. None of the psychological effects of menopause identified in table 7.4 are directly related to the physical changes that accompany menopause.

Depression may be associated with menopause, but menopause does not *cause* depression. Menopause comes at a time when some women are losing their full-time jobs as mothers and wives, when some middle-aged men are attracted to younger women, and when other aspects of the aging process (wrinkles, graying hair, and so on) are also appearing. Therefore, it may be these other factors, rather than menopause itself, that cause depression. Indeed, many women handle menopause in very positive ways, as suggested by the quotes from two of the four women at the beginning of this section. It has been estimated that approximately 20 percent of women go through menopause with no intense symptoms at all, whereas 15 percent experience symptoms that are sufficiently severe to warrant treatment (Women's Medical Center, 1977). Thus, the majority of middle-aged women do not experience any significant declines in mental health because of menopause (Matthews et al., 1990).

The incidence of insomnia, depression, and anxiety may be traced to the meaning or psychosocial significance individuals attach to menopause (Newman, 1982). Generally those who have the greatest psychological difficulty greatly value their roles as mothers and their capacity to bear children. They also express fears of growing old (Newman, 1982). Holte (1978) compared menopausal adjustment across different cultures. Women who displayed the poorest adjustment to menopause belonged to cultures organized around a patriarchy (social power was primarily in the hands of males). Following menopause, these women had more restricted and less important social roles (Bart, 1971). These cultures interpreted the inability to bear children as a role loss and relegated postmenopausal women to a lowered social status. In other cultures, women actually increased their social standing and prestige following menopause. Bart (1971) reported that in such cultures the role of grandmother, for example, was important and valued. Age, wisdom, and the beneficial effects of experience give older, postmenopausal women a special role and status in some cultures. Our own society seems to make menopause a major negative life stressor.

Many middle-aged and older women undergo hysterectomies, a sort of artificial menopause. In a *simple hysterectomy,* the uterus and cervix are surgically removed, while in a *total hysterectomy* the ovaries and fallopian tubes are removed as well. Hysterectomy is one of the most common operations performed in the United States (Morgan, 1978). In 1987 the figure had reached some 800,000 women per year. A hysterectomy is performed for various reasons. The most common involves the slippage and improper positioning of the uterus. A hysterectomy also may be performed to eliminate fibroid tumors, which as many as 25 percent of all women experience. Such tumors are not cancerous, but they may cause abnormal bleeding. The third most common reason for a hysterectomy is cancer, which, if detected early by a Pap test, is not necessarily life threatening (Block, Davidson, & Grambs, 1981; Gambert, 1987).

One of the most controversial aspects of menopause concerns the use of *hormone replacement therapy* (HRT). HRT involves replacing the estrogen that a woman's body no longer produces; physicians usually prescribe it only in severe cases, using the lowest dosage for the shortest possible period of time. Schmitt and his associates (1991) have noted the many benefits and risks of HRT. On the positive side, HRT may be used to reduce hot flashes, relieve vaginal itching and dryness, and prevent osteoporosis. On the negative side, the chances for endometrial, uterine, and breast cancer increase with HRT. To reduce the cancer risk, estrogen is often administered along with a second hormone called *progestin.* Unfortunately, progestin may cause the reoccurrence of cyclical bleeding. And, at present, the risks associated with long-term progestin treatment are unknown. This is important, because much of the danger associated with HRT occurs when the medication is taken for long periods of time. Many women, in fact, receive HRT for ten years or more.

Do men experience biological changes related to their sexuality as they go through middle adulthood? We explore this question next.

## The Male Climacteric

The **male climacteric** occurs during the sixties and seventies in most men when they experience a decline in sexual potency or fertility. The male climacteric differs in two important ways from menopause: it comes later and it progresses at a much slower rate. Men experience hormonal changes in their fifties and sixties, but not to the extent that women do. For example, testosterone production declines about 1 percent a year beginning during middle adulthood, but men do not lose their capacity to father children. Consequently, the male climacteric may have less to do with hormonal change than with the psychological adjustments. This conclusion gains credibility when one considers that testosterone therapy does not relieve the symptoms associated with the male climacteric (Burt & Mecks, 1985; Katchadourian, 1987).

The male climacteric manifests itself in many ways. For example, the influence of psychologically erotic stimuli may decline with increasing age. Thus, although physical stimulation remains effective in producing sexual arousal, psychological stimulation loses some of its power. For instance, a spouse's nudity may not arouse as it did in earlier years. Couples often mistakenly view this as evidence that advancing age means waning sexuality (Katchadourian, 1987). Also, the time necessary for erection and ejaculation, as well as the refractory period that follows ejaculation, grows greater with age, while the intensity of orgasm declines with age (Masters et al., 1991). On a more positive note, Stevens-Long and Commons (1992) have commented that the male climacteric ". . . does alleviate the primary male sexual problem: premature ejaculation. It may open up a whole range of sexual pleasures and activities if men can approach sex with greater patience and humor" (p. 276).

## Sexuality in Late Adulthood

Several experts (Comfort, 1980; Masters et al., 1991) have concluded that aging induces a moderation of the sexual response for both men and women. Thus, it takes longer for both men and women to become aroused. Erections are softer, not maintained as long as in younger years, and are angled less upright. Climax is less intense, contractions fewer, and the volume of ejaculation diminished in comparison to younger years. A similar pattern holds for women's arousal and climax. With reduced levels of estrogen, the vaginal walls become thinner and less elastic and the vagina itself shrinks, becoming shorter. However, even when actual intercourse is impaired by infirmity, physical health, or hospitalization, other sexual needs still persist among the elderly, including closeness, physical touching, emotional intimacy, sensuality, and being valued as a man or a woman. These needs are a vital part of an older person's sexuality.

A direct correlation exists between health and sexual activity. Generally, sexual intercourse is an important part of therapy and treatment following a major illness or surgery and is itself minimally risky to health (Gambert, 1987). Following heart attacks or open-heart surgery, most physicians encourage resuming sexual intercourse within eight to twelve weeks. Patients encounter few physical problems, although they often feel fearful of having a heart attack during intercourse. Sexual intercourse is not terribly taxing, does not lead to an increase in the risk of heart attack, and is roughly comparable to such physical labor as a brisk walk or ascending a flight of stairs (Gambert, 1987)!

Fortunately, many elderly people go on having sex without talking about it, free from the destructive social stereotypes of the dirty old man and the asexual, undesirable old woman. Among people between 60 and 71 years old, almost 50 percent have intercourse on a regular basis. Fifteen percent of those over 78 years old regularly engage in intercourse (Comfort, 1980). Bear in mind that many individuals who are now in their eighties were reared when there was a Victorian attitude toward sex. In early surveys of sexual attitudes, older people were not asked about their sexuality, possibly because everyone assumed they didn't have sex or thought it would embarrass them to ask them about sex.

Most of the published work in the area of sexuality and aging suggests that there are no known age limits to sexual activity (e.g., Kaplan, 1974; Masters & Johnson, 1970; Masters et al., 1991). Adults who have always placed a high priority on their sexual lives approach old age with the same values (Pfeiffer, 1983). Healthy older people who want to have sexual activity are likely to be sexually active in late adulthood (Comfort, 1980). Katchadourian (1987) suggests: "If you want to stay sexually alive, you must keep sexually active. Men and women who remain sexually active are more likely to maintain their sexual vigor and interest into their older years—another illustration of the adage, '*Use it or lose it*' " (p. 73).

The results of a recent national survey of a large number of married people over 60 years of age provide convincing evidence that older adults maintain their sexual activity (Marsiglio & Donnelly, 1991). As shown in table 7.5, 53 percent of the entire sample and 24 percent of those 76 years old or older had intercourse at least once a month. And, most people who are sexually active reported having sex about four times per month. Furthermore, Marsiglio and Donnelly (1991) found that an older person's sense of self-worth and his/her spouse's health status were among the most powerful predictors of sexual activity in their sample.

The greatest obstacles to continued sexual expression are the lack of an available partner, severe health problems, and the belief that society does not condone this mode of expression in old age. However, societal attitudes are changing. Ludeman (1981), for example, noted the greater acceptance of masturbation by older women without available partners. Nearly 50 percent of older adult females masturbated when faced with the lack of a suitable male partner. Comfort (1980) suggested that

*TABLE 7.5*

**Descriptive Data on Sexual Frequency Patterns for Married Persons 60 Years of Age and Older**

| | Percent Having Sex at Least Once within the Past Month (N = 807) | | Mean Frequency of Sex among Those Sexually Active within the Past Month (N = 423) | |
|---|---|---|---|---|
| Sociodemographic/Health Variables | % | N | M | N |
| Total | 53 | 807 | 4.26 | 423 |
| Gender | | | | |
| Male | 54 | (427) | 4.15 | (229) |
| Female | 51 | (380) | 4.41 | (194) |
| Age | | | | |
| 60–65 | 65 | (340) | 4.54 | (221) |
| 66–70 | 55 | (206) | 4.52 | (111) |
| 71–75 | 45 | (140) | 3.51 | (62) |
| 76 and older | 24 | (121) | 2.75 | (29) |
| Race | | | | |
| White | 53 | (711) | 4.34 | (373) |
| Black | 55 | (68) | 2.88 | (39) |
| Other | 43 | (28) | 3.54 | (11) |
| Educational level | | | | |
| Less than 12 years | 46 | (288) | 4.02 | (130) |
| High school graduate | 54 | (322) | 3.88 | (176) |
| Some college | 58 | (84) | 5.30 | (49) |
| College graduate | 62 | (113) | 4.77 | (68) |
| Personal health status | | | | |
| Excellent/good | 58 | (524) | 4.27 | (299) |
| Fair | 45 | (202) | 4.60 | (91) |
| Poor/very poor | 36 | (61) | 2.97 | (24) |
| Spouse's health status | | | | |
| Excellent | 58 | (466) | 4.29 | (271) |
| Fair | 46 | (165) | 4.90 | (76) |
| Poor/very poor | 36 | (49) | 3.48 | (17) |

*From W. Marsiglio and D. Donnelly. "Sexual Relations in Later Life: A National Study of Married Persons" in* Journal of Gerontology: Social Sciences, *46: 338–344. Copyright © 1991 The Gerontological Society of America.*

when a partner is not available, masturbation should be viewed as an acceptable release of sexual tension. He believes that explicit discussion of masturbation with the elderly may relieve anxiety caused by earlier prohibitions.

Most certainly, it is incorrect to assume that sexuality disappears in old age. This holds true even when we examine the sexual needs of unique subpopulations of the elderly, those living in nursing homes. See Research Focus 7.4 for more information about this topic.

## Sexuality and the Institutionalized Elderly

Solnick and Corby (1983) found that most nursing homes and elder care institutions were nominally aware of the sexual needs of their elderly patients. Staff generally felt that physical health problems were a great obstacle to sexual activity, and they largely ignored the needs of the elderly who desired expression of their sexuality. One manifestation of this attitude toward the elderly is the maintenance of sex-segregated floors or wings of the institution. Another example of this attitude is the tendency of institutional personnel to "infantilize" sexual forms of expression. Elderly who express an interest in, genuine caring for, and emotional attachment to each other are often teased, ridiculed, and held up to public scrutiny. For instance, staff might ask a woman how her "date" behaved at the movie shown in the social hall, or they might ask a man to explain his interest in his "girlfriend" or account for her wavering loyalty if she sits next to someone else at mealtime. Adult men and women who display a healthy lifelong interest in their sexuality need *not* be treated as adolescents simply because they reside in an institution. They are entitled to the same privacy and respect that other community-residing elderly receive.

Institutionalization of elderly adults does not necessarily mean the demise of their sexual interest (McCartney, Izeman, Rogers, & Cohen, 1987). Even institutionalized elderly with dementia may maintain the competency to initiate sexual relationships although well-intentioned staff may thwart such interests (Lichtenberg & Strzepek, 1990). Following is one example of guidelines written to help staff determine the competencies of institutionalized elderly to engage in intimate relationships:

1. Patient's awareness of the relationship
   a. Is the patient aware of who is initiating sexual contact?
   b. Does the patient believe that the other person is a spouse and thus acquiesce out of a delusional belief, or are they cognizant of the other's identity and intent?
   c. Can the patient state what level of sexual intimacy they would be comfortable with?
2. Patient's ability to avoid exploitation
   a. Is the behavior consistent with formerly held beliefs/values?
   b. Does the patient have the capacity to say no to any uninvited sexual contact?
3. Patient's awareness of potential risks
   a. Does the patient realize that this relationship may be time limited (placement on unit is temporary)?
   b. Can the patient describe how they will react when the relationship ends (Lichtenberg & Strzepek, 1990, p. 119).

# Sexual Dysfunction in Late Adulthood

The older male has to contend with some obstacles to sexual functioning. One of the most common is the **Widower's syndrome,** which affects men who have not had sexual intercourse for a lengthy period of time following the loss of a spouse (Gambert, 1987). A widower with this syndrome may have both the desire and the opportunity for sexual activity, but his physiological system fails to respond (incomplete penile erection occurs). A comparable condition has been reported among husbands whose wives had Alzheimer's disease (Litz, Zeiss, & Davies, 1990). A second factor to consider among older males is the impact of a variety of common drug treatments and diseases (Gambert, 1987). Drug treatments that may cause impotence include: (1) some of the psychotropic drugs used to treat mental disorders such as depression; (2) alcohol, if used excessively; (3) many of the drugs used to treat high blood pressure (antihypertensive medications); (4) drug treatments that employ steroids; and (5) drugs used to treat diabetes. Diseases that may cause impotence include various illnesses that affect the vascular and endocrine (hormone) systems as well as diabetes, kidney disease, prostate cancer, and neurological lesions in the brain or spinal cord (Gambert, 1987).

In most instances, the older female's sexual problems do not stem wholly from biological causes. For example, many older women do not have sexual intercourse because of the lack of a suitable partner. A spouse may not be physically healthy or may have recently died. Today's older women find it particularly troubling, given their cohort's sexual attitudes, to accept sexual relationships outside of marriage or to engage in masturbation. However, such restrictive attitudes are less common among their older male counterparts (Pfeiffer, 1983).

## Summary

Our relationships with others are extraordinarily important to us as adults. Those who do not have emotional attachments or social ties often suffer from loneliness. It may be important not only to develop an emotional attachment but also to have a network of social ties to adequately round out one's life as an adult. Emotional attachments give us comfort and security, and social ties provide us with a sense of group identity and integration. In new relationships, physical attraction, perceived similarity of the loved one, self-disclosure, romance, and passion seem to be important; security, loyalty, and mutual emotional interests are more germane to enduring relationships.

Intimacy is a very important ingredient in such close relationships as spouse, lover, or close friend. Erik Erikson believed that people should develop intimacy after they have developed a stable and successful identity. Intimacy is a part of development in middle and late adulthood as well as early adulthood. Indeed, building a network of close interpersonal ties appears to be closely linked with life satisfaction.

Marriage follows a developmental sequence of courtship, early years of marriage, childrearing years, postchildrearing years, years as an aging couple, and widowhood. The choice of a mate may be influenced by similarities and complementary needs. Early communication patterns set the tone in a marital relationship. Although not all couples have children, those who do face increased responsibilities and demands. One particularly difficult task is successfully juggling career and family pressures. The time comes later in a couple's life when their children become independent and leave home. Debate focuses on whether the "empty nest" increases or decreases a couple's happiness. The time from retirement until the death of a spouse is the final stage of the marriage process. Considerable adjustment is required at this point in development. Eventually, one spouse dies and the surviving spouse must adjust to being a widow or widower. The initial process usually consists of a period of grieving.

Parenting involves a number of interpersonal skills and emotional demands, yet our society provides little formal education for this task. Many parents have mixed emotions and romantic ideas or illusions about having a child. The developmental course of parenting is affected by the parent's gender, age, and emotional commitment. Various meanings have been attributed to the roles, expectations, and emotional fulfillment of grandparenthood. Grandparenting is also affected by gender, age, and personal commitment. Furthermore, researchers have documented different interaction styles among grandparents as well as great-grandparents.

The diversity of lifestyles includes an increase in the number of single adults. Single adults are often concerned with establishing intimate relationships with other adults, confronting loneliness, and finding a place in a marriage-oriented society. Unique issues face homosexual adults, as well as the large number of formerly married adults affected by divorce. Divorce is a process that all family members find complex and emotionally charged. The most stressful impact seems to occur during the period just after the separation, but over the course of several years the divorced adult seems to adjust to being single. Divorced mothers may be particularly vulnerable to stress because of increased economic and childrearing responsibilities. The effects of divorce on children are mediated by a variety of factors, including postdivorce family functioning and the availability of support systems, particularly for women. Marital separation in later life may be more traumatic than in earlier adulthood because of a greater commitment to the marriage, fewer resources, and more uncertainty about the future. The number of stepfamilies is increasing; it is estimated that in the 1990s, one-fourth to one-third of all children under age 18 will have lived in a stepfamily at some point.

Sexuality consists of biological, behavioral, and attitudinal components. Premarital sex is prevalent among young adults, and sexual activity is a source of great pleasure among young married couples. Menopause—the end of menstruation—is surrounded by many myths. The majority of women cope with menopause without having to undergo medical intervention, and for some women, menopause can be a positive event. Although males do not experience comparable rapid hormonal changes during middle age, they do seem to undergo a climacteric, involving a gradual decline in sexual interest, potency or fertility, and sexual functioning.

Sexual activity and enjoyment may continue among many individuals in late adulthood. However, many elderly adults who have strong sexual interests do not always have the opportunity to fulfill their needs in this important area of life.

## Review Questions

1. How do adults experience intimate relationships, attachment, and love across the adult years? Why are such relationships important?
2. Describe Erikson's ideas about intimacy. Discuss why he believed we must go through the intimacy stage in early adulthood.
3. Outline the developmental course of marital relations. Suggest some of the major issues involved and adaptations that have to be made at each stage of marriage.
4. What is the empty nest? How does this concept relate to the upswing hypothesis?
5. Discuss the special problems associated with widowhood.
6. Discuss the reasons why some adults choose to adopt a single lifestyle.
7. What is the impact of divorce on both men and women?
8. How does adjustment differ when separation or divorce occurs in later life?
9. What are the most important characteristics of the grandparenting role? Discuss the meaning of grandparenting to both grandparents and grandchildren from intact families as well as from divorced families.
10. Describe the strengths and weaknesses of each of the major family forms.
11. Discuss the biological aspects of sexuality in adulthood, placing special emphasis on menopause and the male climacteric.
12. Describe the behavioral and attitudinal components of sexuality through the later adult years.

## For Further Reading

Masters, H. H., Johnson, V. E., & Kolodny, R. C. (1991). *Human sexuality.* Boston: Little, Brown.

Sheehy, G. (1993). *The silent passage: Menopause.* NY: Pocket Books.

# 8

# *Work, Leisure, and Retirement*

*The one important thing I have learned over the years is the difference between taking one's work seriously and taking one's self seriously. The first is imperative and the second is disastrous.*
—Margot Fonteyn

*A perpetual holiday is a good working definition of hell.*
—George Bernard Shaw

## *Introduction*

In this chapter we explore one of the most important domains of adult development—work. Work, for both men and women, can promote a sense of satisfaction and well-being in life as well as meet basic needs (Stein, Newcomb, & Bentler, 1990). It helps us buy food, shelter, and clothing, and it can help us support a family. Work can also contribute to psychological satisfaction, since it is the primary setting in which adults develop skills, show competence, apply knowledge, and generally build self-esteem. Other motives that may undergird an adult's strong interest in working include the intrinsic interest of the work, the chance to learn or use new ideas, and the opportunity to socialize and develop relationships with other people. Most adults in our society spend at least one of every three waking hours working.

We first examine the social and historical contexts of work, then we outline the changes that take place in work across the adult years. Such changes include occupational choice, finding a place in the world of work, adjusting to work, reaching and maintaining occupational satisfaction, and working in late adulthood. We evaluate the varied meanings of work, looking in detail at the achievement motive, intrinsic motivation, the work ethic, and the impact of unemployment. Then we examine perhaps the greatest change in the labor force in the last thirty-five years: the increasing number of working women. We also pay special attention to the career development of men and women in early adulthood.

Not only do people need to learn how to work well, but they also need to develop leisure activities. We'll discuss the nature of leisure activities, leisure at midlife, and leisure in retirement. In the last part of the chapter, we explore factors related to retirement, discuss changing policies in relation to retirement, and describe theories of retirement and the factors predictive of successful adjustment to retirement.

## *The Social and Historical Contexts of Work*

Robert J. Havighurst (1982) described the important role of work in all cultures and its evolution in the United States. The society of the United States was *preindustrial* in the nineteenth century. The majority of families farmed land, worked together, and functioned as a unit. Some townspeople also worked as family units, with one or more sons learning from their fathers to be blacksmiths or carpenters, for example. But by the end of the nineteenth century, the United States was becoming urbanized and industrialized. By 1910, only one-third of the men were farmers or farm laborers.

The year 1910 is often considered the beginning of the Industrial Revolution in the United States. Factories multiplied, and the labor force changed so dramatically that by 1950 half of all male workers were involved in some form of manufacturing or construction. In an industrial society, machines that operate with mechanical energy substantially increase productivity. Coal, petroleum, and natural gas allowed worker productivity to rise, along with the profits of industrial owners.

At the present time, we are making a transition to a *postindustrial* society. Approximately 65 to 70 percent of all workers are engaged in delivering services. It is estimated that by the year 2000, only 10 percent of the labor force will be involved in manufacturing and producing goods for the other 90 percent. The emerging workplace will require highly trained workers to utilize sophisticated technology.

The term *services* can refer to many different activities. In earlier times, common services included domestic work, transportation, and the distribution of goods, whereas in the postindustrial society we are witnessing a significant increase in jobs related to human services (such as education and health) and professional and technical services—data processing, computer applications, and communication, for example.

Havighurst (1982) believes that a major increase in the cost of energy is likely to lower the material standard of living. People may respond by working longer hours and/or more years to increase production of goods and services so that they can maintain their standard of living. The elderly would then be encouraged to remain in the labor force as long as they could remain productive. The average age of voluntary retirement could rise to 70, 75, or older (Chen, 1987). In the 1980s the percentage of men over the age of 65 who continued to work full-time was significantly lower than the percentage at the beginning of this century. Douvan (1983) reported a decline of nearly 70 percent in America's work force over the age of 65 since 1900. One important change among the elderly is a significant increase in part-time employment. The U.S. Bureau of Census reported in 1986 that of the more than 3 million people in the United States over the age of 65 who worked, 54 percent were part-time employees. The percentage of older part-time workers continues to show a dramatic increase from 1960 to the present.

Let's look at work over the life cycle, remembering that earlier in American history, many adolescents engaged in work experiences within their families. In today's industrialized society, schooling has replaced family apprenticeships as workers require direct education and training to fill newly created technologically sophisticated jobs. During the twentieth century, vocational choices have broadened considerably.

*One change in employment patterns among older adults is the increase in part-time work.*

## *Work over the Life Cycle*

In this section, we examine career exploration, planning, and decision making. Then we discuss entry into an occupation as individuals attempt to find their places in the world of work. Subsequently, we evaluate the flexibility of careers in middle adulthood, occupational satisfaction, and work in late adulthood.

### Occupational Choice

When you think about choosing a career, you usually think about a single choice and a commitment to a single career throughout your life. Research indicates, however, that more than half of today's workers will experience at least one major career change (Griese, 1987; Shirom & Mazeh, 1988). Some career changes will challenge and enhance our lives. Other career changes will be forced upon us as corporations reduce the size of their work force and "downsize." In one large-scale national survey, it was found that 42 percent of employees at small, medium, and large companies could identify downsizing and permanent work force reductions since they had been hired (Galinsky, 1993). Still other career changes will be self-determined, for instance, as when a particular career choice proves unsuccessful. Some occupations are best suited to us at one point in our lives, but as we change, they no longer are appropriate.

## The Career of the Professional Athlete: Preparation for Retirement?

Few careers are as intense, emotionally involving, and physically demanding as that of the professional athlete. In the early years of childhood and adolescence, outstanding athletes are advantaged in terms of leadership, autonomy, sense of self, and self-esteem; they are admired, sought by peers, the object of media attention, and recruited by colleges and professional teams (Baillie & Danish, 1992). Yet, after years of outstanding success, those selected to participate at the professional level may have an extremely short-lived athletic career. In one study (Pitts, Popovich, & Bober, 1986) of football players in the National Football League, the average length of a professional career was only 3.2 years! The majority of players end their careers due to injury and report difficulties in adjusting to retirement in the areas of finance, marriage-divorce, substance abuse, and identifying new career paths (Baillie & Danish, 1992; Shahnasarian, 1992). Shahnasarian (1992), for example, suggests that the competitive demands and all-consuming nature of a professional sports career with its focus on each game during lengthy regular season and preseason games, the competition for a place on the team and a contract, as well as physical conditioning and training during the off-season, mean that there is little opportunity, encouragement, or time for players to devote to career development beyond their identification as professional athletes. Most athletes enjoy significant earnings early in adult life; thus their departure from a professional sport means financial difficulties when their playing days are over (Shahnasarian, 1992). Only a handful of professionals in any sport ever realize personal and financial success and a continued career in the same field in upper management or as a scout or coach. In the case of professional football players, Shahnasarian notes that "young men—most retiring in their mid-20s—who have committed a lifetime to pursuing a passion and a dream too often one day find that they are ill-prepared to make the career transition from football" (pp. 300–301).

Retirement from a career as a professional athlete in early adulthood is a difficult life transition leading to predictable stresses. Research studies suggest that a gradual transition for athletes is easier to manage than a precipitous transition to retirement (Baillie & Danish, 1992). There is then more time to prepare and develop career plans beyond the individual's limited but powerful identity as a professional athlete. Retirement is not only hard on the athlete but also on the athlete's family. When retirement is the result of a permanent injury, the stresses are further compounded and life satisfaction indicators are significantly diminished (Baillie & Danish, 1992; Shahnasarian, 1992). Experts have advocated that counseling programs be established to help players focus on retirement, financial planning, and alternative careers. These programs recognize that the majority of professional athletes need to participate in career counseling. They are unprepared for retirement (financially, emotionally, and socially), are anxious to have a more gradual transition out of their sport, and are accepting of the need to be "resocialized" from the world of sports into the world of the ordinary citizen (Baillie & Danish, 1992).

---

The latter case is illustrated in Research Focus 8.1, which discusses professional athletes who must "retire" from sports in their late twenties, at the end of a successful career, and describes some of the adjustments that must be made by young athletes who experience retirement from a career early in their adult lives after a lifetime of training, preparedness, and commitment to a career. Unlike the professional athlete who must find a new career following retirement, some occupations provide continuity and longevity once a career choice has been made, such as in law, teaching, or sales.

At some point toward the end of adolescence or the beginning of early adulthood, individuals enter an occupation. Most career choice theorists and counselors believe that, before deciding upon a particular career, it is wise to explore a wide number of occupational alternatives. Of all decisions in life, career choices often appear to be the most unplanned; yet they are among the most significant decisions of our adult lives (Bolles, 1988; Super, Kowalski, & Gotkin, 1967). We will briefly examine three theories of occupational choice proposed by Donald Super, Eli Ginzberg, and John Holland. All three theorists believe that exploration of alternative career paths is the most important aspect of career development.

***Super's Theory*** Donald Super (1969, 1975, 1980) has consistently maintained that occupational choices are influenced mostly by self-concept. People select particular careers or vocations that best express their self-concepts. This theory suggests the presence of five stages in vocational development, with each stage reflecting predictable changes in self-concept as one's vocational choice is seen as more or less successful (Super, 1980). Super suggests that occupational choice is a continuous developmental process from adolescence to old age, with the person making modifications, reassessments, and redirection throughout the life span as self-concept becomes clearer and more distinct.

Super refers to the first stage of career development as *implementation.* At this stage, individuals, usually adolescents, simply try out a number of part- or full-time jobs to explore the world of work. Part of the exploration involves finding the boundaries of acceptable work-role behavior: dress, communication, punctuality, social networks, supervisor expectancies, reward structures, and so forth. In this stage, exploration is healthy and a reflection of adolescent self-concept. In one investigation, Super and his colleagues (Super et al., 1967) studied young adults after they left high school. The investigators found that more than half of the position changes made between leaving school and the age of 25 involved floundering and unplanned changes. In other words, the young adults were neither systematic nor intentional in their exploration and decision making about careers.

The second stage, the *establishment stage,* involves the transition to a specific career choice. Again, this stage mirrors a young adult's self-concept. Super predicts considerable stability in vocational choice for those at this stage. There will be little movement away from the specific career selected, although some young adults will try to move up the career ladder by changing positions within a company or moving to a different company. If an adult considers a career change, it is usually in midlife that he or she becomes serious about a completely new vocation. Such changes occur after an individual takes stock of the opportunities for self-development within the initially chosen career.

For the majority of people who stay within the career they chose in young adulthood, the *maintenance stage* describes the period from roughly the midforties to the midfifties. This is a time when most people either achieve the levels of occupational success they hoped to attain or recognize that they will not reach these levels. Super describes this decade of vocational development as early preparation for the disengagement expected with retirement. Individuals remain occupationally involved, committed, and focused, but with reduced intensity on personal achievement and success.

About ten to fifteen years prior to actual retirement, Super believes the individual enters the *declaration stage.* This stage reflects an active readiness for retirement as individuals prepare themselves emotionally, financially, and socially. A distance from one's lifelong career begins to emerge. For workers who have made work a central focus in their lives, this stage represents a significant challenge.

The last stage in Super's model is *retirement.* The individual achieves a physical separation from work and begins to function in life without a career or vocation. Super's theory has been criticized for its narrow focus on self-concept as the prime factor responsible for occupational choice. Super largely ignores the role of factors such as social class, education, family, and chance. Moreover, his theory implies that most young adults are articulate, mature, and reflective individuals who are able to reason, evaluate, and rationally compare alternative career pathways. Such assumptions have not been fully tested empirically and rarely are characteristic of women's career development. In fact, one investigation suggests that Super's theory may be irrelevant in accounting for the career development of women (Ornstein & Isabella, 1990). Additionally, Super's approach implies that career choices are stable and predictive throughout adulthood; however, the stages leave no room for the possibility of career change (forced or voluntary), nor for the many entries and exits into the work force characteristic of women's career pathways (Ornstein & Isabella, 1990).

***Ginzberg's Theory*** Eli Ginzberg (1971, 1972) has also developed a stage theory of occupational choice. The essential principle underlying the *fantasy, tentative,* and *realistic stages* is the emergence of more and more realistic vocational decisions. Fantasy stages occur as a child imagines and practices various occupations for a few hours, days, or weeks. The tentative stage begins as the early adolescent explores career involvement. Adolescents may closely monitor adults (models) in various careers; they also read about and discuss occupations with family members and friends. The realistic stage begins as the young adult (from high school graduation to the midtwenties) carefully and rationally analyzes career choices. This stage involves a realistic assessment of the necessary education, apprentice period, and personal qualities (values, attitudes, and aptitudes) required to pursue particular careers. The process of realistic assessment is initiated in young adulthood but continues through the life span. Ginzberg's theory has been criticized for being overly rational in its presentation of occupational choice, with too much emphasis placed on cognitive processes. Ginzberg makes no provision for career change in midlife as a part of this theory.

***Holland's Theory*** Holland's (1973, 1985) theory of career choice is quite different from the stage views of Super and Ginzberg. Holland suggests that career selection is based on the best fit between an individual's personality and the demands of the vocation. A good match between an individual's personality and a specific vocation will lead to job satisfaction and stability, whereas a bad match will lead to job dissatisfaction and the search for a different career. In Holland's view, adults look for careers that are most compatible with their personalities. Psychological tests can help assess an individual's personality profile and match it against the prototypical personality of an individual in a particular career. Holland has identified six basic personality types along with the kinds of careers that best match these personalities (Holland, 1973):

The *artistic* personality (creative, emotionally expressive, innovative, original, reflective): This personality might enjoy being an architect or a designer, or working in fashion-related industries.

The *conventional* personality (concern for conformity, efficiency, somewhat shy and inhibited): This person might become a bookkeeper, secretary, receptionist, or typist.

The *enterprising* personality (high energy and motivation, need to be in control, strong, outgoing, and socially gregarious): This personality thrives in business, management, private companies, and sales work.

The *investigative* personality (strong curiosity, intellectual, rational): People of this personality type make good researchers and scientists.

The *realistic* personality (concrete, materialistic, mechanical, practical, asocial): This person might be a computer programmer, an engineer, or a mechanic.

The *social* personality (cooperative, helpful, social orientation, understanding of human relations): People of this type enjoy being counselors, personnel managers, psychologists, teachers, and social workers.

Some critics of Holland's approach suggest that few adults have the capacity to see themselves, their personalities, and the demands of specific jobs as he suggests. Do adults insightfully, carefully, and deliberately compare potential careers to their own unique personal qualities? Moreover, few people are as accurate in their individual self-assessment as Holland suggests. Critics have also found Holland's theory limited in that it ignores the developmental changes in self-knowledge that occur throughout the life span. Changes in self-knowledge can lead to career changes (Vondareck, Lerner, & Schulenberg, 1986). Yet, for the initial choice of a career, most counselors in the high schools have tended to utilize Holland's approach, matching personality traits among students with particular types of occupations. Many computer-assisted guidance programs in the high schools employ a Holland-type system (Sampson, Reardon, & Lenz, 1991).

## Career Exploration, Planning, and Decision Making

To ensure that students in high school engage in career exploration, educators have adopted a variety of approaches (Osipow, 1987). Some counseling programs are self-oriented (i.e., students are left to their own devices to read about, discuss, and question particular career options). Others are more directive. They bring students to resource centers with computer-assisted career-information packages that can be examined in stepwise fashion (Sampson, Reardon, & Lenz, 1991). Still others have mandated that students enroll in specific credit-bearing courses on career exploration (Hamdani, 1974). Studies confirm that self-directed programs alone rarely have

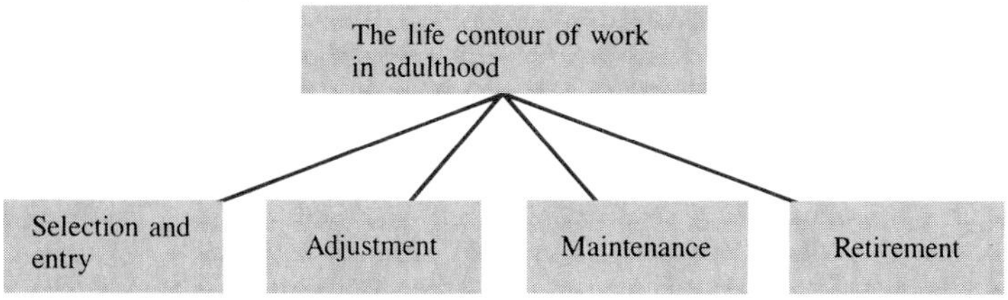

The life contour of work in adulthood

Selection and entry | Adjustment | Maintenance | Retirement

**Figure 8.1** The life contour of work in adulthood.

beneficial effects on students' career exploration and decision making (Corbin, 1974; Hammer, 1974). It is not enough for students to engage in career exploration without any guidance. Most high schools provide students with directed career guidance and placement in their educational programming offering. They offer discussion, seminars, and interpretative analysis of the profiles that students obtain from computer-assisted occupational information software programs that match student traits to specific career pathways (Osipow, 1987; Sampson, Reardon, & Lenz, 1991). Many college placement centers have expanded their programs of résumé writing and interview skills to provide occupational exploration services to students from freshman through graduating seniors.

Career exploration, planning, and decision making are important activities for adolescents and young adults. These processes, however, should not be restricted to any single portion of the life span. Indeed, occupational orientation is lifelong and can be conceptualized to consist of four major stages: *selection and entry, adjustment, maintenance,* and *retirement* (see figure 8.1). These stages are readily identifiable in careers that move in an orderly progression; they become more obscure in disorderly work patterns or changes in career choices that require some form of readjustment.

## Entering an Occupation

At some point during the late teens or twenties, one usually *enters an occupation.* For the first several years, an occupation may take an inordinate amount of a person's time, so that other aspects of life, such as marriage and family, become secondary. Havighurst (1982) believes that getting started in an occupation is more difficult for middle-class than lower-class people because success in an occupation is essential to maintaining middle-class status. Many lower-class individuals, however, are socialized to work long and hard at their jobs. Valliant and Valliant (1981), for example, regularly interviewed a group of 465 lower-social-class men about their work as they aged over a thirty-five-year period. The most industrious participants in childhood remained so in adulthood. They also derived the greatest success from their work, had the warmest social relationships, and the best overall adjustment (mental health).

## Adjustment to the Occupational World

*Adjustment* is the key concept in the second stage of the occupational cycle (figure 8.1). This is the period that Daniel Levinson (1978) calls the *age-30 transition* in men. According to Levinson, once a man has entered an occupation, he must develop a distinct occupational identity and establish himself in the occupational world. Along the way, he may fail, drop out, or begin a new career path. He may stay narrowly on a single track or try several directions before settling firmly on one. This adjustment phase lasts several years. A professional may spend several years in academic study, whereas an executive may spend his early years in lower- or middle-management jobs. Hourly workers typically need several years to explore the work world and move beyond apprentice status to a permanent occupational role. The level of attainment a man reaches by his early thirties varies. One executive may be on the bottom rung of the corporate ladder; another may be near the top. An hourly worker may be an unskilled laborer without job security or a highly skilled craftsperson earning more than many executives or professionals.

The occupational cycle for women, even more so than for men, is also marked by a series of adjustments. Women pursuing careers are faced with the same challenges in embarking on a career as men, yet they also may experience an intense need to balance the competing demands of marriage and family (Betz & Fitzgerald, 1987, 1993; Fitzgerald & Betz, 1984). In our society, men rarely have to decide whether to delay marriage and childrearing in favor of furthering their careers.

Those women who marry, bear children, and become committed to full-time mothering ("traditional women"), subordinating the work role to the family role, are becoming increasingly rare. Osipow (1983) reports that traditional women are strongly motivated by needs of acceptance and love. In the past two decades, increasing numbers of women ("careerists") have developed committed, permanent ties to the workplace that resemble the pattern once reserved for men alone. Osipow (1983) finds careerists strongly achievement-oriented.

Studies show that most women work out of economic need first and foremost, although they may find considerable satisfaction in their careers (Maymi, 1982). Nearly 67 percent of working women in Maymi's study were either single, divorced, separated, widowed, or married to husbands earning less than $10,000 per year. Increasing numbers of women are combining the commitment to both work and family, and recent research shows no sign of this trend changing. Fassinger (1985) found that high-ability women who were juniors and seniors in college showed a strong interest in blending career *and* family in early adulthood.

Tangri and Jenkins (1992) reported three different career orientations among working women. Among the types identified were role innovators and traditionals. Role innovators tended to be most like Fassinger's high-ability women; they displayed strong independence, came from advantaged family circumstances, and were very individualistic. Role innovators also were the strongest achievement-oriented women in the study in terms of their careers; however, they also were the most doubtful about realizing their personal career goals, perhaps in part due to the very high expectations that they established for themselves and their careers initially. The second career type was labeled traditional. Traditional women valued the family above careers and felt that their career should not jeopardize childrearing goals or the maintenance of the household. For traditional women, their husbands' success was

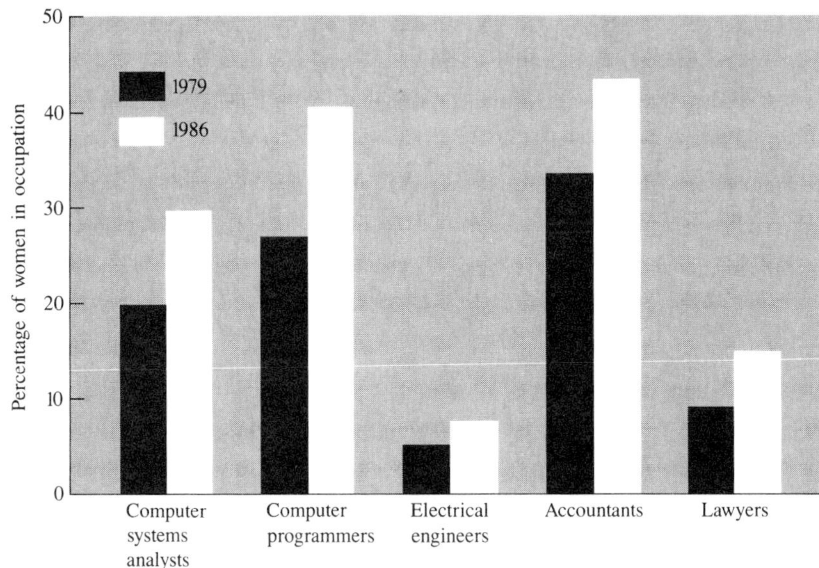


**Figure 8.2** Five professions in which women have been historically underrepresented: 1979–1986. *Source: Data from the U.S. Bureau of the Census.*

used as a vehicle to project their own achievement orientation. Traditional women felt very confident about the likelihood of their succeeding in their self-chosen careers, which were most often "people centered" occupations. Tangri and Jenkins (1992) also reported that the roles ascribed to women in the study tended to be extremely consistent over a fourteen-year period, with some women becoming perhaps more highly traditional or more highly role innovative but with little change from one category to another.

Perhaps no better index of the impact of women in the work force exists than that provided by the increasing number of occupations in which women are now employed. Figure 8.2 shows five professions in which women have made sizable gains in employment over a seven-year period (1979–1986). Given the important jobs that need to be filled in our society, we would think that the sex of a qualified applicant would be irrelevant; indeed, this is the stance our laws take in prohibiting sex discrimination in hiring, salary, and promotion. However, as we shall see, the promises of equal opportunity and equal pay for equal work and equality between husbands and wives in family responsibilities as yet remain unfulfilled (Noble, 1993).

## Occupational Satisfaction and Midlife Career Change

In middle adulthood, most men reach their highest status and income levels in their careers; women, if they have been employed without interruption for family responsibilities most of their adult lives, do likewise. Those who remain in their careers from early adulthood to retirement generally become increasingly satisfied with their work through their midsixties (Rhodes, 1983). Satisfied employees are usually somewhat more productive, whereas dissatisfied workers show both decreased productivity and increased absenteeism (Iaffaldano & Muchinsky, 1985; Rhodes, 1983). What leads employees to be satisfied or dissatisfied with their work?

The factors that lead to occupational satisfaction are different for younger and older workers (Warr, 1992). Younger workers seem concerned with salary, job security, opportunity for advancement, and relationships with both supervisors and coworkers (Nord, 1977). By midlife, established workers focus on different factors: autonomy on the job, the opportunity for individual challenge and mastery, personal achievement, freedom to be creative, and the need to see one's work as contributing to a larger whole (Clausen, 1981). These factors emerged in one recent national study of 3,400 workers, when workers were asked to identify the *most* important reasons in their having selected their current job. Across small, large, and medium-sized companies there was consistency in workers' rankings of those factors that led them to take a position with their current employer (Galinsky, 1993). These ratings of importance are summarized in figure 8.3 and show that factors such as salary and fringe benefits are not nearly as important as characteristics of the job that will enable workers to create a balance in their lives at home and in pursuits outside of work. Most workers spend considerable effort to derive a balance between work responsibilities and family responsibilities. We know very little, however, about how this balance is achieved for younger, middle-aged, and older workers (Human Capital Initiative, 1993). Clearly, it is an important concern among workers and apparently important to achieve. Thus, employees were most concerned about flexibility, personal autonomy, and social interaction on the job. It is the quality of the work environment that appears to be of greatest concern to today's workers and research investigators wonder whether these considerations will continue to dominate workers' attitudes in the future (Galinsky, 1993).

Middle-aged workers find job security and rising to positions of influence—external signs that validate their success—very satisfying. Most older workers are satisfied with their work, have derived recognition for their abilities (enhanced self-esteem), and will not change companies even if offered higher salaries (Havighurst, 1982; Nord, 1977; Tamir, 1989). Middle-aged and older adults are quite reflective and accurate in their assessment of their contributions and the skills necessary for continued occupational success (Fletcher, Hansson, & Bailey, 1992). Middle-aged as well as older employees seem to be able to gauge their own work performance accurately, assess their ability to learn new skills for continued occupational success, and apply their knowledge of the organization to serve their needs far better than younger workers. Thus, middle age becomes a kind of "plateau" for many employees according to Bardwick (1990).

Warr (1992) has studied this plateau by examining the phenomenon of occupational well-being in relation to age. *Occupational well-being* was operationally defined along two broad parameters: (1) job anxiety versus contentment, and (2) job enthusiasm versus depression. Across a wide variety of different kinds of occupations, those who experienced the highest degree of well-being in their jobs were both young workers and older workers. Middle-aged workers showed the lowest level of

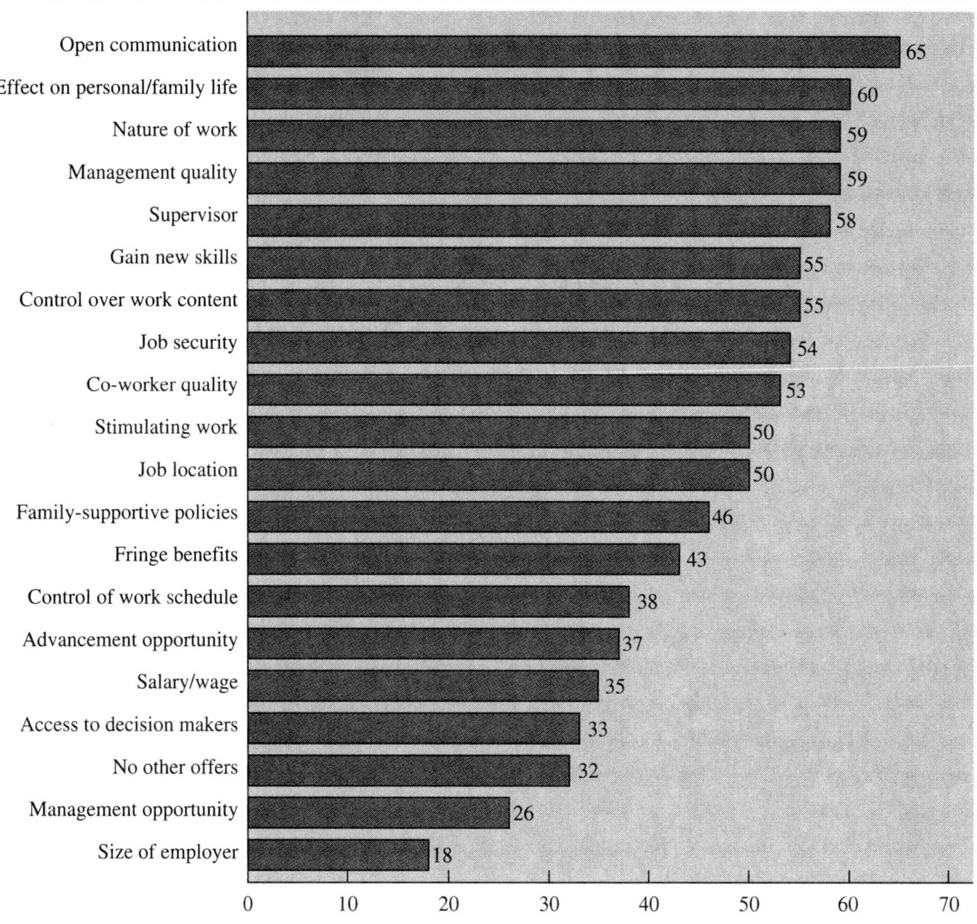


**Figure 8.3** What workers want. Reasons considered to have been "very important" in deciding to take a job with a current employer, from *The National Study of the Changing Workforce.* *Source: Data from Families and Work Institute.*

occupational well-being; the data reflected a clear U-shaped curve across the 1,686 people studied. In Warr's sample, new workers found occupations both novel and interesting and experienced a sense of belonging with their coworkers. Investigators have speculated that by middle age, people often experience boredom in occupations and recognize some of the limitations of their careers as well as the diminished likelihood of advancement, which together promote diminished job satisfaction (Warr, 1992). By later life, among those workers who remain in their occupations, job satisfaction increases as individuals come to terms with their role in the company, their contributions, and the opportunities afforded to them through work (Warr, 1992).

There are, of course, interesting exceptions to these trends; for instance, some people in middle adulthood start over and select a new career. Many men and women who have had relatively routine jobs deliberately seek change to find work that is more interesting and rewarding. For some, a change is brought about by disappointment in a "dead-end" career; for others, changing jobs represents the need for new challenges, and for still others it is a response to increased job stress. Perhaps this helps describe the shift made by traditional women from housework to careers. At present, just over 50 percent of women aged 40 to 59 are in the work force, many of them having obtained jobs as they were raising or immediately after raising a family. Approximately 10 percent of men change the nature of their work between the ages of 40 and 60, either for their own reasons or because they lose their jobs (Havighurst, 1982). And some people change jobs because they feel they are not physically fit for the work required of them (e.g., police officers, professional athletes, and armed forces personnel).

## Psychological Factors in Midlife Career Change

What are some of the factors that motivate individuals to change their careers at midlife? Daniel Levinson (1978) maintains that one important challenge in midlife involves adjusting idealistic hopes to realistic possibilities in light of how much time is left in an occupation. Middle-aged adults often focus on how much time they have left before retirement and the speed with which they are reaching their occupational goals. If individuals believe they are behind schedule, or if they now view their goals as unrealistic, then some reassessment and readjustment is necessary. Levinson (1978) comments that many middle-aged men feel a sense of sadness over unfulfilled dreams. Levinson and his colleagues also found that many middle-aged men feel constrained by their work, bosses, wives, and children. Such feelings may lead to rebellion, which can take several forms—extramarital affairs, divorce, alcoholism, career change, or even suicide. In one investigation, the incidence of extramarital affairs among thirty-two women and twenty-seven men was reported to be related, in part, to a mismatch between vocation and personality profile (Wiggins & Lederer, 1984). Levinson notes that a person in middle age wants desperately to be affirmed in the roles that he or she values most. At about age 40, Levinson's subjects fixed on some key event in their careers (e.g., a promotion or an award) as carrying the ultimate message of affirmation or devaluation by society.

It is important to consider the deeper meanings of career change during the middle years. Midlife career changes are often linked to changes in attitudes, goals, and values (Thomas, 1977). Though some people hang onto their jobs despite intense dislike for their work, others change careers even when their jobs are still satisfactory. The decision to remain with a career is in itself no guarantee that an individual has not revised personal attitudes, goals, and values. Even if nothing in the individual's external life changes, the individual may change. Middle-aged people begin to see themselves, their life situations, and their careers more introspectively, reflectively, and sensitively. Levinson (1978) notes the importance of these internal psychological changes that give different meanings to life, work, and self.

One additional stress on careers in midlife is the existence of fiscal events that influence career decisions. For example, in some families, midlife is a time of

## The Relationship Between Personality Attributes and Upward Occupational Mobility

The California Longitudinal Study compared data collected on the personality attributes of individuals when they were in junior high school with the degree to which the individuals showed upward occupational mobility by the time they reached midlife. Some of the individuals who came from working-class backgrounds ended up with middle-class occupations at midlife. Were there any clues from the personality characteristics of these individuals that were predictive of upward occupational mobility?

John Clausen (1981) found that men who moved from working-class backgrounds into middle-class occupations exceeded their nonmobile peers from comparable backgrounds in dependability, productivity, personal effectiveness, aspiration levels, and intellectual capacities and interests in the junior high school years. The picture that emerged for the working-class mobiles was that of pleasant, dependable, conventional working-class boys who worked productively to get ahead. This contrasted with the more rebellious, self-defensive, less conventional middle-class boys who seemed less pleasant and less dependable. The upwardly mobile working-class boys were also more nurturant and secured more education than their peers who remained in the working class. Further, the upwardly mobile boys continued to increase their intellectual skills and interests as they moved up the occupational ladder. In general, at midlife they more closely resembled men who came from middle-class families than they did their former working-class peers who were employed in blue-collar jobs. Thus, a combination of personality characteristics, the socializing influence of higher education, and the requirements of white-collar jobs differentiated these boys from their peers. Furthermore, it was these upwardly mobile men who were the most satisfied with their occupational success.

financial strain as children enter college. In other families, a reorientation toward the retirement years causes concerns to mount about the adequacy of the family's financial resources for retirement (Heald, 1977). And, with the advent of the empty nest, women often embark on new occupations, complete or extend their education, or resume with greater intensity interrupted careers or those in which they were marginally involved through part-time employment (Black & Hill, 1984).

Of particular interest are the factors related to occupational mobility in adulthood. What factors contribute to the likelihood that an individual from a working-class background will take on a middle-class occupation in adulthood? Data from the California Longitudinal Study (Clausen, 1981) allow us to address this question. See Research Focus 8.2 for information about the relationship between personality attributes in adolescence and middle adulthood and occupational status at midlife.

## Work in Late Adulthood

Productivity in old age seems to be the rule rather than the exception. People who have worked hard throughout their lives often continue to do so in old age. Given the changing demographics of our population, our society will want to determine how to invigorate the work force with older, productive, and vital workers (Human Capital Initiative, 1993). With lower birth rates and fewer young workers to support retirees, we will clearly need older workers to maintain our productivity. Furthermore, it would be wasteful to have nearly one-third of our adult population out of our work force (Human Capital Initiative, 1993).

Some older workers keep schedules that would exhaust younger workers, and many continue to demonstrate highly creative skills, sometimes outperforming their young and middle-aged adult coworkers. Older workers, despite identifiable declines in cognitive processes, have developed special strategies to maintain their success on the job. In some cases, they compensate for declines in motor performance or speed of processing by applying their expertise and acumen developed over many years (Human Capital Initiative, 1993). Corporations have yet to identify the special talents of the older worker and the possibility that such workers could function in new roles to improve overall quality and productivity. Moreover, older workers are less likely to be chosen for training programs since, in the minds of employers, there is minimal "return" on such an investment (Human Capital Initiative, 1993).

In general, there is a modest but positive relationship between age and productivity that favors the older worker. Younger workers have less commitment to their employers than older workers who have invested a lifetime with a company. Thus, older workers have 20 percent less absenteeism than younger workers. There is considerable evidence that older workers are more reliable and derive greater satisfaction from their jobs than do younger workers (Human Capital Initiative, 1993). Older workers also have fewer disabling injuries as well as a lower rate of accidents than young adult workers (Sterns, Barrett, & Alexander, 1985). However, fatal injuries or permanently disabling injuries show a U-shaped function across age (Sterns et al., 1985). In addition, older workers are at increased risk for certain safety problems and injuries. When comparable accidents occur on the job, younger workers have a greater possibility of recovery and a smaller likelihood of permanent disability. The older worker experiencing severe injury may become disabled, preventing further employment, or may suffer disability, dysfunction, or even death. Thus, the consequences of accidents and on-the-job injury are far more serious for older than younger workers (Sterns et al., 1985).

Older workers also experience differential levels of stress when compared to younger workers in certain settings. For example, in one investigation, three age groups of workers (19–28; 30–44; and 53–59 years old) were compared on their adjustment to working a night shift (Harma, Hakola, & Laitinen, 1992). The oldest workers in this sample clearly had the most difficulty in adjusting to night shift work, particularly when consecutive night shifts were required, and led to their early retirement (Harma, Hakola, & Laitinen, 1992). For those older workers fortunate enough to have sufficient financial resources, early retirement is a predictable outcome (Human Capital Initiative, 1993).

Current changes in federal law eliminating nearly all mandatory retirement will continue to alter the way that we all think about the older worker and the meaning of work. At present we have identified some of the factors that contribute to an older adult's decision to continue work or to retire, which include health, finances, nonwork options, role expectations, the meaning of work, and the importance of work roles (Human Capital Initiative, 1993). A rational approach for employers is to encourage older workers to continue in most occupations if they so choose. The limitations of declining health and disease, however, may make it difficult for older workers to maintain occupational roles, even if they would like to continue in their jobs (Human Capital Initiative, 1993; Sterns et al., 1985).

## Job Performance and Aging

Research concerning job performance and aging is difficult to understand without examining the methods used in research studies. Overall it appears that older workers, despite declining cognitive and sensory processes, are able to maintain high-quality levels of productivity similar to younger workers (Human Capital Initiative, 1993). Many studies suggest that older people perform as well as or even better than younger workers; there are also studies, however, reporting an advantage for younger workers (Stagner, 1985). McEvoy and Cascio (1989) concluded that there remains a general cultural belief that older workers perform less ably than when they were younger, a belief that has persisted for more than three decades.

A careful analysis of the research on aging and job performance reveals that researchers often employ dramatically different methodologies (McEvoy & Cascio, 1989; Stagner, 1985). Some studies use objective measures of workers' performance, whereas others rely on the subjective performance ratings of supervisors. Studies relying on the subjective evaluations of executives and supervisors may contain an inherent negative bias against the older worker. And, perhaps surprisingly, even older workers themselves seem to accept negative stereotypes, frequently believing that they are less effective and productive despite objective evidence to the contrary (Stagner, 1985). Objective assessments reveal a much more positive view of the performance of older workers.

It is important to understand how older workers are able to remain effective in their jobs. Certainly some compensatory strategies are developed by older workers to permit them to perform as they did when they were younger. It is also true that wisdom about work conducted for many years also gives older employees an advantage on the job (Human Capital Initiative, 1993).

# *The Meanings of Work, the Achievement Motive, and Unemployment*

In addition to exploring the developmental course of work in the adult years, it also is important to examine the meaning of work for adults. Virtually all workers view their jobs as a way of earning a living, but as we will see, work has other meanings as well. In this section we examine these meanings, as well as the achievement motive and the implications of unemployment.

## The Meanings of Work

A majority of individuals report that they would continue to work even if they inherited enough money to live without working or won millions in the lottery

*TABLE 8.1*

| *The Relationship between the Functions and Meanings of Work* | |
|---|---|
| ***Work Function*** | ***Work Meanings*** |
| Income | Maintaining a minimum sustenance level<br>Achieving some higher level or group standard |
| Expenditure of time and energy | Something to do<br>A way of filling the day or passing time |
| Identification and status | Source of self-respect<br>Way of achieving recognition or respect from others<br>Definition of role |
| Association | Friendship relations<br>Peer-group relations<br>Subordinate-superordinate relations |
| Source of meaningful life experience | Gives purpose to life<br>Creativity, self-expression<br>New experience<br>Service to others |

*From E. Friedmann and R. J. Havighurst,* The Meaning of Work and Retirement. *Copyright © 1954 The University of Chicago Press, Chicago, IL. Reprinted by permission.*

(Morse & Weiss, 1968). Some people view their jobs as a measure of prestige or status, whereas others may see their jobs as their prime contact with the outside world and a way to develop social relationships beyond the family. The challenge of work varies in each occupation. A salesperson worries about cracking a tough customer; the assembly-line worker complains about the monotony of his job, yet brags that he is the best at his job in the plant; the executive discusses her immense responsibilities in the corporation. But there are some common threads of meaning that run through jobs with diverse functions. Table 8.1 presents a list of some of the meanings individuals assign to their jobs and links these meanings with more universal functions of work.

In table 8.2, the data from two studies conducted by Robert Havighurst (Friedmann & Havighurst, 1954; Havighurst, McDonald, Perun, & Snow, 1976) reveal that skilled craftpersons and white-collar groups stress the nonfinancial meanings of work to a much greater degree than workers in heavy industry. It may be that the meanings of work described in table 8.2 become more relevant as we move up the occupational and skill ladders.

We know that some individuals value their work, or the role that they fulfill, so greatly that they choose to work long after others have retired. The decision to continue to work is certainly also related to health, finances, and job satisfaction. What is emerging, however, are other models of work among older adults; for example, there has been significant growth in part-time employment among older adults. And many productive older workers trade their high involvement in careers for volunteerism when they retire (Human Capital Initiative, 1993). We need to recognize that volunteerism, an increasingly common activity chosen by older

*TABLE 8.2*

| Meanings of Work[a] | | | | | | | | |
|---|---|---|---|---|---|---|---|---|
| | Category of Worker (Percent Choosing) | | | | | | Social Scientists | |
| Meanings | Steelworkers | Miners | Photoengravers over 65 | Salespersons | Senior Physicians | College Administrators | Male | Female |
| 1. Income for my needs | 28 | 18 | 11 | 0 | 0 | 4 | 6 | 5 |
| 2. Routine: Makes time pass | 28 | 19 | 15 | 21 | 15 | 1 | 1 | 1 |
| 3a. Self-respect | | | | 12 | 7 | 14 | 12 | 8 |
| 3b. Prestige | | | | 11 | 13 | 11 | 14 | 5 |
| 3a + 3b | 16 | 18 | 24 | | | | | |
| 4. Association with peers | 15 | 19 | 20 | 20 | 19 | 11 | 10 | 17 |
| 5. Self-expression; new experience; creativity | 13 | 11 | 30 | 26 | 15 | 27 | 39 | 41 |
| 6. Service to others; useful | N.D.[b] | 16 | N.D. | 10 | 32 | 31 | 17 | 22 |

[a]*The interview or questionnaire format varied from one group to another, making strict comparisons questionable. The data are reported in percentages within groups, assuming each respondent to have given his/her favored response.*

[b]*N.D. = No data*

*Source: Friedmann and Havighurst, 1954 (table 26); Havighurst, McDonald, Perun, and Snow, 1976 (table 7.2); and Havighurst, 1982, p. 782.*

people, is an activity that makes a valuable contribution to society. The importance of volunteerism in promoting the quality of life for older people is also a possibility for future investigation (Human Capital Initiative, 1993).

## The Culture of the Work Environment

The meaning of work, and the workplace itself, is undergoing rapid change that some have likened to the transition that occurred during the Industrial Revolution. Today, technology and the rapid changes in the ecology of the work environment mean that occupations rarely remain the same for workers. Being able to adjust to change, being able to transition from one job to another within the horizontal structure of an organization, and developing a commitment to lifelong learning are essential requirements for today's workers. Corporations value workers who are productive and assess worker productivity, in part, within the context of employees' ability to adjust to change. Corporations value workers' ability to get along with an increasingly diverse work force (ethnic, racial, gender, and age) and to participate collegially as members of a team. Corporations expect workers to be responsive to suggestions from both vertical and horizontal components of the organization to maintain and improve quality. With women expected to comprise nearly 70 percent of the new workers entering the work force in the next five years, organizations must help workers to develop sensitivity to women's concerns to ensure an environment that is free of bias and harassment. The benefits of such goals are many, and, certainly, productivity is one.

Large corporations, their employees, and workers' unions have recognized that employees are being displaced by technology. Employers, therefore, are initiating collaborative efforts to provide retraining programs and on-site education or career/job counseling. The message communicated through worker retraining is that not only displaced workers but *all* employees are significant and valued; corporations expect that, in return, their employees, young and old, will become strongly motivated to achieve the goals and priorities of the corporation, thereby enhancing productivity and quality.

We find that many of the changes in corporate attitudes and corporate culture are designed to ensure strong motivation, organizational commitment, worker satisfaction, and ultimately quality and productivity. There has been considerable emphasis on management innovations such as team building, quality circles, and Total Quality Management (TQM) approaches. Some of the changes have come about from comparisons with the success of the Japanese companies; other sensitivities have emerged from research in human resource management and still others from programs established decades ago among pioneering corporations committed to the Total Quality Management movement.

As the nature of work and the work environment change, it may be that the meaning and significance of work to employees also undergoes similar change. As we have previously discussed, young workers in organizations tend to be concerned with extrinsic factors such as salary, job security, and continuity in their careers, whereas workers with more seniority focus on intrinsic rewards such as independence, quality of work issues, and the authority to set tasks and achieve them in line with corporate priorities (Galinsky, 1993; Hall and Rabinowitz, 1988). Those workers who welcome change, those who can manage change, and those who initiate and sustain change may be most able to derive the highest degree of personal success and pleasure from their careers (Belasco, 1991). Evidence is already mounting that today's workers are questioning the value of company loyalty and increasingly placing greater value on personal needs and family concerns (Noble, 1993). Those companies embarking on the latest innovations in management science would do well to pay close attention to the survey data provided in figure 8.3 identifying the concerns of employees today (Galinsky, 1993). As but one example, consider that nearly 90 percent of all employees live with and care for other family members; 50 percent care for dependents including children, elderly parents, or spouses with health problems (Galinsky, 1993). We recognize that under such burdens it is difficult for workers to manage competing roles, although the decision usually is made in favor of career or employer rather than in favor of family needs (Galinsky, 1993). When these conflicts arise, however, workers' productivity and efficiency appear to be negatively affected (Human Capital Initiative, 1993).

Next let's look at what many psychologists consider to be a traditional motive in our culture—achievement—and evaluate its relationship to work.

## The Achievement Motive and Work

The **achievement motive** refers to the need to maintain or increase one's competence in activities in which a standard of excellence is involved. If a person is strongly motivated to achieve, he or she will show considerable effort and persistence in succeeding. There is some controversy about how effectively we can measure achievement motivation. The most common strategy has been to use a personality test (e.g., the **Thematic Apperception Test** or **TAT**) that requires the individual to tell a story about some pictures likely to elicit achievement themes. However, it seems that the person's story responses about achievement may not correspond closely with actual achievement behavior. Nonetheless, the concept of achievement motivation is thought to be an important part of our orientation toward work.

As a rule, the higher the adult's achievement motivation, the more likely she or he is to choose work that is characterized by risk and challenge. Starting one's own business would be one example. David McClelland, the architect of much of the early research in the achievement motive (e.g., McClelland, Atkinson, Clark, & Lowell, 1953), has suggested the need for achievement-motivation training to improve the performance of small businesses and to increase the hiring of minorities (McClelland, Constanian, Regaldo, & Stone, 1978). Achievement is also differentially reported among older adults, some of whom are motivated to help themselves overcome losses in areas of functioning central to their self-esteem and basic identity (Brandtstadter, Wentura, & Greve, 1993). Through effort and achievement, such losses may be overcome through "tenacious goal pursuit," according to Brandtstadter, Wentura, and Greve (1993).

What kind of psychological profiles do highly achievement-oriented adults reveal? One effort to investigate this question focused on the interrelationship of work orientation, mastery, and competitiveness (Spence & Helmreich, 1978). The investigators developed self-report procedures to measure separately each of the following motives: (1) *work orientation,* the desire to work hard and do a good job; (2) *mastery,* the preference for difficult and challenging activities; and (3) *competitiveness,* the motivation to beat other people. The highest-achieving adults are consistently high on work and mastery motives but low on the competitive motive. Such a pattern was revealed among college students with the highest grades, business executives with the highest salaries, and scientists who made the most significant contributions (Spence, 1979). Why? It may be that competitiveness can impede achievement, since it is related to **extrinsic motivation** (wanting to outperform one's peers). Some psychologists believe that extrinsic motives can decrease an individual's interest in the activity he or she is working on and consequently reduce success (Deci, 1975; Lepper & Greene, 1975). By contrast, **intrinsic motivation** (doing something for the pleasure in the activity itself rather than for external rewards such as money or compliments from others) is thought to be an important aspect of work (Deci & Ryan, 1985, 1987). Among employees who have made a job change within the past five years, the importance of intrinsic motivation and the lesser importance of direct compensation and fringe benefits have been noted. Such employees place extrinsic factors in the bottom half of twenty reasons considered important in their choice of an employer (Galinsky, 1993).

## Unemployment

Unemployed workers face stress whether the job loss is temporary, cyclical, or permanent. The psychological meaning of job loss may depend on a number of factors, including the individual's personality, social status, and resources. This was the conclusion of an investigation by Terry Buss and F. Stevens Redburn (1983) that focused on how the shutdown of a steel plant in Youngstown, Ohio, affected workers. For example, a 50-year-old married worker with two adolescent children, a limited education, no transferable job skills, and no pension would not react the same way to the shutdown as a 21-year-old apprentice electrician.

Is there any evidence that one type of worker experiences more difficulty with unemployment than others? In the Buss and Redburn (1983) study, managers and steelworkers were compared in 1978 and 1979. Managers were less affected in 1978, one year after the plant closing. The steelworkers felt more helpless, victimized, and distrustful; they tended to avoid social interaction and were more aggressive. They were also more depressed and showed a greater degree of perceived immobility. Over time, the steelworkers were less trustful and continued to feel immobile, helpless, and stressed. Furthermore, they also reported more health problems and increased their alcohol intake.

In contrast, the managers seemed to cope much better with unemployment. Except for a lack of trust, their psychological profiles either continued to improve or remained the same. However, in the second wave of interviews conducted in 1979, the managers began to report more family problems and a higher tendency to consume over-the-counter drugs. Nevertheless, the steelworkers were still more severely affected by the plant closing, probably because they had fewer job options and less hope for similar employment in the future. Professional managers viewed themselves as likely to become employed in a similar capacity, although not necessarily with the same company. With hope for the future, perhaps more financial resources in the form of savings, and a greater sense of control, managers were less likely to feel helpless, depressed, and distressed. Although unemployment has stressful effects on both laborers and managers, managers seem to handle it better.

Being unemployed in the 1990s may be as bad, or in some cases even worse, than was true in the Great Depression of the 1930s. The unemployed in the 1930s had a strong feeling that their jobs would reopen. Because many of today's workers have been replaced by technology and corporate downsizing, expectations that their jobs will reappear are not very realistic. This suggests that many individuals will experience a number of different jobs during their adult years—not a single occupation, as in the past. The tendency for workers to enter and exit several occupations throughout adulthood means that, in the future, more workers will experience job loss and will need to anticipate the event and its economic, emotional, and social consequences not only for themselves personally but also for their families (McLloyd, 1989).

As noted earlier, to be successful, workers need to view their education as a lifelong process, not something completed during two to four years in young adulthood and marked by the receipt of an associate or baccalaureate degree or terminating at the end of a lengthy apprenticeship in the trades. The older, less educated workers, particularly those with lowest self-esteem, have been reported to have the most difficulty coping with job loss and unemployment (Kinicki, 1989). There are job counseling programs and "executives-out-of-work" self-help groups that meet to assist those for whom the loss of a job is most debilitating. Such interventions are directed at providing unemployed workers a commonsense analysis of the situation, offering specific help in résumé writing and interviewing; understanding the resources available to assist in job searching, such as networking; identifying the generic skills that they have acquired and can apply to any work setting; and giving emotional support to help them begin to reorganize their personal lives. Kinicki and Latack (1990) believe that to be successful in coping with job loss, unemployed workers should be able to distance themselves from the loss itself and to begin to place work in balance with other activities in life.

## *Women and Work*

*Were women meant to do everything—work and have babies?*
—Candice Bergan

The most significant change in labor force participation in the past few decades is the increase in the employment of women between the ages of 20 and 65, including married women with children. By 1987, 55 percent of females 20 years of age and older were in the labor force, a figure that has increased approximately 14 percent since 1960 (U.S. Department of Labor, 1989). Data suggest that nearly 70 percent of women with children under the age of 18 currently are employed while more than 50 percent of women with children under the age of six are working (Coleman, 1988).

Although some women are entering previously all-male occupations, the majority of women still have not achieved parity with men in the occupational marketplace in terms of pay or job advancement. The difference between the average salaries for women and men is still substantial: Women earn on average less than 30 percent of the income paid to men (Congressional Caucus for Women's Issues, 1987). While women have entered the work force in greater numbers than ever before, many of the jobs they take are low-paying, low-status positions such as clerical jobs, sales clerk jobs, and part-time positions (Jacobs, 1989; Wright, 1982). In the past few decades, women usually entered the job market while in their forties. They are thus limited in how far they may rise in their occupations, unlike their male counterparts who have a twenty-year head start.

Reskin and Roos (1990) also provide strong evidence that women entering careers today are choosing many more "traditionally male" occupations. They identified thirty-three occupations where women made significant progress from 1970 to 1980. These occupations included such fields as typesetting, where the rate of increase in women employees was 38.9 percent compared to an overall growth in the nation's work force of 4.6 percent. A number of sociocultural factors are at work in opening job opportunities for women. According to Reskin and Roos (1990), these factors include the following:

- Growth in occupations requiring special technical skills (e.g., in the computer field) with no readily available pool of trained workers
- Financial penalties for companies that fail to achieve sex equity in traditionally male-dominated fields (e.g., the insurance industry)
- Technological advances that reduce the importance of physical strength in many jobs (e.g., typesetting, which is now largely computer controlled)
- Training and education of women to increase their employability
- Legal mandates against sex discrimination that have influenced the attitudes of employers

Despite new job opportunities for women, they face a variety of problems in the world of work. For example, women who enter careers in middle age are hampered by the lack of mentors. **Mentors,** readily available to younger adults, are experienced, successful workers about ten to fifteen years older than the fledgling workers they help start on the road to career success. Mentors impart advice, guidance, and perspective through an intense, open, and emotionally close relationship. With males more likely to become managers and executives, many more men than women serve as mentors. As researchers have discovered, when men become mentors to women, the mentoring process is likely to become disrupted by sexual attraction (Roberts & Newton, 1987). Middle-aged women are less likely to have the benefit of a mentor, given their late entry into the work force, and thus are at a distinct disadvantage on the job.

Two recent reports document some of the other special problems middle-aged and older women experience in the work force (Herz, 1988; U.S. Department of Labor, 1989). For example, delaying a full-time career until middle age restricts a woman's options in terms of pensions, Social Security benefits, and retirement. Thus, many older women may find themselves forced to continue to work well beyond the age they would choose to retire.

Therefore, despite the appearance of substantial gains in employment for women, we must interpret such progress cautiously. As mentioned previously, many of the traditionally male occupations showing dramatic growth in hiring women have been jobs that offer low pay, low status, or less desirable working conditions. Some feminists argue that when traditional male occupations do become open to women, it is usually because these fields are having trouble attracting males to fill the jobs, or because the fields show less earning potential, loss of prestige, and diminished power in society (Reskin & Roos, 1990). The recent surge of women into the field of medicine is a good example. This career is no longer as attractive as it used to be, as evidenced by the more than 50 percent decline in applications to medical school in the past ten years. Doctors cite overregulation, excessive malpractice insurance costs, preset fee schedules, and excessive overhead as factors that restrict the appeal of medicine (Reskin & Roos, 1990). The promise of the Clinton administration to revamp the health care system, provide health insurance coverage to all Americans, and lower costs through such mechanisms as increasing use of Health Maintenance Organizations (HMOs) to provide services further threatens the independence of many in the medical profession. The increase in the percentage of women entering traditionally male occupations such as medicine, therefore, must be interpreted cautiously; nearly 50 percent leave such positions within ten years for gender-neutral or traditional female jobs such as teaching or social work (Jacobs, 1989; Reskin & Roos, 1990). There remain many occupations in which males are entrenched, and many fields, such as the corporate world, in which women rarely match men's rate of career advancement.

## Tracks for Women and Men

Most men begin work in early adulthood and work more or less continuously until they retire, unless they return to school or become unemployed. Unstable patterns of work are much more common among low-income than middle-income workers, although a continuous pattern of work is still the norm among low-income male workers.The pattern of work for men and the career choices made typically are most directly influenced by family circumstances and by the aspirations parents established (King, 1989).

Although the majority of college women anticipate having both a career and marriage, many are unrealistic about the difficulties this combination poses (Shields, 1973). The difficulties women feel in combining a family and career seem to result more from role overload than role conflict. Women who cope with time pressures and conflicts by redefining their own and their families' responsibilities are more satisfied than those who attempt to meet all of these demands alone (Osipow, 1983). Galinsky (1993) has identified that there is little "equity" among women and men in dual-career families when work in the home is analyzed. Figure 8.4 shows that there were four areas in the household in which women assumed a disproportionate share of the work: cooking, cleaning, shopping, and paying the bills. Men only took greater responsibility for household repairs. Women clearly have far greater household responsibilities than men despite the fact that these data were derived from dual-earner families (Galinsky, 1993). Diamond (1988) confirms that women experience stress in their careers in ways not encountered by men, for whom the process is far more simple, direct, and culturally sanctioned.

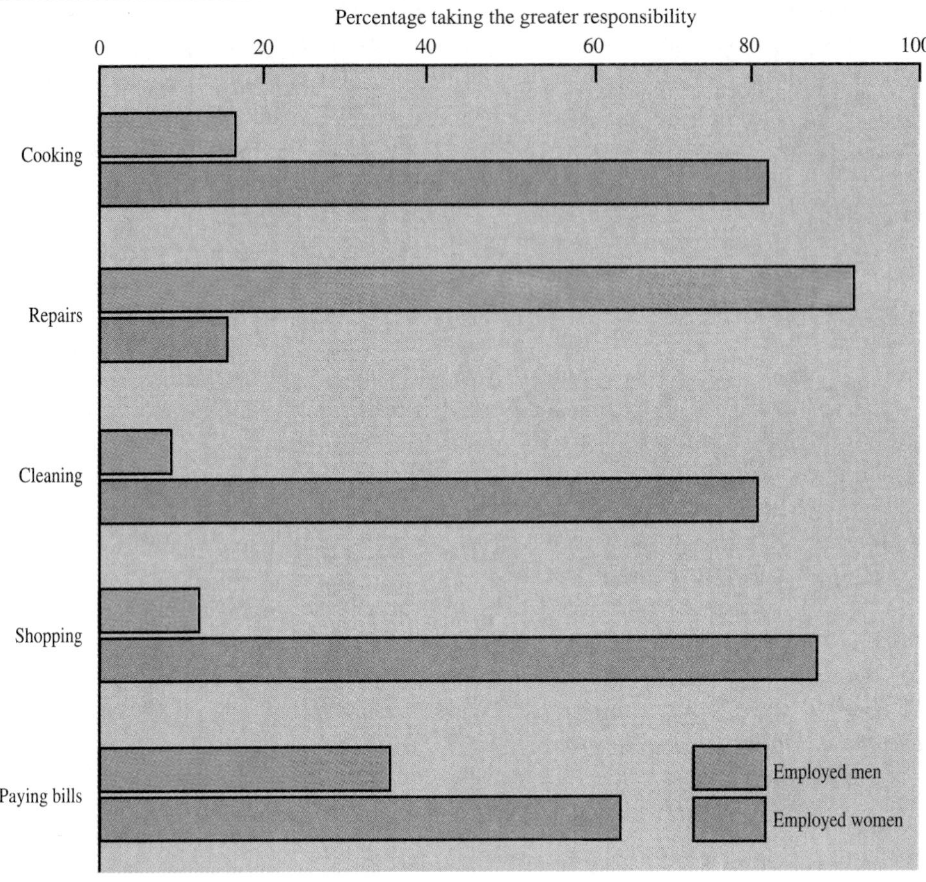


**Figure 8.4**
A woman's work. Comparison of women and men in dual-earner families with respect to who takes the greater responsibility for household work.
*Source: Data from Families and Work Institute.*

Women who return to higher education or careers after marrying and having children show high levels of commitment. Women who are employed have higher levels of life satisfaction and feelings of adequacy and self-esteem than full-time homemakers (Coleman & Antonucci, 1983). However, the psychological benefits of employment are greater for educated middle-class women and the liabilities greater for less well-educated lower-class women.

The most common path for both working-class and middle-class women is to work after finishing high school or college; to marry and cease working when having children; then, when children are a little older, to return to part-time work to supplement the husband's income. As the children begin to leave home, women return to school to update earlier skills or to retrain to better compete for a full-time job. Women in their forties and fifties are relatively free of home and family responsibilities and better able to assume full-time employment.

For professional or career women, the picture is different, since they have committed themselves to maintaining their professional skills. Researchers have identified four career patterns among professional women (Golan, 1986; Paloma, Pendelton, & Garland, 1982). These patterns include: (1) the *regular career pattern*—the woman who pursued her professional training immediately after graduation and who continued to work with no or minimal interruption throughout the years; (2) the *interrupted career pattern*—the woman who began work in the regular pattern but interrupted her career for several years, usually for childrearing, and then went back to work full-time; (3) the *second career pattern*—the woman who started her professional training near or after the time the children left home or after a divorce; and, (4) the *modified second career pattern*—the woman who started her professional training while the children were at home but old enough not to need full-time mothering, then started to work, possibly part-time, until the last child left home, at which time the woman shifted to a full-time career.

Thus far, we have discussed a number of aspects of work, but as adults, we must not only learn how to work well, we also need to learn how to relax. With the kind of work ethic our country has embraced, it is not surprising to find that many adults view leisure as boring and unnecessary. When elderly people find it necessary to reduce their workloads or retire, they often find themselves with more free time than they know how to handle. Let's now look at the nature of leisure in adulthood.

## *Leisure*

*The end of labor is to gain leisure.*
—Aristotle

Aristotle recognized the importance of leisure, stressing that we should not only work well but use leisure well. In our society, the idea that leisure is the opposite of work is common. Some see leisure as wasted time and thus antithetical to the basic values of our society: work, motivation, and achievement. John Neulinger (1981), a leading investigator of leisure in the United States, poses this dilemma: Is humanity's ultimate goal a life of leisure? Clearly, most of us would disagree that leisure is what motivates us or is the measure of our life's success. Yet the puzzle remains: What is leisure? How important is it in our lives?

The word **leisure** has usually been used in four different contexts. Burrus-Bammel and Bammel (1985) recognize the *classical* view that leisure is a state of mind. Free time alone is neither a necessary nor sufficient condition for leisure; rather, it is how one chooses to define tasks and situations that is the critical variable (Neulinger, 1981). Thus, some persons define their work as leisure, while others define specific nonwork activities and time away from work as leisure. Generally, the higher one's occupational status and income, the greater the identification with work rather than leisure (Burrus-Bammel & Bammel, 1985; Neulinger, 1981). Viewing work as leisure may also be influenced by the nature of the rewards derived—intrinsic or extrinsic. Intrinsic rewards characterize leisure in that the activity itself is rewarding. Leisure may also depend on *social class*. Historically, only the elite were free to choose and pursue self-selected activities, while those from lower social classes were destined to a life of constant work. Leisure may also lead to particular kinds of *activity* apart from work roles, such as recreation, entertainment, education, or relaxation. Finally, leisure may refer to the availability of *free time* (Burrus-Bammel & Bammel, 1985; Kraus, 1978). For example, our industrial society provides leisure time to retired workers or to employees who choose activities during nonwork hours.

It seems that attitudes toward leisure are becoming more positive in our society (Clebone & Taylor, 1992). For example, among four generations of women within the same family, attitudes were sampled to investigate patterns and transmission of beliefs in a number of areas including leisure. Overall, the results indicated that at each succeeding generation, women displayed increasingly more positive attitudes to a variety of areas and toward leisure specifically.

## The Nature of Leisure Activities

Ninety years ago the average work week was seventy-one hours. Only in the last several decades has the work week averaged thirty-five to forty hours. We have even created flextime so that workers can complete their week's work without being on the job from 9:00 A.M. to 5:00 P.M. For example, some industries give employees the option of working twelve-hour shifts for three consecutive days with the next four days off. Others let employees set the length of their work days as long as they work a specific minimum number of hours each week. Other companies allow employees to take leaves without pay or to choose part-time employment for significant parts of the year. Workers with such choices have more free time than cohorts in previous generations did. Are we experiencing a growth in leisure activities?

## The Role of Television

Within the last twenty-five years, social scientists have devoted much time to investigating the activities that adults pursue in their leisure. One emerging trend is that adults are becoming increasingly reliant on television over other forms of mass media as a key form of leisure and entertainment (Bell, 1992; Pepper, 1976). Television viewing has partially displaced other leisure activities and consistently appears as one of the most popular leisure choices (Burrus-Bammel & Bammel, 1985). Table 8.3 displays a list of the rankings of preferred leisure-time activities for a representative group of community-dwelling elderly adults (McAvoy, 1979).

Note that a list of preferred leisure activities may not reflect how older adults actually spend their leisure time. McAvoy (1979), for instance, reported that older adults actually preferred other activities, including travel, hobbies, gardening, and driving for pleasure, to watching television. Yet television watching remains the most common leisure activity for older adults next to visiting friends

*TABLE 8.3*

**Leisure Time Activities of Elderly Community-Residing Adults**

| Category | Rank |
|---|---|
| Visiting friends | 1 |
| Watching television | 2 |
| Reading | 3 |
| Gardening | 4 |
| Hobbies | 5 |
| Driving | 6 |
| Walking | 7 |
| Indoor games | 8 |
| Organization and club meetings | 9 |
| Caring for animals | 10 |

*From L. McAvoy, "The Leisure Preferences, Problems, and Needs of the Elderly" in* Journal of Leisure Research, *11:40–47, Copyright © 1979 National Recreation and Park Association, Alexandria, VA. Reprinted by permission.*

(Moss & Lawton, 1982). According to one recent estimate, the typical viewing time for older adults is an average of more than forty hours each week or nearly six hours each day (Bell, 1992).

Recent surveys suggest there are few realistic portrayals of aging and older adults on most television programs (Bell, 1992; Burrus-Bammel & Bammel, 1985). Television presents a highly distorted view of the elderly. Most programs portray older adults living in middle-class settings, without minority representation, free from health concerns, and able to maintain considerable freedom and independence and an active lifestyle (see Research Focus 8.3). Bell recently reported the results of his analysis of the images of aging by studying five prime-time television programs in 1989 in which older persons played a major character: "Murder, She Wrote," "Golden Girls," "Matlock," "Jake and the Fatman," and "In the Heat of the Night." These shows reflected a change in the television stereotypes of the elderly of the 1970s. Earlier the elderly were stereotyped as more "comical, stubborn, eccentric, and foolish" than other television characters. Bell (1992) reported that the elderly on prime-time television in 1989 were stereotyped more positively, appearing powerful, affluent, healthy, socially and mentally active, and widely admired. Bell (1992) does not applaud this overly positive image of the elderly versus the images from the 1970s. Rather, he levels strong criticism at a medium that continues to perpetuate stereotypes of how people age in our society.

Positive distortion, which Palmore (1990) has termed an instance of stereotyping or *positive ageism,* ignores the problems of loneliness, poverty, illness, and dependence among the elderly. By ignoring the diversity of ways in which people grow old and the special problems among widows, minorities, or the isolated and lonely elderly, television may be creating in older people the sense that their own aging is largely negative in comparison to what they see.

## Prime-Time Women

Recently the National Commission on Working Women published an analysis of the image of older women portrayed in television programming (Steenland, 1987). Women over 50 comprise a significant segment of our society, yet on television, the diversity of their experience and living conditions is glossed over in convenient stereotypes. Television portrays older women as having sufficient resources (economic, social, physical mobility, and health) to indulge in leisure pursuits. The image of older women portrayed on television presents a distorted and biased image of females in our society and their individual aging.

Let's examine the stereotypes of aging in our society and try to better understand how television contributes to ageist attitudes. First, consider some basic census data:

1. Among women 50 years of age and older, 13 percent live at or below poverty levels.
2. Among women 65 years of age and older, 80 percent currently receive no pension.
3. The normative age for widowhood is 56 years—an age that does not qualify a widow for either Social Security or Medicare.
4. Women over age 65 represent 71 percent of the elderly living at or below poverty and 80 percent of the elderly living alone.

Now, let's examine the image of the older women (50 years of age or more) on prime-time television. Until the 1970s, the image of the older woman was clear: either she was nonexistent, invisible, or outnumbered significantly by younger characters. The data show that despite the presence of Granny on the "Beverly Hillbillies," Maude, and Edith Bunker on "All in the Family," 91 percent of all older characters on television were male. In the late 1970s, the Screen Actors Guild reported a study showing a positive correlation between age and increasing unemployment rates for actresses. You may recall the characters of older women on TV who were largely "powerless, befuddled, inflexible, and feeble," as well as devoid of sexuality, romance, substance, and power.

Currently the situation has apparently improved with older women now constituting 20 percent of all the women characters on television. Just as earlier older female images were largely negative, today's older television personalities are portrayed in similarly distorted, although positive, ways. The older female character is "powerful, creative, appealing and affluent" (Steenland, 1987). In the spring of 1986 there were nineteen female characters over the age of 50 on prime-time television; their demographic characteristics are presented in table 8.A along with comparable figures for older women nationwide.

For older women such as those on "Dynasty;" "Facts of Life;" "Golden Girls;" "Hotel;" "Knots Landing;" "Murder, She Wrote;" "Who's the Boss;" and other programs "never has life been so good" (Steenland, 1987). The women are predominantly wealthy or middle-class; their power, beauty, money, active lifestyles, and need for adventure draw men to them. They remain independent, creative, mobile, and self-sufficient. The ability of viewers to differentiate age among the television characters is particularly hampered since physical age differences are nonexistent and irrelevant. Steenland

## The Therapeutic Benefits of Pets

Not all older adults are so attracted to television. Many other leisure activities, such as the routine care of pets, become increasingly important as people grow older. For the widowed or single individual, pets can play a therapeutic role, allowing pet owners to organize each day (Soares, 1985). Routine pet care may also help to increase the number of interactions between the pet owner and other people (Brickel, 1980–1981; Miller, Staats, & Partlo, 1992). Ory and Goldberg (1983) reported that among married older women (67 to 75 years of age), those with strong attachments to pets were happier than those with weaker attachments or with no pets. Kidd and Feldman (1981) also reported that compared to those without pets, older pet owners (65 to 87 years of age) scored higher on measures of happiness, self-confidence, responsibility, and dependability. Miller, Staats, and Partlo (1992) found among a group of 250 pet owners (50 to 90 years old) that pets provided far more "uplifts" than hassles. Additionally, pets served slightly different roles for older men and women. Women more so

### Table 8.A

**A Comparison of Prime-Time Older Women and Their Real-Life Counterparts**

| | *Prime-Time Older Women* | *National Statistics on Older Women* |
|---|---|---|
| Age (50+) | 20 percent of all women characters | 38 percent of all women |
| Marital status | 68 percent widowed | 32 percent widowed |
| | 16 percent divorced | 6 percent divorced |
| | 16 percent married | 52 percent married |
| Economic status | 26 percent millionaires | 0.2 percent income $75,000+ |
| | 68 percent middle class | 11 percent income $20,000+ |
| | 5 percent working class | 76 percent income $5,000–$20,000 |
| | 0 percent poor | 13 percent poor |
| Employment | 57 percent employed | 48 percent employed |
| | 20 percent own corporation | 2 percent own corporation |
| | 80 percent managers or professionals | 23 percent managers or professionals |
| Race | 89 percent White | 89 percent White |
| | 11 percent Black | 9 percent Black |
| | 0 percent Asian | 1 percent Asian |
| | 0 percent Hispanic | 1 percent Hispanic |

notes the physically active, youthful, and vibrant appearance of prime-time characters regardless of whether they are 50 or 75. And in the television culture, as many opportunities for older women exist as for women half their age (Steenland, 1987). Only "Golden Girls" has addressed some of the unique problems of older women, faced the conflicts of widowhood and death, presented some of the economic concerns of women in our society (for example, the four central characters pool their resources to meet the pressures of financial obligations), and made age itself an important variable.

With a few exceptions, television presents a distorted view of aging. The elderly are free from discrimination, free from the ageist attitudes that diminish a woman's inherent worth as she grows older, free from economic hardships, and, through the efforts of screenwriters and makeup specialists, free from the physical changes, losses, and health concerns that are realities for every aging woman! Older women who watch prime-time characters on television must surely wonder, "What in the world is wrong with me?"

than men reported pets to be associated with uplifts, freedom, and positive use of leisure time. Men on the other hand associated pets with decreases in social interaction as well as hassles over time and money (Miller & Staats, 1992).

Brickel (1980–1981, 1985) notes that pets may help to meet the dependency needs and increase the responsiveness of the elderly. Pets also provide a concrete anchor for those whose lives have undergone major change or loss (Brickel, 1985). Pets may even serve as family substitutes, providing comfort and support to those experiencing the negative consequences of aging: death of loved ones, sickness, and feelings of loneliness (Brickel, 1985). Some research suggests that the ability to care humanely for pets gives meaning, purpose, and a sense of control over one's environment to the elderly (Banzinger & Roush, 1983). And caring for pets provides a sense of independence for elderly adults who can take care of something rather than be taken care of by others (Banzinger & Roush, 1983). This view is further echoed by James, James, and Smith (1984) who note that the reciprocity involved in pet care leads elderly adults to avoid becoming wholly dependent on others.

*Pets may help promote health, emotional well-being, and responsiveness among older adults.*

Pets have also been shown to have positive health benefits in other areas (National Institute of Health, 1988). Friedmann, Katcher, Lynch, and Thomas (1980) indicated that owning a pet was the best predictor of survival one year after leaving a coronary care unit in the hospital. Of fifty-three pet owners, only 6 percent died within one year, whereas of twenty-eight nonpet owners, 28 percent died within the same period. Pets provided a regularity and predictability in routine care that gave a sense of order to these heart attack patients' lives. Even the presence of minimal-care pets such as goldfish have been reported to help reduce their owners' blood pressure, decrease their sense of anxiety, and increase their leisure satisfaction (Riddick, 1985).

Among the institutionalized elderly, pets can produce similar benefits (National Institute of Health, 1988). For severely depressed residents, pets reduce anxiety, elicit responses (such as care and stroking) when the human environment has been rejected, provide physical reassurance, and help maintain reality, even among those who are terminally ill (Brickel, 1982, 1985; Muschel, 1984). In nursing homes, pet visitations two or three times each week helped break the cycle created by institutionalization: helplessness, hopelessness, dependency, and despair. Some institutions have maintained cats or dogs for a considerable time for this purpose. Others have developed similar programs using tropical fish, or feeders that attract wild birds (Banzinger & Roush, 1983). In these pet therapy programs, investigators have demonstrated that institutionalized older people become less depressed, become more communicative, and evidence higher rates of survival than controls who do not participate in such programs (Langer & Rodin, 1976; National Institute of Health, 1988).

## Sports Participation

Sports play an extremely important role in the leisure activities of Americans, either through direct participation or vicariously through attending sports events, watching televised competitions, reading newspapers or magazines, discussing sports with friends, and so forth. Active participation in physical sports declines somewhat with increasing age (Ostrow, 1980). Thus, in old age, individuals need to make adjustments in sports activities, reducing the intensity but not necessarily the frequency of their participation (Burrus-Bammel & Bammel, 1985; Schmitz-Secherzer, 1976). For example, rather than jogging five miles each day, older adults may reduce the length of their run, the frequency of their run, or both. Research suggests that the more physically active individuals have been in young adulthood and middle age, the more likely they will continue to be involved in physical activities in old age (Bortz, 1980; McCauley, 1992; McCauley, Lox, & Duncan, 1993). Benefits to the individual extend to a variety of psychological domains including reductions in anxiety (Petruzzello, Landers, Hatfield, Kubitz, & Salazar, 1991), and increases in morale (Hill, Storandt, & Malley, 1993), and personal efficacy (McCauley, Courneya, & Lettunich, 1991).

We have seen in earlier chapters, of course, that regular physical activity is one successful way to slow down aging and maintain health. Physical exercise can improve overall fitness, endurance, muscle tone, flexibility, strength, cardiac output, and respiratory efficiency, no matter what age we begin (Blumenthal, Emery, Madden, Schniebolk, Walsh-Riddle, George, McKee, Higgenbotham, Cobb, & Coleman, 1991; Burrus-Bammel & Bammel, 1985; Hill, Storandt, & Malley, 1993). Moreover, in some investigations, regular exercise has been related to increases in longevity (Schnurr, Vailant, & Vailant, 1989), physiological capacity and cardiovascular fitness (Hill, Storandt, & Malley, 1993), and aerobic capacity (Blumenthal et al., 1991). In one recent study, the ability to initiate and maintain involvement in a moderate exercise program over a five-month period was found to enhance feelings of self-efficacy and control. Older adults from 45 to 65 years of age enhanced their beliefs about their personal capacity, endurance, and motivation for physical exercise (McAuley, Lox, & Duncan, 1993). Similar to other research, enhanced self-efficacy leads older adults to engage in more health-promoting behaviors and additional commitments to exercise (McAuley, 1992). Despite the short-term nature of the intervention, the participants continued to demonstrate enhanced self-efficacy perceptions nine months following program completion (McAuley, Lox, & Duncan, 1993). Physical exercise such as walking has also been found to have beneficial effects on the symptoms of older people with depression, particularly somatic symptoms (McNeil, LeBlanc, & Joyner, 1991).

It is difficult for both younger and older people who have remained sedentary to turn over a new leaf. Thus, most older people tend to enjoy leisure activities they have pursued over most of their adult lives and rarely turn to new activities (Cutler & Hendricks, 1990; Schmitz-Secherzer, 1976). Mishra (1992) has found that men with a high level of life satisfaction are more likely to engage in active leisure pursuits and to seek out friends and join volunteer organizations. Sports activities and group participation allow older adults to escape the rigors and pressures of everyday life, even if only for a few hours per week. One critical feature of successful aging is to make the necessary adjustments within physically demanding activities (Burrus-Bammel & Bammel, 1985).

## Leisure at Midlife

Roger Gould (1972) believes that middle age is a time of questioning how time should be spent and of reassessing priorities. Midlife seems to be a time when adults want more freedom and the opportunity to express their individuality.

Leisure may be a particularly important aspect of middle adulthood because of the many changes experienced at this point in development: physical changes, changes in relationships with spouse and children, changes in self-knowledge, and career changes. With college expenses ended, mortgages paid off, and women embarking on careers, couples find themselves with more spendable income, more free time, and more opportunity for leisure. For many people, midlife is the first time in their adult lives that they have the opportunity to diversify their leisure interests. Neulinger (1981), in *The Psychology of Leisure,* reminds us that younger adults are more constrained by social and financial pressures and family obligations than middle-aged adults. In midlife, adults may select from a number of intrinsically interesting, exciting, and enjoyable leisure activities. Their participation is largely on their terms, at their pace, and at times they select. Younger adults, by contrast, must often carefully program their leisure activities to match social convention and center them around the "right" people for social and/or career success.

Adults at midlife need to start preparing both financially and psychologically for retirement. Many programs that help workers prepare for retirement (preretirement counseling) begin in middle age and include leisure education (Connolly, 1992; Knesek, 1992). In our society, with its strong work ethic, people need to be educated about how to use their leisure time and to begin to develop leisure pursuits. Constructive and fulfilling leisure activities developed in middle adulthood are important to this preparation. Leisure activities that can be continued at some level into retirement may help to ease the transition.

## Leisure Activities in Retirement

What do people do with their time when they retire? Studies reveal that they engage in many more activities with an increase in free time (Pepper, 1976). Some of these activities are listed in table 8.4, which summarizes data from five different investigations of leisure activities in retirement (Harris, 1976; McAvoy, 1979; Nystrom, 1974; Roadberg, 1981; Schmitz-Secherzer, 1979). The most common leisure activities chosen by elderly retirees were reading or writing, television, arts and crafts, games, walking, visiting family and friends, physical activity, gardening, travel or camping, organization and club activities, and outings. Of all the data emerging on older people's retirement activities, perhaps the most interesting are those suggesting that, compared to a decade ago, older people today are choosing activities far more like those of people twenty years younger than themselves (Horn & Meer, 1987).

*TABLE 8.4*

*A Synthesis of Research on Leisure Participation: Percentages of Respondents Rating Various Leisure Activities as Important*

| *Activities* | *A* | *B* | *C* | *D* | *E* |
|---|---|---|---|---|---|
| Reading/writing | 37 | 36 | 55 | 67 | 51 |
| Television | 28 | 36 | 89 | 69 | 78 |
| Arts/crafts | 26 | 26 | 40 | 46 | 37 |
| Cards/games | 23 | — | 56 | 29 | 16 |
| Walking | 16 | 25 | — | 31 | 47 |
| Visiting family/friends | 19 | 47 | 63 | 75 | 56 |
| Physical activity | 10 | 3 | — | — | — |
| Gardening | 9 | 39 | 40 | 49 | 27 |
| Travel/camping | 19 | — | — | — | 29 |
| Organizations/clubs | 2 | 17 | 51 | 29 | 8 |
| Outings/driving | 9 | — | 66 | 32 | 29 |
| N | 245 | 2797 | 65 | 540 | ? |

*A Roadburg, 1981*

*B Harris, 1976*

*C Nystrom, 1974*

*D McAvoy, 1979*

*E Schmitz-Secherzer, 1979*



Cutler and Hendricks (1990) have identified gender differences in the choice of leisure activities. Women tend to engage in sociocultural and home-centered activities whereas men seem to prefer outdoor activities (fishing, hunting), sports (playing and observing), and travel. When retirees are asked to reflect on their lives and consider things that they might wish to do differently or areas that they might reprioritize, most people feel that they have adequately balanced and prioritized their lives in terms of leisure as well as friendships, family, work, religion, and health. It is only in the area of education and the development of their intellect that today's retirees feel that they would have liked to have devoted more time if they could live their lives over again (DeGenova, 1992).

Between the ages of 60 and 70, many people retire from their occupations. For a person whose job is the central focus of life, retirement can be a difficult and unwelcome experience. For others, retirement is problematic because it is the result of declining health. And still other retirees relish their new freedom and fill their lives with enjoyable leisure activities, volunteerism, and friendships. One goal for our society is to rethink when and why people retire in view of the increasing retiree/worker ratios (Human Capital Initiative, 1993).

## RETIREMENT

In the early part of this century, most individuals did not have a choice between work and retirement. The Social Security system in 1935 established benefits to workers who retired at the age of 65; most private pension plans have adopted a comparable

*Do middle-aged and older adults possess the physical and mental abilities necessary to fulfill the rigorous and demanding duties of a law-enforcement officer?*

age. Social Security, now involving more than 90 percent of our nation's work force, was originally designed to *supplement* a worker's personal savings and investments for retirement (Parnes, Crowley, Haurin, Less, Morgan, Mott, & Nestal, 1985). However, for many workers Social Security income has become their only means of support. In 1993, a retired worker with a spouse received $1,106 per month in benefits from Social Security. Reduced benefits may begin as early as age 62 with provision for total disability benefits at any age (Parnes et al., 1985).

The development of a retirement option for older workers is a late-twentieth-century phenomenon. It has emerged for two basic reasons: (1) a strong industrial economy that provides sufficient funds to support the retirement of older workers and (2) the institutionalization of retirement nationwide through public and private pension systems (Palmore, Burchett, Fillenbaum, George, & Wallman, 1985). Today's workers will spend nearly 10 to 15 percent of their total lives in retirement. In 1967, the Age Discrimination Employment Act (ADEA) made it federal policy to prohibit firing, forcibly retiring, or failing to hire workers strictly on the basis of age. In 1978, Congress further extended the mandatory retirement age from 65 to 70 in business, industry, and the federal government. In 1986, legislation banned mandatory retirement in all but a few specific occupations (Church et al., 1988). These **Bona Fide Occupational Qualifications (BFOQ)** permit mandatory retirement only by demonstrating that *all* workers in a specific job

## Police Officers and Mandatory Retirement: Application of the Bona Fide Occupational Qualification

In some jobs, there are compelling reasons for mandatory or forced retirement at specific ages. Such designated jobs are called positions of Bona Fide Occupational Qualification (BFOQ). Employers must show, if challenged in court, that a BFOQ job cannot be handled safely and efficiently by older workers. Church et al. (1988) reviewed some of the challenges that have proven successful in demonstrating age discrimination (for example, when the job was not BFOQ and employers forced retirement to save the company money). Age discrimination is also evidenced by factors such as selective dismissal of or failure to hire qualified older workers. The work of police officers is particularly enlightening in helping us see what the courts accept as a valid BFOQ occupation.

In one case, *Equal Employment Opportunity Commission v. Missouri State Highway Patrol* (748 F.2d 447 1984), an officer challenged the policy mandating forced retirement at age 60 for all officers. The courts ruled in favor of the highway patrol department policy (BFOQ) based on evidence that at age 60, most individuals would not be physically able to keep up with the demanding routine of a police officer. The safety of the public might be jeopardized by continuing to employ police officers over this age. Nearly 90 percent of older police officers, according to experts, would not have the aerobic capacities needed to handle standard emergency situations typically encountered on the job. Further, older officers would be at a disadvantage in terms of vision, auditory response, reaction time, physical endurance, and physical strength. And any person over the age of 60 would be far more at risk for heart attack. The importance of individual differences in such global descriptions was noted in the record; that is, some 60-year-olds are physically fit and capable of meeting the demands of the Highway Patrol officer. However, the court accepted the difficulty faced by the Highway Patrol in developing, utilizing, and interpreting a battery of tests to measure physical abilities to help them screen which of the 60-year-olds could remain on the job. The policy was justifiable, and the selected age was consistent with expert opinion on the specific behavioral demands and physical requirements of the job of a police officer.

The right of police departments to maintain mandatory retirement policies at similar or even younger ages has been further supported by the courts. A state police officer challenged the right of the Commonwealth of Massachusetts to force his retirement at age 50 [*Massachusetts Board of Retirement* v. Murgia (427 US 307, 1976)]. The Supreme Court accepted the retirement policy of Massachusetts as "rationally" based on the performance demands of the job of a police officer, despite the fact that the officer currently was in excellent health, able to handle the requirements of the job on all dimensions, and faced serious psychological and economic hardships due to forced retirement at such a young age. In a similar case, *Equal Employment Opportunity Commission* v. *Commonwealth of Pennsylvania* (645 F. Supp. 1545, 186), the court accepted that the demanding job of police officer made mandatory retirement throughout the department appropriate and necessary. All officers had to be prepared to respond to crises, even though such crises materialized infrequently, if at all, for most of the police force. However, the demands that routinely emerged and presented obvious difficulties for older officers included "assisting stranded motorists in snowstorms, pushing disabled vehicles off the roadway, chasing suspects on foot, chasing suspects by vehicle at speeds of seventy to eighty miles per hour, subduing suspects, and removing victims of accidents from wrecked vehicles" (cited in Church et al., 1988, p. 102).

classification, because of age, could not continue to function safely and efficiently (Church et al., 1988). Some of the jobs covered by the Bona Fide Occupational Qualifications include police officers, firefighters, airline pilots, and foreign service officers (the latter having to retire at age 60 because of the hardship and difficulty encountered in "the rigors of overseas duty"). Employers may not fire older workers who have seniority and higher salaries just to save money. The courts, in vigorously defending workers' rights not to suffer age discrimination, have carefully evaluated the justifications made by employers claiming mandatory retirement in BFOQ jobs (see Research Focus 8.4). Recently, for example, research investigators have questioned whether there are sufficient data to support mandatory retirement at age 60 among airline pilots (Stuck, Van-Gorp, & Josephson et al., 1992). The authors found no published studies relating declines in cognitive functioning to increases in age among airline pilots. They argued further that there are no validation studies to support a link between tests of cognitive ability and safety performance among experienced airline pilots; that is, there is no evidence that declines on tests of cognitive ability relate in any way to the job performance of older pilots. With mandatory retirement in our country virtually disappearing, and experts continuing to question the remaining BFOQs, such as airline pilots, Belbin (1983) suggests that most older individuals will be confronted with the decision of *when* to retire rather than being forced to retire (Human Capital Initiative, 1993). In the next section, we look at factors related to retirement and the different phases that people go through when they retire.

## Factors Related to Retirement

A number of factors influence the decision to retire, including financial security, health status, attitude toward work, job satisfaction, and personal interests (Human Capital Initiative, 1993; Palmore et al., 1985). However, it must be recognized that these factors operate in a complex fashion to influence retirement decisions of employees. The factors influencing retirement decisions have been found to overlap one another and to be unique to each individual life situation (Henretta, Chan, & O'Rand, 1992). Table 8.5 summarizes the ratings of important and most important reasons workers give for having chosen to retire. Please note that more than 50 percent of the respondents indicated a single factor led to their retirement decision, 23 percent identified two reasons, 16 percent cited three reasons, and 6 percent cited four or more variables. Social Security benefits and pensions were often mentioned as reasons, but rarely identified as the most important factor in a retirement decision; health and loss of job were the two most important variables cited by workers (Henretta, Chan, & O'Rand, 1992). Workers at all social class levels engage in some preretirement planning and thinking and researchers are beginning to explore the possibility of racial and ethnic differences in attitudes toward retirement. Among black professionals, for instance, those who did the least planning were individuals who were highly committed to their work, had few financial investments, and tended to use their work and coworkers as their primary social basis (Richardson & Kilty, 1992). In the case of a fixed age for retirement, evidence has revealed a *preretirement role-exit process* in which men begin to evaluate their jobs as increasingly burdensome (Ekerdt & DeViney, 1993).

It is not uncommon for an individual to retire from one job, become restless, and then pursue another job. Elderly women, more than men, are likely to continue to look for work in old age (Herz, 1988; U.S. Department of Labor, 1989). For example, Frank Baird, a 72-year-old motel manager, found that he could not tolerate the inactivity of retirement:

> "They gave me a gold watch—a beautiful thing—six months pay, a new car, and a fabulous pension," Baird explained. "We spent three months traveling, playing golf,

*TABLE 8.5*

**Cross-Classification of "Most Important" and "Important" Reasons for Leaving Last Job**

| Most Important Reason | | | Proportion Mentioning Other Reasons | | | | | | | | |
|---|---|---|---|---|---|---|---|---|---|---|---|
| | N | % | Wanted to Retire | Health | Lost Job | Compul-sory | Social Security | Care for Others | Pension | Didn't Like Job | Spouse Retired |
| Wanted to retire | 763 | 47.4 | — | 8.0 | 1.6 | 6.3 | 29.5 | 1.8 | 34.1 | 1.7 | 1.6 |
| Health | 401 | 24.9 | 25.4 | — | 2.7 | 5.5 | 12.5 | 4.0 | 13.2 | 0.2 | 0.7 |
| Lost job | 160 | 9.9 | 9.4 | 6.9 | — | 3.1 | 6.2 | 0 | 2.5 | 0.6 | 0 |
| Compulsory | 139 | 8.6 | 21.6 | 7.9 | 5.0 | — | 17.3 | 3.6 | 14.4 | 0 | 2.7 |
| Social Security | 49 | 3.0 | 47.0 | 12.2 | 2.0 | 10.2 | — | 2.0 | 40.8 | 0 | 2.0 |
| Care for others | 40 | 2.5 | 17.5 | 5.0 | 0 | 0 | 2.5 | — | 7.5 | 0 | 2.5 |
| Pension | 29 | 1.8 | 51.7 | 0 | 3.4 | 0 | 24.1 | 6.9 | — | 0 | 3.4 |
| Didn't like job | 24 | 1.5 | 54.1 | 0 | 4.2 | 0 | 8.4 | 4.2 | 20.8 | — | 0 |
| Spouse retired | 6 | 0.4 | 83.3 | 0 | 0 | 0 | 33.3 | 16.6 | 50.0 | — | 0 |
| Other | 123 | 7.6 | 22.0 | 8.9 | 4.9 | 4.1 | 11.4 | 2.4 | 12.2 | 3.2 | 0 |
| Percent citing as a reason | | | 56.6 | 28.5 | 11.2 | 12.4 | 21.8 | 4.7 | 23.4 | 2.5 | 1.5 |
| Percent most important responses that are only response | | 48.2 | 59.8 | 76.2 | 56.1 | 30.6 | 75.0 | 37.9 | 37.5 | 16.7 | |

From J. C. Henretta, C. G. Chan, and A. M. O'Rand, "Retirement Reason Versus Retirement Process: Examining the Reasons for Retirement Typology" in Journal of Gerontology: Social Sciences, 47:1–7. 

fishing, and getting lazy. At first, I thought it was great. You know, for years you look forward to the freedom, the leisure time, the no hassles. But let me tell you, friend, it gets old. After six months I was bored stiff, and my wife, she was getting fed up too. You know, she had her friends and her activities and didn't need me underfoot. Then I found this job, and it's great. I love it! New people, people from all over, and I am able to make their stay a little more pleasant. Don't ever retire, friend, if you've got a job, stick with it. Retirement is for the birds. Unless you're a lazy bird." (Van Hoose & Worth, 1982, p. 317)

Still, many individuals look forward to retirement and relish the time when they will no longer have to work long hours. The feelings of Katy Adams, a retired teacher, express this sentiment:

"I don't feel any great loss at all. No, no. I taught math and science for thirty-one years, and if I hadn't taken time out to raise two daughters, I would have made it forty. I loved every minute of it, but now it is time to take a rest. After all that time I have earned it, don't you think? Why would I want to go on teaching? I have my retirement, my insurance, and my health. Now I just want to enjoy it." (Van Hoose & Worth, 1982, p. 317)

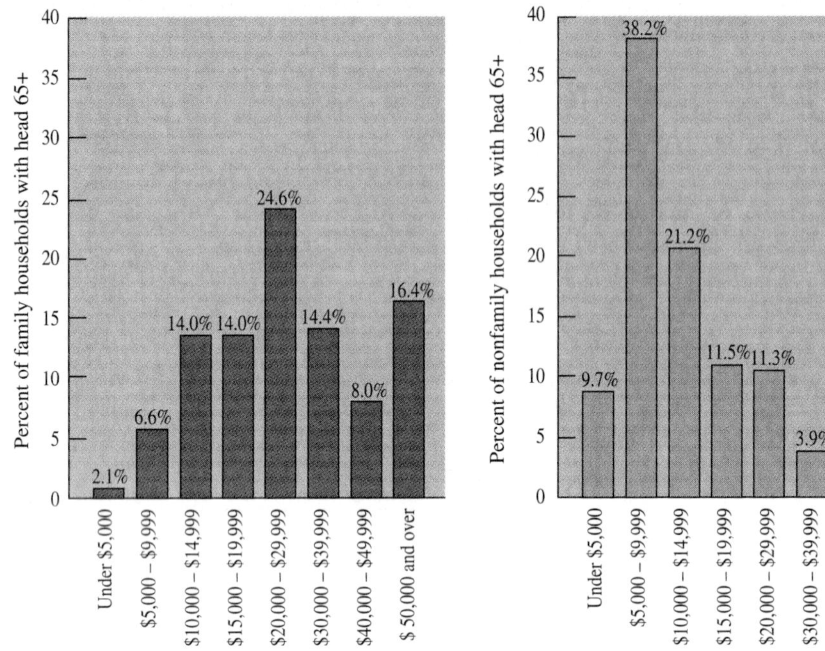


**Figure 8.5** Percent distribution of family income: 1990.
*Source: Data from U.S. Bureau of the Census.*

Many older people continue to work. In fact, a growing segment of our nation's work force is comprised of the elderly, a trend that will continue unabated (Herz, 1988; Human Capital Initiative, 1993). Working in the later years is certainly related to a host of factors, among which are health and finances. If we examine the data in figure 8.5, for example, it reveals the financial importance of continued employment on a full or part-time basis for those over the age of 65. Employing the elderly makes good sense for many reasons, but recently employers have come to understand the value of older workers in simple economic terms. The estimate in 1991 was that there were 6 million unemployed people in our society over the age of 55 who were ready to join the work force. U.S. census data suggest that there are 13.5 million people over the age of 55 already working.

Data were analyzed from three companies (Days Inn of America, Travelers Insurance Corporation, and B & Q, Great Britain's largest do-it-yourself hardware chain) that had policies of hiring people over 50 and were willing to share their business records to evaluate the success of these companies' policies of hiring older workers (Teltsch, 1991). Travelers, recognizing demographic trends suggesting that a smaller and smaller number of young people would be available for jobs, began a job bank project for older people, including recruitment of their own retirees for full-time or part-time reemployment. They reported more than 250 of their own former employees elected to come back to work. Such workers proved the value, economically, of the rehiring process. And, at Days Inn of America, older workers not only learned their job responsibilities well, they displayed less absenteeism and lower rates of job turnover in comparison to younger workers. Although older workers did take longer to learn new procedures and spent somewhat longer time on the telephone talking with callers, they actually had a higher rate of success in getting customers to commit to a reservation. In the B & Q company, older workers were found to be more familiar with household and construction problems and were better able to direct customers to products that were helpful and sold by the hardware chain (Teltsch, 1991).

When given a choice, most people appear to elect to retire as soon as they can afford it (U.S. Department of Labor, 1989). More than 50 percent of those initially filing for Social Security retirement benefits in 1987 were under 65 years of age. And nearly 67 percent of federal government employees choose to retire prior to age 62 (U.S. Department of Labor, 1989). One of the reasons may be that the U.S. Civil Service Commission has encouraged earlier retirement through rules that allow employees to retire after twenty-five years of service. Some industrial firms and labor organizations have developed programs that allow employees to retire when they are in their midfifties. Another reason many people choose to retire is the planning and financial preparation they devote to their retirement. Tax-deferred savings programs, employer pension programs, and personal investments help workers plan to retire. Most people realize the limitations of relying solely on Social Security benefits to meet all their retirement needs. *Thus, today, we note two contrasting trends: an increase in the number of older people in the work force and an increase in the number of people choosing early retirement.* It appears that older women, who comprise an increasing segment of the aging population, are responsible for the increase of elderly people in the labor market. And at the same time, the number of employed males aged 65 or older has steadily declined as they elect early retirement (Herz, 1988).

According to Palmore, George, and Fillenbaum (1982), early retirement at ages under 65 is influenced strongly by subjective factors such as self-perceptions of health, attitudes toward work and retirement, and perception of the adequacy of one's retirement income. Studies show that those who voluntarily leave their careers early for reasons other than ill health enjoy their retirement as long as they have made adequate preparation for their financial needs (Parnes et al., 1985). Elder and Pavalko (1993) have recently monitored the pattern of retirement decisions and exit from the work role by studying Terman's original population of gifted individuals as they reached their later years. Nearly half of the men gradually reduced their work time while about 30 percent left the work force abruptly; only 16 percent of the men returned to their work roles after either a gradual or abrupt retirement decision (Elder & Pavalko, 1993).

## Phases of Retirement

Some social scientists believe that many people go through a series of phases before and during retirement. One such perspective has been developed by Robert Atchley (1976, 1983). Atchley (1983) reports that people's attitudes toward retirement

**Figure 8.6** Seven phases of retirement.

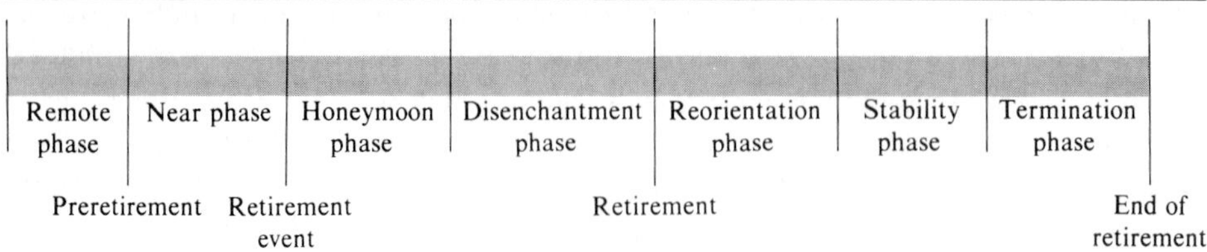


are generally positive regardless of sex or age. The only group who seem somewhat less enthusiastic about retirement are those who would like to work but because of other factors (forced retirement, adverse labor market, financial needs, or poor health) cannot maintain their jobs (Atchley, 1983; Parnes et al., 1985).

Atchley (1976) initially suggested that people go through seven phases of retirement: remote, near, honeymoon, disenchantment, reorientation, stability, and termination. The sequence of these phases is shown in figure 8.6.

Most individuals begin work with the vague belief that they will enjoy the fruits of their labor at some point in the distant future. In this *remote phase* of retirement, most people do virtually nothing to prepare themselves for retirement. As they age toward possible retirement, they often deny that they will eventually quit working.

Only when workers reach the *near phase* do they sometimes participate in preretirement programs. Preretirement planning programs help workers make the transition to retirement and are becoming more common in American businesses. Preretirement programs may help individuals decide when they should retire by familiarizing them with the benefits and pensions they can expect to receive. These programs also discuss more comprehensive issues, such as physical and mental health. Only about 10 percent of the labor force is involved in such preretirement programs, and these programs have a decided emphasis on benefits, pensions, and health insurance. In one investigation (Atchley, 1976), individuals who had participated in a retirement preparation program had higher retirement incomes, engaged in more activities after retirement, and held fewer stereotyped beliefs about retirement than their counterparts who did not participate in a preretirement program. As indicated in figure 8.6, there are five remaining phases after retirement in this model of the retirement process. Of course, not all people go through all of these phases, nor do they necessarily follow them in the order indicated in the figure. How significant each phase is in the retired person's adjustment depends upon such factors as his or her preretirement expectations and the reality of retirement in terms of money, available options, and the ability to make decisions (Williamson, Munley, & Evans, 1980).

It is not unusual for people to initially feel euphoric during the *honeymoon phase* just after their retirement. They may be able to do many things they never had time for before, and they may derive considerable pleasure from leisure activities. However, people who are forced to retire, or who retire because they are angry about their jobs, are less likely to experience the positive aspects of this phase of retirement. The honeymoon phase eventually gives way to a routine. If the routine is satisfying, adjustment to retirement is usually successful. Those whose lifestyles did not entirely revolve around their jobs before retirement are usually able to make the retirement adjustment and develop a satisfying routine more easily than those who did not develop leisure activities during their working years.

Even individuals who initially experience retirement as a honeymoon usually feel some form of letdown or, in some cases, feelings of depression. Preretirement fantasies about the retirement years may be unrealistic. Atchley calls this the *disenchantment phase.* For some, the disenchantment with retirement centers on the experience of loss—loss of power, prestige, status, income, and purpose. Many retired persons also experience the loss of specific work roles (and their own importance) as well as the loss of routine and diminished work-related friendships (Jacobs, 1989).

At some point, most individuals who become disenchanted with retirement begin to reason realistically about how to successfully cope with it. The major purpose of this *reorientation phase* is to explore, evaluate, and make some decisions about the type of lifestyle that will likely lead to life satisfaction during retirement. The *stability phase* of retirement is attained when individuals decide upon a set of criteria for evaluating choices in retirement and how they will perform once they have made these choices. For some, this phase may occur after the honeymoon phase, whereas for others the transition is slower and more difficult.

According to Atchley (1983), at some point the retirement role loses its significance and relevance in the eyes of the older person. The autonomy and self-sufficiency developed in the stable phase may begin to give way to dependency on others, both physically and economically. This final phase of retirement is called the *termination phase.* Because people retire at different ages and for a variety of reasons, there is no immutable timing or sequencing to the seven phases of the retirement process described by Atchley.

Some experts question the need for a phase approach. They see retirement, like other life transitions, as a lengthy process of adjustment. Ekerdt, Bosse, and Levkoff (1985), for example, evaluated the adjustment of 293 men to retirement over a three-year period. Examination of life satisfaction and leisure activities at six-month intervals revealed little support for a phase approach to retirement. The men simply took different amounts of time to examine and make choices about this new era in their lives. These authors suggest that retirement is best conceptualized as a process of adjustment.

## Retirement Adjustment Styles

Other experts studying retirement consider the importance of factors such as previous lifestyle or the importance of work for the individual. Hornstein and Wapner (1985), for instance, questioned whether all individuals experience retirement in the same fashion suggested by phase theorists such as Atchley. Through in-depth interviews of twenty-four individuals obtained one month prior to and six to eight months following retirement, Hornstein and Wapner identified four distinctive retirement styles. The first style they called *transition to old age.* Individuals who typified this style felt that retirement was a time to disengage or wind down rather than undertake new activities. One respondent reported it was too late to create new hobbies or interests: "If you've never been a gardener, you're not going to become one now." The adults in this group believed that retirement marked a transition to old age, much like the rites of passage marked transitions at other periods of development. For them, retirement was the shedding of pressure-filled work roles and the adoption of a restful and enjoyable lifestyle as they moved into old age.

A second style, the *new beginning,* viewed retirement as a welcome opportunity; a chance to live life on one's own terms and to have the freedom to devote time and energy to oneself. For individuals in this group, retirement was marked by feelings of renewal, revitalization, enthusiasm, and increased vigor. These individuals responded to retirement enthusiastically: "It's a whole new life. There's so much I want to do that I almost don't know where to start." People with this style view the future positively as a time to gain control over long-overdue goals and pleasures (hobbies, interests, volunteerism, and so on) and to become the person they always wanted to be. Retirement for these individuals is a new beginning and wholly unconnected to becoming old.

A third style was that of *continuation.* For individuals who adopted this style, retirement carried no major personal impact. These adults were able to continue working, despite having retired. They either changed positions, shifted careers, or devoted greater time to a special skill, hobby, or interest. Thus, work remained a central organizer in their life structure because they voluntarily chose this activity. These individuals differentiated preretirement and retirement not by activity, but by the lessened pace and intensity of the work role. Retirement for people with this style was essentially a nonevent that signified neither an end nor a beginning.

The last retirement style, *imposed disruption,* represented a significant role loss. The people with this style saw retirement in largely negative terms (loss of work, the inability to continue achievement). For the individuals representing this style, work was a role in which they had invested significant parts of their self-identity; without work, a crucial part of their identity was terminated. Although in time retirement becomes a period in which substitute activities evolve, an underlying sense of frustration and loss remains. Nothing seems to replace work for these individuals and retirement is never truly accepted well. Table 8.6 summarizes these four unique styles of adapting to retirement. Hornstein and Wapner (1985) help us see that the transition to retirement depends on a person's previous orientations to work, to life, and to self.

Braithwaite, Gibson, and Bosly-Craft (1986) have also examined the differential styles of adjusting to retirement. Their research focused on the elderly who really never come to terms with their retirement and continue to have problems coping. Those poorly adjusted to retirement generally showed (1) poor health, (2) negative attitudes toward retirement, (3) difficulty making transitions and adjustments throughout the life span, and/or (4) inability to confront job loss. The first two traits predicted retirements characterized by low levels of activity and involvement, physical and mental health problems, insufficient income, and low levels of life satisfaction. The latter two traits were problems for the short term only; these individuals usually made more adaptive responses to retirement over time.

*Retirement for some means a continuation of mentally-challenging skills such as the Japanese board game* Go *and social participation with friends.*

*TABLE 8.6*

| Dimensions of the Four Modes of Adaptation to Retirement | | | | |
|---|---|---|---|---|
| ***Dimension*** | ***Group 1—Transition to Old Age*** | ***Group 2—New Beginning*** | ***Group 3—Continuation*** | ***Group 4—Imposed Disruption*** |
| Significance or central meaning of retirement | End of working life; time to slow down; beginning of transition to last phase of life (old age) | Beginning of new phase of life; time to live in accordance with *own* needs, not those of others | No major significance except as time to continue preretirement activities in more self-chosen way | Loss of most highly valued activity; period of frustration, lack of focus |
| Style of making the transition itself | Gradual disengagement from work; transition taken as very meaningful | Rapid disengagement from work; desire to plunge ahead into retirement itself | Minimal sense of transition | Abrupt break with work; "in shock," at a loss for how to proceed |
| Dominant emotions during the transition period | Reflectiveness; introspection | Excitement; enthusiasm; revitalization; sense of freedom | Quiet satisfaction | Depression; anger; powerlessness |
| Attitude toward work | Enjoyable but pressured; often frustrating in recent years | In many cases, unsatisfying; in others, satisfying but pressured and draining | Either highly valued and satisfying or not very meaningful, no real investment | Main source of self-definition and identity; allowed time to actualize valued parts of self |
| Relation of retirement to sense of self | No change—continuity of self before and after | Retirement allows for birth of new part of self | No change—continuity of self before and after | Retirement represents loss of valued part of self |
| Orientation toward time | Past is satisfying but over; future is constricted; focus is on present | Relief that past is over; future is expanding, filled with opportunity; focus is on actualization of future in present | Future is expanding but based on past; focus is on continuing past in present and future | Past is highly valued; future is constricted; present is "a void," focus is on maintaining past in the present |

*From G. A. Hornstein and S. Wapner, "Modes of Experiencing and Adapting to Retirement" in* International Journal of Aging and Human Development, *21(4):302–303.* 

## Adjustment to Retirement: Activities and Lifestyles

There is no evidence that one single lifestyle will bring about a successful adjustment to retirement. However, it is important that retirees feel that they have choices and control in the way they experience retirement. The fewer choices a person perceives, the greater the dissatisfaction with retirement. If social contacts are sought and maintained, individuals in retirement will be happy. On the other hand, some retirees derive considerable pleasure from having the freedom to spend time alone. Larson, Zuzanek, and Mannel (1985) reported that among retired persons, 50 percent of the waking day was spent alone. Even among married couples in retirement, 40 percent of the waking day was spent in solitude. The investigators hypothesize that the social

| *Dimension* | *Group 1—Transition to Old Age* | *Group 2—New Beginning* | *Group 3—Continuation* | *Group 4—Imposed Disruption* |
|---|---|---|---|---|
| Extent of change in overall life focus | Preretirement focus abandoned | Preretirement focus replaced with new focus | Preretirement focus maintained in slightly changed form | Attempt to maintain preretirement focus despite changed circumstances |
| General level of activity (postretirement) | Tired, less energy than before; generally passive | Highly active, energetic | Moderately active; no real change | Largely immobilized (in a psychological sense); passive, low activity |
| Nature of retirement goals and activities | No clear sense of direction; too late to start major new projects; mainly continuation on diminished level of earlier activities and hobbies in satisfying way | Either clearly articulated specific goals for new projects and activities or movement toward articulation of such goals | Clearly articulated goals but no new activities; previously valued activities continued in generally same form | Some goals, but not experienced as satisfying; frustrated attempt to find activities to substitute for work; mainly involved with daily activities, hobbies in nonsatisfying way |
| Attitude toward old age | Inevitable next stage of life; no choice but to accept it | Denial of connection between retirement and old age; no sense of identification with "old people," "retirees"; feel younger, not older | No particular feelings about it; no clear sense of connection between retirement and old age | Feel as if others see them as old; feel they are not old and should be working; apprehension about idea that retirement is connected to old age |

needs of some older individuals are less intense than those of younger people, since time spent alone was not viewed negatively by the retirees themselves.

In contrast, a study by Hooker and Ventis (1984) reported that satisfaction with retirement among thirty-four men and forty-two women, all between the ages of 53 and 88, was directly proportional to the total number of activities in which they were involved. Moreover, when such activities were perceived by retirees to be "useful," satisfaction in retirement was enhanced. Hooker and Ventis provide support for the **busy ethic,** a theory of successful retirement developed by Ekerdt (1986). Ekerdt believes that in retirement individuals must transfer or channel the work ethic into productive, useful activities. By keeping busy, retirees remain productive within the freedom provided by retirement. Among the most common busy activities are community service, skill development and enhancement, profitable hobbies, and education. The retiree retains the feeling of being useful and a contributing part of society. In addition, these activities provide justification for taking time out for oneself (e.g., scheduling vacations between volunteer activities or resting after a morning of running errands for a friend). The busy ethic also provides a way to distance oneself from the effects of aging. Recently the impact of continued employment among retirees choosing to engage in work was studied (Mor-Barak, Scharlack, Birba, & Sokolov, 1992). Those who used their retirement to engage in other work roles were able to create significantly larger social networks of friends. Van-Tilburg (1992) reported that among recent retirees who did not work, the size of social networks decreased with the loss of many friends from work. However, those friendships that remained, although smaller in number, became more intensified and emotionally supportive and were sustained through reciprocity.

The importance of work friends in later life is the focus of recent research using a *convoy model* of social support (Antonucci & Akiyama, 1991b; Bosse, Aldwin, Levenson, Spiro, & Mroczek 1993; Francis, 1990). The convoy model (see earlier in the text for a discussion of social convoys) suggests that older individuals take with them into aging close friends, family, neighbors, and relatives who define their immediate social support network. Convoys provide one direction for the busy ethic by offering the older person an opportunity to contribute directly to the welfare of others in the social convoy, for example, reciprocity. Morgan, Schuster, and Butler (1991) report that from middle age through age 85 plus people report giving more support to others than they receive when both instrumental and emotional support are considered. These results have been extended to blacks as well as whites; however, black women were less likely than white women to provide instrumental support to others but in old age were more likely than white women to receive instrumental support (Silverstein & Waite, 1993). Personal problems are infrequently discussed with former coworkers and coworker confidants are characteristic of less than 25 percent of retirees (Bosse, Aldwin, & Levenson, 1990; Depner & Ingersoll-Dayton, 1988). Convoys allow coworkers to maintain their self-esteem, "provide continuity between past and present and forge an integrated continuous sense of self" and help in adapting to the discontinuities in later life (Francis, 1990). Retired men appear to experience consistent levels of qualitative support from their most trusted coworkers; yet, the overall number of coworkers with whom retirees maintain contact and exchange support is quantitatively smaller in size (Bosse, Aldwin, Levenson, Spiro, & Mroczek, 1993). Ekerdt (1986) and colleagues (Ekerdt & DeViney, 1990) suggest, through the busy ethic, retirees are viewed as still a valuable and contributing part of society. Of course, not all retirees adhere to this ethic (see, e.g., Hornstein & Wapner, 1985), nor should they.

## Adjustment to Retirement: Predictive Factors

Who adjusts best to retirement? Overall, older adults who adjust best to retirement are healthy, have adequate incomes, are active, are well educated, have extended social networks including both family and friends, and usually were more satisfied with their lives before they retired (Palmore et al., 1985). Older adults with inadequate incomes, poor health, and other stresses that occur at the same time as retirement, such as the death of a spouse or health concerns, have the most difficult time adjusting to retirement (Stull & Hatch, 1984). Women appear to be more vulnerable than men in making a positive adjustment to retirement given the economic disadvantages that they have experienced throughout their work lives (Perkins, 1992). Increasingly, our society is also encountering women who have been previously married but who enter retirement as single persons, alone, economically disadvantaged, and at greater risk of adjusting poorly to retirement (Hatch, 1992). Like their male counterparts, women may experience retirement as a loss in self-image, productivity, usefulness, and social opportunity. Women who cope best are those with higher levels of education and those with better health status (Szinovacz & Washo, 1992).

Overall, about 15 percent of older people have major difficulties adjusting to retirement. The most frequent difficulties in adjustment are found among workers whose health limitations force a retirement decision (Henretta, Chan, & O'Rand, 1992; Ruchlin & Morris, 1992). In recent years, investigators have also focused their interest on retired workers in business, retirees who were college professors, and retired professionals who leave their employment voluntarily (Cude & Jablin, 1992; Dorfman, 1992). Among retired professors, their perception of the importance of their own scholarship, academic work, or creative effort was the most consistent predictor of their adjustment to retirement. For workers in business, however, a paradoxical finding emerged. Those workers who were most strongly committed to their work roles and business organizations, for example, those who had developed a strong identification with the organizational culture and established a deep employee commitment to the company, had the most difficulty in disengaging from work and accepting retirement. Cude and Jablin (1992) suggest that while organizational commitment leads to productive workers with high morale, acceptance of retirement is more difficult for such workers. These individuals may benefit most from preretirement education and attempts to socialize them into acceptable retirement roles.

Not all workers, of course, have such difficulties. Hall and Rabinowitz (1988) have distinguished between two broad classes of employees: (1) those for whom work represents indeed an intense commitment (highly involved career track) and (2) those for whom work is less intense, an activity or means to an end (less involved career track). Based on analysis of workers at a Motorola assembly plant, Hall and Rabinowitz (1988) charted the likely paths adopted by those highly involved career track workers and those less involved career track workers. Highly involved workers value job enhancement, increased responsibility, career movement, and phased retirement, whereas those with less involved career tracks value more extrinsic rewards, reduction in work assignments, and complete retirement. These latter workers would not be predicted to have much difficulty accepting, enjoying, and welcoming retirement (Hall & Rabinowitz, 1988). For some employees work is an end in itself while for others it is a means to other life opportunities.

Research by Toni Calasanti (1988) focused on the importance of the type of job held by workers in determining their adjustment to retirement. In the past, most investigators were concerned with assessing the degree to which blue-collar versus white-collar workers adjusted to retirement. Today, however, there seems to be a greater variation in salary *within* blue- and white-collar groups of workers than *between* these groups. Also, the distinction between white- and blue-collar jobs has become blurred. White-collar

*Table 8.7*

**Types of Products Produced by Core and Peripheral Industries Involved in the Manufacture of Nondurable Goods**

| Products of Core Industries | Products of Peripheral Industries |
|---|---|
| Food | Textiles—knitting mills |
| Tobacco | Textiles—floor coverings |
| Paper | Apparel |
| Printing, publishing | Tanned and finished leather |
| Chemicals and petroleum | Miscellaneous plastic products |

workers, for example, possess less authority and perform more routinized jobs than they did in the past, whereas the opposite trends have been observed for blue-collar workers.

Calasanti (1988) suggests that to best understand retirement, researchers should begin with the *dual economic model.* This model proposes the existence of two types of firms: *core firms* and *peripheral firms.* Core firms are large and monopolistic. They produce many and varied products so that their income is never totally dependent on one product. Core firms wish to maintain a stable work force because they make use of complex technology and employee training is costly. Thus, employees of such firms receive high wages, command great amounts of power and prestige, and possess the ability to unionize. Peripheral firms make up the competitive sector of our economy. They are usually small, produce one product, and are affected by short-term swings in the national economy. Workers in peripheral companies earn lower salaries and possess less prestige and power than their counterparts in core firms. Both women and blacks are overrepresented in peripheral firms. See table 8.7 for a list of the types of manufactured nondurable goods that are produced by companies within core and peripheral firms in our economy.

Calasanti (1988) compared the responses of retirees from core and peripheral firms on several measures of life satisfaction, happiness, and estrangement. Results showed that the amount of satisfaction and happiness displayed by retirees from core firms was most highly related to their health and physical condition. Retirees from peripheral firms, however, based their satisfaction and happiness primarily on their financial well-being rather than their health. Surprisingly, the educational levels of the retirees from both core and peripheral firms was found to be unrelated to the amounts of satisfaction and happiness they experienced during retirement. Calasanti's work suggests that adjustment to retirement is (1) critically dependent on which portion of the economic sector (core or peripheral) one belongs to during adulthood, and (2) somewhat independent of the demographic factors (e.g., educational level) that in the past have been found to be successful predictors of retirement satisfaction.

## Theories of Retirement

There are three types of theories about the effects of retirement on the retiree (Palmore, 1984; Palmore et al., 1985). Some, such as Atchley's, consider retirement to have particular influences in phaselike fashion. Other theories consider retirement a "crisis," with retirees experiencing generally negative transitions due to loss (e.g., the loss of occupational role identity). A third class of theories views retirement from the standpoint of continuity or positive adaptation. In continuity theories, one's occupational identity, though important, is not the sole basis for one's self-concept or feelings of worth. In fact, for many older Americans, retirement is a challenge for positive adaptation. New leisure roles, the intensifying of long-standing friendships and the development of new ones, time for self-indulgence, hobbies, family, and travel are positive aspects of retirement. Retirement, in this view, is not a decision or a single event but a long-term process that presents continual opportunities and challenges as retirees structure, define, and construct adaptive responses.

## Summary

Work has been an important part of all cultures throughout history. In the last hundred years, substantial changes in the nature of work have taken place. In our postindustrial society we have witnessed a significant increase in jobs related to human services, jobs that usually require extensive training and education. In the future, changes in the nature of work are likely to be influenced by energy costs.

Virtually all vocational theories stress the importance of the exploration of a wide array of career alternatives. At some point in the late teens or twenties, individuals usually enter an occupation. Doing so signals the beginning of new roles and responsibilities. Career expectations are high and the demands are real; established workers may serve as mentors in socializing new workers to occupational success. In middle adulthood, most men attain the highest status and income in their careers; women do likewise if they have been employed most of their adult years. But there are some interesting exceptions in middle adulthood of people who start over and select a new career for various reasons. One aspect of midlife career change involves adjusting idealistic hopes to realistic possibilities in light of how much time is left in an occupation. Of particular interest are the factors related to occupational mobility in adulthood. Many individuals continue their work into late adulthood, and productivity in old age is often the rule rather than the exception.

Almost all workers see their jobs as a way of earning a living. But work also has other meanings for most workers—prestige, contact with the outside world, and social relationships. The achievement motive is one of the most important human motives involved in work. As a rule, the higher the adult's achievement motivation, the more likely he or she will choose work characterized by risk and challenge. Our work ethic—the intrinsic worth involved in doing the best possible job regardless of financial reward—seems currently to be very strong. Nonetheless, worker productivity is either stagnant or decreasing. One explanation for this suggests that workers believe they are the least likely to benefit from increased productivity.

No change in the labor force has been as great as the increased participation of women. Though discrimination has been reduced, it has not been eliminated. Early adulthood is a critical time in a woman's decision making about work. The timing of decisions about marriage, childrearing, education, and the commitment to work have long-term implications for the lives and careers of women.

We not only need to learn how to work well, we also need to learn how to relax. Although television viewing dominates the leisure time of older adults, many actually prefer a variety of other activities if given a choice. Sports, experienced either directly or vicariously, also play an important role in the leisure activities of many adults. Constructive leisure activities in midlife may be helpful in making the transition from work to retirement. Pets are one leisure interest that assist both community-residing adults in retirement and older adults in institutions.

By 62 years of age, many workers choose to retire—men far more so than women. In a recent analysis of predictors of early retirement, subjective factors such as health, attitudes toward work and retirement, and adequacy of current finances were all significant predictors. With the virtual elimination of mandatory retirement, the roles of health, finances, personality, lifestyle, commitment to work, and the nature of the job become critical predictors of when people choose to retire. Some social scientists believe that we go through a series of phases before and after retirement—the remote, near, honeymoon, disenchantment, reorientation, stability, and termination phases. Others see retirement as a continuous process of adjustment with distinctive styles of adaptation rather than a single event with a phaselike mode of adaptation.

## Review Questions

1. Describe the social and historical contexts of work.
2. What are the main theories of occupational choice? Describe the roles of exploration, planning, and decision making in occupational choice.
3. Discuss the developmental course of work once one enters an occupation.What is the changing nature of the work environment likely to mean to workers embarking on careers today?
4. What are some of the different meanings of work for men and women? How is the nature of work different for men and women?
5. Discuss the achievement motive and work. What are today's workers likely to value in their search for a successful career?
6. What factors influence the psychological meaning of job loss? How do they operate?
7. Describe the changing role of women in the labor force. Discuss the achievement orientation and career development of females in early adulthood.
8. Describe the importance of leisure in adult life, in particular during the middle adult years. Outline the kinds of leisure activities adults engage in after they retire.
9. What changes would you recommend in social policy regarding work and retirement given the increasing ratios of retirees to workers? Explain.
10. Describe the factors promoting successful retirement. What factors help determine successful adjustment to retirement?

## For Further Reading

Gerson, K. (1986). *Hard choices: How women decide about work, career, and motherhood.* Berkeley, CA: University of California Press.

Neulinger, J. (1981). *The psychology of leisure.* New York: Thomas.

Okun, B. F. (1984). *Working with adults: Individual, family, and career development.* Monterey, CA: Brooks/Cole.

Palmore, E. B., Burchett, B. M., Fillenbaum, G. G., George, L. K., and Wallman, L. M. (1985). *Retirement: Causes and consequences.* New York: Springer.

Turner, B. F., & Troll, L. E. (Eds.). (1993). *Women growing older: Psychological perspectives.* Thousand Oaks, CA: Sage Publications.

9

# Personality and Moral Development

*How many cares one loses when one decides not to be something, but to be someone.*
—Coco Chanel

*The meeting of two personalities is like the contact of two chemical substances; if there is any reaction, both are transformed.*
—Carl Jung

## *Introduction*

In this chapter we attempt to define personality and survey a number of theoretical perspectives used in studying adult personality development. We begin our discussion with Erik Erikson's and Daniel Levinson's stage theories of adult personality development. Next, we turn our attention to a number of longitudinal studies that have examined the stability of a variety of personality traits over the adult years. Then, we describe the contextual or life-events view of adult personality and discuss the importance of individual variation in adult personality. We end this chapter with a discussion of another important aspect of adult personality: the development of morality. We devote special attention to the relationship between moral development and an adult's ability to cope with significant life events.

## *What Is Personality?*

*So many of us define ourselves by what we have, what we wear, what kind of house we live in and what kind of car we drive. . . . If you think of yourself as the woman in the Cartier watch and the Hermes scarf, a house fire will destroy not only your possessions but your self.*
—Linda Henly

First of all, what is personality? It is hard to find agreement on an answer to this question because the answer often hinges on the theoretical view one adopts. Personality is sometimes thought of as a person's most revealing or dominant characteristic. Thus we might describe one person as having a "shy personality" and another person as being an "extrovert." Following are three more formal definitions of personality:

> [Personality is] the dynamic organization within the individual of those psychophysical systems that determine his characteristic behavior and thought (Allport, 1961, p. 28).

> [Personality is] a person's unique pattern of traits (Guilford, 1959a, p. 5).

> [Personality is] the most adequate conceptualization of a person's behavior in all its detail (McClelland, 1951, p. 69).

*Personality traits such as independence generally remain enduring characteristics of adults and older persons.*

As Walter Mischel (1981) concludes, a common theme runs through these and other definitions of personality, namely that **personality** refers to distinctive patterns of behavior, thought, and emotion that characterize each person's typical adaptation to situations in his or her life.

Personality psychologists often differ substantially in their views of human behavior. Sigmund Freud (1949) emphasized the importance of unconscious motives outside the adult's awareness, the sources of which lie deeply buried in the past. B. F. Skinner (1990), in contrast, stressed the importance of learned behavior in understanding personality. He suggested that the things a person does—his or her overt behaviors, not his or her unobservable, unconscious wishes—are the primary sources of personality. Clearly, great variability exists in the way theorists view personality.

Disagreement also exists about how effectively we can measure personality. To assess the validity of various personality theories, we need to state the theories in scientifically testable terms. Behavioral theories are stated in perhaps the most testable terms, whereas psychoanalytic theories are stated in the least testable terms. For behaviorists, personality is observable behavior. Many theorists, however, believe that the behavioral view leaves out much of the richness and complexity of personality. Psychoanalytic theorists believe that the internal dynamics of a person's mind, not observable behavior, constitute the core of personality. But it is not easy to measure the internal dynamics of personality.

How do we measure something so global and yet so rich in diversity as an adult's personality? Many psychologists suggest a simple procedure: ask the person about his or her personality. However, people do not always perceive themselves in objective terms. Some personality psychologists believe that we must study people under carefully controlled experimental conditions; others argue that we can only understand individuals by studying them under naturalistic, lifelike conditions. Furthermore, as Kogan (1990) has stated that to truly understand the course of adult personality development, it is absolutely necessary to use research designs that can separate the effects of age from generational and sociohistorical influences. One astute observer of personality in adulthood, George Valliant (1977), stressed that lives are ". . . too human for science, too beautiful for numbers, too sad for diagnosis, and too immortal for bound journals" (p. 11).

## *The Stage Approach to Adult Personality Development*

*We grow neither better or worse as we get old, but more like ourselves.*
—Mary Lamberton Becker

Recall that one of the major issues in our study of adult lives is the extent to which a person develops in a stage or nonstage manner. A number of personality theories have emphasized stages of child development while virtually ignoring possible stages of adult development. The assumption in such theories—the most prominent being Freud's (1949) psychoanalytic theory—is that the major changes in personality development occur during childhood, *not* adulthood. Freud, for example, asserted that an individual enters the final stage of personality development during adolescence.

Other stage theories, however, are not so narrow in focus. Life-span developmental theories emphasize the series of stages that unfold throughout the life cycle. The most prominent of these views is the psychosocial theory of Erik Erikson, who has described life-span personality development in terms of eight stages.

### Erik Erikson's "Eight Stages of Man"

One serious problem with traditional psychoanalytic thinking arises from the fact that Freud neglected the importance of culture. He failed to see that each society socializes children and adults in very different ways. The strong influence that culture exerts on the timing and dynamics of each stage is a theme reflected in the work of Erik Erikson.

Erikson's theory (Erikson 1963, 1968, 1982; Erikson, Erikson, & Kivnick, 1986) is particularly important because it traces the development of rational or ego processes, and because it casts a life-span frame of reference on development. Erikson accepted the basic outline of Freud's theory. He thought that psychologists should study the **psychosexual development** of the child. That is, we should be interested in how developing individuals deal with pleasurable body sensations. At the same time, however, Erikson saw the need to pay closer attention to the individual's **psychosocial development** across the entire life span. That is, Erikson believed that we should place our strongest emphasis on the lifelong relationship between the developing individual and the social system of which she is a part. Borrowing from the terminology used in chapter 6, it seems reasonable to suggest that Erikson envisioned a dialectic relationship between the individual and society. Both the society and the individual *change* each other and *are changed by* each other.

However, Erikson did not view individuals or societies as changing in a random or chaotic manner. Instead, Erikson's theory is based on the premise that development throughout life is influenced by an underlying genetic plan common to all members of our species. The guiding impetus for growth according to this genetic plan is what Erikson called the **epigenetic principle.** Epigenesis operates in a social and cultural context, not in a vacuum. Furthermore, Erikson believed that human cultures are structured to help the individual along the epigenetic pathway. His theory emphasizes the interaction between epigenesis (genetics) and culture (environment) in understanding human development. Erikson's views on this matter are beautifully summarized in the following passage:

> "The human personality develops in stages predetermined in the growing person's readiness to be driven toward, to be aware of, and to interact with a widening social radius; and society, in principle, tends to be constituted so as to meet and invite this succession of potentialities for interaction and attempts to safeguard and encourage the proper rate and the proper sequence of their unfolding." (Erikson, 1963, p. 270)

Erikson postulated eight stages of development—sometimes called the *Eight Stages of Man.* Each stage centers around a salient and distinct emotional concern stemming from biological pressures within the person (epigenetic principle) and sociocultural expectations outside the person (environment). The concerns or conflicts at each stage may be resolved in a positive and healthy manner or in a pessimistic and unhealthy way. Each conflict offers a polarity and overshadows all the others for a unique time period. Earlier stage conflict must be resolved satisfactorily for the successful resolution of conflicts appearing at later stages of development.

Erikson did not believe that successful resolution of a stage crisis is always completely positive in nature. Some exposure and/or commitment to the negative end of a conflict is often inevitable. However, in a healthy solution to a stage crisis, the positive resolution of the conflict is dominant.

Erikson's stages of psychosocial development are listed in table 9.1. The table also indicates (1) the social sphere within which each conflict occurs, (2) the self-definition that arises during the course of each conflict, and (3) the virtue (psychological strengths) that may evolve if an individual resolves a conflict in a positive manner.

The first stage, *trust versus mistrust*, corresponds to the oral stage in Freudian theory. An infant is almost entirely dependent upon parents for food, sustenance, and comfort. The caretaker is the primary representative of society to the child. And, Erikson assumed that the infant is incapable of distinguishing himself from his caregiver(s). When responsible caretakers meet the infant's needs with warmth, regularity, and affection, the infant will develop a feeling of trust toward the world and in himself. The infant's trust consists of that comfortable feeling that someone will always be around to care for his or her needs, even though the caretaker occasionally disappears. Alternatively, a sense of mistrust or fearful uncertainty can develop if the caretaker fails to provide for these needs.

*TABLE 9.1*

| An Overview of Erikson's Theory of Psychosocial Development | | | | |
|---|---|---|---|---|
| ***Epoch of the Life Span*** | ***Psychosocial Crisis*** | ***Sphere of Social Interaction*** | ***Self-Definition*** | ***Virtue*** |
| Early infancy | Trust vs. mistrust | Mother | I am what I am given | *Hope*—the enduring belief in the attainability of primal wishes in spite of the urges and rages of dependency |
| Late infancy/early childhood | Autonomy vs. shame | Parents | I am what I will to be | *Will*—the unbroken determination to exercise free choice as well as self-restraint in spite of the unavoidable experiences of shame, doubt, and a certain rage over being controlled by others |
| Early childhood | Initiative vs. guilt | Family | I am what I can imagine | *Purpose*—the courage to pursue valued goals while guided by conscience and not paralyzed by guilt |
| Middle childhood | Industry vs. inferiority | Community, school | I am what I learn | *Competence*—the free exercise of dexterity and intelligence in the completion of a serious task |
| Adolescence | Identity vs. confusion | Nation | I am who I define myself to be | *Fidelity*—the ability to sustain loyalties freely pledged in spite of the inevitable contradictions of value systems |
| Early adulthood | Intimacy vs. isolation | Community, nation | We are what we love | *Love*—the mutuality of devotion greater than the antagonisms inherent in divided function |
| Middle adulthood | Generativity vs. stagnation | World, nation, community | I am what I create | *Care*—the broadening concern for what has been generated by love, necessity, or accident |
| Late adulthood | Integrity vs. despair | Universe, world, nation | I am what survives me | *Wisdom*—a detached yet active concern for life bounded by death |



*Autonomy versus shame and doubt* is the second stage and corresponds to the anal stage in Freudian theory. The infant begins to gain control over bowels and bladder. Parents begin imposing demands on the child to conform to socially acceptable methods for eliminating wastes. The child may develop the healthy attitude of self-control over his or her own actions (not just bowel and bladder) or may develop the unhealthy attitude of shame and doubt because he or she is incapable of control.

*Initiative versus guilt* corresponds to the phallic period in Freudian theory. The child is caught in the midst of the Oedipal or Electra conflict, with its alternating love-hate feelings for the parent of the opposite sex and with fear of fulfilling the sexual fantasies that abound. The child may discover ways to overcome feelings of powerlessness by engaging in various activities. If so, a healthy attitude of being the initiator of action results. Alternatively, the child may fail to discover such outlets and feel guilt at being dominated by his or her primitive urges.

*Industry versus inferiority* coincides with the Freudian period of latency. This stage represents the years of middle childhood when the child is involved in the absorption of knowledge and the development of physical skills as the child is drawn into the social culture of peers. If children view themselves as basically competent in these activities, feelings of productivity and industry will result. On the other hand, if children view themselves as incompetent, particularly in comparison with peers, then they will feel unproductive and inferior.

*Identity versus identity confusion* is roughly associated with Freud's genital stage. The major focus during this stage is the formation of a stable personal identity. For Freud, the important part of identity formation resided in the adolescent's resolution of sexual conflicts; for Erikson, the central ingredient is the establishment of a sense of mutual recognition between the adolescent and the society of which he or she is a part. The adolescent needs to view society as decent, moral, and just. And the adolescent must come to believe that his or her existence is valued by society-at-large. Mutual recognition of this sort leads to feelings of personal identity, confidence, and purposefulness. Without mutual recognition, the adolescent may feel confused and troubled.

Most of Erikson's work on identity formation has focused on young men. Ann Constantinople (1976) was one of the first psychologists to study identity formation in women. She discovered that both males and females showed positive identity growth throughout the college years. She also found that women possessed a better sense of personal identity than men when they entered college. But at the end of the college years, men, rather than women, displayed a more positive identity! Differences in the manner in which males and females were socialized in the 1960s may explain these results. Men were usually expected to become independent during adulthood, to "become their own person." Conversely, women were socialized to find husbands and develop an identity as a wife. Because of important sociohistorical change (the growth of the women's movement during the 1970s and 1980s), fewer women rely on a male figure as a basis for their own identity (Skolnick, 1986). Thus, sex differences in identity formation are gradually dissipating. However, some women may still find identity formation more difficult than men do. Consider the following statement made by an adult female college student: "I have always been somebody else's something: my father's daughter, my husband's wife, my children's mom. Now I can begin to be me."

Erikson described three stages of adult personality development. These stages, unlike the earlier ones, do not have parallels in Freudian theory. The first of these adult stages occurs during early adulthood and is termed *intimacy versus isolation.* Young adulthood usually brings a job and the opportunity to form an intimate relationship with a member of the opposite sex. If the young adult forms friendships with others and has a significant, intimate relationship with one individual in particular, a basic feeling of closeness with others will result. A feeling of isolation may result from the inability to form friendships and an intimate relationship.

As we have indicated, the early adult years are a time when individuals usually develop an intimate relationship. At the same time, however, young adults maintain a strong need for independence and freedom. Development during early adulthood, then, often involves an intricate balance of intimacy and commitment on the one hand and independence and freedom on the other. Keep in mind, however, that intimacy and independence are not just concerns in early adulthood; they remain important themes that must be worked and reworked throughout the adult years.

The chief concern of middle-aged adults is to resolve the conflict of *generativity versus stagnation.* The concept of generativity refers to the concern adults have for members of their own generation as well as future generations. Generativity may manifest itself as the desire to help children and adolescents unlock their human potential. Or it may be expressed as the need to become a caring and productive member of one's own generation. Thus, generative adults may conceptualize themselves as caring, giving, and productive. It is during this stage that adults may experience a midlife crisis. For example, some adults may feel a sense of stagnation because they are without children or because they have jobs that have no meaning either for themselves or society. Certain occupations seem to engender generativity, such as teaching, nursing, and social work; however, it is the reflective view of each adult that is the final determinant of generativity or stagnation at this stage.

The ability of the members of our society to deal with the crisis of generativity versus stagnation is captured in the following remarks made by Erikson:

> The only thing that can save us as a species is seeing how we're not thinking of future generations in the way we live. . . . What's lacking is generativity, a generativity that will promote positive values in the lives of the next generation. Unfortunately, we set the example of greed, wanting a bigger and better everything, with no thought of what will make it a better world for our great-grandchildren. That's why we go on depleting the earth: we're not thinking of the next generations. (quoted in Coleman, 1988)

In a recent study, McAdams, de St. Aubin, and Logan (1993) examined age differences in generativity among young (aged 22 to 27), midlife (aged 37 to 42), and older (aged 67 to 72) adults. McAdams et al. collected data on four different dimensions of generativity: *generative concern*—the extent to which an individual feels concerned about the welfare of future generations; *generative strivings*—the specific things that an individual would like to do that would help and nurture—the next generation; *generative action*—a listing of the specific generative behaviors that an individual has actually performed; and *generative narration*—the degree to which salient past memories reflect the basic theme of generativity. Erikson's theory suggests that generativity should peak during middle adulthood and progressively decline throughout old age. Results were partially supportive of Erikson's position. As expected, younger adults displayed, by far, the lowest levels of generativity. Middle-aged adults scored higher than younger but *not* older adults. Thus, it would seem as if the daily

*Table 9.2*

**Some of the Strivings Reported by Younger, Midlife, and Older Adults**

| Age of Participant | Examples of Responses to the Statement "I typically try to . . ." |
|---|---|
| 26-year-old woman | "make my job more interesting"<br>"figure out what I want to do with my life"<br>"be well liked"<br>"make my life more interesting and challenging"<br>"keep up with current events"<br>"make others believe I am completely confident and secure" |
| 40-year-old woman | "be a positive role model for young people"<br>"explain teenage experience to my son and help him work through difficult situations"<br>"provide for my mother to the best of my ability"<br>"be helpful to those who are in need of help" |
| 68-year-old woman | "counsel a daughter who was recently let go from a job due to cutbacks"<br>"help another daughter with her sick child"<br>"help as a volunteer at a nonprofit organization"<br>"offer financial aid to someone, friend or relative, if needed" |

*From D. P. McAdams, E. de St. Aubin, and R. L. Logan, "Generativity Among Young, Midlife, and Older Adults" in* Psychology and Aging, *8:221–230. Copyright 1993 by the American Psychological Association. Reprinted by permission.*

lives of midlife and older adults, much moreso than younger adults, are guided by a need to be generative. This conclusion is illustrated by the responses (see table 9.2) of different-aged adults to the open-ended question, "I typically try to . . ." Finally, McAdams et al. (1993) reported that, within each age group, participants who scored the highest on the generativity measures also displayed the greatest amounts of life satisfaction and happiness.

In the later years, adults enter the stage of *ego integrity versus despair.* This is a time when individuals face their own deaths by looking back at what they have done with their lives. The older person may develop a positive outlook on each of the preceding periods of emotional conflict and resolution. If so, his retrospective glances will reveal a picture of a life well spent, a significant and meaningful life, and the person will be satisfied (ego integrity). However, the older person may have resolved one or more crises in a negative way or been unable to exercise control over life decisions. If so, retrospective glances will yield doubt, gloom, and despair over the worth of one's life. Erikson's own words best capture the richness of his thoughts about the crisis of ego integrity versus despair:

> A meaningful old age, then . . . serves the need for that integrated heritage which gives indispensable perspective on the life cycle. Strength here takes the form of that detached yet active concern with life bounded with death, which we call *wisdom* . . .
>
> To whatever abyss ultimate concerns may lead individual men, man as a psychosocial creature will face, toward the end of his life, a new edition of the identity crisis which we may state in the words, "I am what survives me." (1968, pp. 140–141)

Robert Butler (1963) has given a special name to the older adult's tendency to look back in time and analyze the meaning of his or her life: the **life review.**

## Childhood Attachment and Well-Being in Older Adulthood

Two recent studies have examined the relationship between childhood experiences and psychological functioning during older adulthood. Anderson and Stevens (1993) proposed that the presence of an affectionate partner (e.g., a spouse, close friend, etc.) will diminish the importance of the recalled quality of early parental experiences on the physical and psychological well-being of older adults; whereas the absence of an affectionate partner during old age will result in the opposite set of outcomes. In other words, if no attachment figure is currently available, it is very likely that older adults will symbolically reinstate their parents as the most significant attachment figures in their current lives. Thus, elderly adults who remember their parents as uncaring and cold will display low levels of subjective physical health and high levels of anxiety, depression, and loneliness. Anderson and Stevens also hypothesized that the lack of an affectionate partner will have a much greater effect on older men than women. This is because women seem to display a greater degree of versatility and fluidity in their interpersonal affairs than do men. They are more capable of developing a revised sense of self that transcends their early experiences.

To test these hypotheses, Anderson and Stevens administered a number of standardized measures of health care utilization, psychosomatic symptoms, subjective physical health, self-esteem, depression, and loneliness to 267 adults between 65 and 74 years of age. The attachment status of the participants was determined by their responses to a variety of questions concerning their current marital status, presence of close friends and confidants, and the degree of tension experienced with close relationships. The quality of early parental experiences was measured by participants' rating on the *Parental Bonding Instrument.* This test contains statements pertaining to the quality of early maternal/paternal care such as: "Seemed emotionally cold to me," "Appeared to understand my problems," and "Did not seem to understand what I needed or wanted."

In general, the results of this study were consistent with both the hypotheses upon which it was based. Early experiences with parents have a long-lasting effect on the elderly. This effect, however, was found to be much stronger for unattached older adults, especially elderly males. The only exception was that early parental experiences were related to participants' scores on the psychological but *not* the biological indices of health. Table 9.A contains information about the responses given by unattached men and women on the different tests of physical and psychological health. Note that the results are broken down in terms of participants' memory of the care they were given by their mothers in comparison to their fathers.

Krause (1993), in a related study, estimated the effects of early parental loss on the psychological health of older adults. The participants in this research were 519 adults

At first glance, it seems obvious that Erikson conceptualized the crises that make up the human life span in a linear manner. Moving through the Eriksonian stages seems akin to climbing a ladder. The bottom rung consists of the crisis of trust versus mistrust, while the top rung is represented by the crisis of ego integrity versus despair. This is *not* the picture of the life span, however, that Erikson tried to paint. Erikson envisioned the life span in a cyclical or circular manner. He thought the individuals who are just beginning life (infants and very young children) may be profoundly influenced by individuals who are about to leave life behind (the elderly). Erikson has stated his thoughts on this matter in the following way: "And it seems possible to paraphrase the relation of adult integrity and infantile trust by saying that healthy children will not fear life if their elders have integrity enough not to fear death" (1963, p. 268).

Research Focus 9.1 presents information about the relationship between early experience with parents and subjective well-being during later adulthood. The research described in this box would seem to be a natural extension of Erikson's nonlinear model of personality development.

*TABLE 9.A*

***Correlations Between Measures of Physical and Psychological Health for Unattached Males (n = 51) and Unattached Females (n = 84).***

| | *Health Care Utilization* | *Psychosomatic Symptoms* | *Subjectively Assessed Health* | *Self-esteem* | *Anxiety* | *Depression* | *Attachment* | *Social Integration* | *Reassurance of Worth* |
|---|---|---|---|---|---|---|---|---|---|
| ***Men*** | | | | | | | | | |
| Paternal care | .10 | –.07 | .24* | .33* | .34* | .26* | .39* | .33* | .48* |
| Maternal care | –.05 | .09 | .21 | .48* | .39* | .28* | .47* | .30* | .59* |
| ***Women*** | | | | | | | | | |
| Paternal care | .09 | .10 | –.03 | .09 | .04 | –.03 | .21* | .17 | .08 |
| Maternal care | .04 | .17 | .04 | .18* | .17 | –.05 | .27* | .20 | .20* |

**indicates a statistically significant correlation*

*From L. Anderson and N. Stevens, "Association between Early Experiences with Parents and Well-Being in Old Age" in* Journal of Gerontology: Psychological Sciences, *48:109-116. Copyright © 1993 The Gerontological Society of America.*

approximately 72 years of age, 122 of whom had experienced the loss of a parent because of death, divorce, or separation before 16 years of age. Participants in the "parental loss group" showed diminished feelings of personal control over their lives, had lower levels of formal education, and experienced much higher levels of financial strain.

In general, we think of parents as exerting a profound effect on the psychological health of children and adolescents. For some reason, we seem to believe that we can outgrow the effects of childhood experiences as we age. The research described here casts doubt on these assumptions.

## Daniel Levinson's "The Seasons of a Man's Life"

Daniel Levinson's (1980, 1986, 1987, 1990) vision of adult development was first set out in his well-known book, *The Seasons of a Man's Life* (1978). This book grew out of his research on the personality development of forty middle-aged men. Levinson used biographical case material to illustrate the stages of personality development in adulthood. His interviews were conducted with hourly workers, business executives, academic biologists, and novelists. Though Levinson's major interest was midlife transition, he described a number of phases, stages, and transitions in the life cycle, as indicated in figure 9.1.

The most important concept articulated by Levinson is the individual's **life structure.** The term *life structure* refers to the ". . . underlying pattern or design of a person's life at any given time" (Levinson, 1986, p. 41). A person's life structure is revealed by the choices he makes and by the relationships he enters into. For example, a person may choose to devote a significant amount of time and energy to his occupation and forsake his relationships with his wife, children, and fellow coworkers.

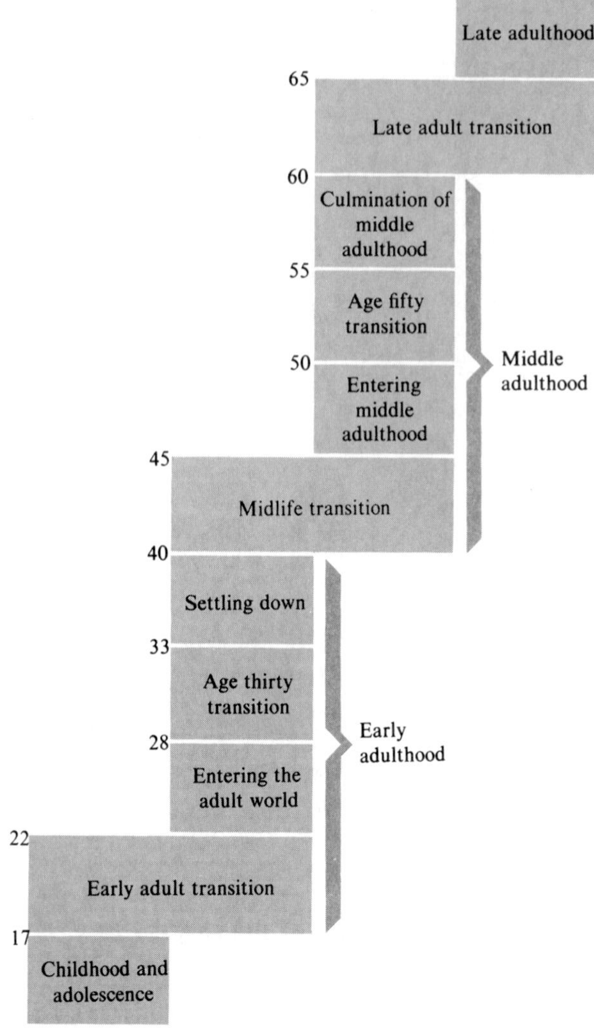


**Figure 9.1**
Development periods in the eras of early and middle adulthood.

Another individual may choose to use her time and energy to help others acquire new competencies and job skills and to become closer to her family. Levinson reminds us that the choices we make concerning marriage and family and occupation are the two most important facets of our life structure. The relationships we have with others, as well as with our work, ". . . are the stuff our lives are made of. They give shape and substance to the life course. They are the vehicle through which we live out—and bury—various aspects of ourselves and by which we participate, for better or worse, in the world around us" (Levinson, 1986, p. 6). Finally, Levinson argues that the life structure changes and evolves over the different periods of the adult life span.

According to Levinson, the human life cycle consists of four different **eras,** each of which has a distinctive character. Like Robert Havighurst (1972), Levinson emphasizes that developmental tasks must be mastered during each of these eras. The eras partially overlap one another, a new era begins as an old era comes to an end. These periods of overlap are referred to as **transitions** and last for approximately five years. As Levinson notes, "The eras and cross-era transitional periods form the macrostructure of the life cycle, providing an underlying order in the flow of all human lives yet permitting exquisite variations in the individual life course" (1986, p. 5).

The first era, *preadulthood,* lasts from conception to about 17 years of age. During this time, the individual grows from a highly dependent infant to beginning to be an independent, responsible adult. The years from 17 to 22 comprise the *early adult transition.* It is at this time that the developing person first starts to modify his relationships with family and friends to help build a place in the adult world.

The next era, *early adulthood,* spans the approximate ages of 22 to 40. This is an era that is characterized by the greatest energy, contradiction, and stress. The major tasks to be mastered are forming and pursuing youthful aspirations (fulfilling a *dream*), raising a family, and establishing a senior position in the adult world. This period can be immensely rewarding in terms of love, occupational advancement, and the realization of one's major life goals. But, due to the demands of parenthood, marriage, and occupation, this era can also be marked by major stressors. We may be terrorized by our own ambitions as well as by the demands of family, community, and society.

The *midlife transition* lasts from about 40 to 45 years of age. By the time many individuals enter this transitional period, they realize they have not accomplished what they set out to do during the early adulthood era. This realization leads to feelings of disappointment and forces the individual to recast earlier life goals. Alternatively, some individuals meet or even exceed their initial dreams. These individuals may soon realize, however, that their outstanding accomplishments did not insulate them from feelings of anxiety and crisis. These negative emotions emerge from several different sources. For example, individuals start to experience themselves as old and physically vulnerable. They become aware of their own aging, as well as the aging (and deaths) of their parents. They begin to view themselves as next in line for death. And they view themselves as the oldest surviving members of their families. Individuals still want to accomplish much, but they feel they have little time left. In essence, these are the characteristics of what other psychologists such as Gould (1972, 1980) and Sheehy (1976, 1981) refer to as the *midlife crisis.* The successful resolution of the midlife transition leads men to refine their goals and prove themselves while separating themselves from mentors and parents—a process that Levinson calls *BOOM* (Becoming One's Own Man).

In the final analysis, Levinson suggests that the midlife transition is a time of crisis and soul-searching that provides us with the opportunity to either become more caring, reflective, and loving or more stagnated, depending on how we accept and integrate the following polarities of adult existence: (1) being young versus old, (2) being masculine versus feminine, (3) being destructive versus constructive, and (4) being attached versus separated from others.

The third era, *middle adulthood,* lasts from about 45 to 60 years of age. This is the time period during which most individuals have the potential to have the most profound and positive impact on their families, their professions, and the world they live in. Individuals no longer concern themselves with their own ambitions. They develop new long-range goals that help them to facilitate the growth of others. This is the time during which adults have the capacity to become mentors to younger individuals. They take pride in the competence and productivity of younger individuals rather than being threatened by them. Furthermore, as individuals enter middle adulthood, they are more able to reap the benefits of family life. In essence, Levinson's ideas about middle adulthood correspond to Erikson's notion of generativity.

The *late adult transition* occurs from ages 60 to 65. It is during this time that older adults experience anxiety because of the physical decline they see in themselves and their agemates, and because they are now "old" in the eyes of their culture. In the *late adulthood era* (65 years of age to death), the individual must develop a way of living that allows him to accept the realities of the past, present, and future. During this era, the individual must come to grips with a crisis that is similar to the Eriksonian idea of ego integrity versus despair.

Levinson (in press) has expanded upon his original work and has argued that his theoretical viewpoint holds true for women as well as men from different cultures, classes, and historical epochs. In a review of four doctoral dissertations, Priscilla Roberts and Peter Newton (1987) found that several aspects of Levinson's model applied to the personality development of young and middle-aged women. This was especially true for Levinson's suggestion that a significant transition occurs at about 30 years of age. There was, however, a major sex difference with regard to the type of dreams that were constructed during early adulthood. Recall that a "dream," in a Levinsonian sense, refers to a set of aspirations that allows an individual to break away from the preadult world and establish an overarching goal for his/her adult life, and that the dreams of young men focus on career-related issues (e.g., rising to a position of power within a law firm). Roberts and Newton (1987) reported that women's dreams were far more complex. In fact, women were likely to experience a *split dream* in which they expressed a concern with both interpersonal relationships *and* occupational accomplishments. Most importantly, women with split dreams tended to have unstable lives. These women were likely to experience a sense of dissatisfaction with either their family lives or their careers. They took longer to settle into an occupation and established fewer mentor relationships. And, even though a large number of these women were married, they found their husbands to be obstacles to their own development. Overall, these results are somewhat supportive of Gilligan's (1982) view that women are more likely to seek a balance between interpersonal attachment and individual accomplishment than are men. It is most unfortunate that our culture, as it presently stands, does not present women with the opportunity to fulfill both of these components of their dreams.

Finally, please note that Levinson's publications, like Erikson's, are not research reports in any conventional sense. They include no statistics to speak of and no quantified results. However, the data reported by Levinson are consistent with the clinical tradition, and the quality and quantity of the rich biographical reporting are certainly intriguing.

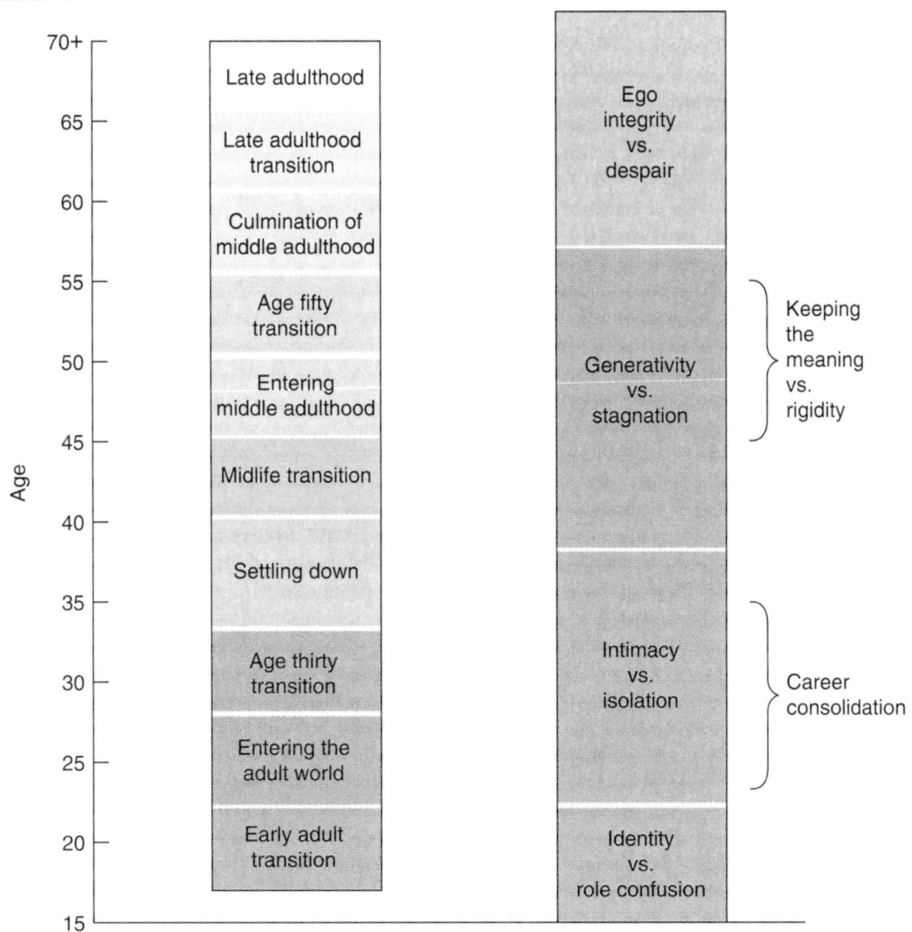


**Figure 9.2** A comparison of the adult stages of Levinson and Erikson.

## Conclusions and Criticisms about Adult Stage Theories

There seems to be reasonable agreement between Erikson and Levinson about the nature of stages in adulthood. Both would concur with a general outline of adult development that begins with a shift from identity to intimacy, followed by a change from career considerations to generativity, and finally marked by the shift from searching for meaning in life (in the face of death) to some final integration. Thus, although each theorist labels the stages differently and views the processes responsible for developmental change uniquely, the underlying themes of adult development are remarkably similar. See figure 9.2 for a comparison of these viewpoints.

Stage theories have a strong intuitive appeal. But, they suffer from four major limitations. First, stage theories are extremely difficult to verify through empirical research (Miller, 1983). For example, how does one find out whether an individual has experienced a particular stage of development? You might follow Erikson's and

Levinson's technique of probing the depths of an individual's personality by conducting a series of long open-ended interviews. Or, you might decide to develop a questionnaire or survey that asks adults how they feel about themselves. The former method would be extremely costly, time consuming, and information could be collected from a rather small (and perhaps nonrepresentative) number of participants. The latter method is certainly more cost effective and may be used to test large numbers of participants. But, could a researcher really capture the essence of the stages and crises articulated by Erikson or Levinson in an objective paper-and-pencil questionnaire? Given these problems, it should come as no surprise that there is considerable debate about whether stage theories are, in fact, truly researchable.

Second, these theorists have a tendency to focus too extensively on stages as *crises* in development, particularly in the case of the midlife crisis. For example, David Featherman (cited in Gallagher, 1993) argued that only about 5 percent of the adult population experiences a midlife crisis, and that those individuals who suffer from crisis at midlife have typically experienced traumas and psychological upheavals throughout their entire lives. Ronald Kessler, the noted sociologist, has maintained that middle age is the "best" time of life. He stated that:

> When looking at the total U.S. population, the best year is fifty. You don't have to deal with the aches and pains of old age or the anxieties of youth: Is anyone going to love me? Will I ever get my career off the ground? Rates of general distress are low—then incidence of depression and anxiety fall at about age thirty-five and don't climb again until the sixties. You're healthy. You're productive. You have enough money to do some of the things you like to do. You've come to terms with your relationships, and the chance of divorce is very low. Midlife is the "it" you've been working toward. You can turn your attention toward being rather than becoming. (Kessler, quoted in *Gallagher, 1993,* p. 51)

George Valliant (1977) also believes that only a minority of adults experience a midlife crisis:

> Just as pop psychologists have reveled in the not-so-common high drama of adolescent turmoil, the popular press, sensing good copy, has made all too much of midlife. The term *midlife crisis* brings to mind some variation of the renegade minister who leaves behind four children and the congregation that loved him in order to drive off in a magenta Porsche with a twenty-five-year-old striptease artist. Like all tabloid fables, there is much to be learned from such stories, but such aberrations are rare, albeit memorable, caricatures of more mundane issues of development. As with adolescent turmoil, midlife crises are much rarer in community samples than in clinical samples. (pp. 222–223)

Valliant's claims about adult personality development were based on data collected during a thirty-year longitudinal research project called the Grant Study. The subjects in this study were initially interviewed when they were students at Harvard University.

Third, there is an increasing tendency for theory and research on adult development to emphasize the importance of personal life events (e.g., a change in occupational or marital status) and major sociocultural factors (e.g., a war or economic depression) rather than using stages or phases to organize development. Alice Rossi

*Over time, different lifestyles and activity patterns have decidedly different consequences on the aging process.*

(1984) observed that most of the individuals studied by Levinson were born right around the time of the depression. What was true for these individuals when they reached age 40 may not be true for the members of more recent cohorts when they reach 40. Rossi suggests that the men studied by Levinson may have been burned out at a premature age (because of the pressures put upon them by their generation) rather than moving through a normal developmental pattern that all adults go through upon entry into midlife.

What events or societal changes do you think have occurred during the latter part of this century that may have led to the birth of the midlife crisis? Do you think that changes in society will heighten or diminish the tendency for members of future cohorts to experience a crisis at midlife?

## The Trait Approach to Adult Personality

*So we talked about some old times and we had ourselves some beers*
*Still crazy after all of these years.*
—Paul Simon

The degree to which personality is stable or changes is a major issue in adult development. This issue can be approached in many different ways. We may evaluate the extent to which childhood personality characteristics predict adult personality characteristics. For example, is an introverted child also an introverted adult? Is a neurotic adolescent also a neurotic adult at midlife? We can ask whether an achievement-oriented woman in early adulthood is still striving hard to be successful at the age of 50. Or to what extent is a depressed 30-year-old still depressed at the age of 70? Further, rather than looking only at the stability of a single personality characteristic, such as introversion, we may evaluate how one or several characteristics present at specific points in the life cycle predict other characteristics at a later point in life. We might also be interested in how social experiences, family experiences, and work experiences predict personality characteristics later in life.

To the extent that there is consistency or continuity from one period of time to another in some attribute of personality, we usually describe personality as being *stable.* In contrast, to the extent that there is little consistency from one period of time to another, we refer to *change* or *discontinuity* in personality.

Personality theorists are often categorized by whether they stress stability in personality across time as well as across situations. Personality theorists called **personologists** or traditional **trait theorists** argue for consistency and stability, whereas contextual, life-events, or stage theorists are likely to maintain that personality changes over time.

## Characteristics of Traits

What is a trait? What are the major assumptions that underlie the trait approach to personality? To help answer these questions, it may be useful to consider the ideas of Paul Costa and Robert McCrae (1980). These psychologists, two of the most influential researchers studying adult personality, have listed a set of principles underlying the trait approach:

1. Traits may be regarded as generalized dispositions to thoughts, feelings, and behaviors that endure over substantial periods of time.
2. Traits have relatively little to do with the determination of single, specific behaviors. Specific behaviors are usually controlled by situational influences. Traits do, however, show an appreciable influence over behaviors that are averaged over long periods of time and over a range of diverse situations.
3. Traits, by their inherent nature, are highly interactive (e.g., trait anxiety is the tendency to experience fear when threatened, sociability involves the tendency to act friendly when in the presence of other people, and so forth). Thus, trait theory recognizes the importance of the *Person X Situation* interaction.
4. Traits are not merely reactive. Traits possess dynamic, motivating tendencies that seek out or produce situations which allow for the expression of certain behaviors. For example, a person who is open to experience may react with interest when presented with a new idea and may actively seek out new situations (by attending lectures, reading books, changing an occupation, and so on) that lead to new experiences.

5. The enduring quality of generalized traits may manifest itself by the emergence of seemingly different types of behaviors that occur at different times in the adult life span. For example, an anxious person may be afraid of rejection in high school, economic recession in adulthood, and illness and death in old age.
6. Traits need not be purely inherited or biologically based. The origin of personality traits can (and should) remain an open question.
7. Traits are most useful in describing and predicting psychologically important global characteristics in individuals. Since traits are sensitive to the generalities in behavior, trait theory is especially useful in giving a holistic picture of the person. It is this feature of trait theory that makes it the ideal basis for the study of personality and aging. If one adopted a radical interactionist or contextual model of personality, one would never attempt to address such global matters as how personality changes with age.
8. The aims of trait theory are compatible with the aims of longitudinal and sequential research. If traits are assumed to endure over time, they must be measured over time. And the influence of cohort and time of measurement on the assessment of traits must be differentiated from age and true developmental relationships.

Now that we have a general understanding of the trait approach, let's look at some of the major studies of personality development that shed light on the stability-change issue as it relates to personality in the adult years.

## The Kansas City Study

One of the earliest longitudinal studies of personality in adulthood was conducted by Bernice Neugarten on a large sample of people aged 40 to 80 (Neugarten, 1964, 1973, 1977; Neugarten & Gutmann, 1968). This study took place over a ten-year period in Kansas City, Missouri. The Kansas City Study was not completely grounded in the trait approach, but the results derived from this research have important implications for trait theory. Dependent measures included a number of projective tests, questionnaires, and several types of interviews designed to gain information about the participants. Neugarten concluded that personality is continuous or stable in a number of respects but that some age-related changes occur as well. The most stable characteristics of personality were socioadaptive characteristics, such as coping styles, methods of attaining life satisfaction, and the strength of goal-directed behaviors. Some consistent age-related differences occurred in various intrapsychic personality dimensions that reflect different feelings about the extent to which one can control one's environment. For example, 40-year-olds felt that they had considerable direct or active control over their environments and risk taking was not a primary concern. However, 60-year-olds were more likely to perceive the environment as threatening and sometimes dangerous. They also had a more passive view of the self. This personality change in adulthood was described by Neugarten as moving from *active to passive mastery.*

*Adults in the later years often choose to spend time reflecting on memories and experiences from the past.*

Movement from active mastery in midlife to a more passive orientation in late adulthood seems to be a salient characteristic of adult development in a number of diverse cultures. Groups of individuals such as Navajo Indians, isolated groups in Israel, and the Mayans of Mexico also seem to move from an active, controlling view of their interactions with the world to a more passive, receptive, less controlling orientation as they age (Gutmann, 1977).

According to Neugarten, older adults also seem more concerned about inner life than middle-aged adults. Older adults in her study were found to be more introspective and self-reflective than younger adults. Neugarten refers to this change in the personality of older adults as **interiority** (Rosen & Neugarten, 1964).

In addition to the growth of passive mastery and interiority, a shift in sex-role expressiveness seemed to occur in late adulthood in the participants of the Kansas City Study. More specifically, it was found that significant sex-role reversals began to take place as people grew older—men became more tolerant and expressive of their nurturant impulses, and women became more tolerant and expressive of their aggressive tendencies (Neugarten, 1973).

With regard to trait theory, the Kansas City data seem to suggest age-related changes on two important personality dimensions: introversion-extroversion, and masculinity-femininity. With age, adults become more introverted, men become more feminine, and women become more masculine. These conclusions seem consistent with David Gutmann's (1977) ideas of adult sex-role development, which were discussed earlier.

## The Normative Aging Study and the Baltimore Longitudinal Study

As already mentioned, two of the strongest advocates of the trait approach to personality are Paul Costa and Robert McCrae. The majority of their research comes from two massive longitudinal studies derived from the Normative Aging Study, which is associated with the Veterans Administration Outpatient Clinic in Boston, and the Baltimore Longitudinal Study of Aging, which is being conducted by the National Institute on Aging. The participants in both of these studies were thousands of relatively well-educated, primarily white, mostly healthy men. They ranged from 20 to 80 years of age. Data collection began in the late 1950s to mid-1960s and is ongoing. Most importantly, the way the data were collected allowed for cross-sectional, longitudinal, and sequential analyses. Thus, the effects of age, cohort, and time of measurement could be determined. Finally, participants in both of these studies were administered an extensive battery of standardized psychometric personality tests. These personality tests, called **self-report inventories,** are designed in such a way that a participant is required to report his or her opinions, feelings, and activities on a wide range of topics.

Costa and McCrae's research (Costa, 1986; Costa & McCrae, 1977, 1978, 1980, 1982, 1985, 1986; McCrae & Costa, 1984, 1987, 1990) has yielded two important findings. First, they discovered that personality can best be conceptualized as consisting of five independent dimensions or factors: *neuroticism, extroversion, openness to experience, agreeableness,* and *conscientiousness.* These five dimensions make up what Costa and McCrae call the **five-factor model** of personality (see figure 9.3). The vast majority of the research on this model involves an analysis of the dimensions of neuroticism, extroversion, and openness to experience. Each of these dimensions of personality contains six different facets. **Neuroticism** encompasses how anxious, stable, depressed, self-conscious, impulsive, and vulnerable the individual is; **extroversion** measures the individual's attachment, gregariousness, assertiveness, activity, excitement-seeking, and positive emotions; and **openness to experience** pertains to the individual's openness with respect to fantasy, aesthetics, feelings, actions, ideas, and values.

The second major finding of this research is that these three dimensions of personality remain remarkably stable over the adult years. This is especially true when the data from these studies are analyzed in a longitudinal or sequential manner rather than a cross-sectional manner. This is not to say that the men did not change in a number of ways. In fact, some of the men and their lives changed a great deal. For example, men who were found to be open to experience were likely to change occupations, live eventful lives, and experience good as well as bad in very forceful ways. Individuals who were rated high in neuroticism found

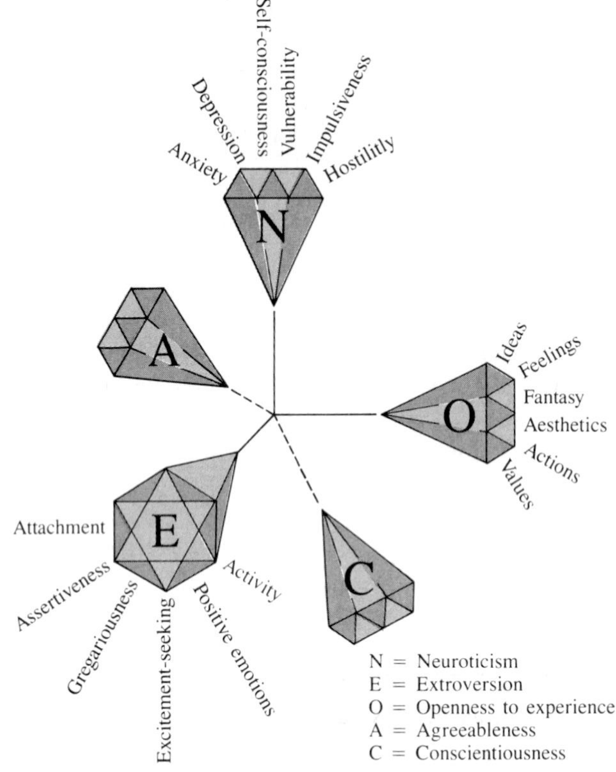


**Figure 9.3** An illustration of Costa and McCrae's five-factor model of personality.

new things about which to complain, worry, and become dissatisfied. What endured over time, of course, were the general orientations or dispositions (i.e., the traits) that the men used to structure their lives.

One potential problem associated with the self-report methodology is that the stability of personality may be a personal illusion. An individual may construct an image of himself in which he believes the major facets of his personality are stable; but, in fact, his personality may have changed to a considerable extent over time. To address this issue, Costa and McCrae (1988) analyzed the self-reports of the participants' in the Baltimore Longitudinal Study as well as ratings of the men's personalities made by their wives. Results showed that, over time, the wives' ratings of the husbands' personalities remained stable on all of the traits within the five-factor model. In a similar set of studies, Conley (1985) found that the traits of neuroticism and extroversion remained stable over periods between 20 to 45 years regardless of whether the participants' self-reports, or ratings made by their spouses or peer acquaintances were considered during data analysis.

Perhaps the results of these studies can be best summed up by examining the following excerpts from a recent interview with Paul Costa:

> I see no evidence for specific changes in personality due to age. What changes as you go through life are your roles and the issues that matter most to you. People

may think that their personality has changed as they age, but it is their habits that change, their vigor, their health, their responsibilities and circumstances—not their basic personality.

There is no evidence for any universal age-related crises; those people who have a crisis at one point or another in life tend to be those who are more emotional. Such people experience some degree of distress through most of life; only the form of the trouble seems to change. After twenty-five, as William James said, character is set in plaster. (quoted in Goleman, 1987)

Other psychologists who have analyzed various aspects of the data collected in the Baltimore Longitudinal Study have reported the same findings as Costa and McCrae. Douglas and Arenberg (1978) found that when these data were analyzed in a cross-sectional manner, there were several traits on which young and older adults differed. For example, older adults were found to be submissive, restrained, or serious-minded—this appears to be an increase in introversion. But more sophisticated statistical analyses revealed that these differences were really due to cohort differences between the participants. The only differences in personality that were found to be due to age (rather than cohort and/or time of measurement) were that the men (1) became less masculine as they aged, and (2) displayed a lower activity level (preferred a slow pace in their lives).

## The Seattle Longitudinal Study

K. Warner Schaie and his associates have been involved in a large-scale longitudinal study in the Pacific Northwest, with a great many participants from the city of Seattle, Washington. As mentioned previously, this research project has produced a wealth of data about intellectual development during adulthood. In this section, we highlight a number of important findings about personality that this research has yielded.

Schaie and Parham (1976) used a variety of methods to analyze the data collected during 1963 and 1970 on a large number of men and women who ranged from 21 to 84 years of age. All of these participants completed a self-report inventory that measured sixteen different personality traits. When the data were analyzed cross-sectionally, many traits (most notably introversion) seemed to change with age. Older adults were found to be more reserved, less outgoing, and so forth. Upon closer scrutiny, however, these age-related differences were found to be due to cohort effects—adults born in earlier generations were more introverted than those born in later generations. In fact, the only dimension of personality that was found to change with age was excitability. This means that older adults were more likely than young adults to become frazzled, annoyed, and frustrated by many of the events of everyday life.

In a more recent study, Schaie and Willis (1991) examined data that was collected on 3,442 participants relative to the personality traits of *behavioral rigidity, attitudinal flexibility,* and *social responsibility* in 1956, 1963, 1970, 1977, and 1984. The participants ranged from 22 to 84 years of age and were from ten different birth cohorts between 1896 to 1959. Given the complex nature of this study,

Schaie and Willis were able to examine the separate (and interactive) influence of age and cohort on personality development. As would be expected, cross-sectional analyses showed that individuals became more rigid and inflexible as they aged, whereas the longitudinal data showed that most traits remained stable until the late sixties, and then displayed small negative age changes thereafter. Furthermore, more sophisticated sequential methods of data analysis indicated that the age differences obtained in the cross-sectional analysis were, in reality, due to cohort or generational influences. This finding led Schaie and Willis (1991) to conclude that, over the last seventy years, there has been a substantial positive change toward more open and flexible behaviors, attitudes, and personality styles in successive generations of individuals. The continuation of this trend would mean that future generations of individuals will be better capable of adapting to changes that will take place in our fast-paced society.

There was, however, one rather disheartening result of the Schaie and Willis (1991) research. Specifically, they found a downward trend across cohorts in the trait of social responsibility. This prompted Schaie and Willis to suggest that ". . . our results . . . support those who see a societal trend of increasing individual adaptation, but lowered concern for the needs of others" (p. 283).

## Berkeley Older Generation Study

The Berkeley Older Generation Study is a longitudinal study of approximately 420 men and women who were first interviewed in Berkeley, California, in 1928 and 1929. The participants in the study have been tested over a fifty-five-year time span that has encompassed their young adulthood, midlife, and older years. In a recent study, Field and Millsap (1991) analyzed the information gathered from the surviving participants in this study during the years of 1969 and 1983. In 1969 two distinct age groups were interviewed: a group of young-old adults (individuals who averaged 65 years of age), and old-old adults (individuals who averaged 75 years of age). In 1983, a group of forty-seven old-old adults (average age of 79) and twenty-one oldest-old (average age of 89) were reexamined. Given this design, Field and Millsap were able to compare the stability of personality for members of two cohorts across a fourteen-year time span.

All of the participants were administered a rather intensive open-ended interview that assessed the traits of: *intellect, extraversion, agreeableness, satisfaction,* and *energetic.* These traits, except for energetic (the degree to which a person feels fresh, energetic, restless, etc.) were very similar to the traits of openness to experience, extraversion, agreeableness, and neuroticism that play a dominant role in Costa and McCrae's model of adult personality development.

The results of this study tell an interesting story. When data from all subjects were taken as a whole, satisfaction and agreeableness remained stable. In fact, satisfaction was, by far, the most stable trait. With regard to this finding, Field and Millsap (1991) commented that it seems very hard for younger persons to understand the continuing satisfaction that older people derive from life considering the

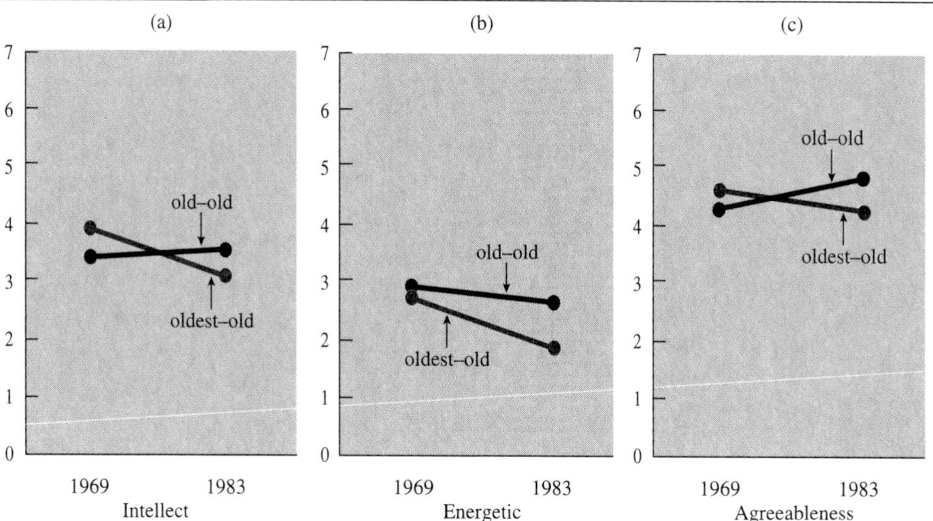


**Figure 9.4**
Significant change over time: Comparing the old-old and the oldest-old persons.

fact that old age is accompanied by significant losses in the interpersonal and physical domains. On the other hand, moderate declines were noted for intellect, energetic, and extraversion. However, as illustrated in figure 9.4, traits of intellect, agreeableness, and energetic changed in a different manner for individuals who, between 1969 and 1983, made the transition from young-old to old-old, and from old-old to oldest-old. Figures 9.4a and 9.4b shows for example, that scores on the dimensions of intellect and energetic declined over time for the people who became the oldest-old but not the old-old. And, figure 9.4c shows that individuals who made the transition to the status of old-old increased in agreeableness, while those who became the oldest-old exhibited stability on this trait. Field and Millsap maintained that the trait of agreeableness is, in all probability, very similar to Erikson's notions of generativity and ego integrity—traits that would be expected, from an Eriksonian position, to increase and stabilize over the later years of life.

In conclusion, Field and Millsap argued that there is a:

> . . . normative developmental increase in *agreeableness,* accompanied by what may be a normative decline in *extraversion,* as well as relative stability in two other traits, *satisfaction* and *intellect,* in advanced old age.
>
> These findings help shatter the common stereotype that personality "rigidifies" in old age, or that people become more conservative or cranky as they age. (p. 307)

Overall, the data obtained by Field and Millsap, as well as other personologists mentioned in this section, have shown that adult personality is remarkably stable over the adult years. There may be profound individual differences, however, in the stability (or instability) of personality over time. Research Focus 9.2 presents some rather surprising data about the mortality rates of older adults who exhibit a stable versus unstable pattern of personality.

## *Stability of Personality and Survival Rates in Old Age*

Developmental research has documented a great deal of interindividual variability with regard to the stability of personality. Some individuals exhibit significant changes in personality while others do not. Hagberg, Samuelsson, Lindberg, and Dehlin (1991) wondered if interindividual differences in the stability of personality were related to survival rates during older adulthood. They suggested that a change in personality could be the end product of a fragile individual personality structure coming into contact with a number of harsh psychological (e.g., loss of a loved one) and/or biological (e.g., illness) stressors. This led them to hypothesize that older adults who displayed stability in personality would live longer than those adults who exhibited a significant change in their personality.

To test their hypothesis, Hagberg et al. employed a unique measure of personality called the *Rod and Frame Task (RFT)*. In the *RFT*, a participant is asked to look into a darkened chamber that contains an illuminated square-shaped frame inside of which is positioned a straight illuminated glass rod. The frame is tilted, by the experimenter, twenty degrees to the right or the left and the participant is asked to turn a knob so that the rod rotates to a true vertical position. There are two distinct patterns of performance on the *RFT*. First, some individuals (see Figure 9.A) are categorized as *field independent*. They are capable of aligning the rod in a true vertical position without being influenced by the tilted frame. Second, other people (see Figure 9.B) are labeled as *field dependent*. They align the rod in a vertical position relative to the tilted frame, but they think they are positioning the rod in a truly vertical manner. In other words, the terms field independent and field dependent signify the degree to which an individual's perceptual judgments are affected by the elements within his visual environment. The perceptual styles of field independence versus field dependence have been found to be related to the personality traits of extroversion, locus of control, and flexibility as well as self-concept and identity status.

**Figure 9.A** A field-independent response on the rod-and-frame task.

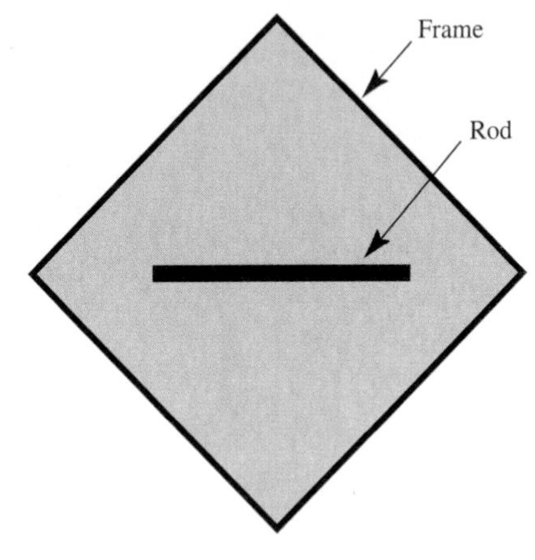


**Figure 9.B** A field-dependent response on the rod-and-frame task.

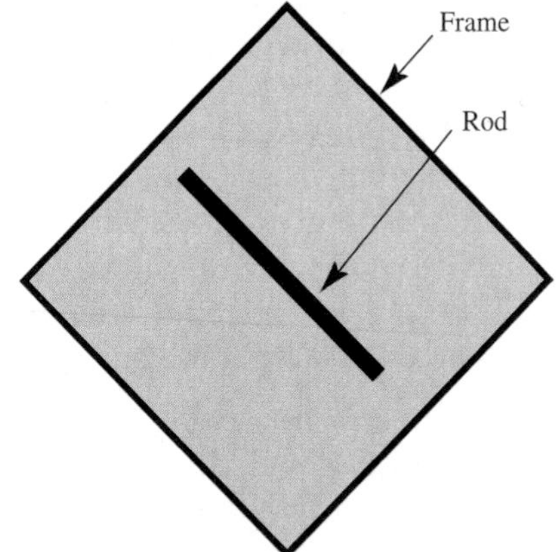


## Conclusions about the Stability of Adult Personality

Costa (1994) has observed that adult personality is characterized largely by stability and continuity rather than extensive change and reorganization. The adult personality seems to be an organized system of traits that resists major alteration. Can you imagine how difficult it would be to adapt to the changing demands of our lives if our core personalities (as well as the personalities of our friends and

**Figure 9.C** The relationship between stability of performance on the rod-and-frame task and survival rates for older males and females.

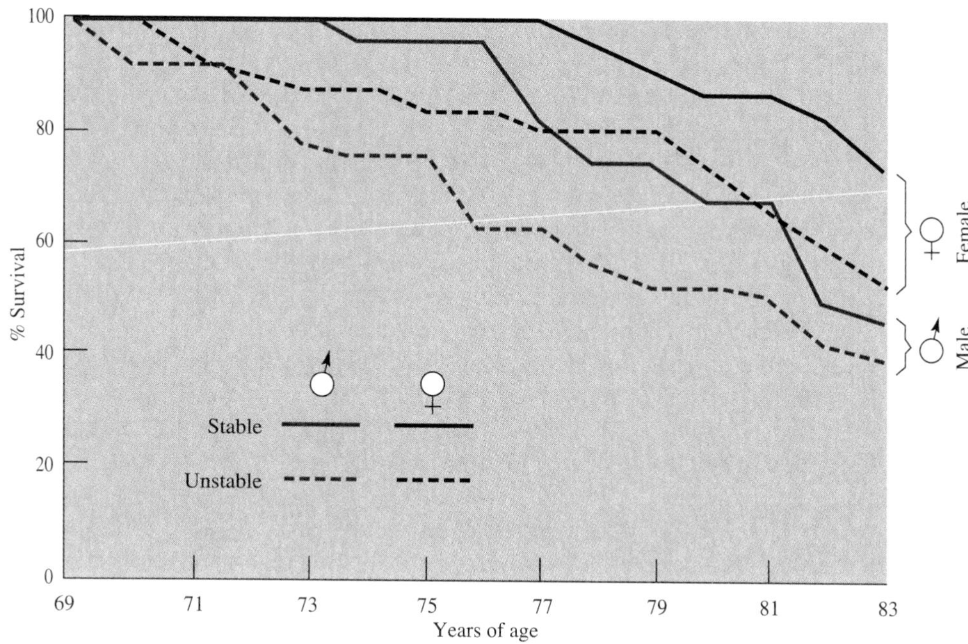


Hagberg et al. (1991) conducted a longitudinal design in which they administered the *RFT* to 113 men and 79 women every second year during a six-year period. Testing began when each participant was 67 years of age. The proportion of survivors was calculated when the participants should have reached 69, 71, 73, 75, 77, 79, 81, and 83 years of age. It was found that about 20 percent of the older adults displayed an unstable pattern of performance on the *RFT* (i.e., they changed from field independence to field dependence (or vice versa) over the six-year testing period). These "unstable" participants (see Figure 9.C) were less likely to survive than the elderly adults who displayed a consistent pattern of performance on the *RFT*. This finding held true for both males and females. Finally, whether participants were classified as field independent or dependent was found to be unrelated to survival rates.

Hagberg et al. concluded that human personality is a tremendously intricate system. In fact, personality is probably so complex that various sorts of perturbations (psychological stress, disease, etc.) that accompany the aging processes, as well as aging itself, can have a significant destabilizing effect. This would help explain why personality change is a sensitive predictor of mortality.

family members) underwent frequent change? With regard to this matter, Krueger and Heckhausen (1993) have recently shown that individuals across the adult life-span tend to have subjective conceptions about adult personality development that are characterized by the growth and/or stability of personality traits until about 60 years of age, followed by a slight decline thereafter. In fact, Krueger and Heckhausen (1993) found that elderly adults were much more optimistic about late-life personality development than were younger or middle-aged adults.

Second, Schaie and Willis (1986) maintained that many of the apparent personality differences between young, middle-aged, and older adults are really caused by generational (cohort) differences rather than age-related differences. Thus, one of the most salient predictors of an adult's personality may be her year of birth rather than mere chronological age. The only personality differences that seem to be due primarily to age are that men seem to become a little more feminine as they age, while women become a little more masculine, and that many older adults decrease their activity levels or their pace of life.

Third, Schaie and Willis (1986) argue that despite the inherent stability of adult personality, the potential for change still exists. For example, even when psychologists find correlations as high as +.70 between personality inventory scores separated by long periods of time in test administration, about 50 percent of the variability in the participants' test scores remains unexplained. Obviously, a portion of this variability is caused by imperfections in the test and the conditions under which it was administered. But another source of variability is probably the real shifts that occur in the personality trait in question. According to Schaie and Willis: "The *average* score for a given trait is likely to remain the same, which means that the people whose scores on the trait increase are balanced by people whose scores decrease. As they grow older, people experience a variety of nonnormative events, changing them in different ways. There is very little *general* change, but there is quite a bit of *individual* change" (1986, p. 157).

Furthermore, the trait approach to adult personality is not totally antagonistic to the stage perspective. For example, it is possible that a specific individual may go through adulthood with a constellation of stable, enduring personality traits; yet this adult may use these stable traits to tackle the different tasks and psychosocial crises that writers like Erikson and Levinson have identified. A person may deal with an identity crisis in adolescence, a midlife crisis at age 40, and a life review at age 75 with the same stable degrees of openness to experience, introversion-extroversion, and neuroticism.

In conclusion, developmentalists should concentrate their energies on both change and stability as well as on the interdependence between the individual and the events of his or her life.

## *The Contextual or Life-Events Framework*

*Everything happens to everybody sooner or later if there is enough time.*
—George Bernard Shaw

An alternative to the stage and trait approaches to adult personality development is the **life-events framework** or contextual model. In the earlier versions of this perspective (e.g., Holmes & Rahe, 1967), it was suggested that major life events produce taxing circumstances for individuals, forcing them to change their personalities. Events such as the death of a spouse, marriage, and divorce were thought to produce increasing degrees of stress and therefore were likely to have an influence on the individual's personality.

More sophisticated versions of the life-events framework (Brim & Ryff, 1980; Dohrenwend, Krasnoff, Askensay, & Dohrenwend, 1978; Hultsch & Plemons, 1979) emphasize the factors that mediate the influence of life events on adult development—physical health, intelligence, personality, family supports, income, and so forth. Some individuals may perceive a life event as highly stressful while others perceive the same event as a challenge.

We also need to consider the sociocultural circumstances within which life events occur. For example, divorce may be more stressful after many years of marriage, when individuals are in their fifties, than when they have only been married a few years and are in their twenties (Chiriboga, 1982b). Also, individuals may be able to cope more effectively with divorce in 1990 than in 1950 because divorce is more commonplace in today's society.

Bernice Neugarten and Nancy Datan (1973) were among the first psychologists to suggest that understanding the nature of adult personality development depends on an analysis of the sociohistorical and personal circumstances within which adult life occurs. They suggested that chronological age has little, if any, bearing on adult personality. For example, Neugarten (1980a, 1980b, 1989) proposed that the admonition "*Act your age*" has become progressively less meaningful since the middle part of this century. We are constantly aware of adults who occupy roles that seem out of step with their biological ages (e.g., the 28-year-old mayor, the 60-year-old father of a preschooler, and the 70-year-old college student).

Neugarten also has deep-seated doubts about an increasing number of popular books such as Gail Sheehy's widely read *Passages* (1976) or *Pathfinders* (1981) that emphasize predictable, age-related life crises. People who read such books worry about their midlife crises, apologize if they don't seem to be coping with them properly, and appear dismayed if they aren't having them. These crisis theories, Neugarten maintains, do not really define the typical pattern of adult development. It may be that adults change far more, and far less predictably, than many oversimplified stage theories or crisis theories suggest. As Neugarten (1980b) has asserted:

> My students and I have studied what happens to people over the life cycle. . . . We have found great trouble clustering people into age brackets that are characterized by particular conflicts; the conflicts won't stay put, and neither will the people. Choices and dilemmas do not sprout forth at ten-year intervals, and decisions are not made and then left behind as if they were merely beads on a chain. (p. 289)

Neugarten (1968) argued that the social environment within which the members of a particular generation evolved can alter their **social clock**—the timetable according to which individuals are expected to accomplish life's tasks, such as marrying, establishing a career, and even experiencing a monumental crisis at midlife. Social clocks provide guides for our lives. Sociohistorical events and trends unique to specific cohorts "set" the social clock for that cohort.

In earlier periods in our society, it may have been reasonable to describe life as a series set of discrete, predictable stages or crises. More people seemed to experience the same life events at the same ages. People knew the "right age" for marriage, the first child, the last child, career achievement, retirement, and even death. In the last few decades, however, Neugarten (1989) has argued that chronological age has become nearly irrelevant as an index of such significant events within adult development.

During the latter part of this century, our social time clocks have changed dramatically. New trends in work, family size, health, and education have produced phenomena that are unprecedented in our history. We see, for example, a significantly longer empty nest period after the children leave home that may require major readjustments in the parents' relationship. Also, we see an increase in the numbers of great-grandparents as well as those who start new families, new jobs, and new avocations when they are 40, 50, or 60 years old (Neugarten, 1980a, 1989).

The life tasks that we used to associate with one particular stage of adult development seem to reoccur over the entire course of the adult life span. Neugarten has articulated this point in a most eloquent manner:

> Most of the themes of adulthood appear and reappear in new forms over long periods of time. Issues of intimacy and freedom, for example, which are supposed to concern young adults just starting out in marriage and careers, are never settled once and for all. They haunt many couples continuously; compromises are found for a while, then renegotiated. Similarly, feeling the pressure of time, reformulating goals, coming to grips with success (and failure)—these are not the exclusive property of the forty-eight to fifty-two-year-olds, by any means. (Neugarten, 1980a, pp. 289–290)

## Applying a Life-Course Perspective to Life Events

It is important to make connections between age or life stage, the probability of certain events taking place, and the power of the event as a stressor (Brim & Ryff, 1980). Some events, such as a serious automobile accident, are not necessarily age-linked and have a low probability of occurring. Therefore, we are seldom prepared for such events psychologically. However, other events, such as menopause, retirement, or the death of a parent have stronger ties with age. This allows us to anticipate the events and to develop coping strategies that may help alleviate some of the stress these events engender (Neugarten, 1989; Pearlin & Lieberman, 1977). Figure 9.5 shows how a life-course perspective can be applied to life events (Hultsch & Plemons, 1979). This figure considers variations in the probability of certain events, their timing and sequencing, the motivational factors stimulated by the events, the coping resources available for dealing with them, and adaptational outcomes.

The life-events framework described in figure 9.5 has four main components: antecedent life-event stressors, mediating factors, a social/psychological adaptation process, and consequent adaptive or maladaptive outcomes. From this perspective, all life events, regardless of whether they are positive (marriage, being promoted at work) or negative (divorce, the death of a spouse), are viewed as potentially stressful. Factors that may mediate the effects of life events on the individual can be categorized as internal (physical health or intelligence) or external (salary, social support network). Social-psychological adaptation refers to the individual's coping strategies, which may produce either a positive or negative outcome.

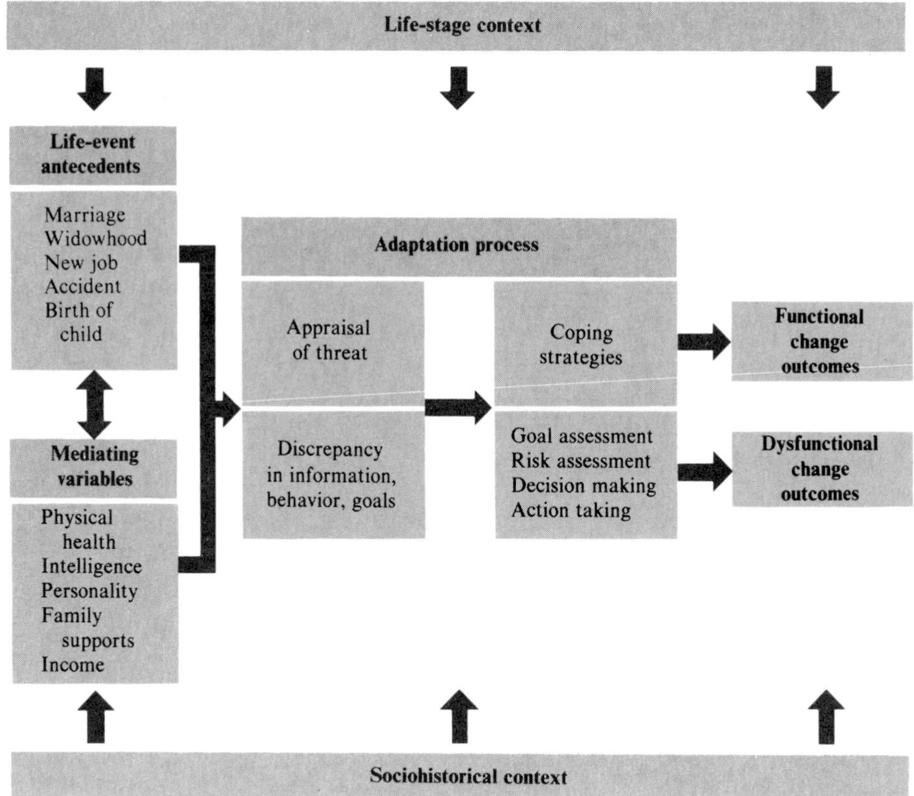


**Figure 9.5** A life-events framework.

As indicated in figure 9.5, it is also important to consider both the life stage and the sociohistorical context in which a life event occurs. Two timelines that are important in our lives, then, are **individual time** and **historical time.** An event (such as the death of a spouse) that occurs at age 30 may have a different impact on the individual than if it occurred at age 73. Similarly, an event (such as a woman being promoted over a man at work) would have a different impact if it occurred in 1990 rather than 1950.

The life-events framework provides valuable insights into adult development (Kogan, 1990). Like all the other theories described in this chapter, however, it is not without flaws (Dohrenwend & Dohrenwend, 1978; Lazarus & DeLongis, 1983; Maddi, 1986). One of the most significant drawbacks of the life-events framework is that it may place too much emphasis on change. It does not recognize the stability that, at least to some degree, characterizes adult development. Another potential drawback is that this perspective may place too much emphasis on major life events as the primary sources of personality change. Enduring a boring and tense job, a dull marriage, or living in poverty do not qualify as major life events. Yet the everyday pounding we take from these types of conditions can add up to a highly stressful life. Some psychologists (e.g., Lazarus & Folkman, 1984) believe that we can gain greater insight into the source of life's stresses by focusing on daily hassles and uplifts rather than focusing so much on the catastrophic experience of major life stressors.

## Recognizing Individual Variation

Broadly speaking, there are two theoretical approaches to the study of personality development—one focuses on similarities, the other on differences. The stage theories of Erikson and Levinson attempt to describe universal forms of intraindividual change that take place during adult development. The life-events framework, as championed by Neugarten, focuses on the interindividual variability that is characteristic of adult personality change.

In an extensive investigation of a random sample of 500 men at midlife, Michael Farrell and Stanley Rosenberg (1981) discovered a wide range of individual differences in adult personality. They concluded:

> While some studies have found middle age to be the apex of satisfaction and effectiveness, others found it to be a period of identity crisis and discontent. . . . Both our research design and our findings suggest a more complex model [than the universal stage model], one anchored in the idea that the individual is an active agent in interpreting, shaping, and altering his own reality. He not only experiences internal and external changes, he gives meaning to them. The meaning given shows a wide range of variation. (p. 2)

Think about yourself and other people you know. You have certain things in common with others, yet you differ in many ways. Individual variation must be an important aspect of any viable model of adult development.

## *Moral Development*

*Being entirely honest with oneself is a good exercise.*
—Sigmund Freud

In this section, we look at another important aspect of personality in adulthood—*moral development.* It has long been recognized that morality represents a central feature of personality. Freud (1949), for example, regarded the superego (one's sense of morality) as one of the primary structures of personality.

Moral development is a multidimensional construct. Most psychologists, conceptualize morality as possessing three interrelated aspects. The first component is *moral reasoning:* how do people think about rules of ethical conduct? For example, an individual may hear a story in which the central character is faced with the dilemma of whether to steal to save the life of another person. Then the individual may be asked how the character should resolve the moral conflict. In this procedure, primary emphasis is placed on the individual's rationale used to justify the character's moral decision.

A second issue in moral development involves the *moral behavior* of individuals in real-life situations. Here the primary concern is whether an individual would, for example, actually steal to help another. In this case, psychologists are concerned with factors that lead to rule transgression or behavioral control.

A third domain of interest is *moral emotion:* how do individuals feel after making a moral decision and engaging in a particular behavior? Psychologists often are particularly interested in emotions that follow either altruistic behavior (helping others, donating to charity) or rule violations (stealing, cheating, lying).

In the following section, we describe Lawrence Kohlberg's theory of moral development. Kohlberg's theory, which is one of the most important and influential theories of morality, focuses primarily on the first of the just-mentioned aspects of morality—moral reasoning. But as we shall see, Kohlberg's theory has important implications for how adults adjust to emotionally charged life events and how adults behave in moral contexts.

## Kohlberg's Theory

Kohlberg (1958, 1987, 1990) argued that morality is not formed all at once, early in life. Instead, moral development unfolds in a series of discrete stages. Kohlberg's stages of moral development have much in common with Piaget's stages of cognitive development. For example, the stages develop in an invariant or unchangeable sequence, and they develop in the same way for all individuals (i.e., the stages are universal). Furthermore, Kohlberg claimed that the stages that comprise moral development are qualitatively different from one another. Finally, Kohlberg maintained that each stage represents the integration and elaboration of the previous stage in the sequence.

## Levels and Stages of Moral Development

Kohlberg (1987) proposed that moral development involves three different *levels* (preconventional, conventional, and postconventional) with two different *stages* within each level. An individual's level and stage of moral development are measured by evaluating that individual's response to a number of hypothetical moral dilemmas. One of Kohlberg's well-known dilemmas, "Heinz and the Drug," is presented below:

> In Europe a woman was near death from cancer. One drug might save her, a form of radium that a druggist in the same town had recently discovered. The druggist was charging $2,000, ten times what the drug cost him to make. The sick woman's husband, Heinz, went to everyone he knew to borrow the money, but he could only get together about half of what the drug cost. He told the druggist his wife was dying and asked him to sell it cheaper or let him pay later. But the druggist said no. The husband got desperate and broke into the man's store to steal the drug for his wife. Should the husband have done that? Why? (Kohlberg, 1969, p. 379)

A person's stage of moral development is determined by his or her answer to the question "Why?" not to the question about what Heinz should have done. In other words, it is the *type* of reasoning a person uses to justify his or her judgment that counts; whether the person thinks Heinz should or shouldn't have stolen the drug is unimportant. Put somewhat differently, Kohlberg's theory places primary emphasis on the *structure* of moral judgment, not the *content* of moral judgment. The former refers to the underlying rule-system that gives rise to a specific moral decision; the latter refers to the decision itself.

The first two stages comprise the **preconventional level** because the individual interprets moral problems from the point of view of physical or material concerns (punishment and reward, the maintenance of power and wealth, and so on) or his own hedonistic wishes. At the preconventional level, then, rules and social expectations are viewed as something external to the self.

*Table 9.3*

**An Overview of the Levels and Stages That Comprise Kohlberg's Theory of Moral Development**

| Level and Stage | What Is Right | Reasons for Doing Right | Sociomoral Perspective |
|---|---|---|---|
| ***LEVEL I—PRECONVENTIONAL***<br>Stage 1—Heteronomous morality | To avoid breaking rules backed by punishment, obedience for its own sake, and avoiding physical damage to persons and property. | Avoidance of punishment, and the superior power of authorities. | *Egocentric point of view.* Doesn't consider the interests of others or recognize that they differ from the actor's; doesn't relate two points of view. Actions are considered physically rather than in terms of psychological interests of others. Confusion of authority's perspective with one's own. |
| Stage 2—Individualism, instrumental purpose, and exchange | Following rules only when it is to someone's immediate interest; acting to meet one's own interests and needs and letting others do the same. Right is also what's fair, what's an equal exchange, a deal, an agreement. | To serve one's own needs or interests in a world where you have to recognize that other people have their interests, too. | *Concrete individualistic perspective.* Aware that everybody has his own interest to pursue and these conflict, so that right is relative (in the concrete individualistic sense). |
| ***LEVEL II—CONVENTIONAL***<br>Stage 3—Mutual interpersonal expectations, relationships, and interpersonal conformity | Living up to what is expected by people close to you or what people generally expect of people in your role as son, brother, friend, and so on. "Being good" is important and means having good motives, showing concern about others. It also means keeping mutual relationships, such as trust, loyalty, respect and gratitude. | The need to be a good person in your own eyes and those of others. Your caring for others. Belief in the Golden Rule. Desire to maintain rules and authority which support stereotypical good behavior. | *Perspective of the individual in relationships with other individuals.* Aware of shared feelings, agreements, and expectations which take primacy over individual interests. Relates points of view through the concrete Golden Rule, putting yourself in the other guy's shoes. Does not yet consider generalized system perspective. |

*From Lawrence Kohlberg, "Moral Stages and Moralization" in* Moral Development and Behavior, *Thomas Lickona (ed.). Copyright © 1976 by Holt, Rinehart and Winston. Reprinted by permission of Thomas Lickona.*

The third and fourth stages make up the **conventional level.** At this level, the individual's understanding of morality depends on her (or his) internalization of the expectations that other individuals such as friends, family, or society have of her. Maintaining these expectations leads to interpersonal trust and loyalty as well as the preservation of the social system of which the individual is a part. At the conventional level, therefore, the person has identified with or internalized the rules and expectations of other individuals or of a more generalized social system.

| Level and Stage | What Is Right | Reasons for Doing Right | Sociomoral Perspective |
|---|---|---|---|
| Stage 4—Social system and conscience | Fulfilling the actual duties to which you have agreed. Laws are to be upheld except in extreme cases where they conflict with other fixed social duties. Right is also contributing to society, the group, or institution. | To keep the institution going as a whole, to avoid the breakdown in the system "if everyone did it," or the imperative of conscience to meet one's defined obligations. | *Differentiates societal point of view from interpersonal agreement or motives.* Takes the point of view of the system that defines roles and rules. Considers individual relations in terms of place in the system. |
| ***LEVEL III—POSTCONVENTIONAL, OR PRINCIPLED*** Stage 5—Social contract or utility and individual rights | Being aware that people hold a variety of values and opinions, that most values and rules are relative to your group. These relative rules should usually be upheld, however, in the interest of impartiality and because they are the social contract. Some nonrelative values and rights like *life* and *liberty,* however, must be upheld in any society regardless of majority opinion. | A sense of obligation to law because of one's social contract to make and abide by laws for the welfare of all and for the protection of all people's rights. A feeling of contractual commitment, freely entered upon, to family, friendship, trust, and work obligations. Concerns that laws and duties be based on rational calculation of overall utility, "the greatest good for the greatest number." | *Prior-to-society perspective.* Perspective of a rational individual aware of values and rights prior to social attachments and contracts. Integrates perspectives by formal mechanisms of agreement, contract, objective impartiality, and due process. Considers moral and legal points of view; recognizes that they sometimes conflict and finds it difficult to integrate them. |
| Stage 6—Universal ethical principles | Following self-chosen ethical principles. Particular laws or social agreements are usually valid because they rest on such principles. When laws violate these principles, one acts in accordance with the principle. Principles are universal principles of justice: the equality of human rights and respect for the dignity of human beings as individual persons. | The belief as a rational person in the validity of universal moral principles, and a sense of personal commitment to them. | *Perspective of a moral point of view from which social arrangements derive.* Perspective is that of any rational individual recognizing the nature of morality or the fact that persons are ends in themselves and must be treated as such. |

The **postconventional level** consists of the fifth and sixth stages in Kohlberg's sequence. At this level, the individual becomes capable of distinguishing between basic human rights and obligations, which remain constant over different cultures and historical epochs, versus societal and legal rules, which can change over socio-historical contexts. In other words, the postconventional reasoner can construct a set of universal moral principles by differentiating his or her moral point of view from the rules and expectations of significant others and society. Table 9.3 provides a more complete description of the different stages and levels that make up Kohlberg's theory. Also, table 9.4 provides examples of the type of moral reasoning generated by an individual at each of Kohlberg's stages.

*TABLE 9.4*

**Responses at Each Stage Level to the "Heinz and the Drug" Dilemma**

| Pro | Con |
|---|---|
| **Stage 1** | |
| It's not really bad to steal the drug. It's not like he did not ask to pay for it first. The drug really isn't worth $2,000; at most it costs about $200. Also, letting your wife die would be the same as killing her—and God's commandments say that killing another person is wrong. | Heinz shouldn't steal; he should buy the drug instead. Also, if he steals the drug he'd be committing a big crime and the police would put him in jail for a long time. Finally, God's commandments say that stealing is wrong. |
| **Stage 2** | |
| Heinz should steal the drug because he'd be lonely and sad if his wife dies. He wants her to live more than anything else. Anyway, if he gets sent to jail (that would make him sad), but he'd still have his wife (and that would make him really happy). | Heinz should not steal the drug if he doesn't like his wife a lot. Also, the druggist isn't really a bad person; he just wants to make a profit from all his hard work. That is what you are in business for, to make money. |
| **Stage 3** | |
| If I were Heinz, I'd steal the drug for my wife. Heinz could not be so heartless as to let his wife die. The two partners in a marriage should naturally expect that they will come to each other's aid. Also, you can't put a price on life: and, any decent person should value life above anything else. | Heinz shouldn't steal. If his wife dies, he cannot be blamed. After all, everybody knows that Heinz is not cruel and heartless, he tried to buy the drug legally. The druggist is the selfish one. He deserves to be stolen from. |
| **Stage 4** | |
| When you get married, you take a vow to love and cherish your wife. Marriage is not only love, it's an obligation as well. Marriage is like a legal contract that must be obeyed. Also, by stealing the drug and going to court, Heinz will be able to show the members of his society how dumb the laws about stealing are. This might lead to positive changes in the judicial system. | It's a natural thing for Heinz to want to save his wife, but it is still always wrong to steal. If everybody took the law into their own hands—like Heinz wants to do—his society would be in total chaos. In the long run, nobody in Heinz's society will benefit from this; not even Heinz and his wife! |
| **Stage 5** | |
| The law is not set up to deal with the unique circumstances of the Heinz case. Taking the drug in this situation is not correct from a "legal" point of view. But, there may be a set of basic human rights (such as the right to life) that must be preserved regardless of what the law may happen to say. The law of the land should protect peoples' basic rights. It certainly isn't in this case. Therefore, Heinz should steal the drug. | You cannot completely blame Heinz for stealing; but extreme circumstances do not really justify violating the law. This is because the law represents a commitment that Heinz and the other members of his society have made to one another. |
| **Stage 6** | |
| Heinz has to act in terms of the principle of preserving and respecting life. It would be both irrational and immoral to preserve the druggist's property right to the drug at the expense of his wife's right to life. After all, people invented the concept of personal property; it is a culturally relative concept. Alternatively, the right of a person to claim their right to life should be absolute. | Heinz is faced with the decision of whether to consider the other people who need the drug just as much as his wife. Heinz ought to act not according to his own feelings toward his wife but on his consideration of all of the lives involved. |

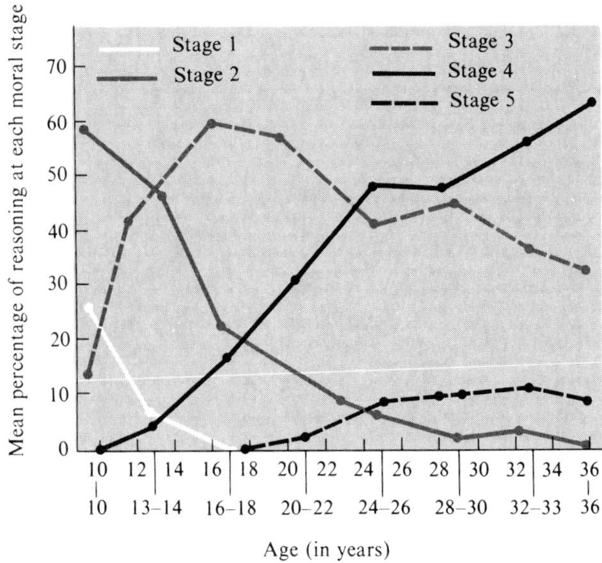


**Figure 9.6** Age-related changes in moral reasoning.

## Age-Related Changes in Moral Reasoning

Kohlberg's initial research (Kohlberg, 1958) led to the conclusion that individuals completed the moral stage sequence by the end of adolescence. However, longitudinal data collected by Kohlberg and Kramer (1969) showed that the adolescents who had attained postconventional morality during high school regressed to a preconventional level in their college years. Such a clear violation of the stage criterion of invariant progression forced Kohlberg and his associates to undertake major changes in the theory and measurement of moral development.

Using a revised and more stringent scoring system, Colby, Kohlberg, Gibbs, and Lieberman (1983) reanalyzed Kohlberg and Kramer's longitudinal data and found no evidence of regressive stage movement—the principle of invariant progression had been reconfirmed. Furthermore, Colby et al. (1983) analyzed the data from a twenty-year longitudinal study of moral development that began in the late 1950s. The results of this study are illustrated in figure 9.6. This figure shows the mean percent of moral reasoning displayed by the participants at each of the first five stages in Kohlberg's theory across the entire twenty years of the study. As you can see, there is a clear relationship between age and moral reasoning. Over the twenty-year period, reasoning at stages 1 and 2 decreased. Stage 3 peaked in late adolescence or early adulthood and declined thereafter. Reasoning at stage 4 did not appear at all among the 10-year-olds in the study; yet it was reflected in 62 percent of the judgments of the 36-six-year-olds. Stage 5 moral reasoning did not appear until the age of 20 to 22. Furthermore, it never rose above 10 percent of the total number of the participants' judgments. Similar results have been obtained by Armon (1991).

Based on these results, Kohlberg (1987) suggested that children and young adolescents reason at the preconventional level; most older adolescents and adults reason at the conventional level; and a small percentage of adults (mostly middle-aged and older) reason at the postconventional level. Therefore, it seems as if adulthood (not adolescence, as originally suggested) is marked by the ability to construct a universal set of moral principles. Kohlberg's discovery that moral development occurs during all epochs of the life span—childhood, adolescence, and adulthood—as well as his claim regarding the existence of distinct adult moral stages have been viewed positively by developmentalists.

## Determinants of Moral Development

What causes a person to move from one moral stage to the next? There is no reason to believe that chronological age, by itself, is a prime determinant of moral change. Some researchers (Kuhn, Langer, Kohlberg, & Haan, 1977; Tomlinson-Keasey & Keasey, 1974) have shown that the attainment of postconventional morality depends on formal operations; however, formal operation, by itself, is not sufficient to automatically produce postconventional morality. Roodin, Rybash, and Hoyer (1984, 1985) have suggested that advanced moral reasoning depends on the growth of postformal styles of thinking within the domain of personal knowledge. In fact, it seems that postconventional morality has much in common with Paul Baltes's concept of wisdom. Before his death, Kohlberg (1990) tried to establish a link between postformal thinking and postconventional reasoning.

In addition to logical thinking, psychologists have examined a number of other factors responsible for the transitions in moral development. After all, if moral development is nothing more than logical thinking applied to moral problems there should be no need to have a theory of moral development separate from cognitive/intellectual development. Kohlberg (1976) suggested that moral development is also heavily dependent on the *sociomoral perspective* a person brings to a moral problem (refer to table 9.3). These stages of sociomoral perspective-taking are actively constructed through the reciprocal interactions that take place between an individual and his or her social environment. Moral development should thus be promoted by social environments that (1) give the individual a broad range of role-taking experiences, so that the person becomes aware of the thoughts, feelings, and attitudes of other people and/or adopts the perspectives of various social institutions; and (2) place the individual in real-life positions of moral responsibility (e.g., a physician who is forced to make important health-care decisions).

## The Importance of Moral Development

Why do psychologists attach so much importance to Kohlberg's theory? What is the practical significance of being a postconventional rather than a conventional moral reasoner? Should one try to promote moral development in adults, and if so, how? These important questions can be answered in a variety of ways.

First, as individuals progress through the different moral stages, they should be able to make better or more effective decisions about the moral dilemmas that occur within their own lives. This does not mean that advanced (postconventional) moral reasoners are better people than lower-level moral reasoners. Instead, it means that postconventional reasoners bring a broader, more all-encompassing, and balanced point of view to a moral problem. A postconventional point of view does not have its primary

## Research focus 9.3

# Moral Reasoning and Coping

A sophisticated series of studies about the relationship between life experiences and adult moral development was conducted by Edward Lonky, Cheryl Kaus, and Paul Roodin (1984). Their research had its basis in John Gibbs's reformulation of Kohlberg's theory of moral reasoning.

Gibbs (1977, 1979) proposed the existence of two distinct phases of moral development: the **standard phase,** and the **existential phase.** The standard phase consists of the four stages that comprise the first two levels (preconventional and conventional) of Kohlberg's theory. Gibbs used the term *standard* to mean normal or expected. That is, it is the norm for the majority of adults to progress through the first four stages in Kohlberg's theory. This is because these stages are directly tied to changes in logical thinking and perspective-taking that occur in the vast majority of adults. The existential phase incorporates the stages that make up the last (postconventional) level in Kohlberg's theory. Gibbs argued that these two stages (5 and 6) do not meet the criteria that define true developmental stages. Gibbs maintained that (1) postconventional morality is displayed in only a very small percentage of adults in our Western culture and is absent in a variety of non-Western (or traditional) societies; and (2) unlike the first four stages, stages 5 and 6 of Kohlberg's theory are subject to reversals and regressions.

More specifically, Gibbs argued that existential or postconventional morality only develops when an adult comes to grips with the core needs that underlie human existence. These core needs, initially identified by Erich Fromm (1955), are *relatedness* (the need to overcome feelings of aloneness), *transcendence* (the need to surpass passivity and demonstrate competence), *rootedness* (the need for warmth, protection, and security), *identity* (the need to control one's own destiny and be aware of oneself as a separate entity), and *meaning* (the need for a guiding set of principles and beliefs).

Gibbs (1979) argued that these core needs are experienced within the context of salient life events and experiences. He also noted that once an individual experiences a need, she seeks a mode of coping with it. Coping may be characterized as either **affirmative** (essentially positive) or **abortive** (essentially negative and nonproductive). An affirmative mode of coping lays the basis for mutual love, productive creativity, egalitarian community, responsive individuality, and a system of reason and devotion. An abortive mode of coping generates an obsession with power or submission, wanton destructiveness, in-group chauvinism, herd conformity, and rationalizing ideology.

These speculations led Lonky et al. (1984) to wonder if an abortive coping style would be related to a fixation at the standard phase of moral development, while an affirmative mode of coping would be associated with the existential phase of moral development. They studied a group of adult women who had experienced a major loss or separation (the death of a loved one, divorce, and so on) during the past twelve months. These women participated in a semistructured interview that assessed the manner in which they coped with their negative life experiences. The researchers also measured the women's level of moral reasoning. Results indicated that women in the standard phase of moral development (conventional reasoners) tended to deal abortively with the needs they experienced within the context of these life events; whereas women in the existential phase (postconventional reasoners) dealt with the same needs in an affirmative manner. Lonky et al. also showed that affirmative coping was related to the personality trait of openness to experience as identified by Costa and McCrae (1980) and a problem-solving, action-oriented coping style labeled *problem-focused coping* by Lazarus and Folkman (1984).

Lonky et al. (1984) recognize that it is not possible, based on the design of their research studies, to determine if coping determines moral reasoning or vice versa. But these researchers have established an important link between these two psychological constructs.

---

roots in self-centered interests or social/interpersonal expectations. Thus, it allows individuals to more fully consider the conflicting claims that surround a moral dilemma.

Second, it has been shown that a person's level of moral reasoning is related to a person's *moral behavior.* In a review of the literature, Kohlberg and Candee (1984) have shown that as individuals progress through the moral stages, they engage in more consistent instances of moral action: honesty, altruism, and political and civil rights activism. Furthermore, they are less likely to comply with immoral orders given by authority figures.

Third, Kohlberg's theory may provide valuable information about how adults comprehend and cope with real life sociomoral issues. For example, Rybash and Roodin (1989) have discussed the manner by which different moral orientations influence adults' understanding of the right to self-determination in medical contexts (that is, the right to accept or reject medical treatment for a life-threatening illness). Research Focus 9.3 contains more detailed information about the relationship between coping and moral reasoning.

## Alternatives and Criticisms to Kohlberg's Theory

A number of studies have validated Kohlberg's claims about the invariance and universality of his moral stage theory (see Colby & Kohlberg, 1987; Demetriou, 1990; Harkness, Edwards, & Super, 1981; Li & Lui, 1991; Snarey 1985; Tietjen & Walker, 1985). However, no theory escapes criticism.

Carol Gilligan (1982) believes that Kohlberg's view is not as applicable to females as to males. She points out that adult males, on average, score higher (stage 4) than adult females (stage 3) on Kohlberg's measure of moral reasoning. This is not, in her opinion, due to the fact that men are more moral than women. Instead, Gilligan argues, this sex difference in moral reasoning has its basis in the different *orientations* that men and women bring to moral problems. A man's orientation toward morality is based in abstract principles of justice, whereas a woman's orientation toward morality is grounded in her relationships with others. These differences have their basis, according to Gilligan (1985), in the socialization of the sexes during childhood. Thus, Gilligan maintains that women score lower on Kohlberg's assessment of moral stage reasoning because Kohlberg's measure is biased in favor of males (i.e., Kohlberg's test measures a person's understanding of abstract principles of justice, rather than the sense of connectedness that binds individuals together). Research inspired by Gilligan's theory (Gilligan, 1977, 1982; Gilligan & Belenky, 1980; Lyons, 1983) has found that women make moral judgments by focusing on their responsibilities to people: their families, their friends, and themselves. However, several psychologists have not observed the sex differences in moral reasoning reported by Gilligan (Gibbs, Arnold, & Burkhart, 1984; Walker, 1986; Walker, deVries, & Trevethan, 1987). Therefore, Gilligan's viewpoint has not achieved unequivocal support.

Another criticism of Kohlberg's theory that bears on adult development has been raised by Rybash, Roodin, and Hoyer (1983). They argued that the problems encountered by adults in real-life contexts, especially older adults, may have little in common with the hypothetical dilemmas that Kohlberg uses to measure moral development. Elderly participants described problems relating to family and medical matters such as whether to: give advice to an adult child who is having an affair; give financial support to an adult child who keeps on squandering money; move into a nursing home or remain in the home of an adult; discontinue life support for a terminally ill spouse; and so on. This suggests that older adults may be at a disadvantage when using Kohlberg's assessments of moral reasoning. Most interestingly, Rybash et al. found that a significant proportion of elderly indicated that they were *free* from personal moral dilemmas. Consider the following response given by a 73-year-old man:

> At this point in my life I feel that there are no moral decisions I have to make. I have reached a point in my life where I have peace of mind and am content with my life. I'm

*Some of the most significant ethical and moral decisions in our culture are made by older adults.*

> in good health and live each day not worrying about having to make moral decisions. There were times when I was younger that I had to make moral decisions, but now all I have to decide about is where I want to go and what I want to do. You come to this point in your life, and I feel everyone about the same age as me feels the same way. (Rybash et al., 1983, p. 257)

How would you categorize this response? Is it indicative of ego-integrity? Does it represent a healthy disengagement from life?

In a related study, Pratt, Golding, and Kerig (1987) found that older adults were more reflective when they reasoned about real-life problems than about the hypothetical moral problems used in Kohlberg's assessment procedure. Pratt et al. (1987) also reported a great deal of consistency between the stage of moral reasoning used by young and middle-aged adults when they reasoned about real-life versus hypothetical dilemmas, but *no* consistency in stagelike reasoning when older adults reasoned about different types of dilemmas.

## Summary

There are several definitions of personality and wide-ranging theoretical views of how personality should be conceptualized and measured. Some personality theorists adopt a stage perspective. Among the stage theorists, Freud believed that little or no personality change occurs during the adult years, whereas Erikson stressed personality changes throughout the life cycle. Four of Erikson's eight stages are particularly important in terms of personality development in adulthood—identity versus role confusion, intimacy versus isolation, generativity versus stagnation, and ego integrity versus despair. Erikson's theory has stimulated a great deal of interest in themes of personality at different points in adulthood, but it has been hard to develop the empirical data to support his theory.

Daniel Levinson's stage theory focuses on personality change during adulthood and midlife transition. He proposed that the middle-aged adult faces four conflicts: being young versus old, being masculine versus feminine, being destructive versus constructive, and being attached to others versus separated from them. The success of the midlife transition depends on how effectively individuals are able to reduce these polarities.

Despite the richness and intrinsic appeal of stage theories, there are a number of methodological shortcomings in Erikson's and Levinson's work. Furthermore, these theorists may have underestimated the role played by generational factors in adult personality development.

Life-events theorists believe that personality itself often changes because of the unique life events that individuals experience during adulthood. Bernice Neugarten, one of the major pioneers of the life-events framework, has argued that we need to consider the sociohistorical circumstances in which life events occur. She leaves the impression that sociohistorical influences are more important in the personality equation than chronological age. Life-events theorists believe that too much emphasis has been placed on stages of adult development and the concept of predictable life crises at the same points in adult life. In particular, they attack the midlife crisis theorists, arguing that events at midlife only take on crisis proportions when powerful, nonnormative life events occur.

Many theorists also recognize the importance of individual differences in adult personality. Not all people go through stages, crises, or life events in the same way, so there is a great deal of individual variation in adult personality development.

Some developmentalists measure the stability of individual differences in personality by adopting a trait approach. Traits may be best conceptualized as enduring characteristics or dispositions that help to organize a person's thoughts, feelings, and behaviors. Two of the most well-known trait theorists are Paul Costa and Robert McCrae. There are many complex aspects to the question of how stable personality is in adulthood. Some overall themes do appear, however, in the longitudinal studies of personality development: the Kansas City Study, the Normative Aging Study, the Baltimore Study, the Seattle Study, and the Berkeley Older Generation Study. These studies show that adult personality traits such as neuroticism, extroversion, and openness to experience remain remarkably stable over the adult life span. They also revealed that major changes, transitions, and upheavals in adult personality are more apparent than real. Moreover, these studies have also shown that generational or cohort differences can have a significant impact on the structure of adult personality. Finally, the proponents of the trait approach acknowledge that there is always the potential for personality change during the adult years.

A person's sense of morality is an important component of his or her personality. Psychologists have studied three aspects of moral development—moral reasoning, behavior, and feeling. At the core of Lawrence Kohlberg's major theory of moral development is an analysis of how people reason about and understand complex moral dilemmas. Kohlberg believes that moral development occurs in a stagelike sequence. Specifically, his theory proposes the existence of three moral levels (preconventional, conventional, and postconventional), with two stages within each level. Kohlberg also argues that moral development continues during childhood, adolescence, and adulthood. Most adults reason at the conventional moral level, although a small percentage of adults attain postconventional morality.

Adults who reason at the postconventional level seem to cope with negative life events in a much more affirmative manner than conventional reasoners. Moreover, it appears that adults at the postconventional level are more likely to engage in moral action than individuals at lower levels.

Kohlberg is not without his critics. Carol Gilligan has argued that Kohlberg's theory is biased in favor of men. Other psychologists argue that the dilemmas Kohlberg uses to assess moral reasoning are very different from the ones that adults experience in their everyday lives.

## Review Questions

1. Describe the differences between the views of personologists, or traditional trait theorists, and those of stage and life-events theorists.
2. Compare and contrast the stage theories of Erikson and Levinson. What seem to be the strongest and weakest points of these theories?
3. How do the proponents of the life-events framework explain the notion of midlife crisis? Why do life-events theorists attach more importance to sociohistorical influences than stage theorists do?
4. What are personality traits? Briefly describe the three different personality traits that make up Costa and McCrae's five-factor model of personality.
5. What are the findings of the major longitudinal studies of adult personality development?
6. What is the advantage of having a personality structure that remains stable over time?
7. Given all of the information presented in this chapter, do you think that a person's age or year of birth is a more important determinant of his or her personality?
8. Describe the levels and stages that make up Kohlberg's theory of moral development. What level of moral development is unique to adulthood?
9. From the perspective of Kohlberg's theory, what are the factors responsible for moral development?
10. Briefly describe John Gibbs's reformulation of Kohlberg's theory of moral development. Explain how Gibbs's viewpoint may relate both to moral reasoning and coping style.
11. Briefly describe Carol Gilligan's major criticism of Kohlberg's theory.

## For Further Reading

Erikson, E. (1963). *Childhood and society.* (2d Ed.). New York: Norton.

Gilligan, C. (1982). *In a different voice: Psychological theory and women's development.* Cambridge, MA: Harvard University Press.

Levinson, D. J. (1978). *The seasons of a man's life.* New York: Knopf.

McCrae, R. R., & Costa, P. T. (1990). *Personality in adulthood.* NY: Guilford Press.

10

# Coping, Adaptation, and Mental Health

*Life can be so long, so you've got to be so strong.*
—John Lennon

*The person will cope if he can, defend if he must, and fragment if he is forced . . .*
—Norma Haan

## Introduction

In this chapter we examine the interrelationship of coping and adaptation in adulthood and then turn to the many issues surrounding the mental health of older adults. We begin with a discussion of the methods adults use to adapt and cope with life stressors and see how coping strategies may evidence age-related changes. We also explore the importance of individual experiences and the meanings that adults attach to them. And, we will examine some of the common problems with which older individuals must cope: the timing of these events, the severity of these experiences, and the available resources that individuals bring to bear. Next we turn our attention to the mental health of older adults and the most typical mental disorders in older populations—dementia, depression, and suicide. We describe different types of dementia and discuss the importance of distinguishing between dementia and depression. We also explore the burgeoning research on Alzheimer's disease and other dementias: diagnosis, theories of causation, treatment, the impact on family and caregivers, and the importance of respite care.

## Stress, Coping, and Adaptation

Psychologists have long been interested in stress and helping people develop more adaptive ways of coping. The ability to manage stress successfully is a hallmark of positive functioning in adulthood. Most older adults are in good mental health and capable of managing the stresses that they experience, although they may be more likely to be overwhelmed and even clinically depressed in special circumstances such as the death of a spouse or in the caretaking role of a relative with **Alzheimer's disease (AD)** (Cohen, 1990; Gatz, Bengtson, & Blum, 1990). Experts have different theories of stress, different assessment procedures, and different views of the degree to which stress is experienced at critical points in adult life. Richard Lazarus and his coworkers Anita DeLongis (1983) and Susan Folkman (1984) believe that to better understand psychological stress and coping in aging, we should distinguish between two models of stress: the **life-events model** and the **cognitive model.** They further believe that to delineate more effective ways to cope with stress, we should study how adults cognitively appraise, personally interpret, and individually define the stressors of life. In the following sections, we will explore these two models.

## The Life-Events Model of Adaptation and Coping

The earlier work of Hans Selye (1956, 1980) linking stress to physical illness played an important role in focusing attention on the identification of environmental events

*Natural disasters tax the coping skills of individuals throuthout the life span in dramaticlly different ways.*

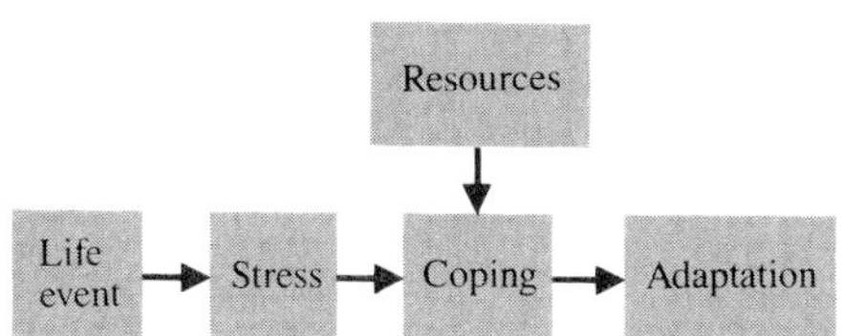


**Figure 10.1** The life events model for coping and adaption

that individuals find stressful and that heighten hormonal and neurochemical reactions that may trigger disease and illness (Endroczi, 1991). From this work, psychologists began an environmental inventory to identify those events that caused emotional stress, to better understand how people interpret and respond to stressful life experiences—physically, psychologically, biologically. Originally, investigators searched for commonalities in the adaptation and coping behaviors that individuals displayed. Key life events mandate change and adaptation among all individuals, young and old (Whitbourne, 1985b); the life-events model is briefly summarized in figure 10.1.

## Measuring Stress Through Life Events

Some psychologists believe that life events can be ranked by the magnitude of stress they produce. It is maintained that the greater the stress produced by specific life events, the greater the likelihood a person will experience physical health problems,

*Table 10.1*

*The Social Readjustment Rating Scale*

| Rank | Life Event | Mean Value | Rank | Life Event | Mean Value |
|---|---|---|---|---|---|
| 1 | Death of spouse | 100 | 23 | Son or daughter leaving home | 29 |
| 2 | Divorce | 73 | 24 | Trouble with in-laws | 29 |
| 3 | Marital separation | 65 | 25 | Outstanding personal achievement | 28 |
| 4 | Jail term | 63 | 26 | Wife begin or stop work | 26 |
| 5 | Death of close family member | 63 | 27 | Begin or end school | 26 |
| 6 | Personal injury or illness | 53 | 28 | Change in living condition | 25 |
| 7 | Marriage | 50 | 29 | Revision of personal habits | 24 |
| 8 | Fired at work | 47 | 30 | Trouble with boss | 23 |
| 9 | Marital reconciliation | 45 | 31 | Change in work hours or conditions | 20 |
| 10 | Retirement | 45 | 32 | Change in residence | 20 |
| 11 | Change in health of family member | 44 | 33 | Change in schools | 20 |
| 12 | Pregnancy | 40 | 34 | Change in recreation | 19 |
| 13 | Sex difficulties | 39 | 35 | Change in church activities | 19 |
| 14 | Gain of new family member | 39 | 36 | Change in social activities | 18 |
| 15 | Business readjustment | 39 | 37 | Mortgage or loan less than $10,000 | 17 |
| 16 | Change in financial state | 38 | 38 | Change in sleeping habits | 16 |
| 17 | Death of a close friend | 37 | 39 | Change in number of family get-togethers | 15 |
| 18 | Change to different line of work | 36 | | | |
| 19 | Change in number of arguments with spouse | 35 | 40 | Change in eating habits | 15 |
| | | | 41 | Vacation | 13 |
| 20 | Mortgage over $10,000 | 31 | 42 | Christmas | 12 |
| 21 | Foreclosure of mortgage or loan | 30 | 43 | Minor violations of the law | 11 |
| 22 | Change in responsibilities at work | 29 | | | |

*From Journal of Psychosomatic Research, 11:213–218. T. H. Holmes and R. H. Rahe, "The Social Readjustment Rating Scale." Reprinted with permission from © 1967 Elsevier Science Ltd., Pergamon Imprint, Oxford, England.*

diseases, and difficulties in emotional or psychological adjustment. Holmes and Rahe's Social Readjustment Rating Scale (table 10.1) has often been used as an index of the stress that specific life events produce.

How do researchers arrive at the stress values of various life events? An event such as marriage is used as an anchor point and assigned a value. In the case of the Social Readjustment Rating Scale, marriage was assigned the value of 50. A sample of adults was then asked how much readjustment would be required if each of the events listed in the table occurred in their lives. This question was asked in relation to marriage; for example, would being fired at work require more or less readjustment than marriage? How about sex difficulties, divorce, or the death of a close friend? The average score for an event was then divided by ten to arrive at the number you see beside each life event in the table. Look at the life events and their readjustment scores and rankings. Do you agree with their order?

Generally, a significant but modest relationship has been found between the degree of stress and the physical illness (Aldwin, Spiro, Bosse, & Levenson, 1989; Ben-Sira, 1991). Many individuals, but not all, who have experienced stressful life events seem to show more physical and health-related problems

(Rabkin & Struening, 1976; Taylor, 1990). Some people handle stress better than others, resisting illness even in the face of highly stressful life events. For example, when business executives have vigorous attitudes toward challenging situations, they experience fewer physical problems and less illness than their counterparts with opposite attitudes (Kobasa, 1979). People who face stress but retain their health probably perceive change as a challenging opportunity, not a threat.

We can ask several questions about the relationship between aging and stress. For example, do we experience an ever-increasing number of stressors as we age? Do we develop more effective strategies for coping with stress as we grow older? Or do older adults, faced with a barrage of stressful experiences, find their adaptive abilities simply overwhelmed?

## The Social Readjustment Scale: Critique

Some believe that the life-events model predicts that the more changes a person has to make, the greater the stress. Others believe that older adults are unable to manage stress as well as younger adults do and therefore are at increased risk for health problems, illness, and disease. Unfortunately, there is not much research bearing on these specific questions.

Still other psychologists believe the life-events model places too much emphasis on change and largely ignores mediating processes such as the personal significance (context) and subjective interpretation (cognitive-emotional) of the events themselves as well as the presence of environmental resources that may be helpful (Ben-Sira, 1991; Rybash et al., 1986; Whitbourne, 1985a). For example, the death of a parent, while stressful, may be interpreted quite differently by a child sixteen years of age and a "child" forty-five years of age. Thus, the same traumatic event may produce different levels of stress for each person. Furthermore, even when faced with comparable stressful events, people do not choose the same coping strategies and solutions. Most people examine their coping resources and strategies in deciding how to face a stressful experience (Lazarus & DeLongis, 1983; Lazarus & Folkman, 1984; Sarason & Spielberger, 1980; Thomae, 1992; Whitbourne, 1985a).

### *The Cognitive Model of Adaptation and Coping*

A second model of coping and adaptation to stress, the cognitive model (see figure 10.2), emphasizes the importance of a person's subjective perception of potentially stressful life events. Thus, not all people see highly ranked stressful life experiences (table 10.1) as traumatic and serious problems in their lives. The process of determining if an event is stressful is called **primary appraisal.** The subjective determination of an event as stressful produces emotional reactions of tension, anxiety, and dread, while events considered nonstressful provide challenge and growth, typically producing emotions of hope, excitement, and joy (Lazarus & Folkman, 1984). Once primary appraisal has occurred, a person can decide how to adapt by choosing resources and determining the costs of using such resources—a process called **secondary appraisal.**

**Figure 10.2**
Lazarus's cognitive model of coping and adaptation

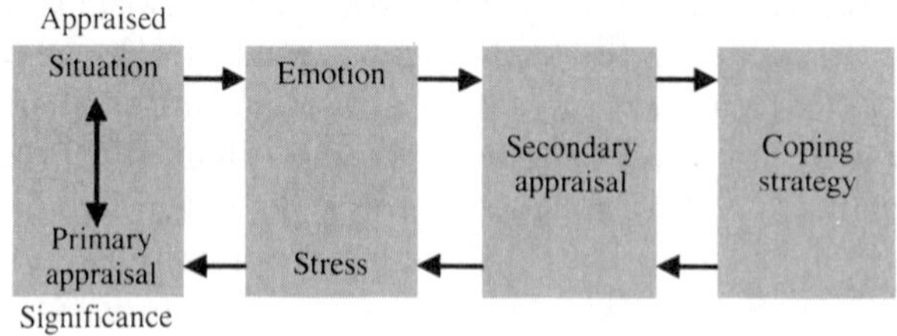


In research on stress in the adult years, Richard Lazarus and his colleagues (DeLongis, Coyne, Dakof, Folkman, & Lazarus, 1982; Lazarus & Folkman, 1984) found an inverse relationship between stressful life events and age for people aged 45 to 64. Does this mean that people experience fewer stressful life events as they age? We cannot conclude that just because the frequency of stressful life events decreases with age, older people experience less stress (Kahana, 1992). We must also take into account the meaning or subjective interpretation of stress (primary appraisal). A simple frequency analysis of the number of stressful life events ignores the different coping demands of younger and older people. Older individuals, for example, may find that a single minimally stressful life event, such as leaving home for a vacation, may overwhelm them if they also have to deal with a chronic infirmity such as arthritis and nonsupportive relatives who question the wisdom of their decision to travel (Kahana, 1992).

## Daily Hassles and Uplifts: The Broken Shoelace Syndrome

**Daily hassles** are the little, irritating annoyances that punctuate our day-to-day existence (DeLongis et al., 1982; Lazarus & Folkman, 1984). Some hassles are transient, such as having a rude and uncaring waiter, whereas others may be chronic, such as having to wait hours in traffic each day as we travel to and from work. Lazarus and his colleagues (Folkman, Lazarus, Pimley, & Novacek, 1987; Monat & Lazarus, 1985) have developed a hassles scale that evaluates the frequency and intensity of everyday stresses such as misplacing belongings, not having enough time for family, filling out forms, or breaking a shoelace. Counterbalancing such hassles are corresponding **uplifts,** or positive experiences, which we also may encounter each day (Lazarus & Folkman, 1984).

In their research, Lazarus and his colleagues have found little difference between men and women in the type and frequency of hassles encountered (Folkman, Lazarus, Dunkel-Schetter, DeLongis, & Gruen, 1986; Folkman, Lazarus, Gruen, & DeLongis, 1986). Interestingly, the measurement of daily hassles is a strong predictor of a person's overall adaptation. The individual's ability to cope with hassles, in fact, is a far better predictor of morale and life satisfaction, psychological symptoms, and somatic illness than the number of major life stresses the person has endured (DeLongis et al., 1982; Kanner, Coyne, Schaefer, & Lazarus, 1981; Lazarus & Folkman, 1984). Why might this be so? Daily hassles seem to have a stronger link with health outcomes because they evaluate proximal aspects of stress, whereas life-event rankings measure distal aspects. *Proximal* aspects are the adult's immediate perceptions of the environment, whereas *distal* aspects are more removed perceptions that may not have common meanings for all people.

In studying the daily hassles of college students, young adults, and middle-aged adults, Lazarus and his colleagues (Folkman et al., 1987; Lazarus & Folkman, 1984) found some age differences. Younger adults often reported more hassles than older adults in two areas: economics or finances and work (although personal-social concerns were also problematic). Younger college students had to cope with academic and social problems—wasting time, meeting high standards, being lonely. Older adults, on the other hand, experienced hassles most often in the areas of environmental and social problems, home upkeep, and health. Lazarus's sample was essentially white, healthy, middle class, and well educated. The daily hassles of adults from other life circumstances probably vary from this pattern.

## Coping and Adaptation: The Timing of Significant Experiences

The extent to which individuals cope and adapt successfully to stressful life experiences has also been related to the timing of such events. Neugarten and Neugarten (1987) have suggested that negative events produce levels of stress that are lower when experienced at predictable points in the life course than when experienced as completely unanticipated or predicted. Neugarten (1968) originally provided convincing evidence that adults construct a kind of social timetable or social clock against which they compare their own social developmental progress; they judge the "right" age for marriage, the "right" time to have children, and the predictable time to experience losses, such as the death of a parent (most often between 40 and 50 years of age). Events that occur "on time" usually cause minimal stress, whereas those that are unexpected produce considerable stress. For example, pregnancy can be a wonderful and exciting time for a married women in her twenties or thirties; the same event can bring considerable stress to an unmarried adolescent girl or a 45-year-old woman with a demanding career and two teenagers. Similarly, the death of a parent is a very different experience for a 55-year-old as opposed to a 15-year-old.

The significance of an illness may also vary according to the time it occurs in a person's life. For example, in one study (Mages & Mendelsohn, 1979), older people who discovered they had cancer often accelerated processes associated with the ending of life such as disengagement from external commitments, increased dependency, and the life-review process. Older adults were also more likely to confront cancer with less anger than younger adults, who feel they should have much of their lives ahead. Young adults with AIDS often approach their extended families to ask them to accept and reinterpret their relationships in an attempt to resolve years of isolation, distancing, and abandonment, a process that ordinarily takes decades for families to accomplish (Ascher, 1993). It is difficult for any young adult, but imperative for those with AIDS, to try to bring rapid resolution of their personal family relationships. They anticipate stresses at memorial events, public death announcements, and in the disposition of their belongings. They wish to bring acceptance to all, long before families are ready, to avoid conflicts between their 'two worlds' (e.g., their biological relatives and their lovers) at the time of death (*U.S. News and World Report,* 1993). Such findings illustrate the importance of considering the personal meanings of stressful events as "off-time" events at different points in adult development (Hultsch & Plemons, 1979; Lazarus & DeLongis, 1983).

## Coping and Adaptation: Life-Threatening Illness

Shelley Taylor (1983) and her colleagues (Taylor, Kemeny, Aspinwall, Schneider, Rodriguez, & Heubert, 1992; Wood, Taylor, & Lichtman, 1985) investigated a variety of illnesses to explore how people cope with life-threatening illnesses such as AIDS and breast cancer. Through her work we see the role of cognitive factors, which help to give hope and a positive approach to managing the events (Rybash et al., 1986). Taylor et al. (1985), for example, reported that women responded to the diagnosis of breast cancer, a life-threatening illness, by undergoing a set of active distortions of reality. Of seventy-eight women interviewed, 95 percent tried to derive a new sense of personal meaning from their illness (e.g., "I was very happy to find out that I am a very strong person"). A second theme in their coping with this life-threatening disease was an earnest attempt to gain "magical mastery" or control over their cancer. For example, many believed dietary changes, lifestyle changes, or maintaining a positive attitude would help them win their battle against the disease. A third theme was the attempt to regain feelings of self-esteem. The women selected a reference group against which to compare themselves so that they would derive a more favorable view of themselves and their disease. Thus, older women felt better off than younger women, married women felt sorry for unmarried women, and those with a poor prognosis consoled themselves that at least they were still alive. The women who coped most successfully with cancer tried to master their dilemma and take charge of their lives regardless of the probabilities and realities of their situations. Olivia Newton-John, popular celebrity and singer, recently disclosed that she, like 182,000 other women each year, had breast cancer in 1992. In her public remarks, the 45-year-old wife and mother of a 7-year-old echoed the preceding research findings, "It really refocused my life. When you go through something like that it really puts everything else in perspective. I was trying to be everything to everybody—I was Mom, I was trying to save the world, and I was running a business. I strongly believe that illness is related to your mind and stress and your feelings."

In a similar fashion, Taylor and her colleagues (Taylor, et al., 1992) reported that gay men who were seropositive for HIV showed a strong "unrealistic optimism," less distress, and more positive attitudes than those who were still free of the virus. That is, the gay men who tested positive distorted the future probabilities that they indeed would develop AIDS; in their beliefs and attitudes, they were far more optimistic that they would not contract the AIDS disease, despite already harboring the virus, than a comparable group of HIV seronegative gay men, who showed more fatalism in their perceptions, believing that they had little control over the virus and the AIDS disease (Taylor et al., 1992). Taylor suggests that unrealistic optimism is characteristic of adaptation and coping with life-threatening illness (Taylor & Brown, 1988). Unrealistic optimism and the active distortion of reality promote positive feelings of self-worth, the ability to care for oneself and others, a level of personal control, and the capacity to cope effectively with the stress of the life-threatening illness as well as other stresses (Taylor & Brown, 1988; Taylor et al., 1992).

## Coping and Adaptation: The Use of Resources and Defenses

Adults use coping strategies to adapt, respond, reduce, or avoid stress and with increasing age actively seek out environmental resources to enhance their coping strategies or to compensate for declining resources of the self (Ben-Sira, 1991 in Kahana, Stange, & Kahana, 1993). Adults rarely respond passively to stress, but attempt to change circumstances when possible and seek resources and help; when they can't, they often invoke cognitive strategies to alter the meaning of stressful circumstances, as did the women with breast cancer and the men who were seropositive for HIV (Taylor, 1983; Taylor et al., 1992; Wood et al., 1985).

Individuals use many common defense mechanisms and unconscious strategies such as repression and denial, to protect the ego from threat and anxiety. Repression and denial in particular are more likely to be adopted in response to extreme stress (Weinberger & Schwartz, 1990). George Valliant (1977), who conducted a longitudinal study of personality and coping, considers denial and distortion of reality to be at the lowest level of adult coping mechanisms (Valliant, 1977). The most mature coping strategies are characterized by altruism; humor (i.e., a method of expressing emotions that is free from consequences); suppression (being optimistic in the face of problems, waiting for a desired outcome, looking for a silver lining); anticipation (planning and preparation for realistic outcomes such as death of a loved one); and sublimation (channeling unacceptable impulses and emotions into socially valued and personally rewarding activities).

It is interesting to contrast Valliant's view that denial and distortion of reality represent immature coping with the views that consider denial to be an acceptable and healthy mode of adjustment in response to specific types of stressful events (Kemp, 1985; Monat & Lazarus, 1985; Taylor et al., 1992). Denial may allow an individual to gain the emotional resources to face reality. For example, on a short-term basis, a victim of a severe spinal cord injury may be helped by denying the extent of the injury and being optimistic that some recovery of function may be gained (Kemp, 1985, Monat & Lazarus, 1985). However, in time, denial must be abandoned in favor of more realistic approaches. Some denial and distortions of reality, then, may be helpful in coping, depending on the stressful event itself and the length of time these strategies are maintained. The use of positive, active distortion, however, is a different kind of defense than simple denial for those with life-threatening illness. People seem to recognize the threat they face, yet display unrealistic optimism as a way to experience feelings of control and maintain self-esteem. Taylor et al. (1992), for example, noted that men who were seropositive for HIV continued to engage in health-enhancing behaviors, including safe sex practices, believing that it was still within their control to defend against AIDS.

It is not an easy task to measure coping resources and strategies apart from specific events (Carver, Scheier, & Weintraub, 1989; Taylor, 1990; Taylor et al., 1992). Recent formulations suggest that to better understand the relationship of stress and coping to aging it is necessary to study both domain-specific stressors and the domain-specific coping responses and resources that people employ (Stephens, Crowther, Hobfoll & Tennenbaum, 1990; Kahana et al., 1993). Too often, coping has been assessed as a trait or style determined from a single measure at one point in time; however, coping may be related to the type of event itself (e.g., life-threatening illness) rather than reflective of a general trait or style (Taylor et al., 1992). In a recent investigation of caretaking of an older parent or relative, three dimensions or domains were identified that could produce stress (Albert, 1991): (1) the type of impairment (physical vs. cognitive-emotional), (2) the location of the caregiving (home vs. outside the home) and (3) the response to parental incompetency (regaining personal autonomy vs. relinquishing autonomy to a surrogate/guardian). Each of these three dimensions, while part of the general domain of caretaking, produced its own unique caretaking stresses and elicited unique coping responses that were related to each of these three domain-specific or unique stresses (Albert, 1991).

Single measurements of coping also may not predict how adults will react across time and in various situations. Folkman and Lazarus (1980) constructed a checklist of coping strategies that described how adults thought, felt, and behaved in a number of specific stressful circumstances. Using this measure, the researchers identified two basic coping strategies used by adults: **problem-focused coping** and **emotion-focused coping.** When people use problem-focused coping strategies, they attempt to obtain additional information to be more effective in problem solving or to actively change the stressful situation or event. When adults use emotion-focused coping strategies, they use behavioral and cognitive techniques to help manage the emotional tension produced by the stressful life situation. This strategy does not necessarily remove the perceived stress, but, rather, helps in managing or reducing the accompanying emotional distress. Most people use both problem-focused and emotion-focused strategies rather than relying solely on one or the other. When coping patterns are charted according to age, some interesting trends emerge. Folkman et al. (1987) reported that

> . . . younger respondents used proportionately more active, interpersonal, problem-focused forms of coping (e.g., confrontive coping, seeking social support, planful problem solving) than did the older people, and the older people used proportionately more passive, intrapersonal emotion-focused forms of coping (e.g., distancing, acceptance of responsibility, and positive reappraisal) than did the younger people. (p. 182)

Carver, Scheier, and Weintraub (1989) suggest that the emotion-focused and problem-focused distinction made by Lazarus may be far too simple and that additional dimensions may need to be considered in examining age-related differences in coping. Interestingly, older adults perceive the sources of stress that they experience as potentially less controllable than younger persons (Blanchard-Fields & Robinson, 1987). Yet, older adults are far more likely to cope successfully with stressors (e.g., by tailoring their coping strategies to fit those situations they believe they can control), than younger adults and adolescents, who more often employ denial and other defensive strategies (Blanchard-Fields & Irion, 1988; Blanchard-Fields & Robinson, 1987). It is more characteristic of older adults to recognize when environmental resources are needed to assist them or to help in managing a difficult situation, although mental health needs are an exception (Ben-Sira, 1991).

## Coping in Action: Caring for an Older Relative

There are, of course, many predictable stressors across the life course, including caring for an elderly parent or other relative who may be ill (Brody, 1985; Wolfson, Handfield-Jones, Glass, McClaran, & Keyserlingk, 1993). Regular visitations between middle-aged adults and their parents are common, independent of need, in both city and rural environments (Krout, 1988). Tensions that surround caregiving include: financial obligations, filial responsibility, and preservation of the personal autonomy, rights, and dignity of the older individual (Cicirelli, 1992; Wolfson et al., 1993). When a spouse is not available, this responsibility falls on middle-aged adults; most often it is a daughter who provides for the care of her widowed mother (Baum & Page, 1991). In the caregiving role, adult children are most likely to care for a parent of the same gender; with the majority of older parents being mothers, the caregiving relationship and responsibilty is assumed by daughters, following this **gender consistency model** (Lee, Dwyer, & Coward, 1993). Providing care to an elderly parent often produces strong feelings of obligation, guilt, and resentment over the time taken from spouse and children. The popular press identifies with the stress experienced by adults with multiple responsibilities to their parents, their spouse, and their own children, labeling them the "sandwich generation." Investigators have identified the intense stress and emotional reactions of middle-aged adults caring for parents as part of a specific syndrome: **caregiver distress** (George, 1990b; Haley, 1991; Knight, Lutzky, & Macofsky-Urban, 1993).

Wolfson et al. (1993) found adult children feeling a strong societal or moral obligation to provide for their elderly parents' financial, emotional, and physical needs, but unable to actually provide as much support as they feel they should. However, in the case of an elderly parent moving in with an adult child, the elderly parent, despite illness or diminished finances, often provides some assistance to the extended household (Speare & Avery, 1993). Elderly parents who move in to live with their adult children do 79 percent of the housework (Ward, Logan, & Spitze, 1992) and contribute direct financial assistance to their adult children, particularly when the adult children are unmarried (Hoyert, 1991; Speare & Avery, 1993). The most common causes of elderly parents moving in with adult children are: (1) inadequate finances to sustain independent living, and (2) the need for direct assistance in managing tasks of daily living. Speare and Avery (1993) also found that it was less common among non-Hispanic whites for elderly parents to move in with their adult children. In this instance, family background (e.g., race and ethnicity) can help to reduce the level of stress encountered in the extended family (Speare & Avery, 1993).

Overall, Lerner, Somers, Reid, Chiriboga, and Tierney (1991) have shown that regardless of the reality in caring for an older parent, siblings report differential "egocentric" perceptions of their own and their siblings contributions. Each believes individually that other siblings contribute less, derive less personal satisfaction from their contributions, and have more freedom to alter their caregiving arrangements. Perhaps even more striking in this study is the belief that other siblings would agree with the egocentric beliefs that each sibling holds about their own contributions and the relative contributions of other siblings to the caretaking arrangements (Lerner et al., 1991).

In examining sources of stress in managing the care of a parent with dementia, Suitor and Pillemer (1993) have confirmed that although important social support is derived from friends and siblings, the interpersonal stress experienced by married daughters in their caretaking roles stems primarily from their own siblings (Suitor & Pillemer, 1993). Another source of stress recently identifed among women who assume a caretaking role is the reduction in income and derived benefits from Social Security (Kingson & O'Grady-LeShane, 1993). This effect is immediate in that women frequently have to give up work or significantly reduce their work schedules to care for an aging parent or relative and is also seen later in the reduced benefits they receive at the time of retirement. Kingson and O'Grady-LeShane (1993) estimated this difference to result in the loss of benefits of $127 per month at retirement among women who have assumed the responsibility of caring for an older parent or relative.

L. P. Gwyther (1992) in a recent review summarized the research findings of studies focused on caregiver distress indicating "that families provide most care; that caregiving has the potential for both positive and negative outcomes (although caregiver burden, stress, and decrements resulting from caregiving tend to be the focus of most studies and interventions); that caregivers and care receivers are too diverse for simplistic, unidimensional approaches; . . . that most modest interventions to support caregivers will be subjectively perceived as satisfactory but will not produce significant changes in the *multiple* dimensions of burden, well-being, health, mental health or capacity to continue family care" (p. 866).

The stressful nature of caring for a spouse with dementia or stroke has also been well documented (Anthony-Bergstone, Zarit, & Gatz, 1988; George & Gwyther, 1986; Gilhooly, 1984; Moritz, Kasl, & Berkman, 1989). It appears that such caregiving contributes to increased levels of depression and hostility. Younger and older women (60 and over) reported increased levels of anxiety when they acted as caregivers (Anthony-Bergstone, Zarit, & Gatz, 1988). Researchers have identified three styles of coping with an ailing parent: *confrontational* (focusing on dealing with anger, guilt, and sadness, and attempting to bring stressful encounters with the parent to an end); *denial* (suppression and eventual repression of negative feelings); and *avoidant* (consistent suppression rather than denial or repression of negative emotions). Stephens, Norris, Kinney, Ritchie, and Grotz (1988) found both avoidance coping strategies and depression among caregivers 60 years of age and over who were responsible for the care of an older spouse or relative recently discharged from a rehabilitation hospital. Avoidance strategies may help people cope with the immediate impact of stress or a short-term problem (Roth & Cohen, 1986). However, if employed consistently as a strategy to deal with problems of extended duration (more than six to nine months), avoidance generally produces negative outcomes (Roth & Cohen, 1986).

The caretaking role of an older relative or parent is intense and demanding; the greater the health problems and overall frailty of the older person the more likely the caretaker experiences feelings of hostility, resentment, and guilt (Light, Niederehe, & Lebowitz, 1994). Franks and Stephens (1992) have tried to refine the concept of stress experienced in caring for an elderly parent by examining the meaning or value assigned to each of the roles (e.g., caretaker, mother, and spouse) that may be in conflict. They suggest that adult daughters will experience stress in the role of caretaker as a direct result of the degree to which each role (e.g., caretaker, mother, wife) contributes to their sense of well-being. For some daughters, role conflicts will not cause as much stress, if a particular role contributes only marginally to a sense of well-being. Such roles may be more easily abandoned (temporarily) in favor of another role that contributes more to their well-being (Franks & Stephens, 1992).

It is also important to note that the experience of stress in caring for elderly adults is by no means restricted to adult children. Significant concern has also been directed at the stress encountered by professionals who provide direct services and supervision through community programs such as respite and day care programs for families with a relative with Alzheimer's disease, and by staff who provide services for the elderly in nursing homes, hospitals, and extended care facilities (Biegel & Blum, 1990; Chapell & Novak, 1992; Montgomery, Kosloski, & Borgatta; 1990). Chapell and Novak (1992) report that nursing assistants in a long-term care institution for the elderly were found to experience significant stress, defined as burden, burnout, and perceived job pressure. The importance of providing specific training to help the nursing assistants cope with elderly residents with cognitive impairment was a major variable in reducing job-related stress. Support from family and friends also provided nursing assistants some help in reducing perceived job pressures and burnout (Chapell & Novak, 1992).

## Coping Effectively with Stress: The Value of Social Support

In other research studies with informal caregivers of the elderly (e.g., relatives), the value of social support has been confirmed, although debate exists regarding the importance of the number of people who might provide support versus the type of social support that is provided (Vitaliano, Russo, Young, Teri & Maivro, 1991; Lawton, Moss, Kleban, Glicksman, & Rovine, 1991). Wheaton (1985) suggests that social support in general serves the informal family caregivers of the elderly as a buffer, protecting against some of the more difficult stresses of coping with a chronic situation that is difficult to manage. Indeed, the recent literature has confirmed that families appear to be able to maintain their caretaking of a frail or ill older parent in the home primarily through social support (Mathews, Werkner, & Delaney, 1989; Pearlin, 1985; Thompson, Futterman, Gallagher-Thompson, Rose, & Lovett, 1993). In one study, different types of social support were compared to evaluate which were most effective in reducing the burden of caretaking on family members (Thompson et al., 1993). Engaging in social interaction for simple fun and recreation was measurably superior to other forms of social support in helping family members manage their stress in caretaking for an older relative. Other types of social support, such as direct aid, physical assistance, emotional support, and validation of self-esteem, were ineffectual in reducing the stress associated with chronic caregiving to an elderly relative in the home. The findings suggest that, in coping with the chronic stress of their roles in the extended family, and to help themselves manage the burden of their complex and demanding roles, it is vital for caregivers to engage in regular pleasant activities with friends and other relatives (Thompson et al., 1993).

## Coping Effectively with Stress: Personality and Social Interaction

Marjorie Fiske (1980) indicates that virtually every individual harbors both deficits and resources within her or his psychological makeup. Fiske believes that we must learn more about the adaptive coexistence of both deficits and resources, because one strong resource may offset or counterbalance several deficits. In an ongoing longitudinal study, Fiske is attempting to assess the balance between inner resources and deficits among men and women at different stages of the life course, the relationship between these dimensions, and the individual's sense of well-being. Looked at separately, the two dimensions are related to life satisfaction in an entirely rational fashion. People with the most resources (such as the capacity for mutuality, growth, competence, hope, and insight) tend to be satisfied with themselves and their lives; those with deficits (psychological symptoms, including anxiety, hostility, and self-hatred) are the least satisfied. But these expected results were found among fewer than one-third of the people studied. Among the other two-thirds, a combination of many positive and negative attributes seemed to increase the individual's sense of well-being.

Well-being and actual physical health among the elderly have been found to be related. We noted earlier that elderly with better health status were able to initiate and sustain more contacts with their families than those in poorer health (Field et al., 1993). Well-being is enhanced with higher levels of social interaction and lowest among adults who have no close confidants and no companions (Cohen & Syme, 1985; Thomae, 1992). Field et al. (1993) hypothesized that feelings of closeness between healthier elderly and their families were possible through the mechanism of reciprocity (i.e., mutual giving and receiving of social, tangible, and emotional support). Such reciprocity was less likely among family members and the elderly who were in poorer health than among those in better health (Field et al., 1993). This result was also recently confirmed in a cross-cultural investigation among the rural elderly in China (Shi, 1993). Elderly Chinese with greater resources such as health, income, and education were more likely to provide than receive assistance in their family social support networks; exchanges were most often in the form of emotional support and/or behavioral assistance (Shi, 1993).

The elderly have been found to maintain social friendship networks established earlier in their lives, with the degree of contact among friends and family for older persons nearly comparable to the levels of earlier ages (Field & Minkler, 1988). Age by itself is not as good a predictor of the type and frequency of social interaction when compared to more powerful variables such as gender, ethnicity, and social class

(Antonnuci & Akiyama, 1991a). Age was related to the size of the social network in one investigation. Social networks were found to contract around age 70 and then increase dramatically as direct help with daily activities from family members became necessary, most typically near age 85 (Wenger, 1984).

## The Search for Meaning: Cognitive Distortion, Social Comparison Processes, and Mastery

The attempt to make sense out of what is happening to us shapes our cognitive appraisal of stressful encounters and our choice of coping strategies. It is part of our continuous search for mastery and control over difficult situations (Bandura, 1982, 1989; Lachman, 1986; Lefebvre-Pinard, 1984; Rodin, 1986; Rybash et al., 1986). The cognitive-affective struggle we call *coping* has important implications for our health, psychological functioning, competence both at work and at home, and the success we find in interpersonal relationships. According to Lazarus and DeLongis:

> . . . the significance of such a process-oriented perspective may be even greater in the study of aging than in midlife because of the presence of widespread losses of roles and relationships. But whether viewed in the context of the entire life course or more narrowly in aging, we must see people as engaged in a life drama with a continuous story line that is best grasped not as a still photo but as a moving picture with a beginning, middle, and end. (1983, p. 24)

As we have seen, adaptation and coping are important ingredients in understanding the adult's subjective experience of stressful events. Recently, psychologists studying coping and adaptation in the elderly have begun to question *how* older people are able to maintain positive self-esteem, feelings of control, and a sense of mastery in the face of an increasing number of forced changes and losses (Brandtstadter, Wentura, & Greve, 1993). Lachman (1986; Lachman & Burak, 1993), for instance, provides support for the notion that older adults continue to maintain a strong belief in their ability to control the external environment. A strong belief in personal control is positively related to other areas of psychological functioning, physical health, and cognitive-intellectual achievements (Lachman & Burak, 1993; Rodin, 1990). Older adults make choices regarding those areas of life that they can still manage and forego areas in which they no longer have as much control. This is, of course, in contrast to younger adults who have minimal control over life tasks such as schooling, work, or residential location (Brim, 1992; Lachman & Burak, 1993). In this sense, older adults, intentionally or unintentionally, adjust aspirations, relinquish goals, lower expectations, and readjust priorities as developmental changes occur (Lachman & Burak, 1993). In the face of age-related developmental change they are able to maintain a positive view of self and their own personal control.

In one account (Brandtstadter et al., 1993), the success of adults in adjusting and coping with the cumulative losses in old age and their attendant threats to self-esteem lies in their use of accommodative and assimilative processes. **Accommodative processes** allow older adults to disengage and lower their aspirations from

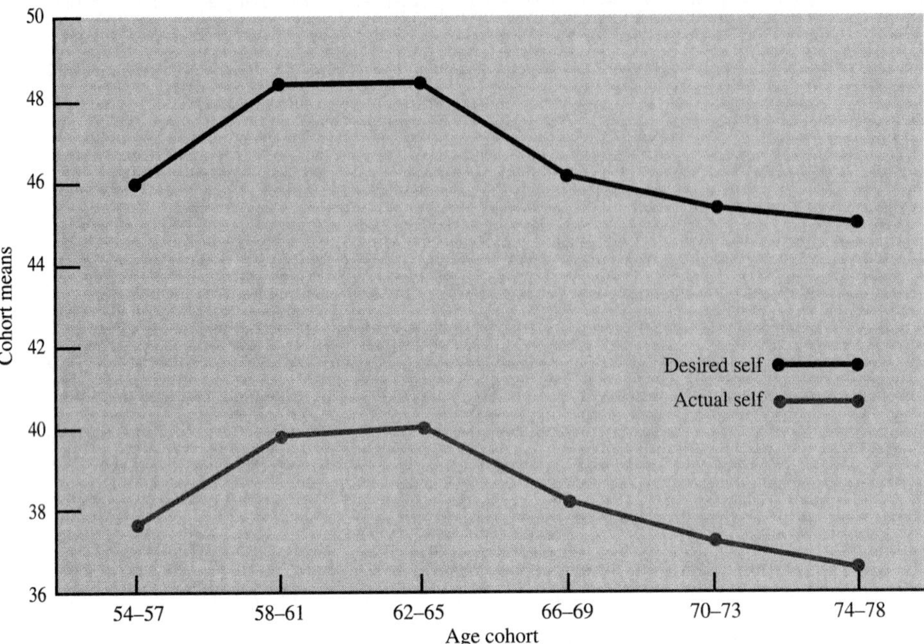


**Figure 10.3** Age differences in ratings of desired self and of actual self (sum scores). By accommodating normative self-conceptions, self-esteem can be stabilized despite perceived developmental losses.

goals that they cannot attain. Accommodative processes become more important with advancing age, since they are relevant to the adjustment and coping process as well as to the self-evaluation and reprioritizing of goals in old age. **Assimilative processes** direct older adults' instrumental behavior, actively engage them, and encourage them to strive to achieve personally derived goals and priorities. Assimilative processes imply a directed, intentional activity that prevents or reduces the developmental losses in domains that are central to the older person's self-esteem and personal identify.

It is in the interplay of these two processes that older adults are able to maintain both a sense of control and a positive view of self (Brandtstadter et al., 1993). Figure 10.3 shows that the interplay between assimilative and accommodative processes contributes to the maintenance of self-esteem across the life span. Based on results of cross-sectional comparisons from 1,256 participants taken in 1991, the figure shows little difference between age groups in their perceived self and their desired self. Older adults recognize losses in different domains yet are able to promote a positive view of self. Brandtstadter et al. (1993) note that self-evaluations in the later years remain virtually unaffected by actual or perceived age-related developmental losses; that is, the data in figure 10.3 show self-evaluations for each age cohort, measured by the difference between actual and desired self, to remain about the same. It is further noted that among successive age cohorts perceived self-deficits do not increase with age (Brandtstadter et al., 1993; Ryff, 1991).

These complementary dual processes of **life management** help to protect the aging self. Older persons are able to manage stress and preserve a positive view of themselves based on subjective interpretations of developmental gains and losses. The process of life managment offers us one way of understanding how older persons effectively cope with the aversive effects of developmental changes as they age and maintain positive self-evaluation and well-being. Life management is not, however, a process of active denial and repression; older persons are well aware of changes and losses that occur. Rather, positive self-evaluations are derived through active processes such as assimilative and accommodative modes of coping. Brandstadter et al. (1993) also have begun to apply this model to help us understand how older people preserve their sense of control. They argue that control at one level may simply be a lowering of aspirations or devaluing goals that are difficult to attain. This process leads to stability or enhancement of the older person's sense of personal control (Brandtstadter et al., 1993; Brandtstadter & Renner, 1992).

In addition to life management, older adults also make use of other coping and adjustment processes such as *social comparisons* to maintain a stable and positive view of self in the face of age-related change (Gibbons & Gerrard, 1991; Ryff & Essex, 1991; Wood et al., 1985). Based on a hypothesized need for self-appraisal, we turn to comparisons with other people to evaluate how we are doing, especially when situations are ambiguous or when external standards against which to compare ourselves are lacking (Heidrich & Ryff, 1993). In two separate studies, Heidrich and Ryff examined the role of social comparison processes in a large sample of elderly women. Those women who were in poorer physical health more frequently engaged in social comparison processes; yet, surprisingly, the results of such frequent comparisons with others led these women to have more positive mental health and better coping. The more frequently social comparisons were utilized, the more positive the mental health of the women, even those in the poorest of physical health. The primary mechanism employed by the older women was "downward comparison" in which they evaluated themselves against a group of women who experienced poorer physical health than themselves; the process of downward comparison has also been reported previously among individuals attempting to cope with life-threatening illnesses (Taylor & Lobel, 1989; Wood et al., 1985).

Heidrich and Ryff (1993) not only found that elderly women's social comparisons resulted in self-enhancement and improved mental health, they documented those areas in which downward comparisons were utilized: physical health, coping with aging, and level of activity. All of these domains are ones in which loss or declines are likely to emerge in old age and document that downward comparisons indeed serve a self-enhancing function. Two areas in which upward comparisons were reported involved friendships and physical appearance. It was hypothesized that these two domains represent ones in which elderly women may be motivated by a continued need for self-improvement, with upward social comparisons serving to motivate or direct them to particular role models or serve as an inspirational function (Heidrich & Ryff, 1993). (See Research Focus 10.1 for a discussion of other research in this area.)

### Research Focus 10.1

## Possible Selves: The Fear of Poor Health

In a recent publication, Karen Hooker and Cheryl Kaus (1994) investigated how adults create a framework in which their own behaviors are linked directly to their health. The study was based on the pioneering work of Markus and Nurius (1986) on *possible selves*: a future view of our self-identity representing a desirable goal in terms of what we might like to become or an undesirable goal or fear of what we might become. Markus and Nurius believe that possible selves provide individuals with heightened motivation to action to either realize those positive goals we seek for our "self" or to avoid becoming what we fear for our "self." The construct of possible selves implies that individuals can shed images that no longer fit the reality of aging (e.g., accepting accumulated losses) as we have just seen in the previous section. As such, possible selves have been closely related to positive adjustment, since they help to preserve well-being (Markus & Herzog,1992) and a sense of personal integrity (Ryff, 1991). Possible selves are both causes of action (Karoly, 1993) and a source of direction in later development (Hooker & Kaus, 1992). Possible selves represent the individual's embodiment of actual life goals (definition of possible selves) and behaviors (actions) that will help attain these goals.

The eighty-four young adults (24–39 years old) and eighty-seven middle-aged adults (40–59 years old) in Hooker and Kaus's study indicated whether they had positive images of a healthy self in the future (e.g., "hoped-for selves") as well as negative images of an unhealthy self (e.g., "feared selves"). In the results obtained by Hooker and Kaus (1994) middle-aged respondents indicated significantly more health-related selves than did young adults. Both young and middle-aged adults did not seem to be considering healthy possible selves as much as unhealthy possible selves. In other words, the goal for individuals was primarily to *avoid* a possible self replete with health problems and health deficiencies. Similar responses have been reported among middle-aged persons (Cross & Markus, 1991; Leventhal, Leventhal, & Schaefer, 1991). Carol Ryff (1991) also noted that fear of declining health and well-being dominated older adults' views of possible selves. In this regard, "dread" directs middle-aged individuals to adopt health-enhancing behaviors (actions), e.g., "I do not want to have these events occur to me." Indeed, when Hooker and Kaus assessed goal-oriented activities and other self-regulatory variables, they found that there were two types of significant predictors of health behaviors: *(1)* actions that were taken to avoid feared health-related selves, and (2) a person's *perception* or *belief* that they were capable of preventing such "dreaded" selves. Leventhal, Leventhal, and Schaefer (1991) noted that though middle-aged and younger adults are similar in their fear of health threats, older adults are more likely to have adopted a greater number of health preventive behaviors. In fact, in an earlier study (Hooker, 1992), older adults reported to have both feared and hoped-for health-related selves. Remaining at issue for future research is the identification of those possible hoped-for health-related selves which may promote specific types of health preventive behaviors, particularly for young and middle-aged adults (Hooker & Kaus, 1994; Leventhal, Leventhal, Schaefer, & Easterling,1993).

## Mental Health in Late Adulthood

Some older individuals lose the ability to cope with the demands and complexities of everyday life. The following sections examine the impact of this loss of coping ability on older adults, their family and friends, and the rest of society. A breakdown in coping strategies and the loss of the ability to function psychologically are two important hallmarks of mental disorders. The importance of understanding and treating mental disorders in older adults has been captured in Seymour Kety's foreword to the *Handbook of Mental Health and Aging* (1980). Specifically, Kety commented that:

> A national health problem that is most severe in terms of its prevalence and cost is a group of mental disorders and dysfunctions which are associated with aging. . . . As the result of progress in medical science, a substantial segment of the population can now look forward to a longer life, but one which may unfortunately be hampered by mental disability. This is a prospect that is both troubling to the individual and costly to society.

> Since mental handicap makes an individual increasingly dependent on the help and care of others, the cost of these services and prerequisites to other members of the family and to the whole of society as well represents a burden which has been estimated at 36.78 billions of dollars per year in the United States. More important, perhaps, is a cost that cannot be measured or tabulated: the loss of human potential and of the affected person's capacity for adaptation and ability to contribute to human welfare. (p. xi)

Recently, experts have commented on the relative lack of change in national policy regarding the mental health needs of older persons (Eisdorfer, 1993; Kiesler, 1992). As but one example of national priorities, it has been noted that currently only 3 percent of Medicare funding is being used to support mental health. In the debate about a new health care policy, universal health insurance, and access to increasingly scarce medical resources, the significance of mental health needs has continued to remain far in the background. Eisdorfer (1993) further remarks that although a significant number of nursing home admissions and hospitalizations among the elderly continue to relate directly to mental health disorders, a minimal amount of outpatient treatment (e.g., individual therapy, group intervention, etc.) is being provided to those 65 years of age and older, a situation that has continued for decades.

Defining *mental health* is not an easy task, although the term has become commonplace in our society. It presumably not only embraces the absence of mental illness, but also reflects one's ability to deal with the issues of life in an effective if not pleasurable or satisfying manner. Although some emphasize a definition that embraces the negative qualities in summarizing adjustment difficulties, others utilize a definition of mental health that is focused on the positive characteristics in adjustment and coping (Birren & Sloane, 1980; Butler, Lewis, & Sunderland, 1991). (See also Research Focus 10.2.) Although not a complete inventory, mental health using positive indicators is marked by coping and adaptation that demonstrates an accurate perception of reality, personal mastery, individual autonomy, positive self-esteem, and a drive toward self-actualization (Birren & Renner, 1980). Because older adults are more likely than younger adults to have some type of physical illness, the interweaving of physical and mental problems is more likely to occur in later adulthood than in younger adulthood (Birren & Sloane, 1980; Gambert, 1987).

Beyond any doubt, there is a need to address the mental health needs of the growing population of older adults. However, it cannot be assumed that growing old increases the risk of mental illness. In one study that used a sequential research design and involved more than two thousand participants ranging from midlife to old age, Aldwin et al. (1989) found no support for the hypothesis that the symptoms of mental illness increase with age. Most interestingly, Aldwin et al. (1989) discovered that with increasing age came greater variability in the extent to which individuals experienced emotional distress. This increased interindividual variability in mental health among the elderly may be due to varying life circumstances. For example, Aldwin et al. (1989) suggested that for some individuals, mental distress may increase with age because of the death of friends

## *Manic-Depressive Disorders and Creativity*

Experts examining psychological adjustment and coping processes have noted that frequently (but *not* always), those who make unique and outstanding contributions to the creative arts demonstrate cycles of manic-depressive behavior during their lives. It is curious that many of the musical geniuses of the past two centuries suffered from bouts of manic-depression, or bipolar affective disorder. DeAngelis (1989) recently examined the suffering and personal anguish this mood disorder brought to the lives of talented composers such as George Frederic Handel, Hugo Wolf, Robert Schumann, Hector Berlioz, and Gustav Mahler. The cyclic effects of intense periods of activity or mania obviously contributed to the immense musical productivity of this group of outstanding and creative composers. Yet their corresponding bouts of debilitating depression, leading at times to suicidal thoughts or behaviors, also affected these composers.

The following diary excerpts and letters reveal how difficult it was for these composers to cope with their manic-depressive episodes. Berlioz, for instance, described his two moods as "the two kinds of spleen; one mocking, active, passionate, malignant; the other morose and wholly passive." Schumann likened his mood swings to two imaginary people, the first "impulsive, widely energetic, impassioned, decisive, masculine, high-spirited, and iconoclastic; the other gentle, melancholic, pious, introspective, and inwardly-gazing." According to musicologist Robert Winter, Gustav Mahler recognized the emergence of the condition as early as age 19, writing, "I have become a different person. I don't know whether this new person is better; he certainly is not happier. The fires of a supreme zest for living and the most gnawing desire for death alternate in my heart, sometimes in the course of a single hour."

Is manic-depression a prerequisite to creative expression in the arts? Are all creative people likely to experience manic-depression? Though many creative people in music, writing, and the visual arts have experienced manic-depression, the percentages rarely exceed 66 percent in any of the samples selected for study. However, even more modest estimates that 25 to 50 percent of a sample of creative persons experience and/or have been treated for manic-depressive disorders represents a "disproportionate rate of affective illness in the highly creative," according to Kay Jamison of Johns Hopkins University of Medicine. However, not all persons who are creative, talented, and gifted in the arts experience manic-depressive disorders. Nor are all those with manic-depression necessarily creative.

Current research and theory suggests that manic-depression stems from biological factors that are expressed psychologically. The condition is apparently triggered when an environmental stressor primes the pump and the affective disorder begins its inevitable progression. The most effective treatments are based on a combination of psychotherapy and the use of lithium, a drug used to level extreme moods. But researchers estimate that fewer than two-thirds of the more than two million adults with manic-depression are diagnosed or treated. Thus, even in the 1990s, many people continue to experience the sufferings described by the composers a century or more ago. Many of these untreated adults are elderly.



and loved ones and the onset of chronic illness; other older adults may show improvements in mental health as the strains caused by an unbearable job or caring for ill parents come to an end. Aldwin et al. (1989) concluded that

> . . . rather than asking whether mental health changes with age, perhaps we should ask what patterns of change are characteristic of different groups of adults, and what are the antecedents and consequences of long-term change or stability in mental health? In this manner we can begin to understand the process of "successful" aging . . . (p. 305)

Let's look at some of the categories of mental disorders that afflict the elderly. These disorders, along with several others not mentioned in this text, are more fully described in the *DSM-III-R (Diagnostic and Statistical Manual of Mental Disorders, Third Edition, Revised)* published by the American Psychiatric Association (1987).

*Table 10.2*

| Acute Brain Syndromes: Preventable and Reversible Causes |
|---|
| Drug toxicity (medications and alcohol, heavy metals, carbon monoxide) |
| Metabolic disorders (salt and water imbalance) |
| Endocrine abnormalities (hyper- and hypoglycemia, thyroidism) |
| Nutritional problems (general malnutrition, vitamin $B_{12}$ deficiency) |
| Heart and lung disease |
| Kidney disease |
| Head injury (tumor and trauma) |
| Infections (central nervous system) |
| Emotional problems (depression) |
| Communication deficit (vision, hearing, aphasis) |

## Categorizing the Mental Health Problems of the Elderly

In categorizing mental health problems, a distinction is usually made between organic and functional disorders. **Organic disorders** are associated with some physical cause, such as brain damage. Authorities estimate that about 10 to 20 percent of organic disorders are reversible or partially reversible and that the number of preventable cases is nearly 25 percent (Gambert, 1987; LaRue, Dessonville, & Jarvik, 1985). By contrast, **functional disorders** are unrelated to physiological problems and are caused by psychological or socioenvironmental factors. Two forms of organic disorders researchers have studied are **acute brain syndromes,** which are reversible, and **chronic brain syndromes,** which are not reversible. An acute brain syndrome is a kind of medical emergency requiring rapid diagnosis and treatment to prevent losses and reverse damage. Like other medical emergencies, acute brain syndrome may come on suddenly, without warning. Clairfield (1988) estimates that only 3 percent of the acute brain syndromes are completely reversible with 8 percent partially reversible. Table 10.2 contains a list of some of the most common causes of acute brain syndromes.

***Delirium*** A special type of acute brain syndrome is **delirium.** Delirium is marked by minimal awareness of self and environment, disorientation, hallucinations, delusions (often paranoid), attentional disorders, and sleep disorders (Lipowski, 1980; Zarit & Zarit, 1983). Its incidence seems correlated with factors related to cerebral metabolism. Delirium often occurs following surgery, accompanying severe malnutrition, or as the result of toxic levels of drugs, drug-drug interactions, electrolyte imbalances, or potassium deficits (Zarit & Zarit, 1983). Acute brain syndrome or delirium may be misdiagnosed as dementia; medical personnel must rule out such problems as those listed in table 10.2 *before* they diagnose an irreversible dementia or organic brain syndrome (Gambert, 1987; Zarit, Eiler, & Hassinger, 1985).

Chronic brain syndromes usually involve permanent brain damage. They may produce a variety of symptoms, such as confusion, suspiciousness, lack of concern for personal and social amenities, and loss of control over bodily functions. Since brain tissue appears unrecoverable once destroyed, it is critical to understand the possible causes of such problems and to undertake rapid intervention, if possible.

David Kay and Klaus Bergmann (1980) concluded that chronic brain syndrome is the most prevalent mental disorder among people aged 65 and over. Of these individuals, 1 to 2 percent are severely impaired and 3 to 4 percent are moderately impaired. The majority live at home rather than in institutions and are cared for by relatives and neighbors.

***Dementia*** Perhaps the most controversial, confounding, and debilitating set of mental disturbances afflicts individuals who have been classified as having some type of dementia. **Dementia** is a global term for any neurological disorder whose primary symptomology is the deterioration of mental functioning; it represents an abnormal clinical condition, a mental disorder that is *not* part of the universal process of aging. **Senility** is a term used by the general public to describe the severe mental deterioration displayed by some older adults; as used by the common person in everyday discussions, senility is nearly identical in meaning to the medical term dementia. On the other hand, **senescence** is a term used to describe normal developmental aging; unless we die early of disease, all of us will experience it. Senescence is the point at which degenerative processes overwhelm the biological capacity of the individual to recover from such losses (Rockstein & Sussman, 1979). Unfortunately, many members of the general public equate senility with senescence. They mistakenly believe and perpetuate an unfounded myth that normal aging is always accompanied by severe mental deterioration and disorganization.

Dementia is estimated to affect a steadily increasing percentage of those over the age of 65 and is present in more than 20 percent of those over the age of 80 (Connolly & Williams, 1993; Gurland & Cross, 1982; LaRue et al., 1985). There are more than seventy different types or causes of dementia (Connolly & Williams, 1993), all characterized by a gradual deterioration of intelligence and cognitive ability, often with associated behavioral changes in areas such as self-care. In an overview of the causes and treatments of dementia, Gary Small and Lissy Jarvik (1982) concluded that dementia is best understood as a clinical syndrome—a cluster of symptoms and signs that should lead to a search for the cause of the disorder. Dementia is present in the elderly whenever the following diagnostic symptoms appear (LaRue et al., 1985, p. 676):

1. Loss of intellectual ability severe enough to interfere with social or occupational functioning
2. Memory impairment
3. Impairment in abstract thinking, judgment, or higher cortical functions, or personality change
4. Clear state of consciousness (no delirium or intoxication)
5. Documented or presumed evidence of an organic cause

Note that it is almost impossible to differentiate a reversible (acute brain syndrome) from an irreversible (chronic brain syndrome) dementia using these five criteria (National Institute of Aging Task Force, 1980; Zarit & Zarit, 1983). A discussion of the several forms of dementia follows. These variants of dementia include Alzheimer's disease, multi-infarct dementia, mixed type, Creutzfeldt-Jakob disease, and AIDS dementia complex.

## *Understanding Alzheimer's Disease*

The symptoms of Alzheimer's disease or AD were first described by a German physician, Alois Alzheimer, in 1907. Alzheimer's disease is a form of dementia. Dementia, as we have discussed, has often erroneously been referred to as senility, an overused and imprecise layperson's term summarizing all of the debilitating personality and cognitive changes that may be observed in the elderly. To complicate things even further, physicians and psychologists may refer to Alzheimer's disease as *senile dementia of the Alzheimer's type* or *SDAT.* We have chosen to use the more general term *Alzheimer's disease* or *AD* in this text. In this section we describe some of the most current research findings regarding AD, the disorder sometimes called the "disease of the century."

### Description of Alzheimer's Disease

Alzheimer's disease is arguably the most severe and devastating of all of the different types of dementia. It is a degenerative brain disease that is the most common cause of cognitive failure in older adulthood (Reisberg, Ferris, deLeon, & Crook, 1985; Selkoe et al., 1987). The elderly person with AD loses the ability to remember, recognize, and reason. In the final stages of the disease, the afflicted person develops profound physical as well as mental disabilities and typically needs institutional care. At present, there is no cure for this disease. Death usually occurs within five to ten years after the initial onset of symptoms, regardless of the age at which it strikes (Reisberg, 1987). It has been estimated that AD is the fourth leading cause of death for adults in the United States (Katzman, 1986) and that approximately 5 percent of the 30 million adults over 65 years of age suffer from AD (Reisberg, 1987; Thompson, 1986). Given the fact that the population of the United States, as well as most Westernized societies, is gradually aging, AD will become still more prevalent in the future and the cost of caring for AD patients will rise dramatically. There are more elderly people in nursing homes than in hospitals (1.3 million versus 1 million). It has been estimated that 58 percent of the residents of nursing homes suffer from AD (Reisberg, 1987).

Several health economists have tried to calculate the monetary impact of AD. It was estimated that in 1985, approximately 80 billion dollars were spent due to AD and related dementias. This estimate includes 13.3 billion dollars spent on direct patient care (Cartwright, Haung, & Hu, 1988). Table 10.3 provides information concerning the societal costs of caring for AD patients as well as those with other life-threatening disorders. The table also contains information about the extent to which the federal government funds research projects designed to find the causes and cures for these disorders. Based on the data in table 10.3, it would seem as if research on AD is underfunded.

In the past, AD was defined as a type of dementia not associated with old age. It was thought to be a neurological disease that occurred during middle age and was thus viewed as a type of "presenile dementia." Furthermore, it was discovered that AD only afflicted an exceptionally small number of middle-aged adults. Thus, AD was thought of as a very rare disorder that the typical older person had little need to worry

*TABLE 10.3*

***Societal Costs of Alzheimer's Disease and Other Illnesses***

| *Disease* | *Estimated Societal Cost* | *1989 Federal Funding* |
|---|---|---|
| Alzheimer's Disease | $51–$79 billion (1985) | $120 million |
| Heart Disease | $88 billion (1989) | $640 million |
| AIDS | $66 billion (1991) | $607 million |
| Cancer | $71.5 billion (1985) | $1.45 billion |

*From* Aging Research and Training News, *March 27, 1989, p. 43, published by Business Publishers, Inc., 951 Pershing Drive, Silver Spring, MD. Reprinted by permission.*

about. It was believed that true senility or dementia was a totally different disease. Senility was thought to be a disorder of old age, and it was believed to be caused by vascular disorders such as cerebral arteriosclerosis (i.e., a hardening of the arteries that feed the brain). In the late 1960s and early 1970s, however, it was discovered that the symptoms and causes of dementia in both middle-aged and elderly adults were identical (Petit, 1982; Wurtman, 1985). This finding revolutionized our ideas about the prevalence and seriousness of AD. Scientists began to realize that AD in old age had been misdiagnosed and misunderstood for an extremely long time. (See Research Focus 10.3 for a brief synopsis of the facts we now know about Alzheimer's disease.)

Some of the most interesting and important findings about AD are the types of brain changes that appear in patients with this disorder. Specifically, AD patients have an excessive number of senile plaques and neurofibrillary tangles. **Senile plaques** are composed of a protein, amyloid, and contain at their perimeter the remaining fragments of dead neurons. **Neurofibrillary tangles** are pairs of filaments in neurons that have become intertwined and twisted around each other. Both plaques and tangles may only be detected from microscopic slides of brain tissue collected through autopsy. Whitehouse (1993) reminds us that it is only through autopsy that a definitive diagnosis of AD versus other forms of dementia can be made. Given the recent discovery that suggests a genetic relationship for certain forms of AD, autopsy is an important step for families to consider and may help research investigators studying this disease (Whitehouse, 1993). The presence of plaques and tangles represent two prominent features of normal aging (e.g., senescence). This suggests that there is a quantitative, rather than a qualitative, difference between the brains of the healthy elderly and those with AD—the brains of AD patients have *more* plaques and tangles than those contained in normal aged brains.These plaques and tangles are spread throughout the brain, but are most concentrated in the hippocampus and the cortex (Cote, 1981; Petit, 1982; Reisberg, 1981; Scheibel & Wechsler, 1986). This has led to the speculation (Cote, 1981) that AD may really be "accelerated, normal aging"! Think about the implication of this statement. If we live long enough—if we begin to approach the upper end of the potential human life span—we may face an ever-increasing risk of suffering from AD.

# Facts About Alzheimer's Disease

**Definition and Scope**
Alzheimer's disease (pronounced Alz-hi-merz) is a disease of the brain that impairs the afflicted individual's memory and ability to reason. Alzheimer's disease (AD) is the most common form of dementing illness. Dementia is a loss of intellectual function (thinking, remembering and reasoning) so severe that it interferes with an individual's daily life and eventually results in death. More than 100,000 people die of Alzheimer's disease annually. This makes AD the fourth leading cause of death in adults, after heart disease, cancer and stroke. Men and women are affected almost equally. The disease was first described by Alois Alzheimer in 1906. Researchers have identified specific biochemical criteria (amyloid plaques and neurofibrillary tangles) and behavioral changes that characterize the disease. The only identified risk factors are age and family history. Most people experience AD after age 65; however, people in their 40s and 50s have been diagnosed.

**Symptoms**
Symptoms of Alzheimer's disease include a gradual memory loss, decline in the ability to perform routine tasks, disorientation, personality changes, difficulty in learning, loss of language skills, and impairment of judgment and planning. The rate of change varies from person to person. The time from onset of symptoms until death ranges from 3 to 20 years. In the severe, advanced stage of the disease, people are totally incapable of caring for themselves.

**Diagnosis**
Early and precise diagnosis is important to determine if suspected symptoms support a diagnosis of Alzheimer's disease, other dementia or a treatable condition. Possible reversible conditions include depression, adverse drug reactions, metabolic changes, nutritional deficiencies, head injuries and stroke.

There is no single clinical test to identify Alzheimer's disease. A comprehensive evaluation to establish diagnosis will include a complete health history, physical examination, neurological and mental status assessments and other diagnostic tests including blood studies, urinalysis, electrocardiogram and chest x-rays. Documenting symptoms and behavioral incidents over time, in a diary fashion, will assist physicians to understand the person's history. Other studies often recommended include: computerized tomography (CT Scan), electroencephalography (EEG), removal from medication, formal psychiatric assessment, neuropsychological testing, and occasionally, examination of the cerebrospinal fluid by spinal tap. While this evaluation may provide a clinical diagnosis, confirmation of Alzheimer's disease requires examination of brain tissue, which is usually done by an autopsy.

**Treatment**
Although no cure for Alzheimer's disease is presently available, good planning and medical and social management can ease the burdens on the patient and family. Health care directives and decisions can be made while the patient has the mental capacity to do so. Physical exercise and social activity are important, as are proper nutrition. A calm and well-structured environment may help the afflicted person to continue functioning. Appropriate medication can lessen agitation, anxiety, unpredictable behavior, improve sleeping patterns and treat depression.

**Causes & Research**
The causes of Alzheimer's disease are not known and are currently receiving intensive scientific investigation. Suspected causes include a genetic predisposition, a slow virus or other infectious agents, environmental toxins and immunologic changes. Scientists are applying the newest knowledge and research techniques in molecular genetics, pathology, virology, immunology, toxicology, neurology, psychiatry, pharmacology, biochemistry and epidemiology to find the causes, treatments and cures for Alzheimer's disease.

**Economic Impact**
During the later stages of the disease, 24-hour care is required for daily activities such as eating, grooming and toileting. The financing of care for Alzheimer's disease—including costs of diagnosis, treatment, nursing home care, informal care and lost wages—is estimated to be more than $100 billion each year. The federal government covers $4.4 billion and the states another $4.1 billion. Much of the remaining costs are borne by patients and their families.

The Alzheimer's Association is the oldest and largest national voluntary health organization dedicated to research for the causes, cure and prervention of Alzheimer's disease and to providing education and support services to Alzheimer patients, their families and caregivers. A nationwide 24-hour information and referral line links families who need assistance with nearby Chapters. Those interested in help may call **800–272–3900.**

A nationwide twenty-four hour information and referral line links families who need assistance with nearby Alzheimer's Association chapters. Those interested in help may call the Alzheimer's Association at 800–272–3900 (Illinois residents call 800–572–6037).

AD is difficult to diagnose since a number of other biological and psychological disorders closely imitate the symptoms of AD. For example, individuals who are clinically depressed or who suffer from curable dementias (described later in this chapter) display some of the same behavioral symptoms as AD patients (Heston & White, 1983; Zarit & Zarit, 1983).) As mentioned earlier, the only way to make a certain diagnosis of AD is by an autopsy (Heston & White, 1983; Whitehouse, 1993). In this procedure, brain tissue is analyzed microscopically to determine the presence and location of excessive plaques, tangles, and cell loss. Prior to a patient's death and autopsy, Reisberg (1987) notes, clinicians make the diagnosis of AD by exclusion of other causes (i.e., all other diagnoses are ruled out and nothing else is known that could explain the symptoms). As yet, there is no clear diagnosis by inclusion, or by a listing of the physical and behavioral symptoms that must be present if AD is to be diagnosed.

## Stages of Alzheimer's Disease

In AD there seems to be a predictable, progressive decline in specific areas of psychological, physiological, and social functioning. Reisberg and his colleagues (Reisberg & Bornstein, 1986; Reisberg, Ferris, & Franssen, 1985) have developed a **Functional Assessment Staging System (FAST)** to categorize these losses. The advantage of such an approach is that it provides clinicians and family members with the information necessary to provide appropriate intervention and to identify the projected course of the disease. Table 10.4 contains a description of FAST. This table lists the approximate time spent in each stage, the functional loss associated with each stage, and the mean duration of each stage. The early stages (1, 2, and 3) are *not* specifically descriptive of AD. For example, stages 1 and 2 are included to inform professionals of the typical patterns seen in normal aging. Stage 3 describes an early confused state that may be characteristic of a number of possible disorders. The patterns that emerge in the remaining four stages clearly reflect AD. A more in-depth description of the clinical manifestations of AD may be found by examining the *Global Deterioration Scale* (table 10.5). The numbers on the far left of the table refer to the FAST stages described in table 10.4.

## Causes and Treatment of Alzheimer's Disease

At present, no one knows the actual cause of AD. Researchers are still uncertain as to whether plaques and tangles are a cause or an effect of AD. Nevertheless, a number of different theories implicating more than forty possible factors have been advanced to account for the development of this disease (Jorm, 1990). McLachlan (1982) has suggested AD is caused by a slow virus that infects the brain. Other researchers have discovered that one type of AD runs in families. They have developed a genetic model to explain the cause of the *early-onset familial* form of AD. Familial or inherited AD accounts for a small number of patients with the disease (Kosik, 1992). However, this variation of AD represents at most 10 percent of the total cases (Jarvik, 1987). In a tremendously important

### *Table 10.4*

***Functional Assessment Staging (Fast Staging) of Alzheimer's Disease: Correspondence of Fast Stages with Normal Human Development and Estimated Time Course of Progression***

| *FAST Stage and Characeristics* | *Clinical Diagnosis* | *Approximate Age at Which Function is Acquired* | *Estimated Mean Duration in Survivors* |
|---|---|---|---|
| 1. No functional decrement | Normal adult | Adult | 50 years |
| 2. Subjective word difficulties | Normal aged adult | — | 15 years |
| 3. Decreased function in demanding employment settings | Compatible with possible incipient Alzheimer's disease in minority of cases | Young adult | 7 years |
| 4. Decreased ability to perform complex tasks such as handling finances or planning dinner for guests | Mild Alzheimer's disease | 8 years to adolescence | 2 years |
| 5. Requires assistance in choosing proper clothing | Moderate Alzheimer's disease | 5–7 years | 18 months |
| 6. (a) Difficulty putting on clothing properly | Moderately severe Alzheimer's disease | 5 years | 5 months |
| (b) Requires assistance bathing | | 4 years | 5 months |
| (c) Inability to handle mechanics of toileting | | 48 months | 5 months |
| (d) Urinary incontinence | | 36–54 months | 4 months |
| (e) Fecal incontinence | | 24–36 months | 10 months |
| 7. (a) Ability to speak limited to about six words | Severe Alzheimer's disease | 15 months | 12 months |
| (b) Intelligible vocabulary limited to a single word | | 12 months | 18 months |
| (c) Ambulatory ability lost | | 12 months | 12 months |
| (d) Ability to sit up lost | | 24–40 weeks | 12 months |
| (e) Ability to smile lost | | 8–16 weeks | 18 months |
| (f) Ability to hold up head lost | | 4–12 weeks | Not applicable |

*From Reisberg, B., "Dementia: A Systematic Approach to Identifying Reversible Causes" in* Geriatrics, *41(4): 30–46, 1986. Copyright 1984 by Barry Reisberg, M.D. Reprinted by permission.*

**TABLE 10.5**

**Global Deterioration Scale for Age-Associated Cognitive Decline and Alzheimer's Disease**

| *GDS Stage* | *Clinical Phase* | *Clinical Characteristics* | *Diagnosis* |
|---|---|---|---|
| 1. No cognitive decline | Normal | No subjective complaints of memory deficit; no memory deficit evidence on clinical interview. | Normal |
| 2. Very mild cognitive decline | Forgetfulness | Subjective complaints of memory deficit, most frequently in the following areas: (a) forgetting where one has placed familiar objects; (b) forgetting names one formerly knew well.<br><br>No objective evidence of memory deficit on clinical interview; no objective deficits in employment or social situations; appropriate concern with respect to symptomatology. | Normal for age |
| 3. Mild cognitive decline | Early confusional | Earliest clear-cut deficits; manifestations in more than one of the following areas: (a) patient may have gotten lost when traveling to an unfamiliar locaton; (b) coworkers become aware of patient's relatively poor performance; (c) word- and name-finding deficits become evident to intimates; (d) patient may read a passage or a book and retain relatively little material; (e) patient may demonstrate decreased facility in remembering names upon introduction to new people; (f) patient may have lost or misplaced an object of value; (g) concentration deficit may be evident on clinical testing.<br><br>Objective evidence of memory deficit obtained only when an intensive interview conducted by a trained diagnostician; decreased performance in demanding employment and social settings; denial begins to become manifest in patient; mild to moderate anxiety accompanies symptoms. | Compatible with possible incipient Alzheimer's disease in a minority of cases |
| 4. Moderate cognitive decline | Late confusional | Clear-cut deficit on careful clinical interview; deficit manifest in the following areas: (a) decreased knowledge of current and recent events; (b) may exhibit some deficit in memory of personal history; (c) concentration deficit elicited on serial subtractions; (d) decreased ability to travel, handle finances, and so on.<br><br>Frequently no deficit in the following areas: (a) orientation to time and person; (b) recognition of familiar persons and faces; (c) ability to travel to familiar locations.<br><br>Inability to perform complex tasks; denial is dominant defense mechanism; flattening of affect and withdrawal from challenging situations. | Mild Alzheimer's disease |

| | | | |
|---|---|---|---|
| 5. Moderately severe cognitive decline | Early dementia | Patients can no longer survive without some assistance; patients are unable during interview to recall a major relevant aspect of their current lives: for example, their address or telephone number of many years, the names of close members of their family (such as grandchildren), the name of the high school or college they attended.<br><br>Frequently some disorientation to time (date, day of week, season) or to place; an educated person may have difficulty counting backward from forty by fours or from twenty by twos.<br><br>Persons at this stage retain knowledge of many major facts regarding themselves and others; they invariably know their own name and generally know their spouse's and children's names; they require no assistance with toileting or eating, but may have some difficulty choosing the proper clothing to wear. | Moderate Alzheimer's disease |
| 6. Severe cognitive decline | Middle dementia | May occasionally forget the name of the spouse upon whom they are entirely dependent for survival; are largely unaware of all recent events and experiences in their lives; retain some knowledge of their past lives, but this is very sketchy. Generally unaware of their surroundings, the year, the season, and so on; may have difficulty counting from ten backward and, sometimes, forward; require some assistance with activities of daily living, for example, may become incontinent, require travel assistance but occasionally display ability to travel to familiar locations; diurnal rhythm frequently disturbed; almost always recall their own name; frequently continue to be able to distinguish familiar from unfamiliar persons in their environment.<br><br>Personality and emotional changes occur; these are quite variable and include: (a) delusional behavior (for example, patients may accuse their spouse of being an impostor, may talk to imaginary figures in the environment, or to their own reflections in the mirror); (b) obsessive symptoms (for example, person may continually repeat simple cleaning activities); (c) anxiety symptoms, agitation, and even previously nonexistent violent behavior may occur; (d) cognitive abulia (that is, loss of willpower because individual cannot carry a thought long enough to determine a purposeful course of action). | Moderately severe Alzheimer's disease |
| 7. Very severe cognitive decline | Late dementia | All verbal abilities are lost; frequently there is no speech at all—only grunting; incontinent of urine; requires assistance toileting and feeding; loses basic psychomotor skills (for example, ability to walk); it appears the brain no longer is able to tell the body what to do. | Severe Alzheimer's disease |

*From Reisberg, B., Ferris, S. H., de Leon, M. J., and Crook, T., "The Global Deterioration Scale for Assessment of Primary Degenerative Dementia" in* American Journal of Psychiatry, *139: 1136–1139, 1982. Adapted with permission.*

study, Peter St. George-Hyslop and his associates (St. George-Hyslop et al., 1987) discovered that the familial type of AD is associated with a defective gene located on chromosome 21. Furthermore, Rudolph Tanzi and his colleagues (Tanzi et al., 1987) found that the gene responsible for the production of *amyloid* (the core material of senile plaques) is also located on chromosome 21. This is most interesting, since it has been well documented that nearly every individual suffering from Down syndrome (most frequently related to extra chromosome material on the 21st pair) begins to develop the biochemical and psychological symptoms of AD by about age 41 (Kolata, 1985; Kosik, 1992; Raskind & Peskind, 1992; Wurtman, 1985). Thus, the excessive amyloid deposition in the brain and accumulation of senile plaque in both AD and Down syndrome patients may have a common origin—chromosome 21. A mutation on chromosome 21 occurs specifically in a gene responsible for encoding an amyloid precursor protein (APP). APP has been found to underlie the accumulation of amyloid in the core material of senile plaque, a neurological landmark of AD (Kosik, 1992). Certain immune proteins, also genetically based, appear to be responsible for helping to destroy brain cells among AD patients (Fackelmann, 1992; Kosik, 1992). Such destruction has been related to immune disorders such as muscular dystrophy, but in the case of AD relates directly to neuronal dystrophy; neuronal cell destruction is seen to be in response to a protein, *tau,* encoded by a single gene (Fackelmann, 1992). However, as Jarvik (1987) has noted, the genes responsible for amyloid production, early-onset familial AD, and Down syndrome are positioned in very different locations on chromosome 21. Thus, the specific relationship between AD, amyloid production, and Down syndrome is still a genetic mystery. A second genetic link has been established in specific types of unusual familial AD in which the disease is present in 50 percent of those family members who are at risk (Raskind & Peskind, 1992).

Another significant finding is that the neurons in the hippocampus and particular areas of the neocortex (e.g., the temporal lobe) are among the most negatively affected parts of the brain in AD patients. These portions of the brain play a crucial role in memory. Furthermore, these brain structures employ acetylcholine as a neurotransmitter. It has been documented that the brains of individuals with AD contain significantly less acetylcholine than those of normal individuals (Weiner, 1991). This has led to the hypothesis that a reduction in the ability to produce acetylcholine may cause AD (Butcher & Woolf, 1986; Coyle, Price, & DeLong, 1983; Jorm, 1990; Weiner, 1991; Wurtman, 1985). Again, however, it is difficult to tell if a decrement in acetylcholine is a cause or an effect of AD.

Because we don't know the specific cause of Alzheimer's disease, it has been difficult to develop effective treatments that cure, delay, or prevent its onset. There is one promising approach, however, as to how some of the cognitive symptoms of AD (memory loss, confusion, and so on) may be relieved or greatly reduced. Initially, there were two variations to this approach. The first variation was based on the idea that the symptoms of AD should lessen if patients could produce more acetylcholine. This led physicians to advise patients with AD to eat foods rich in choline since choline is a food substance that the brain transforms into acetylcholine. Unfortunately, this approach has not produced any significant changes in functioning among AD patients. A number of drugs can also increase acetylcholine levels in the brain. But these drugs are dangerous, and it is not advisable to administer them to humans (Thompson, 1986).

The second variation of the acetylcholine approach was based on the theory that patients' AD symptoms should dissipate if they are given a drug that inhibits the activity of **acetylcholinesterase**. Acetylcholinesterase is the chemical responsible for the synaptic absorption and deactivation of acetylcholine. The inhibition of acetylcholinesterase should allow small amounts of acetylcholine to gradually accumulate on the receptor sites of neurons. These small amounts of acetylcholine would be quickly deactivated if acetylcholinesterase production was at its normal level. Once acetylcholine levels reach a critical threshold, the receptor cell fires—and the person remembers, thinks, and reasons. William Summers and his colleagues (Summers et al., 1986) have gathered impressive results using this strategy with the degree of success directly related to the patients' stage of AD. Summers et al. administered THA (tetrahydroaminoacridine), a drug that inhibits acetylcholinesterase, to a group of AD patients. Compared to a control group, the patients administered THA showed significant improvement on a number of cognitive measures. Furthermore, some of the members of the treatment group were even capable of resuming normal activities such as homemaking, golfing, holding down a part-time job, and so on. THA, like other **palliative treatments,** only treats the symptoms, not the causes, of AD. It helps patients function in a more effective manner. But unfortunately, as with all palliative treatments, the underlying disease progresses and the AD patient ultimately dies. Small (1992) suggests that THA or *tacrine* does offer modest relief of some symptoms of AD, but notes that AD has more than one cause. Tacrine may thus benefit only a small subset of patients (Fackelmann, 1992). Despite the promise of THA, recent clinical trials have revealed an unacceptable incidence of liver damage in patients who have received this drug. Quite clearly, a great deal of work must be done before we can cure AD or even treat its cognitive symptoms.

The picture is somewhat brighter when one considers the noncognitive symptoms associated with AD, such as paranoia. Reisberg (1986, 1987) suggests that these symptoms may be treated by using various drugs that have proven effective in psychiatric settings.

## Providing Care for Alzheimer's Disease Patients: Spouse, Children, and Institutions

It has been well documented that there are profound physical, emotional, and financial costs to the family members and friends of AD patients (Brody, 1985; Zarit, Todd, & Zarit, 1986). Therefore, psychologists also are concerned with providing care and support for the individuals who will survive the patient (Zarit, Anthony, & Boutselis, 1987). It has even been suggested that families have been the

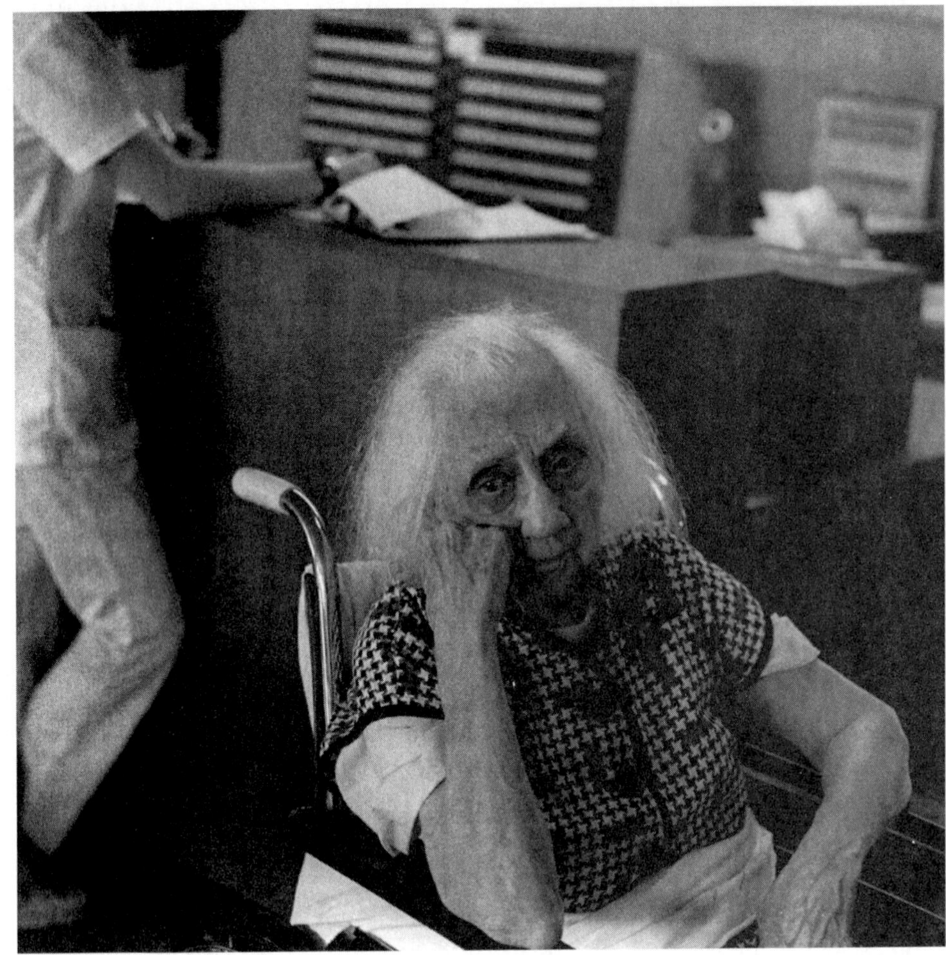

*When the management and personal care of Alzheimer's patients becomes too complex and burdensome, nursing home care is sought by most families.*

"hidden victims" of AD (Zarit, Orr, & Zarit, 1985). Increasing awareness of AD and the availability of community support groups help provide for the needs of concerned relatives. Table 10.6 provides a description of some of the management strategies that may be considered for patients in the different FAST stages.

Other management approaches based on staging of AD patients also have been developed. For example, Baum, Edwards, and Morrow-Howell (1993) have developed a measurement-based approach to the management of AD patients that emphasizes the functional strengths that remain in each of the various stages. Using the Functional Behavior Profile (Table 10.7) it is possible for caretakers and respite programs to prepare programs for AD patients that reduce the rate at which functional behaviors are lost and at the same time encourage activities among family members that will successfully engage the AD patient given the adaptive behaviors still present (Baum et al., 1993). AD patients should continue some active involvement in the immediate environment, whether institution or home, within their overall level of functioning (Baum et al., 1993; Takman, 1992). Various forms

## *Table 10.6*

### *Treatment Implications for AD Patients in Fast Stages*

*Stage 1:* No treatment necessary.

*Stage 2:* No treatment necessary.

*Stage 3:* Advise a withdrawal from overly complex and anxiety-arousing situations; basic living skills remain functionally adaptive.

*Stage 4:* Maximize personally adaptive functional skills, and monitor areas in which concerns arise such as structured travel and leisure activities and wearing identification bracelets and name tags in clothes. Provide financial supervision.

*Stage 5:* Independent living in the community a great risk; need for home monitoring (night and day) and direct supervision such as Adult Day Care. Provide continuous support groups and time off for the caregiver(s).

*Stage 6:* Full-time home health care required to assist in management of bathing and toileting needs. Possible need for psychiatric drugs to combat agitation, paranoia, delusions, and so on. Develop strategies to minimize emotional stress in caregiver(s).

*Stage 7:* Full enrollment in community or institutional setting is mandatory to cope with fundamental loss in daily living skills: self-feeding, swallowing, comprehension and production of language, ambulation, sitting up, smiling. Encouragement to caregivers arriving at this decision.

*From Reisberg, B., Ferris, S. H., de Leon, M. J., Crook, T., and Haynes, N., "Senile Dementia of the Alzheimer Type" in Bergener, M. (Ed.),* Psychogeriatrics: An International Handbook, *pp. 306–334, Springer, New York, 1987. Adapted with permission.*

## *Table 10.7*

### *Items of the Functional Behavior Profile Showing Significant Decline Between Stages of Alzheimer's Disease*

| *Item* | *0.5–1* | *0.5–2* | *1–2* | *0.5–3* | *1–3* | *2–3* |
|---|---|---|---|---|---|---|
| Follows three-step command | | * | * | * | * | |
| Learns complex tasks without difficulty | * | * | * | * | * | |
| Follows two-step command | | * | * | * | * | * |
| Knows the day of the week and/or date | * | * | * | * | * | |
| Independently makes complex decisions | * | * | * | * | * | |
| Problem solves without assistance | * | * | * | * | * | |
| Problem solves with repeated assistance | * | * | * | * | * | |
| Takes responsibility | | * | * | * | * | * |
| Finishes a task | | * | * | * | * | * |
| Performs work that is neat | | * | * | * | * | * |
| Concentrates on a task for a time | | * | * | * | * | * |
| Handles tools or instruments | | * | * | * | * | * |
| Performs fine detail | | | | * | * | * |
| Performs work within a reasonable time | | * | | * | * | |
| Activities appropriate to the time of day | | * | * | * | * | * |
| Makes simple decisions | | * | * | * | * | * |
| Follows one-step command | | * | * | * | * | * |
| Shows enjoyment in activity | | | | * | * | |
| Socializes when others initiate | | | | * | * | * |
| Participates in activities | | | * | * | * | |
| Initiates conversation with family | | | | * | * | * |
| Identifies familiar people | | | | * | * | * |
| Expresses self appropriately | | | | * | * | * |
| Performs activity without frustration | | | | * | * | |
| Makes decisions when given choices | | * | * | * | * | * |
| Continues activities when frustrated | | * | * | * | * | |
| Learns simple tasks without difficulty | | * | * | * | * | * |

*From C. Baum, D. F. Edwards, and N. Morrow-Howell, "Identification and Measures of Productive Behaviors in Senile Dementia of the Alzheimer's Type" in* The Gerontologist, *33(3): 403–408. Copyright © 1993. The Gerontological Society of America.*

of involvment have been suggested including the use of creative arts, such as music representative of earlier time periods in the AD patient's life, movement therapy, art, and individual performance (Aldridge & Aldridge, 1992; Johnson, Lahey, & Shore, 1992; Smith, 1992).

## Respite Care for Alzheimer's Patients

**Respite care** provides those who meet the day-to-day needs of patients with AD an important break or respite from the burden of providing chronic care. Respite care is time away from caretaking and as such it can take many forms: day care, evening care, or brief institutionalization of the patient. The primary goal is relief and rest for the caretakers on a temporary basis and its importance cannot be overstated (Hirsch, Davies, Boatwright, & Ochango, 1993; Lawton, Brody, & Saperstein, 1991). The burden of twenty-four-hour-a-day caretaking of AD patients takes its toll; depression is reported in more than 50 percent of family caretakers and is a primary reason for considering institutionalization (Hirsch et al., 1993). Since many caretakers are themselves older and more frail, they are unable to sustain a community residence for an older AD relative very long without severe emotional and physical costs (Lawton et al., 1991). Cairl and Kosberg (1993) have suggested that support services needed by relatives caring for AD patients in the home must be tailored to fit the type of caregiving being provided, the background and status of the caregiver, and the level of functioning of the AD patient; targeted service interventions following assessments of need are recommended rather than simply utilizing generic community programs (i.e., "one size fits all"). Community-based services such as respite care do not currently qualify for Medicare or insurance reimbursement (Lawton et al., 1991).

In general, it appears that racial and ethnic minorities may differ in their willingness to access community services such as respite care or caretaker support groups. Experts have questioned whether minorities, without such support, are able to cope and adjust to the caretaker role. In one recent study, investigators evaluated African American and white caregivers who were responsible for a relative with diagnosed dementia; 40 percent were AD patients, 17 percent showed multi-infarct dementia and stroke, and 35 percent had dementia that was unspecified (Hinrichsen & Ramirez, 1992). Overall, there were no racial differences among caregivers in their acceptance of the demands of the caretaking role. However, African American caregivers were less willing to consider institutionalization for their relatives and appeared to accept the distress and burden more effectively than white caretakers. African American caregivers reported that they had a greater need for services such as nursing care and training in providing physical therapy than whites.

Henderson, Gutierrez-Mayka, Garcia, & Boyd (1993), in a related study, implemented an AD support group from the evidence suggesting that, in African American and Hispanic communities, such programs are minimally utilized. Henderson

*Table 10.8*

| Implementation of an AD Support Group for Targeted Minorities: Basic Principles |
|---|
| 1. Conduct Targeted Ethnographic Survey |
| a. Develop a community demographic profile |
| b. Develop a list of ethnic minority organizations |
| c. Identify ethnic minority media |
| d. Identify key community members |
| e. Interview those identified as key community members |
| 2. Train Community-Based Support Leaders |
| 3. Announce Ethnic Specific Support Groups |
| 4. Conduct Support Groups |
| 5. Develop Meeting Location at Culturally-Neutral Site |

*From J. N. Henderson, M. Gutierrez-Mayka, J. Garcia, and S. Boyd, "A Model for Alzheimer's Disease Support Group Development in African-American and Hispanic Populations" in* The Gerontologist, *33(3):409–414.* 

et al. developed a community-based program that had a central identity with the targeted African American and Hispanic populations living in two citites and actively recruited minorities directly to an AD support group. Through targeted recruitment and ethnic program identification, significant numbers of both African American and Hispanic caregivers participated in the AD support program with an increase to 114 participants from a near zero level. The program by Henderson et al. (1993) is outlined in table 10.8 and demonstrates the importance of implementing an AD support group that matches the ethnocultural values of a community in order to have ethnic minorities participate extensively in the intervention program.

## The Perspective of Patients with Alzheimer's Disease

Psychologists have recently begun to examine the perceptions of patients who have Alzheimer's disease. This is an important shift in emphasis from studying the caregivers to studying the experience of the elderly with the disease. Some experts believe that to understand the perspective and world in which the Alzheimer's patient lives, we must understand that those with dementia are acting *and* interacting with the disease, not merely passively responding or being shaped by it (Cotrell & Schulz, 1993). What is it like to experience the losses associated with Alzheimer's disease? Do people realize what is happening to them? What fears are common to those who are in the early stages of Alzheimer's disease? What happens when patients relinquish control over routine activities and day-to-day pursuits? In framing these questions, professionals appear to be trying to provide an environment that is more sensitive and more responsive to the needs of those with this disease.

A book-length narrative, *Living in the Labyrinth,* by a remarkable individual, Diana Friel McGowin, who in her late forties was diagnosed with Alzheimer's disease, provides insights into the feelings and reactions she experienced in coping with the disease (McGowin, 1993). Her diary, written on a computer, provides tentative answers to some of the preceding questions. She describes two of the earliest signs of her problems as (1) memory and (2) recognizing/negotiating her regular environment—becoming lost and driving many hours close to home and getting directions from a security guard at a local park.

> "I appear to be lost," I began, making a great effort to keep my voice level, despite my emotional state. "Where do you need to go?" the guard asked politely. A cold chill enveloped me as I realized I could not remember the name of my street. Tears began to flow down my cheeks. I did not know where I wanted to go. He prompted me, his voice soft as he noticed my tears. "Are you heading to Orland, or Windermere?" "Orland!" I sighed gratefully. That was right. I live in Orland, I was certain of it. But where? . . . I felt panic wash over me anew as I searched my memory and found it blank. Suddenly, I remembered bringing my grandchildren to this park. That must mean I lived relatively nearby, surely. "What is the closest subdivision?" I quavered. The guard scratched his head thoughtfully. "The closest Orland subdivision would be Pine Hills, maybe," he ventured. "That's right!" I exclaimed gratefully. The name of my subdivision had rung a bell. . . . Once home a wave of relief brought more tears. I rushed through my home, closing drapes and ensuring all doors were locked. I looked at my bedroom clock. I had been gone over four hours. I took refuge in my darkened master bedroom, and sat, curled up on my bed, my arms wrapped tightly around myself. It was thus that Jack found me when he returned home that evening. I would not at first answer Jack's queries as to why I was so depressed, but as he pressed, a torrent of tears spilled from me. I related all that I could recall of the wretched day's events. Jack had no explanation, but only looked at me with a puzzled expression. (McGowin, 1993, pp. 6–9)

From her personal account, the "patient frame of reference" is made clear. Cotrell and Schulz (1993) have developed another method of understanding the perspective of the Alzheimer's patient based on how people generally cope with chronic illness (Conrad, 1990; Gerhardt, 1990). These concepts include (1) stigma, originating from the shame one feels in having a particular illness and the fear of having to confront directly actual discrimination or rejection from others because of the illness and (2) disruption of self-image, occurring as a result of restricted lifestyle, fewer social contacts, increased reliance on others. McGowin (1993), for instance, writes about the pain and fear of being stigmatized in disclosing the diagnosis of Alzheimer's disease to her family:

> . . . I could not bring myself to confide in my children. I could not even accept it myself. Intellectually, I knew my condition was not cause for shame, yet emotionally I felt ashamed. I was losing my intelligence, losing my memory, and my directional system was really shot to Hades. Embarrassment kept me from confiding in my family and friends. I had no idea of how they would respond. If they were too condescending and made me feel worthless, I would chafe; on the other hand if they displayed a "so what" attitude, I would be devastated. It would break my heart. I wished I could unload this burden, reveal my thoughts to someone, state my innermost

> fears and anxieties, and receive kind support and understanding. . . . What I wanted, no, needed was someone to assure me that no matter what my future held, they would stand beside me, fight my battles with me, or if need be, for me. I wanted assurance from someone that I would not be abandoned to shrivel away. They would give me encouragement, love, moral support, and if necessary, take care of me. (McGowin, 1993, pp. 53–54)

To the categories of stigma and disruption of self-image, experts have also reported that those with chronic disorders have strong fears of desertion, feelings of social isolation (from relatives and friends), and fears of the future (Cohen & Eisdorfer, 1986). These too are recognized by McGowin. And, in the early stages of coping with the disease, she tries to cover up many of her problems in coping. For example, she describes her continuing attempts to hide her difficulties on the job:

> I attempted to bluff my way through small talk with the young stranger. As we walked along together, (he said) he was there to interview for a job as a messenger or courier. Could I help him? I threw in the towel and smiled resignedly at him. "Please forgive me. I know that I know you, but it is just one of those days! I simply can't bring your name to mind. I will be happy to put in a word for you, if you could write down your name and other relevant details." "I don't get it," he muttered. "Your name?" I did not waver. "Diane, I'm your cousin, Rich," he said slowly. Tears began to surface in my eyes, and I embraced my cousin, whispering, "I was just trying to keep anyone from overhearing that one of my relatives is applying. Of course I'll put in a good recommendation with the personnel department. Absolutely!" It struck me that while I may forget relatives, co-workers, or the way to the restroom, I certainly could think fast enough when cornered, and come forth with a believable bluff. (McGowin, 1993, pp. 19–20)

Many people believe that personal reflections and insights such as those of Diana McGowin will ultimately help shape and improve our understanding and treatment of the illness. Through increased sensitivity we will provide more humanized care as well as help focus attention on neglected areas of research (Cotrell & Schulz, 1993). Thus far psychological studies and treatment approaches for Alzheimer's disease have overemphasized the management of disruptive behaviors, controlling the environment, and assessing functional impairments or losses (Cotrell & Schulz, 1993). Little work has been directed at evaluating the positive experiences of the person with Alzheimer's disease, understanding their daily lives—personal pleasures and frustrations, their capacity to experience happiness, joy, and delight. McGowin's narrative begins to suggest the importance of such efforts. And some treatment approaches have begun to create programs that build on the positive skills and abilities that remain among Alzheimer's patients (Sheridan, 1993). Research Focus 10.4 shares some of the recent views on whether to tell a diagnosed person that he or she has Alzheimer's disease.

## *Alzheimer's Dilemma: Whether to Tell People They Have the Disease*

In recent years the doctor-patient relationship has been characterized by increasing openness, directness, and frankness. Physicians and patients speak with each other about cancer or AIDS, yet Altman (1992) suggests that the diagnosis of Alzheimer's disease may be medicine's "last taboo." Telling patients that they have a terminal disease is one of the most difficult tasks for physicians; of all fatal diseases, the diagnosis of Alzheimer's disease is perhaps one of the most devastating of diagnoses to communicate. Because of the special nature of the progressive losses experienced by Alzheimer's patients, physicians realize all too well that the disease ultimately "robs people of one of the most fundamental things that makes them human—memory, personality and the ability to think" (Altman, 1992, p. C3). What do you think . . . should physicians tell patients that they are in the early stages of the disease?

Many people believe it is a physician's responsibility and a patient's right to know of a suspected diagnosis. However, contrary opinions argue that such information will do more harm than good. With a diagnosis of Alzheimer's disease, might persons be inclined to commit suicide? Will they understand how difficult it is to make an early diagnosis? In deciding what to communicate to the patient and the family, physicians must employ exceptional humanity, sensitivity, and judgment; this is the "art" of medicine. Physicians appear to judge the strength of the personalities involved, the strength of the family unit, and the stage to which the disease has progressed. Also of importance is the source of the referral (patient or family) and when an initial diagnosis is sought.

Physicians realize that what is best to share with a person with Alzheimer's disease may not be in the best interest of the family. And, conversely, what family members may wish for themselves to cope best with a relative with Alzheimer's disease may be at odds with a physician's appraisal of what the affected patient can effectively handle. For example, patients may have developed covert strategies to hide their difficulties from family, friends, and coworkers; they may have been coerced into an initial visit by concerned relatives. Other times patients themselves recognize that there are uncommon problems, visit a physician, and then may refuse to share the diagnosis with relatives such as children or a spouse.

Recall that a diagnosis of Alzheimer's disease is difficult to confirm and physicians may be reluctant to voice a label with so much emotional baggage. Often they use general descriptions such as "senile memory problem" or "neurological deterioration" without employing definitive terms. Under such conditions, physicians may rightly be hedging their bets. By the time a clear picture emerges and a more definite diagnosis is possible, the person with Alzheimer's disease may not fully comprehend the diagnosis, and, thus, may have been spared much emotional damage under such conditions. Most patients who can comprehend the diagnosis appear to fear the label Alzheimer's disease and the social stigma attached to it. Perhaps, on such grounds it is argued, it is best to wait for the sake of the patient. Why rush persons into such confrontations and into depressed moods; what is the benefit?

Telling those in early-stage Alzheimer's disease of the suspected diagnosis, on the other hand, has the advantage of allowing all concerned to make sound, responsible decisions. Early in the disease patients can make decisions affecting their finances, their wills, and their health-care options before they become more debilitated. There are opportunities for Alzheimer's patients to exercise good judgment in these matters and to play a central role in deciding what they want for themselves. With an opportunity to understand their situation, perhaps they might wish to do things that they would like, including volunteering for experimental treatment programs or visiting special friends. Also, families can begin to prepare for the changes needed to provide continuous care and begin to think about how to intervene in anticipation of behavioral changes and functional losses that will emerge. Sometimes just being able to prepare for those changes that will ensue is sufficient to help families cope with them.

However, not all Alzheimer's patients necessarily wish their families to know of their situation. Eth and Leong (1992), for example, note that some patients may refuse to share information and insist on strict confidentiality by their physician as a means of "gaining some control over their lives." Thus, families and physicians may have to confront difficult ethical issues to obtain information related to diagnosis and treatment when confidentiality is the wish of the patient. There is little normative statistical data to provide physicians, families, and Alzheimer's patients with clues as to what is best. Most physicians continue to rely on their own professional experience and judgment (Altman, 1992).

## *Other Dementias*

### Multi-Infarct Dementia

Multi-infarct dementia has been estimated to account for 20 to 25 percent of cases of dementia (Gambert, 1987; Zarit & Zarit, 1983). Multi-infarct dementia arises from a series of ministrokes in the cerebral arteries. The condition is more common among men with a history of hypertension (high blood pressure) and arises when the arteries to the brain are blocked (e.g., by small pieces of atherosclerotic plaque dislodging from the artery walls in other parts of the body and traveling to the brain). The clinical picture for multi-infarct dementia is different from that of Alzheimer's disease, since the individual typically shows clear and predictable recovery from the former versus the gradual deterioration of the latter. Symptoms may include bouts of confusion, slurring of speech, difficulty in writing, or weakness on the left or right side of the body, hand, or leg. However, after each such occurrence, rapid and steady improvement usually occurs. Each succeeding occasion leaves a bit more of a residual problem, making recovery from each new episode increasingly difficult. A relatively minor stroke or infarct is usually termed a **transient ischemic attack** or **TIA.** See figure 10.4 for more information about this disorder.

### Mixed Dementia

In some cases, two forms of dementia coexist (Raskind & Peskind, 1992). For example, Alzheimer's disease and multi-infarct dementia have been estimated to co-occur in approximately 18 percent of those cases of diagnosed dementia (Raskind & Peskind, 1992); it is impossible to determine with accuracy the cause of the observed symptoms although autopsy may help to determine cause. Such cases are reasonably common and not the "medical zebras" clinicians report to their colleagues to highlight their diagnostic skills. Obviously, treatment and intervention for a person with mixed dementia presents an especially difficult challenge. Larson (1993) considers elderly people 85 years of age and older particularly likely to have mixed dementia.

### Creutzfeldt-Jakob Disease

This form of dementia is infrequently encountered in clinical diagnosis. It has aroused great interest in those seeking to understand the etiology of AD, because Creutzfeldt-Jakob disease is caused by a *slow-acting virus* and under rare circumstances can be infectious (Raskind & Peskind, 1992). In experimental studies, an analogous slow-acting virus has been found to be transmitted from lower animals to other primates. The analog virus in sheep produces a disease called *scrapie,*

**Figure 10.4**
Recognizing the symptoms of ministrokes or transient ischemic attacks.

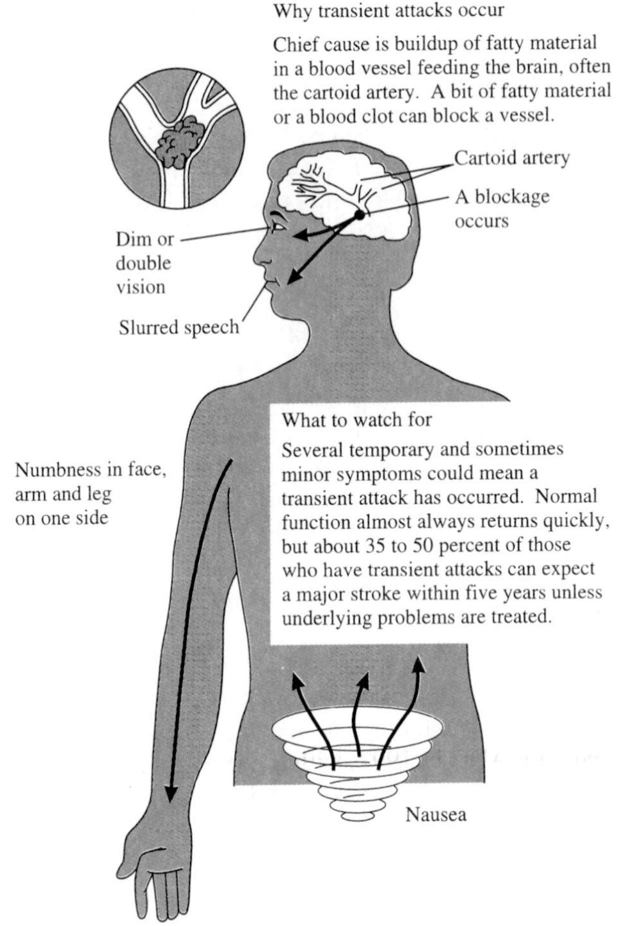


whose symptoms and destruction of brain tissue are similar to the symptoms of Creutzfeldt-Jakob disease. Scrapie can be transmitted directly to chimpanzees and monkeys in laboratory investigations (Cohen, 1988). There is also evidence from work in New Guinea that another rare neurologic brain disorder, *Kuru,* can be virally transmitted from primate to human (Zarit & Zarit, 1983). This leads to the question of whether the more common dementias such as Alzheimer's may also be the product of a virus, transmitted either from animal to human or from human to human. In the latter instance, some support for direct human-to-human transmission of Creutzfeldt-Jakob disease has been reported (Gorman, Benson, Vogel, & Vinters, 1992). The pattern of symptoms in Creutzfeldt-Jakob disease is highly variable, although central nervous system deterioration is commonly present. The rate of decline is rapid and death ensues within two years (Raskind & Peskind, 1992). The emergence of specific symptoms and the rate of progressive deterioration in cognitive functioning, judgment, memory, and personal and social competence depends on the overall rate and extent of neuron loss in the brain, the initial level of intellectual ability, and the availability of a socially supportive and simplified environment in which to live.

## AIDS Dementia Complex

This neurological disorder is characterized by progressive cognitive, motor, and behavioral loss. It arises in concert with the acquired immunodeficiency-syndrome **(AIDS)** and is a predictable part of the infection (Price, Sidtis, & Rosenblum, 1988; Raskind & Peskind, 1992). **AIDS dementia complex (ADC)** is the result of direct brain infection by the human immunodeficiency virus (HIV). An HIV by-product, a protein called gp 120, is responsible for the death of neuron cells, which ultimately produces dementia. Early symptoms include inability to concentrate, difficulty performing complex sequential mental tasks, and memory loss in tasks requiring concentrated attention (reading, meeting the demands of independent living and working). Motor symptoms include clumsiness and weakness in the limbs; behavioral changes include apathy, loss of spontaneity, depression, social withdrawal, and personality alterations. As ADC progresses, mental performance becomes noticeably worse and motor behaviors become impaired. Fine motor responses weaken, walking without assistance becomes difficult, and bowel and bladder control are lost. The terminal phase is marked by confinement to bed, vacant staring, and minimal social and cognitive interaction (Price et al., 1988). Raskind and Peskind (1992) estimate that approximately ten thousand adults in the U.S. over 60 were diagnosed with ADC in 1992, with transmission attributable to male homosexuality and infection via contaminated blood. By learning how the virus invades the brain, scientists hope to learn more about how AIDS itself is transmitted within the body so that they can develop biochemical barriers that prevent the disease from spreading.

## Focal Brain Damage

Zarit and Zarit (1983) have suggested that the sudden emergence of selective (rather than global) impairment of specific cognitive abilities is typical of focal brain damage. Focal brain damage is not considered a dementia and is not marked by progressive deterioration. The likelihood of localized brain damage due to head trauma, stroke, or tumor is a common occurrence among young adult patients but is frequently overlooked among the elderly (Zarit & Zarit, 1983). The defining characteristic of focal brain damage is the rapid and sudden onset of limited, specific cognitive impairments. Once identified, further losses in intellectual function can be prevented with timely and appropriate intervention.

## Dementia Caused by Psychiatric Disorders

The clinical picture of depression in the elderly often mimics dementia; some clinicians have even labeled depression as **depressive pseudodementia** (Kiloh, 1961;

*TABLE 10.9*

***Depressive Pseudodementia versus True Dementia: Differential Symptoms***

| | *Depression* | *Dementia* |
|---|---|---|
| Onset | Rapid; exact onset can often be dated | Insidious and ill-defined |
| Behavior | Stable; depression, apathy, and withdrawal common | Labile; fluctuates between normal and withdrawn and apathetic |
| Mental competence | Usually unaffected; however, may appear demented at times; complains of memory problems | Consistently impaired, tries to hide cognitive impairment |
| Somatic signs | Anxiety, insomnia, eating disturbances | Occasional sleep disturbances |
| Self-image | Poor | Normal |
| Prognosis | Reversible with therapy | Chronic; slow progressive decline |

LaRue et al., 1985; Zarit & Zarit, 1983). Table 10.9 presents the difference in symptoms between true dementia and depressive pseudodementia. At least 30 percent of the elderly diagnosed with dementia have been misdiagnosed and in fact have treatable depressive pseudodementia (LaRue et al., 1985; National Institute on Aging Task Force, 1980). Symptoms such as apathy, psychomotor retardation, impaired concentration, delusions, and confusion in a depressed elderly person may easily be mistaken for dementia, particularly when they are accompanied by complaints of memory loss. Interestingly, clinicians observe that persons with depressive pseudodementia may complain far more about memory loss than those with true dementia. Although some studies suggest the presence of differential brain wave activity during sleep, at present, the only way of definitively identifying depressive pseudodementia from true dementia is by retrospective means (Hoch, Buysse, Monk, & Reynolds, 1992). Thus, if any of the treatments effective in helping depressives produce dramatic improvements in a person's cognitive deficits and other symptoms, then the diagnosis of depressive pseudodementia must be correct (LaRue et al., 1985). Clinicians are thus advised to treat such symptoms not as dementia but as depressive pseudodementia. Given the difficulty of diagnosing either problem prior to treatment, the scientific utility of the concept of depressive pseudodementia has been questioned (LaRue et al., 1985). Caine and Grossman (1992) suggest that those with depressive pseudodementia sometimes may be "coaxed" into more positive cognitive functioning and improved task performance through techniques such as cued recall, whereas elderly with true dementia are unable to benefit from these interventions.

Other reversible dementias may be caused by drugs, toxins, and physical illness. The sedative effects of some drugs (including alcohol) on older persons and drug-drug interactions may also contribute to memory impairment, delirium, or acute brain syndrome/reversible dementia (Cohen, 1988; Schuckit, Morrissey, & O'Leary, 1979; Zarit and Zarit, 1983). Disorders of thyroid metabolism (such as hyperthyroidism) may impair cognitive ability and represent still another reversible cause of the dementia syndrome. And almost any intracranial lesion or tumor may produce memory loss or dementia (Gambert, 1987; Zarit, Eiler, & Hassinger, 1985). Seeking the particular cause of dementia is important because treatment can be somewhat successful in at least 10 to 30 percent of the cases (LaRue et al., 1985; Smith & Kiloh, 1981). Some experts would like to discard labels such as dementia because of the problems in defining and diagnosing it. The next section discusses the issue of depression among the elderly, which seems to be the most common psychiatric complaint among older adults.

## Depression

The actual incidence of depression among older adults varies widely since different methodologies, samples, nationalities, and criteria have been employed in research studies (Anthony & Aboraya, 1992; Koenig & Blazer, 1992; LaRue et al., 1985; Raskind & Peskind, 1992). There is some agreement that about 4 to 7 percent of the elderly experience depression serious enough to require intervention (Anthony & Aboraya, 1992; Gallagher & Thompson, 1983; Gurland & Cross, 1982). Gurland (1976, 1980) initially noted that the highest rates of depressive *symptoms* appear among those older than 65; yet the frequency of depression as a *psychiatric diagnosis* is highest among those 25 to 65 years of age. Some of the inconsistency in the research relating age and incidence of depression has been related to the variety of scales used to screen for symptoms. Kessler, Foster, Webster, and House (1992), for example, noted that the inclusion of many items with a strong somatic component are biased against the elderly, who are far more likely to report symptoms in this domain than are younger persons. And previous studies have examined the relationship of age and depression often using a very narrow age range of older persons (e.g., 65–75), a small number of very old respondents (e.g., 75+ years of age), or a measure of age that combined all individuals over the age of 65 into a single group for analysis (Kessler et al, 1992).

Cross-sectional age comparisons with respondents 18 to 90 years of age revealed that depression is at its lowest level in middle age and reaches its highest level in those over the age of 80 (Mirowsky & Ross, 1992). Contributing factors to the steady increase across the later part of the life span include losses in marriage, employment, economic well-being, health, status, and personal control (Mirowsky & Ross, 1992). Among institutionalized populations, in particular, deteriorating health and associated increases in depression have been found to be predictive of death (Parmelee, Katz, & Lawton, 1992).

It appears that depression among older adults is identical to that experienced by younger adults; however, far fewer older adults recognize the problem or are treated for this mental condition (LaRue et al., 1985). An estimated 80 percent of older adults with depressive symptoms receive no treatment at all (Gallagher & Thompson, 1983). The oft-held assumption among the elderly themselves and their families is that depressive symptoms are a natural consequence of growing older, reflecting the

### *Table 10.10*

**Symptoms of Depression: Diagnostic Criteria for Major Depressive Episodes**

A Major Depressive Syndrome is defined as criterion A.

A. At least five of the following symptoms have been present during the same two-week period and represent a change from previous functioning; at least one of the symptoms is either (1) depressed mood, or (2) loss of interest or pleasure. (Do not include symptoms that are clearly due to a physical condition, mood-incongruent delusions or hallucinations, incoherence, or marked loosening of associations.)

1. Depressed mood (or can be irritable mood in children and adolescents) most of the day, nearly every day, as indicated either by subjective account or observation by others
2. Markedly diminished interest or pleasure in all, or almost all, activities most of the day, nearly every day (as indicated either by subjective account or observation by others of apathy most of the time)
3. Significant weight loss or weight gain when not dieting (e.g., more than 5 percent of the body weight in a month), or decrease or increase in appetite nearly every day (in children, consider failure to make expected weight gains)
4. Insomnia or hypersomnia nearly every day
5. Psychomotor agitation or retardation nearly every day (observable by others, not merely subjective feelings of restlessness or being slowed down)
6. Fatigue or loss of energy nearly every day
7. Feelings of worthlessness or excessive or inappropriate guilt (which may be delusional) nearly every day (not merely self-reproach or guilt about being sick)
8. Diminished ability to think or concentrate, or indecisiveness, nearly every day (either by subjective account or as observed by others)
9. Recurrent thoughts of death (not just fear of dying), recurrent suicidal ideation without a specific plan, or a suicide attempt or a specific plan for committing suicide

*From the American Psychiatric Association:* Diagnostic and Statistical Manual of Mental Disorders, *Third Edition, Revised, Washington, DC, American Psychiatric Association, 1987. Reprinted by permission.*

many losses (spouse, job, friends, family, housing) and the steadily increasing physical health problems that are encountered (Weiner, 1992). Though these events may be a part of the culture of growing old, they are not uniquely restricted to the later part of the life span and may occur at any age; clinical depression demands intervention whenever it is encountered. Older people can expect to find that depressive symptoms improve or even disappear with intensive, brief psychotherapy or drug therapy just as they do in younger adults (Gallagher, Thompson, & Breckenridge, 1986). Weiner (1992) has confirmed, however, that today's cohort of elderly may be embarrassed to seek treatment for depression and reluctant to admit such difficulties to others due to shame, guilt, and fear of public knowledge.

The actual symptoms of depression as identified in *DSM-III-R* are listed in table 10.10. (Research Focus 10.5 discusses recommendations for treatment of depression in the elderly.) Gatz, Smyer, and Lawton (1980) have described some of the problems associated with the treatment of depression in the elderly:

> Two aspects of depression in older adults make it particularly troublesome to treat. The first is that there are often real reasons for feeling depressed, for instance, personal losses that may trigger existential questions. . . . The second difficult aspect of depression is that family and friends do not enjoy being around depressed people. The depressed person tends to be dependent and demanding, thereby discouraging the very people who might be supportive. Thus, the families and caretakers need assistance, and the depressed older adults need interventions that will mobilize their resources while recognizing their concerns as valid. (pp. 11–12)

## *Treatment of Depression in the Elderly*

At a major conference organized by the National Institutes of Health, attention was centered on the complex problems of depression in the elderly (e.g., diagnosis and treatment). Experts concurred that many elderly who are depressed are not diagnosed and remain untreated; those with depression who are untreated have a high risk of suicide. The risk of suicide is greatest among elderly men, who have the highest rate of all age groups. Older persons who commit suicide typically are encountering their first episode of depression that is moderately severe and have seen a physician within one month before their death.

Conference participants concluded that the reported incidence of depression in the population over 65 years of age—3 to 5% for elderly individuals living in the community and 20 to 25% among nursing home residents—is an underestimate. Nearly one-third of all widows and widowers evidence signs of bereavement depression in the first month following the death of a spouse and half of these individuals continue to show signs of depression throughout the next twelve months. Experts considered a change in the DSM-IIIR to include a special diagnostic category of depression in the elderly. They hope that with better diagnosis perhaps we can increase the proportion of depressed elderly who actually receive treatment, which currently stands at only 10 percent. Conference attenders concluded, based on the extant literature, that treatment of elderly persons with major depression should include antidepressant drugs over a six- to twelve-month period. Similarly, there was a weak endorsement of a controversial treatment for depression, electroconvulsive shock therapy, based on research evidence supporting its effectiveness in treating depressed elderly persons. Experts noted that "psychosocial treatments can also play an essential role in the care of elderly patients who have significant life crises, lack social support, or lack coping skills." To date, few comparisons between treatments based on drugs versus psychotherapy have been conducted with populations over the age of 65; for example, less than twenty-five well-designed studies have evaluated drug treatment versus psychosocial treatments. The questions remaining to be answered are: (1) Why have so few studies been conducted comparing the effectiveness of psychosocial therapies versus other treatments? and (2) When can we expect outcome studies to indicate which of the various psychosocial interventions (e.g., counseling, cognitive therapy, etc.) work best in treating depression in the elderly and prevent its recurrence? Conference participants discussed whether the funds provided by drug companies to evaluate their products may have contributed to the imbalance in research on treatment approaches to depression (Adler, 1992).

## *Suicide*

The major consequence of undiagnosed and untreated depression is an increased incidence of suicide among people of all ages. Among the elderly, as we have seen, depression is frequently ignored or accepted as the natural consequence of aging. In fact, older people with depression are at a high risk for carrying out suicidal wishes; they commit 17 percent of *all* suicides yet comprise only 11 to 12% of the population (Koenig & Blazer, 1992). Estimates suggest that one of every six elderly with severe depression actually brings about their own death (Kivela, 1985; Thomas & Gallagher, 1985). Statistics also reveal that nearly 25 percent of those who commit suicide are older than 65, with rates of 18 per 100,000 for those 65 to 74; 22 per 100,000 for those 74 to 85; and 19 per 100,000 for those 85 and older (Church et al., 1988). Figure 10.5 presents the incidence of suicide as a corollary of age. These analyses also suggest that the four greatest risk factors related to suicide among the elderly include (1) living alone, (2) being male, (3) experiencing the loss of a spouse, and (4) failing health. There is *no* evidence that the rate of suicide increases following retirement (Atchley, 1983). Among older adults, the male suicide rate is nearly seven times that of the female rate (Atchley, 1983; Porcino, 1985). However, the incidence of depression is more prevalent

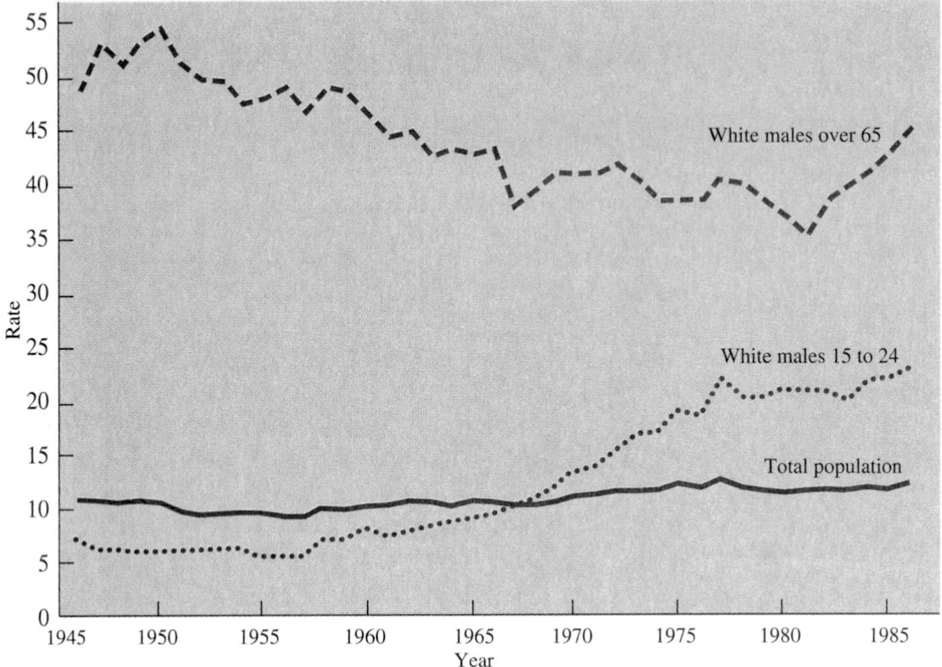


**Figure 10.5** Total and white male suicide rates for ages 15 to 24 and 65 and over per 100,00 population: 1946 to 1986.

among females than males. Analysis by race reveals that white males aged 85 or older have three times the rate of suicide of that of African American males in the same age group (Koenig & Blazer, 1992).

Suicides among the elderly are sometimes preceded by clear signals that, unfortunately, are largely ignored (Achete & Karha, 1986; Koenig & Blazer, 1992). Since older people are usually successful in committing suicide, intervention must be directed at preventing the attempt itself (Achete & Karha, 1986; Blazer, Bacher, & Manton, 1986; Koenig & Blazer, 1992). Mental health professionals must look for signs of extreme despair, overwhelming helplessness, and hopelessness in the elderly. The signs appearing among at-risk individuals, regardless of age, include:

1. Extreme mood or personality changes
2. Discussion of suicide and death
3. Preoccupation with the futility of continuing the struggle of daily living
4. Giving cherished personal possessions to friends and relatives
5. Disturbances in sleeping and/or eating
6. Severe threat to identity and self-esteem
7. Death of loved ones and/or long-term friends

Without a social support network to monitor depressive or presuicidal feelings on a daily basis, it is understandable that suicidal thoughts among the elderly easily become actions (Achete & Karha, 1986; Koenig & Blazer, 1992). It is important to have physicians, mental health professionals, and caregivers share possible plans that might be followed, to help monitor and prevent an older person from carrying them out (Koenig & Blazer, 1992). Suicide techniques used by older people are somewhat more passive than those used by younger groups. They include starvation, single-car automobile accidents, failure to take needed medications, mixing medications, combining medications with dangerous drugs such as alcohol, or overdosing on prescription medications (Church et al., 1988). Koenig and Blazer (1992) suggest that suicide rates in the medically ill, who often successfully employ passive techniques, may not be accurately reflected in current estimates.

## *Schizophrenia*

Schizophrenia is a label for a group of disorders marked by the presence of hallucinations, delusions, inappropriate affect, disturbances in speech, and alterations in logical thought processes. In short, the schizophrenic patient has broken from reality. Although there are a number of older schizophrenics, schizophrenia is *not* a disorder of old age; in one small-scale study of diagnoses of schizophrenia in a clinic population, only 4 percent of males and 26 percent of females showed onset of the disorder after age 45 (Rabins, 1992). Schizophrenia is a chronic condition, then, that most often begins in late adolescence or early adulthood and persists, if untreated, throughout adult life. It is very much out of the ordinary for schizophrenic symptoms to first manifest themselves in very old age (Rabins, 1992). In fact, according to Rabins (1992), it seems as if the symptoms of late-onset schizophrenia are somewhat different from early-onset conditions in that delusions are more marked and vividly experienced, thought disorders are not as debilitating, affect is not as flat, and hallucinations are more often sensory (e.g., tactile, visual, olfactory, or gustatory). With these differences it has been argued that perhaps early-onset and late-onset schizophrenia are different disorders (Rabins, 1992).

Schizophrenia seems to have a genetic and/or biological basis. For example, schizophrenic symptoms have been traced to the overproduction of (or hypersensitivity to) the neurotransmitter **dopamine.** Treatment for schizophrenia usually involves the administration of drugs that block the effects of dopamine. During the course of normal aging, the number of neurotransmitters (including dopamine) manufactured by the brain decreases. This natural reduction in the number of dopamine neurotransmitters would explain why the onset of schizophrenia is inversely related to age (Cohen, 1988). Risk factors identified in developing late-onset schizophrenia include a history of eccentricity and isolation, never married or having children, and being female (Rabins, 1992). Treatment is more effective in removing hallucinations and delusions but apathy and social isolation are difficult to change (Rabins, 1992).

## *Parkinson's Disease*

Tremors of the voluntary small muscle groups are the most noticeable symptoms of Parkinson's disease which is a motor disorder triggered by degeneration of dopaminergic neurons in the brain (Morgan, 1992). Reduced numbers of dopamine neurotransmitters seem to be the primary cause of Parkinson's disease; as such, it is the opposite of schizophrenia (Morgan, 1992). Small muscle tremors occur between three and seven times per second and appear as jerky motions. This neurological disorder produces not only disturbances in psychomotor functioning but in about 45 percent of the cases is associated with depression, and in 15 to 40 percent of the cases, is associated with dementia (Raskind & Peskind, 1992). Dementia related to Parkinson's disease suggests significantly more cognitive impairment in the frontal cortex than in those with the disease who do not experience dementia. The indicators of frontal cortex involvement include greater difficulty on delayed recall of objects, in using cues to create a consistent recall strategy, and attempting to shift cognitive set (Wertman, Speedie, Shemesh, & Gilon; 1993). It is sometimes difficult to differentiate Parkinson's disease and its associated symptoms from simple major depression. At least one investigation has found that rate of speech among matched age controls with major depression is significantly slower than among Parkinson's disease patients (Flint, Black, Campbell-Taylor, & Gailey, 1992). Symptoms of Parkinson's disease include unnatural immobility of the facial muscles, staring appearance of the eyes, and the characteristic tremors or shaking. In the initial phases of the disease, tremors appear in an upper limb and then alternate to the lower limb on the same side. The risk of falling increases among the aged with Parkinson's disease (Ochs et al., 1985).

The standard treatment for Parkinson's disease is the administration of a drug called L-dopa. L-dopa is converted by the brain into dopamine. It is sometimes difficult to determine the correct dosage of L-dopa. For example, if Parkinson's patients are given too much of this chemical, they may display what appear to be schizophrenic symptoms. Conversely, if young schizophrenic patients are given too much of a drug that blocks the effects of dopamine, they may develop what appear to be the symptoms of Parkinson's disease. Another treatment for Parkinson's disease involves transplanting cells into the brain, which helps stimulate the production of dopamine (Raskind & Peskind, 1992). One dopamine-rich center of the brain that helps to trigger neurons that control movement is the *substantia nigra* and is a promising focus of cell transplantation. Researchers are developing, from Parkinson's patients' own skin cells, reengineered cells that become capable of making dopamine when implanted in the substantia nigra of the brain. These forms of treatment, although promising, are still in the initial experimental stages.

## Summary

The ability to cope and adapt to life is an important feature of adult development. One view of stress focuses on the impact of life events, attempting to determine the relative severity of the stresses. However, other experts believe that simply rating stressors does not accurately predict adaptation and adjustment. Lazarus and his colleagues believe that *how* the individual cognitively perceives and understands events is far more significant than a rating of the severity of the stress caused by a life event. Additional support for the cognitive view is found in the concept of daily hassles and uplifts.

Some experts belive that adaptation is best understood by examining the timing of significant life experiences. Neugarten and her colleagues, for example, report that off-time events are more likely to be experienced as stressful than events that are predictable or on-time. Recent studies have confirmed the importance of cognitive distortion and unrealistic optimism as effective coping strategies for people facing life-threatening illnesses such as cancer or AIDS. The care of an older relative demands effective coping by caregivers such as middle-aged daughters who face complex burdens in trying to manage competing priorities on their time and resources. The importance of social support in times of stress was highlighted for both caregivers and for the elderly themselves. In understanding adaptation adults throughout the life span search for meaning and a way to preserve their personal control, a positive view of self, and their sense of mastery. Different life management processes designed to accomplish these goals were identified. The role of possible selves in health-promoting behaviors was also reviewed.

Although we need to address the mental health needs of the elderly, we need not assume that the incidence of mental disorders increases with age. A basic distinction may be made between acute brain syndromes, which are reversible, and chronic brain syndromes, which are not. Chronic brain syndromes include Alzheimer's disease, multi-infarct dementia, mixed dementia, Creutzfeldt-Jakob disease, and the AIDS dementia complex. Dementia and senescence are not interchangeable terms. The former refers to an abnormal condition of aging, the latter to the universal processes of aging. Alzheimer's disease was presented in terms of causes, diagnostic approaches, and the value of staging. The complexities of providing home care and institutional care for patients with Alzheimer's and other cognitive dementias remains a challenge for families, service agencies, and our society.

When Alzheimer's patients remain at home with relatives, respite care provides valuable relief from round-the-clock caregiving; minorities do not readily seek respite care programs. The dilemma of whether to tell a person who has been diagnosed with Alzheimer's about their condition was also discussed.

Many conditions mimic chronic brain syndromes but are in reality reversible features of acute brain syndromes. One of the more common of these conditions is focal brain damage, in which a temporary slowing or obstruction of blood flow to the brain (e.g., a transient ischemic attack) produces the symptoms of chronic brain syndrome. Pseudodementia is another condition that mimics dementia. Pseudodementia is typically caused by undiagnosed and untreated depression.

Depression remains one of the most overlooked and yet common mental health problems of the elderly. Treatment approaches include antidepressant drugs, electroconvulsive therapy, and psychosocial therapies. If untreated, depression in older adults may lead to suicide; the suicide statistics are particularly grim for older men. Both schizophrenia and Parkinson's disease also have implications for those studying aging and the role of neurobehavioral and neurochemical processes.

## Review Questions

1. Discuss two major views of stress.
2. Outline Lazarus's basic ideas about stress and coping.
3. Distinguish between accommodative and assimilative processes as they apply to coping or life management. Give an example of each process.
4. Describe an off-time event and an on-time event and indicate how timing influences stress.
5. Describe some of the coping strategies used by women facing a diagnosis of breast cancer.
6. What are the differences between dementia, senility, and sensescence? Describe how some forms of mental illness have been misdiagnosed in terms of reversible or chronic dementia.
7. List two aspects of depression in elderly adults that make it difficult to treat.
8. What is the relationship between depression and suicide in the later years? Why does this relationship exist?
9. Describe the role of respite care in families dealing with Alzheimer's disease. What are the immediate consequences of caregiving within such families?
10. Provide a "patient's perspective" on Alzheimer's disease. How is this perspective related to the concepts of stigma and disruption of self-image?
11. What are some of the risk factors identified with suicide among older adults?
12. Explain the biological basis of Parkinson's disease. Describe two forms of treatment of the disease.

## For Further Reading


Berenger, M., Haseqawa, K., Finkel, S. T., & Nishimura, T. (1992). *Aging and mental disorders: International perspectives.* New York: Springer.

Birren, J. E., Sloane, R. B., and Cohen, D. (1992). *Handbook of Mental Health and Aging, (2nd edition).* San Diego: Academic Press.

Edwards, A. J. (1993). *Dementia.* New York: Plenum.

Gray, D. D. (1993). *I want to remember: A son's reflection on his mother's Alzheimer's journey.* Wellesley, MA: Roundtable Press.

McGowin, D. F. (1993). *Living in the labyrinth: A personal journey through the maze of Alzheimer's disease.* New York: Delacorte Press.

Richman, J. (1993). *Preventing elderly suicide: Overcoming personal despair, professional indifference, and social bias.* New York: Springer.

# 11

# APPLICATIONS AND THE CONTEXTS OF AGING

*Age only matters when one is aging. Now that I have arrived at great age, I might as well be twenty.*
—Pablo Picasso

*It is sad to grow old, but nice to ripen.*
—Brigitte Bardot

## *Introduction*

This chapter discusses some of the ways the material presented in this text is applicable to real-life situations, to understand the *contexts* in which older persons live their later years. It is important to recognize these contexts, as well as the role of special environments. Although some elderly experience impairments in the later years, our efforts as a society emphasize rehabilitation and preservation of autonomy so that we can optimize the lives of all older persons regardless of the many different environments in which they reside. By examining the contexts of aging, we can better understand the ways in which the elderly experience and derive meaning from their world.

## *Meeting the Health Care Needs of the Elderly*

Public policy has increasingly focused on identifying those programs that must be developed or enhanced to meet the health needs of older adults in the United States (Gottleib, 1992). Census data reveal that one of every eight people in our society is over the age of 65, with older women composing a larger and larger segment of the elderly population and ethnic minorities also projected to show increases of more than 5 percent of this population within the next thirty years (Gottleib, 1992; National Center for Health Statistics, 1987a). Older women and ethnic minorities are adversely affected in terms of access to health care. The situation is mirrored in the demographic profile of our society as a whole; current census reports indicate that in 1992, 37.4 million Americans or 14.7 percent of our total population lacked health care insurance, an increase of 2 million people over the previous year (National Center for Health Statistics, 1993). Women, for example, have fewer financial resources the longer they live and health care consumes an increasingly larger portion of their income. One consequence is that women become more and more dependent both on their own children (where possible) and the health care system to meet their medical, social, and general needs (Gottleib, 1992; Soldo & Agree, 1988). Analogously, many minorities in old age continue to reveal the accumulated effects of socioeconomic disadvantage and routinely encounter financial, social, and cultural barriers to health care (Gottleib, 1992). The health needs of underrepresented elderly are quantitatively and qualitatively different from majority members of our society and their needs increasingly are being met by government programs of public support.

It is difficult for older persons to meet the increased costs associated with health care given the typical decline in yearly income of 30 to 50 percent following retirement (Gottleib, 1992; Soldo & Agree, 1988). Health care coverage costs are partially covered by Social Security, Medicare, and so on for many older adults. Some elderly are able to meet the gap in their health care coverage with personal savings, others rely on private insurance coverage (Medigap policies), and still others depend on special appropriations through government-sponsored programs designed for low-income elderly. Gottleib (1992) reminds public policymakers that there is a considerable range of income among today's elderly. Developing simple comprehensive programs to ensure adequate health care is exceedingly difficult given the disparities in income among the elderly. Further, public policy regarding health care must take into account the mechanisms for continued funding of programs with both the escalating cost of providing health care and the increasing number of enrollees. The anticipated growth in the **dependency ratio** (a larger number of older adults needing support from a smaller number of workers), may mean shifting some of the costs of health care programs directly back to those who utilize program services, the elderly themselves (Gottleib, 1992). Many program changes are possible and will be debated throughout the next decade. However, policymakers agree that health promotion and health prevention are far less expensive to provide to our society than any other public policy program designed to deliver needed health-care services after illness or disability arise. With improved health as individuals age, there is less need for costly intervention, greater derived benefits in terms of overall psychological, social, and physical functioning, and, undoubtedly, improvements in life satisfaction and perceived quality of life (Gottleib, 1992).

The psychological needs of the elderly and the provision for intervention services are important dimensions of the health and well-being that must be addressed. The goal of these programs is to enhance and preserve psychological functioning throughout the later years. Mental health intervention approaches often rely heavily on the concept of functional assessment, that is, the basic abilities necessary for adequate functioning in our society. Functional abilities deemed important in assessments range from physical health through more complex skills and social roles (Kemp & Mitchell, 1992; Lawton, 1986). These functional abilities are outlined in figure 11.1. It is important to understand that different interventions are possible at different functional levels. There are also a number of factors that have limited these interventions from being applied to the older adult population. First, psychologists must be encouraged to work with the elderly, and the elderly must see that they can and do benefit from various types of therapeutic intervention (Gallagher et al., 1986). Second, we must make mental health care both affordable and available as is being done with other health care programs. (Medicare currently pays lower percentages for mental health care than for physical care.) Third, we need to increase the number of geropsychologists (Reveron, 1982). Perhaps this could be accomplished by advocating that courses on aging be part of the undergraduate and graduate programs in fields such as psychology, human services, nursing, and sociology. If students find study of the field of aging and gerontology interesting and challenging, they may become committed to a career working with the elderly. Appendix B discusses specific careers in applied gerontology that are projected to need significantly more professionals in the coming years.

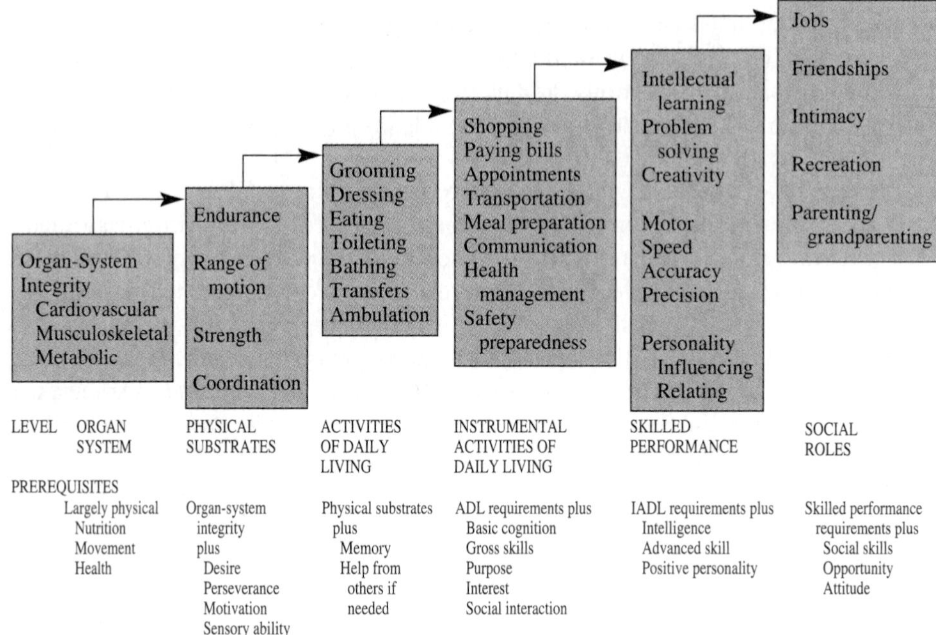


**Figure 11.1** A hierarchical model of functional abilities.

## Health, Mental Health, and Individual Perception

Older individuals may show an increase in health-related problems as they age. Of all the factors predictive of how individuals will adjust to aging and predictive of subsequent mortality, health is the most powerful (Rodin & McAvay, 1992). Among persons 62 years of age and older, perceived health declines with the onset of new illnesses and the associated increase in the number of visits to physicians for care and/or preexisting illnesses that worsen (Rodin & McAvay, 1992). Among older adults, perceived health was also predicted by higher scores on tests used to measure depression and by lower scores on a life satisfaction index, for example, indicators of psychosocial status. Health can be defined in many ways: number of illnesses, chronic conditions, disabilities, restrictions or limitations, physical pain, emotional status, or cardiovascular capacity, to cite but a few of the most common.

There is support for a relationship between certain kinds of functional disabilities (see figure 11.1), the presence of pain, and older persons experiencing depressive symptoms. Williamson and Schulz (1991) found that community-residing people over the age of 55 identified limitations in nine activities—self care, care of others, eating habits, sleeping habits, doing household chores, going shopping, visiting friends, working on hobbies, and maintaining friendships—in association with the degree of pain or discomfort they reported generally throughout the previous week. Older persons who experienced the highest levels of pain were also those who identified the most limitations across these nine areas and, not surprisingly perhaps, were also the most depressed (Williamson & Schulz, 1991). Although other studies have conclusively shown a link between chronic pain and depression, these studies have been conducted with institutionalized elderly. In the more restricted environment of the nursing home, functional disability was not found to play a role (Parmelee, Katz, & Lawton, 1991). However, when community-residing elderly were investigated, a clear relationship was found among functional disability (e.g., the nine areas identified), level of pain experienced, and depression (Williamson & Schulz, 1991).

## Elder Abuse

Older individuals are not immune from the impact of violence in our society. From many sources, increasing attention has been directed at **elder abuse** in hopes of raising awareness of the *physical, financial,* and *emotional* harm that can occur. Although there is a surprising lack of consistency in how elder abuse is defined, (Moon & Williams, 1993), some evidence suggests that passive forms of neglect are more prevalent than active forms of physical violence against the elderly. (See table 7.2 for a list of different forms of elder abuse.) Peretti and Majecen (1991) have indicated that the abusive behaviors which elderly individuals (68–87 years of age) themselves report having endured include: lack of attention, lack of affection, general neglect, derogatory naming, demeaning commentary, exploitation, threats of violence, loud talking, and confinement. Most of these older persons believed that they were targets of calculated exploitation by relatives, friends, and others (Peretti & Majecen, 1991).

Similar to the problems of child abuse or spouse abuse, the abuse of the elderly is an oftentimes invisible phenomenon, occurring within the home and away from public awareness (Eth & Leong, 1992). The House Select Committee on Aging estimates that four of every five cases of elder abuse goes unreported and uninvestigated (Church et al., 1988). Although states have enacted strict and formal reporting guidelines for child abuse, few laws exist to govern the abuse of elders and those that do exist are somewhat imprecise, variable from one jurisdiction to another, and perceived to border on infringement of individual and family rights (Eth & Leong, 1992).

Physicians can play a leading role in the identification of probable incidents of elder abuse (Blakely, Dolon, & May, 1993). When physicians recognize suspected cases of elder abuse and neglect, they are more likely to inform community-based service agencies for the elderly of the problem than report it to the police (Blakely & Dolon, 1991). Generally, however, physicians are reluctant to report their suspicions regarding elder abuse due to a number of reasons: lack of awareness of mandatory reporting laws, insufficient training, minimal knowledge of the life situations of their patients, and ageist attitudes (Blakely, Dolon, & May, 1993). Estimates of elder abuse continue to vary in the range of 1 percent to 10 percent (Pillemer & Wolf, 1986). In one study in a large metropolitan city, a random sampling of incidents of physical violence, verbal aggression, and neglect revealed rates of 32 per 1,000 among older adults (Pillemer & Finkelhor, 1988). This would represent an estimated incidence of 700,00 to 1.1 million cases per year nationwide (Pillemer & Finkelhor, 1988).

Elder abuse is a repetitive pattern of behavior, not an isolated or single occurrence. Those who abuse the elderly are frequently found to have experienced marital problems, financial hardships, alcoholism, drug abuse, and child abuse (Church et al., 1988). Elderly adults are most often abused by their own spouses (Pillemer & Finkelhor, 1988). Previous research (Yin, 1985) suggests that women are more likely to be victims of abuse than men; however, other evidence indicates nearly equal rates of abuse toward older men and women (Pillemer & Finkelhor, 1988). Perhaps somewhat surprisingly, older women are infrequently seen or referred to battered women's shelters, and few such shelters have provisions for special programming for the elderly seeking their services (Vinton, 1992). Another large group who abuse the elderly are relatives who act as caregivers (Pillemer & Wolf, 1986). And it appears that abuse is far more likely among elderly who share living arrangements with a spouse, child, or other relative than among elderly who live alone (Quinn & Tomita, 1986). More recently investigators have identified older adults who are *self*-neglectful to the point of causing abusive outcomes. Self-neglectful elderly are most likely to be male, alcoholic, and to have disabilities such as dementia, most commonly Alzheimer's disease (Vinton, 1991).

Although we can identify those who are likely to abuse the elderly, we still know relatively little about why the elderly are abused (Reinberg & Hayslip, 1991). The causes of elder abuse are varied. Investigators have focused attention on a *recurrent stress pattern* found among both the abused and the abuser (Pillemer & Wolf, 1986). The constant responsibility for the care of an older, frail adult often falls on those who neither choose this role nor the financial, interpersonal, and time demands that are associated with it (Lau & Kosberg, 1979; Reinberg & Hayslip, 1991). Thus, in a recent survey of 184 Alzheimer's patients and their primary caregivers, violence and abuse were very commonly reported (Paveza, Cohen, Eisdorfer, Freels, et al., 1992). Within the past twelve months, 15.8 percent of patients were identified as having become violent toward their caregivers and 5.4 percent of the caregivers reported as having been violent toward the Alzheimer's patient.

Resentment over the lack of freedom and free time have also been regularly reported in the abusive patterns among those who care for the elderly. The commitment that caregivers must make to the elderly person is often not recognized by anyone—neither the elderly person nor others in the immediate family. The sacrifice and effort required of caregivers has not been sufficiently rewarded socially or economically; the absence of reward and recognition leads to further cycles of abuse (Myers & Shelton, 1987). In providing care for an elderly parent, for example, adult children in middle age must make difficult choices: (1) limiting their careers, accepting part-time employment rather than full-time work, or giving up a job to remain at home to provide elder care; (2) postponing vacations or forgoing evenings out with spouse or friends; (3) providing financial assistance, nursing care, or a special diet at a time when most families face the burgeoning costs of their growing children, some of whom will be attending college; and (4) making their own retirement planning and financial savings a secondary concern (Church et al., 1988).

Pillemer (1986) has noted another common factor in the background of the abused elderly: *dependency.* Initially researchers believed that older persons became targets for abuse because they depended on relatives for many of their needs. Their heightened dependency suggested helplessness, weakness, and a lack of personal efficacy (Quinn & Tomita, 1986). However, other data (Pillemer, 1986) revealed that caregivers who abuse the elderly are themselves very dependent on those whom they target for abuse. Abusers may be dependent on their elderly victims for housing, for assistance with routine household tasks, or for financial support. It is this type of dependency that is also implicated in elder abuse.

Research also supports the notion that elder abuse by caregivers represents continuation of a cycle of abuse that has characterized family relationships at earlier periods of development (Steinmetz, 1978, 1981). For instance, experiencing consistent patterns of family violence may create expectations that this behavior is accepted at other points in the life cycle, opening the door to child abuse, spousal abuse, and elder abuse. Among such families, violence and abuse is tolerated and not at all perceived to be deviant.

These explanations, taken as a whole, suggest that elder abuse may be best understood as the result of socialization in the family to accept violence and abuse, long-standing family conflicts, or accumulated stress on the primary caregiver in meeting the needs of a frail older relative. Ethnic and racial factors however, are beginning to be recognized as important factors as well. Griffin and Williams (1992) suggest that in understanding elder abuse among African Americans, there are unique characteristics of the African American family, patterns of socialization, and economic conditions that are more predictive of abuse than those factors which hold for other families. In a similar vein, Moon and Williams (1993) report the strong influence that culture and ethnicity have in defining elder abuse. Among groups of Korean American, African American, and Caucasian elderly women, different definitions of elder abuse were found in their classification of a number of hypothetical scenarios. Older Korean American women generally perceived somewhat less elder abuse in the scenarios whereas older African American women perceived more abuse. For example, the three ethnic groups were asked whether there was elder abuse in a scenario describing the frustration a daughter or daughter-in-law experienced by her mother's/mother-in-law's embarrassing behaviors with guests who visited their home. In the scenario, the daughter or daughter-in-law gave tranquilizers to control the embarrassing behavior, but falsely indicated that they were doctor-ordered medications. Moon and Williams (1993) reported that among these older women, 63 percent of African Americans, 36 percent of Caucasian, and only 10 percent of Korean Americans saw this scenario as one involving elder abuse. In general, most Korean Americans reported that, regardless of the type or frequency of abuse, it would be very difficult for them to reveal to others (e.g., professionals) that elder abuse was occurring in their family. They were reluctant to expose the family to the "shame" of such incidents in this public manner and also were fearful of creating conflict among members of their extended family (Moon & Williams, 1993). It remains for other investigators to continue to explore the meaning of differing definitions and the likelihood of reporting elder abuse as determined by cultural experience, race, and ethnicity. The role of cultural variation needs to be considered in future formulations (Moon & Williams, 1993).

### *Autonomy and Control*

Mental health experts have recognized the importance of providing the elderly with a sense of control and autonomy. Without individual control, human beings experience emotional distress, depression, lowered motivation, reduced feelings of well-being and life satisfaction, and deficits in cognitive and motor performance (Gallagher & Thompson, 1983; Rodin, 1986; Shupe, 1985).

Older people encounter many circumstances that limit their sense of autonomy and control. These include physical impairments, reduced economic resources, and change in residence (Rowe & Kahn, 1987). In some studies, researchers have observed that genuine concern and love may lead a caregiver or human service professional to do too much for an older person. These behaviors may unintentionally produce dependency, helplessness, and hopelessness among the elderly (Rowe & Kahn, 1987). When control and autonomy are given to residents of nursing homes and other institutions, beneficial outcomes are routinely found. Beneficial interventions include providing choice over the *timing* of a move in living arrangements; providing *options* for residents to select in their nursing home environment; giving residents *control* over the length and timing of student volunteer visits; and having residents *care* for pets and plants (Langer & Rodin, 1976; Rodin, 1986). These interventions have been reported to improve health, emotions, subjective well-being and satisfaction, activity levels, eating, and sleeping. Encouraging control and autonomy also means discouraging well-intentioned caregivers from *infantilizing the elderly*—treating them as cute children rather than dignified adults. Overprotecting and infantilizing robs the elderly of their dignity, self-worth, mastery, and sense of achievement.

## Driving and Aging

One of the most important signs of autonomy and control is the freedom afforded adults who can drive a car (Campbell, Bush, & Hale, 1993). For individuals in our society, driving provides the ability to maintain an independent lifestyle whether residing in a rural environment or an urban center. Among the cohort of older people today, men, in particular, associate driving with independence and are most reluctant to forgo their driving privileges (Campbell et al., 1993; National Research Council, 1988, 1992). Scharff (1991) notes, however, that there will be a growing number of elderly women in the coming years who also associate driving with personal freedom and independence. Persson (1993) noted the following communication in her recent work: "Driving is a way of holding on to your life. I was 94 years old, and it was like losing my hand to give up driving." When asked to identify what older people missed most about not driving any longer, they responded most often with the following three words: independence, convenience, and mobility (Persson, 1993). Walker (1991) has projected cohort differences among today's elderly drivers and those who will become 65 years of age in the coming decades: more and more women reaching old age will routinely possess a driving license and will have had many years of experience behind the wheel. Only a few decades ago, most elderly drivers were

*Driving is a demanding activity that necessitates the complex integration of a variety of physical, sensory, and cognitive abilities.*

males; women who held driving licenses were small in number, often learning to drive later in life. In one recent study, nearly 40 percent of adults over 65 had never driven a car (Marottoli, Ostfeld, Merrill, Perlman, Foley, & Cooney, 1993). By the year 2000, drivers 55 years of age and older will comprise 28 percent of the driving population and by 2050 will comprise 39 percent of all drivers (Malfetti, 1985; Persson, 1993).

Society is increasingly concerned about the safety of older drivers because of the increased likelihood of impairments in physical, visual, and cognitive capacities (Campbell, Bush, & Hale, 1993). There is no unified approach or interpretation to assessing the driving skills of older individuals, nor is there agreement regarding the use of the results of vision screening tests currently required by all states for older person's license renewal (Persson, 1993). Investigators have found that the physical skills necessary for safe driving decline dramatically by age 75 (Persson, 1993). However, even in late middle age there is evidence that driving is problematic. The National Research Council (1988) noted that for adults 65 to 74, vehicular crashes are the leading cause of accidental death and the second leading cause (next to falls) for those adults 75 and over (Persson, 1993). Studies have shown that with increasing age older drivers have difficulty in reading signs, particularly at night (Kline, Ghali, Kline, & Brown, 1990; Kline, Kline, Fozard, Kosnik, Schieber, & Sekuler, 1992). The Canadian government has recommended that a ratio of letter size to distance be established in recognition of this problem for older drivers as well as the creation of minimum levels of illumination for signs at night (Charness & Bosman, 1990). However, when visual images or pictorial signs are used instead of lettered signs, no age differences are reported among younger, middle-aged, or older drivers (Kline, Ghali, Kline, & Brown, 1990).

Visual acuity and peripheral vision show loss beginning in the 50's and it becomes more difficult to engage in *dual processing tasks.* Driving demands this type of complex task performance in which physical and visual-cognitive processing of complex and dynamic information is required such as that required in yielding the right of way at an intersection (Kline et al., 1992; Persson, 1993). In one investigation, drivers from 22 to 92 years old were surveyed to evaluate any visual difficulties they encountered in routine driving tasks (Kline et al., 1992). There was a relationship with age such that older drivers experienced more problems with routine tasks: unexpected vehicles, vehicle speed, dim displays, windshield problems, and sign reading. These data, plotted as a function of age, are presented in figure 11.2 and suggest that the declines in visual functioning reported in other studies are related to the perceived experiences of older drivers. Kline et al. (1992) also report that these data in figure 11.2 were related to the types of automobile accidents more frequently found among older drivers.

The decision to stop driving completely is a difficult one for older persons to make. Campbell, Bush, and Hale (1993) found that nearly 50 percent of those drivers who had ceased driving completely, despite the vast majority maintaining a valid license, identified medical reasons for their decision. Specific factors in their decision to stop driving included visual impairments (macular degeneration, retinal hemorrhage), deficits in functional ability (e.g., the ability to physically carry through other daily living tasks), Parkinson's disease, stroke and stroke-related residual paralysis or weakness, and episodes of losing consciousness, and Alzheimer's disease (Campbell et al., 1993; Gilley, Wilson, Bennett, Stebbins, Bernard, Whalen & Fox 1991; Kline et al., 1992; Legh-Smith, Wade & Hewer 1986; McLay, 1989). Marottoli et al., (1993) confirm that older adults may decide to stop driving based on their own assessment of their abilities, their age, the presence of neurologic disease, cataracts, and other limiting disabilities. However, social and economic factors also play a role (Campbell et al., 1993; Marottoli et al., 1993). Among a group of older drivers (Marottoli et al., 1993), 40 percent had stopped driving within the past six years due to physical or visual impairment, increased physical disability, and social factors (economics and retirement). Though all of these factors combined to predict total cessation of driving, the single best predictor of driving cessation was a social factor, "no longer working." In another investigation, Persson (1993) asked elderly adults to identify the reasons for their having stopped driving. The reasons included: advice from a physician, increased anxiety while driving, trouble seeing pedestrians and other cars, medical conditions, and advice from family and friends.

Perrson (1993) reports that 42 percent of the older adults still driving drive more than five thousand miles per year. Older drivers who drive more than five thousand miles have higher incomes and are reported to be male and still employed, and relatively younger and less disabled than older adults who drive less miles or do not

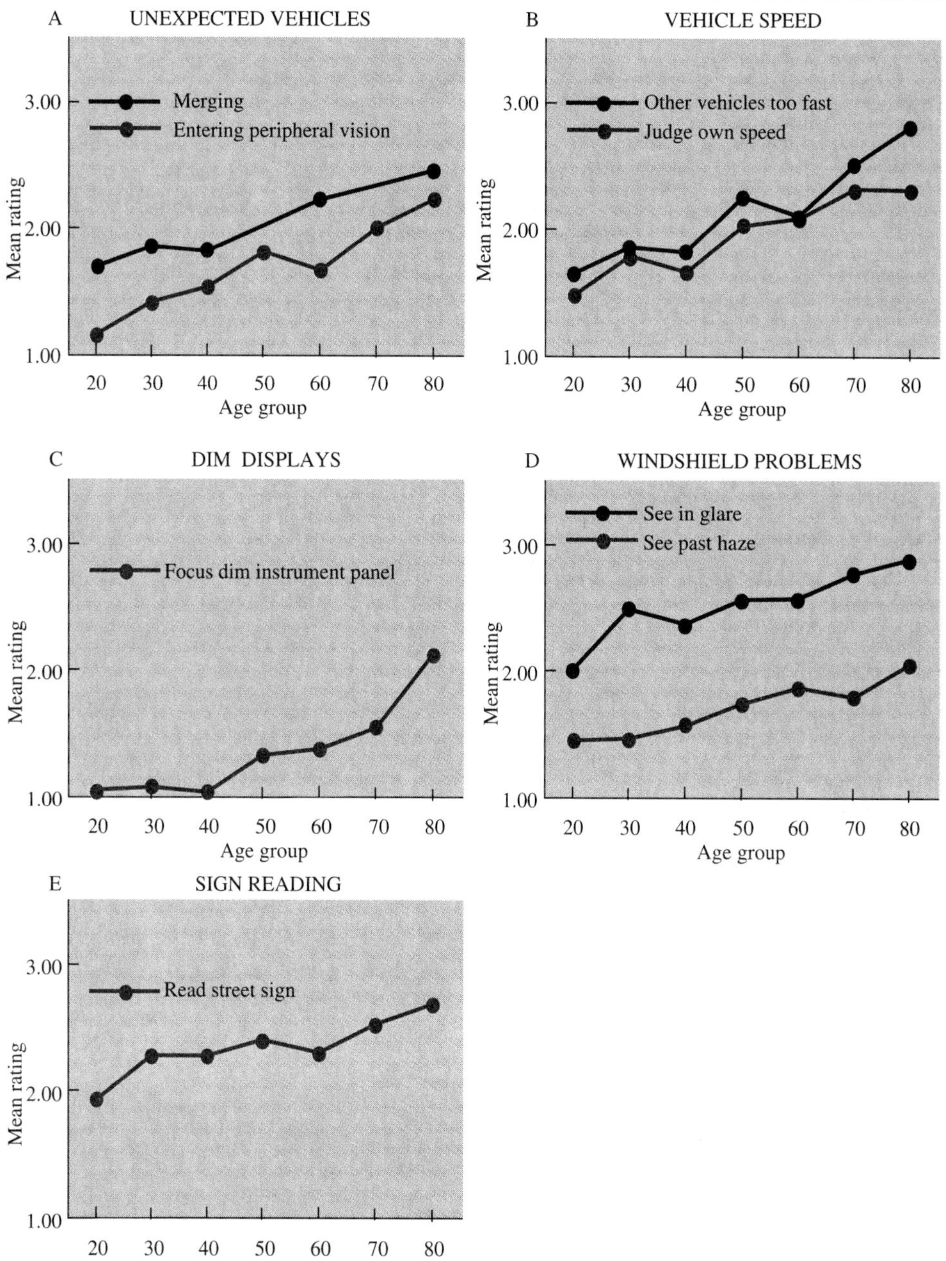


**Figure 11.2** Mean reported difficulty on visual driving tasks as a function of age.

drive at all (Marottoli et al., 1993). Other studies suggest that older drivers *voluntarily* adjust the frequency, length of trips, speed, time of day (e.g., daylight hours rather than evening), miles driven, and avoid peak traffic or superhighways (Kosnik, Sekuler, & Kline, 1990; Marottoli et al., 1993). Although older individuals can and do make the decision to stop or reduce their driving themselves, little research has examined how the elderly perceive their own driving skills. Some studies report that older drivers believe that they are both safer and more skilled than other drivers of a similar age (Svenson, 1981; Persson, 1993). It is interesting that older individuals apparently ignore factors related to safety such as hearing loss or cognitive difficulties in making assessments of their own driving skills and abilities. One of the respondents in Persson's investigation jokingly remarked, "I can barely hear, barely see, and barely walk. Things could be worse though. At least I can still drive." Perhaps this reflects a bias in the typical sample surveyed, that is, community-residing and ambulatory older adults (Campbell et al., 1993). The point in much of the research is that while most older adults voluntarily decide to stop driving, there is evidence that many elderly individuals with identical problems and circumstances believe that they still can continue and indeed do so. For example, consider the presence of medical conditions such as **syncope** (pronounced sin-cō-pea) (losing consciousness). Florida, along with thirteen other states, requires patients with this condition to have a 12-month driving suspension. Yet, a recent analysis revealed that 65 percent of those older people with syncope continued to drive (Campbell et al., 1993).

It remains difficult to limit the independence and autonomy of older drivers even when conditions appear to warrant cessation of driving privileges. Yet, it should be clear from the national statistics on automobile accidents that older persons *are* increasingly at risk with a higher rate of accidents than any other age group, except teenagers (Insurance Institute for Highway Safety, 1992). Persson (1993) notes that the advice of a physician to stop driving is one of the most authoritative voices to which older adults are sensitive. Physicians can play a critical role in managing this problem. It must be realized that with increased age there truly are concomitant declines in some of the basic skills and abilities needed to be successful in the complex task of driving a car.

## *Crime*

The biological decrements, physical limitations, and functional impairments of older persons may contribute to a sense of growing vulnerability and increased fear. One of the most striking manifestations of the older person's sense of vulnerability is the fear of being the victim of a crime. The fear of crime, if sufficiently powerful among older people, has been hypothesized to become a deterrent to travel, social contacts, and the pursuit of an active lifestyle among elderly persons (Lindquist & Duke, 1982). In one survey, nearly one-quarter of all those 65 years of age and older expressed a generalized fear of being the victim of a crime (National Institute on Aging, 1982). Other research studies have supported the view that older adults do report greater fear of crime (Lewis & Salem, 1986; Moeller, 1989; Ortega & Myles, 1987). At all ages women are more fearful of crime than men (Ferraro & LaGrange, 1992).

*As adults age, they become increasingly fearful about the prospect of being a victim of crime.*

The studies examining older persons' fear of crime contrasts sharply with actual crime reports, which reveal that becoming a victim of crime is *less* likely among those 65 years of age and older than among younger adults, as can be seen in table 11.1. These statistics show clearly that the rate of victimization is lowest among older persons than it is for any other age group.

Violent crime represents a small percentage (6%) of offenses against the elderly (Bureau of Justice Department Statistics, 1987). More common are nonviolent crimes such as fraud, vandalism, purse snatching, pickpocketing, and harassment. The incidence of such nonviolent crime is likely low due to underreporting. Older people may fear retribution, believe the criminal justice system cannot help them, or wish to avoid the publicity that causes personal shame and embarrassment. More crimes against the elderly occur in or near their homes as compared to younger victims (Church et al., 1988).

The factors that predict crime victimization of the elderly include age (over 65), race (African American), sex (male), and residential status (urban metropolitan center). Thus, for the older African American male living in the inner city, the fear of crime is based on reality (Jackson, 1988). More than 60 percent of our nation's population of elderly reside within the boundaries of a metropolitan city and are likely targets for criminals as they walk the streets, ride public transportation, or enter large apartment buildings (Church et al., 1988). Given their physical limitations and reduced functional reserve, most elderly residents will not resist or protest when a crime is perpetrated. In fact, when older people protest, they more often require subsequent medical treatment than younger people who experience

*TABLE 11.1*

***Age Distribution of Victim and Type of Crime: 1980–1985***

| | *Age of victim* | | | |
|---|---|---|---|---|
| | *12-24* | *25-49* | *50-64* | *65 and older* |
| Victimization rate | | | | |
| Crimes of violence | 67.5 | 34.0 | 11.3 | 6.0 |
| Rape | 2.0 | .8 | .1[a] | .1[a] |
| Robbery | 11.4 | 6.0 | 3.4 | 2.7 |
| Assault | 54.2 | 27.1 | 7.8 | 3.2 |
| Aggravated | 18.4 | 9.1 | 2.7 | 1.0 |
| Simple | 35.8 | 18.0 | 5.1 | 2.3 |
| Crimes of theft | 126.5 | 82.4 | 46.1 | 22.3 |
| Personal larceny with contact | 3.5 | 2.8 | 2.8 | 3.1 |
| Personal larceny without contract | 123.0 | 79.6 | 43.4 | 19.2 |
| Household crimes | 371.4 | 242.6 | 164.4 | 102.7 |
| Burglary | 144.3 | 86.9 | 59.4 | 44.0 |
| Household larceny | 196.8 | 136.5 | 92.3 | 53.7 |
| Motor vehicle theft | 30.3 | 19.3 | 12.7 | 5.1 |
| Number of victimizations | | | | |
| Crimes of violence | 3,429,700 | 2,703,500 | 375,300 | 154,200 |
| Rape | 99,000 | 65,600 | 4,600[a] | 1,900[a] |
| Robbery | 579,300 | 480,300 | 113,800 | 69,000 |
| Assault | 2,751,400 | 2,157,500 | 256,900 | 83,400 |
| Aggravated | 934,100 | 727,200 | 89,300 | 24,600 |
| Simple | 1,817,300 | 1,430,400 | 167,600 | 58,800 |
| Crimes of theft | 6,423,800 | 6,553,900 | 1,527,200 | 576,400 |
| Personal larceny with contact | 176,700 | 225,500 | 92,500 | 79,600 |
| Personal larceny without contact | 6,247,100 | 6,328,400 | 1,434,700 | 496,900 |
| Household crimes | 2,708,700 | 10,195,400 | 3,151,300 | 1,809,500 |
| Burglary | 1,052,300 | 3,651,300 | 1,138,300 | 775,100 |
| Household larceny | 1,435,600 | 5,733,900 | 1,768,800 | 945,300 |
| Motor vehicle theft | 220,700 | 810,200 | 244,200 | 89,100 |
| Number of persons in age group[b] | 50,792,400 | 79,549,900 | 33,091,500 | 25,811,700 |
| Number of households in age group[b] | 7,293,100 | 42,018,500 | 19,172,300 | 17,614,400 |

*Note: The victimization rate is the annual average of the number of victimizations for 1980–1985 per 1,000 persons or households in that age group. Detail may not add to total because of rounding. [a]Average annual estimate is based on ten or fewer sample cases. [b]Annual average for 1980–1985.*
*Source: Elderly Victims, Bureau of Justice Statistics, Washington, DC, November 1987.*

identical violent crimes. Tragically, older persons who experience a violent crime believe strongly that they will be victimized again. They become worrisome, fearful, and obsessed with protecting themselves from another incident.

In recent years, social scientists have questioned the methods used in studies showing that fear of crime is more prevalent among older adults. Many of these earlier studies, for example, have used single-item questions as indicators of fear of crime, relying on two widely available simple measures from national surveys: (1) "How safe do you feel or would you feel being out alone in your neighborhood at night?" and (2) Is there any area right around here—that is within a mile—where you would be afraid to walk alone at night?" Ferraro and LaGrange (1992) note that the reliability and validity of these two global questions have not been determined. In addition, such general questions do not differentiate between fear of different types of crime and may be viewed quite differently by older persons who go out at night versus those who do not. Ferraro and LaGrange (1992) note that these questions also appear to confuse *risk* of crime (a realistic appraisal of probability) with *fear* of crime (an emotional response to a hypothetical situation). Using the second question as an index of fear of crime is also problematic, since it appears to be reflective of safety in the neighborhood at night (Ferraro & LaGrange, 1992).

Adults at different ages across the life span were recently sampled in a telephone survey that was more sensitive both to the actual fear of different types of crime (e.g., robbery, car theft, rape, murder, property damage, etc.) and the likelihood that these crimes might actually occur (Ferraro & LaGrange, 1992). Results were clear and unambiguous; the fear of crime was *not* greater among older adults. In fact, younger adults (18 to 24 years of age) were more fearful of most crimes than were older persons. Among those 75 years of age and older, the fear of some types of crime (e.g., fear of property crime) was the lowest of any age group (Ferraro & LaGrange, 1992). These results, if replicable, call into question conventional wisdom that aging and fear of crime are directly related. It must be recognized that the measures of fear were uniquely constructed by Ferraro and LaGrange and have not been used in other studies. And the sampling, conducted in 33 larger metropolitan areas and 117 smaller areas and counties, undersampled small towns and rural communities.

## *Alcoholism*

Among today's elderly Americans, the excessive use of alcohol is the most common drug abuse problem, excluding tobacco use (Atkinson, Ganzini, & Bernstein, 1992). Older adults generally show symptoms of alcoholism similar to those found among younger persons (e.g., amount consumed, alcohol-related social and legal problems, alcohol-related health problems, behavioral signs of drunkenness, and self-recognition of alcohol problems). However, some age differences between older and younger alcoholics have been reported (Curtis, Geller, Stokes, & Levine, 1989). For example, given the increased biological sensitivity of older persons to drugs, intoxication may occur at lower levels; additionally, older persons more often than younger persons self-report depressive symptoms along with alcoholism (Atkinson et al., 1992). With increasing age, the body becomes less able to tolerate the effects of alcohol. Nearly 10 percent of alcoholics receiving treatment for their condition are over age 60, with a gender difference showing far more males than females (Rivers, Rivers, & Newman, 1991). Demographic surveys indicate that older men are two to six times more likely than older women to be alcoholic (Atkinson et al., 1992).

Paradoxically, statistics reveal that with increasing age, beginning at age 50, the number of people classified as alcoholics decreases (Simon, 1980). Those who develop alcoholic behaviors in early adulthood **(early-onset alcoholism)** often do not survive to reach middle or old age, or they develop multiple health problems that force them either to abstain or to prepare for imminent death (Atkinson et al., 1992). However, among those who continue to use alcohol, the rate of alcoholism holds between 4 and 10 percent (Department of Health and Human Services, 1990). Early-onset alcoholics who reach old age are beset with a variety of physical health problems including liver damage, high blood pressure, heart disease, and alcohol-based organic brain syndrome. The latter condition, called **Korsakoff's syndrome,** is marked by behavioral disorientation, confusion, delusions, and irreversible memory disorder. Alcohol-based organic brain syndrome is related to the destruction of brain cells and the correlated incidence of malnourishment, vitamin deficiency, and inadequate protein. Alcoholics typically forgo basic nutritional needs in favor of gratifying their substance dependency. Like all substance abuse treatments, the goals for elderly alcoholics are to attain stabilization or reduction of alcohol consumption, treat coexisting problems, and establish appropriate social intervention (Atkinson et al., 1992). Higher rates of success are reported with treatment in this older population, in contrast to that reported among young adult alcoholics (Atkinson & Schuckit, 1981; Liberto, Oslin, & Ruskin, 1992).

In recent years, experts have concurred that the incidence of alcohol-related problems in the elderly has been regularly and consistently underestimated (Adams & Waskel, 1993; Caracci & Miller, 1991). In one study, a group of new admissions to a hospital was screened for alcoholism. Positive identification of alcoholism was reported to be 27 percent among adults under 60 years of age and 21 percent for those 60 years of age and older. In another investigation of alcohol-related hospitalizations, the rate per 10,000 individuals aged 65 years of age and older was reported to be 54.7 for men and 14.8 for women (AARP, 1993).

There is also increasing evidence that older problem drinkers turn to alcohol in response to negative life events, chronic stress, and social resource deficits (Brennan & Moos, 1992; Moos, Mertens, & Brennan, 1993). Older adults with prior incidents of alcoholism in their developmental history are more likely to experience recurrence of the syndrome when faced with stressors in late life (Atkinson et al., 1992; Liberto et al., 1992). There is also evidence that older African Americans have higher rates of alcoholism than other minority group elderly persons (Atkinson et al., 1992; Curtis, Geller, Stokes, & Levine, 1989). **Late-onset alcoholism** emerges initially in middle-to-late life, often in response to multiple stressors (e.g., loss of spouse, relocation, physical disability), and accounts for between one-third to one-half of all elderly alcoholics (Liberto et al., 1992). The existence of late-onset alcoholism was disputed for many years. Atkinson, et al. (1992) have confirmed the phenomenon, which may emerge in one of three forms: (1) as an increase in consumption over earlier periods in development, (2) as a relapse reflective of earlier patterns of overuse, or (3) as a first-time phenomenon. In reviewing studies, Atkinson, et al. (1992) note that the incidence of initial drinking problems among those 60 years of age and older has been reported in studies across a wide range with rates varying between 29 percent to 68 percent. Late-onset alcoholism appears to be more common among older women than older men and is also associated with higher socioeconomic status (Atkinson et al., 1992). This form of alcoholism continues to be underdiagnosed by professionals and under-recognized by family members and friends (Beresford, Blow, Brower, Adams, & Hall, 1988; Department of Health and Human Services, 1990). Underdiagnosis is particularly likely in elderly Hispanic populations, where symptoms such as frailty, depression, senility, or unsteadiness may be seen as "normal" aging, not alcoholism (Lopez-Bushnell, Tyra, & Futrell, 1992).

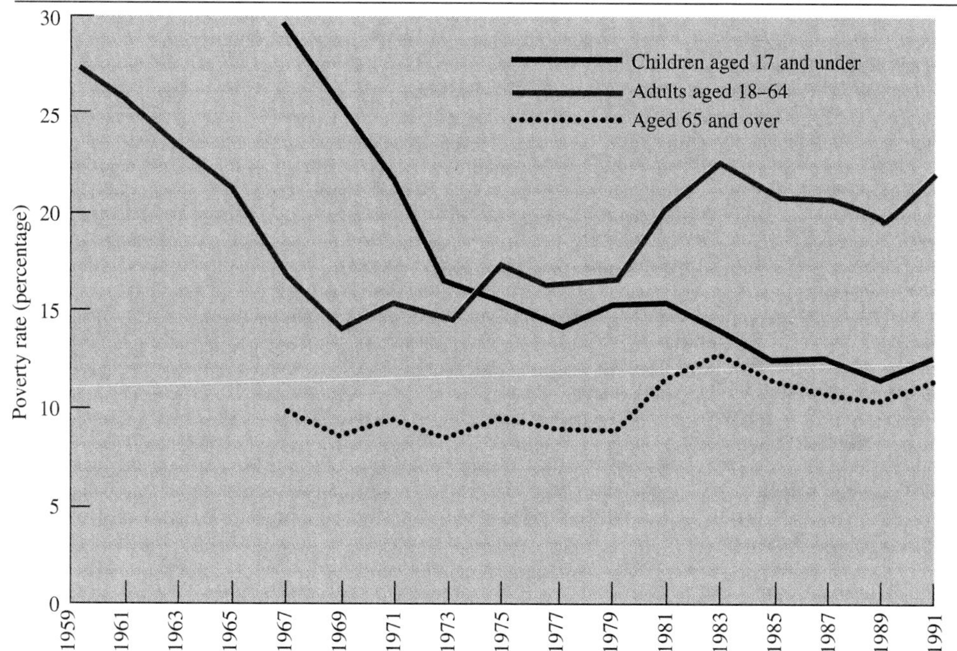


**Figure 11.3** Trends in official poverty rates among the old and the young.
*Source: U.S. Department of Commerce, Bureau of the Census, Poverty in the United States: 1991, Current Population Reports, Series P-60, No. 181, Government Printing Office, Washington, DC, 1992.*

## *Elderly in Urban and Rural Communities*

There is consistent concern over the welfare of the elderly in our communities (Quinn & Smeeding, 1993). Recent census data suggest that although the overall number of older people living in poverty has declined from 1966, the percentage of older persons comprising those living in poverty has remained consistently between 10–12 percent since 1981 (U.S. Department of Commerce, 1992). These trends, mentioned earlier in the text, are presented in figure 11.3.

Overall, the elderly are generally more comparable economically, than other age groups (Quinn & Smeeding, 1993). Two points, however, need to be recognized in these data. First, there are many elderly for whom poverty and disadvantage remain realities: women who live alone and minorities. More than 25 percent of those older women living alone live in poverty. Among minorities, who currently comprise 20 percent of today's elderly population, poverty rates are two to three times higher for older adult African American and Hispanics (Van Nostrand, 1993a). When taken together, 50 percent of older Hispanic women who live alone live in poverty, compared to almost 60 percent of older African American women living alone (Quinn & Smeeding, 1993). The census data examining poverty can also be analyzed within the various subgroups of those over age 65 (see table 11.2). The data in table 11.2 reveal that the oldest old are most likely to be living in poverty (Quinn & Smeeding, 1993). And, as we have seen previously in figure 11.3, it appears that there have been economic changes for successive cohorts of older adults that may be directly related to their having higher educational attainment, better economic histories, and higher average incomes. Therefore, the elderly show lower rates of poverty than adults 18–64 and children 17 and under (Ruggles, 1992). These data suggest that poverty, though

*TABLE 11.2*

| *Poverty Rates Among Subgroups of the Elderly, 1990* | | | | |
|---|---|---|---|---|
| *Category of Elderly* | *All Aged 65+* | *Aged 65 to 74* | *Aged 75 to 84* | *Aged 85+* |
| Total | 12.2 | 9.7 | 14.9 | 20.2 |
| Males (Total) | 7.6 | 6.4 | 9.3 | 12.6 |
| Male, Married | 5.3 | 4.2 | 7.2 | 11.4 |
| Male, Widowed | 13.8 | 13.2 | 14.3 | 13.9 |
| Females (Total) | 15.4 | 12.3 | 18.3 | 24.1 |
| Female, Married | 5.7 | 4.7 | 8.1 | NA |
| Female, Widowed | 21.4 | 19.5 | 22.1 | 24.4 |

*Note: Estimates show percentage of persons who are poor in each age group.*
*Source: U.S. Congress, House Committee on Ways and Means, 1992 Green Book: Material and Data on Programs Within the Jurisdiction of the Committee on Ways and Means, U.S. Government Printing Office. Washington, DC, 1992.*

not absent from our elderly population, is differentially distributed across this heterogeneous age group (Quinn & Smeeding, 1993). Those least likely to experience poverty, as shown in table 11.2, are older couples for whom poverty is reported to be only about 5 percent (U. S. Department of Commerce, 1992).

Others have noted that some of the reported differences in poverty among the elderly may reflect, in part, alternative methods of classification (McLaughlin & Jensen, 1993). The definitions of poverty used in studies often vary from study to study, with recent analyses sometimes including rates of "deep poverty," defined as a level of poverty that is 50 percent or less of the poverty threshold (McLaughlin & Jensen, 1993).

Regardless of how the data are arrayed and defined, they indicate considerable diversity in the living conditions of elderly people. In addition to financial conditions, it is also important to compare the living conditions experienced by older people in urban and rural settings. The elderly represent nearly 15 percent of rural populations but only 12 percent of urban populations (Van Nostrand, 1993b).

Recent social and economic analyses suggest that the elderly in urban settings have experienced significant declines in both health and welfare (Ford, Haug, Roy, Jones, & Folmar, 1992). In one analysis, comparison of 65- to 76-year-olds across a twelve-year period revealed more chronic illnesses, more psychological distress, more need for assistance with daily living activities, more visits to physicians, and more medical care. Today's new cohort of urban dwellers 65 to 76 years of age also showed significantly more impairment, disability, and disadvantage than their predecessors (Ford et al., 1992). Retired men who live in the suburbs surrounding urban areas have been found to experience the highest levels of well-being when compared to those living in other locations (Reitzes, Mutran, & Pope, 1991). However, when poor health occurs, it has a greater negative impact on these retired men living in the suburbs than it does for those living in urban areas.

Poverty among the rural elderly is far more prevalent than among urban elderly. And, poverty is far more common among rural African Americans than among urban African Americans (Van Nostrand, 1993b). The growing economic difficulties encountered by elderly minorities in rural environments, particularly African Americans in the South, has also been documented (Angel & Hogan, 1992; Lichter, 1989).

*TABLE 11.3*

***Average Percentage of Total Family Income from Various Sources for Elderly Individuals by Poverty Status and Residence***

| | *Total U.S.* | | *Rural* | | *Urban* | |
|---|---|---|---|---|---|---|
| Income Type | Poor | Nonpoor | Poor | Nonpoor | Poor | Nonpoor |
| Earnings | 0-.9 | 17.5 | 2.1 | 13.9 | 0.0 | 18.8 |
| Social Security | 76.0 | 46.4 | 78.4 | 51.3 | 74.6 | 44.7 |
| Supplemental Security Income | 10.2 | 1.2 | 10.6 | 1.0 | 10.0 | 1.2 |
| Retirement & Survivor Benefits | 3.9 | 15.5 | 2.2 | 13.0 | 4.9 | 16.0 |
| Interest/Dividends | 5.7 | 15.5 | 4.0 | 15.0 | 6.7 | 15.7 |
| All Other Sources | 3.3 | 4.1 | 2.7 | 5.8 | 3.8 | 3.6 |

*From D. K. McLaughlin and L. Jensen, "Poverty among Older Americans: The Plight of Nonmetropolitan Elders" in* Journal of Gerontology: Social Sciences, *48 (2): 44–54. Copyright © 1993 The Gerontological Society of America.*

Elderly individuals residing in rural environments have been found to be less likely to have additional sources of income beyond Social Security benefits, which are, on balance, lower than benefits received by urban elderly (McLaughlin & Jensen, 1993). Such differences may be traced to the restricted type and availability of jobs for adult workers. Among the rural elderly, jobs are likely to pay lower wages, to be nonunionized, to offer no pension benefits, and to be seasonal (McLaughlin & Jensen, 1993). The differences in sources of family income among rural and urban residing elderly are presented in table 11.3. It has also been reported that these differences are even greater when the oldest old are examined (McLaughlin & Jensen, 1993). Thus, the rural elderly who have generally experienced employment options with limited income and have received less education will more likely encounter poverty in old age when compared to the urban dwelling elderly who have been more advantaged throughout their lives in terms of income, employment, and education. One additional variable, marital status, plays a significant role in understanding the rural elderly. Married women may derive significant retirement benefits from their husbands' earlier employment, but these women are "dependent on the continuation of a marital union for their economic well-being. Moreover, divorced and widowed women with little or no labor force experience must rely totally on the benefits associated with their spouse's employment, on other family members, or on the government for income during their later years" (McLaughlin & Jensen, 1993, p. S45). Sorenson and McLanahan (1987) have also noted that many pension and retirement benefits are not necessarily continued following the death of a husband. Until fairly recently, older women, particularly rural elderly women, did not work independently outside of the home and derived no pension or retirement benefits of their own. For them, the death of a spouse meant a significant reduction in income.

## THE CHOICE OF HOUSING

The majority of older individuals in our society know exactly where and how they want to live as they age (Deets, 1993). The overwhelming preference (84%) of adults 55 years of age and older is to live in their own homes and never move. Nearly

75 percent of the elderly in one recent study by the American Association of Retired Persons (1993a) believed that they could stay in the same home, in the same community, in which they currently reside, a phenomenon identified as *aging in place.* Aging in place indeed is not a new phenomenon and perhaps is related to our American ideals emphasizing the importance of independence and personal autonomy.

Most older persons live in their own homes and the rural elderly are more likely to own a home than those elderly living in urban areas (Van Nostrand, 1993a, 1993b). Investigators have noted that for older persons, their home serves as a personal symbol of continuity with the past as well as a vehicle for coping with the possibility of a threatening future (Elias & Inui, 1993; Sixsmith & Sixsmith, 1991). Being able to continue to live in one's home despite physical and functional losses in old age serves to confirm the older person's "undiminished stature, sturdiness, functionality, permanence, and presence in the community" (Elias & Inui, 1993). One reflection of how important continued home ownership is for older persons is the data on home equity conversion. A home equity conversion consists of converting a home's value (less mortgage, if any) to cash to help meet current living expenses. Few elderly participants choose such programs; those who do participate have low current income, few other assets, and have recognized significant obstacles in moving to another residence (Reschovsky, 1990).

Not all older persons can remain in their current residence, and Kendig (1990) has documented that those who move are typically renters who are victims of redevelopment, eviction, or conversion to condominium or cooperative apartment ownership that they cannot afford. Only a small percentage (13%) of older adults prefer to move from their current housing arrangement, and when they change residence, they expect to do so to be able to move closer to family (AARP, 1993a). The loss of one's home substantially alters the routines of living for older persons. Such disruptions challenge the social, psychological, physical, and economic well-being of the elderly. Through stable and consistent residential arrangements, older people derive a sense of structure, security, integrity, and comfort. When these arrangements must be altered, older adults are severely challenged to regain a sense of stability and security in their personal identity (Elias & Inui, 1993; Sixsmith & Sixsmith, 1991). Researchers found that the unique associations of older people to the question, "What is home?" centered on responses that emphasized good neighbors, memories, and having friendly people around (Sixsmith & Sixsmith, 1991). Certainly in the social construction of the "home," older people derive considerably more meaning from the concept than do younger persons.

## Housing Quality

Lawton (1985) and Mikelson (1990) have documented the fact that older people live in older homes requiring considerable maintenance and upkeep. Yet, there is surprisingly little home repair and modernization among older home owners (Parmelee & Lawton, 1990; U. S. Department of Commerce, 1989). Repair and maintenance includes the need for *vital repair,* such as roofing and plumbing, as

**TABLE 11.4**

*Home Upkeep Activity by Homeowners, by Age of Household Head*

| | Age of Household Head | | | |
|---|---|---|---|---|
| | <60 | 60–64 | 65–69 | 70–74 |
| Quantity of home upkeep | | | | |
| Mean | $466.2 | $435.1 | $368.1 | $275.7 |
| Median | 142.0 | 113.7 | 84.0 | 101.5 |
| Percent who engaged in any home upkeep | 80.1 | 76.0 | 73.1 | 75.4 |
| Number of jobs done by households that engaged in upkeep | | | | |
| Mean | 2.6 | 2.5 | 2.3 | 2.3 |
| Median | 2.0 | 2.0 | 2.0 | 2.0 |
| Size of upkeep jobs | | | | |
| Mean | $207.3 | $221.4 | $221.0 | $160.2 |
| Median | 140.1 | 110.3 | 145.5 | 93.7 |
| Number of observations | 256 | 200 | 171 | 130 |

*From J. D. Reschovsky and S. J. Newman, "Home Upkeep and Housing Quality of Older Homeowners" in* Journal of Gerontology: Social Sciences, *46 (5): 288–297. Copyright © 1991 The Gerontological Society of America.*

well as *discretionary repair,* such as kitchen and bathroom modernization. Though home repair expenses are high, it is not the cost of the repairs alone that seems to keep older people from initiating repair and maintenance projects (Reschovsky & Newman, 1991). In one investigation, Reschovsky and Newman (1991) examined the variables underlying the relationship between aging and the decreased likelihood of home repair. Age was found to be the best predictor of whether or not home repairs were undertaken, with larger repairs performed by fewer and fewer older households. Household income was only found to predict the *number* of home repairs that were undertaken (Reschovsky & Newman, 1991). Generally, vital repairs were undertaken by homeowners at all ages; however, lower upkeep by older home owners was found only for discretionary repairs. These relationships may be seen in table 11.4. The results of this investigation also suggest that elderly residents in isolated, rural environments are less likely to engage in home upkeep than elderly residents in suburban or urban environments (Reschovsky & Newman, 1991). Older homes are often difficult to resell and their values may be depressed, particularly if they are in areas where prices are declining (Boehm & Ihlanfeldt, 1986). Such older homes were originally designed for different generations with different lifestyles and are generally smaller in size and have fewer modernizations such as air conditioning or energy-saving features (e.g., storm windows or efficient furnaces).

## Independent Living and the Need for Assistance

Older adults are increasingly concerned about their ability to pay their property taxes and utility, home maintenance, and repair cost. They believe that as they age, failing health and declining power of their income due to inflation will present serious problems (AARP, 1993b). These fears are based, in part, on reality. The probabilities that

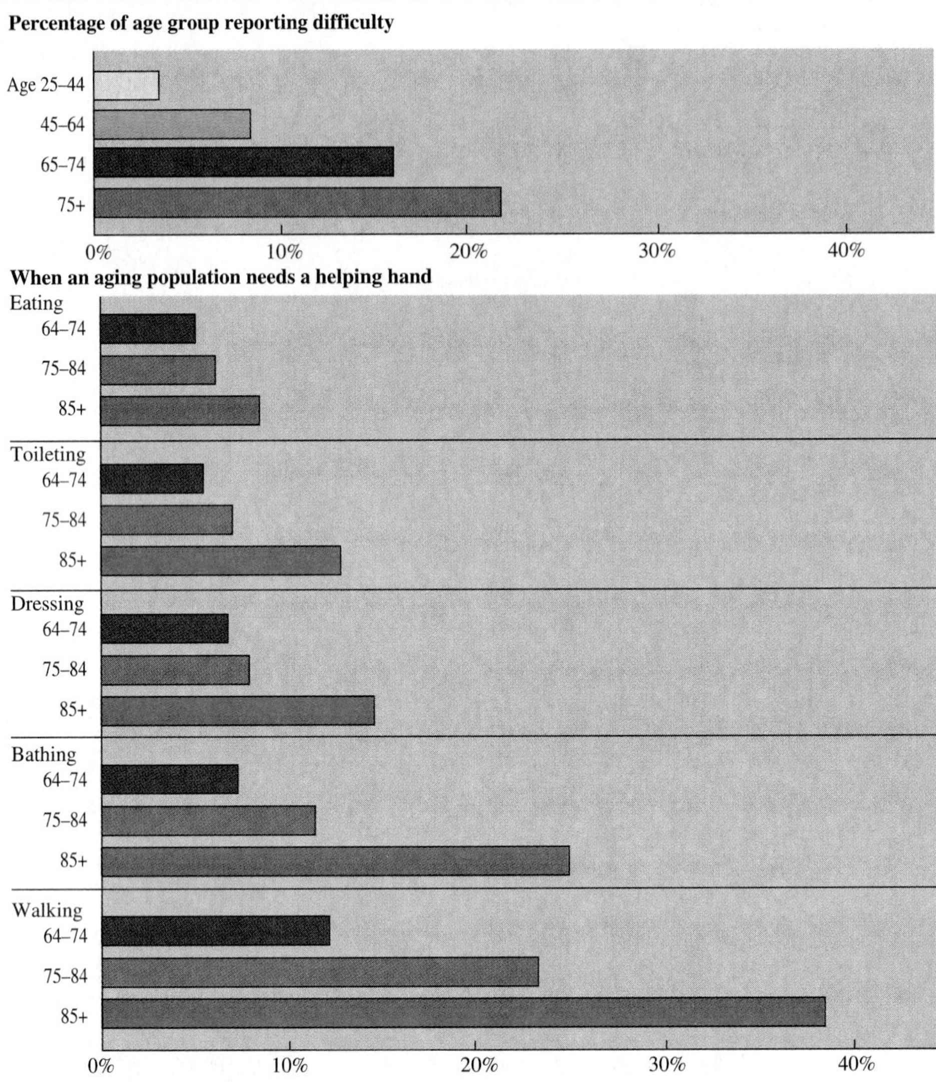


**Figure 11.4** Major activity limitations by age.
*Source: National Center for Health Statistics.*

older adults will live where they would like and as they wish may be viewed in context with the data in figure 11.4. In this figure, it is clear that with increasing age there is less likelihood that fully independent, autonomous living will occur.

As people grow older, their ability to lead an independent life is challenged. Older people may require increasing help from concerned relatives, friends, or neighbors. The assistance provided includes transportation to church, the doctor's office, or the market; it may also include assistance in cleaning a home or apartment, preparing meals, and balancing the checkbook. Figure 11.4 also reveals the type of assistance that older persons need to maintain their functional abilities or routine **activities of daily living** (ADL). Many also require ongoing assistance with transportation, which might entail trips to and from supermarkets, stores,

*Delivering prepared food (Meals on Wheels) is a service found throughout communities in our society.*

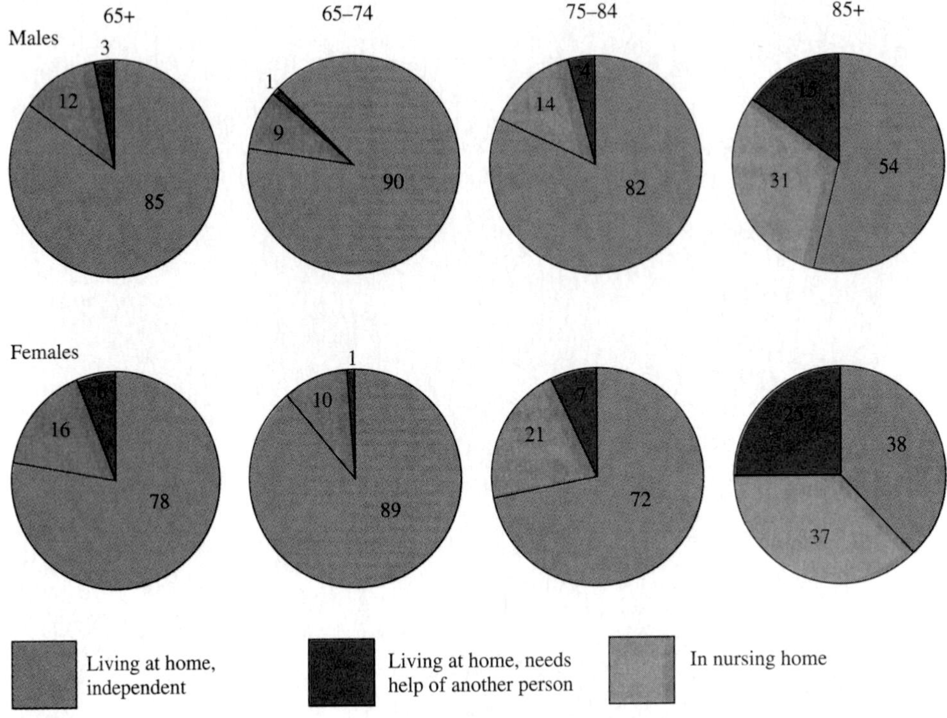


**Figure 11.5** Percentage of the older population that live at home independently, live at home but require the help of another person, or reside in a nursing home.

church, and physicians' offices. The burden of providing these services to older males usually falls to a spouse, while for elderly females, who typically outlive their husbands, adult children are most likely to provide such services (Cicirelli, 1981).

Guralnik and Simonsick (1993) have illustrated in figure 11.5 the percentage of older men and women requiring assistance and living independently among both community-residing and nursing home residents. By age 65, 22 percent of the women and 15 percent of the men needed help in living at home or had already moved to an institution. By age 85, the figures show that 62 percent of women and 46 percent of men needed help at home or already were residing in a nursing home (Guralnik & Simonsick, 1993). More positively, of course, many older adults, at all ages, are able to maintain independence and freedom of choice in their residence.

To understand how older individuals live, it is necessary to examine the many interactive factors that influence their choice of housing. One of the more important influences is the presence of physical, cognitive, emotional, sensory and social disabilities (Guralnik & Simonsick, 1993). The domain that is most often assessed to determine the impact of such disabilities is routine self-care activities such as dressing, bathing, using the toilet, eating, and moving from bed to chair. A number of simple tests can be used to assess these simple activities of daily living, which are a part of the larger functional abilities presented earlier in figure 11.1. Professionals

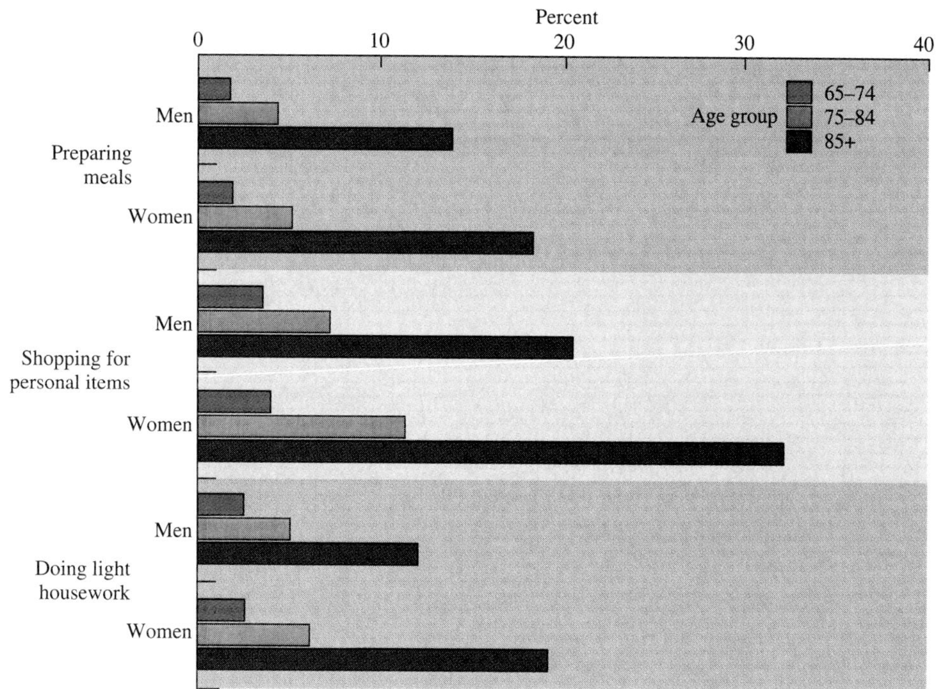


**Figure 11.6** Percentage of population dependent in three instrumental activities of daily living in the United States, 1984. Dependence is defined as having difficulty or being unable to perform a specific activity by oneself because of a health problem.
*Source: Data from Fulton et al., 1989.*

employ such assessment instruments or tests of the activities of daily living to help identify: (1) the specific types of assistance that may be needed by an older person to function independently or to maintain an autonomous lifestyle, (2) those elderly who are frail and require assistance with self-care activities to be able to live independently, and (3) those older adults who have disabilities severe enough to require institutional care. Guralnik & Simonsick (1993) estimate, for example, that there are between 5 to 8.1 percent of noninstitutionalized persons over the age of 65 who regularly receive help from another person in performing one or more ADL tasks. Figure 11.6 presents three illustrations of specific tasks used to assess the activities of daily living and the need of older persons for assistance. These data show a substantial increase as a function of age in the number of elderly adults requiring assistance to enable them to continue to live independently in the community. The data in figure 11.6 also reveal the disportionate number of women at the two older age ranges needing direct assistance reflective of sex differences in survivorship in old age. Also represented is the changing nature of the type of assistance that older people require. Figure 11.7 illustrates the increasing dependency among elderly women, with the oldest group of women in the sample needing the most assistance. These data suggest that the process of living independently becomes progressively more difficult with age and is associated with physical declines that, taken together, often make the decision to move from independent living in a home or apartment a virtual necessity.

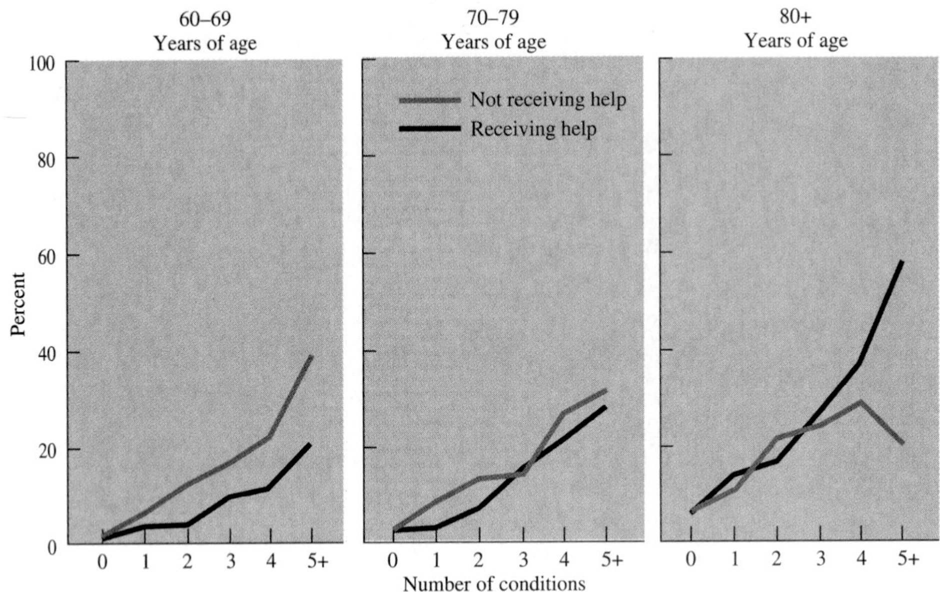


**Figure 11.7** Prevalence of difficulty in one or more activities of daily living by number of chronic conditions and age group, in women 60 years of age and over. *Source: Data from J. M. Guralnik, A. Z. LaCroix, and D. F. Everett, et al., 1989 (25).*

## Relocation and Change of Residence

Some older adults decide to give up their homes voluntarily and move. In this society and in others (e.g., Great Britain), studies have shown that older people migrate most often to locations that are perceived as highly desirable and that have a high density of other older residents (Rogers, Watkins, & Woodward, 1990). Not all such relocations are to warmer climates such as our Sun Belt. Some elderly migrate and relocate to coordinated retirement communities; others remain in the same region of the country.

Across a number of investigations (Beland, 1984; Bradsher, Longino, Jackson, & Zimmerman, 1992; Zimmerman, Jackson, Longino, & Bradsher, 1993), the decision to consider a change in residence has been found to be related to age, widowhood, social class, and physical problems requiring medical supervision. Bradsher et al., (1992) reported that following the death of a spouse, the likelihood that older people will move increases significantly. And, a clear linkage was reported between death of a spouse, health, and moving. That is, when widows experience significant declines in health, there is a greater probability of their making a move from their current residence (Bradsher et al., 1992). Other studies that predict residence choices among the elderly have revealed the importance of perceived health status, traveling distance to social community supports and to physicians, as well as the time it takes to reach the nearest relative, familiarity with the neighborhood, and number of years in residence (Lawton, 1980, 1985). Interestingly, neither the degree of assistance required nor the extent of physical disabilities alone predict either when older persons will decide to leave their residence or the type of residence to which they will choose to move (supervised residence, nursing home, and so on). Research Focus 11.1 describes some of the factors recently identified in an older person's decision to relocate to a regional migration center.

## Choosing a Retirement Community: The Case of Cape Cod

Studies of interstate retirement migration show that more than 60 percent of older adults relocate in the Sun Belt. Cuba and Longino (1991), however, were interested in those who choose to retire closer to home, so-called regional "migrants," who relocate to regional centers or retirement centers, such as the popular resort communities in Cape Cod, Massachusetts. The investigators examined two questions: (1) Why is a regional resort community attractive to older retired migrants? and (2) Are there important differences among those choosing regional retirement resorts? From a total sample of 151 retirees 60 years of age and older, Cuba and Longino identified 61 percent who were relocating to Cape Cod either from within the state of Massachusetts or relocating interstate (e.g., including all five New England states as well as Pennsylvania, New Jersey, and Maryland).

Retirees who move to Cape Cod cite the physical environment and associated amenities (outdoor activities, natural beauty, mild climate, change of seasons) as major reasons for their decision to relocate. Migration was seen as relocation to a *familiar destination,* since 95 percent of those interviewed had previously spent some time on the Cape prior to their retirement. More than one-third had spent some time as summer residents prior to retirement relocation. Cuba and Longino report that, indeed, retirees were familiar with the Cape, knew what to expect in terms of lifestyle, climate, leisure activities, and experienced few unexpected "surprises" in the cost of living or access to services after moving. Retirees who were from the Northeast also were familiar with the social and cultural values of Cape Cod; relocation was comfortable, since it preserved and capitalized on older persons' former New England traditions. Thus while seeking a change, regional migration was chosen over Sun Belt locations because these retirees were "wary of shifting the cultural parameters that have bounded their experience and lifestyle."

Other Sun Belt destinations were seen as too hot, too formal and structured, too focused on organized leisure activities, too full of old persons, and quite simply *too far away.* This latter factor, relative closeness of the Cape to retirees' previous communities, permitted continuity with retirees' previous residence, family, and friends. In some cases, a move to Cape Cod actually resulted in a move closer to friends, children, and grandchildren. Retirees considered proximity to significant others one of the most important factors in their choice of the Cape over other regions in the country. And, a third factor identified in this study of regional migration in the Northeast was the importance of "amenities" such as beaches, oceans, mild climate, and easy access to recreational sports facilities such as tennis, golf, nature walks. The amenities available on Cape Cod preserved preretirement lifestyles, contact with retirees' previous communities, and access to a familiar urban environment, for example, the city of Boston, which is only two hours away. Yet, retirement did produce a subtle shift for most retirees from a suburban to rural environment living. This shift was welcomed but, somewhat unexpectedly, was perceived by retirees as actually preserving *continuity* in their lives, continuity between preretirement and postretirement living.

Those who retired to Cape Cod and remained in their home state of Massachusetts (intrastate migrants) differed somewhat from those who were interstate migrants. The fundamental difference was that out-of-state migrants had to make more adjustments in retirement than intrastate migrants: acquiring knowledge of new state laws, a new political context, different taxes, and acquiring a new identity as a resident of the state of Massachusetts. Interstate migrants appeared to have considered more alternatives such as moving to the Sun Belt prior to deciding to move to Cape Cod than did intrastate retirees. And, not surprisingly, out-of-state retirees reported that they felt that their lifestyles had changed far more during retirement and relocation on the Cape than did those who relocated from within the state of Massachusetts.

Cuba and Longino conclude that choosing a regional retirement community affords older people a greater degree of continuity in their lives than a move to a completely different region of the country. Since most of the retirees in this study had spent at least some time vacationing or visiting friends on Cape Cod during other points in their lives, retirement migration to a familiar environment was easier and smoother, particularly for those who moved intrastate, than relocation to a completely different region of the country.

Cuba and Longino (1991) provide important insights into the process of regional migration in retirement. Through their work, they have identified those factors that influence older people's relocation decision: (1) distance from one's previous community (family and friends), (2) continuity of living, (3) familiarity with the region, and (4) access to amenities such as natural beauty of the environment, climate, and recreational opportunities.

Adapted from L. Cuba, and C. F. Longino, (1991). "Regional Retirement Migration: The Case of Cape Cod" in Journal of Gerontology: Social Sciences, 46 (1): S33-S42. 

## Living with an Older Parent

As parents age, we find a kernel of truth to the notion that adult children become parents to their own parents. The data previously presented in figure 11.4 clearly reveal that older persons increasingly can expect to need assistance as they grow older. This need for assistance can be provided in the home of adult children or by home health care workers in a parent's own residence. If the need for assistance is substantial, then full-time nursing care may be required by paid nurses or, alternatively, through nursing home placement. The need for daily care and assistance serves to remind adult children that a parent is mortal, like other human beings, and is moving closer to the end of life. Blenkner (1965) has used the term filial maturity to reflect this growing understanding of our parents as possessing qualities like other adults and like ourselves in many ways.

The adoption of filial responsibility roles brings about basic tensions, although few adult children ever totally reject their parents at this point in life. Many families, rather than placing an elderly parent in a group or institutionalized living arrangement, may elect to have a parent live with them. Few adult children, however, anticipate the physical and emotional demands of the decision to provide care for a parent. Tobin (1978) suggests that routine day-to-day care is most often provided by daughters for their mothers, whereas sons usually assist a parent by hiring housekeepers or home health aides. And, in such arrangements, it is the emotional support, the daily worries, and the physical closeness of daughters living near their mothers that most often leads to tension and resentment between siblings over caretaking responsibilities.

Unmarried adult children who provide day-to-day assistance to an elderly parent are more likely to move into the residence of an elderly parent, whereas the reverse holds for married adult children (Bernard, 1975; Tobin, 1978). Spitze, Logan and Robinson (1992) found that the greater the number of children in the family, the higher the probability that an elderly parent currently living alone would move into the home of one of their children when self-care assistance was needed. The number of children in the family, however, was not a factor in the parents' move from a child's home to another living arrangement such as an institution.

Widows usually move in with their married daughters rather than their married sons (Bernard, 1975; Sussman, 1985). The stresses in the family are great as both adult children and their parents forgo freedom, independence, and personal autonomy in favor of maintaining an interdependent relationship. With these added stresses, it is difficult to maintain such living arrangements for more than a few years; yet, families often feel guilty when they can no longer continue to care for parents at home (Tobin & Lieberman, 1976). Caretaking demands escalate and few adult children are trained to deliver self-help care, health care, and medical or nursing care. In fact, Roodin, Rybash, and Hoyer (1985) have suggested that it is the increase in these demanding responsibilities over the years, as well as the accumulated physical burden of doing so, that provides caregivers a rationale for placing a parent in a nursing home or residential institution.

## *Life in the Slum Hotel*

An estimated 146,000 poor older persons reside in run-down hotels or rooming houses in the blighted sections of cities (Carp, 1976). Though SROs (single room occupancies) house a very small percentage of all older persons, residents' lifestyles reflect the same staunch desire for privacy, independence, and autonomy that the elderly residing in more desirable homes show.

An ethnography of a slum hotel in a large western city (Stephens, 1976) shows how the elderly who are near the bottom of the economic ladder live. Approximately 30 percent of the occupants of this particular hotel were elderly.

> Isolation in one form or another was the hallmark of this social environment. For the most part, the ninety-seven elderly males avoided not only the eleven elderly females but each other as well. These people were virtually required to relinquish their needs for intimacy to survive in the hotel. The two principal reasons for developing or maintaining relationships were common economic interests or shared leisure activities. Relationships among residents seemed to require some justification; simple social interaction never seemed to be enough.
>
> The prime source of income for many older residents involved "hustling"—scavenging, peddling, pushing drugs, or shoplifting. In some cases, two or more residents developed relationships which facilitated hustling schemes. It was also necessary for a "hustler" to let others know of hustling successes since hustling was a key determinant of social status along three dimensions: its profitability, its dependability as a source of income, and the degree of autonomy it provided. Besides socializing over successful hustling feats, residents also related to one another through drinking or better activities.
>
> Only minimal social activity took place at the hotel, and it served as the focal point for little physical activity other than sleep. Most residents had to go outside the hotel for food and routine health needs. Some took meals at the least expensive places in the neighborhood, where muggings were frequent. The rooms had no cooking or refrigeration facilities, but some residents cooked using a hot iron braced by two bibles as a hot plate. . . . (Williamson, Munley & Evans, 1980, pp. 259–260).

Locked into this situation by poverty, ill health, and a desire to maintain independence, many older residents of this hotel planned to die there.

## Types of Residences for the Elderly

Income plays an important role in the living conditions of the elderly. Only about 1 percent of aged families and one-tenth of 1 percent of unrelated elderly people have annual incomes of $50,000 or more. For such individuals, housing options are virtually unlimited. At the other extreme, homeless individuals with a mean income of $3,250 live in places such as the slum hotel described in Research Focus 11. 2. Currently, two of every five older persons living at or below the poverty level identify housing as their primary expense; these expenses typically exceed 45 percent of the limited, fixed incomes of the poor (Church et al., 1988). Of course, most of the elderly fall between these two extremes.

The vast majority of older adults live in an individual private home (75% are home owners) with only 5 percent residing in institutional settings (Parmelee & Lawton, 1990). The changing life situations of the older people who live in individual homes require modification of the residence for reasons of health, safety, or mobility. Such *adapted housing* is recognizable by the addition of grab bars in the bathroom area, handrails in hallways, and ramps to accommodate wheelchairs (see figure 11.15). Nearly 10 percent of those homes headed by an individual over 65 showed such modifications (Parmelee & Lawton, 1990).

One way to help older Americans in meeting their housing needs has been to provide subsidized living arrangements, which was briefly discussed earlier in the text. Subsidized housing or *planned independent housing* has been established largely in multiunit arrangements for the elderly. Such living arrangements are created for the elderly who need support for housing and who can maintain an autonomous lifestyle. Planned independent housing makes no provision for any supportive services (Parmelee & Lawton, 1990).

At the other extreme, for elderly with sufficient economic assets, are residential options (Branch, 1987; Cohen et al., 1988; Gottlieb, 1992; Tell et al., 1987) such as living in a *Continuity Care Retirement Community (CCRC)* or *LifeCare Community (LCC)*. To enroll in a CCRC or LifeCare Community, older adults must pay a substantial initiation or entrance fee and sign an additional contract that establishes a regular monthly fee. The initial entrance fee, ranging between $50,000 to $300,000, is a one-time payment for purchase of an apartment or condominium. Residents also agree to pay a monthly fee, ranging between $400 to $3,000, which is guaranteed to remain constant regardless of the amount and type of medical and nursing care residents might require throughout the remainder of their lives (Gottlieb, 1992). CCRCs were formerly called "LifeCare Communities" because they provided the elderly assurance that they would be protected fully throughout their lives against all future long-term care costs, such as the escalating costs of medical care and nursing care, increased property taxes, and home maintenance and repair costs (Parmelee & Lawton, 1990). Thus CCRCs offer a full range of living options and support services on-site or by contract, which includes medical care, personal assistance, and both intermediate and skilled nursing care (Gottlieb, 1992). Those considering this option are economically advantaged, better educated, and older (but rarely over 85). The typical enrollment is by single, unmarried, and childless individuals in their late seventies (Sherwood, Ruchlin, & Sherwood, 1989). Tell et al. (1987) predicts the number of available CCRCs to increase to fifteen hundred nationwide within the next ten years. The CCRCs nationwide are owned by the not-for-profit sector entities, such as religious organizations, as well as profit-based entities (Gottlieb, 1992).

*Congregate housing* is a type of planned housing, chiefly apartments, that permits elderly residents to live independently but have easy and direct access to support services. Residents live in individual apartments with a twenty-four hour-a-day electronic system in each room to call a central office in case of medical emergencies such as falling or heart attack. Congregate housing is considered by some to be a form of communal or community housing; one of its most distinctive features is the provision of meals for all residents in a common dining room (Parmelee & Lawton, 1990). In some respects, this type of living provides considerable security, safety, and a simplified routine for residents, since they interact within a somewhat limited, supervised, managed environment. Congregate housing represents an intermediate housing alternative that provides living arrangements common to both independent housing and institutions. The support services for residents are not coordinated by those who manage the congregate housing facility but are made available chiefly through the wider community. Evidence suggests that residents in congregate housing appear to function independently longer than comparably aged

*TABLE 11.5*

**Nursing Home Population Distributed by Age**

| Age | Percentage of entire elderly population who reside in nursing homes |
|---|---|
| 65–74 | 1.5 percent |
| 75–84 | 6.0 percent |
| 85 + | 23.0 percent |

*Source: Data from D. K. Churck, M. A. Siegel, and C. D. Foster,* Growing Old in America, *1988.*

persons residing in traditional homes (Carlin & Mansberg, 1984; Heumann & Boldy, 1982). Congregate housing, originally modeled after demonstration programs in Great Britain, is operated on both a for-profit and a not-for-profit basis (Parmelee & Lawton, 1990).

*Single Room Occupancy (SRO)* hotels for the elderly represent a housing choice for older persons primarily in inner cities (Erikson & Ekert, 1977; Lawton, 1980). They offer a high level of independent living and freedom of lifestyle within a managed and supervised living arrangement; residents, chiefly poor and often single older adults, are provided a moderate degree of security and protection. Such hotels have been located in large metropolitan cities in areas that increasingly are considered dangerous and often are targeted by city planners for urban renewal. Sanjek (1984) noted that between 1970 and 1983 nearly 89 percent of such SRO hotels have disappeared; many times these decaying areas become replaced with new, expensive apartments or condominiums. Some SRO hotels provide daily housekeeping and have become residences for working-class male elderly. Still others have become residences for middle-income occupants, providing more extensive services and coordinated activities to both male and female elderly residents (Erikson & Ekert, 1977).

*Residential care homes* for the elderly offer assistance with basic day-to-day care to help them maintain independent functioning. These facilities are usually rather small and provide not only room and board, similar to congregate housing facilities, but also self-care assistance and twenty-four-hour-a-day supervision. Residential care homes include both licensed and unlicensed facilities and offer support services so that the older adult can maintain as much autonomy as possible (Parmelee & Lawton, 1990). In many ways residential care homes are much like small college dormitories in terms of the services that are provided; residents who choose them, while needing intervention and assistance, do not require the sophisticated levels of care offered by a nursing home facility.

*Nursing homes* offer specialized medical and nursing care to the moderately and severely disabled elderly. Trunzo (1982) first noted that nursing homes may be the *only* housing alternative for some of our nation's elderly. There are more than 1.6 million elderly over the age of 65 who reside in such facilities, as seen in table 11.5 and represented in the bar graphs in figure 11.8 (National Center for Health Statistics, 1987). While the overall percentage of elderly in nursing homes continues to represent about 5 percent of those over 65, it is noted that this percentage

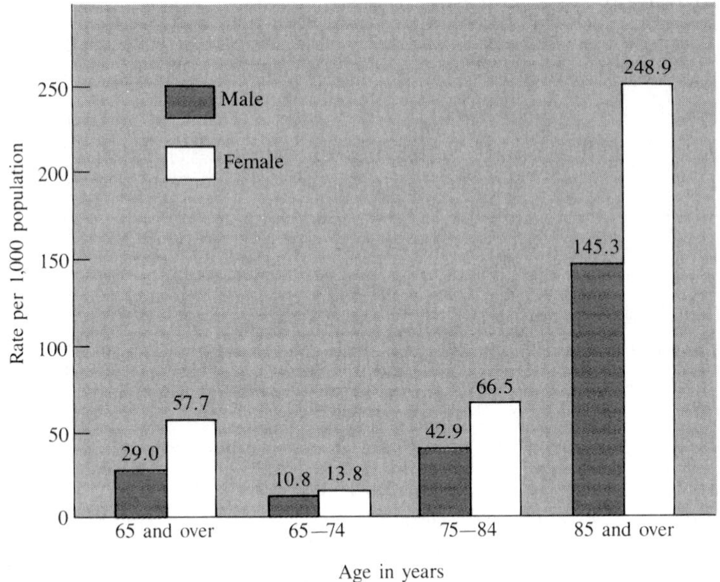


**Figure 11.8** The number of nursing home residents per 1,000 of the population of individuals sixty-five years of age and over: by sex and age in the United States. *Source: Use of Nursing Homes by the Elderly: Preliminary Date from the 1985 National Nursing Home Survey, National Center for Health Statistics, May 14, 1987.*

reflects a dramatic increase in the actual number of elderly in nursing home facilities (Parmelee & Lawton, 1990). For example, given the growth in the population over 65 from 1977 to 1987, there was a 17 percent increase in the sheer number of older people living in nursing homes (Parmelee & Lawton, 1990). As we will see later in this chapter, nursing homes provide different levels of care, depending on the disability and functional level of the elderly seeking admission. With more governmental monitoring and regulation, there are fewer homes providing shoddy, substandard care.

In recent years, a significant number of nursing home admissions (3%) come directly from mental health facilities or involve adults whose institutionalization is based on mental health needs (Parmelee & Lawton, 1990). The ability of nursing homes to meet the mental health needs of their elderly residents remains a serious concern, since most facilities have tended to emphasize medical, nursing, and health services, not psychological or social intervention. Parmelee and Lawton (1990) note that with the increase in psychiatric-based admissions, the social milieu of the nursing home itself is undergoing rapid change.

*Homelessness* is in some ways a housing alternative for the elderly, but it is rarely a choice; rather, it can be one of the consequences of being old, being poor, and being alone. For some of the elderly in our society, homelessness is unavoidable. Jonathon Kozol (1988) helped sensitize our society to the plight of the homeless families in America by vividly portraying the conditions in which they live. U. S. Census data suggest that there are between 1 and 2.5 million homeless people overall. Cohen et al., (1988) have estimated that about 25 to 30 percent of all homeless people are over the age of 60 and others confirm a range between 15 and 28 percent for those over the age of 50 (Elias & Inui, 1993).

Although some homeless elderly have been found to adapt and cope successfully with their environments, life for many of the homeless elderly is marked by constant vigilance and significant stress in managing the high risks of such a lifestyle (Elias & Inui, 1993). Investigators have described the dangers that homeless elderly men encounter on the street and in the shelters where they seek food, showers, and beds (Elias & Inui, 1993). Often public shelters offer support, safety, and a sense of community as well as a respite to regain sobriety (Elias & Inui, 1993).

The explanations offered for homelessness in a society as advantaged as our own are often unsatisfying. Martin (1990) has identified some of these, which include: (1) loss of jobs and income and the nonaffordability of suitable housing, and (2) characteristics of the homeless themselves such as having mental health problems, abusing drugs and alcohol, and having experienced violence. The homeless elderly men in most research studies have reasonably positive social ties to others like themselves and strongly endorse and follow a norm of "reciprocity" (Cohen et al., 1988; Elias & Inui, 1993). They show positive adjustment to the realities of living with extremes of poverty, violence, and crime (Elias and Inui, 1993). The simple truth is that the homeless elderly have become a nearly invisible entity in our society. Though some programs have been developed to assist homeless families and children, most programs consistently ignore the elderly homeless.

## The Consequences of Different Housing Choices

The relationship of the environment to an older person's perception, attitudes, and behavior has been a focus of considerable research. Research investigators have emphasized the significance of understanding the "meaning" of home for the elderly, viewing the older adult's residence as a "transactional experience" (Elias & Inui, 1993). For older persons, their residence and social construction of "home" is a negotiated meaning that is thought to allow the preservation of independence, self-identity, and preparation for death (Elias & Inui, 1993; Sixsmith & Sixsmith, 1991). It is important to know the way in which residential choices and the design, management, and general atmosphere of such facilities have an impact on older people. By studying the many environments in which older people live, we can better understand how to design and structure these residences to improve their lives, enhance their sense of well-being, maintain their independent functioning, and sustain their sense of autonomy and personal control.

Lawton and his colleagues have been central in developing theoretical models of how the environmental design of housing choices affects the day-to-day lives, social interaction, and psychological functioning of the elderly (Lawton & Nahemow, 1973; Lawton, 1985, 1977, 1980; Parmelee & Lawton, 1990). This work is based on

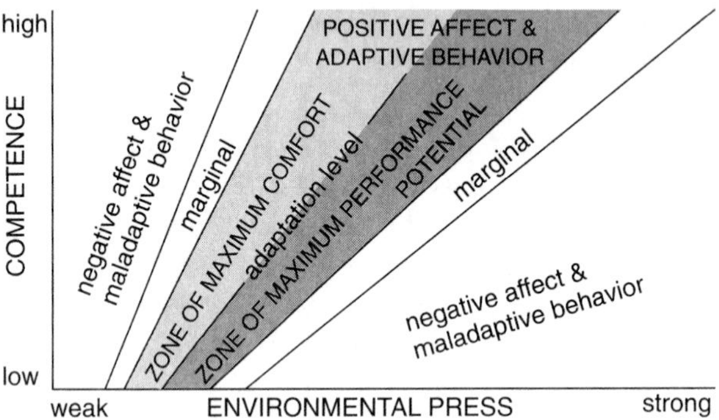


**Figure 11.9** Behavioral and affective outcomes of person-environment interactions based on the competence–environmental press model. This figure indicates that an individual of high competence will show maximum performance over a larger range of environmental situations than will a less competent person. The range of optimal environments occurs at a higher level of environmental press (A) for the most competent person than it does for the least competent person (B). *(Source: "Ecology and the Aging Process" (p. 661) by M. P. Lawton and L. Nahemow, 1973, in C. Eisdorfer and M. P. Lawton, Eds.,* The Psychology of Adult Development and Aging, *Washington, DC: American Psychological Association. Copyright © 1973 by the American Psychological Association. Reprinted with permission of the publisher and author.)*

the importance of interacting dimensions descriptive of the *person-environment congruence.* According to this view, an ideal match between the housing choices of the elderly and the individual occurs when there is just the right balance between what the person needs in terms of assistance and intervention and the ability of the residence, its structure, and its services to meet these needs. If too much assistance and too many services are provided to persons who do not need or do not want them, the environment is seen as overbearing, intrusive, and limiting. In such instances, older persons are denied the opportunity to create for themselves a sense of personal mastery and self-efficacy. Without the opportunities for mastery and self-efficacy, individuals feel less competent, overprotected, and overcontrolled by their environment—ultimately they experience a loss of self-esteem (Lawton, 1985, 1990; Lawton & Parmelee, 1990).

This simple example of Lawton's person-environment congruence hypothesis can be extended to determine the possible effects that any housing alternative may have for older persons as shown in figure 11.9. As illustrated in this figure, older persons will adapt more easily to environments whose *demand quality* fits the individual's range of competence. In such settings, older persons experience a level of *environmental press* sufficient for them to display competent behavior. The environmental press cannot be excessive, nor can it be too weak; otherwise, competence cannot be shown by older persons in their regular interactions with the environments in which they live. However, with an opportunity to display competent behavior, older persons display high levels of positive adaptation and function at or near their maximum performance potential (e.g., competence), regardless of the type of housing they encounter. It is difficult to fit environments to individuals; older persons need regular sustained challenges to maintain positive feelings of self-esteem, mastery, and self-efficacy. The process of fit requires careful individual assessments of an older persons' abilities, the self-care assistance they require to preserve their functioning, and the level of support from the environment (Lawton, 1975, 1977, 1980, 1990; Parmelee & Lawton, 1990). It is simply not possible, under the assumptions outlined in figure 11.9 for a simple "one size fits all" solution to match older persons to environments.

In creating person-environment congruence for older persons, it is important to preserve choices (Lawton, 1990). No matter how structured or supportive the environment, older individuals appear to feel more competent when they can exercise choice (Lawton, 1990). Choice is framed in the context of balancing the needs of older persons to have an environment that provides security (i.e., safety, protection, assistance, freedom from fears) as well as personal autonomy (i.e., the freedom to seek self-selected tasks and goals without the assistance of others). This idealized balance may lead to high levels of life satisfaction, personal mastery, and feelings of self-efficacy, but it is neither easy to create nor easy to sustain.

Lawton (1990), for example, noted that often severely disabled elderly choose to continue to live in their own home under exceptional conditions to preserve this balance between security and autonomy. He first reported that severely disabled older persons created an area in their home, usually the living room, that functioned as a *control center.* The control center for the severely disabled elderly appeared to contain all of the minimum pieces of furniture, self-care features, and necessary communication systems to permit total living within an exceptionally small space. The control center, according to Lawton (1990), is exemplary of older persons' choice of an environmental arrangement that, for them, maximizes the balance between autonomy and security. From the control center, an older, severely disabled person can continue to derive a sense of mastery, self-esteem, freedom of choice, and continuity of self-identity that enables him or her to have reasonably positive feelings about competence, despite the disabilities with which he or she must deal:

> The control center began with a chair, usually a comfortable one, that also met good ergonomic specifications, in terms of ease of access and steadiness. The chair invariably faced the living room window, with a maximum possible view of front porch, sidewalk, and street. The same chair orientation enabled the front door to be monitored. A telephone, television set, and usually a radio extended psychological space far beyond the living room. Table surfaces on either side of the chair afforded the enriching objects of personal preference, whether photographs, letters, knickknacks, food, medicine, or reading material. The control center was completed by some arrangement for toileting, whether by a urinal or nearby commode, or for the few who were lucky enough to have a ground-floor bathroom, a pathway to it alongside convenient places to grab while in transit. (Lawton, 1990, p. 640)

## Caregiving Burden and Institutional Settings

The decision to institutionalize an elderly parent or relative presents many conflicts. It often follows a number of years of trying to handle the increasing physical and emotional demands of caregiving (George, 1992). Caregiving by family members for a disabled older relative is a natural response to an immediate need for assistance (Gatz et al., 1990). Caregivers are assumed to be motivated by altruistic reasons (e.g., feelings of empathy and attachment), social norms (e.g., reciprocity and ethical responsibility), and "self-serving" motives, which include avoidance of guilt, fear of public censure, or a sense of indebtedness (Gatz et al., 1990; Schulz, Biegel, Morycz, & Visintainer, 1989). Yet, the direct consequences of accepting the responsibility to care for an impaired or disabled elderly relative are rarely understood until caregiving is well underway (George, 1992a; 1992b). Caregiver burden, which includes the negative impact on physical health and finances, as well as the diminished time and involvement in friendships, leisure activities, and the larger community is simply difficult to anticipate (George, 1992a, 1992b). Evidence in recent studies suggests that caregivers of impaired older adults are increasingly at risk of mental health problems such as depression (Clipp & George, 1990; Cohen & Eisdorfer, 1989; George, 1992a, 1992b).

Most of what we know about the burden of caregiving comes from studies almost exclusively concerned with caring for an impaired parent or relative with dementia. There is very little information about the process of caring for an older parent or relative with a chronic physical illness (Gatz et al., 1990; George, 1992a, 1992b). Daughters who provide much of the caregiving to their mothers show concern for the time constraints that caregiving places on other areas of their lives as well as frustration and anxiety over the complexity and uncertainty of the situation. Mothers who receive such care, although they experience feelings of love and care from their daughters, also feel both anger and helplessness at their own condition and remorse over the burden that they bring to their child (Walker, Martin, & Jones, 1992).

Following the decision to institutionalize a close relative or parent, caregivers are significantly unburdened from the extraordinary physical demands (feeding, bathing, dressing, wandering, safety, incontinence, and behavioral/cognitive deficits) and the emotional demands that they have accepted for many months and years (Takman, 1992). With institutionalization of an AD patient, for example, comes freedom from the former demanding role of physical caregiving. Older spouses, understandably, will make the decision to institutionalize a disabled husband or wife sooner than middle-aged children will decide to institutionalize a parent or relative. Middle-aged children in comparison to older spouses are stronger and more able to deal with the physical demands of caregiving for a parent or older relative. The immediate impact of institutionalization on caregivers, freed from the day-to-day responsibilities of providing assistance to an impaired elder, is a gain of one hour and forty-seven minutes per day, representing the time formerly spent in the role of caregiver (Moss et al., 1993). How is this increase in time used? Caregivers spend additional time in family interaction, recreational activities, and activities outside of the home. Institutional placement, though offering freedom to former caregivers as well as relief from stress and physical demands, brings emotional turmoil to the extended family and the elderly person (Beland, 1984). But as families discover, once the institutionalization decision is made, it is usually viewed as a wise choice, if not the most emotionally satisfying to all family members.

The decision to institutionalize an older parent or elderly relative is usually the result of a lengthy process of increasingly complex burdens on caregivers and increased feelings of conflict for the elderly individual. The extended family wrestles with the decision to institutionalize a disabled older relative, as does the older person about to be institutionalized. There are frequent family discussions of the matter with those living nearby and far away who may have a stake in sharing the decision (Beland, 1984).The steps prior to and just following institutionalization and the immediate impact on elderly persons themselves have been studied for some time (Tobin & Lieberman, 1976; Stein, Linn, & Stein, 1985). The initial period of anticipation of a move to a nursing home is marked by a variety of concerns by the elderly individual, including: (1) orientation and adjustment to the new facility, (2) family and dependency concerns, (3) quality and availability of medical care, (4) provision of tender loving care, and (5) availability of sufficient space (Stein et al., 1985).

The actual move to an institution may lead to a period of confusion, disorientation, and withdrawal that lasts about two months (Borup, 1983; Tobin & Lieberman, 1976). The somewhat difficult and uncooperative nursing home residents who nonetheless perceive quality care and a concerned staff during this initial phase show better adjustment and longer survival rates than their more docile, more cooperative counterparts (Simms, Jones, & Yoder, 1982; Tobin & Lieberman, 1983). In one study, levels of stress were higher among elderly planning a move to a poorer-quality nursing home than among those planning a move to a better facility (Stein, Linn, & Stein, 1986). And in a three-month follow-up, these anticipated differences were found to be predictive of the residents' overall adjustments. Better-quality nursing programs provided residents more of the "tender loving care" they hoped to receive, whereas poorer-quality programs, as residents predicted, did not meet their needs or expectations (Stein et al., 1986). With the public interest in nursing homes and the deficiencies discovered by state monitoring and the media, the nursing home industry certainly will continue to be regulated and closely monitored. The projected growth of the older population emphasizes the need for quality nursing home care.

## Nursing Home Living

Only about 5 percent of the elderly reside in nursing homes at any time in our society. Yet this relatively small percentage represents an increasingly large number of people. For example, given the projections listed in table 11.6, we can estimate that by the year 2000 about 1,800,000 individuals 65 years of age and older will reside in nursing homes (Haber, 1987). However, only a small percentage of nursing home residents remain there permanently; the majority are institutionalized only

*TABLE 11.6*

| *Anticipated Population Growth of Americans Aged 65 and Older (2000–2080)* | | |
|---|---|---|
| *Year* | *Total U.S. population* | *Percent older than sixty-five* |
| 2000 | 267,915,000 | 13 percent |
| 2030 | 304,807,000 | 21 percent |
| 2050 | 309,488,000 | 22 percent |
| 2080 | 310,762,000 | 24 percent |

*Source: U.S. Bureau of the Census, Current Population Reports, Series P-25, no. 962: 7, May 1984.*

temporarily. Three times as many residents are discharged from nursing homes as die in such facilities (Haber, 1987). The chances that an older person will spend some time in a nursing home are directly related to increased age. One estimate is that 43 percent of adults will likely spend some time in a nursing home (TIAA, 1992). The average cost of nursing home care per day nationwide is about $80, which results in a total cost over a twelve-month period of more than $29,000 per year (TIAA, 1992). Some private facilities have considerably higher rates, between $3,500 and $4,500 per month. For a typical older person living alone with an annual income between $9,700 and $15,000, even a relatively short seventeen-week stay in a nursing home would have severe financial consequences (Church et al., 1988).

Nursing homes may be divided into three classifications (Bould et al., 1989; Haber, 1987): (1) proprietary homes, (2) voluntary nonprofit nursing homes, and (3) government facilities. **Proprietary homes** represent a business arrangement in which the overall goal is to secure a profit for those providing the building, maintenance, and day-to-day costs of this service. Rates are competitive to attract prospective clients as well as to ensure a profit. Proprietary homes operate in the free-market economy; elderly individuals and their families may select a facility that provides the environment, services, and care they are seeking. **Voluntary nonprofit nursing homes** are usually designed for those with a specific religion, fraternal, or union affiliation. The voluntary nonprofit home must by law establish rates that generate no excess capital. The most common type of voluntary nonprofit nursing home is the religiously affiliated, although all faiths and beliefs are accepted into the facility. Residents are provided a specific social and moral climate as well as traditional nursing services, meals, and other services comparable to those found in the proprietary homes. **Government nursing homes** are run by the federal government, individual states, or local counties. This third category has the fewest number of nursing homes (Haber, 1987).

In addition to the three types of nursing homes, three kinds of services or levels of nursing care are provided (Haber, 1987). The most highly intensive nursing care is found in a **skilled nursing facility.** This category of care requires careful adherence to standards established by the federal government and enforced by each state. The next level of care is **intermediate (ordinary) nursing care,** which

*TABLE 11.7*

*Average Costs Per Day for Non-Medicaid Patients in Nursing Homes in Different Regions of the United States*

| *Ownership and region* | *Level of Care* | | |
|---|---|---|---|
| | *Skilled* | *Intermediate* | *Residential* |
| Ownership | | | |
| Proprietary | $58.67 | $47.28 | $28.00 |
| Voluntary nonprofit | 66.37 | 50.57 | 35.82 |
| Government | 68.27 | 48.25 | 41.81 |
| Census region | | | |
| Northeast | 79.85 | 63.33 | 29.73 |
| North Central | 57.06 | 46.01 | 35.84 |
| South | 53.19 | 43.83 | 29.63 |
| West | 58.22 | 47.44 | 28.52 |

*Source: Nursing Home Characteristics: Preliminary Data from the 1985 National Nursing Home Survey in* Advancedata, *National Center for Health Statistics, March 27, 1987.*

is less intensive than that provided in a skilled nursing program. A **residential care facility,** which meets the least restrictive set of standards, offers a minimal level of nursing care. Residential care is largely routine maintenance and personal assistance in meeting day-to-day needs. Residential care may include provision for some rehabilitation, if needed, and other simple intervention services.

The costs of residential care are lower than those in the other two categories (Bould et al., 1989). Table 11.7 summarizes data comparing the costs of skilled, intermediate, and residential private nursing homes for those elderly patients who are nonsubsidized by Medicaid (National Center for Health Statistics, 1987). Nursing costs in the northeast United States are substantially higher for skilled care, moderately higher for intermediate care, and roughly comparable to other regions for residential care. These costs reflect the availability of nursing homes relative to demand and population; they are most available in the north central region, and least available in the northeast region (Haber, 1987). More than 75 percent of the nursing homes in our country are proprietary, 18 percent are voluntary nonprofit, and the remaining 7 percent are government run. In 1979, there were only 3,600 nursing homes designated as skilled nursing facilities, with only 2,100 accredited by Medicare and Medicaid (Haber, 1987). Those who must often obtain nursing home placement are elderly persons who are unmarried, widowed, and who have no close family or relatives (National Center for Health Statistics, 1987).

The nursing home industry has been subject to increasing scrutiny and regulation in recent years (Liptzin, 1992). One of the most important changes has been the establishment of federal requirements for nursing homes to continue their participation in Medicare and Medicaid programs. Public Law 100-203, the **Nursing Home Reform Act of 1987,** will gradually help to phase out the distinctions between skilled nursing facilities and intermediate care facilities; a single set of regulations will govern all nursing home facilities (Liptzin, 1992). Because of past abuses and the need to establish minimum care requirements, the new law will require participating nursing homes to ensure for their residents that the following conditions are being met (Liptzin, 1992):

1. a physician visits each resident at least once every sixty days
2. at least a part-time medical director is on staff
3. a full-time social worker is on staff for facilities with more than 120 beds
4. licensed nurses on staff twenty-four hours a day with a Registered Nurse on duty each day
5. qualified activities director on staff
6. qualified dietitian on staff
7. mandatory training programs for nurses and nurse's aides

In addition, the Nursing Home Reform Act of 1987 requires a complete assessment of each resident at the time of admission and after *any* significant change in condition. There must be an annual written treatment plan describing the care to be provided to meet each resident's nursing, medical, and psychosocial needs. This annual treatment plan is prepared by an inter-disciplinary team, which includes the resident's attending physician, other professionals, and, where possible, the nursing home resident. The annual treatment plan is subject to periodic review and revision. It must be sensitive to issues of quality of life, freedom from restraints (chemical and physical), freedom from physical and mental abuse (including involuntary seclusion), provide residents the right to privacy and confidentiality, notification of legal rights/responsibilities and informed consent regarding treatment, notification of services available, and freedom from involuntary transfer and discharge (Liptzin, 1992). While these goals are laudable, Public Law 100–203 has thus far only established draft regulations for implementation. The draft regulations regarding implementation of the new law may prove to be more difficult than actual passage of the federal law itself. Numerous questions have been raised about phasing in implementation of the new federal law. Many who have voiced criticisms are concerned that in order to monitor nursing home compliance with these regulations, it will require highly intrusive regulation by government into the privileged domain of delivering clinical care to the elderly (Liptzin, 1992).

## *Economics of Aging and Long-Term Health Care*

### Pensions

Having a pension from an employer has a tremendous impact on the financial well-being of an older adult (Burkhauser & Salisbury, 1993). In several European countries, such as Sweden, Germany, France, Great Britain, the Netherlands, and in Australia, nearly all older persons receive a substantial pension. In the United States, however, pensions are relatively small and usually provided to only a minority of older adults (Quinn & Smeeding, 1993). Figure 11.10 displays a comparison of the *minimum* old age benefits provided to retired adults in each of seven countries as well as in the United States, using computations expressed as a percentage of the adjusted median income for that country. These data in figure 11.10

**Figure 11.10** Poverty and benefit adequacy among the U.S. elderly in a cross-national context.[a,c]

*Source: Luxembourg Income Study as in Smeeding, et al. (1993).*

[a]*Income is adjusted using the simple LIS equivalence scale that counts the first person as 1.0 and all other persons as 0.5 regardless of age. Elderly heads are 65 and over.*

[b]*Poverty rates are percentages of persons aged 65 and over whose disposable after tax incomes fall below the specified percentage of adjusted median income. The U.S. poverty line was 40.7 percent of adjusted income in 1986.*

[c]*Minimum benefits as published by the Organization for Economic Cooperation and Development (OECD) were compared with adjusted median income after adjusting for national price changes. For the United States, the figures include the Supplemental Security Income benefit, plus the Old Age and Survivors Insurance disregard; plus Food Stamps as indicated in U.S. Congress, House, Committee on Ways and Means, 1992 Green Book: Background Material and Data on Programs within the Jurisdiction of the Committee on Ways and Means (Washington, DC: U.S. Government Printing Office, 1992).*

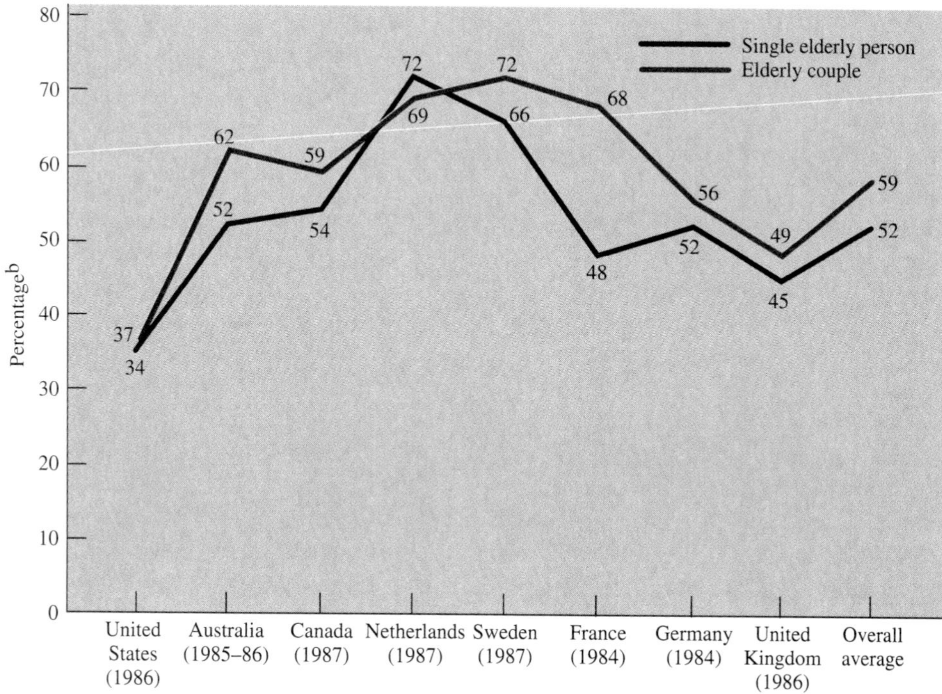


suggest that the United States provides *fewer* older persons a minimum level of support when compared to retirees in each of these other countries. Thus, although Social Security provides a base of financial support for older adults in our society, it leaves many individuals in retirement to live a meager life if this is all they have to draw upon.

It is increasingly important that people anticipate the need for multiple levels of support to sustain them into old age. Table 11.8 identifies the combination of traditional "passive" economic supports available to older people, which includes Social Security, pensions, earnings, and assets (Gottlieb, 1992; Soldo & Agree, 1988). There is considerable disparity in such passive sources of income as a function of both marital status and race. Table 11.8 shows Social Security to be the single most important source of income for retirees. For instance, among unmarried older persons Social Security accounted for more than 50 percent of the total retirement income of African Americans (70%), Hispanics (74%), and whites (54%) according to Snyder (1993).

*TABLE 11.8*

*Shares and Median Value of Aggregate by Marital Status, Gender, Race, and Hispanic Origin*

| *Income Share and Amount* | *White* | *Black* | *Hispanic* |
|---|---|---|---|
| ***Married Men and Their Wives*** | | | |
| Total number (in thousands) | 521.2 | 40.3 | 12.5 |
| Median amount | $18,240 | $11,980 | $12,700 |
| Total income | 100.0% | 100.0% | 100.0% |
| Social Security | 34.5 | 44.1[a] | 42.4[a] |
| pensions | 19.9 | 23.3 | 10.4[a,b] |
| earnings | 19.8 | 25.1[a] | 31.0[a] |
| assets | 21.1 | 3.6[a] | 10.0[a] |
| other | 4.7 | 3.9 | 6.2 |
| ***Married Women and Their Husbands*** | | | |
| Total number (in thousands) | 335.1 | 21.8 | 7.9 |
| Median amount | $17,780 | $10,790 | $13,040 |
| Total income | 100.0% | 100.0% | 100.0% |
| Social Security | 37.3 | 48.3[a] | 44.9[a] |
| pensions | 16.2 | 21.7[a] | 19.4 |
| earnings | 24.5 | 24.6 | 25.9 |
| assets | 18.0 | 2.0[a] | 8.3[a] |
| other | 4.0 | 3.4 | 1.5[a] |
| ***Unmarried Men and Women*** | | | |
| Total number (in thousands) | 239.0 | 41.5 | 11.3 |
| Median amount | $9,940 | $5,570 | $5,210 |
| Total income | 100.0% | 100.0% | 100.0% |
| Social Security | 40.3 | 53.8[a] | 52.9[a] |
| pensions | 18.8 | 14.4 | 12.6[a] |
| earnings | 14.0 | 21.8[a] | 17.9 |
| assets | 20.0 | 3.6[a] | 9.1[a] |
| other | 6.9 | 6.3 | 8.5 |

*Source: data from Richard V. Burkhauser and Dallas L. Salisbury (eds.),* Pensions In a Changing Economy, *Copyright © National Academy on Aging, Department of Health and Human Services, Washington DC; and data from New Beneficiary Survey, 1982.*
*[a]Significantly different from whites at the 0.95 level of confidence.*
*[b]Significantly different from blacks at the 0.95 level of confidence.*

Many married women, in particular, come to discover that the impact of the death of a spouse may mean the end of supplemental pensions and other types of income supports. Often retirement plans, pensions, and the like are established for the employee's benefit and following death do not necessarily transfer directly to a spouse.

## Health Care Costs

When major health problems strike older people, they often require medical or nursing care. Nursing home care and reimbursement policies are linked to current health-care policies, which are designed to contain hospital and medical costs. National health-care policy requires that each patient with a specific medical condition or **Diagnostic Related Group (DRG)** conform to the average cost and length of treatment in a hospital comparable to other patients with this condition (Church et al., 1988).

Hospitals receive federal support for each patient in a specific DRG based on this average. If some patients require longer stays or more complex treatment, the hospital must absorb the differential in cost between the patient care provided and that reimbursed by federal programs such as Medicare (Church et al., 1988).

Treating patients within the norms of the DRGs for comparable conditions is difficult. Hospital stays and medical costs above these DRG averages must be provided by the hospital, corporation, and physician; those under the averages still receive the same reimbursement. The result is that patients are now discharged as soon as practically possible and sent home or to a nursing home facility. The most commonly treated medical conditions among nursing home residents (Gambert, 1987; Haber, 1987) include circulatory diseases (40%), mental disorders and various forms of dementia (20%), endocrine, nutritional, and metabolic diseases (6%), and neoplasms including cancer (2.5%). Additional surveys reveal that nearly half of the residents in nursing homes suffer severe forms of mental disorder, often in conjunction with other medical problems, and almost one-third have lost bladder control (AARP, 1986). Nursing home placement may become necessary when older people live alone or far away from friends or relatives. This explains, in part, why women occupy more than 75 percent of the available beds in nursing homes (U.S. Bureau of the Census, 1983).

## Long-Term Care

The elderly who, through illness or accident, require long-term care experience significant economic hardships. *Long-term care* includes medical intervention, social support services, and personal care assistance to help chronically ill or disabled elderly cope with basic day-to-day activities. Long-term care is less frequently referred to as custodial care. The day-to-day care activities with which older persons need assistance include personal care such as dressing, bathing, toileting, and walking. Some long-term care is delivered in the home and includes help with cooking, shopping, or help with self-feeding. Other long-term care is provided in specialized centers such as those providing physical rehabilitation or supervised day care for a person with Alzheimer's disease. If you are familiar with community-based programs such as visiting nurse programs, home health aide services, or respite programs for Alzheimer's disease caregivers, then you already recognize some of the many types of long-term care programs. Table 11.9 illustrates the differences between long-term care and acute care, using an example of the treatment and delivery of services to an older person who has experienced a stroke. As is true for any impairment, the goal of long-term care is to help the older person regain skills and maintain as much independent functioning as possible. Table 11.10 shows that among adults over the age of 65, there is an increasing probability with advancing age that some long-term care services will be required; current estimates are that nearly 60 percent of adults will require such services at least once in their lives (TIAA, 1992). The cost of long-term care for the elderly is substantial and many people have little knowledge of the economics until such services are needed. Figure 11.11 compares the typical costs incurred for long-term home care and long-term nursing home care over a six-year period. Note that the costs for these services vary somewhat across service providers and across regions of our country.

*Table 11.9*

*Types of Care*

This chart shows the possible types of care given to someone who has suffered a stroke. It illustrates the differences between acute care and long-term care.

| | *Acute Care* | *Long-Term Care* |
|---|---|---|
| ***Care objectives*** | Improve patient's ability to function | Maintain patient at current level of function |
| ***Where care is received*** | Hospital and rehabilitation unit | At home |
| ***Who provides care*** | Physicians, nurses, therapists | Family member, home health aide |
| ***Type of care*** | Medication, X rays, IV feedings, physical therapy | Help with bathing and dressing, shopping and housework |
| ***Length of care*** | 4 weeks in hospital and rehabilititation | Ongoing |
| ***Who pays for care*** | Medicare and private supplemental insurance | Patient most likely pays out of pocket |



*Table 11.10*

*Percentage of Persons over 65 Years of Age Reporting Difficulty with Selected Personal Health Care Activities (1984)*

| | *Personal care activity* | | | | | | |
|---|---|---|---|---|---|---|---|
| *Age* | *Bathing* | *Dressing* | *Eating* | *Transferring* | *Walking* | *Getting outside* | *Using toilet* |
| 65 years and over .... | 9.8 | 6.2 | 1.8 | 8.0 | 18.7 | 9.6 | 4.3 |
| 65-74 years ......... | 6.4 | 4.3 | 1.2 | 6.1 | 14.2 | 5.6 | 2.6 |
| 65-69 years ......... | 5.2 | 3.9 | 1.2 | 5.3 | 12.2 | 4.9 | 2.2 |
| 70-74 years ......... | 7.9 | 4.8 | 1.1 | 7.1 | 16.6 | 6.6 | 3.0 |
| 75-84 years ......... | 12.3 | 7.6 | 2.5 | 9.2 | 22.9 | 12.3 | 5.4 |
| 76-79 years ......... | 9.8 | 6.4 | 2.1 | 7.5 | 19.5 | 9.9 | 4.1 |
| 80-84 years ......... | 16.8 | 9.7 | 3.2 | 12.4 | 29.0 | 16.8 | 7.8 |
| 85 years and over .... | 27.9 | 16.6 | 4.4 | 19.3 | 39.9 | 31.3 | 14.1 |

*Source: National Health Interview Survey, National Center for Health Statistics, 1984.*

Long-term care for the chronically ill elderly is most frequently delivered in nursing homes, where costs continue to escalate year after year. The typical nursing home stay is about seventy-five days, but long-term care needs may find a small number of older people staying six to seven years or longer. Who pays for such services? Medicare and Medicaid are federally subsidized programs that provide the basic coverage older people need, but they rarely cover the complete costs of such services such as long-term care as seen in Figure 11.12. It is important to understand how these two programs differ from each other and the eligibility criteria established for program enrollees.

***Medicaid*** **Medicaid** is a federal insurance program that provides matching funds to the states to pay for the medical care of lower-income elderly over the age of 65 who are at or near the level of poverty. Medicaid is provided to states only when minimum basic benefits are offered, although individual states may establish restrictions

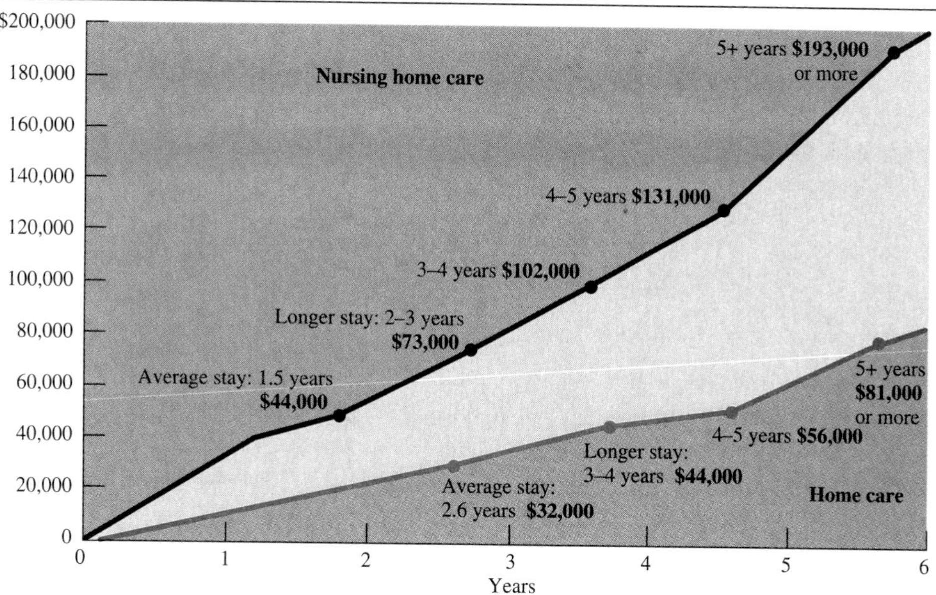


**Figure 11.11** How much does long-term care cost? Expected cost of long-term care.

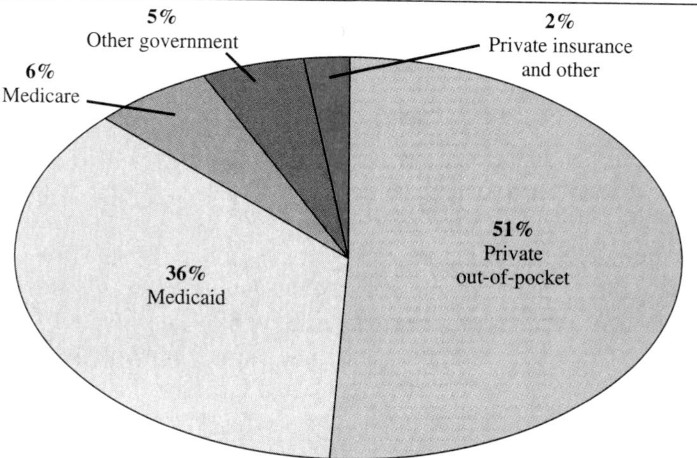


**Figure 11.12** Long-term care costs.
*Source: Data from Select Committee on Aging, U.S. House of Representatives, June 1991.*

on the types of services offered and the level of support offered to older persons (Gottleib, 1992). Medicaid typically covers about two-thirds of the cost of the medical health services of poor elderly, including some psychiatric services (Rivlin & Wiener, 1988). Medicaid may be applied to meet the long-term care costs of the poor, but historically has met about only about 36 percent of such costs (TIAA, 1992). Gottlieb (1992) estimates that Medicaid reimburses nearly 42 percent of the cost of all skilled and intermediate nursing home expenses in our country, but a surprisingly small percentage of all long-term costs.

If older people have significant assets, of course, Medicaid cannot help with long-term care expenses. However, when such assets are depleted due to long-term care costs or reach a minimum level, a process called **spending down,** older people become eligible for Medicaid. Currently the spouse of a person receiving Medicaid payments may receive $984 per month in income and hold $13,296 of assets, excluding a couple's home (TIAA, 1992). Data from national studies suggest that at the time of nursing home admission, about 35 percent of the elderly qualify for Medicaid, about 15 percent will qualify within the first twelve months by spending down, and another 10 percent will qualify after the first year of spending down (LifePlans, 1990).

***Medicare*** **Medicare** is part of the Social Security system (Title XVIII) and provides some support, but not complete coverage, for medical services for *any* individual over age 65. Currently, 32 million people are covered by Medicare including not only the elderly but also any individuals with end-stage renal disease and disabled younger persons who pay a monthly premium for coverage (Gottlieb, 1992). Medicare, as a broad-based program under the Social Security system, will pay for hospitalization for each illness up to 150 days, less deductibles, as long as the older person is receiving needed medical treatment. There are no limits to the number of hospital stays that will be covered as long as sixty days have elapsed between discharge and readmission. Medicare will also cover nursing home services (a maximum of a hundred days) for a medical condition as long as a physician has "prescribed" such services (Gottlieb, 1992; TIAA, 1992).

Older persons under Medicare have coverage for hospitalization, as just described, under provisions of the specific *Hospital Insurance, Part A program.* This program is funded from Social Security payroll taxes paid by workers and their employers and has resulted in the Part A Hospital Insurance Trust Fund (Gottlieb, 1992). A low monthly premium extends the benefits of the hospital coverage offered to older persons under a voluntary *Supplemental Medical Insurance, Part B program.* Nearly 97 percent of those who are eligible for Hospital Insurance, Part A elect to have extended coverage under the Supplemental Medical Insurance, Part B program (Gottlieb, 1992). A Part B Trust Fund has been created from general revenue from the federal government, monthly premiums, and the trust fund interest (Gottlieb, 1992). Physicians receive reimbursement through rates established by the government based on customary, prevailing, and reasonable rates, which is a fee for services that integrates the usual costs of specific services in a community, the lowest cost of specific services, the charge of specific services by other physicians, and a historical review of charges for similar services (Gottlieb, 1992). There are no limits on medical or surgical benefits (e.g., lifetime costs, costs per illness, or number of visits for treatments), although psychiatric-related treatments, particularly outpatient services, until very recently were restricted to those provided under the direct supervision of a physician. Currently, clinical social workers and psychologists may receive direct reimbursement as independent providers.

*Table 11.11*

**Comparison of Home Care and Nursing Home Costs**

| *Nursing Home Costs* | |
|---|---|
| | *U.S. Average* |
| Daily Cost | $80 |
| | x 7 |
| Weekly Cost | $560 |
| | x 52 |
| Annual Cost | $29,120 |
| ***Home Care Costs*** | |
| | *U.S. Average* |
| ***Home Health Aide Visit*** | $45 |
| (4 hours a day) | x 4 |
| 4 visits per week | $180 |
| ***Registered Nurse Visit*** | $60 |
| (1 day a week) | |
| ***Total cost per week*** | $240 |
| | x 52 |
| ***Annual Cost*** | $12,480 |

*From Long-Term Care—A Guide for the Educational Community. Copyright © 1992 Teachers Insurance and Annuity Association (TIAA).*

Medicare does not cover an older person's long-term health-care needs, since it specifically excludes personal home care services as well as custodial care regardless of whether it is provided in a hospital or in a nursing home (Haber, 1987; Rivlin & Wiener, 1988; TIAA, 1992). One of the most underutilized covered services has been treatments for psychiatric disorders, which totaled about 2.5 percent of all expenditures (Gottlieb, 1992).

Most older persons consider supplemental nursing home insurance coverage, yet few obtain this protection. Nursing home insurance policies are expensive and many adults believe that Medicare or Medicaid will meet both their hospital and nursing home needs (AARP, 1986; TIAA, 1992). Table 11.11 shows comparative national figures on the current costs of nursing home care, in-home care, and an illustration of a typical long-term care scenario, which includes four years of home care and an additional two years of nursing home care (TIAA, 1992). Those who do seek private insurance for nursing home care find the costs very high. Insurance policy charges range from $318 to $684 per year for those aged 65; yet the same policy costs $728 to $1,496 for those 79 years old. Insurance companies do not accept those most likely to use nursing home services—older people with prior illnesses, prior nursing home utilization, and chronic disabilities. Many policies may specifically exclude disorders such as Alzheimer's disease. Finally, most policies provide a *fixed* daily rate of reimbursement (indemnity) rather than meeting the costs of services required. The reimbursement rate varies from $10 to $120 per day. These rates do not increase year by year to take inflation and the generally escalating costs of nursing home stays into account. When people purchase policies ten to fifteen years in advance of their use, they often discover that their own projections of nursing home costs are far out of line with current charges (Rivlin & Wiener, 1988).

Increasingly, nursing homes are regularly and systematically reviewed by governmental agencies. Investigative reports of nursing homes have reinforced the need for vigilance and careful monitoring. More than one-third of nursing homes investigated were reported to be seriously deficient in at least one major area. Medicare and Medicaid programs will not provide reimbursement to unaccredited nursing homes (i.e., to homes that fail federally mandated inspections). Haber (1987) notes that nearly one-third of the available skilled nursing facilities, therefore, are not eligible for this reimbursement. Many, however do not have major deficiencies in service delivery; they simply cannot meet the minimum requirements for availability of physicians, pharmacists, and various rehabilitation professionals (such as occupational and physical therapists). Further concern has been directed at ensuring compliance with Public Law 100–203, which includes patients' rights such as the right to privacy, access to information (open access to medical files), a lifestyle in keeping with the resident's mental and physical capacities, safety, and maintenance of personal items (Haber, 1987).

## *Cognitive Impairment and Environmental Intervention*

### Community and Home Care

Not all older persons will need the specialized services provided by an institutional environment. George (1992) has emphasized the significance of understanding when and how home care and community services are accessed for the cognitively impaired elderly. Sommers, Baskin, Specht, and Shiverly (1988), for instance, originally reported that following discharge from a state mental hospital, those older adults without sufficient social support and having a high degree of cognitive impairment were most likely to enter nursing homes rather than community-based alternatives. Based on this and other work, George (1992) identified two general hypotheses that examine the relationship between decisions to access community and home care living arrangements for cognitively impaired older persons. The *substitution hypothesis* is based on the premise that formal services will be used by older persons who lack informal sources of support (e.g., friends, family, etc.) or whose social networks are unable or unwilling to provide such services (George, 1989, 1992; Noelker & Bass, 1989). As one form of supplementation, community programs may offer replacement services directly to the impaired elderly when social supports are lacking. Another form of substitution consists of respite services that permit the continuation of informal assistance from social networks such as family to delay as long as possible or avoid institutionalization completely (George, 1992; Greene, 1983).

Alternatively, the *supplementation* or *linking hypothesis* places the formal services accessed to help the cognitively impaired elderly as secondary to the contributions provided by family members (George, 1992). Caregivers may target specific supplementary formal services for the impaired older adult for which caregivers are not trained or are unable to provide, so-called *task differentiation.* Or caregivers may simply link the impaired older adult to appropriate formal programs and services. George (1992) suggests the need for further research to understand the conditions under which substitution versus supplementation choices are accessed by family members providing care to the cognitively impaired older person. Although some investigations of the elderly have explored this concern in the area of physical disabilities, no comparable research deals with mental impairments. Evidence suggests that knowledge of community-based services alone is not sufficient to predict actual use or access of such services. Some studies suggest, however, that family caregivers can actually be *trained* to access specific direct community services for the cognitively impaired elderly as well as to access intervention programs such as respite care, social support groups, and case management training programs to help the caregivers themselves (George, 1992, Greene & Monahan, 1987). In general, such training and intervention appears to decrease the risk of institutionalization of care recipients, although not all studies show that accessing formal services reduces the likelihood of institutional placement (Coelrick & George, 1986; George, 1992).

## Environmental Design for the Cognitively Impaired Elderly

Regnier and Pynoos (1992) have developed a set of twelve principles to enhance the institutional settings and home environments in which cognitively impaired elderly, such as those with dementia, live. These principles can help professionals responsible for the architecture, interior design, and aesthetics of institutions focus on critical dimensions of the immediate environment that are known to influence both the behavior and quality of life of cognitively impaired older persons. For example, when cognitively impaired residents with AD are able to see their bathroom and toilet from bed, incidents of incontinence are significantly reduced (Brink, 1993). The "L" design or "toe-to-toe" placement of beds provides more privacy for residents than placing them side by side (see figure 11.13) (Brink, 1993; Regnier & Pynoos, 1992). Such principles are outlined and briefly discussed in table 11.12 (for a more complete account see Regnier & Pynoos, 1992, pp. 763–792). It is hoped that regardless of the type of housing for impaired elderly, better, safer, and more secure environments will emerge that encourage and sustain the capacity for independent living.

*Nursing homes vary in the kinds and quality of services they offer.*

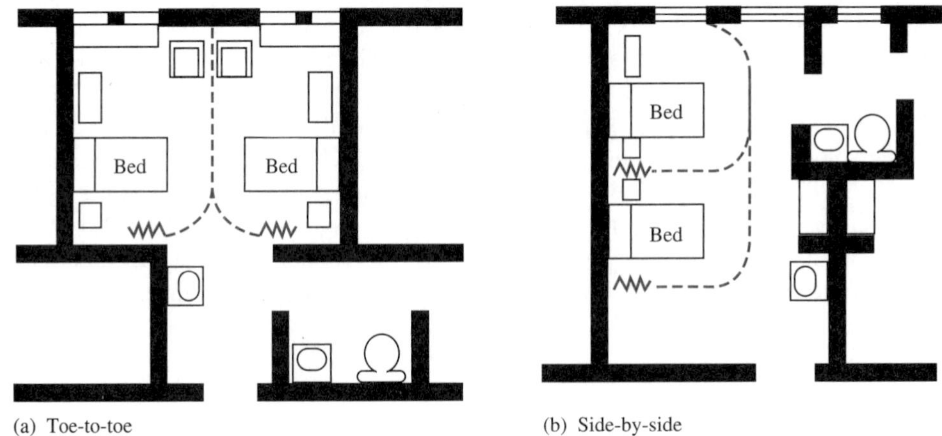


(a) Toe-to-toe

(b) Side-by-side

**Figure 11.13** Two basic room configurations are commonly utilized in skilled nursing facilities today. (a) Two-bed room, toe-to-toe, (b) two-bed room, side-by-side. Configuration (a) provides more privacy.

**TABLE 11.12**

| Twelve Environment-Behavior Principles for Cognitively Impaired Older Persons |
|---|
| 1. **Privacy:** *Provide opportunities for a place of seclusion from company or observation where one can be free from unauthorized intrusion.* Privacy may be illustrated by having one's own room and the time to be away from others, free from unnecessary surveillance. |
| 2. **Social Interaction:** *Provide opportunities for social exchange and interaction.* For cognitively impaired individuals, social interaction can be therapeutic and even the wide corridors of institutions can become "streets" for social activity, viewing others, and opportunities for friendly exchange. |
| 3. **Control, Choice, and Autonomy:** *Promote opportunities for residents to make choices and control events that influence outcomes.* Older persons need to have a sense of control and mastery over the environment in which they live. |
| 4. **Orientation and Way Finding:** *Foster a sense of orientation within the environment that reduces confusion and facilitates way finding.* Provide an environment that is easy to negotiate and easy to understand for those with cognitive impairments. |
| 5. **Safety and Security:** *Provide an environment that ensures each user will sustain no harm, injury, and undue risk.* |
| 6. **Accessibility and Functioning:** *Consider manipulation and accessibility as the basic requirements for a functional environment.* Utilize environmental features that are easy to manipulate (doors, windows) and require simple decision choices. |
| 7. **Sensory Aspects:** *Changes in visual, auditory, and olfactory senses should be accounted for in environments.* Plan to meet the needs of older residents to sustain social and successful physical interaction with their environment such as providing sufficient audition and illumination. |
| 8. **Stimulation and Challenge:** *Provide a stimulating environment that is safe but challenging.* Stimulating environments minimize boredom and passivity and challenge the older person to maintain their alertness and awareness. |
| 9. **Familiarity:** *Environments that use historical reference and solutions influenced by tradition can provide a sense of familiarity and continuity.* Encourage the use of personal objects, particularly in new settings, to provide the older impaired individual a familiar frame of reference and a sense of continuity regarding the self. |
| 10. **Aesthetics and Appearance:** *Design environments that appear attractive, provocative, and noninstitutional.* Avoid appearance of living conditions that depersonalize and stigmatize residents; build on residential models to humanize and individualize the living experiences. |
| 11. **Personalization:** *Provide opportunities to make the environment personal and mark it as the property of a single, unique individual.* Maintain self-identity through individualizing the space that the individual occupies; demonstrate the older person's uniqueness. |
| 12. **Adaptability:** *An adaptable or flexible environment can be made to fit changing personal characteristics.* With flexibility environments can be adapted to the changes encountered by the elderly to permit them to "age in place" rather than to have to move to new settings; this permits redesign within existing structures, for example, to enhance safety. An illustration of such an environment is found in figure 11.14, which displays the relatively simple but essential adaptations necessary to help the cognitively impaired older adult successfully, and with as much autonomy as possible, negotiate the task of bathing. |

*From V. Regnier and J. Pynoos, "Environmental Intervention for Cognitively Impaired Older Persons" in* Handbook of Mental Health and Aging, 2d ed. *Copyright © 1992 Academic Press, Orlando, FL.*

**Figure 11.14** An older person's ability to continue using a bathtub can be enhanced through the installation of such features as a hand-held shower, grab bars, a bench-type seat, nonskid strips on the bottom, and lever-type control handles. (See page 445.)

## Wandering and Cognitive Impairment

Institutional and home care for cognitively impaired elderly must also address the difficulties and the safety concerns that are associated with wandering. Wandering is a common problem among older persons with dementia and a special burden on those providing home care (Martino-Saltzman, Blasch, Morris, & McNeal, 1992). The U.S. Veterans Administration (1985, p. VIII-6) considers wandering to be "so imprecise as to defy definition," including "pacing, trying doorknobs, entering other people's rooms, talking about going 'home,' attempting to leave or leaving an institution against advice, getting lost on a walk, or simply talking in a way that someone considers disoriented." In a recent investigation, nursing home residents with dementia and identified as wanderers were compared with a comparable group of residents in the same nursing home who were not wanderers. Martino-Saltzman et al. (1991) identified four types of travel patterns, which may be seen in figure 11.15 from their analysis of more than ten thousand events that were videorecorded in the nursing home over a one-month period, twenty-four hours each day. Although based on a small sample of dementia residents, overall, the results summarized in table 11.13 suggest that with more severe dementia, direct patterns of travel were less frequent, and lapping was significantly more common. The groups primarily traveled independently within the nursing home for specific or directed reasons.

Pacing and its relationship to cognitive impairment in the elderly has also been reported by others (Cohen-Mansfield, Werner, Marx, & Freedman, 1991). Pacing, when examined across the twenty-four-hour period of study, was found to increase

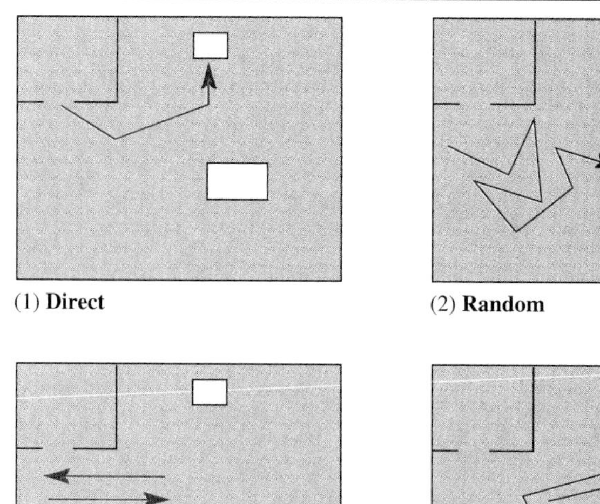


**Figure 11.15** Travel patterns of nursing home residents identified as wanderers and nonwanderers. Lapping was more common among wanderers.

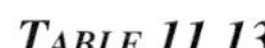

*TABLE 11.13*

***Characteristic Wandering Patterns among Nursing Home Residents with Different Levels of Dementia***

| *Pattern of Travel* | *Mild/No Dementia* | *Moderate Dementia* | *Severe Dementia* |
|---|---|---|---|
| Direct | 94.7% | 92.5% | 72.0% |
| Random | 0.2% | 1.0% | 1.7% |
| Pacing | 1.5% | 0.0% | 0.03% |
| Lapping | 3.6% | 6.5% | 26.0% |

*Adapted from Martino-Saltzman, Blasch, B. B., Morris, R. D., and McNeal, L. W. (1992). Travel behavior of nursing home residents perceived as wanderers and nonwanderers.* The Gerontologist, *31 (5), 666–672.*

most dramatically in the evening hours from 7:00 to 10:00 P.M., consistent with other observations of "sundowning" in dementia patients; in the present study, the peak for nondirective travel was 7:15 P.M. Table 11.14 shows the distribution of nondirective travel (e.g., random, pacing, and lapping) across the day and evening hours.

These findings suggest that the overall travel of wanderers, particularly those with severe dementia and the difficulties presented to nursing homes may be overestimated (Martina-Saltzman et al., 1992). With the greater likelihood of lapping, it may be desirable to design and utilize structured or protected walking environments given the need for patients to engage in such autonomous behaviors. Regnier and Pynoos (1992) describe an institution that has incorporated AD wandering gardens that provide to "restless patients" the chance to walk unencumbered in a safe, controlled area.

*Table 11.14*

*Percentage of Nondirective Independent Travel Events at Selective Time Periods for Nursing Home Residents with Various Levels of Dementia*

| | *Level of dementia* | | |
|---|---|---|---|
| *Time period* | *Mild/none (n = 12)* | *Moderate (n = 11)* | *Severe (n = 9)* |
| 10 pm–4 am | 4% | 1% | 31% |
| 4 am–7am | 2% | 13% | 26% |
| Breakfast | 2% | 5% | 19% |
| 9 am–12 noon | 2% | 7% | 31% |
| Lunch | 4% | 5% | 15% |
| 2 pm–5 pm | 7% | 6% | 32% |
| Dinner | 4% | 8% | 23% |
| 7 pm–10 pm | 15% | 12% | 31% |
| Total | 5% | 7% | 28% |
| Total excluding meal times | 7% | 8% | 31% |

## Restraints

In view of safety and legal concerns, most nursing home staff understandably take a very conservative approach to control of wandering using electronic monitoring, drugs, or physical restraints. In 1989, as many as 40 percent of nursing home residents were restrained for part of each day to beds, chairs, or wheelchairs using lengths of cloth tied at the waist, hips, chest, arms, or legs. This practice had declined to about 22 percent by 1992, according to the American Health Care Association (Brink, 1993). Advocates have justified the use of restraints to protect residents from falling, helping to maintain needed medical treatment, controlling wandering, and protecting staff and other residents from aggressive behaviors. Burton, German, Rovner, Brant, and Clark (1992) recently studied the use of restraints among elderly persons admitted with "mental illness" to a nursing home facility. The more severe the cognitive impairment and the more difficulty in managing independent daily living skills, the more likely staff were to employ physical restraints (Burton et al., 1992). There were also clear differences in the use of restraints among the eight nursing homes studied by Burton et al. (1992), with high-use institutions tending to restrain persons who needed assistance in walking and low-use homes not engaging in this practice. Burton et al. (1992) suggest that it is staff attitudes which predominately account for differences among high- and low-use nursing homes; in high-use homes, staff try to protect residents from falling and are quick to provide assistance with daily living tasks such as walking and dressing. They report considerable latitude in staff adoption of the use of physical restraint rather than mandated policies of the nursing home (Burton et al., 1992). It is important to understand the variables that predict adoption of restraints in institutional care facilities and the risks/benefits associated with their use. Research Focus 11.3 provides some insights on these issues.

## The Use of Restraints in Nursing Homes

The use of restraints in nursing homes is controversial and but one of many practices under which nursing home residents will soon receive federal protection under a Bill of Rights, established in 1987 under the Omnibus Budget Reconciliation Act. Although penalties for nursing homes that fail to comply are still evolving, the Bill of Rights presently specifies that residents have the right to a physician, to be informed about treatment, to refuse treatment, to complain without fear of reprisal, and the right to be free of restraints (Brink, 1993). Investigators (Burton, et al., 1992; Miles & Irvine, 1992) suggest that many considerations govern the use of restraints by staff. Schnelle, Simmons, and Ory (1992), for example, reported that staff failed to provide release from physical restraints (wrist, mittens, vest, and geri-chairs) among nursing home residents who were perceived by them to be verbally aggressive, physically aggressive, and generally unpleasant. The continuous use of restraints for any extended period must be monitored carefully. Restrained residents require as much as 15 percent more time from nursing home staff than those who are unrestrained, and restraints over extended periods limit independence such as toileting and may contribute to painful pressure sores (Brink, 1993). Miles and Irvine (1992), using an ex post facto analysis, reported that the ultimate risk inherent in using restraints continuously without supervision and without regular monitoring in nursing homes was death. Their analysis revealed that death was most likely to occur to a nursing home resident who was female, about 81 years old, and diagnosed with dementia. Miles and Irvine (1992) estimated that about 1 in 1,000 nursing home deaths could be linked directly to the use of restraints and advocated a dramatic reduction in their use; they suggest short-term use of restraints only to ensure medically necessary therapy for acutely ill, delirious older persons. From their analysis of case records, a composite scenario has been developed to illustrate the way in which restraints can accidentally cause death:

> "A nurse or aide applies a vest or strap restraint. While unobserved for ten minutes to several hours the patient slides off the bed or chair so that the restraint bears her weight and prevents her from sliding further down to a weight-bearing surface. She is confused and unable to use her arms or legs to return to a safe position in her bed or chair. Her weight, transmitted through the restraint, creates a force about her chest. As she struggles, the restraint gathers, thus concentrating the pressure around her chest. She asphyxiates, usually because she cannot inhale, less often because the restraint slides up and gathers to act as a ligature on her neck" (p. 765).

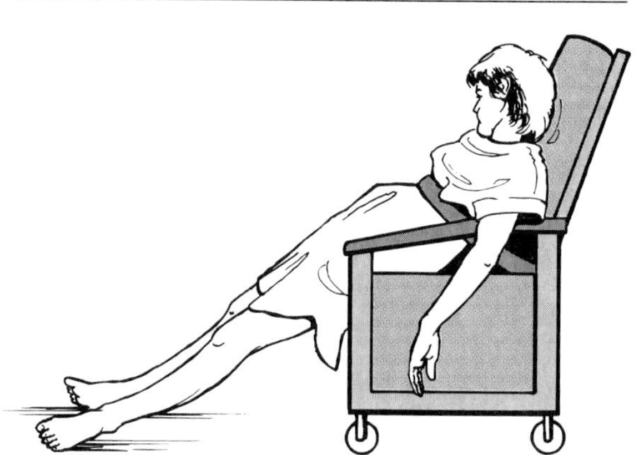

An illustration of such a situation is provided in figure 11.A.

Miles, S. H. and Irvine, P. (1992) Deaths caused by physical restraints. *The Gerontologist, 32* (6), 762–766.

## AGING IN SPECIAL POPULATIONS: REHABILITATION

Rehabilitation is a growing field devoted to appraising, intervening, and ameliorating the effects of disabilities. Most of the disabilities experienced by older adults are chronic and have little chance of being cured. They include conditions such as stroke, Parkinson's disease, osteoarthritis, rheumatoid arthritis, multiple sclerosis, diabetes, coronary artery disease, and cancer, as well as conditions occurring early in development such as mental retardation or cerebral palsy (Kemp, 1985). A disability (1) is caused by a physical injury or exists as the result of a physical or mental illness, (2) produces long-term interference in day-to-day function, and (3) produces a clear disruption in a person's typical style of social or physical response to the environment (Kemp, 1985).

The underlying theme of rehabilitation is the concept of *normalization,* meaning that as much as possible every citizen, regardless of age and disability, is entitled to participate fully in every aspect of life. Thus, intervention is designed to maximize individual functioning and promote independence, personal autonomy, self-worth, and positive self-concept. In implementing this approach, rehabilitation programs for the elderly face a variety of challenges. Older adults often have multiple chronic illnesses as well as mental disorders such as depression. Health professionals and the elderly themselves maintain negative attitudes toward older people (ageism), perhaps because of their slower rate of progress as compared to younger persons in rehabilitative programs (Kemp, 1985). The goals of rehabilitation for younger people include improving functioning to enable a person to lead an independent, community-based lifestyle with social supports from friends and family, but the goals are somewhat different for the elderly. With severe arthritis, heart disease, or stroke, an older person may not be able to resume independent living. A rehabilitation program for an elderly person may be more concerned with preserving some degree of independence in a supervised residence (Kemp, 1985).

Failing health and increased disabilities, you may recall from our earlier discussion, are among the predictors of suicide among the elderly (Blazer, 1982). In old age, disabilities often emerge without any warning and without any opportunity to develop coping resources to deal with them (Kemp, 1985). Some experts believe a series of adjustments or phases are experienced when a disabling condition suddenly strikes (Athelstan, 1981; Steger, 1976). The initial phase is one of *shock,* when the total impact of the disability is not yet fully understood. Next, a phase of *defensive retreat* emerges, in which the individual realizes what has occurred. The individual is terrified and in crisis as he or she seeks to cope. Often, primitive defense mechanisms are adopted in this stage; the person may deny and regress to protect him or herself against the fear, anxiety, and depression that arise from the reality of the disability. As we have seen earlier in this text, individuals under stress frequently distort reality; older adults, for instance, may believe a disability was not correctly diagnosed or will not be permanent. Such beliefs may continue for many months or even years. Final recognition of the reality of the disability and its permanence occurs during the *acknowledgment* phase. The final phase, *adaptation,* reflects the attempt to face the difficult challenges the disability presents—becoming as well-integrated as possible into the mainstream of social action (Kemp, 1985).

For some elderly adults, the emergence of late-onset disability may not neatly follow the progressive pattern just outlined; rather, the disability may represent just one more loss in a lengthy string of other loss experiences (Kemp, 1985). Whereas the presence of high-functioning role models (e.g., athletes with diabetes) helps the younger adult to look ahead, older individuals have few such role models. Older adults may compare their current functioning with a disability to their previous functioning without the disability. Such comparisons frequently produce negativism and depressive reactions (Kemp, 1985). Rehabilitation goals for older persons center on both normalizing and preserving functional integrity within the limits of the disability.

Rehabilitation requires a variety of contextual assessments, including the current family situation, other social supports, type of home environment, perception of the disability by the person, relatives, and friends, and a variety of other personality, cognitive, and emotional evaluations. It is important to examine the person's view of the rehabilitation goals as well as their motivation for improvement. With this background, intervention in the forms of therapy and family involvement can help improve the ability of the disabled older adult to function (Kemp, 1985).

## Summary

To help promote the health of the elderly, we must focus on maintaining and preserving a sense of autonomy and personal control in their lives. It is difficult to do so under the complex conditions that influence aging among widows, minorities, and single persons in our society. It is important to recognize the elderly individual's perception of vulnerability and their encounters with abuse experienced in a variety of living conditions. Elder abuse is increasingly common. Investigators have found it to be cyclical and related to dependency, to inadequate recognition of the sacrifices made by the caretaker, and to a lack of reward or appreciation from the older adult who receives the care. The fear of crime, rather than the actual incidence of crime, may itself limit older people's freedom and autonomy. Such fears become more prevalent among the elderly who have been victimized by crime, whose lifestyles sometimes become dominated by the threat of the crime occurring a second time. Alcoholism among elderly individuals is less of a mental health problem than it is for younger adults. However, alcoholic behavior, whether early or late onset, leads to increasingly complex medical problems.

Those older persons who live in rural environments generally encounter more poverty and lower-quality housing, whereas the elderly in urban centers experience poorer-quality health and social services. The ability of older persons to care for themselves is inversely related to age. Many types of housing are available for older persons, but most elderly prefer to reside in their own homes. The cost of independent home ownership is substantial for those on fixed incomes. Vital repairs are routinely undertaken, but income determines both the frequency of discretionary repairs and the expenditures allocated. Although a variety of housing alternatives are available for older persons needing assistance, there is a growing concern for the homeless elderly in our society. The living arrangements of older persons have an impact on the way in which older persons understand and manage their environments. Significant consequences are inherent in the residential choices that older persons make.

Caring for an elderly parent is emotionally demanding and requires an immense commitment of personal energy and resources. Home care is often a prelude to nursing home care. The economics of aging suggest that long-term care and general health-care costs are critical considerations in the financial planning, security, and well-being of older adults. Custodial, residential, and skilled nursing homes involve different levels of nursing care and intervention. Psychological, physical, and economic factors must be evaluated in a nursing home placement. Only 5 percent of our elderly reside in nursing homes at any time; for every person who dies in a nursing home, three are able to return to and live in the community.

Rehabilitation must be a goal for special older populations. Rehabilitation is a critical strategy for those with chronic arthritis, diabetes, stroke, and other disabilities. Through rehabilitation, elderly individuals may spend their later years in as normal a way as possible within the limits of their disabilities. Rehabilitation has become a vital intervention strategy for the elderly.

## Review Questions

1. Discuss the optimization of the later years in terms of the health needs and the mental health needs of the elderly. What are some considerations that must be recognized in terms of service delivery?
2. Describe the patterns of elder abuse reported in our society and the factors that lead to abuse within families. What impact does culture and social class difference play in such situations?
3. Develop a public policy based on the discussion of driving and old age in the test that could form the basis of new legislation to regulate the driving of older persons. What are some of the critical psychological factors that must be recognized?
4. Describe two views and accompanying relevant research that examines older persons' fear of victimization and crime.
5. Explain the relationship between growing older in rural versus urban areas and the likelihood of experiencing poverty.
6. What factors underlie older persons choices of housing options? Describe these housing options.
7. Outline those conditions that might contribute to an older person moving to a different housing option. What are considerations that should be taken into account in making such transitions successful?
8. Describe the typical transfer of an elderly individual into a nursing home. What factors are most likely to be worrisome to the older person making such a move? What can be done to reduce these fears?
9. What are the fundamental goals of Public Law 100-203 and how are these implemented in practice?
10. Describe the features of long-term care and the available funding mechanisms for older persons receiving such treatment. What is the difference between Medicare and Medicaid?
11. Discuss the principles of environmental design applicable to older persons with cognitive impairments.
12. How do institutions balance their responsibilities and the need of older persons for freedom and personal independence? Discuss the special issues of restraints and wandering.
13. What is the relationship between rehabilitation and normalization? Discuss the challenges facing individuals responsible for implementing rehabilitation services for the elderly.

## For Further Reading


Armstrong, A., & Donahue, M. R. (1993). *A widow's passage to emotional and financial well-being.* Chicago, IL: Dearborn Financial Publishing.

Beles, R. P., Gift, H. C., & Ory, M. C. (1994). *Aging and quality of life.* New York: Springer.

Estes, C. L., & Swan, J. H. (1993). *The long-term care crisis: Edlers trapped in the no-care zone.* Thousand Oaks, CA: Sage.

Gatz, M., Popkin, S. J., Pino, C. D., & VandenBos, G. R. (1985). Psychological intervention with older adults. In J. E. Birren & K. W. Schaie (Eds.), *The handbook of the psychology of aging* (2nd ed.). New York: Van Nostrand Reinhold.

Golant, S. M. (1992). *Housing America's elderly: Many possibilities, few choices.* Thousand Oaks, CA: Sage.

Gubrium, J. F. (1993). Speaking of life: *Horizons of meaning for nursing home residents.* Hawthorne, NY: Aldine.

Pillemer, K. A., & Wolf, R. S. (1986). *Elder abuse.* Dover: Auburn House.

Sheridan, C. (1993). *Failure-free activities for the Alzheimer's patient.* San Francisco: Elder Books.

# 12

# HOW WE DIE

*This is the end*
*My intimate friend*
*The end.*
—Jim Morrison

*While others may argue about whether the world ends in a bang or a whimper,*
*I just want to make sure mine doesn't end with a whine.*
—Barbara Gordon

## *Introduction*

The process of dying and the event of death is as much an integral part of the human life cycle as the process of birth. In this chapter, we evaluate different ways in which death is defined, survey the sociohistorical and sociocultural contexts of death, and comment on the practice of euthanasia as well as legal issues surrounding end-of-life decisions. We describe attitudes toward death at different points in the life cycle, noting in particular attitudes toward death and the dying process in the adult years. In our discussion of facing death, we critically evaluate Elisabeth Kübler-Ross's theory on the stages of dying, and then outline the phases of dying suggested by E. Mansell Pattison. We also focus on the need for open communication and discuss the process of denial. Next, we turn to the contexts in which people die—hospitals, hospices, and at home—and evaluate how we cope with the deaths of those we love. We also examine grief, including stages of grief, impediments to successful grieving, and coping with being a widow or widower. Finally, we detail various forms of mourning, consider the importance of death education, take a critical look at our society's funeral rituals, and consider deaths issues that are difficult to resolve.

## *Ethical, Medical, and Legal Issues*

*No matter what the intervention, the mortality rate remains one per person.*
—Jack Denaro

### Definitions of Death

In previous decades, death was a simple matter. The cessation of biological functioning—the termination of the heartbeat, the cessation of breathing, the absence of blood pressure, rigidity of the body (*rigor mortis*)—was a clear and specific sign of death. With advances in technology in medicine and in corollary terminology, it has become increasingly complex for a physician to make the medical pronouncement that a patient is dead. We understand that death has fundamental properties, including the cessation of essential biological functions such as circulation and respiration (Kalish, 1985). We also know that death is irreversible. But if a patient is dependent on some sort of specialized medical treatment, how can we determine exactly *when* he or she is no longer really living?

*TABLE 12.1*

| *Harvard Criteria for Brain Death (Modified)* |
|---|
| 1. *Unreceptivity and unresponsivity*<br>Even the most intensely painful stimuli do not evoke a vocal or other response. |
| 2. *No movements or breathing*<br>Observation covering a period of at least one hour by a physician is adequate to satisfy the criterion of no spontaneous muscular movements or spontaneous respiration or response to stimuli. The total absence of spontaneous breathing may be determined by turning off a respirator for three minutes and observing whether there is any effort on the part of the individual to breathe. |
| 3. *No reflexes*<br>The pupil will be fixed and dilated. It will not respond to a direct source of bright light. Eye movement and blinking are absent. Swallowing, yawning, coughing and vocalizing are absent. As a rule, the stretch or tendon reflexes cannot be elicited. |
| 4. *Flat electroencephalogram*<br>Of great confirmatory value is the presence of a flat or isoelectric electroencephalogram. There should be an absence of EEG activity in response to pinch or noise stimuli. Furthermore, a minimum of ten minutes recording time should be observed. All of the above tests should be repeated at least twenty-four hours later with no change in results. Also, the presence of hypothermia (body temperature below 32.2° C/90° F) and central nervous system depressants such as barbiturates must be ruled out. |

*From "A Definition of Irreversible Coma: Report of the Ad Hoc Committee of Harvard Medical School to Examine the Definition of Brain Death" in* Journal of the American Medical Association, *205:307–340. Copyright © 1968 American Medical Association. Reprinted by permission.*

Physicians today accept brain death indicators as binding, legal criteria for death. At least thirty-seven states and Puerto Rico have enacted laws defining brain death as equivalent to cardiopulmonary death (Kaufman & Lynn, 1986). The medical community, led by Harvard Medical School, developed four neurological criteria to define brain death in 1968. These criteria are outlined in table 12.1. **Brain death** means that all electrical activity in the brain has ceased for a specified period of time as determined by an electroencephalogram (EEG). The absence of blood flow to the brain, determined by cerebral angiography—monitoring the passage of injectable dye through the arteries—confirms this fact. If an individual's heartbeat has stopped but is restored through cardiopulmonary resuscitation (CPR), then a person who has technically died can be revived. This is because lower brain stem centers (such as the medulla) that monitor heartbeat and respiration may die somewhat later than higher brain centers. However, when the higher brain centers have been deprived of oxygen for more than five to ten minutes, the individual will either never recover mental and motor abilities or will recover them only with severe impairment (Weir, 1986).

The major criticism of the Harvard criteria for determining brain death has been that they are too stringent to be of much use in actual practice (Collaborative Study, 1977). In one investigation of more than 503 neurological patients who were likely brain dead, only 19 actually met all of the criteria completely (Black, 1983a, 1983b). The Medical Consultants of the President's Commission on Ethics in Biomedical and Behavioral Research has formulated new guidelines for determining brain death (1981); they are presented in Research Focus 12.1. The modifications suggest that the Harvard criteria may not be applied routinely to infants and young

## Current Brain Death Criteria

Guidelines for Brain Death Proposed by Medical Consultants on the Diagnosis of Death to the President's Commission for the Study of Ethical Problems in Medicine and Biomedical and Behavioral Research

Statement: An individual with irreversible cessation of all functions of the entire brain including the brain stem is *dead.* The determination of death must follow accepted medical standards.

1. *Cessation* is determined by evaluation of a *and* b:
   a. *Cerebral functions are absent*—Deep coma with unreceptivity and unresponsivity; confirmation by flat EEG (no electrical activity) or blood flow analysis/angiography showing no circulating blood to brain for at least ten minutes may be done to confirm evaluation.
   b. *Brainstem functions are absent*—No pupillary reflex to bright light in either eye; no extraocular movements (no eye movements when head turned from side to side or when ear canals are irrigated with ice water); no corneal reflex when the cornea is lightly touched; no gag reflex when a tongue depressor is touched against the back of the pharynx; no cough reflex; no respiratory (apnea) reflexes. Note that some primitive spinal cord reflexes may persist after brain death.
2. *Irreversibility* of death is determined when evaluation discloses a *and* b *and* c:
   a. The cause of coma is determined and is sufficient to account for the loss of brain functions.
   b. The possibility of recovery of any brain function is excluded.
   c. The cessation of all brain functions persists during a reasonable period of observation and/or trial of therapy; and confirmation of this clinical judgment, when appropriate, is made with EEG or blood flow data (cessation of blood flow for at least ten minutes).

*Conditions Limiting the Reliable Application of the Above-Mentioned Criteria:*

a. *Drug and metabolic conditions*—If any sedative is suspected to be present, there must be toxicology screening to identify the drug.
b. *Hypothermia*—Temperature below 32.2 degrees C/90 degrees F.
c. *Developmental immaturity*—Infants and young children under the age of five have increased resistance to damage and greater potential for recovery despite showing neurologic unresponsiveness for longer periods of time than adults.
d. *Shock*—Produces significant reduction in cerebral blood flow.



children under five; that all tests need not be repeated at least twenty-four hours later, but *may* be repeated in accord with accepted clinical-medical judgment; and that the presence of fixed pupils (nonresponsive to bright light) may be differentiated from widely dilated pupils, which may or may not indicate brain death (*Hospital Law Manual,* 1982). In addition, several specific conditions make the application of brain death criteria invalid: drug or metabolic intoxication, hypothermia, developmental immaturity, or shock.

Others have suggested that more qualitative criteria should be recognized. For example, minimal electrical brain stem activity sufficient to control respiratory reflexes or heartbeat may *not* be sufficient to meet the *psychological* definition of living (Veatch, 1981). Can primitive reflexes at the level of the medulla be sufficient to engage a person in the experience of life—the conscious, reflective, and personally involving experience of living, self-care, and social interaction? Questions of ethics, medical responsibility, law, and personal values make the issue of defining death a central concern to society. Despite having the legal right to pronounce a person brain dead, no more than 13 percent of a sample of nearly 650 neurosurgeons and no more than 2 percent of 1,410 internists would simply turn off a respirator without also obtaining consent from either family members or colleagues (Pinkus, 1984).

The need for a precise definition of death assumes greater importance because of recent advances in medical science that have the potential to sustain essential biological functions for a prolonged time period. Physicians and hospital staff have the ability to "pull the plug" and terminate life-sustaining technological interventions. But family members rarely discuss the conditions under which they would like their lives to be continued using so-called heroic life-support measures. Ideally, each person should have a chance to communicate with a physician regarding their status, their chances of survival, and the possibility of recovery. Since this is impossible for those who unexpectedly become brain dead through accidents or sudden illnesses such as cerebral hemorrhage, we are sometimes forced to judge how a person would feel or react to the use of life-sustaining interventions. Physicians may hear a family member say, "Dad was always an active person. For him to simply remain flat in bed, unconscious, hooked to a respirator, is totally contrary to his view of life and living. Please unhook this machine and let him die." Should a physician act in accordance with such statements from the family? What if not all family members agree?

Bringing closure to these debates has been difficult for physicians, ethicists, and clergy. Recently experts have recognized from investigations that even when brain death of the entire brain occurs (i.e., meeting the criteria in Research Focus 12.1), there is no assurance that all brain functioning has ceased (Halevy & Brody, 1993). Halevy and Brody (1993) reviewed studies showing that despite meeting the criteria of brain death, there remains brain activity in rare instances that includes continuation of neurohormonal functioning, cortical functioning consistent with deep coma and indexed by EEG, and brain stem functioning as revealed through evoked potentials. Based on their analysis, they suggest that any further attempt to try to dichotomize the distinction between life and death based on brain functioning is "biologically artificial." Brain death is not a fixed, finite event or end point; rather, it is on a continuum. Death is best conceptualized as a process in this view, with the process potentially able to be prolonged or extended due to life support and other medical interventions.

Halevy and Brody (1993) suggest that we need to consider three questions regarding death and three different answers in response: (1) When can funeral directors begin their services?—when there has been no evidence of any blood flow (e.g., absence of any blood pressure); (2) When can care be unilaterally withheld?—when there is irreversible cessation of conscious functioning; and (3) When may organs be harvested?—when current brain death criteria have been satisfied. This revises the way we conceptualize life and death and avoids the impossible task of creating a single criterion and a single definition that is satisfying theoretically and speaks practically to the three important preceding questions (Halevy & Brody, 1993). For example, accepting only absence of blood flow as a single, certain indicator of death would effectively terminate any transplantation, since tissues and organs would at that point not be viable. And, although the loss of conscious functioning would be sufficient grounds for some to withhold extraordinary intervention and life support, it would not be appropriate to call for the services of a funeral director. In contrast with past views of brain death criteria to determine death, Halevy and Brody (1993) have broken new ground in their criticism and reconceptualization. Death is a process, not an event; how and when we intervene is determined by the nature of the concerns that we bring to the process of death itself.

One of the most troubling of interventions occurs when individuals have incurred severe brain damage and coma but also show signs of a "sleepwakefulness" cycle without any detectable signs of awareness, a condition called **persistent vegetative state–PVS** (Multi-Society Task Force on PVS, 1994). Karen Ann Quinlan experienced this phenomenon in her early adulthood following cardiopulmonary arrest in 1975. She died 10 years later never having regained consciousness and became a classic example of the difficulty families have in removing a relative from a respirator/ventilator (Kinney, Korein, Panigrahy, Dikkes, and Goode, 1994).

PVS is a clinical condition marked by a complete unawareness of the self and the environment. Individuals are unconscious yet maintain a sleep-wake cycle and preserve functioning of the autonomic system in the brain-stem as well as function of the hypothalamus (Multi-Society Task Force on PVS, 1994). PVS may be temporary or permanent but is always characterized by the absence of ". . . any behaviorally detectable expression of self-awareness, specific recognition of external stimuli, or consistent evidence of attention or intention or learned responses" (Multi-Society Task Force on PVS, 1994, p. 1500). Thus individuals show no evidence of sustained, reproducible, purposeful, or voluntary behavioral responses to visual, auditory, tactile or noxious stimuli; show no evidence of language comprehension or expression; have bowel and bladder incontinence; and have variably preserved cranial nerve and spinal reflexes (Multi-Society Task Force on PVS, 1994, p. 1499). PVS is said to be present if such conditions are present one month following acute brain trauma and nontraumatic brain injury or are evident for one month in persons with degenerative or metabolic disorders. Recovery of consciousness from a posttraumatic vegetative state is unlikely after twelve months. And, any recovery from a nontraumatic persistent vegetative state after three months is exceedingly rare for adults or children (Multi-Society Task Force on PVS, 1994). Those with degenerative disorders (e.g., dementia) or metabolic disorders also show very low likelihood of regaining consciousness after remaining in PVS for a few months. Life span estimates of those experiencing PVS is typically from two to five years with survival of more than ten years highly unusual (Multi-Society Task Force on PVS, 1994).

The distinctions outlined in Table 12.2 distinguish PVS from other conditions which can also cause unconsciousness: (1) coma following a traumatic or nontraumatic injury (with death occurring prior to attainment of stable brain-stem function sufficient to produce PVS), (2) end stages of neurological diseases such as Alzheimer's Disease, and (3) coma produced from untreatable tumors and vascular

*Table 12.2*

***Characteristics of the Persistent Vegetative State and Related Conditions.****

| *Condition* | *Self-Awareness* | *Sleep-Wake Cycles* | *Motor Function* | *Experience of Suffering* | *Respiratory Function* | *EEG Activity* | *Cerebral Metabolism* | *Prognosis For Neurologic Recovery* |
|---|---|---|---|---|---|---|---|---|
| Persistent vegetative state | Absent | Intact | No purposeful movement | No | Normal | Polymorphic delta or theta, sometimes slow alpha | Reduced by 50% or more | Depends on cause (acute traumatic or nontraumatic injury, degenerative or metabolic condition, or developmental malformation) |
| Coma | Absent | Absent | No purposeful movement | No | Depressed, variable | Polymorphic delta or theta | Reduced by 50% or more (depends on cause) | Usually recovery, persistent vegetative state, or death in 2 to 4 weeks |
| Brain death | Absent | Absent | None or only reflex spinal movements | No | Absent | Electrocerebral silence | Absent | No recovery |
| Locked-in syndrome | Present | Intact | Quadriplegia and pseudobulbar palsy; eye movement preserved | Yes | Normal | Normal or minimally abnormal | Minimally or moderately reduced | Recovery unlikely; persistent quadriplegia with prolonged survival possible |
| Akinetic mutism | Present | Intact | Paucity of movement | Yes | Normal | Nonspecific slowing | Unknown | Recovery very unlikely (depends on cause) |
| Dementia | Present but lost in late stages | Intact | Variable; limited with progression | Yes but lost in late stages | Normal | Nonspecific slowing | Variably reduced | Irreversible (ultimate outcome depends on cause) |

**From the Multi-Society Task Force on Persistent Vegetative State, "Medical Aspects of the Persistent Vegetative State" in* New England Journal of Medicine, *330(21): 1499–1508.* 

conditions e.g., stroke. In Table 12.2, it is evident that PVS has distinguishable clinical features and a definitive prognosis to help physicians and families make decisions regarding withholding or withdrawing various treatments and interventions. Such decisions are difficult when placed in the context of other behavioral signs that may be observed in a relative such as the shedding of tears, occasional smiles, vocal grunts, moans or screams, random limb movement, and continuation of some central nervous system reflexes. Table 12.2 distinguishes PVS from locked-in syndrome, akinetic mutism, and dementia. Locked-in syndrome describes the extremely rare condition in which a person is conscious yet due to severe total paralysis is unable to communicate with others (Multi-Society Task Force on PVS, 1994). Akinetic mutism is a yet even more rare disorder with pathologically slowed or virtually absent bodily movements and a total loss of speech (Multi-Society Task Force on PVS, 1994). With the recency of PVS as a clinically distinguishable syndrome, the exact incidence of PVS is hard to estimate. But, it appears that PVS draws an important distinction that will assist our society in managing the ethical and legal implications of medical intervention such as the consequences of decisions to provide, withdraw, or withhold medical treatment (e.g., mechanical ventilation or tubal feeding).

From clinical observation it appears that it is possible to differentiate with reasonable certainty *persistent* vegetative states (PVS) from *permanent* vegetative states. The latter condition means that an irreversible condition is most likely present, a condition from which the individual will not recover consciousness or, if consciousness were regained, severe disabilities would be present (Multi-Society Task Force on PVS, 1994). While guidelines are still being formulated, physicians suggest that if PVS continues for three months or more, recovery is extremely unlikely. As a result of the distinction between persistent and permanent vegetative states, the boundaries and outcomes of ethical and legal decisions become more clearly defined.

## Decisions Regarding Health Care

Health care decisions for older individuals cannot always be made with their full, clear, and unequivocal participation; in catastrophic illness and emergency situations, they are unable to respond and may be comatose or irrational. Even when older persons are apparently able to communicate effectively, they may be influenced by current conditions or context. Cohen-Mansfield, Droge, & Billig (1992), for example, asked ninety-seven elderly patients who were hospitalized about their views regarding three different hypothetical treatments that might arise when they themselves were cognitively intact, confused, or comatose. Two results are of special interest. First, 12 percent of the respondents showed no consistent pattern in their responses and no underlying systematic approach to resolving these hypothetical dilemmas; such respondents were lowest in overall education and highest in their incidence of depressive symptoms. Second, treatment preferences were influenced by the personal values of the elderly as well as their religious beliefs and prior experience with illnesses of others (Cohen-Mansfield, Droge, & Billig, 1992). Often, health care decisions will determine not just health and medical intervention for the elderly, but ultimately will determine treatment that will prolong life or hasten death.

***Living Wills, Medical Directives, and Durable Powers of Attorney*** The **living will** was created to help ensure the right of all individuals to choose whether heroic measures will be used to sustain their lives. This document, presented in figure 12.1, allows individuals the choice of how, when, and under what circumstances life-sustaining treatments will be provided or withheld. It establishes a contract between the person, the medical community, and close relatives.

A living will should, in principle, make life-sustaining treatment a less complex decision for physicians and family members. In actual practice, many difficulties may arise. For example, if one relative objects to the wishes outlined in a living will at the time of a medical crisis, the will may not be enforced (Society for the Right to Die, 1987). Another possible complication is that physicians, relatives, and the patient may be at odds regarding treatment outcomes. Additionally, in many gray areas, the person's wishes and acceptable medical treatment standards may conflict. For instance, a patient may not want to accept tubal feeding to sustain life, yet a physician may be unwilling to withhold nutrients and water knowing the consequences will be death.

The **medical directive** (see figure 12.2) has been proposed to deal with such problems. It anticipates specific conditions not covered in detail in the living will. The medical directive, sometimes called an *advance directive,* has been seen as empowering the individual to make decisions regarding treatment *before* special conditions exist, such as brain injury, stroke, or other extreme conditions, rather than having family members or physicians make such choices. Also accepted by the courts is a **durable power of attorney**, which specifies a surrogate decision maker (relative, physician, lawyer, or friend) whom an individual legally designates to elect health care choices if the individual becomes decisionally incapacitated.

High (1993) notes that within the past fifteen years, every state has come to accept ". . . legally binding living wills or powers of attorney for health care decision making in the event of a terminal illness or decisional incapacity necessitating surrogate decision makers" (p. 342). Yet, despite state legislation providing legal acceptance of living wills, durable power of attorney, and advance medical directives, surprisingly few older persons have actually used these options. High's (1993) review of studies showed at most an 18 percent rate among people 60 years of age and older, with usage sometimes as low as 0 to 4 percent. Even with deliberate educational intervention such as free legal assistance and lecture/discussion presentations, elderly individuals were only slightly more willing to complete a living will or advance directive. Among a sample of 293 older people (65–93 years old) living independently and participating in an educational intervention explaining advance directives, the overall percentage increase in the sample was modest—22 percent to 32 percent, which can be compared to the 76 percent of

**Figure 12.1** Living will declaration.
*Source: Society for the Right to Die; 250 West 57th Street; New York, NY 10107.*

**INSTRUCTIONS**

# CALIFORNIA DECLARATION

If I should have an incurable and irreversible condition that has been diagnosed by two physicians and that will result in my death within a relatively short time without the administration of life-sustaining treatment or has produced an irreversible coma or persistent vegetative state, and I am no longer able to make decisions regarding my medical treatment, I direct my attending physician, pursuant to the Natural Death Act of California, to withhold or withdraw treatment, including artificially administered nutrition and hydration, that only prolongs the process of dying or the irreversible coma or persistent vegetative state and is not necessary for my comfort or to alleviate pain.

If I have been diagnosed as pregnant, and that diagnosis is known to my physician, this declaration shall have no force or effect during my pregnancy.

**ADD PERSONAL INSTRUCTIONS (IF ANY)**

Other instructions:

**DATE AND SIGN THE DOCUMENT AND PRINT YOUR ADDRESS**

**NOTE: YOUR WITNESSES MUST SIGN ON THE NEXT PAGE**

Signed this _____ day of ____________________, 19____.

Signature ____________________________________

Address ____________________________________

____________________________________

**Figure 12.1**
continued.

**WITNESSING PROCEDURE**

**WITNESSES MUST SIGN AND PRINT THEIR ADDRESSES**

The declarant voluntarily signed this writing in my presence. I am not a health care provider, an employee of a health care provider, the operator of a community care facility, an employee of an operator of a community care facility, the operator of a residential care facility for the elderly, or an employee of an operator of a residential care facility for the elderly.

**WITNESS #1**

Witness ______________________________

Address ______________________________

______________________________

The declarant voluntarily signed this writing in my presence. I am not entitled to any portion of the estate of the declarant upon his or her death under any will or codicil thereto of the declarant now existing or by operation of law. I am not a health care provider, an employee of a health care provider, the operator of a community care facility, an employee of an operator of a community care facility, the operator of a residential care facility for the elderly, or an employee of an operator of a residential care facility for the elderly.

**WITNESS #2**

Witness ______________________________

Address ______________________________

______________________________

**IF YOU ARE A PATIENT IN A NURSING HOME, A PATIENT ADVOCATE MUST ALSO SIGN**

## STATEMENT OF PATIENT ADVOCATE OR OMBUDSMAN

I further declare under penalty of perjury under the laws of California that I am a patient advocate or ombudsman as designated by the State Department of Aging and that I am serving as a witness as required by Section 7178 of the Health and Safety Code.

Signature: ______________________________

*Courtesy of* ***Choice In Dying*** 11/93
200 Varick Street, New York, NY 10014 1-800-989-WILL

**PAGE 2**

**Figure 12.2** The medical directive. *Copyright 1990 by Linda L. Emanuel and Ezekiel J. Emanuel. The authors of this form advise that it should be completed pursuant to a discussion between the principal and his or her physician, so that the principal can be adequately informed of any pertinent medical information and so that the physician can be appraised of the intentions of the principal and the existence of such a document which may be made part of the principal's records. This form was originally published as part of an article by Linda L. Emanuel and Ezekiel J. Emanuel, "The Medical Directive: A New Comprehensive Advance Care Document" in* Journal of the American Medical Association *June 9, 1989; 261:3290. It does not reflect the official policy of the American Medical Association. Copies of this form may be obtained from the Harvard Medical School Health Publications Group, P.O. Box 380, Boston, MA 02117 at 2 copies for $5 or 5 copies for $10; bulk orders also available.*

### The Medical Directive: An Introduction

As part of a person's right to self-determination, every adult has the freedom to accept or refuse any recommended medical treatment. This is relatively easy when people are well and can communicate. Unfortunately, during severe illness, people are often unable to communicate their wishes at the very time that many critical decisions about medical interventions need to be made.

The Medical Directive states a person's wishes for or against types of medical interventions in several key situations, so that the person's wishes can be respected even when he or she cannot communicate.

A Medical Directive only comes into effect if a person becomes incompetent, or unable to make decisions or to express his or her wishes. It can be changed at any time up until then. Decisions not involving incompetence should be discussed directly with the physician.

The Medical Directive also allows for appointing someone to make medical decisions for a person should he or she become unable to make his or her own; this is a proxy or durable power of attorney. The Medical Directive also allows for a statement of wishes concerning organ donation.

A copy of the completed Medical Directive should be given to a person's regular physician and to his or her family or friend to ensure that it is available when necessary.

Medical Directives should be seen not only as legal protection for personal rights but also as a guide to a person's physician. Discussion of Medical Directives with the physician can help in making plans for health care that suit a person's values.

* * *

A person's wishes usually reflect personal, philosophical, and religious views, so an individual may wish to discuss the issues with his or her family, friends, and religious mentor as well.

Before recording a personal statement in the Medical Directive, it may be helpful to consider the following question: What kind of medical condition, if any, would make life hard enough that attempts to prolong life would be undesirable? Some may say none. For others the answer may be intractable pain. For other people the limit may be permanent dependence on others, or irreversible mental damage, or inability to exchange affection.

Under such circumstances as these, the goal of medical treatment may be to secure comfort only, or it may be to use ordinary treatments while avoiding heroic ones, or to use treatments that offer improved function (palliation), or to use all appropriate interventions to prolong life independent of quality. These points may help to clarify a person's thoughts and wishes.

### Durable Power of Attorney

I understand that my wishes expressed in these four cases may not cover all possible aspects of my care if I become incompetent. I also may be undecided about whether I want a particular treatment or not. Consequently there may be a need for someone to accept or refuse medical interventions for me in consultation with my physicians. I authorize:

______________________________

______________________________

as my proxy(s) to make the decision for me whenever my wishes expressed in this document are insufficient or undecided.

Should there be any disagreement between the wishes I have indicated in this document and the decisions favored by my above-named proxy(s), I wish my proxy(s) to have authority over my Medical Directive/I wish my Medical Directive to have authority over my proxy(s). (Please delete as necessary.)

Should there be any disagreement between the wishes of my proxies,

______________________________

shall have final authority.

**Organ Donation**

I hereby make this anatomical gift to take effect upon my death.

I give: ________ my body; ________ any needed organs or parts; ________ the following organs or parts ____________________ to the following person or institution: ________ the physician in attendance at my death; ________ the hospital in which I die; ________ the following named physician, hospital, storage bank, or other medical institution ____________________; for the following purposes: ________ any purpose authorized by law; ________ transplantation; ________ therapy; ________ research; ________ medical education.

**My Personal Statement** (use another page if necessary.)

______________________________

______________________________

______________________________

Signed ____________ Date ____________

Witness ____________ Date ____________

Witness ____________ Date ____________

*TABLE 12.3*

| Reasons for Not Executing an Advance Directive | | |
|---|---|---|
| ***Living Will (n = 151)*** | ***n*** | ***(%)*** |
| Deference to others and putting it off | 75 | 50% |
| Barriers and difficulties in getting documents executed | 30 | 20 |
| Accept/rely on present arrangements or state of affairs | 27 | 18 |
| Other reasons | 19 | 12 |
| ***Surrogate Appointment or Health-Care Proxy (n = 63)*** | | |
| Deference to others and putting it off | 31 | 49 |
| Barriers and difficulties in getting documents executed | 07 | 11 |
| Accept/rely on present arrangements or state of affairs | 15 | 24 |
| Other reasons | 10 | 16 |

*From D. M. High, "Advance Directives and the Elderly: A Study of Intervention Strategies to Increase Use" in* The Gerontologist, *33:342–349. Copyright © 1993 The Gerontological Society of America.*

this sample who had filed a legal will directing disposition of their assets (High, 1993). Table 12.3 provides the reasons given for not using the option of an advance directive (a living will or a surrogate appointment/health care proxy) despite having participated in an educational intervention designed to increase use (High, 1993).

High (1991,1993) has recently questioned the assumption underlying living wills, durable powers of attorney, and medical directives, that is, that individual self-determination is better than interdependent decision making among family members. Individual autonomy in our culture has been elevated to the exclusion of family participation (High, 1991). Some believe that family members' judgments are biased in choosing health care options for relatives and that families will make poor decisions or be unwilling to carry out the wishes of loved ones, preferring to have independent verification of an individual's specific health-care choices (Zweibel & Cassel, 1989). High (1991) questions whether 'outside' agents such as institutions, lawyers, or medical personnel should be given such powers under the illusion that it is the individual's self-determination at work when a decision is made. Outside agents are assumed to be capable of *substituted judgments* that are closest to those which the individual would have made. Is the converse true, however, that the elderly will be served less well when family members participate in health-care decision making (High, 1991)? There is a presupposition that family members cannot and will not provide the direction and autonomy established by the individual needing health care choices; however, this belief has not been supported (Horowitz, Silverstone, & Reinhardt, 1991). Currently, the courts require an individual's family to prove (i.e., provide evidence) what an individual's health care choices might be, preferably in terms of the individual actually anticipating a specific medical situation (High, 1991, 1993). However, there is no burden of proof on the state to show that a family's decisions would be biased or contrary to the wishes of the individual (Annas, 1990; High, 1993; Kapp, 1991; Pearlman, 1991).

Kapp (1991) has recently summarized the benefits of *family-shared decision making* regarding medical decisions and concludes that such processes (1) are empowering to the older person, (2) alleviate emotional strain on both the older individual as well as family members and (3) are helpful to those having to make substituted judgments about health care choices for the older person. Legal remedies, based on property law, exist that could be helpful in mediating those special instances in which family members disagree about health-care decisions, when the possibility of coercion has arisen in making treatment choices, or where a conflict of interest appears. Most family relationships permit intimate moral relationships to flourish and genuine care and concern are communicated in open dialogue (Lambert, Gibson, & Nathanson, 1990). "The family can be presumed to be the best decision maker, not only regarding knowledge about and concern for the relative but because family members embody the social nexus of values shared by the family unit" (High, 1991, p. 617). It is through such dialogue that society will ensure the autonomy that older individuals need to govern their health care choices (High, 1991; Jecker, 1990; Kapp, 1991).

***DNR Orders*** The state of New York in 1988 passed a **Do Not Resuscitate Act** that has become a model for other states seeking guidance in this complex health-care area. Do Not Resuscitate (DNR) orders in the charts of hospitalized patients specifically direct that physicians and hospital staff *not* initiate resuscitation measures (such as CPR, electric shock, medication injected into the heart, open chest massage, or tracheotomy) when breathing or heartbeat has stopped. Similar DNR orders apply to nursing home residents for whom transfer to a hospital for these procedures will not be permitted. Hospital and nursing home residents themselves can request and consent to a DNR order *orally,* provided two witnesses are present, one of whom is a physician. DNR orders can also be made in writing prior to or during hospitalization as long as two adults are present to sign as witnesses (just as a living will provides). Limits on DNR orders can also be established in advance (e.g., do not resuscitate if a terminal illness or irreversible coma exists).

The obligations and choices physicians have in following DNR orders are also specified. A physician given a DNR order has three choices: (1) enter the order as given in the chart and follow the specifications; (2) transfer a patient requesting DNR orders to another physician; or (3) bring the DNR order to the attention of a mediation panel in the hospital or nursing home (mediation panels cannot overrule a patient's request for a DNR). For individuals who are incapacitated or mentally unable to elect a DNR decision, a list of those who may make this decision on the patient's behalf has been established. These proxy decision makers may include (1) a person previously designated to make a DNR decision; (2) a court-appointed guardian; (3) the closest relative; or (4) a close friend. The proxy decision must represent the patient's own wishes, religious and moral beliefs, or best interests. Any family disagreements regarding DNR decisions must be mediated. For those with no one to serve as proxy, a DNR decision may be made if two physicians agree that resuscitation would be medically futile. DNR orders may be changed by informing the relevant health-care staff of the changes using appropriate notification procedures (New York State Department of Health, 1988).

## Euthanasia

**Euthanasia,** or mercy killing, is the act of putting to death an individual with a terminal illness, a massive disability, or an intensely painful disease. **Active euthanasia**—death induced by positive action such as the injection of a deadly drug or the administration of a drug overdose—may be contrasted with **passive euthanasia**—death induced by the failure to act or the withdrawal of a life-sustaining medication or machine. Physicians, in taking the Hippocratic Oath, have vowed to act "to benefit the sick" by choosing treatments believed "most helpful to patients." Any form of euthanasia is antithetical to these principles. Similarly, it is illegal for laypersons to engage in euthanasia in every country worldwide, although the Netherlands exempts a few specific conditions (Cutter, 1991; Levinson, 1987). Cutter (1991) notes that in the Netherlands, a physician may assist in a patient-requested suicide and not be prosecuted as long as

1. at least two physicians agree the request by the patient is legitimate and understandable given the current situation,
2. the patient's condition is intolerable and no hope for improvement exists,
3. no relief is apparent or likely to emerge in the immediate future,
4. the patient is competent to make such a request, and
5. the patient has made the request repeatedly over an extended period of time.

In our society, we neither encourage nor support legally the practice of euthanasia. Leading ethicists have raised questions about euthanasia: As our medical technology becomes more and more sophisticated, are we adding to life or merely prolonging death? Could families be spared agonizing decisions, painful memories and guilt, and considerable financial expense if euthanasia were legal? Should hospitals and the health-care system use increasingly scarce resources and expensive nursing and medical care for patients with little or no hope of recovery? These decisions are becoming a matter of joint responsibility among all concerned: patient, physician, and family members. Research Focus 12.2 presents one illustration of the ethical difficulties in prolonging life.

In complex situations like the one illustrated in Research Focus 12.2, it appears that physicians, the elderly person, and family members engage in sharing moral responsibility for treatment decisions (Slomka, 1992). However, it is important to examine the type of decisions that are made and the degree of responsibility accepted by individuals. For example, when a decision is made to withdraw a life-sustaining treatment, such as tube feeding that has already been initiated, and the outcome will be the death of the individual, the moral responsibility is typically shared among family members. Yet, when a decision is made to withhold treatment that could delay a person's death, such as in cases of DNR orders, the moral responsibility appears to be assigned to the right of choice or individual autonomy of the older person (Slomka, 1992). Slomka (1992) raises the possibility that the assignment of moral responsibility in either the case of withdrawing treatment or withholding treatment is designed to assist all participants in an illusion of choice; that is, physicians, family members, and older persons near death negotiate a set of meanings about impending death, share moral responsibility differentially for the failure of medicine, in order to eventually accept death.

## *The Ethics of Prolonging Life*

Many clinical, ethical, and legal issues arise when we ask whether it is justifiable to withhold or discontinue aggressive life support to allow severely ill or injured persons to die. In our pluralistic society, the attempt to resolve these issues generates new conflicts within medical ethics, the law, and the general perceptions of the public.

**The Refusal to Prolong Life: A Case Study**

A 47-year-old woman suffers from a progressive spinal muscular atrophy called **Kugelberg-Welander's disease.** She has deteriorated to the point where she cannot move or eat by herself. She is intelligent and utterly lucid, knows she has an untreatable fatal disease, realizes she must remain on a respirator with a tracheotomy for the rest of her life, and recognizes that she could live for quite a while. Should a doctor respect this woman's lucid, repeated, and unvacillating demand to disconnect the respirator?

Many would hold to the principle that the will of the patient, not the health of the patient, should be the supreme law. The Vatican Declaration on Euthanasia gives additional support to self-determination. It proposes that

> One cannot impose on anyone the obligation to have recourse to a technique which is already in use but which carries a risk or is burdensome. Such a refusal is not the equivalent of suicide; on the contrary it should be considered as an acceptance of the human condition, or a wish to avoid the application of a medical procedure disproportionate to the results that can be expected, or a desire not to impose excessive expense on the family or community. (Vatican Congregation for the Doctrine of the Faith, 1980)

These clear and reasonable principles may conflict sharply with strongly held clinical perceptions and certain dominant values in our culture. For example, a doctor may be repulsed by the thought of disconnecting a respirator from the intelligent, conscious, and lucid patient described above; particularly when her prognosis is for continued life over an extensive period of time. This reluctance may stem from bonds to this woman forged during preceding fights for life. Distressed family members may also offer sharp dissent when a patient refuses or wants to discontinue life support.

Clinical ethics involve more than the deductive application of principles to cases of this sort. Physicians may experience the "executioner syndrome" when a lucid patient asks to discontinue life support; the physician must weigh the patient's desires against the personal perception that to do so would be to become a killer.

From D. J. Roy, D. Verret, and C. Roberge, "Death, Dying, and the Brain: Ethical Moments in Critical Care Medicine" in *Critical Care Clinics,* 2 (1): 168–169. Copyright © W. B. Saunders Co., Philadelphia, PA. Reprinted by permission.

## *Sociohistorical and Sociocultural Views of Death*

*For certain is death for the born*
*And certain is birth for the dead*
*Therefore over the inevitable*
*Thou shouldst not grieve.*
—Bhagavad Gita

Historically, the relationship between death and age has changed considerably (Kalish, 1985). In earlier times, death occurred with equal probability among young infants and young children, adolescents, young adults, and older individuals. As we have advanced in the treatment of disease and improved the likelihood that infants will reach adulthood and old age, growing old has acquired a parallel meaning: aging means drawing close to death (Kalish, 1985). Life expectancy has increased from 47.3 years for a person born in 1900 to more than 75.7 years for a person born in 1991 (Van Nostrand, 1993a). Over the years, death has become closely associated with old age, although with the increase in AIDS-related death throughout the life span, including infancy and childhood, our society is beginning to recognize that death is not only an old age phenomenon (Callan, 1990).

## The Different Meanings of Death

The recent change in the causes of death has led to a variety of different meanings for death in our society. Kalish (1985) notes that death has become an important *organizer* of time. Older individuals are more likely than younger people to use their current age to mark their probable longevity (Keith, 1981–1982; Reynolds & Kalish, 1974). Some authors (e.g., Shneidman, 1992) have noted how aging makes one appreciate the importance of time and the fleeting or transitory nature of life itself. Death also is important as a passage or *transition* (Kalish, 1985). Nearly 75 percent of an American sample of older adults reported they believed in and hoped for some form of life after death (Argyle & Beit-Hallahmi, 1975; Kalish, 1976; Kalish & Reynolds, 1981). Finally, death is a significant *loss* experience: loss of immediate experience, of memories of past events, people, and places; loss of being able to achieve, produce, or create; loss of body, mind, personal identity, and physical existence (Kalish, 1985). In the eyes of current experts, individuals anticipating their own death and the attendant losses begin to grieve for themselves, often leading to depression, hopelessness, and isolation (Shneidman, 1992).

## Attitudes toward Death

Just as each person must come to terms with death, each society in history has had to confront death. The ancient Greeks faced death as they faced life—openly and directly. To live a full life and die with glory was the prevailing attitude among the Greeks. Currently, our society largely avoids or denies death. Such denial can take many forms:

- The tendency of the funeral industry to gloss over death and to fashion lifelike qualities in the physical appearance of the dead
- The adoption of euphemistic language for death, such as *passing on, passing away,* and *no longer with us*
- The persistent search for the fountain of youth in cosmetics, plastic surgery, vitamins, and exercise
- The rejection and isolation of the aged, who remind us of the inevitability of death
- The appealing concept of a pleasant and rewarding afterlife, suggesting we are immortal
- Emphasis by the medical community on prolonging biological life even among patients whose chances of recovery or quality lifestyle are nil
- The failure to discuss emotional reactions to death with our children
- The attempt to cover up emotions at funerals and afterward as mourners adopt a "stiff upper lip" or are encouraged to "get over it quickly and get on with life."

Though Americans are conditioned from early life to live as though they were immortal, this idea cannot easily be maintained elsewhere in the world. People are more conscious of death in times of natural disaster, plague, and war. Death crowds the streets of Calcutta and poverty-stricken villages of Africa. Children live with malnutrition and disease, mothers lose as many babies as they see survive into adulthood, and it is the rare family that remains intact, insulated from death. Even in geographical areas where life is better and health and maturity may be reasonable expectations, the presence of dying people in the house, the large attendance at funerals, and the daily contact with those who are dying help prepare the young for the fact of death and provide them with guidelines about how we die. In the United States, we encounter death relatively late in childhood. In one recent study, Dickinson (1992) asked 440 college students to identify their first experience with death. The average age reported by the students was nearly 8 years and centered on the death of a relative for 57 percent of the sample or the death of a pet for 28 percent of the students. Even years later, students recalled vividly their reactions, most typically crying, the reactions and comments of others, as well as very specific details of the funeral (Dickinson, 1992).

Most societies throughout history have had philosophical or religious beliefs about death, and most societies have some form of ritual that surrounds death. For example, elderly Eskimos in Greenland who could no longer contribute to their society might walk off alone, never to be seen again, or might be given a departure ceremony at which they are honored, then ritually killed. Freuchen (1961) describes such a departure ceremony among one Eskimo tribe:

> In some tribes, an old man wants his oldest son or favorite daughter to be the one to put the string around his neck and hoist him to his death. This was always done at the height of the party where good things were being eaten, where everyone—including the one who was about to die—felt happy and gay, and which would end with the angakok conjuring and dancing to chase out the evil spirits. At the end of his performance, he would give a special rope made of seal and walrus skin to the "executioner" who then placed it over the beam of the roof of the house and fastened it to the neck of the old man. Then the two rubbed noses, and the young man pulled the rope. Everybody in the house either helped or sat on the rope so as to have the honor of bringing the suffering one to the Happy Hunting Grounds where there would always be light and plenty of game of all kinds. (pp. 194–195)

In most societies, death is not viewed as the end of existence; although the body has died, the spirit is believed to live on. This is true as well in most religions: Ardent Irish Catholics celebrate a wake as the arrival of the dead person's soul in God's heavenly home; the Hindu believes in the continued existence of the person's life through reincarnation; Hungarian gypsies gather at the bedside of a dying loved one to ensure support and an open window so that the spirit can leave and find the way to heaven. Perceptions of why people die are many and varied. Death may be punishment for one's sins, an act of atonement, or the action of a higher being or deity (Kalish, 1985). In some societies, long life is the reward for having performed many acts of kindness (Cavanaugh, 1993), whereas in other cultures longevity is linked to having wisely conserved one's energy and vitality in youth.

## A Developmental View of Death

In general, we adopt attitudes toward death consistent with our culture, our family values, and our cognitive and emotional maturity (Kastenbaum, 1985). Clearly, attitudes toward death change as we ourselves age.

Children two or three years old are rarely upset by the sight of a dead animal or by hearing that a person has died. Children at this age really do not understand death cognitively or emotionally. They may even blame themselves for the deaths of those closest to them, illogically believing that they caused the death by disobeying the person who died. For young children, death is equated with sleep. They expect that someone who has died will wake up, return to be with them, and come back to life. Five-year-olds, for example, do not believe that death is final and expect those who have died to come back to life (Speece & Brent, 1984). Although few cross-cultural comparisons of children's understanding of death have been conducted, given the Piagetian cognitive characteristics of preoperational thinking, children up to 7 or 8 years of age do not appear to understand that death is universal, inevitable, and irrevocable. Most preoperational children (those of preschool age) assume that dead people continue to experience the same life processes as they did when they were alive. The dead simply have "moved away" and continue to live in Heaven, working, eating, bathing, shopping, and playing. Preschoolers believe that those who die continue to have concrete needs, feelings, and experiences as they did when they were alive (Blueband-Langner, 1977). Children older than 7 or 8 years of age view death as an event that will occur for some people, but not all. Usually by age 9 or so, children recognize both the finality and universality of death (Nagy, 1948).

Adolescents typically deny death, especially the possibility of their own death. The topic is avoided, glossed over, kidded about, neutralized, and controlled as adolescents distance themselves from death. Adolescents do, nonetheless, experience a good deal of anxiety about death.

The awareness of death increases with age, yet older persons also show a greater acceptance and less fear of death than younger or middle-aged individuals (Woodruff-Pak, 1988). In her review of research, Woodruff-Pak (1988) confirms that adolescents and young adults are most fearful of death, although older people are most concerned about the circumstances surrounding their death (Kalish, 1976; Kastenbaum, 1992). DeVries, Bluck, and Birren (1993) have also reported that in comparison to younger adults, middle-aged respondents tend to focus more detail and attention on the process of dying than on the event of one's death; Kastenbaum (1992) finds that older adults are most concerned not about death but rather the context and situation in which they will die. Kalish (1985) notes that the elderly show (1) greater knowledge of the limits of their life and a more realistic assessment of their longevity; (2) an awareness that many significant life roles are no longer available; (3) a sense of achievement in being able to live beyond normal life expectancy, or alternatively, a sense of loss if unable to reach expected years of survival; and (4) a sense of sadness, loss, and emptiness as loved ones and close friends die—but also *relief and guilt* as they continue to escape death.

Fear of death and death anxiety, however, may not represent a single, unidimensional construct for individuals at any age (Gresser, Wong & Reker (1987–88). Even adults participate in active denial and avoidance of death. Kastenbaum (1985) has noted that nearly 25 percent of all patients near the end of life deny that they are dying and Callan (1990) noted a strong belief in invulnerability among gay men with AIDS.

## Death Education

Death education has become important in helping people who are facing death, as well as their friends and relatives, to cope not only with the emotions and anticipated losses associated with death but also with the death itself—the rituals, such as funerals, and the intense feelings of grief, bereavement, and mourning. Death education allows people an opportunity to learn about themselves, the relationships they have developed and are about to lose, and the meaning of their own existence. It is not always possible to anticipate and prepare for a loved one's death, and often death educators deal with people after a sudden or unexpected death. Regardless of the circumstances, death education is playing an increasingly important role in adjustment to death and loss. For some it is an antidote to the denial and avoidance of death that has been a part of our Puritanical cultural traditions; for others it provides a model for how we could change to provide continuous death education throughout the life span, that is, to view death as a natural part of our living and existence.

Despite the appearance of an age-related decline in death anxiety, some researchers suggest that age itself is *not* the best predictor of death anxiety; rather, they suggest that better predictors are past experiences and confrontations with death (Kastenbaum, 1992; Shneidman, 1992). Numerous therapeutic programs have recognized the need to provide an opportunity for children and adolescents to discuss their responses to the deaths of people close to them (Attig, 1992; McDonald, 1981). Sandler, West, Baca, and Pillov et al. (1992) provided therapeutic death education for children and remaining family members who had experienced the death of a parent. The education intervention was designed to prevent mental health problems and results indicated clear support for the program's effectiveness. Through open exchange guided by a mental health professional, children and the remaining family members enhanced the warmth and openness in their relationships despite feelings of loss, sadness, and abandonment. The discussion sessions offered to all family members an opportunity to derive mutual social support and a forum for exchanging grief-related issues and feelings. Among the older children, reductions in behavioral acting out, depression, and other such problems were noted.

In death education programs, whether for children or adults, professional counselors emphasize honest and open exchange as the best strategy to help people cope with death. Most of us have grown up in a society in which death is rarely discussed. In one investigation that examined the attitudes of thirty thousand young adults, more than 30 percent said they could not recall any discussion of death during their childhoods; an equal number said that although death was discussed, the discussion took place in an uncomfortable atmosphere (Shneidman, 1992). It has also been found that the majority of young people initially became aware of death sometime between the ages of 5 and 10

(Dickinson, 1992). More than half of the respondents said that the death of a relative, typically a grandparent, represented their first personal confrontation with death. Generally, the more freedom there was to discuss death, the more mature (emotionally and cognitively) were the attitudes toward death. It seems that even religious orientation plays a role. The data suggest a *curvilinear* pattern, with strong or weak religious *beliefs* leading to less fear of death but moderate beliefs associated with higher levels of death anxiety (Feifel & Nagy, 1981; Kalish, 1985; Nelson & Nelson, 1973).

Middle adulthood, you may recall, is a time when men and women begin to think more intensely about how much time is left in their lives. Middle age may be a time for talking with other family members about death as life insurance needs grow, as wills are written or revised, as one's children reach early adulthood, and as one's parents age and die. Certainly the elderly have considerable direct experience with death as friends and relatives become ill and die. With middle age comes experience with death and loss, which leads to a greater differentiation between the concept of death and the concept of dying than at younger ages (DeVries, Bluck, & Birren, 1993). Both men and women respondents, even in middle age, however, displayed far more knowledge and detail in their understanding of death than they did in their understanding of dying (DeVries, Bluck, & Birren, 1993).

Kastenbaum (1981) suggests that the elderly may experience **bereavement overload** from the cumulative effects of having to cope with the deaths of friends, neighbors, and relatives in a short time span. The elderly are forced to examine the meanings of life and death much more often than those in middle age or young adulthood. Bereavement overload has also been reported among gay men coping with the cumulative effects of multiple losses of close friends and lovers (Neugebauer, Rabkin, & Williams et al., 1992). The greater the number of losses, the more common and intense bereavement reactions (Neugebauer et al., 1992). There are also, of course, considerable individual differences. Some elderly are able to see their lives draw to a close and recognize that there is not much else to live for, whereas others cling passionately to life, savoring each activity, personal relationship, and achievement (Kastenbaum, 1969; Kalish, 1987).

How are death education programs structured? No single approach has proven successful above all others. Many experts believe that effective approaches must offer individuals, both young and old, an opportunity to personalize the learning that occurs, that is, *experiential* or *person-centered death education* (Attig, 1992). Personally experiencing the death of a friend or loved one makes people especially primed for learning about the event—emotionally and intellectually; however, an immediate personal experience with death is not required to participate in experiential or person-centered death education programs. These programs are heavily existential and require participants to share their experiences, inner feelings, and thoughts with methods such as storytelling, to tell of personal encounters with death, as a way of counteracting the tendency to "impersonalize" the event and the learning that occurs. Skilled death educators help individuals to confront death by examining how the experience sheds personal insight into the meaning of life itself (e.g., its finite nature and its uncertainty), what it means to be human (e.g., our vulnerability), and how to respect other persons' lives in leading a humane existence (Attig, 1992).

Other death education programs are far more *didactic* or *instruction-centered* in that people enroll as they might for a course and study the subject matter of death; they are not required to involve themselves personally with the material presented. There are formal lectures and discussions, multimedia presentations, and class trips to hospitals, nursing homes, funeral homes, cemeteries, and hospices. Without some opportunity to reflect on the meaning and experiential component of death, didactic death education programs appear to result in minimal change in attitudes about death (Attig, 1992; Durlak & Riesenberg, 1991).

In one recent study (Hutchison & Scherman, 1992), both didactic and experiential (person-centered) approaches were compared among two groups of adults. At both the conclusion of the study and at an eight-week follow-up, Hutchison and Scherman (1992) reported that didactic death education produced lower scores on the Death Anxiety Scale. There are, as you might imagine, countless problems in evaluating empirical studies in this field, particularly in comparisons between the two approaches. First, those who participate in death education programs represent a sampling bias and controls are difficult to find for comparative purposes. It is also important to realize that there are multiple indicators of program outcome and success; however, research investigators have relied on single measures of program effectiveness, most often attitudinal change rather than behavioral change (Durlak & Riesenberg, 1991). In most of the studies, death education effects are evaluated on a short-term basis and little is known about the long-term persistence of any changes. Durlak and Riesenberg (1991), however, suggest that long-term follow-up is particularly needed. What are participants' changes in attitudes among participants in death education programs going to mean about their future contact with those who are near death? How do they approach preparation of a will or an advance medical directive or the choice of becoming an organ donor?

## *Facing Death*

*Death, the only immortal who treats us all alike, whose pity and whose peace and whose refuge are for all—the soiled and the pure, the rich and the poor, the loved and the unloved.*
—Mark Twain

In his book *The Sane Society,* Erich Fromm (1955) comments, "Man is the only animal that finds his own existence a problem which he has to solve and from which he cannot escape. In the same sense, man is the only animal who knows he must die" (p. 23). It is this knowledge that we will someday die that gives meaning to life, that causes us to establish priorities, and that demands that we use our time wisely. Over the centuries, philosophers, theologians, poets, and psychologists have attempted to explain the phenomenon of death and theorized about why all people must die and whether some form of existence exists beyond life on earth.

Most dying individuals want the opportunity to make some decisions regarding their death. Some individuals want to complete **unfinished business;** for example, resolving problems and mending fences in personal relationships. When asked how they would spend their last six months of life, younger adults described activities

## Swan Songs: Characteristics of Last Compositions

In an article in the journal of *Psychology and Aging,* D. K. Simonton from the University of California at Davis reported the results of his analysis of the final musical works of 172 classical composers. He wondered whether there would be any unique characteristics in the very last musical work or "swan song" of each of these composers.

In a series of complex computer analyses performed on these varied pieces, Simonton surprisingly discovered some commonalities in these final musical compositions. Seven basic variables were used to compare earlier works with the last work of the composer: melodic originality and variation, repertoire popularity, aesthetic significance, listener accessibility, performance duration, and thematic size. Unlike earlier investigators' attempts to examine swan songs, Simonton was able to rule out statistically contaminating factors such as the average age at which the last composition was written and individual differences in terms of fame, reputation, and success. In examining each individual composer's last musical work, or swan song, and comparing it to earlier compositions, Simonton found that the last work was somewhat shorter in length. Swan songs were also typically far more simple in their organization or structure. Also, the swan songs have become some of the most enduring, well-recognized, and cherished pieces in the field of classical music. These musical finales are characterized by a degree of aesthetic significance that earlier works do not have. Examples of legendary swan songs include Mozart's *Requiem,* Tchaikovsky's *Sixth Symphony,* and Schubert's *Unfinished Symphony.* As composers near the end of their lives, their musical works seemed to reveal personal contentment, inner harmony, and acceptance rather than depression, sorrow, or tragedy.

The ability of composers to construct such enduring works at the end of their lives remains puzzling. The swan song structure found by Simonton is understated in its aesthetic beauty and simplicity. Yet the simplicity is not that of a country melody or peasant folk tune. What emerges is the elegance of a musical composition that is not too complex, not too simple; music that is "just right." The swan song demonstrates that the composer knew how to produce a work that presented the pure essence of a feeling, mood, or theme in the clearest and most direct fashion. It might be argued that this happened because the composers knew that their lives were nearly over. However, most of the composers did not know they were near death; they did not consciously attempt to produce a final composition. The swan song phenomenon is even more striking when juxtaposed against possible "false alarms"; many of the composers produced musical works against the backdrop of serious disease that brought them to the brink of death. Yet during these near brushes with death, the musical compositions created are similar to those produced at other times throughout their careers. It is only the swan song that contains the unique qualities that separate it from a composer's earlier musical compositions.

such as traveling and accomplishing things they previously had not done; older adults, in contrast, described more inner-focused activities such as contemplation and meditation (Kalish & Reynolds, 1981). Research Focus 12.3 describes such a shift in focus among classical musical composers nearing the end of life.

In the next section, we examine the often-cited psychological stages of dying developed by Elisabeth Kübler-Ross and then explore the dying phases or dying trajectories. We also consider the concept of appropriate death, as well as the variety of coping strategies individuals develop to deal with the stress of knowing they are dying.

# PSYCHOLOGICAL STAGES OF DYING

## Kübler-Ross's Theory

The most widely cited view of how people cope with death was developed by Elisabeth Kübler-Ross (1969, 1981). This view, however, has received little empirical support and has been the subject of much theoretical criticism (Kastenbaum, 1981; Shneidman, 1980, 1992). Kübler-Ross's theory, which suggests the existence of stages in dealing with the dying process, helped focus professional concern on death education and counseling—topics that had been largely ignored. In her psychiatric work with hospitalized patients dying from cancer, Kübler-Ross first identified and reported the existence of five stages: denial/isolation, anger, bargaining, depression, and acceptance.

In the first stage, a common initial reaction to terminal illness is **denial/isolation.** The individual denies that death is really going to occur, saying, "No, it can't happen to me," "It's not possible," or "There must be a mistake, an error in the laboratory or in the diagnosis." Denial is like shock and is considered a transitory defense. It is eventually replaced with increasing acceptance when the individual confronts such matters as finances, unfinished business, and arrangements for surviving family members.

In the second stage, **anger,** the dying individual recognizes that denial can no longer be maintained; anger, resentment, rage, and envy are expressed directly. Now the issue becomes, "Why me?" At this point, the individual becomes increasingly difficult to care for as anger is displaced and projected onto physicians, nurses, hospital staff, family members, and God. The realization of loss is great, and those who symbolize life, energy, and competent functioning are the targets of the dying individual's resentment and jealousy.

In the third stage, **bargaining,** the individual develops hope that death can somehow be postponed or delayed. Some individuals enter into a brief period of bargaining or negotiation—often with God—as they try to delay their deaths. Psychologically, these people are trying to buy a few more weeks, months, or years in exchange for leading a reformed life or for choosing a life dedicated to God or the service of others.

In the fourth stage, **depression,** the dying individual begins to accept the certainty of his or her death; as she or he recognizes the growing severity of specific symptoms, a period of depression or preparatory grief may appear. The dying individual is often silent, refuses visitors, and spends much of the time crying or grieving. Shneidman (1992) finds individuals at this point mourning their own death, the loss of their special talent and abilities, the loss of their former sense of contentment and well-being, and the loss of their experiences (past, present, and future). Attempts to cheer up dying individuals at this stage should be avoided, says Kübler-Ross, because of the dying person's need to contemplate and grieve over their own impending death.

In the fifth stage, **acceptance,** the individual develops a sense of peace, a unique acceptance of fate, and in many cases, a desire to be left alone. This stage may be devoid of feeling; physical pain and discomfort are often absent. Kübler-Ross describes this stage as the last one before undertaking a long journey and reaching the end of the struggle.

No one has yet been able to provide independent confirmation that people actually go through all five stages in the order described by Kübler-Ross (Kastenbaum, 1981; Schulz & Alderman, 1974; Shneidman, 1973, 1980, 1992). Theoretically and empirically, the stages have raised many questions, although Kübler-Ross feels that she has often been misread and misinterpreted. For instance, she maintains that she never intended the stages to represent an invariant sequence of developmental steps toward death. And she has consistently recognized the importance of individual variation in how we face death (Kübler-Ross, 1974). Nevertheless, Kübler-Ross still believes that the optimal way to face death lies in the sequence she has proposed.

Other investigators have not found the same five stages (Metzger, 1979); many report that a single stage (e.g., depression or denial) dominates the entire dying experience, while still others identify dying patients as being in two or three stages simultaneously (Kalish, 1985; Shneidman, 1973, 1980). The fact that Kübler-Ross used primarily interview data with many young or middle-aged adults without sophisticated statistical evaluations provides yet another criticism of her work. Marshall and Levy (1990) suggest that among such respondents, the experience of anger, bargaining, and depression would be far more likely than among older individuals. Even in Kübler-Ross's earliest work, it is clear that many patients remained at one of the first stages (denial or anger) and never passed through all five stages of the sequence. Moreover, some patients move backward or regress into stages already completed (Shneidman, 1973, 1992). We are left with a provocative and historically important theory of dying, but one that has few developmental or stage properties. In the minds of many critics, the theory, other than serving to stimulate interest and research on the topic of death and dying, has had little utility.

## An Appropriate Death

In a certain sense, the ways in which people face death may simply reflect how they face life. The concept of an **appropriate death** (Weisman, 1972) suggests that individuals should be granted the freedom to face dying as they choose, a death that fits one's expectations and style of coping. An appropriate death permits people to die with dignity on their own terms (Kalish, 1985). There is no mandate to move through a set of stages, no requirement to push to acceptance, no social pressure to face death in a prescriptive way. By permitting individuals an appropriate death, we allow them to maintain a sense of hopefulness. Hopefulness refers to the positive anticipation of the future: birthdays, wedding anniversaries, visits from friends or relatives, seeing the new year arrive. As studies suggest, hopefulness provides one means of control or mastery over terminal illness and allows the process of living to coexist with the process of dying (Kastenbaum, 1981). Some dying persons continue to participate in living each day, *resisting* rather than denying death. Their spirit and hope should not be confused with outright denial; resisting death implies a choice and involves an active decision. With an appropriate death, individuals can maintain their dignity, their self-esteem, their identity, and their individuality. Kalish (1981) notes that "different people die in different ways and experience a variety of feelings and emotions during the process . . ." (p. 186). Kalish (1985) also identified three factors necessary to permit an appropriate death: (1) a warm, intimate personal relationship with family, friends, or health professionals; (2) an open environment in which emotions, information, and the terminal condition can be discussed by all involved; and (3) a sense of meaning derived from this experience, from one's life, or from religion.

**Figure 12.3** Acute, chronic, and terminal phases of the dying process. *From* The Experience of Dying *by E. Mansell Pattison. © 1977 by Prentice-Hall, Inc. Published by permission of Prentice-Hall, Inc., Englewood Cliffs, NJ.*

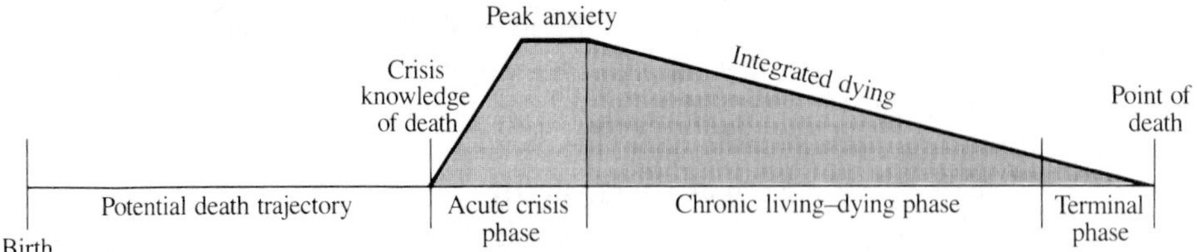


## Pattison's Phases of the Living-Dying Interval

The **trajectory of life** has been defined by E. Mansell Pattison (1977) as our anticipated life span and the plan we make for the way we will live out our life. When an illness or serious injury occurs and leads to a revision of our anticipated life span, the life trajectory must be revised because we perceive that we are likely to die much sooner than we had anticipated. Pattison calls the time interval between our discovery that we will die sooner than we had thought and the time when we actually die the *living-dying interval.* The living-dying interval is characterized by three phases: acute, chronic, and terminal. The goal of those who counsel individuals in the living-dying interval is to assist them in coping with the first or acute phase, to help them to live as reasonably as possible through the second, or chronic phase, and to move them into the third or terminal phase (see figure 12.3). Pattison sees a pattern to the phases. Depending on the nature of the illness, different people may spend vastly different periods of time in each phase. For example, some illnesses allow a pattern of chronic living-dying for only a few weeks; others allow a more protracted period of months or even years, such as may occur with a slow, lingering illness or disease or with someone who has a deteriorating heart condition.

Pattison describes each phase in terms of the individual's reactions and coping needs. In the *acute phase,* individuals face what is probably the most severe crisis in their lives—the realization that they will die sooner than they thought and will not get to accomplish and experience all they had hoped. People in this stage feel immobilized, experience high levels of anxiety, and call into play a number of defense mechanisms to deal with the extreme fear and stress they are confronting. In this phase, people need a great deal of emotional support from others and need help to deal rationally with the fact that they are going to die.

In the *chronic phase,* Pattison believes that individuals begin to confront directly their fear of dying. Fears about loneliness, suffering, separation from loved ones, and the unknown often surface. Health professionals can assist dying people by helping them put life into perspective, working through some of the defense mechanisms, and allowing open discussion of death and basic fears.

In the *terminal phase,* individuals begin to withdraw as their hope of getting better gives way to the realization that they are probably going to get worse. At the end of this phase, individuals turn inward, distancing themselves from people and everyday experience.

Just as Kübler-Ross's stages are neither fixed nor invariant for all people, Pattison's dying phases do not represent a single trajectory descriptive of every person's death; each person spends different amounts of time in each of the three phases. Some have questioned the need to describe the time spent in each phase of Pattison's dying trajectory, preferring to examine the *process* of dying; for some people dying is rapid and sudden with little time to prepare, for others it is preparation that lasts for years.

Marsall and Levy (1990) have considered that a dying person is involved in a *dying career,* which begins with the realization that one's time left to live is limited and finite. The dying careers of seventeen people (21 to 71 years old) who were coping with AIDS were recently documented by McCain and Gramling (1992). The dying career was marked from the initial diagnosis of being HIV seropositive, through the diagnosis of AIDS, to impending death. McCain and Gramling (1992) identified three processes involved in the dying career of these individuals: (1) living with dying, (2) fighting the sickness, and (3) getting worn out. Each of us begins his or her dying career from the time that we realize emotionally that indeed we are all mortal. As each generation dies before us (i.e., great-grandparents, grandparents, and parents) we come to understand that our own time is drawing closer; with the death of parents, we have no one left to stand before us: our generation's death is next and our dying career nearer to its end.

## *Communicating with the Dying Person*

To help the dying person and the family cope more effectively with death, health-care professionals, as we have seen in the section on death education, are placing increasing emphasis on effective communication, openness, and understanding. We discuss these issues in this section. We'll then examine the contexts in which people die—another important issue death education programs address—in the next section.

### Listening to the Dying Person

It is generally agreed that the situation is optimal when the dying person knows she is dying and significant others also recognize this fact. Research has consistently revealed that people believe dying persons have the right to know their condition and prognosis (Kalish, 1985). This is in contrast to **mutual pretense,** when the dying person, friends, relatives, and staff pretend that the person will recover (Glaser & Strauss, 1965). With mutual pretense, people are isolated from each other at a time when they should be close and able to freely express their thoughts and feelings (Kalish, 1985). Richard Kalish (1981) describes the advantages of an open-awareness context for dying persons:

1. Dying individuals can close life in accord with their own ideas about proper dying.
2. They can complete some plans and projects, make arrangements for survivors, and participate in decisions about a funeral and burial.

### *Research Focus 12.4*

## *Open Communication with the Dying Person*

My 81-year-old aunt was extremely ill and had been for two years; the indications were that she would probably not live for many more weeks. My home was 800 miles away, but I was able to get to visit her and my uncle for a couple of days. It bothered me to see her hooked into a machine that held her life; the ugly wig she had worn during the past couple of years had been discarded, and there were only a few wisps of hair left, but at least they were hers. Her teeth had been placed in the drawer by her bed since she couldn't take solid food and at this point she was not concerned about how she looked.

My uncle and I were in her room talking with her as she moved in and out of awareness. He was standing at the foot of the bed and I was sitting next to her, holding her hand. He began to talk to her about coming to visit me as soon as she could get up and around again, probably next summer. I noticed that she tuned his comments out. Then I found a pretext to get him out of the room.

When we were alone, I stood up and kissed her, I'd like to say that it was easy, but it really wasn't. I told her that I loved her, and I realized that I had never said that to her before, hadn't even thought about it, hadn't even consciously thought that I loved her. I just . . . loved her.

Then I said, "Bea, I have to leave now. I may never see you again, and I want you to know how much I love you." Her eyes were closed and she was breathing strangely, but she winced at my words, and I became frightened that I'd said too much, so I hesitated. "Well, I hope that I'll see you again, but I might not." And I left.

She died before I could visit again, and I always wondered whether I should have said what I did, but it seemed important to say it. Even if it pained her to hear me, she knew it was true, and she had not shrunk from painful situations before. It had been easy for me over many years to talk and write about death and dying, but it was very difficult for me to be in the situation where someone I loved was dying. I did what I have told other people to do, and it wasn't at all natural—I had to force myself. But when I heard, three weeks later, that she had died, I considered myself fortunate to have had the chance to be with her before she died and to have been both caring and honest. (p. 172)



3. They have the opportunity to reminisce, to converse with others who have been important in their lives, and to be near to death conscious of what life has been like.
4. They have more understanding of what is happening within their bodies and of what the medical staff is doing.

It may be easier to die when people we love can converse freely with us about what is happening, even if it entails considerable sadness. Research Focus 12.4 describes a circumstance in which open communication with a dying person occurs and proves beneficial.

For the dying person, external accomplishments and continued achievements become less possible. The focus of communication thus needs to be directed more at internal processes, past experiences, endearing memories, and personal successes. A caring relationship is a very important aspect of the dying person's life. But such caring does not have to come from a mental health professional; a concerned nurse, an attentive physician, an interested chaplain, a sensitive spouse, or a caring friend all provide important communication resources for the dying person. In such interactions and communications, we should try to emphasize the person's strengths and preparation for the remainder of life. When hospital-based adult volunteers, who were assisting families in coping with impending death and subsequent bereavement,

## Research Focus 12.5

### The Denial of Dying

Denial can be a protective mechanism that enables people to cope with the torturous feelings that accompany the realization that they are going to die. People who are dying can either deny the existence of information about their impending death or they can reinterpret the meaning of the information to avoid its negative implications. There are three forms of denial (Weisman, 1972). The first involves the denial of facts. For example, a woman who has been told by her physician that a scheduled operation is for cancer believes that the operation is for a benign tumor. The second form of denial involves implications. A man accepts the fact that he has a disease but denies that it will end in death. A third form of denial involves extinction, which is limited to people who accept a diagnosis and its implications but still act as if they were going to live through the ordeal. This last form of denial does not apply to people whose deep religious convictions include some form of belief in immortality.

Another classification includes the categories of *brittle* and *adaptive denial.* Brittle denial involves anxiety and agitation. The individual often rejects attempts to improve his or her psychological adaptation to impending death. However, adaptive denial occurs when the individual decides not to dwell on this aspect of his or her life but to emphasize strengths and opportunities during what remains of life. Adaptive deniers want help and support. Such adaptive denial fits well with the ideas of perceived control and the elimination of learned helplessness.

In discussing the role of denial, Richard Kalish (1981) concluded that denial can be adaptive, maladaptive, or even both at the same time. One can call on denial to avoid the destructive impact of shock by delaying the necessity of dealing with one's death. Further, denial can insulate a person from coping with feelings of anger and hurt, emotions that may intrude on other behaviors and feelings because they are so intense.

felt that appropriate caring relationships and open communication had been established among involved family members, health-care professionals, and the dying person, they strongly believed that the illness and the person's death had been very well managed (Couldrick, 1992).

Likewise, the need for open disclosure of dying is vitally important and has an impact among the institutionalized elderly (Lavigne-Pley & Levesque, 1992). Older individuals who are institutionalized do not want to be kept in the dark regarding the condition of roommates, acquaintances, or friends who reside with them. Of twenty-five institutionalized elderly in one exploratory investigation, twenty-one reported that they wanted to be informed of the impending death of a well-known peer. When asked if the institutional staff had provided or withheld this information in the past, twenty of the twenty-five residents reported having an experience in which the staff did not identify for them when a peer was dying (Lavigne-Pley & Levesque, 1992). One of the consequences of withholding information about the impeding death of a well-known peer was that residents believed that the staff who cared for them were essentially indifferent to the death of an elderly person (Lavigne-Pley & Levesque, 1992).

## Denial of Death in the Dying Person

Not all people close to death are able to communicate openly. Denial is characteristic of some individuals' approach to death. In fact, it is not unusual for some dying individuals to continue to deny death right to the end. Life without hope is unbearable, and denial serves to protect them from the tortuous reality that they are going to die. Research Focus 12.5 describes denial in coping with impending death.

Some psychologists believe that the more denial an individual has, the more difficulty he or she will have facing death and dying in a peaceful and dignified way. Others feel that not confronting death until the very end may be highly adaptive (Kalish, 1981, 1987; Lifton, 1977; Shneidman, 1973, 1992).

Denial of death takes many forms (Weisman, 1972). For example, a man scheduled for an operation for cancer of the colon denies the facts and believes that the operation is only for benign polyps. Refusing to acknowledge the implications of a disease or a life-threatening situation is another form of denial. For example, a woman may accept the fact that she has a severe kidney disease but deny its life-threatening consequences. Finally, we may deny our own mortality; that is, even if we accept biological death, we maintain faith in our spiritual immortality.

Denial can be used adaptively to delay dealing with one's death and thus delay the shock, and it can insulate an individual from having to cope with intense feelings of anger and hurt. Yet, denial does have maladaptive features. For example, it may keep us from seeking medical diagnosis and treatment when life-threatening symptoms appear, or it may block communication and other forms of adjustment to dying.

The use of denial must be evaluated in terms of its adaptive qualities for the individual (Kalish, 1981). Taylor and her colleagues (1992) have reported that denial and active distortion was characteristic of a group of gay men, all of whom had tested positive for the AIDS virus. Compared to a group of gay men who had not tested positive for the virus, those who were HIV positive believed that they would not develop AIDS, despite the evidence that they were carrying the virus. Taylor and her colleagues (1992) suggest that such "unrealistic optimism" helped these men cope with the predictable progression of the disease . . . and ultimately death. Denial, avoidance, and active distortion are common among people facing the inevitability of death. Such strategies help people cope and actively manage the stress that is related to the knowledge that their own death is inevitable (Taylor et al., 1992).

## *The Contexts in Which We Die*

### Home and Hospital

Most people in the United States, Canada, and England die in some type of health-care institution, typically a general hospital (Cartwright, Hockey, & Anderson, 1973; Kalish, 1985; Lerner, 1970; Marshall, 1980). The majority of individuals, when asked where they would want to die, indicate a preference to be at home (Kalish & Reynolds, 1981); very few young adults asked to imagine their death scene actually visualize themselves dying in a hospital (Kastenbaum & Norman, 1990). However, dying people do feel they may be a burden at home, recognize the problem of limited space, and know they may place undue stress on family members. Those who are dying also worry about the competency and availability of emergency medical treatment if they remain at home. Hospitals offer a number of advantages to the dying person and the family: professional staff members are available and advanced medical equipment is accessible. Yet a hospital may not be the best location for the dying person to engage in meaningful, intimate relationships or to retain autonomy. Dying at home is a choice many elderly individuals cannot elect, since they typically require extensive medical care, are often in failing condition, and require sophisticated nursing skills (Kalish, 1985).

## Hospice Programs

The **hospice** provides an alternative to dying at home or in a hospital. The hospice blends institutional care and home care and provides some significant innovations designed to humanize the end-of-life experience for the dying individual as well as all who interact with this person. Many experts on the care of the dying view the hospice as a unique and humanistic program for the care of the terminally ill, particularly the elderly (Kastenbaum, 1985). The hospice movement has attracted interest among many health-care providers in the United States; by 1987 there were nearly two hundred hospices nationwide (Kitch, 1987). The hospice program emanates from the pioneering work in London, England, of Dr. Cicely Saunders, medical director of St. Christopher's Hospice (Saunders, 1977). When medical treatments are no longer effective and when hospitalization is inappropriate, the hospice may be chosen (Kalish, 1985).

Most hospice programs advocate two goals: (1) the control of pain for dying individuals, many of whom have cancer, and (2) the creation of an open, intimate, and supportive environment to share the ending of life with loved ones and those providing care. The hospice maintains the humanity, dignity, and personal identity of each dying individual. Pain control is under the direction of the patient and medications that preserve alertness are employed. Thus, patients do not need to wait until they are overwhelmed with pain to ask for assistance. In one hospice program, pain is managed by the dying person, using standing physician orders for drugs that are administered in conjunction with both staff assessments of consciousness and a log or pain diary that is kept (McCracken & Gerdsen, 1991). In the hospice, the dying patient remains an integral part of his or her family. The family is welcomed at any time and the entire staff is skilled in death education and counseling. Staff not only help the patient, but also help the family in discussing their feelings over the impending death, the meaning of the loss, and the significance of the dying person in their own lives.

McCracken & Gerdsen (1991) have developed a hospice program that promotes a "comfortable and satisfying death" by administering care and support as tailored to three phases of death: (1) realization of terminal status, (2) imminent death, and (3) *postvention* following death, that is, intervention with survivors up to one year after the person's death. Staff regularly provide psychosocial assessments of the needs of the dying person and the family, paying special attention to their emotional needs and day-to-day problems. All are preparing for the actual death, and staff members provide special support at that time. The formalized postvention bereavement program that extends for up to one year is an important component of this specific hospice program. Postvention programs help survivors to recognize their feelings, cope with grief and its concomitant manifestations, anger and guilt

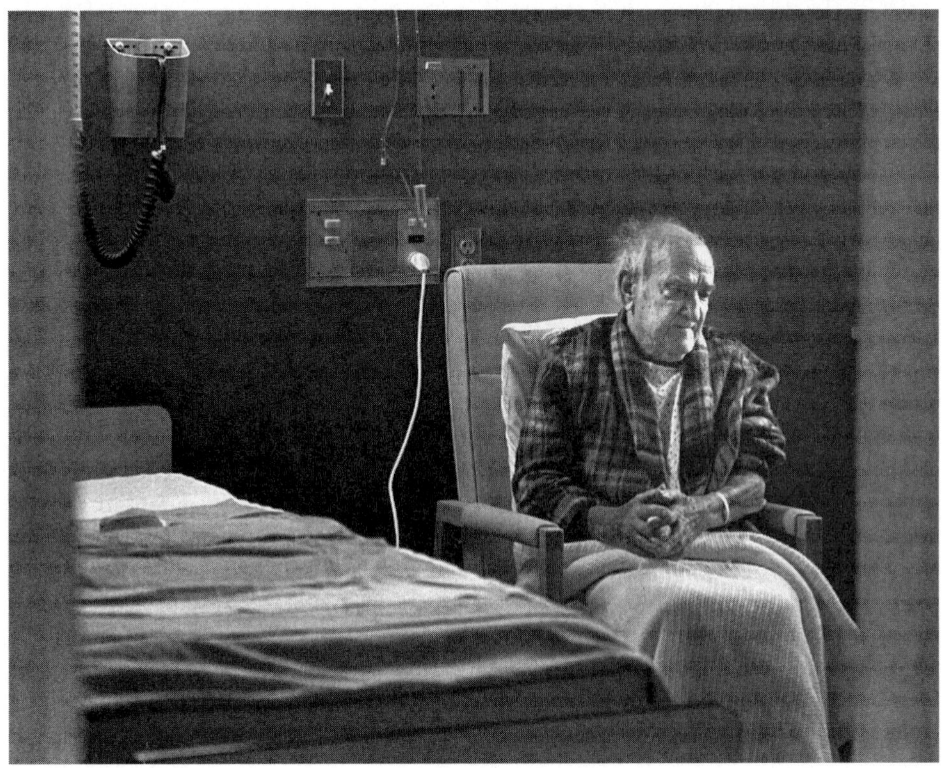

*Hospices offer medical care within a personalized, supportive setting (top). Hospitals primarily offer medical care (bottom).*

(Shneidman, 1992). Hospice staff postvention assistance includes conducting a memorial service, providing educational literature, encouraging identification and discussion of feelings, and formalized educational/support groups with regular meetings (McCracken & Gerdsen, 1991).

Many hospice programs also provide counseling and support to staff members, who themselves need a regular opportunity to share their feelings (Stephenson, 1985). Robbins (1992) found that even volunteers in hospice programs derive benefits from the training, support, and experience in managing death. In her investigation, hospice volunteers, when compared to controls who were hospital volunteers, displayed strong beliefs that their hospice work had made them more capable and competent in dealing with death. Robbins (1992) also found that hospice volunteers who were most experienced (four years or more) were better able to cope with death, as evidenced by their scores on a Coping with Death Scale, than volunteers who had less hospice involvement (two to four years) or recent trainees (less than two years). In a similar vein, nursing home workers have been reported to be more able to manage death and death anxiety as a function of their contact and experience with death and dying than a matched comparison group without such work experience (DePaola, Neimeyer, Lupfer, & Fiedler, 1992).

The hospice program encompasses a philosophy of care for the terminally ill that has already helped to humanize the care of dying patients in all contexts (Hayslip & Leon, 1988; Kastenbaum, 1985; Koff, 1981). Despite agreement on the underlying philosophy of hospice care, however, it should be noted that programs may differ substantially in actual practice. For example, some hospice programs will provide services, personnel, and support, as needed, in the dying person's home. This, of course, is contingent on the person's medical needs and the presence of other caregivers such as family and friends. And, within individual programs, hospice staff do not uniformly agree on fundamental issues such as the appropriateness of hospice treatment for all terminally ill people or the degree to which dying persons should have control over their own lives (Rinaldi & Kearl, 1990).

To date, only a few research studies have been conducted on the effects of hospice care or the impact of hospice care on relatives and hospice personnel (Kalish, 1985; McCracken & Gerdsen, 1991; Mor, 1982; Morris, 1982; Rinaldi & Kearl, 1990; Robbins, 1992). Most hospice patients studied have been terminally ill with cancer. Hinton (1972, 1979) reported that with hospice care, patients showed less anxiety, less depression, less hostility, and more acceptance of the efforts of the staff than patients in traditional hospitals. Patients appreciated the chance to talk about death, which may have also reduced the guilt of family members and led to more satisfaction with the treatment provided (Lack & Buckingham, 1978).

Current concern over the high cost of health care makes the hospice program a cost-effective option for insurance providers. Hospice care receives the strong endorsement of those at the local, state, and national levels who establish health-care priorities (Mor, 1982). More than fifteen hundred community groups nationwide are involved in establishing hospice programs (Stephenson, 1985). Currently, considerable emphasis has been directed at subsuming hospice programs physically within hospitals. It may be possible to provide hospice services on a separate floor or ward of a hospital, but there are risks in maintaining the integrity and distinctiveness of the program (DeSpelder & Strickland, 1992). With hospice treatment now covered under Medicare, hospitals have a strong financial incentive to incorporate these programs into their services.

## *Coping with the Death of a Loved One*

*To everything there is a season, and a time to every purpose under heaven. A time to live and a time to die . . .*
—Ecclesiastes

Loss comes in many forms in our lives—divorce, the death of a pet, loss of a job. No loss, however, is greater than the loss that comes from the death of someone we love and care for—a parent, a sibling, a spouse, a relative, or a friend. In rating life stresses, the death of a spouse is consistently identified as the most stressful life experience (Holmes & Rahe, 1967).

Significant loss can lead to bereavement, grief, and mourning (Kalish, 1985). The term **bereaved** describes the status of a person who survives the death of a loved one. **Grief** refers to the feelings associated with loss and usually encompasses the deep sorrow, anger, guilt, and confusion that often accompany a loss. The process of grieving is considered essential to full recovery from the loss of a significant person in our life. Grief is one of the most powerful of human feelings and produces intense emotional pain and suffering. **Mourning** is the overt expression of grief by the bereaved as defined by cultural, social, and religious custom. Mourning is expressed in various rituals—how we dress, what burial customs we follow, whether we say prayers, and so forth.

### Forms of Mourning and the Funeral

There are many cultural differences in mourning. For example, **sati** is the ancient and infrequently practiced Hindu ritual of burning a dead man's widow alive to increase his family's prestige, enhance the importance of the village, and create an image of the widow as a goddess in whose memory prayers will be offered at the site of the funeral pyre (*India Today,* 1987). Other cultures hold a ceremonial meal for the mourners; in still others, mourners wear black armbands for one year following a death. In the United States, the funeral offers a variety of options through which survivors can express their loss. According to Kalish and Reynolds (1981), there is also evidence that in the United States, certain aspects of mourning vary from one ethnic group to another (see table 12.4).

The funeral industry has been charged with taking advantage of the bereaved at a time when they are most vulnerable. Undertakers have offered expensive but needless rituals, services, and goods to those who can ill-afford such luxuries (Baird, 1976; Mitford, 1963). Many states now require "truth in services" at the time funeral arrangements are being made. The bereaved must be informed in writing of the exact

### *Table 12.4*

**Responses of 434 Persons in the Greater Los Angeles Area Regarding the Length of Time Following the Death of Spouse Before it Would be Appropriate for a Person of Respondent's Age, Sex, and Ethnicity to do Each of the Indicated Actions.**

| | Percent of Black Americans | Percent of Japanese Americans | Percent of Mexican Americans | Percent of "Anglo" Americans |
|---|---|---|---|---|
| ***To remarry*** | | | | |
| Unimportant to wait | 34 | 14 | 22 | 26 |
| 1 week–6 months | 15 | 3 | 1 | 23 |
| 1 year | 25 | 30 | 38 | 34 |
| 2 years | 11 | 26 | 20 | 11 |
| Other (including never; depends) | 16 | 28 | 19 | 7 |
| ***To stop wearing black*** | | | | |
| Unimportant to wait | 62 | 42 | 52 | 53 |
| 1 day–4 months | 24 | 26 | 11 | 31 |
| 6 months + | 11 | 21 | 35 | 6 |
| Other/depends | 4 | 11 | 3 | 11 |
| ***To return to his/her place of employment*** | | | | |
| Unimportant to wait | 39 | 22 | 27 | 47 |
| 1 day–1 week | 39 | 28 | 37 | 35 |
| 1 month + | 17 | 35 | 27 | 9 |
| Other/depends | 6 | 16 | 9 | 10 |
| ***To start going out with other men/women*** | | | | |
| Unimportant to wait | 30 | 17 | 17 | 25 |
| 1 week–1 month | 14 | 8 | 4 | 9 |
| 6 months | 24 | 22 | 22 | 29 |
| 1 year + | 11 | 34 | 40 | 21 |
| Other/depends | 21 | 19 | 18 | 17 |
| ***What do you feel is the fewest number of times he/she should visit his/her spouse's grave during the first year—not counting the burial service?*** | | | | |
| Unimportant to do | 39 | 7 | 11 | 35 |
| 1–2 times | 32 | 18 | 19 | 11 |
| 3–5 times | 16 | 18 | 12 | 18 |
| 6 + times | 13 | 58 | 59 | 35 |
| (Don't know, etc.) | (11) | (6) | (3) | (19) |
| ***What do you feel is the fewest number of times he/she should visit his/her spouse's grave during the fifth year after the death?*** | | | | |
| Unimportant to do | 52 | 8 | 20 | 43 |
| 1–2 times | 30 | 17 | 39 | 35 |
| 3–5 times | 9 | 16 | 22 | 15 |
| 6 + times | 10 | 30 | 18 | 6 |
| (Don't know, etc.) | (14) | (6) | (4) | (22) |

*From R. A. Kalish and D. K. Reynolds, "An Overview of Death and Ethnicity" in* Death and Ethnicity: A Psychocultural Study. *Copyright © 1976 Baywood Publishing Company, Inc., Farmingdale, NY. Reprinted by permission.*

*The members of this Tibetan family are conducting a ritualistic ceremony as a memorial on the first anniversary of the death of a loved one.*

charges for each specific funeral expense (see table 12.5 for examples). It is hoped that by providing charges in writing, the bereaved may choose desired options appropriately, avoid unnecessary funeral costs, and understand more completely the charges incurred (Federal Trade Commission, 1978). An average funeral costs more than $3,500 according to the American Association of Retired Persons (1992). This figure, however, does not include fees for the clergy, limousine, flowers, newspaper notices, and so on, nor cemetery fees such as burial plot, marker, or the costs of opening and closing a grave (AARP, 1992). Annual increases are projected to be 4 to 6 percent.

Because it is difficult for the bereaved to make funeral decisions, some elderly individuals are deciding *in advance* exactly what funeral arrangements they wish to have. Funeral homes have adopted **prior-to-need** or **pre-need** (Rowse, 1988) funeral plans so that survivors may be spared the difficulty of making and paying for such services at a time when they are intensely grieving. Cemeteries also have their own pre-need plans to cover the cost of burial expenses. More and more people have opted for prior-to-need arrangements. In one study, more than a million people over 65 years of age purchased such arrangements for themselves in 1990 in the United States (AARP, 1992). Most bodies in the United States are placed in caskets in the ground or in mausoleums; in-ground burial adds about $1,000–2,000 in cemetery charges (AARP, 1992). About 14 percent of those who die are cremated, with Florida and California reporting nearly 25 percent (AARP, 1988). Individuals who are cremated typically have their ashes spread in the crematorium's garden; others

### *TABLE 12.5*

**Itemization of Funeral Services and Merchandise (February, 1994)**
**Services and Merchandise Provided and Price Range**

**Funeral Home Expenses and Mortician Charges**

1. *Direct Cremation* $900–1000 This charge includes transfer of remains to funeral home, required authorizations, services of funeral director and staff, unfinished wooden box or heavy cardboard container, transportation of the body to local crematory, and return of the remains to the funeral home. The direct cremation charges do not include the crematory charge.
2. *Direct Burial Costs* $950–1495 (Average = $1,221) This charge includes an immediate burial, transfer of remains to funeral home, required authorizations, funeral services and staff, transportation of the body to local area cemetery. This charge includes the least expensive casket (cloth-covered hardwood) but does not reflect cemetery charges or preparation-of-remains charges.
3. *Preparation of Remains* $660 Charges for embalming ($275), use of preparation room ($95), topical disinfectant ($85), custodial care ($45), dressing/casketing ($22), and cosmetology ($18).
4. *Arrangements and Supervision* $761 Funeral director, staff, equipment, and facilities needed to respond to initial request for service, arrangement conference, coordination of service plans and final disposition of the deceased. These are nondeclinable professional services provided by funeral director and staff during visitation (two days), funeral service, and graveside ceremony.
5. *Charge for Facilities* $206 Use of funeral home for visitation (two days) and funeral service.
6. *Cemetery Service* $202
7. *Livery Charge* $414 Hearse and flower vehicle within ten miles with $1.10 per mile charge for each mile beyond ten miles. Average costs include transfer of remains to funeral home ($100), hearse to cemetery ($132), limousine for family ($107), and flower vehicle ($75).
8. *Merchandise* Charge for casket ($695–8,995) and charge for outer interment receptacle, liner, or vault ($645–1,228).
9. *Additional Services and Merchandise* $155 Charges for memorial cards, acknowledgment cards, register book, death notices, and cemetery equipment.
10. *Copies of Death Certificate* $15–20 per copy

**Cemetery Expenses**

1. *Interment Costs* $300–600 Opening and closing of grave, rental and setting up chairs, replacement of grass, administrative fees.
2. *Cemetery Plot* $500–2,500 Costs vary greatly by location and size (e.g., individual, couple, or family plot).
3. *Perpetual Maintenance* $400 Costs to maintain the cemetery and gravesites (lawnmowing, road upkeep, etc).
4. *Marker, Memorial, or Monument* $500–5,000 Costs vary depending on size, material, and artwork.

*Sources: National Funeral Directors Association (1994); AARP (1993); AARP (1994).*

wish their ashes taken to specific locations. Cremation societies offer to provide all such arrangements for a lesser fee than funeral directors. Some people prefer to donate their bodies to medical schools for research (AARP, 1988). A viewing of the body occurs in about 75 percent of deaths, a practice that many experts concur helps avoid denial (Swanson & Bennett, 1982-1983). Obviously, having an open casket is a personal choice for families and raises additional costs as funeral directors must perform such services as embalming, applying facial makeup, and preparing the body. Though the funeral industry has been charged with exploiting the bereaved in the purchase of unnecessary services and merchandise, other factors may also come into play, including a sense of guilt on the part of survivors, their reluctance to ask about various options, and their desire to bury their loved one "in style."

## The Grieving Process

Researchers have identified several phases of grief. However, validation of each phase has been controversial (Kalish, 1985). One view suggests there are three phases of grief: *shock, despair,* and *recovery* (Worden, 1982). Another identifies four phases: *numbness*—downplaying the significance of the loss; *yearning*—attempting to recover or search for the person we have lost; *disorganization and despair*—accepting and no longer pining over the loss; and *reorganization*—recovery from the loss (Parkes, 1970, 1972).

Drawing from Parkes's approach, the work of Pincus (1976), and the pioneering work of Pollack (1961), it appears that the first phase of grief is marked by feelings of shock, disbelief, numbness, and considerable weeping and agitation. This stage occurs very soon after the death and usually lasts no more than three days. Survivors may experience panic, faint, and even shriek or moan.

During the second phase, survivors feel a painful longing for the dead and memories and visual images of the deceased are often on their minds. People actually experience hallucinations and report seeing, hearing, being held, kissing, touching, and even talking to the deceased. Survivors feel intense psychological pain. The desire to recover the dead is very strong, and some may even contemplate suicide as a way to rejoin their loved one. Insomnia, compulsive pacing or walking, intense sadness, irritability, and restlessness are common. Private conversations, fantasies, and dreams of the deceased are also characteristic of this phase. If such responses persist and survivors continue to ignore reality, the grief process may be difficult to complete. This phase emerges soon after death, peaks two to four weeks later, and may subside after several months but can persist for as long as one or two years.

The third phase is the realistic appraisal of what the loss means. It is characterized by the *separation reaction* of survivors, which produces both disorganization and despair as it becomes clear that the deceased is no longer physically close and will never return. Common responses include heightened anxiety and fear for one's safety and protection. Survivors may even express anger toward the deceased for leaving them and making them experience such sorrow, or they may channel their anger (displaced aggression) toward health professionals who cared for the dead. Finally, in this phase, the experience of guilt occurs (Pincus, 1976; Pollack, 1978; Stephenson, 1985). Survivors may regret what they did not do for or say to the deceased. They may even feel that if they had acted more quickly, recognized the signs of serious illness earlier, or found a better physician or hospital then the death would not have happened. Guilt may also appear in a form of *idealization* or *sanctification* (Lopata, 1979), in which a spouse identifies only the most positive image of a mate who has died. The dead spouse's faults are ignored and their strengths overdramatized. The deceased is remembered without flaws or human weaknesses; they are recalled with only positive emotion and wonderful memories.

*In the case of a young person dying of AIDS, an AIDS quilt serves as a concrete tie between victims and survivors dealing with the grief and sorrow that accompanies such untimely deaths.*

The last phase (*reorganization* and *recovery*) usually occurs within a year after the death. It is marked by a resumption of ordinary activities, a greater likelihood that the deceased will be recalled with pleasant but realistic memories, and the resumption of social relationships—maintaining ongoing friendships as well as establishing new ones. One component of this phase is the survivor's *identification* with the deceased. Identification involves adopting the personal traits, behaviors, speech, mannerisms, gestures, habits, and concerns of the deceased (Stephenson, 1985). Worden (1982) notes that through such identification the dead person becomes a part of the mourner, internalized so that the dead is still a part of the living. This too is a necessary part of grieving and helps to pave the way for continuing life. At this point, survivors realize that they can continue to live without the dead. They recognize the sources of pleasure, love, and support derived from relatives, friends, and community.

Grief is one of the most powerful emotions ever experienced. Therapists and counselors recognize the immense energy and commitment that those who are grieving must expend to arrive at some resolution of their loss. The term **grief work** is an apt description of the intensity and duration of this process. It is difficult, all-consuming, and pervasive work for those who mourn (Worden, 1982).

## Outcomes of the Grieving Process

Grief can be experienced in many ways—as anger, guilt, or idealization. One of the most common is through **grief pangs.** These feelings include somatic distress occurring in waves and lasting twenty minutes to an hour, a tight feeling in the throat, shortness of breath, the need to sigh, an empty feeling in the stomach, lack of physical strength, tension, sobbing, or crying (Frederick, 1983–1984; Lindmann, 1944; Parkes, 1964; Stephenson, 1985; Worden, 1982). The sadness and deep sorrow that grieving people experience are sufficient to meet the criteria for clinical depression or physical illness (Frederick, 1983–1984). Frederick notes, for example, that the experience of intense grief produces heightened levels of *corticosteroids* (hormones), which may account, in part, for the psychological and physical symptoms of grief. It has also been reported that among the recently bereaved, the rate of death and the incidence of serious illness are dramatically higher (Stephenson, 1985). Kalish (1985) speculates that this may be the result of psychological stress, grief, and the impact of the loss as well as the physical stress of caretaking and visiting the hospital, which may lead to inadequate sleep, exercise, and poor nutrition.

Resolution of grief leads to a renewal of interest in living and in the self. Often after a year or so, people come to terms with the death and begin to make major decisions affecting their lives. They may repaint a room, buy new furniture, or travel to emphasize that life must continue. Regression may also be a consequence of mourning; some people need to return to an earlier stage to gather their resources and try to cope with loss (Pincus, 1976; Worden, 1982). In addition, grief work may be arrested and remain incomplete as individuals deny their loss, their feelings, and their need to bring resolution to their grief. Experts have reported the existence of **delayed grief reactions** in some personal histories. Delayed grief emerges long after the deaths of those we love. It may emerge as a heightened reaction to the death of someone we barely know, of a relative with whom we were not very close, or even of the loss of a family pet (see Research Focus 12.6).

Finally, at special times that remind us of a loss, we may experience **anniversary reactions.** On birthdays, at family gatherings, on holidays, or on the anniversary date of the person's death, we may feel particularly lonely and yearn for the relationship we have lost. One form of grief, **anticipatory grief,** actually begins prior to death. This form is the anticipation of a death that is virtually guaranteed to occur. The grief work may begin weeks or months in advance of the actual death. As yet, there is no evidence that anticipatory grief makes adapting to the actual loss easier (Marshall, 1980; Stephenson, 1985).

## The Delayed Grief Reaction

John Dacy, psychologist, professor at Boston College, and author has allowed us to share a particularly tragic encounter with delayed grief reaction from his own life. In a discussion of grief, he related the following story:

> I would like to relate an experience of mine that seems relevant to this question about the role of grief. In April 1957, I joined the United States Navy and sailed to the Mediterranean for a six-month tour of duty on an oil supply ship. In early November I returned home to a joyful reunion with my family. After this wonderful weekend at home, I returned to my ship. Two days later I received a telegram informing me of a tragedy: my mother, two younger brothers and two younger sisters had been killed in a fire that had destroyed our house. My father and four other brothers and sisters had escaped with burns.
>
> On the long train ride home from the naval port, I recall thinking that, as the oldest, I should be especially helpful to my father in the terrible time ahead. I was also aware of a curious absence of dismay in myself. In our upstate New York town, the catastrophe was unprecedented, and expressions of grief and condolence were myriad. People kept saying to me, "Don't try to be so brave, it's good for you to let yourself cry." And I tried to, but it just wouldn't come.
>
> At the funeral, the caskets were closed, and I can remember thinking that maybe, just maybe, this was all just a horrible dream. I distinctly remember one fantasy about my brother Mike, who was born on my first birthday and with whom I had recently become especially close. I imagined that he had actually hit his head trying to escape, and wandered off to Chicago with a case of amnesia, and no one was willing to admit that they didn't know where he was. I knew this wasn't true, but I secretly clung to the possibility. After a very difficult period of time, our family gradually began a new life. Many people generously helped us, and eventually the memories faded.
>
> Several times in the years that followed, I went to doctors because of a stomach ache, a painful stiff neck, or some other malady, which couldn't be diagnosed physically. One doctor suggested that I might be suffering from an unresolved subconscious problem, but I doubted it.
>
> Then one night in 1972, fifteen years after the fire, I was watching the original version of *The Waltons* on TV, the episode in which the father is lost at Christmas. Although dissimilar from my own experience, this tragedy triggered an incredible response in me. Suddenly it occurred to me, "My God, half my family is really gone forever!" I began sobbing and could not stop for over three hours. When I finally stopped, I felt weak and empty, relieved of an awful burden. In the days that followed I believe I went through a clear-cut "delayed grief" reaction. Therefore, the answer to the question above, at least in my experience, is clear: grief work really is essential, and we avoid it only at the cost of even greater pain. My father died recently, and my reaction was immediate and intense. I cannot help but feel that my emotional response this time was considerably more appropriate and healthy.



## Making Sense Out of the World

One of the most important aspects of grieving is that it stimulates many people to strive to make sense of their world and to search for new meanings in life (Lieberman & Peskin, 1992). Among one group of recently bereaved spouses, 27 percent reported themselves to have grown from the experience as indexed by having created new ways of responding, new methods of completing tasks, rethinking about the self differently, and discovering components of their individual identity in the process of grieving. Edmonds and Hooker (1992) published an investigation in which forty-nine college students, all of whom had recently experienced the death of a close family member, were asked to complete measures assessing their grief-distress as well as the significance of the loss in terms of its personal meaning (existential), its religious meaning, and its meaning in terms of life goals. A significant inverse relationship was found between level of grief and personal or existential meaning. Further, college students indicated a positive change in life goals as well as a correlated change in existential meaning of the loss. The higher the levels of grief experienced, the more likely that students redefined their relationship with God and the significance of their religious ideology (Edmonds & Hooker, 1992). In conclusion, the authors state that bereavement can bring about positive changes in one's life and grief itself may be an impetus for individual growth in the search for personal (existential) meaning of the loss (Edmonds & Hooker, 1992).

Grief is an overwhelming emotion with which younger individuals have little prior experience. It is particularly difficult to grieve alone or in secrecy. Yet, in recent years, death due to AIDS has led to such private grief, which offers little help, since it often cannot be fully shared with other friends or family (Ascher, 1993). Without the opportunity to talk, experience, and fully explore the range of emotions that are associated with the loss, friends and relatives of those who have died of AIDS remain remorseful over a long period of time. They often ruminate over the years in which a gulf distanced the loved one from themselves. As Ascher (1993) notes, grieving for those who die of AIDS means realizing that it is too late to ever re-create the years of separation and too late to "remedy failed love." Whether we are young or old, coping with death is difficult. Age itself is of little benefit, as can be seen in the description that Richard Kalish (1981) has written of the process of searching for personal (existential) meaning:

> A common occurrence during the grieving period is to go over, again and again, all the events that led up to the death. This can become a virtual preoccupation with some individuals, but almost all of us partake of it to some extent. In the days and weeks after the death, the closest family members will share experiences with each other—sometimes providing new information and insights into the person who died, sometimes reminiscing over familiar experiences. . . .
>
> When a death is caused by an accident or a disaster, the effort to make sense of it is pursued more vigorously. As added pieces of news come trickling in, they are integrated into the puzzle. The bereaved want to put the death into a perspective that they can understand—divine intervention, a curse from a neighboring tribe, a logical sequence of cause and effect, or whatever it may be. . . .
>
> Eventually each of us finds an adequate "story of the dying and death"— of our father, mother, or of a friend. Versions of the death may differ—whether the physician really did all she could to save the patient, whether Aunt Bella showed up frequently at the hospital or not, whether the operation succeeded or didn't quite succeed, whether father was ready to die or would have lived longer if possible—but each person's version satisfies him [or her] and that version, with slight modifications, becomes the official version for the teller. (pp. 227–228)

## Types of Death That are Difficult to Resolve

Coping with death is never easy. However, some deaths prove to be more problematic than others. According to Richard Kalish (1981, 1985), some of the most troublesome types of death include:

- Suicides or deaths due to self-neglect or carelessness
- Unexpected deaths, such as deaths of young people, those recently married, or those close to achieving significant goals

- Deaths that forced the bereaved to care for the dying person in a manner that proved to be distressing
- Deaths in which the bereaved believes he or she was partly or fully responsible, such as a child's drowning in a swimming pool
- Homicides
- Unconfirmed deaths with no body found
- Deaths so drawn out over time that the survivors become impatient for death to occur

In the remainder of this section, we briefly describe some of the types of deaths that place the greatest burden on our coping skills.

***Death of a Child*** The death of a young child produces such intense grief and is such a devastating loss that parents may not ever recover; local support groups for those who have experienced such a loss (parents, siblings, grandparents, friends, and relatives) are particularly helpful (Klass, 1988; Rando, 1986). The unexpected death of a child is even more difficult. If the death is due to an accident, parents experience enormous guilt, accepting responsibility far in excess of what is appropriate. If the death is anticipated, parents are encouraged to be honest and open with their child rather than engaging in mutual pretense (Stephenson, 1985). Parents may alleviate the child's fears of loneliness, separation, and pain rather than dealing with the concept of death itself (Stillion & Wass, 1979), and parents are encouraged themselves to begin the process of anticipatory grief work (Sahler, 1978).

The death of an adult child for an elderly parent can also be devastating (DeSpelder & Strickland, 1992; Goodman, Rubinstein, Alexander, & Luborsky, 1991). It is unexpected to survive a child, and for some older parents it is the most difficult death to encounter—generating fears of isolation, insecurity regarding their own care, as well as intense guilt and anger over the loss of a lifetime identity as parent (DeSpelder & Strickland, 1992; Hocker, 1988; Schatz, 1986). Cultural differences in how elderly women (61 to 93 years of age) coped with the death of an adult child were recently reported by Goodman, Rubinstein, Alexander, and Luborsky (1991). Jewish women in the study appeared to be more grief-stricken and more depressed than other women in having lost what was for them a fundamental direction, focus, and identity in their lives. Among Protestant and Catholic women, the investigators found somewhat more acceptance and an ability to place the death of their adult child into a larger perspective so that they could move beyond the loss and continue with their own lives (Goodman et al., 1991). These qualitative differences in cultural orientation between Jewish and non-Jewish women in coping with the loss of an adult child were also supported when quantitative indicators of well-being, affect, generativity, and personality were examined. Jewish women in this study were far more intense in interpreting the meaning of the death of an adult child, expressing their grief, and preparing themselves for the future than Protestant or Catholic women; culture, ethnicity, and religion clearly play an important role in how coping is actualized (Goodman et al., 1991).

***Death of a Sibling*** The death of a sibling is difficult to resolve for brothers and sisters, especially while still in childhood. Not only do they feel the loss deeply, there may be cognitive distortions as to the meaning of the loss. Younger children, as we described earlier in this chapter, may not fully comprehend death, may not have the language to express their own concerns, and may not have ready listeners in parents, who themselves are intensely grieving. Various experts (Pollack, 1978; Stephenson, 1985) suggest that with the death of a sibling, young children simply do not have much chance to deal with the guilt they experience. The rivalry and ambivalence expressed normally by all siblings heightens the guilt in the surviving siblings not only in childhood but also throughout adulthood.

***Death of a Parent*** The death of a parent shows persistent long-term effects whether it occurs in childhood, adolescence, or adulthood. Children are faced with separation and loss as well as a reduction in the love, affection, and attention they have received. Parental death often means other significant life changes such as moving, reduction in standard of living, changes in friends, and stepparenting. Krause (1993) has recently identified that early parental loss has lifelong effects persisting well into late life. When young children experience the death of a parent, they often have no one to replace the lost parent; in single-parent families they usually assume adult roles, including work and financial support, far earlier than children from two-parent, intact homes. Krause (1991a, 1991b) has already shown that the financial strain experienced and increased social isolation has deleterious effects well into late adulthood. Among a sample of 519 older adults participating, Krause (1993) provided support for a model showing that early parental loss was related to lower levels of educational attainment, leading to financial difficulties later in life and ultimately contributing to a reduced sense of personal control in late adulthood.

Even for older adults, the death of a parent demands enormous grief work. The loss is intense and the loss of attachment bonds and emotional security are irreplaceable. The deaths of elderly parents are somewhat easier to manage for adult children than the death of parents who are younger. There is some evidence that in the former instance, adult children have an opportunity to prepare themselves for the death as they witness parents becoming older and frail (Moss & Moss, 1983–1984; Norris & Murrell, 1990). Regardless of circumstances, most adult children believe that a parent who has died did not live long enough (Moss & Moss, 1983–1984). The death of a parent signifies that all humans are mortal and that our turn will also come; adult children realize that there is no other older generation standing between them and death.

***Death of a Spouse*** The death of a spouse is exceptionally difficult and leads to overwhelming bereavement and challenges (Lieberman & Peskin, 1992). One's entire social network and social support system must be reconstructed (Lieberman, Heller, & Mullan, 1990). Additionally, spouses must begin to confront themselves, their strengths and weaknesses, and their futures, which creates a heightened sense of the closeness of their own death (Lieberman & Peskin, 1992).

Widows provide each other with a great deal of social support.

Bereavement is not always debilitating, as we have discussed, and investigators are beginning to identify the "existential" growth that occurs among some widows and widowers (Lieberman, 1992; Yalom & Lieberman, 1991).

There are more than 12 million widowed people in the United States. Recent statistics suggest that by age 65, roughly 50 percent of the women in the United States are already widowed; only 20 percent of males are widowers at the same age (Campbell & Silverman, 1987). By age 75, nearly 67 percent of all females and 25 percent of all males have experienced the death of a spouse (Meyers, 1990). Widows outnumber widowers by a 5:1 ratio (Campbell & Silverman, 1987; Kalish, 1985). The death of a spouse is usually unpreventable, may shatter a long-standing attachment bond, require the pursuit of new roles and status, lead to financial hardship, and leave the survivor without a major support system (Lieberman & Peskin, 1992; Osterweis, Solomon, & Green, 1984). Following the death of a spouse there is an increased risk of mortality, attenuated ability to activate the immunogenic system, and increased risk of various physical and psychological disorders (Bradshaw et al., 1992; Osterweis et al., 1984).

Widows generally have greatest difficulties in managing new roles, such as finances, insurance, home maintenance, lawn and garden care, and upkeep of the family car, and dealing with unbearable loneliness. Most widows experience a significant reduction in income and support following the death of their husbands. Widowers, on the other hand, must cope with new responsibilities in the home: cooking, doing laundry, cleaning, and coping with their personal sense of isolation (Kalish, 1985). Widows appear to provide considerable social support for each other, whereas widowers are often more isolated (Connidis, 1989; Connidis & Daviesa, 1990, 1990b).

Young surviving spouses experience different kinds of adjustment problems than do surviving older spouses. Young survivors must often deal with childrearing as single parents, cope with the demands of grandparents, and manage a work role as well as the complexities of dating. Older survivors must deal with the loss of security and support (physical, emotional, and financial) as well as manage the difficulty in maintaining social contacts. In the early phases of bereavement younger surviving spouses appear to undergo far more intense grief reactions, whereas older surviving spouses show better earlier adjustment but more intense feelings of grief months later (Wisocki & Averill, 1987). Adjustment problems include depression, increasing physician consultations, hospitalization, increases in smoking and drinking, pathological grief reactions, nutritional deficits, and higher mortality rates (Kaprio, Kosenvuo, & Rita, 1987; Rosenbloom & Whittington, 1993; Zisook, 1987; Zisook, Shuchter, & Lyons, 1987). Rosenbloom and Whittington (1993), for example, noted that among recent widows, bereavement reactions and high levels of grief significantly changed the social meaning that eating had formerly occupied in their lives, that is, as a social, shared, and emotionally satisfying experience. The data revealed that widows found eating less pleasurable and the loneliness difficult to manage at mealtimes; widows ate less, experienced significant reductions in nutrients, and lost weight—an average of 7.6 pounds. As the widows' grief diminished, these trends began to be reversed (Rosenbloom & Whittington, 1993). Bereavement has also been reported to be related to difficulty sleeping and in early morning awakening (Hoch et al., 1992). Such symptoms are also associated with depression (Hoch et al., 1992).

The experience of widowhood changes dramatically depending on sociohistorical circumstances (Lopata, 1987a). The modernization of societies has enabled many widows to live independently, free from the control of the patriarchal family, and able to maintain themselves economically through paid employment and/or the Social Security system in the United States. Some widows are unable to reengage in social relations, and friendships enjoyed with other couples may wane after the death of a spouse.Yet many widows are able to create support systems with each other and eventually reimmerse themselves in their families, their neighborhoods, support networks, occupations, or volunteer organizations.

Lopata (1987b) also suggests that widowhood may be experienced in many different ways. Some widows are passive, accepting changes produced by the death of a husband. Others display personal abilities, long dormant, that may blossom in widowhood. Some stay in pockets of comfortable social support, whereas others expand, seeking new resources, new friendships, and new social roles. Among recent elderly widows, Bradsher, Longino, Jackson, and Zimmerman (1992) have documented the greater likelihood of changing residence when health and functional disability occur. Chronic functional disabilities and deteriorating health seem to lead widows to move their residence, since they do not have the additional support from a spouse to manage the routine tasks of the household and daily living (Bradsher et al., 1992).

Recent studies have shown that some widows and widowers show little grieving and yet are able to adapt successfully to the loss (Lieberman & Peskin, 1992). In one investigation, 37 percent of a group of widows showed no grief reactions either at the time of death or twelve months later. When compared to other widows who grieved primarily at the time of death, throughout the twelve month period, or who showed delayed grief, the most well-adjusted widows were those who showed little grief at the time of the death of their husbands (Lieberman, 1992). Current interest is being directed at such results, which challenge conventional wisdom. Research investigators believe that perhaps widows who can derive significant social support, develop mastery over the social context in which they continue to have to live, and who themselves are positive copers and have adjusted to life crises successfully in the past are the ones who actively manage the loss of a spouse in a most effective manner (Liberman & Peskin, 1992).

***Suicide*** The impact of suicide on survivors is enormous, particularly on a surviving spouse. In many investigations, the impact of suicide on middle-aged and younger spouses appears to produce heightened and more intense bereavement reactions such as denial, major depression, uncontrollable grief, physical symptoms requiring medical examination, and even hospitalization (Farberow, Gallagher-Thompson, Gilewski, & Thompson, 1992). Such studies, while consistent and revealing, have focused on immediate reaction to the suicide in short-term follow-ups and have not typically included older surviving spouses. Farberow et al., (1992) completed a two-and-a-half-year longitudinal investigation examining the impact of suicide among surviving spouses (55 years of age and older). Comparisons were made between similar-aged respondents who were coping with the natural death of their spouse, and married older persons who were still living. The longitudinal nature of the study confirmed that older surviving spouses experience lengthy and intense feelings of bereavement when compared to earlier studies of younger individuals. Independent of type of death, the older spouses in this study were still experiencing bereavement reactions such as grief, depression, anxiety, and alienation at the end of the two-and-a-half-year period. Survivors of the natural death of their spouse showed gradual decline and relief from grief both six months following death and then again after eighteen months. Grief reactions among those whose spouse had committed suicide, however, remained high consistently throughout the first year and did not show any appreciable decline until eighteen months had passed. This extended period of grief was also seen in their rankings of their own mental health, depression, and distress, which showed little improvement until a year after the suicide (Farberow et al., 1992). At the end of the thirty months of the study, both bereaved groups of older spouses were functioning at nearly similar levels and reported continued feelings of loss, isolation, and sadness.

## Summary

Although death is inevitable, it remains an uncomfortable topic in our culture. It may seem easy to identify when an individual has died, but recent medical advances have made the determination complex. For example, brain death can occur even though critical organs like the heart and lungs continue to function. Today we are faced with ethical questions concerning the practice of euthanasia and when we should prolong a person's life. Several states are enacting laws to determine when a dying person may not be resuscitated. Controversy continues over the definition of brain death and its relation to the process of death versus the event itself. Depending on what decisions need to be made about the process of death, competing definitions may be entirely acceptable.

It is important to consider the sociohistorical and sociocultural contexts of death. There is more avoidance and denial of death in American culture than in many other cultures. Experience and contact with death and dying may contribute to cultural differences and individual differences in attitudes toward death and dying.

Elisabeth Kübler-Ross has suggested five psychological stages of dying: denial and isolation, anger, bargaining, depression, and acceptance. Researchers have been unable to verify that dying people go through the stages in the sequence prescribed; however, Kübler-Ross's main contribution is the humanization of the dying process. E. Mansell Pattison has suggested three phases of what he calls the living-dying interval: acute, chronic, and terminal. The dying process is multifaceted and involves much more than descriptive stages or phases. For example, denial is an important aspect of the coping process for the dying person. By itself, denial is neither good nor bad. For many dying people, adaptive denial may be helpful. An open system of communication with the dying is often an optimal strategy. Above all, we should avoid stereotypes about dying and the aged. The dying person is a unique individual, with strengths and ongoing challenges to face. For those people near death and with limited ability to participate in their environment, it may be best to emphasize their own inner personal resources.

The contexts in which people die are also important. Hospitals ensure medical expertise and sophisticated equipment, but more intimacy and autonomy is usually possible at home. An alternative to home or hospital is the hospice, a humanizing institution that many experts believe offers the best blend of home and hospital benefits. The hospice movement began in the 1960s and continues to expand. It stresses patient control and management of pain as well as a philosophy based on open communication, family involvement, and extensive support services.

The loss of someone we are attached to is among the most stressful of life events. Coping with the death of a loved one has been described in terms of bereavement—the state of loss—and mourning, the overt, behavioral expression of bereavement and grief. Mourning takes many forms, depending on the culture. In the United States, the mourning process usually involves a funeral, which is followed by burial or cremation. In recent years, controversy has arisen about the funeral industry.

Grief may be seen as a series of phases—shock, despair, and recovery. However, people do not have to go through each phase to cope adaptively with grief. One of the most common ways of experiencing grief is through grief pangs. Denial is also part of grief, just as it is part of the dying process. One aspect of the grief is existential and involves making sense out of the world and trying to solve the puzzle of death. One of the most intense losses we can suffer is the death of a spouse. Longitudinal study of bereavement in older surviving spouses shows how lengthy the process is for the elderly. Suicide has an immense impact on survivors, and bereavement among widows and widowers is both more intense and more extended than when death is due to natural causes.

## Review Questions

1. At present, what is the biological definition of death?
2. Explain the difference between *death* and the *process of dying.* What is the significance of the difference?
3. Do you believe that euthanasia should be practiced? Explain.
4. Discuss the sociohistorical contexts of death.
5. What are common attitudes about death in young childhood, adolescence, and early, middle, and late adulthood?
6. Describe and critically evaluate Kübler-Ross's five psychological stages of dying. How important is it to complete all five stages?
7. Describe how denial can affect the dying person.
8. What are some of the recommended strategies for communicating with a dying person?
9. Describe the contexts in which people die—in hospitals, hospices, and at home—including the benefits and disadvantages of each.
10. Outline the phases of grief that people go through, how they try to make sense out of the world when someone close to them dies, and how grief may be particularly intense in the case of a widow or widower.
11. What kinds of death make it particularly difficult to resolve the grief process?
12. Discuss various forms of mourning and the ongoing controversy over the funeral industry.

## For Further Reading


Burnell, G. M. (1993). *Final Choices: To live or die in an age of medical technology.* New York: Plenum Press.

Irish, D. P., Lundquist, K. F., & Nelson, V. K. (1993). *Ethnic variations in dying, death, and grief: Diversity in Universality.* Bristol, PA: Taylor & Francis.

Kastenbaum, R. (1985). Dying and death: A life-span approach. In J. E. Birren & K. W. Schaie (Eds.), *The handbook of the psychology of aging* (2d ed.). New York: Van Nostrand Reinhold.

Shneidman, E. S. (1980). *Voices of death.* New York: Harper and Row.

Siegel, R. K. (1980). The psychology of life after death. *American Psychologist, 35,* 911–931.

Stephenson, J. S. (1985). *Death, grief, and mourning: Individual and social realities.* New York: Free Press.

Wass, H., & Neimeyer, R. A. (1994). *Dying: Facing the facts* (3d ed.). Bristol, PA: Taylor & Francis.

*Appendix A*

# *Developmental Research Methods*

*It is the theory which decides what can be observed.*
—Albert Einstein



## *Introduction*

Imagine that you are a researcher studying whether creativity declines with age. You suspect that many opinions about aging and creativity are rooted in negative prejudices and stereotypes of the aged, or are based on socially accepted behavior standards for people of different ages. You are interested in obtaining objective, scientific evidence on creativity across the life span. How should you proceed?

One approach might be simply to ask people of different ages to rate their creativity (using a seven-point scale, for example). But your goal is to gather objective, scientific data on creativity, not subjective impressions that doubtlessly are influenced by conventional wisdom as well as the egos of your participants. Another approach might be to collect ratings on people's creativity from friends and relatives. This might solve the ego problem, but conventional wisdom and subjective judgments would remain troublesome factors. Moreover, how well can friends and relatives judge a person's creativity? (Do your friends and relatives know exactly how creative you are?) Another approach might be to use a questionnaire or structured interview. Rather than simply asking people about their creativity, you might ask them about a variety of items such as lifestyle (are they unconventional?), work habits (do they waste many idle hours until spurred by a creative burst?), and motivations (do they enjoy following orders and being told what to do, or do they prefer to set their own tasks and goals?). Responses could be scored or weighted for creativity, and a total creativity score derived. Unfortunately, participants might guess the purpose of your study and try to produce answers that appear creative.

Perhaps it would be better to test people's ability to find creative solutions to problems rather than to ask them about creativity. Indeed, it might be useful to find a standardized test of creative problem solving that many samples of people have taken. This approach seems promising, but you must ensure the reliability and validity of your creativity test. Does the test give consistent estimates of creativity if the same individual is tested twice? This demonstrates reliability. Does the test truly measure creativity, or simply intelligence? This question involves validity.

Even if a test shows high reliability and validity with young adults, the test might not be as reliable and valid for elderly people. Further, age differences in creative problem solving might not reflect age per se, but, rather, extraneous factors such as educational background or health. Some of these factors might be controlled by a longitudinal design, testing the same individuals every ten years from ages 20 to 70. But do you have fifty years to complete your study? And how many of the participants you test today will still be available fifty years from now?

The problem of extraneous factors and the difficulty of conducting longitudinal designs might lead you to use archival or historical data. For example, you might investigate the typical ages at which people have produced great artistic or scientific achievements. Unfortunately, the evidence provided by archival investigations is highly indirect; many factors in addition to creativity determine at what age someone might produce a great artistic or scientific accomplishment. (Indeed, it is arguable that many social and cultural factors, including conventional wisdom about aging and creativity, may influence the time course of creative achievement in adults.) Further, the accuracy and completeness of archival data is always a concern.

Faced with all of these problems, you might wish to add animal models in your research. With animals, it is possible to control many factors (diet, experiences in infancy, and so forth) that cannot be controlled in humans. Also, many animals have a relatively brief life span, making longitudinal research more feasible. But how do you devise a creativity test that animals can complete? And can results obtained with animals be generalized to humans?

What, then, should you do to investigate aging and creativity? There is no one right answer—only alternative approaches with varying advantages and disadvantages. Furthermore, there is ample room for your own creativity in selecting, combining, and even modifying approaches to suit your own research goals. Indeed, the need for creativity in science is an integral part of its challenge and appeal.

Since the fundamental task of science is measurement (McCain & Segal, 1988; Shaughnessy & Zechmeister, 1990), we begin this chapter with a discussion of two basic issues involved in measurement: the reliability of measurements and the validity of measurements. Then we discuss several basic techniques used for collecting observations: the structured interview and questionnaire, standardized tests, and behavioral research. Next, we consider some of the basic ways to describe and interpret measurements. Then we explore the topic of research design, considering first simple correlational designs and then more powerful experimental designs. We also discuss the role played by quasi-experimental designs in developmental research. The appendix closes with a section on sampling, a critical problem in all psychological research but particularly important in research on adult development and aging.

## *Basic Issues of Measurement*

Measurement—a major task of science—sounds simple. However, to make accurate and meaningful measurements is far from simple. Let's look at two basic issues we must consider when making scientific measurements.

### Reliability of Measures

Suppose you are assisting on a research project focusing on age changes in reaction time, the amount of time it takes to respond to a simple stimulus. You are asked to construct a task that will measure the reaction times of all the adults participating in this research study. After a great deal of thought, you develop the following **reaction-time task.** You ask each participant to sit individually at a table and you place a set of earphones on his or her head. Directly in front of each participant on the table is a telegraph key. You tell the participants that every now and then they will hear a beeping sound delivered to both ears via the earphones. You instruct the participants to press the telegraph key as quickly as possible whenever they hear a beep. Within this context, you define reaction time as the amount of time it takes a participant to press the key after the beep has initially sounded. Furthermore, you decide to measure the participants' reaction times by using a handheld stopwatch that measures time in hundredths of seconds. You plan to start the watch when the participant hears the beep (you will also wear a pair of earphones connected to the same sound source as those worn by each participant). And you plan to stop the watch when the participant presses the key.

Suppose that you tell the principal investigator of the research project about your plan to measure reaction time. You assume that she will be very impressed with the task you have developed. However, she seems very concerned about the *reliability* of your measure. What exactly is the principal investigator worried about? How can you reassure her? Essentially, the concept of **reliability** refers to the degree to which measurement is consistent, stable, and accurate over time. Given your inexperience at measuring reaction time, there are many reasons why the measurements you collect might be inconsistent and unstable. For example, were all of the participants instructed to press the button by using the index finger on their preferred hand? Did some of the participants position their fingers directly on top of the telegraph key before some of the trials but place their fingers on the table before some of the other trials? If the participants positioned their fingers in different locations before each trial, you would collect very unreliable data. (Remember, you want to measure the time it takes to press the key—not the time it takes to move your finger to the key and *then* press the key!) Also, when did you plan to begin measuring the participants' response times—as soon as they begin to perform the reaction-time task or after several practice trials? Until a participant becomes familiar with the experimental task and apparatus, his or her reaction times could vary considerably from trial to trial. Finally, the principal investigator may wonder how accurately you can measure reaction time by using a handheld stop watch. Is it possible for you to start your watch at the *exact* split second the beep sounds and stop the watch at the *exact* instant the participant depresses the telegraph key? Even if you could accurately measure reaction time at the beginning of the experimental session (which is extremely doubtful), might you become increasingly tired, bored, and/or absentminded as you measured more and more reaction times.

As you can now see, there are a number of points to consider in measuring reaction time reliably. Other types of measurement can pose much greater problems of reliability. Suppose, for example, that you were asked to determine an elderly adult's level of life satisfaction. How reliable would your estimations be? How many sources of measurement error would exist?

## Assessing Reliability

How can we assess the reliability of various measures? There are a variety of techniques, but all are based on the assumption that reliable observations are repeatable.

**Test-retest reliability** can be assessed by obtaining the same set of measurements on two different occasions. The question is whether measurements (frequently numerical scores of some kind) on occasion 2 are predictable from observations gathered on occasion 1. Thus, after a familiarization period, we could administer 100 reaction-time trials to participants on day 1 and 100 trials on day 2; if the test is reliable, we should be able to compute the reliability of the participants' reaction times. Of course, test-retest reliability is meaningful only when the variable we are measuring is assumed to be stable over time. Were we observing the momentary moods of individuals, we probably would not wish to assess test-retest reliability. For example, if a person were judged to be happy on day 1 and sad on day 2, this need not imply low test reliability. It could simply mean that the person's mood had changed.

**Interrater reliability** should be assessed whenever measurements involve a subjective, judgmental component. This is frequently the case in studies where observational data are collected. The technique is simply to use two or more observers independently, then assess the agreement among these observers. High agreement implies high reliability.

**Interitem reliability** can be examined whenever measurements entail multiple items. A common procedure for assessing interitem reliability is to divide the items into halves (for instance, the odd-numbered items versus the even-numbered items) and to determine the extent to which measurements (average scores) on one half are predictable from measurements on the other half. High predictability implies high reliability.

## Ways of Improving Reliability

How do we improve the reliability of measurements? One method is to take many different measures of the same individual or behavior. However, an even better way is to refine and standardize the procedures and tools used for measurement. In our initial example of measuring reaction time, we could improve reliability by making multiple assessments of reaction time, particularly if the assessments were made by different research assistants. It obviously would also be helpful to use a carefully planned and standardized set of procedures for assessing reaction time (e.g., instructing participants to place the index finger of their preferred hand on the telegraph key). Finally, the use of high-precision equipment would be beneficial (a computer with an internal clock would be programmed to record the exact time—in milliseconds—between the onset of the beep and the depression of the key). Future scientific advances should ultimately provide the refinements and standardization needed to produce truly reliable measures of physical, intellectual, and social behaviors.

Reliability is a concern in all psychological research. However, reliability problems are particularly bothersome in developmental research, especially when individual differences are at issue. If a group of people is given an IQ test at age 18 and again at age 45, it is probable that some individuals will show gains from the first test to the second, whereas others will show losses. Are there true differences between the gainers and the losers in intelligence, or are we simply seeing the effects of an unreliable measuring instrument? Although statistical methods can be applied to this problem, reliability remains questionable. Furthermore, envision a situation where every person tested at age 45 scores exactly ten points higher on the IQ test than they scored at age 18. Since we could exactly predict a person's IQ at age 45 from his or her IQ at age 18, we would conclude that the test used to measure IQ is highly reliable—it possesses a perfect level of test-retest reliability. However, it is obvious that not one of our participants has the same IQ score at both times of testing, making the test's stability questionable. Therefore, since the concept of reliability entails both the *predictability* and the *stability* of measurements, separate measures of predictability and stability should be developed and used.

## Validity of Measurement

In our example of measuring reaction time, the principal investigator questioned the reliability (essentially, the repeatability) of the measurement. What if she also doubted the **validity** of the measure itself? A measure is valid if it actually measures what it purports to measure. The measure of reaction time, therefore, is valid if it really measures the amount of time it takes adults to make a simple motor response once they hear a sound. The principal investigator might suggest that the task you developed to measure reaction time could actually measure how well participants can *hear* the beep rather than to react to it. If older adults have trouble hearing, they will have difficulty reacting to the beep. Thus, to make certain that the measure of reaction time is valid, all of the prospective participants in the study will have to be screened for auditory sensitivity.

Although there are many different types of validity, the type we are currently addressing is **construct validity.** Constructs are abstract entities that cannot be directly observed but are presumed to influence observable phenomena. Intelligence is a construct, so are anxiety, creativity, memory, self-esteem, and other aspects of personality and cognition. We often attempt to observe phenomena that we believe might reflect these constructs. The question of whether the observed phenomena actually do reflect the constructs is the issue of construct validity.

Even when observations are highly reliable, they do not necessarily imply high construct validity. Were we to devise a test of creativity, we might be able to demonstrate high test-retest reliability as well as high interitem reliability. However, the test could still be vulnerable to the charge that it really measures intelligence, not creativity—or to the charge that creativity may not even truly exist.

Students of adult development and aging must consider whether a given test or measurement might have reasonable construct validity for young adults but not for elderly people. For example, a test of long-term memory might be reasonably valid for college students who are accustomed to memory tests. But the same test might be intimidating to elderly people who might not have taken a memory test for decades. Hence, the performance of elderly people might reflect anxiety more than memory per se.

# *Basic Techniques Used for Collecting Measurements*

## Interviews and Questionnaires

Many inquiries on adult development have been based on the techniques of interview and questionnaire. An *interview* is a set of questions asked face-to-face. The interview can range from being very structured to very unstructured. For example, a very unstructured interview might include open-ended questions such as, "Tell me about some of the things you do with your friends," or "Tell me about yourself." On the other hand, a very structured interview might question whether the respondent highly approves, moderately approves, moderately disapproves, or highly disapproves of his friends' use of drugs. Highly unstructured interviews, while often yielding valuable clinical insights, usually do not yield information suitable for research purposes. However, unstructured interview questions can be helpful in developing more focused interview questions for future efforts.

Structured interviews conducted by an experienced researcher can produce valuable data. However, structured interviews are not without problems. Perhaps the most critical of these problems involves the response bias of social desirability. In a face-to-face situation, where anonymity is impossible, a person's responses may reflect social desirability rather than her actual feelings or actions. In other words, a person may respond to gain the approval of the interviewer rather than say what she actually thinks. When asked about sexual relationships, for example, a person may not want to admit having had sexual intercourse on a casual basis. Skilled interviewing techniques and built-in questions designed to help eliminate such defenses are critical in obtaining accurate information in an interview.

Researchers are also able to question adults through surveys or questionnaires. A *questionnaire* is similar to a highly structured interview except that adults read the questions and mark their answers on a sheet of paper rather than responding orally to the interviewer. One major advantage of questionnaires is that they can easily be given to a very large number of people. A sample of responses from five thousand to ten thousand people is possible to obtain. However, a number of experts on measurement (for example, Bailey, 1987; Shaughnessy & Zechmeister, 1990; Simon & Burstein, 1985) have pointed out that surveys and questionnaires have been badly abused instruments of inquiry. For example, survey items should be concrete, specific, and unambiguous; often they are not.

Another problem with both interviews and surveys or questionnaires is that some questions may be retrospective in nature; that is, they may require the participant to recall events or feelings that occurred at some point in the past. It is not unusual, for example, to interview older adults about experiences they had during adolescence or young adulthood. Unfortunately, retrospective interviews may be seriously affected by distortions in memory. It is exceedingly difficult to glean accurate information about the past from verbal reports. However, because of the importance of understanding retrospective verbal reports, 1978 Nobel Prize winner Herbert Simon and others are developing better ways to gain more accurate verbal assessments of the past (Ericsson & Simon, 1984).

## Behavioral Research

Regardless of advances in our understanding of verbal reports, they probably will never be adequate, by themselves, as a basis for psychological research. Apart from problems of response set or memory, verbal reports obviously depend on conscious awareness. Yet many aspects of cognition, personality, and social behavior apparently are subconscious. Thus we must go beyond what people tell us about themselves and examine how they behave.

**Behavioral research** does not depend on participants' verbal reports regarding the issue under study. For example, a questionnaire might be based on verbal reports of memory problems as experienced by the elderly. In contrast, a behavioral study of memory might actually assess the accuracy of verbal recall by the elderly. (For instance, the researcher might present a list of words, followed by a test of verbal recall for these words.) Both approaches involve verbalization on the part of participants, but only the questionnaire involves verbalization *about* memory itself. Interestingly, evidence exists that indicates that reports of memory problems are not strongly associated with true deficits in performance on memory tasks. Marion Perlmutter (Perlmutter, 1978; Perlmutter, Metzger, Nezworski, & Miller, 1981) has collected both questionnaire and performance data on memory in young and elderly adults. Overall, she found that older adults report more memory problems on a questionnaire and that they also perform more poorly on some (but not all) memory tasks. But reported memory problems have proved to be a poor basis for predicting actual memory performance in this type of research (Perlmutter, 1986). For example, a person reporting many memory problems might actually perform very well on a memory test, and vice versa.

## Behavioral Research in Laboratory versus Field Settings

In behavioral research, it is frequently necessary to control certain factors that might determine behavior but are not the focus of the inquiry. For example, if we are interested in studying long-term memory in different age groups, we might want to control motivation as well as the conditions of learning (study time, distracting noises, etc.). Even extraneous factors such as temperature and time of day might be important. Laboratories are places that allow considerable control over many extraneous factors. For this reason, behavioral research is frequently conducted in laboratories.

However, costs are also involved in conducting laboratory research, and some of these costs are especially high when developmental issues are being addressed. First, it is impossible to conduct research in a laboratory without letting the participants know they are in an experiment. This creates problems of **reactivity.** Reactivity occurs when participants think they should behave in a specific manner because they are in an experimental setting. Second, the laboratory setting is unnatural and might cause unnatural behavior on the part of participants. This problem can be particularly severe with elderly participants, who may find the laboratory setting even more unnatural than young adults do. Finally, certain phenomena, particularly social phenomena, are difficult, if not impossible, to produce in the laboratory. The effects of "job-related stress on marital satisfaction," for example, might be difficult (and unethical) to investigate in a laboratory setting. Because of these problems with laboratory research, many psychologists are beginning to conduct *field* or *observational* research in real-world settings. Such settings can include job sites, shopping malls, senior citizen centers, nursing homes, or any other place where appropriate observations can be made. The main drawback of field research is limited control over extraneous factors. However, this drawback is frequently outweighed by the benefits of low reactivity, natural contexts, and access to interesting phenomena that are difficult to observe in the laboratory.

Though they are often presented as dichotomous, laboratory and field research are really two points on a continuum, a continuum that can be labeled **naturalism**

**versus control.** If some laboratory experiments employ conditions or tasks of a decidedly natural character, these experiments belong in the middle area of the continuum. For example, a laboratory study of memory might examine recall of events from one's past. A laboratory study of social behavior might bring middle-aged parents and their adolescent offspring together to discuss problems in their family. Researchers find that many benefits of field studies can be enjoyed in the laboratory *if* the activities of the participants are to some degree natural. This is an important lesson for psychologists interested in adult development and aging. It is frequently necessary to conduct developmental research within some form of laboratory-like context (perhaps a simple room with few distracting stimuli). This does not mean that the tasks performed by participants must be unnatural and uninteresting. Such tasks might put elderly people who are unaccustomed to performing artificial and irrelevant tasks at an unfair advantage.

## Laboratory Research with Animal Models

Although laboratory and field research can be thought of as two points on a continuum, laboratory research with human participants is not the end point of this continuum. The end point is laboratory research with animal participants, because such research allows far more control than is possible with humans. We can control an animal's genetic endowment, diet, experiences during infancy, and countless other factors that cannot be controlled when humans are studied. We can also investigate effects of treatments (brain lesions or restricted diet, for example) that would be unethical to attempt with humans. Moreover, with some animals it is possible to track the entire life course in a very short period of time. (Laboratory mice live at most a few years.)

A major disadvantage of animal research is, of course, that it may well not generalize to humans. Indeed, many aspects of human development—language, for example—are simply impossible to study except with humans. Nevertheless, some aspects of animal development do generalize to humans and promise to teach us much about development across the life span. For example, there is an amazing degree of similarity in the structure and function of the brain in humans and rats. Furthermore, a team of researchers (Selkoe, Bell, Podlisny, Price, & Cork, 1987) have discovered that the same brain changes that accompany normal aging in humans (and abnormal aging such as Alzheimer's disease) occur in a wide variety of animals (e.g., rats, dogs, and polar bears) as well. This suggests that researchers may be able to construct animal models that will shed a great deal of light on both normal and pathological age-related changes in the human nervous system.

## Standardized Tests

Standardized tests attempt to measure an individual's characteristics or abilities *as compared to* those of a large group of similar individuals. Such tests may take the forms of questionnaires, interviews, or behavioral tests. To maximize reliability, a good test should have a reasonably large number of items and should be given in an objective, standardized manner. The **standardization** of tests actually refers to two different qualities: the establishment of fixed or standard procedures for administration and scoring, and the establishment of norms for age, grade, race, sex, and so on. Norms are patterns or representative values for a group. Hence, the performance of an individual can be assessed relative to that of a comparison group (people of the same age, sex, and so on).

Many standardized tests have good reliability but their construct validity can be questioned. IQ tests, for example, show impressive reliability, but there is considerable uncertainty about what such tests actually measure (Gardner, 1983, 1985; Sternberg, 1985). The problem is compounded by the possibility that a single test might measure different things at different ages; for example, an IQ test might measure intellectual ability in young adulthood, but anxiety in old age. This possibility is critical in interpreting developmental research that shows that IQ performance can change with age.

There are standardized tests for intellectual functioning, for psychopathology or mental illness, for life satisfaction, creativity, and many other aspects of personality and cognition. Such tests are used for a wide variety of purposes and are invaluable in developmental research. However, when using any test, it is important to consider construct validity. That is, does the standardized test truly measure the construct in question, whether it is intelligence, creativity, or schizophrenia?

## Physiological Research

There is no question that a biological level of analysis offers a great deal of information about adult development and aging. This is not to say that psychological and sociocultural factors are unimportant; indeed, there is good reason to believe that there are multiple determinants of adult development. Moreover, physiological factors and psychological-sociocultural factors *interact* during the course of adult development. Biological research frequently suggests strategies to remove or reverse certain types of behavioral change, which is sometimes desirable.

## *Basic Strategies for Describing and Interpreting Measurements*

In most scientific studies, a vast number of measurements allow researchers to collect considerable amounts of raw data. For this data to be understood, they must be described and interpreted objectively. In this section, we summarize some of the statistical techniques that developmentalists use to make sense out of raw data.

## Measures of Central Tendency and Variability

Most people are familiar with the procedure of averaging. Given a set of $n$ scores (where $n$ refers to the total number of scores in a data set), we add their values and divide by $n$. The result is called the **mean,** which is by far the most common—but not the only—measure of **central tendency.** Another such measure is the **median,** which is a value in the middle of the distribution of scores (so that as many scores fall above the median as fall below it). The **mode** is the most frequently appearing score in the set.

Measures of central tendency such as the mean provide important but incomplete information. Reporting the mean score is like telling another person that the score of a baseball game is 3–1 but failing to tell the person which team is ahead and which inning it is. For this reason, we often need information on the **variability** of scores as well as their mean. The simplest measure of variability is the **range,** which is a comparison between the lowest and highest scores in a data set. A much more meaningful measure of variability is the **standard deviation.** The standard deviation is a mathematical index of the degree to which every score in a distribution of scores differs from the mean score. The more the scores in a distribution vary from the mean, the larger the standard deviation. The less the scores in a distribution differ from the mean, the smaller the standard deviation.

Means and standard deviations are reported frequently in research on adult development. There are several reasons for this, but none is more important than the relevance of these measures to individual differences in the course of adult development. For example, it is possible that a group of young adults and a group of older adults would both remember the same mean number of items on a test of memory ability (each group could recognize, on average, twenty words from a list of thirty-five). However, we might discover that the standard deviation for the older group was 7.4, while the standard deviation for the younger group was 3.1. These results would suggest that there is much more variability in the performance of older subjects than in that of the younger subjects. This important point would be obscured if the investigator only reported the mean score.

## Correlation Between Variables

To understand the concept of correlation, one must first understand the meaning of the term **variable.** A variable is something that can vary, that is, take on different levels or values. Age, for example, is a variable because it can take on values between 0 and 100 years or more. Other common variables are IQ, height, weight, and years of education. Some variables can take only two different values (biological sex, for example, can take on only male or female).

A **correlation** is a measure of the relationship or strength of association between two variables. During adulthood, for example, there is usually a correlation between a person's age and the number of grandchildren he has; generally, the older the adult, the greater the number of grandchildren.

Correlations can be either positive or negative. A **positive correlation** exists when high values of one variable are associated with high values of the other. During the adult years, the variables of age and onset of chronic illness are positively correlated—the older a person is, the more likely she is to develop a chronic illness such as arthritis. A **negative correlation** exists when high values of one variable are associated with low values of the other. In contemporary American society, there is a negative correlation between age and years of education—young adults in their thirties, on the average, have completed more years of formal education than older adults in their seventies and eighties. This is because of the relative lack of educational opportunity available to many individuals during the early part of the twentieth century.

Remember that a positive correlation is not necessarily reflective of a "good" finding, nor is a negative correlation reflective of a "bad" finding. For example, there is obviously nothing "good" about the finding that as individuals grow older they are more likely to encounter a greater number of health problems.

Whether positive or negative, correlations can vary from weak to strong. A correlation is strong if the values of one variable are predictable from the values of the other. A perfect correlation exists when the values of one variable are perfectly predictable from the values of the other. The strength of a correlation can be measured quantitatively by computing the **Pearson product moment correlation coefficient,** which is abbreviated as *r.* A perfect correlation will yield an *r* of either +1.0 or –1.0, depending upon whether the association between the variables is positive or negative. As the association becomes weaker, the *r* score drops in absolute value from 1.0 to .90, .60, .40, and so on, all the way down to 0.00, which is a noncorrelation. Perfect correlations (1.0) are seldom obtained, but even moderate correlations (say, those with *r* values of .30 to .60) can be very meaningful.

An example should help illustrate the importance of correlations and how they can be interpreted. One study involved measurement of IQ on individuals at two points in their lives, once in late adolescence and again in middle age (Eichorn et al., 1981). The striking result was that IQ in late adolescence and IQ in middle age were strongly correlated, with *r* values of about +.80. Despite these high correlations, it was also true that about half of the subjects showed changes of at least ten points in IQ between the two testings. These IQ changes are at least as important as the stability in IQ implied by the high correlation. To be sure, a strong correlation implies significant predictability of scores on one variable (IQ in middle age) from scores on another (IQ in adolescence). But significant predictability is not perfect stability. Even strong correlations allow for interesting discrepancies between the values on two variables.

Two final points need to be made about correlational analyses. First, measures of correlation, such as Pearson's *r,* reflect the strength of the **linear** association between variables. This is fine in many cases, but sometimes there are **curvilinear** associations between variables. For example, it doubtlessly is true that most people have little personal income in childhood but that their income increases and then falls again as they grow older. Such a curvilinear association between age and income cannot be measured by Pearson's *r.* Second, correlational techniques are typically used to measure the relationship between two variables at a time. Thus, we could examine the correlation between: IQ and income; income and years of education; and, IQ and years of education. Correlational analyses are not usually called upon to examine how income and years of education, taken together, predict IQ scores.

## Multiple Regression

*Multiple regression* is a powerful statistical method that allows an investigator to go beyond correlational analyses. Using this technique, a researcher can set up a complex model in which she can determine if a number of variables, in combination with each other (or independent of each other), predict another variable. For example, a psychologist could determine how age, years of education, social class, gender, and need for achievement predict IQ scores. And, she could also find out if age predicts IQ independent of years of education, social class, gender, and need for achievement. Finally, multiple regression may be used to measure curvilinear relationships. Thus, a regression model could be developed that describes the finding that marital satisfaction progressively declines as children move through adolescence but begins to increase once children leave home and attend college.

## Factor Analysis

To understand adult development, it is sometimes necessary to examine many variables and to assess the pattern of correlations between these variables. For example, we might be interested in examining the variables of age with mathematical ability, creativity, health, income, occupational status, and life satisfaction. That would give us seven variables in all, among which there are twenty-one possible correlations. How do we make sense of so many correlations? How do we get a view of the forest, not just the trees?

*Factor analysis* can be useful for producing a kind of summary of many correlations. The goal is simply to reduce a large number of correlations to a smaller number of independent sets called **factors.** Put somewhat differently, this procedure discovers what variables are significantly correlated with one another but totally uncorrelated with all the other variables. For example, if health, exercise, life satisfaction, and income all correlated with one another but were mathematically independent of all of the other variables, we might want to say that these variables make up a factor which we could label as "general well-being" or "vigor." Through this process, we would replace four original variables with a single derived factor.

A potential problem with factors derived from patterns of correlations is their meaning. Once we identify and label a factor as representing *x* (well-being or vigor, for example), there is a tendency to believe that *x* truly exists (that there is, in fact, a separate "trait" of well-being or vigor and that people differ on this trait). In reality, a factor is only a summary of a pattern of correlations among variables. Our label for a factor is just that, a label. It can be wrong or misleading.

## Significance Tests

Suppose we conducted a study to determine if early retirement results in high levels of life satisfaction. We might ask a group of adults who opted for early retirement and a group of their age-mates who are still working to complete a standardized measure of life satisfaction. After collecting the data, we discover that the mean scores for the early retirees versus the workers were 101 and 77, respectively. At this point we might wonder if there is a *significant* difference between the two groups on the measure of life satisfaction. Or we might wonder if there is a *significant* relationship between the participants' work status (working versus retired) and their scores on the measure of life satisfaction.

To determine the **statistical significance** of the results of a research study, it is first necessary to *determine the probability of obtaining the observed results by pure chance alone.* This is accomplished by employing any of a number of sophisticated statistical techniques. Although it is not within the scope of this text to show you how to obtain these probability estimates, you should know how these probability estimates are interpreted. If a researcher determined that the probability of obtaining the observed results by pure chance is $^{5}/_{100}$ (.05) or less, she would conclude that the two groups in her study reflected differences so great that they are unlikely to have occurred by chance alone. Thus, differences this substantial would be viewed as "significant." Conversely, if the researcher determined that the probability of obtaining the observed results by chance is high (say $^{80}/_{100}$ [0.8] or more), she would conclude that the differences between the groups in her study were "not significant" and that the two groups responded in much the same way. Specifically, psychologists consider probabilities of $^{5}/_{100}$ (.05) or less as indicative of statistical significance. To return to our original example, if we discovered that the probability of obtaining the observed differences between the workers and early retirees on the life satisfaction measure by pure chance was $^{1}/_{100}$ (.01) or less, we would conclude that (1) the two groups differ significantly on their responses to the life satisfaction measure, and (2) there is a significant relationship between work status and life satisfaction.

## *Basic Strategies for Research Design*

In preparing to conduct a research project, it is especially important to consider design principles. The research design will determine the relationships assessed and/or the comparisons made. It will also determine how valid our conclusions can be. In general, there are two types of research designs: correlational and experimental designs.

### Correlational versus Experimental Strategies

It often is said that the experiment is the principal tool of any research scientist. Yet the vast majority of studies on adult development and aging are not true experiments; rather, they are correlational studies. What is the difference between the two? Why are correlational strategies so often used to study development? Do developmental researchers pay a price for not performing true experiments?

A **correlational study** is one in which associations among variables are merely observed. An **experimental study** also assesses associations between variables; but, in an experiment, a distinction is made between **dependent variables,** which are measured or observed, and **independent variables,** which are manipulated by the experimenter. Thus, both the manipulation of independent variables and the observation of dependent variables are the critical features of experiments.

A concrete example may help to clarify the differences between a correlational versus an experimental study. Suppose we develop the hypothesis that living in a dull, nondemanding social environment causes a deterioration in the memories of older adults; whereas living in a stimulating, demanding social environment causes older adults to maintain their memories. We could investigate this hypothesis by conducting a correlational study. This might entail administering a standardized test of memory to two groups of older adults who live in two different types of environments: a nondemanding environment (perhaps a nursing home), and a demanding environment (living independently at home and being actively involved in a senior citizens center, doing volunteer work, etc.). From this study we might discover that the demandingness of the social environment is positively correlated with memory performance; that is, as the demands of the environment increase, participants' scores on the memory test increase. Regardless of the strength of this correlation, however, we could *not* conclude that changes in the environment cause differences in memory. It may be that older people who remember and think well are likely to choose to live at home, whereas people who have more difficulty remembering and who are not self-sufficient wind up in nursing homes. Thus, it could be that the ability to remember determines the type of environment in which a person lives, rather than vice versa. The real purpose of a correlational study is to make accurate *predictions* (not to determine cause-effect relationships). For example, from this study we could predict that people who live in nursing homes often have poor memories, but we would not know why they have poor memories.

To determine cause-and-effect relationships, it is necessary to perform an *experimental study.* In order to conduct an experimental study, it is necessary to manipulate an independent variable. Ellen Langer and her associates (Langer, Rodin, Beck, Weinman, & Spitzer, 1979) conducted an experiment that bears on the hypothesis described in the preceding paragraph. The investigators randomly divided a sample of the residents of a nursing home into different groups or conditions. In the *contingent condition,* residents were told that they would be visited several times during the next few weeks and would be asked a number of questions such as, "What did you have for breakfast two days ago?" These residents were given a poker chip for each memory question they answered correctly. The poker chips could be exchanged for gifts at a later date. The participants in the contingent condition thus lived in a demanding social environment. In the *noncontingent condition,* residents were asked the same memory questions over the same time period. At the end of the questioning session, these residents were given some poker chips as a "momento." (Care was taken to equate the number of chips given to members of the contingent and noncontingent groups.) Residents in the noncontingent group were told that the number of chips they received did *not* depend on the accuracy of their memory. They were also allowed to exchange their chips for gifts. The participants in the noncontingent condition, therefore, lived in a nondemanding social environment.

After three weeks of treatment, all participants were administered a number of memory tests. Results indicated that the residents from the demanding environment (the contingent condition) performed significantly better on the memory tests than those from the nondemanding environment (the noncontingent condition). Thus, the initial hypothesis was confirmed. In this experiment the manipulated independent variable was whether participants received poker chips under contingent or noncontingent conditions. The observed or measured dependent variable was the way the participants scored on the memory tests. But could other factors besides the conditions to which the participants were assigned account for the results of this experiment? How do we actually know that it was the independent variable that produced the differences between the participants in the two conditions?

One approach to this problem is to match the two groups on **extraneous variables** that are suspected to be important. For example, we could give IQ tests to all participants, making sure that the groups were matched with respect to IQ. Such matching can be useful, but **random assignment** is a much more powerful technique. In an experiment, individuals are always assigned to a specific group on a random basis. If assignment to groups is random and if the number of participants is reasonably large, we can assume that all extraneous factors will be randomly distributed in the two groups. This includes extraneous factors that we could never have thought of in advance, as well as the more obvious factors that might be handled through matching.

## Manipulations Between and Within Subjects

Random assignment of participants to different groups is one way to manipulate an independent variable. Such manipulations are **between-subject manipulations.** There are also **within-subject manipulations,** which involve observing each participant in an experiment under two or more conditions. For example, if we suspect that a certain drug improves memory in patients with Alzheimer's disease, we might measure memory ability in each individual after administration of this drug and also after administration of a placebo. Each individual then could be examined under the drug condition and later under the placebo condition to determine the effect of the drug. Counterbalancing would be advisable in such an experiment—we would test one-half of the sample first in the drug condition and later in the placebo condition, and we would test the remaining sample first in the placebo condition and later in the drug condition. Counterbalancing controls the effects of the time at which variables are manipulated within subjects.

## Quasi-Experimental Strategies in Developmental Research

All "true" experiments involve the manipulation of variables. Unfortunately, some variables are difficult if not impossible to manipulate. Age is one of these variables. *Since we cannot manipulate a person's age, we cannot perform true experiments to examine the effects of age on a person's behavior.* Despite the fact that most studies involving age are not true experiments, they often resemble true experiments in the ways in which they are designed or analyzed; age is treated as an independent variable even though it is not actually manipulated. Thus, we look for *effects of age*—actually, *effects related to age*—on one or more dependent variables. Because they are similar to true experiments, but also because the independent variable—age—is not truly manipulated, such studies are called **quasi-experiments.**

Let's consider what it means to say that a person's age cannot be manipulated. Suppose we are conducting a study on adult development and succeed in finding individuals who are willing to serve as participants. We can observe their behavior under a variety of conditions that are under our control. For example, we might present one of several different types of instruction, or administer several different types of drugs. It is up to us, the experimenters, to decide which conditions or treatments each participant will receive. But we can't decide each participant's age; we cannot alter the number of years each person has lived.

Of course, we can assign any one participant to a group of similarly aged individuals and compare this group to another group of younger or older individuals. We can also plan to test our participants not only today but again several years from now. Using these strategies, we can compare functioning at different ages and gather evidence about effects and phenomena that are *related* to age. But clearly these strategies do *not* entail the actual manipulation of age. They simply allow us to take advantage of differences and changes in age that occur independently of our study and that are beyond our control.

## The Problem of Internal Validity

Perhaps you feel that the difference between an experiment and a quasi-experiment is rather subtle and has no practical importance. If so, you are right about the subtlety but wrong about the importance. The difference is critical, and it is clarified by the concept of internal validity.

The concept of internal validity concerns the role played by an independent variable in an experiment (or quasi-experiment). An experiment possesses **internal validity** if the results of the experiment reflect the influence of the independent variable rather than the influence of any extraneous or uncontrolled variables.

Internal validity is a concept that was developed by Donald Campbell and Julian Stanley in their classic book, *Experimental and Quasi-Experimental Designs for Research* (1963). Campbell and Stanley enumerate several threats to internal validity and show that quasi-experimental studies, which include most studies of adult development and aging, are much more vulnerable to these threats than are true experiments.

One of the most serious threats to internal validity is **selection.** This threat is especially troublesome when different-aged groups are compared. In such cases, the procedures used to select groups can result in many extraneous differences among these groups, *differences that do not pertain to age per se.* For example, a young-adult group and an elderly group might differ with respect to years of education, health status, and so on. These differences between the members of these different cohorts may make the results of a research study very difficult to interpret.

A second threat to internal validity is **history.** This is especially serious when we test the same individuals at different ages. The problem is that between one time of testing and another, many events can have a profound effect on the person's behavior; also, of course, the person is growing older between testings. Possible historical effects include attitudinal changes (social attitudes toward aging, for example), economic events (increases in social security), and social changes (the development of new senior citizen's centers), among others. These changes might have a positive effect on an aging population if, as individuals grow older, they (1) are looked upon more positively, (2) have more money to spend, and (3) have more opportunities for social and intellectual stimulation. Thus, these individuals are likely to function in a more adaptive psychological manner not because they are getting older, but because of positive sociohistorical changes.

A third threat to internal validity is **testing.** Taking a test on one occasion can affect test performance on a subsequent occasion. Obviously, the testing threat can accompany the history threat whenever we test the same individuals at different ages. However, the testing threat is especially serious when we are measuring some type of behavior that can change with practice. (Many types of intellectual performance can change with practice.)

Suppose that we had a machine that could make someone 20 years old, or even 90 years old, by turning a switch (and that we could bring the person back to his or her original age with no harm done). We could take a sample of subjects and randomly assign half of them to a 20-year-old condition and the other half to a 90-year-old condition, and then compare them on many different dependent measures (e.g., creativity). Random assignment would take care of all extraneous differences between the two age groups (the selection threat). History would not be a factor because we could test all subjects on the same day. Further, we would test each subject only once, thus avoiding the threat of testing. Under these ideal conditions, we could solve all problems of internal validity. Unfortunately, we have no ideal situation. In developmental research we must live with threats to internal validity and compensate for them as best we can.

Next we consider several different types of quasi-experimental designs that are used in research on adult development and aging. We will see that different designs compensate for different internal validity threats. We will also see that the time span of a research design is a critical factor in determining what kinds of threats it can handle.

## *Quasi-Experimental Designs for the Study of Adult Development and Aging*

Discussion of quasi-experimental research designs can be complicated. Let's start with the simplest designs: the cross-sectional and longitudinal designs, which are the basis for all developmental research. Then we'll describe more complex designs called sequential designs, which are actually further elaborations of the basic cross-sectional and simple longitudinal designs. There are ways in which all of these designs compensate, or fail to compensate, for the various threats to internal validity. Table A.1 provides a summary of each design, its susceptibility to internal validity threats, and other distinguishing features. It may be helpful to consult this table throughout the discussion that follows.

*TABLE A.1*

| *Summary of Quasi-Experimental Designs in Adult Development and Aging* | | | |
|---|---|---|---|
| ***Design*** | ***Description*** | ***Threats to Internal Validity*** | ***Other Properties*** |
| Simple-Cross Sectional | Two or more age groups are compared at one time of testing | Selection, especially cohort effects; differences between groups might reflect differences in time of birth | Easy to conduct; can be useful as a pilot study |
| Simple Longitudinal | A single group of subjects is tested repeatedly at different points in time | Time-of-testing (history) effects: historical changes might produce effects that appear to be age-related changes; repeated testing might influence measures (testing effects) | Time-consuming; subjects may drop out of study prior to completion—selective dropout (this threatens generalizability of findings); allows assessment of individual differences in developmental change |
| Cohort-Sequential | Two or more longitudinal comparisons are made on different cohorts | Time-of-testing and testing effects as for simple longitudinal (can remove testing effects with independent samples) | Extremely time-consuming; requires two time periods to examine change over one time period; allows separate examination of age-related effects and cohort effects |
| Time-Sequential | Two or more cross-sectional comparisons are made at different times of testing | Cohort effects, since every cross-sectional comparison is possibly influenced by cohort as well as age | Time-consuming, but not as time-consuming as cohort-sequential designs; allows separate examination of age effects and time-of-testing (history) effects |
| Cross-Sequential | Two or more cohorts are compared at two or more times of testing | Neither time-of-testing nor cohort effects are independent of age-related changes | Time-consuming; provides no clear information on age-related changes |

## Cross-Sectional and Longitudinal Designs

Consider two different ways in which we might examine the impact of aging on behavior. First, we might perform a **cross-sectional study,** comparing groups of people in different age ranges. A typical cross-sectional study might include a group of 18- to 20-year-olds and a group of 65- to 70-year-olds. A more comprehensive cross-sectional study might include groups from every decade of life from the twenties through the nineties. The investigators could compare the different groups on a variety of dependent variables, such as IQ performance, memory, and creativity. They could collect data in a very short time; even a large study can be completed within a few months. The major purpose of a cross-sectional study is to measure *age-related differences.* As we shall see, a cross-sectional study allows us to determine if one age group of subjects differs from other age groups. Cross-sectional studies, however, do *not* allow us to measure age-related change (i.e., the extent to which age-graded factors, by themselves, cause developmental change).

Another way we might explore the effects of aging on behavior is to perform a **longitudinal study.** In this case, we would take a single group of subjects, all the same age, and test them today and on one or more occasions in the future. For example, we might decide to examine creativity at ages 50, 57, 64, and 71. Longitudinal studies clearly take a long time to complete. Furthermore, the purpose of a longitudinal study is to measure *age-related changes,* not age differences. As we shall see, simple longitudinal studies are not always successful in measuring such changes.

One advantage of cross-sectional designs, then, is time efficiency. Further, cross-sectional designs are virtually free of two important internal validity threats. There is no history threat because all subjects are tested at the same time. There is no testing threat because it is necessary to test each individual subject only once. For these reasons, cross-sectional designs are enormously popular. However, as mentioned earlier, cross-sectional designs are highly susceptible to the internal validity threat of *selection.* We often do not know the extent to which the results of a cross-sectional study reflect the effects of age versus the effects of countless extraneous factors. Many extraneous factors involved in cross-sectional designs pertain to **cohort effects.** Cohort effects are caused by a subject's time of birth or generation but not actually to her or his age. For example, cohorts can differ with respect to years of education, childrearing practices, health, and attitudes on topics such as sex and religion. These cohort effects are important because they can powerfully influence the dependent measures in a study concerned with age. Cohort effects can look like age effects, but they are not.

Since cross-sectional designs do not allow random assignment of individuals to age groups, there is no way to control cohort effects or other extraneous variables. Our only approach to controlling these variables is through *matching.* For example, if our young subjects are all college students, we might make sure that all our elderly subjects are also college students. Unfortunately, matching for extraneous variables is sometimes impossible. (We may be unable to find an adequate number of elderly college students who are willing to participate in our study.) Further, we can only match for the extraneous variables whose importance we recognize. Finally, matching can have the unwanted side effect of producing unusual or *nonrepresentative* groups—elderly people in college may differ in many ways from the average person of their age. Selection poses a serious threat to cross-sectional studies, and matching is not truly adequate to remove it.

Figure A.1 contains a diagram of a simple cross-sectional study that addresses the issue of whether IQ changes from 50 to 60 to 70 years of age. This study, if it were conducted in the year 1990, would employ participants of different ages (50, 60, and 70) representing different cohorts according to the year in which they were born (1920, 1930, and 1940). Interpreting the data obtained in this study would be impossible because changes in age are *confounded* (i.e., confused with) changes in cohort. For example, we might find that 70-year-olds have lower IQ scores than 50-year-olds. But we would not know if this is because of the ages of the participants, the amount of education received by individuals born in 1920 versus those born in 1940, or some other extraneous factor.

Although longitudinal studies are time-consuming, they are valuable because they remove the threat of selection, or cohort effects. This is because individuals from a single cohort form the subject pool for a longitudinal study. Further, longitudinal

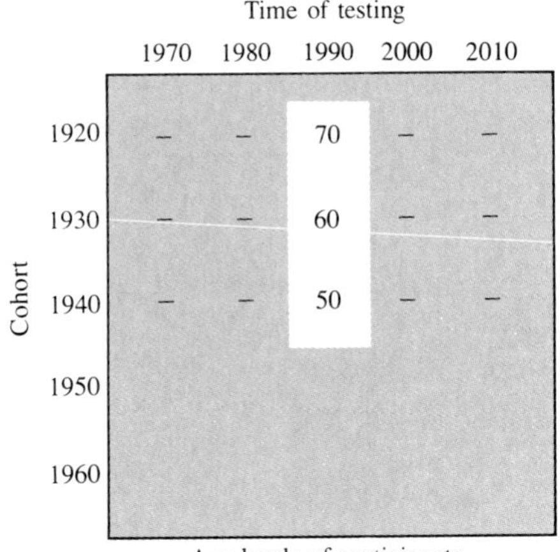


**Figure A.1** A cross-sectional design measures age-related differences between different cohorts.

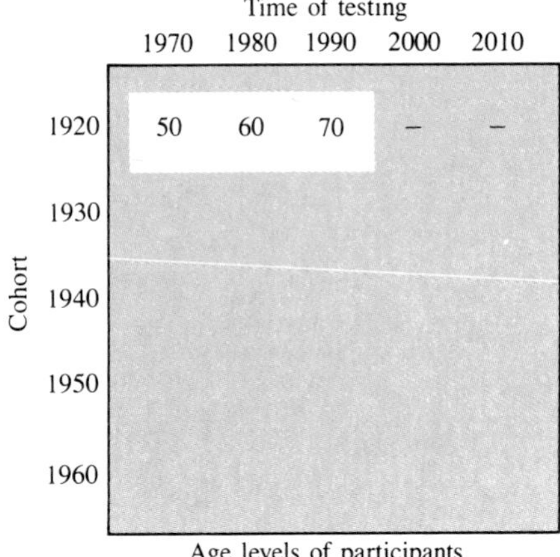


**Figure A.2** A longitudinal design measures age-related changes within a cohort.

studies have the great advantage of allowing us to track changes that take place within individual subjects over a long time interval. If one's primary concern is the study of intraindividual change over the course of development, longitudinal designs are indispensable.

Unfortunately, the threats of history, testing, and selective dropout are especially troublesome in longitudinal designs. *Selective dropout* refers to the possibility that over the course of a longitudinal study, participants who either perform poorly on a particular test, or are unmotivated or ill, will be less likely to undergo repeated testing. To illustrate, consider the longitudinal study diagrammed in figure A.2. This study measures IQ changes in individuals from the 1920 birth cohort as they move from 50 to 60 to 70 years of age. The study begins in the year 1970 and concludes in the year 1990. The same participants are retested at ten-year intervals. Interpreting the data obtained in this study would be very difficult. For example, we might find that the participants display higher IQ scores at age 70 than age 50. This finding might be due to any number of facts; for example, it could be true that (1) people actually become more intelligent as they age; (2) between 1970 and 1990 our society has changed so that life has become more stimulating, enriching, and enjoyable for the typical older person; (3) the subjects became more familiar with the IQ test each time they were tested; or (4) at the end of the study in 1990, we were left with a very biased group of participants—those who were exceptionally bright, motivated, healthy, and so on.

It may be possible to remove the threats of testing and selective dropout by adding new or independent samples of participants at each testing. For example, we could collect data on a group of randomly selected 60-year-olds in 1980 and compare their IQ performance to those participants tested for the second time in 1980. And we could also add another group of randomly selected 70-year-olds in 1990. This procedure, however, would still not remove the history threat.

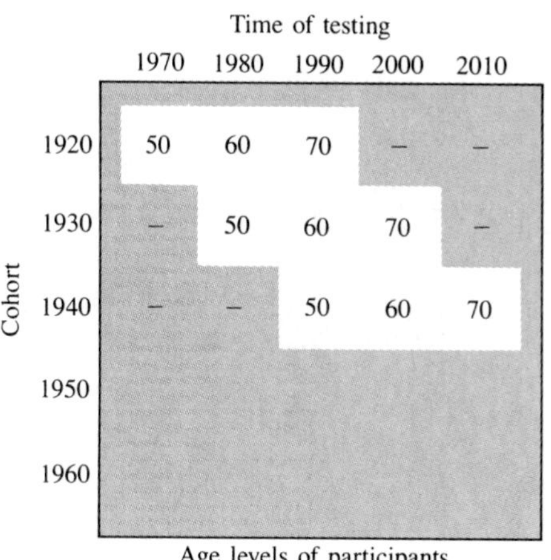


**Figure A.3** A cohort-sequential design involves two or more longitudinal studies covering the same age ranges over different time eras.

## Cohort-Sequential Designs

Sequential research designs may be used to correct some of the inadequacies of cross-sectional and longitudinal research. A **cohort-sequential design** entails two or more longitudinal studies, each covering the same range of ages, conducted over differing lengths of time. An example of a simple cohort-sequential design is shown in figure A.3. Three different cohorts are selected; a cohort born in 1920, a second cohort born in 1930, and a third born in 1940. A sample from each cohort is tested on three different occasions—first when the participants are 50 years old, again when they are 60 years old, and a third time when they are 70 years old. As in the simple longitudinal design, independent samples could also be drawn at the different times of testing to control the threats of testing and selective dropout.

The cohort-sequential design corrects for the major drawback associated with the simple cross-sectional design; that is, by conducting a cohort-sequential study, we can estimate the relative importance of age effects in comparison to cohort effects. For example, we can compare performance by the 1920 versus 1930 versus 1940 cohorts by looking across the rows in figure A.3. This tells us something about how cohort-related factors might influence our measure. We can also compare the performance of individuals from each of the three age groups. This is accomplished by looking at the diagonals in figure A.3—we could calculate the average score of all of the 50-year-olds and compare it to the average score for all groups of 60-year-olds, and so on. This tells us how age influences our measure independently of cohort. Further, the design allows us to assess interactions between cohort and age. We can see if the age effect is constant across the two cohorts, or if it varies between the cohorts. This can obviously be very important if there are different rates of aging in different cohorts.

The main weakness of cohort-sequential design is that it doesn't compensate for the history threat. We would have no understanding, in other words, of how the historical changes that occurred from 1970 to 2010 affected the behavior of our

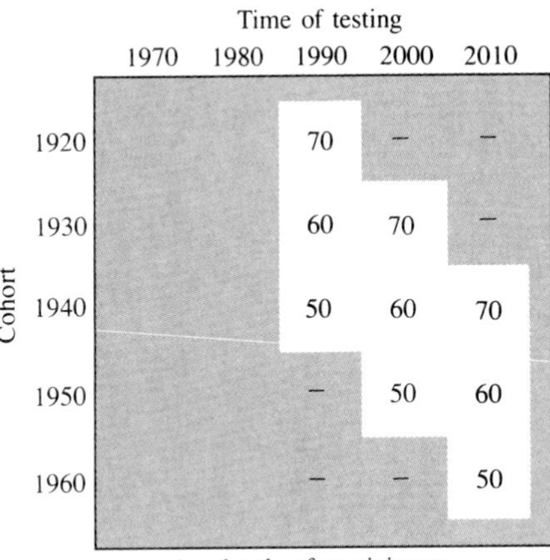


**Figure A.4** A time-sequential design differentiates age effects from historical changes.

participants. Another weakness of the design is that it takes a great deal of time to complete. As you can see from figure A.3, to study aging and cohort effects on IQ at 50, 60, and 70 years of age, we need forty years to collect the data.

## Time-Sequential Designs

The **time-sequential design** corrects for the major limitation of the longitudinal design. This design is capable of differentiating age effects from historical changes (or time-of-testing effects). Time-sequential designs involve two or more cross-sectional studies, each covering the same range of ages, conducted at different times. An example is shown in figure A.4. According to this figure, in 1990, we examine performance of three age groups: 50-, 60-, and 70-year-olds. In 2000 and also in 2010, we again examine the performance of individuals at these three age levels (these are, of course, entirely *new* samples of participants).

The strength of the time-sequential design is that history effects—or time-of-testing effects—can be examined explicitly, in addition to differences related to age. That is, looking at the columns in figure A.4, we can examine differences between performance in 1970, 1980, and 1990; this tells us directly about history effects. Independent of history, we can look at the diagonals to examine differences between the 50-, 60-, and 70-year-olds; this gives us information relevant to aging. Furthermore, we can examine the interactions between age and time of testing. If age-related differences in 1980 are smaller than age-related differences in 1970 and 1990, it might support some interesting conclusions about history-related changes in the course of adult development.

Another advantage of the time-sequential design is that it is more time efficient than the cohort-sequential design. In our example (figure A.4), age and history effects can be studied over a twenty-year span (compared to a forty-year span for the cohort-sequential design). Also, note that the time-sequential design (figure A.4) takes the same length of time to conduct as the longitudinal design (figure A.2)!

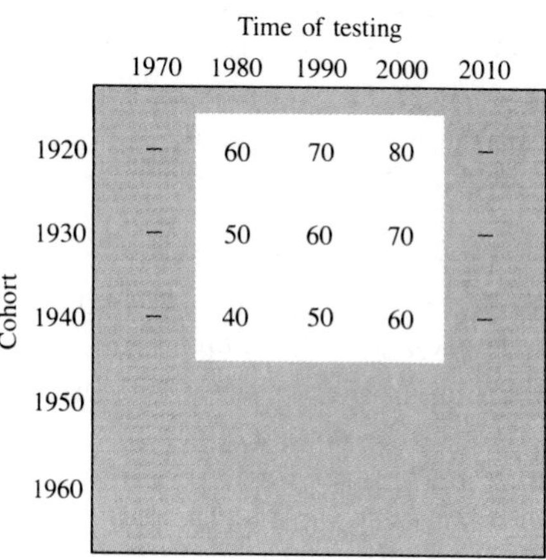


**Figure A.5** A cross-sequential design combines the cross-sectional and longitudinal designs.

The disadvantage of the time-sequential design is that it does not consider cohort effects. At each time of measurement, we must be concerned with the possibility that differences between our age groups may, in part, reflect differences in their respective cohorts.

## Cross-Sequential Designs

**Cross-sequential designs** are a kind of hybrid combination of cross-sectional and longitudinal designs. They are not fundamentally relevant to adult development and aging because they do not separate age effects from either cohort or history effects. Rather, cross-sequential designs separate cohort and history effects from each other.

The technique used in a cross-sequential design, illustrated in figure A.5, is to examine two (or more) cohorts, covering different age ranges, at each of two (or more) times of testing. Differences among cohorts can be examined independently of differences among times of measurement. Unfortunately, neither of these differences can be separated from age. The cohorts differ on an age dimension, and subjects must obviously be older at the second testing than the first.

Perhaps this is a good time for you to stop and review the various quasi-experimental designs in adult development and aging. Going over them once or even twice probably won't be enough. Take some time to study the material in table A.1, which summarizes the main characteristics of each of these quasi-experimental designs.

## Schaie's Most Efficient Design

We can summarize the preceding discussion by saying that the cohort-sequential design is a useful extension of simple longitudinal designs and that the time-sequential design is a useful extension of cross-sectional designs. Furthermore, we could conclude that these sequential designs are far superior to the simple cross-sectional and longitudinal studies from which they are derived. However, the various sequential designs are still less than perfect. History or time-of-testing effects threaten the internal validity of cohort-sequential designs. Cohort effects threaten the internal validity of time-sequential designs. So what are we to do to ensure the internal validity of our research?

One answer is to use *both* the cohort-sequential and time-sequential designs, and then even to add the cross-sequential design for good measure. Incorporating all of these designs at once is more difficult than performing one of them alone. K. W. Schaie (1965, 1977), an authority on sequential designs, has developed the **most efficient design** to combine the best features of the other designs.

The most efficient design is illustrated in figure A.6. Individuals in five different cohorts are studied: 1900, 1910, 1920, 1930, and 1940. Measurements are made at five different times: 1950, 1960, 1970, 1980, and 1990. Finally, it is necessary to collect data from new, independent samples of each cohort at each of the different times of testing (though retesting of the original samples is also recommended). If all this is accomplished, it is possible to perform a cohort-sequential analysis, a time-sequential analysis, and a cross-sequential analysis all at once, as shown in figure A.6.

Such analyses provide a wealth of interesting comparisons. Certain patterns can reveal strong evidence for age-related changes, cohort differences, and history effects. Consider the following possible outcome in a study of creativity: The cohort-sequential analysis may suggest a strong effect of cohort but only a weak effect of age. The time-sequential analysis supports only weak effects of time of testing and age. Finally, the cross-sequential analysis supports, again, a strong effect of cohort but only a weak effect of time of measurement. In this hypothetical case, we would have clear indications that cohort is an important variable but that age and time of measurement are not.

We must always be mindful of the tremendous difficulty of collecting the data that permit such complex analyses. Faced with this difficulty, it may frequently be advisable to first conduct simple cross-sectional studies, controlling as much as possible for extraneous, cohort-related variables known to be important. Examining the effects of different treatments in such designs can also help isolate the specific ways in which younger groups differ from older groups at a particular time in history. Subsequently, once important differences between younger and older groups have been isolated, longitudinal and even sequential strategies can be carried out, allowing a much more complete understanding of the causes of these differences.

Stated somewhat differently, cross-sectional studies seem to be the logical starting point in developmental research. If this type of research establishes reliable age differences in behavior, then other types of designs should be carried out to determine the underlying causes of the apparent age difference.

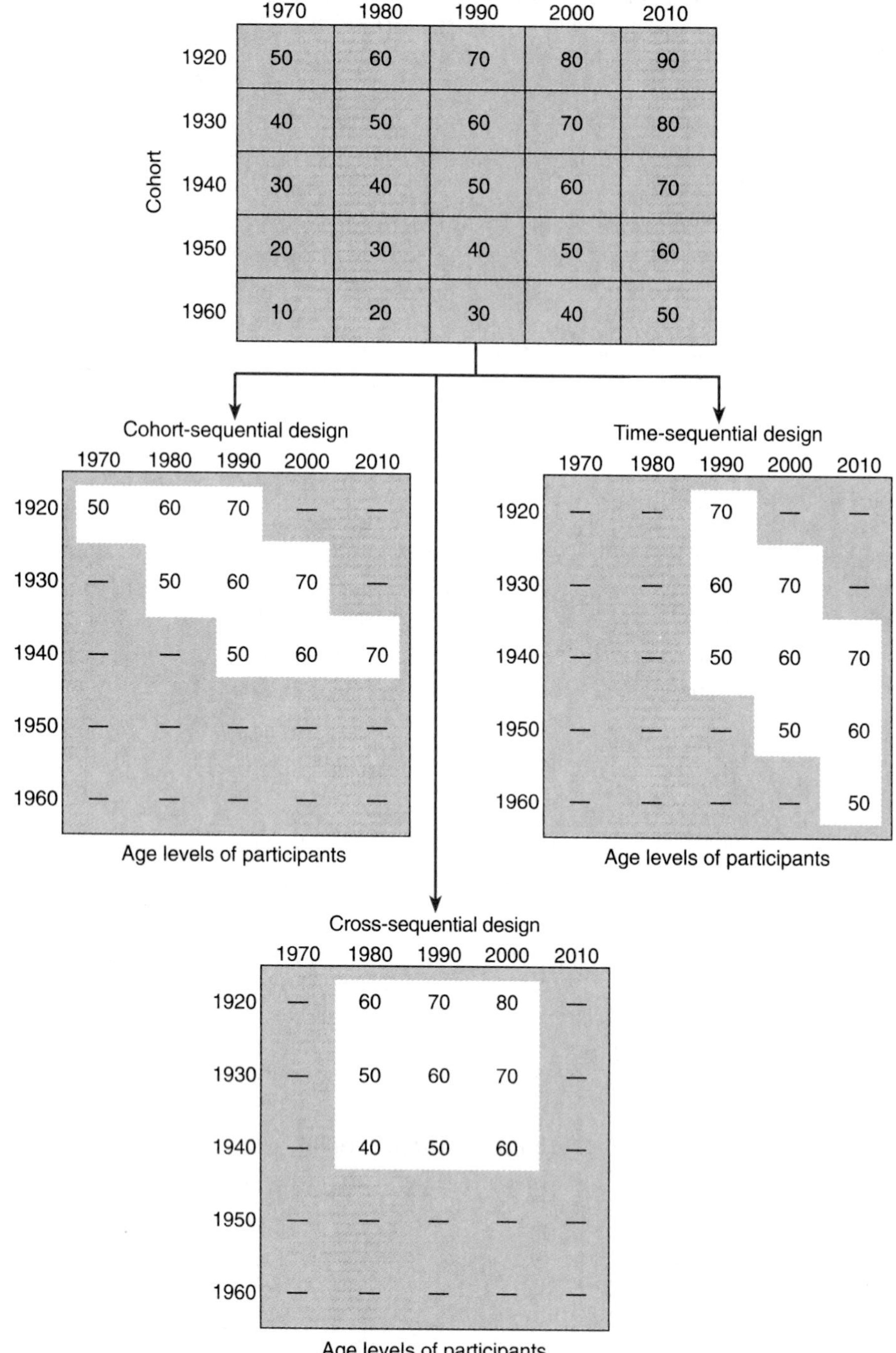


**Figure A.6** Schaie's "most efficient" design.

## *Problems of Sampling in Developmental Research*

When we decide to study a certain group of individuals (say, 70-year-olds who have recently retired), we obviously cannot collect measurements on everyone in that group. Rather, we must study a sample of the entire population of individuals in the class. Although we study only a sample, we want to generalize our findings to the rest of the population. Thus, the sampling procedures form a very important aspect of research methodology.

A **representative sample** has the same characteristics as the larger population to which we want to generalize our findings. The best way to achieve a representative sample is through the technique of random sampling, a technique in which every member of the population has an equal chance of being in the sample that we study. For example, the ideal way to find a representative sample of recently retired 70-year-olds would be to compile a list of every such individual in the world and then to pick randomly a number of these individuals to be in our study. Obviously, truly random sampling can rarely be employed. Indeed, we often must struggle to find people with certain characteristics who are willing to participate in our studies.

Investigators of adult development seldom can be sure that their samples are representative. This fact produces two consequences, one pertaining primarily to cross-sectional designs and the other primarily to longitudinal designs.

### Nonrepresentative Samples in Cross-Sectional Designs

In cross-sectional designs, the problem of nonrepresentative samples adds to problems of internal validity. Specifically, selection threats may be due partially to nonrepresentative sampling. If we find differences between a group of young subjects and a group of elderly subjects but do not know whether either sample is representative, it is difficult to be sure if either age or cohort is responsible for the differences. Perhaps these differences occurred because we selected a group of young adults with below-average intelligence for individuals of their age and a group of older persons with above-average intelligence for individuals of their age. The solution to this problem is to measure various extraneous variables (IQ, for example) that are suspected to be important. We must measure the IQs of the two groups and relate them to the norms for their age groups. Though not ideal, this approach is much better than ignoring these issues.

### Nonrepresentative Samples in Longitudinal Designs

The problem of sampling in longitudinal studies is not just a hypothetical problem; it has been shown to occur. It frequently takes the form of selective dropout. As we have already mentioned, selective dropout refers to the fact that some participants drop out of a longitudinal study before all of the testings are complete. The problem is that those who drop out of a study are likely to differ significantly from those who continue until the end. Indeed, it has been shown that people who return for testing in a longitudinal study often have greater intellectual abilities than those who do not

(Riegel & Riegel, 1972). Further, longitudinal declines in intellectual ability are more likely to occur among those who drop out of a study after several testings than among those who remain (Eisdorfer & Wilkie, 1973; Wilkie & Eisdorfer, 1973). Finally, Cooney, Schaie, and Willis (1988) have shown that participants who leave a longitudinal study for health reasons are largely responsible for producing the selective dropout effect. As a result, the data collected in a longitudinal study may reflect aging among adults of superior ability and good health, not aging among adults of average or below-average ability and health.

At another level, sampling problems can threaten the external validity of longitudinal research (Campbell & Stanley, 1963). **External validity** refers to the degree to which we may generalize the results of a scientific study. When we use nonrepresentative samples, we often do not know whether age trends observed in one longitudinal study are representative of age trends in the population at large. The external validity of cross-sectional designs, of course, may be threatened for the same reason.

## Summary

Two basic problems of measurement are reliability and validity. Although the problem of reliability is serious, effective methods for assessing reliability (e.g., the test-retest method) and for increasing reliability (e.g., collecting data on multiple items) do exist. The problem of validity is more troublesome because many psychological concepts, such as creativity and self-concept, are highly abstract. When we attempt to evaluate such abstract concepts, it is often arguable that we are not truly measuring what we think we are measuring.

Among the basic measures used for collecting observations are the interview and questionnaire, behavioral research, standardized tests, and physiological research. Each has strengths and weaknesses. Interview and questionnaire studies can often be conducted when other sorts of studies are impossible or, at best, impractical. However, these types of studies are especially susceptible to the problem of reactivity, particularly the problem of response bias. Moreover, interviews and questionnaires are highly dependent upon the subjects' conscious impressions of themselves, and these impressions can be at variance with actual behavior.

Behavioral measures are many and varied. They can be collected in laboratory settings or in the field. Behavioral studies in the laboratory allow impressive control over many extraneous variables. However, they often can be artificial, even anxiety provoking, to subjects. Further, laboratory studies produce problems of reactivity, and they cannot be used to study certain kinds of real-world phenomena. Field studies allow fewer controls, but they can be very naturalistic, can reduce problems of reactivity, and can reveal real-life phenomena that are not reproducible in the laboratory. Standardized tests are useful for comparing a particular sample of subjects to representative samples of subjects tested previously. However, the validity of such tests is often questionable. Further, it is frequently the case that no previously developed test can measure exactly what we want to measure. Physiological measures can be invaluable for an increased understanding of behavioral data, and they can suggest ways to reduce or remove age-related differences in behavior when this is desirable.

Among the basic strategies for summarizing data are measures of central tendency and variability. Correlations are used to determine the degree to which two variables are related to each other. However, many studies produce so many correlations that interpretation is difficult. In these cases, factor analysis can be useful for reducing many correlations to a smaller number of factors. Significance tests are used to determine if the results of a study are due to chance.

In terms of research design, correlational studies must be distinguished from true experiments. Experiments involve the manipulation of independent variables and actually provide evidence for cause-effect relationships between independent and dependent variables. Quasi-experiments are similar to true experiments, but quasi-experiments do not involve the actual manipulation of independent variables. Since age cannot be manipulated, studies of this variable are considered to be quasi-experimental. Three threats to internal validity, threats that are problematic in such quasi-experimental studies, are selection, history, and testing.

Several types of quasi-experiments are used to study adult development and aging. Simple cross-sectional and longitudinal designs are limited in their usefulness. Cross-sectional designs suffer from cohort effects, whereas longitudinal designs suffer from both testing and history effects. Among the sequential designs, the cohort-sequential design allows independent assessment of age and cohort effects but does not solve the problem of history effects. The time-sequential design allows independent assessment of age and history effects but does not solve the problem of cohort effects. The use of both designs together, along with the cross-sequential design as well, can in principle allow us to distinguish age, cohort, and history effects. A greater investment of time and resources is necessary to use all these designs together, however.

Researchers must frequently sample their participants from different age groups (cohorts), and this sampling can introduce bias; samples may be nonrepresentative. The problem of sampling is unavoidable, but we must keep it in mind when we are interpreting the data in studies of adult development and aging. Particularly vexing is the problem of selective dropout or experimental mortality, which occurs when participants drop out of a longitudinal study. Those who drop out are likely to suffer systematically from those who remain. This can threaten the generalizability of longitudinal studies.

## Review Questions

1. How can we assess reliability? How can we improve the methods we use to assess reliability?
2. What are the central issues involved in the validity of measurement?
3. Describe the basic types of measures used for collecting information about adults. Include the advantages and disadvantages of each type.
4. What are the basic strategies for summarizing measurements?
5. Explain the logic behind the technique of factor analysis.
6. Provide an overview of correlational and experimental strategies in research design. Include in your answer information about manipulations between and within subjects.
7. Discuss quasi-experimental designs and the problem of internal validity.
8. Compare and contrast the simple quasi-experimental designs (cross-sectional and longitudinal) with the complex quasi-experimental designs (sequential designs) used to study adult development and aging.
9. What are some of the main sampling problems in conducting research with adults?

# CAREERS IN BASIC AND APPLIED GERONTOLOGY

*It is not enough for a great nation merely to have added new years to life—our objective must also be to add new life to those years.*
—John Fitzgerald Kennedy



## GERONTOLOGY: BASIC AND APPLIED

*Gerontology* is the scientific study of aging, where aging is understood to encompass "the regular changes that occur in mature, genetically representative organisms living under representative environmental conditions as they advance in chronological age" (Birren & Renner, 1977). Concern for the elderly was heightened in this country in the 1930s when social scientists were consulted in developing policies for social security and retirement; their opinions were sought to understand how such policies might affect older persons—psychologically, socially, and economically. Scientific interest in the elderly may be marked by the founding of the Gerontological Society of America in 1945. The major journal of this organization, *The Journal of Gerontology,* first appeared in 1946, and one year later the American Psychological Association created a separate Division of Maturity and Old Age (Division 20) for professionals interested in this area. Since these formative days, the field of gerontology has grown, and interdisciplinary and multidisciplinary perspectives are commonly adopted in research, assessment, treatment, and services. Gerontologists are conducting many studies of early adulthood, the middle-age years, as well as the changes associated with the young-old, the old-old, and the frail elderly. Aging and a life-span developmental perspective have much in common today.

There continues to be confusion in the minds of professionals who work with the elderly in a variety of capacities as to whether the study of aging should be considered a discipline by itself, a separate profession, or simply representative of a broad-based orientation (Huyck & Hoyer, 1982).

A field of study is termed a *discipline* when it involves a specialized body of knowledge and, often, special techniques of discovery. Traditionally, universities have been organized around relatively "bounded" disciplines, represented by departments bearing their respective names: biology, economics, mathematics, philosophy, or psychology. However, the boundaries separating such disciplines are shifting rapidly as new fields emerge that cross departmental structures or evolve from a synthesis of a number of different fields, for example, biochemistry, cognitive neuroscience, information sciences, international relations, mathematical economics, and public policy analysis. The fact remains that there is nothing intrinsic about the disciplines themselves; they have been changing in universities for centuries as scholars debate which ones are needed for a college education. For example, over a hundred years ago, faculty debated the legitimacy of studying the "Modern Languages" rather than Greek and Latin.

There is already a sufficiently stable and growing body of knowledge describing the special characteristics of older adults. Those who see gerontology as a separate discipline emphasize that this field requires an *inter*disciplinary approach. To understand and describe human aging requires crossing traditional disciplinary boundaries, blending them, and even creating new ones. The fact that a field is interdisciplinary in no way denies the validity of the body of knowledge that is subsumed within it. To understand human aging, we may adopt a multidisciplinary approach as well, examining those fields that have the potential to help us understand the complexities of aging. We welcome the contributions not only of fields such as biology, chemistry, psychology, and sociology but also law, medicine, economics, and anthropology. To focus exclusively on only one discipline would result in a biased and limited view of the complexities of aging. Gerontology thus requires a multidisciplinary approach, integrating and applying results from traditional fields as well as an interdisciplinary approach blending traditional fields of knowledge and utilizing the contributions from newly emerging fields.

A *profession* involves the application of specialized knowledge. Professionals determine the boundaries of their expertise: what they should know and how to apply it. At present there is certainly a vital and dynamic interdisciplinary knowledge base in gerontology, a base that professional gerontologists should know. Very little consensus exists, however, as to what a professional gerontologist could or should do. In what settings should this unique knowledge be applied and what professional responsibilities might be assumed by someone who uses the label of professional gerontologist?

This brings us to a final option, to consider gerontology as a pervasive *orientation* or a general point of view that can be applied to relevant disciplines and professions that already exist. Through a gerontological orientation, disciplines may emphasize age as a relevant dimension or begin to include it in their approaches. There are few disciplines that would not be amenable to a gerontological view. For instance, the field of marketing has begun to recognize the changing demographics of our aging society in its efforts to promote products and increase sales. Anthropologists too have begun to explore different cultures for evidence of universal patterns of aging as well as for those special features that mark a culture's distinctive approach to the process of aging. Rural sociologists have studied how older people age, how they retire, and how they spend their free time. Economists have examined spending habits of older persons, their savings for retirement, and their expenditures for goods and services. Political scientists have become interested in the patterns of voting behavior by age group and the growing segment of elderly people who will have increasing control and power in determining national policies through their choice of representatives.

## *Careers in Basic and Applied Gerontology*

As a rapidly growing field, gerontology has many career possibilities. Generally, studies show that there will be an 8 to 11 percent higher projected need for professionals working in the field of gerontology than for all other jobs combined in our society through the year 2005 (American College Testing, 1993). Some of these careers are described in this appendix briefly (cf. Swanson, 1989) and suggestions for further information from professional organizations are listed.

### Gerontologist

*Gerontologists* typically follow basic careers in research under the aegis of the federal or local government. They specialize in the study of aging, the unique problems of the aged, and the impact that this has on governmental programs, social policy, and planning for delivery of services. Gerontological research requires data collection, assessments of its validity, and analysis of results. Gerontologists require different levels of education, depending on the role one assumes on a research team. Research problems of interest to gerontologists include the effects of a growing population of older people on our social institutions, including our economic welfare and health and Medicare systems (ACT, 1993). Most often, sociological or demographic research and social services and community needs analysis are prime examples of the types of research in which gerontologists become involved.

Gerontologists working for the federal government are employed in the Department of Health and Human Services, as well as the Bureau of the Census. For additional information contact:

Gerontological Society of America
1275 "K" Street, NW
Suite 350
Washington, DC 20005–4006

## Geriatric Physician

*Geriatric physicians* are medical doctors who specialize in treating the elderly and in understanding some of their unique problems. Physicians in this specialty, following graduation from medical school, will complete a residency of three to four years duration under the supervision of experienced geriatric physicians and pass competency examinations in the field of geriatric medicine. Geriatric physicians provide diagnosis of the medical problems of the elderly and direct treatment, routine care, and referrals to other physicians. They discuss treatment options with the older adults and provide recommendations and referrals (e.g., extended care facilities, nursing home placement) when medical or physical disabilities severely limit the capacity for independent living. For additional information contact:

American Medical Association
515 North State Street
Chicago, IL 60610

## Rehabilitation Counselor

*Rehabilitation counselors* work directly in helping the elderly with disabilities to preserve as much functioning as possible, regardless of the type of disability or extent of loss, so that they may participate fully in life. They not only evaluate the extent of disabilities but they also arrange for other interventions such as medical care, job training, or recreational therapy. They routinely conduct interviews with their clients to help in their evaluations and are regularly consulted by physicians, psychologists, and occupational therapists. In their work with older persons, they provide direct counseling, develop support groups, and coordinate services including housing and institutionalization, if necessary. The primary emphasis of rehabilitation counseling is on "normalization," that is, engaging individuals regardless of age and condition in as many day-to-day living experiences as possible. Rehabilitation counselors work for private and community agencies, vocational rehabilitation centers, governmental agencies at the federal, state, and local level, and group homes. There are two associations to contact for more information.

American Rehabilitation Counseling Association
5999 Stevenson Avenue
Alexandria, VA 22304–3300

National Rehabilitation Counseling Association
1910 Association Drive
Suite 206
Reston, VA 22091–1502

## Geropsychologist

*Geropsychologists* specialize in providing intervention, assessment, and support to older adults. Geropsychologists are particularly trained to undertake assessments of intellectual functioning, emotional status, physical capabilities, social status, and a variety of mental health indicators in the elderly. They are also able to interpret such assessments and direct elderly individuals and their families to seek appropriate interventions, which include both individual and group counseling as well as community support groups, and therapeutic activities such as physical therapy, dance-movement therapy, or recreation therapy. For additional information contact:

American Psychological Association
750 First Street, NE
Washington, DC 20002–4242

## Medical Social Worker

*Medical social workers* coordinate a wide variety of support services to elderly persons and their immediate families as a function of a severe or longer-term illness or disability. They focus where appropriate on recovery, rehabilitation, and adjustment. Medical social workers are very much needed by older persons and their families. They coordinate health care, nutrition, legal, financial, and home care services. Medical social workers may assist in helping arrange a move from home to institutional living or assist a widow in finding transportation to the local supermarket or provide meals to a home-based elderly person following discharge from a hospital. Helping the elderly find economic assistance—Medicare, Medicaid, and Social Security—is also within the scope of the social worker's role, as is accessing or even creating needed community-based services. The medical social worker may be based in a hospital outpatient or social services department, health maintenance organization, home health agency, nursing home, long-term health care facility, department of public health, government agency at the state, local, or national level, private practice setting, or volunteer agency. With this profession expected to need almost as many new workers as nursing, there appears to be many opportunities for those interested in helping the elderly through a career in medical social work. For additional information contact:

National Association of Social Workers, Inc.
7981 Eastern Avenue
Silver Spring, MD 20910

## Nursing

*Nursing* is a profession that provides to the elderly preventative services as well as intervention for chronic and acute health problems. Depending on training and education, nursing can entail different levels of skill and rather different types of health services in specific settings. There is not sufficient room to begin to summarize these differences, except to indicate that there will be a critical shortage of 500,000 to 1,000,000 nurses by the year 2000. For additional information on specific types of nursing careers, contact any statewide board responsible for licensing of this profession or contact:

National League for Nurses
10 Columbus Circle
New York, NY 10019

or

American Nurses' Association
240 Pershing Road
Kansas City, MO 64108

## Respiratory Therapist

*Respiratory therapists* provide assessment and intervention for those elderly before and after surgery as well as for those with lung and breathing disorders that may emanate from pneumonia, bronchitis, emphysema, et cetera. Under the direct supervision of a physician, respiratory therapists employ sophisticated equipment in their therapy and carefully monitor patients' progress to preserve as much as possible of a high quality of life. Although most of the assessments conducted by respiratory therapists occur in hospitals, some treatment is delivered in physicians' offices, in nursing homes, and in aged persons' homes. For additional information contact:

American Association for Respiratory Care
11030 Ables Lane
Dallas, TX 75229

or

National Board for Respiratory Care
11015 West Seventy-Fifth Terrace
Shawnee Mission, KS 66214

## Physical Therapist

*Physical therapists* provide rehabilitation through programmed experiences to older adults who have experienced a loss of functioning in some specific part of the body, although the practice of therapy is focused on the "whole person." Swanson (1989) defined physical therapy as "the science and art of applying the therapeutic properties of exercise, heat, cold, water, electricity, ultrasound, massage, . . . for the purposes of restoring function, relieving pain, preventing disability, and promoting healing following disease, injury, or other disabling conditions of the muscles, nerves, joints, or bones, or loss of body part. Where physical therapy cannot restore, relieve, or heal, it teaches adaptation" (p. 223). Physical therapists develop treatment plans, deliver direct services, and monitor/assess the effectiveness of their treatments. Recommended treatments are based on patient need and may include a home visit to determine if special modifications are required. Physical therapists work in hospital settings, nursing homes, rehabilitation centers, community health centers, and, more recently, in established private practices. For additional information contact:

American Physical Therapy Association
1111 North Fairfax Street
Alexandria, VA 22304

## Home Health Aide

*Home health aides* provide direct services to the elderly residing in their home. As paraprofessionals, they assist the elderly and/or disabled with basic self-care tasks and provide assistance in managing simple home-making skills. They are brought into the home of the aged to assist with tasks such as bathing, dressing, preparing meals, and walking, and they oversee prescribed physical exercises, monitor basic health, and check blood pressure, heart, and respiratory functions. Home health care workers share knowledge with the elderly about techniques for managing short-term and long-term disabilities. Through such services and regular visits, the home health care worker monitors progress of the older adult and provides social contact and emotional support to those who might otherwise be hospitalized or placed in a residential care facility. Home health care workers are employed by local and regional community health and welfare agencies, state and local governments, hospitals, volunteer agencies, and the "for-profit" private health care companies. For additional information contact:

National Home Caring Council
519 C Street, NE
Washington, DC 20002

## Recreational Therapist

*Recreational therapists* (activity directors) attempt to engage elderly persons in a range of activities that include arts and crafts, gardening, drama, art, dance or movement, music, and organized social interactions to keep them engaged, involved with others, and experiencing positive emotions. Recreation therapists plan, organize, and directly lead such programs that for the elderly, will help them become resocialized following disabling conditions or will enhance their interpersonal interactions and self-image. Considerable emphasis is placed on group activities and parallel activities such as crafts, through which social support, social exchange, and personal achievement are reinforced. Recreational therapists are employed most often by nursing homes but may also be found working in hospital settings, mental health centers, senior centers, community recreation centers, rehabilitation centers, adult day care programs, and community agencies for the elderly. For additional information contact:

National Therapeutic Recreation Society
3101 Park Center Drive
Alexandria, VA 22302

or

National Council for Therapeutic Recreation Certification
49 South Main Street
Suite 5
Spring Valley, NY 10977

## Audiologist

*Audiologists* are trained to assess and identify the presence and severity of hearing loss, problems with balance, and related problems. Their expertise extends to rehabilitation of hearing impairments, which includes assessing (and sometimes dispensing) the benefits of hearing aids and consulting about strategies or solutions to hearing losses. Audiologists who work with the elderly may work in hearing and speech centers, hospitals and rehabilitation centers, private practices, college and university clinics, home health agencies, long-term and outpatient care facilities, health departments, and community centers. For additional information contact:

American Speech Language Hearing Association
10801 Rockville
Pike Rockville, MD 20852

## Speech Pathologist

*Speech pathologists* are health care professionals trained to identify, assess, and treat disorders of speech, language, and voice. Speech pathologists are sought by physicians, psychologists, social workers, occupational therapists, and rehabilitation counselors when older individuals experience a stroke or cerebral event that causes various forms of aphasia or ataxia or other communication disorders. They offer specific training and practice to help older persons regain language and communication functions in those cases where damage to the brain can be reversed. Speech pathologists may work in private practice settings, in long-term care facilities such as nursing homes, in home health programs, as well as in hospitals and medical settings, rehabilitation centers, and government agencies. For additional information contact:

American Speech-Language Hearing Association
10801 Rockville Pike
Rockville, MD 20852

## Art Therapist

*Art therapists* provide art activities to older adults with mental and physical impairments as a vehicle to stimulate communication (nonverbal) and expression as well as provide insight and resolution of emotional conflicts. Art is a common activity for older persons who are unable to speak due to stroke or emotional problems and can be a clinical tool in helping to understand and provide rehabilitation to such persons. Art therapists combine extensive training in both art and psychology. They plan activities, utilize arts and crafts materials, and offer instruction. Art activities can be individual or group projects and as such provide the opportunity for social exchange. Art therapists work directly as members of treatment teams in psychiatric centers, outpatient clinics, community mental health centers, nursing homes, hospitals, rehabilitation centers, adult day care programs, and in private practices. For additional information contact:

American Art Therapy Association, Inc.
505 East Hawley Street
Mendelein, IL 60060

## Movement (Dance) Therapist

*Movement (dance) therapists* use movement psychotherapeutically to enhance the emotional and physical well-being of older persons. Therapists both diagnose and treat those elderly with psychological, hearing, visual, and other physical impairments. A movement therapist is trained in both psychology and dance and participates as a member of a health care team to offer recreational and therapeutic programs. The elderly are encouraged to use dance and movement as a form of communication, to improve their self-concept, enhance their self-awareness, and build greater confidence in their overall physical and social competence. Through movement (dance) therapy, the elderly can maintain mobility, flexibility, overcome inactivity and social isolation, and restore functioning in the safe, secure, and protected environment created by the therapist. Therapists involve the older person in social exchange and help to preserve physical functioning, for example, small and large muscle groups. Movement (dance) therapists work in hospitals, community mental health centers, senior centers, adult day care centers, extended care facilities, rehabilitation centers, and nursing homes. Through dance or movement activities, therapists direct the older person in ways that are beneficial to their overall physical and mental health. For additional information contact:

American Dance Therapy Association, Inc.
2000 Century Plaza
Suite 108
Columbia, MD 21044

## Music Therapist

*Music therapists* utilize music to create a therapeutic environment for the aged through which rehabilitation of various physical, emotional, and behavioral disorders can occur. As a member of a health care team, these therapists help older adults and those with hearing and visual impairments, physical disabilities, and emotional difficulties such as depression. Activities include group singing, playing musical instruments, and musical games, all of which are designed to provide preservation, restoration, or enhancement of an older person's physical and mental health. For additional information contact:

National Association for Music Therapy, Inc.
505 Eleventh Street, S.E.
Washington, DC 20003

or

American Association for Music Therapy
66 Morris Avenue, P.O. Box 359
Springfield, NJ 07081

## Occupational Therapist

*Occupational therapists* help older workers maintain, develop, or regain those daily living and work skills that have been lost due to disability or disease. Through their own assessments of an older person's skills and abilities, as well as in consultation with other health professionals, occupational therapists develop programs of activities to build the skills the older person needs. Often with impaired older persons such skills involve basic motor functions, self-care (including dressing, bathing, and cooking), as well as cognitive skills. Occupational therapists may also direct their rehabilitation programs to help an older person by identifying specialized equipment or devices to assist those who are permanently disabled or direct them to a different type of work or hobby, one that may better fit the current physical or mental status of the affected individual. This field, by the year 2005, is expected to show a 55 percent increase in new workers given the demand for rehabilitation and long-term services (American College Testing, 1993). Occupational therapists working with the aged are found most often in settings such as hospitals, outpatient clinics, community mental health centers, nursing homes, adult day care programs, residential care facilities, and home health agencies. For additional information contact:

American Occupational Therapy Association
P.O. Box 1725
1383 Piccard Drive
Suite 300
Rockville, MD 20849–1725

# Glossary

## A

**Abortive coping** A form of adjustment to life events which is predominantly negative, nonproductive, and limiting to human growth. (p. 329)

**Acceptance** The fifth and final stage of Kübler-Ross's psychological stages of dying. In this stage, said to be characterized by peace, acceptance of one's fate, and desire to be left alone, dying patients end their struggle against death. (p. 466)

**Accommodation** The process of eye muscle adjustments that allows the eye to have the greatest clarity of image (resolution); the ability to focus and maintain an image on the retina. (p. 77)

**Accommodative processes** Processes involved in helping older persons adjust to cumulative losses and threats to self-esteem by disengagement and the lowering of aspirations from goals which are unattainable. (p. 349)

**Acetylcholine (ACH)** A neurotransmitter necessary for brain activation, responsiveness, and communication. Comprised essentially from choline, it travels from the axon across the synaptic cleft and to the dendrites of another cell. (p. 72)

**Acetylcholinesterase (ACHE)** The substance responsible for the deactivation of acetylcholine; limits the length of time a neuron is stimulated. (p. 365)

**Achievement motive** The need to maintain or increase one's competence in activities in which a standard of excellence is involved. (p. 259)

**Active euthanasia** Inducing death in an incurably ill person by some positive action, such as injecting a lethal dose of a drug. (p. 457)

**Active mastery** A style of relating to the environment that changes with age in different ways for men and women. It allows the adult more direct control over the environment. (p. 42)

**Activities of daily living (ADL)** The basic functions necessary for individuals to maintain independent living which include: feeding, meal-preparation, bathing, dressing, toileting, and general health and hygiene. The long-term needs of the elderly are assessed by reference to such functions with an eye to providing intervention where necessary. (p. 406)

**Activity theory** A theory of aging which states that activity and involvement in late adulthood are often associated with life satisfaction. (p. 45)

**Acute brain syndrome** A form of organic brain disorder which has a sudden onset and is potentially reversible. (p. 355)

**Affirmative coping** A form of adjustment to life events which is positive, productive, and enhancing to human growth. (p. 329)

**Age by experience paradigm** A methodology used to assess the role of age and expertise on some aspect of cognitive ability. (p. 188)

**Ageism** The unwarranted assumption that chronological age is the primary determinant of human traits, abilities, and characteristics and that one age is superior to another. (p. 34)

**Age structure** The percentage of males and females within various age intervals in a given society. (p. 26)

**Agnosia** The inability to visually recognize familiar objects. (p. 71)

**AIDS** Acquired immune deficiency syndrome. The failure of the body's immune system which leaves afflicted individuals vulnerable to a variety of diseases and ultimately leads to death. (p. 375)

**AIDS dementia complex** A set of cognitive dysfunctions associated with brain infection caused by the HIV virus. (p. 375)

**Alpha rhythm** Brain wave patterns detected by using an electroencephalogram that has a frequency of 8–12 cycles per second. (p. 75)

**Alzheimer's disease (AD)** Irreversible dementia characterized by progressive deterioration in memory, awareness, and body functions, eventually leading to death. (p. 336)

**Amyloid** The chemical substance that is found in the senile plaques associated with Alzheimer's disease. (p. 73)

**Androgynous** Acceptance of both male and female characteristics in oneself. (p. 41)

**Anger** The second of Kübler-Ross's stages of dying. In this stage dying persons realize that denial of death cannot be maintained, causing them to become angry, resentful, and envious. (p. 466)

**Anniversary reactions** Feelings of loneliness that occur on holidays, birthdays, etc., following the death of a loved one. (p. 482)

**Anticipatory grief** Feelings of grief, loneliness, and despair that precede the death of a loved one. (p. 482)

**Aphasia** A breakdown or loss of an individual's language abilities. (p. 71)

**Apparent memory deficits** Memory losses that can be attributed to faulty encoding and retrieval processes; these are potentially reversible through intervention or instruction. (p. 121)

**Appropriate death** A mode of coping with death that approximates the wishes and ideals of the dying person. (p. 467)

**Ascending reticular activating system (ARAS)** A brain system that controls levels of awareness or consciousness. (p. 69)

**Assimilative processes** Help to direct older adults to specific activities and goals which are personally derived and effectively reduce the impact of the cumulative impact of developmental losses central to self-esteem and personal identity. (p. 350)

**Attention** A process that controls both the content and the amount of information that is encoded. (p. 98)

**Autobiographical memory task** A task in which a person is asked to recall a personal life experience. (p. 113)

**Autoimmune theory** The idea that biological aging is the result of the diminishing capacity of the body's autoimmune system to identify foreign material. (p. 54)

**Autoimmunity** A condition that is caused by a failure of immune mechanisms to detect normal cells or by mistakes in the formation of antibodies that make them react to normal cells as well as foreign ones. (p. 55)

**Automatic information processing** Information processing that does not draw on limited attention capacity. (p. 101)

**Axon** The part of the neuron that transmits information. (p. 71)

## *B*

**Bargaining** The third of Kübler-Ross's stages of dying. In this stage dying patients hope that death may be postponed by negotiating with God. (p. 466)

**Behavioral research** Research that obtains the direct observation and recording of behavior, including experimental approaches. (p. 499)

**Benign senescent forgetfulness** The normal, non-pathological memory loss associated with aging. (p. 120)

**Bereaved** The status of a person or family who has survived the death of a loved one. (p. 476)

**Bereavement overload** The inability to work through the deaths of loved ones which occur close to one another in time. (p. 463)

**Beta rhythm** Fast brain rhythm that characterizes an attentive, alert state. (p. 75)

**Between-subjects manipulations** The random assignment of subjects to groups in an experiment. (p. 508)

**Biological age** The relative condition of an individual's organ and body system. (p. 13)

**Bona fide occupational qualifications (BFOQ)** Legislation that mandates that workers in selective job classifications retire at a specific age due to the abilities or traits demanded for successful performance, e.g., police or airline traffic controllers. (p. 274)

**Brain death** That point at which all electrical activity has ceased in the brain as determined by an EEG. (p. 445)

**Brain stem** The primitive part of the lower brain that controls the basic biological processes associated with respiration and heartbeat. (p. 69)

**Busy ethic** A theory of retirement that suggests that people need to channel their work ethic into productive, useful leisure activities in old age. (p. 285)

## *C*

**Caregiver distress** The intense stress and negative emotional reactions common to those adults caring and providing for the emotional, social, intellectual, and physical needs of an elderly person in their own families. (p. 345)

**Cataracts** Opacity in the lens of the eye that can cause blindness if not corrected. (p. 80)

**Cellular theories** Theories or proposals about the nature of biological aging that give explanatory emphasis to the various processes or malfunctions that take place within the cells of the body. (p. 53)

**Central tendency** The manipulation of a given set of scores to determine the mean, median, or mode. (p. 502)

**Cerebellum** A primitive part of the brain that controls balance and motor programming, and simple conditioning. (p. 69)

**Cerebrum** The largest and evolutionarily most recent part of the brain. (p. 69)

**Chronic brain syndrome** Forms of organic disorders that are nonreversible and which may produce a variety of emotional and cognitive symptoms. (p. 355)

**Chronological age** The number of years since a person's birth. (p. 13)

**Cochlea** The primary neural receptor for hearing. (p. 80)

**Cognitive model** A model of coping and adaptation developed by Lazarus with an emphasis on the subjective perception of potentially stressful life events; cognitive processes underlie subjective perception through primary and secondary appraisal. (p. 336)

**Cohort** A group of people born in the same time period; a generation one is born into. (p. 140)

**Cohort effects** Differences in behaviors that are found among people born at different times in history. (p. 512)

**Cohort-sequential design** A complex research design which allows a research investigator to distinguish between age effects and cohort effects. (p. 514)

**Concrete operational stage** The third stage of Piaget's theory of mental development which highlights a type of thinking limited to concrete ideas and experiences. (p. 165)

**Construct validity** The extent to which a psychological test or assessment measures a hypothetical entity, e.g., intelligence. (p. 498)

**Contextual model** The model that suggests that adults, like historical events, are ongoing, dynamic, and not directed towards an ideal or end-state. (p. 16)

**Contextual perspective** The viewpoint that suggests that the effectiveness of a person's memory depends on the context or setting within which the person is required to learn and remember information. (p. 155)

**Continuity of functioning** The notion that the same processes control psychological functioning throughout the life span. (p. 6)

**Contrast** The difference in brightness between adjacent parts of a visual stimulus. (p. 78)

**Contrast sensitivity** An individual's ability to perceive visual stimuli that differ in terms of both contrast and spatial frequency. (p. 77)

**Contrast threshold** The minimal amount of contrast needed to perceive spacial frequency differences in gratings. (p. 78)

**Conventional level** The third and fourth stages of Kohlberg's theory of moral development in which moral thought is based on the desire to preserve good interpersonal relations (stage 3) and to comply with formalized rules that exist in society (stage 4). (p. 324)

**Convergent thinking** A type of thinking that is designed to reveal a single correct answer for a problem. (p. 151)

**Corpus callosum** A band of nerve fibers that connects the brain's two hemispheres. (p. 69)

**Correlation** A relationship or association between two variables that can be either positive or negative and vary from weak to strong. (p. 503)

**Correlational study** A type of research in which associations between variables are merely observed. (p. 506)

**Cortex** The outer covering of the cerebrum. (p. 69)

**Cross-sectional study** A study in which individuals of different ages are observed at different times to obtain information about some variable, usually contaminated by cohort effects. (p. 511)

**Cross-sequential design** A complex research design that allows an investigator to distinguish time of testing effects from cohort effects. (p. 516)

**Crystallized intelligence** The type of intelligence that involves skills, abilities, and understanding gained through instruction and observation. (p. 128)

**CT scan** An advanced, noninvasive technique used to determine a two- or three-dimensional representation of the human brain. (p. 75)

**Curvilinear** The reflection of the association of variables that is represented by a curved line when plotted on a graph. (p. 504)

## *D*

**Daily hassles** The little irritating annoyances that punctuate our daily existence. (p. 340)

**Dark adaptation** The visual adjustment required when one enters environments of different illumination; particularly difficult for the elderly when going from a brightly lit to a dimly lit environment. (p. 77)

**Delayed grief reaction** A delayed and heightened reaction to the death of a loved one that is elicited in response to the death of someone to whom the individual is not emotionally attached. (p. 482)

**Delirium** A form of acute brain syndrome marked by minimal awareness of self and environment and the presence of hallucinations, delusions, and distortions. (p. 355)

**Delta rhythms** The brain wave associated with deep sleep. (p. 75)

**Dementia** An organically-based disorder of late adulthood characterized by a deterioration of intelligence and behavior. (p. 356)

**Dendrites** The component of a neuron that receives information. (p. 71)

**Denial/isolation** The first of Kübler-Ross's psychological stages of dying. In this stage dying persons react to terminal illness with shock, denial, and withdrawal. (p. 466)

**Dependency ratio** A reflection of the number of workers in the U.S. relative to the number of people deriving support from these workers, most typically children under the age of 15 and elderly persons 65 years of age and older. (p. 387)

**Dependent variables** The values that are measured as a result of experimental manipulations. (p. 506)

**Depression** The fourth of Kübler-Ross's stages of dying. In this stage dying person's become silent, spend much time crying, and want to be alone in an effort to disconnect themselves from objects of love. (p. 466)

**Depressive pseudodementia** Depression that mimics dementia. (p. 375)

**Development** Refers to a form of change that is organized and adaptive (positive) in nature. (p. 4)

**Developmental psychology** The study of age-related interindividual differences and age-related intraindividual change. (p. 3)

**Diagnostic related group (DRG)** National health care definitions of specific medical conditions to permit construction of average costs and lengths of treatment in a hospital for insurance reimbursement purposes. (p. 426)

**Dialectical view** The belief that individuals are constantly changing organisms in a constantly changing world. (p. 16)

**Discontinuity of functioning** The belief among stage theorists that development is abrupt, with different processes controlling psychological functioning across the life span. (p. 6)

**Disengagement theory** A theory of aging that argues that with increasing age, older individuals withdraw from society and society withdraws from individuals. (p. 45)

**Divergent thinking** A type of thinking closely related to creativity that produces many different answers to a single question. (p. 151)

**Divided attention** The ability to simultaneously attend to two different pieces of environmental information. (p. 98)

**Do not resuscitate act** Specific orders that direct physicians to not initiate heroic measures (e.g., electric shock) when breathing or heartbeat has stopped. (p. 456)

**Dopamine (DA)** A neurotransmitter implicated in Parkinson's Disease and schizophrenia. (p. 381)

**Dual-task** A person's ability to perform two tasks at once. (p. 99)

**Durable power of attorney** Legal appointment of a surrogate (relative, friend, or lawyer) designated to make health care choices in the event a person becomes decisionally incompetent or incapacitated. The surrogate is legally authorized to act to accept or refuse any medical interventions not specified in advance by the person. (p. 451)

## *E*

**Early-onset alcoholism** The development of alcoholism through adolescence to middle age. (p. 399)

**Effortful information processing** Information processing that draws on limited attentional resources. (p. 101)

**Ego mastery styles** The style adopted in coping with self and others that reflects the underlying organization of values and beliefs that govern external behavior. (p. 42)

**Elder abuse** Both active and passive forms of mistreatment of older persons such as physical, psychological, financial/material damage as well as violations of constitutional rights and failure to provide safe and satisfactory living environments. (p. 389)

**Electroencephalogram (EEG)** A machine used to measure the electrical activity of the cortex. (p. 75)

**Emotion-focused coping** Behavioral and cognitive strategies designed to help manage the emotional tensions produced by stressful life situations. (p. 344)

**Empty nest syndrome** A group of symptoms typified by anxiety and depression thought to be experienced by parents associated with their children's leaving home. (p. 205)

**Encapsulation model** A model of adult cognitive development designed to explain age-related changes in processing, knowing, and thinking. (p. 179)

**Encoding deficit** A memory failure that may be traced to the inability to acquire to-be-remembered information. (p. 118)

**Epigenic principle** In Erikson's theory, the belief that all growth has an underlying structure that determines the occasions during which specific psychosocial crises may occur. (p. 295)

**Episodic memory** The memory for the details of personally experienced events, such as the ability to accurately recall details about the source or the context of remembered information. (p. 102)

**Eras** Major portions of the life span according to Daniel Levinson. (p. 302)

**Error catastrophe theory** The theory that errors occur in the RNA responsible for the production of enzymes that are essential to metabolism, resulting in a reduction of cell functioning and possible death. (p. 53)

**Estrogen** The primary female sex hormone, the depletion of which is associated with menopause. (p. 229)

**Euthanasia** The act of painlessly putting to death people who are suffering from incurable diseases or severe disability. (p. 457)

**Exceptional creativity** Another term for creative genius. (p. 151)

**Existential phase** The term Gibbs uses to describe the last two stages in Kohlberg's theory of moral development. (p. 329)

**Experimental study** A study in which an independent variable is manipulated and a dependent variable is observed. (p. 506)

**Explicit memory task** A task in which a subject is directly instructed to consciously remember a previous event or experience. (p. 109)

**External validity** The extent to which one may generalize the results of an experiment. (p. 520)

**Extraneous variables** Variables that are not measured nor manipulated but are suspected to be important. (p. 508)

**Extrinsic motivation** The initiation and maintenance of an activity or behavior in order to achieve an external goal or outcome. (p. 259)

**Extroversion** One of the dimensions of Costa and McCrae's five-factor model of personality. (p. 311)

## *F*

**Factor analysis** A statistical technique that produces a summary of many correlations. (p. 130)

**Factors** The identification through factor analysis of a set of variables that may be grouped together. (p. 505)

**Filial maturity** Adults' growing ability to view their parents as separate persons and personalities. (p. 205)

**Filial piety** The cultural belief in eastern society that the elderly possess a higher status and command a higher respect than younger people. (p. 39)

**Five-factor model** Costa and McCrae's belief that adult personality consists of five stable and independent personality traits: neuroticism, extroversion, openness-to-experience, agreeableness, and conscientiousness. (p. 311)

**Flashbulb memories** Vivid, detailed, and long-lasting mental representations of personally experienced events. (p. 116)

**Fluid intelligence** The basic information-processing abilities of the mind independent of life-experience and education; measured by relational thinking tasks such as block design and digit-symbol substitution. (p. 128)

**Formal operations** The fourth stage in Piaget's theory of intellectual development in which individuals are capable of abstract, hypothetical thinking. (p. 165)

**Free radical theory** A theory that suggests that aging is due to deleterious and short-lived chemical changes occurring within the cells of the body. (p. 53)

**Free recall** A test of long-term memory in which an individual is asked to recall as many items as possible from a given list. (p. 105)

**Frontal lobe** A portion of the cortex. (p. 69)

**Functional age** An individual's level of capacity relative to other people of the same age for functioning in a given environment. (p. 14)

**Functional assessment staging system (FAST)** Reisberg's conceptualization of the predictable, progressive declines in patients with AD. (p. 360)

**Functional disorders** Maladaptive behavior caused by psychological rather than biological factors. (p. 355)

## *G*

**Gender consistency model** The assumption of caregiving roles and responsibilities by adult daughters of their elderly mothers and the reverse by sons for their fathers. (p. 345)

**Genetic switching theory** A theory or proposal that attributes biological aging to the cessation of operation of selected genes. (p. 53)

**Genetic theory** A theory that suggests that aging occurs because certain genes are programmed to "switch off" and stop producing DNA. (p. 53)

**Genuine memory deficits** Memory impairment that is due to the brain's inability to store new information. (p. 121)

**g Factor** Spearman's term for general intelligence. (p. 127)

**Glare** The reflection of light that has the capacity to limit vision; begins to limit vision in middle-age. (p. 77)

**Glaucoma** An increase in pressure within the eye that may lead to blindness if left untreated. (p. 80)

**Government nursing home** Nursing homes that are subsidized by the federal, state, or local governments. (p. 432)

**Gratings** Visual stimuli that differ in contrast and spatial frequency. (p. 78)

**Grief** The sorrow, anger, guilt, and confusion that usually accompany a significant loss. (p. 476)

**Grief pangs** The somatic experience of grief, which includes tightness in the throat, nausea, difficulty in breathing, and sobbing. (p. 482)

**Grief work** The process of arriving at resolution of the loss of a loved one. (p. 210)

## *H*

**Hemispheres** The division of the cerebrum into two halves. (p. 69)

**Hidden poor** Those individuals who could be classified as poor on the basis of their own income but who reside with friends or relatives who are not poor. (p. 35)

**Hierarchical integration** One of the criteria used to identify cognitive stages; current stages incorporate (and extend) the characteristics of preceding stages. (p. 163)

**Hippocampus** A portion of the limbic system involved with memory processes. (p. 69)

**Historical time** The sociohistorical context within which a life-event occurs. (p. 321)

**History** A potential threat to the internal validity of a quasi-experiment; it is most likely to occur when the same individuals are tested at different times. (p. 509)

**Hormonal theory** The theory that aging pacemakers in control centers in the brain stimulate a series of hormonal changes that cause one to age. (p. 54)

**Hospice** An institution characterized by a philosophy of caring and counseling for the terminally ill and their families. (p. 473)

**Hypothetical construct** A process or entity that is inferred from observation. (p. 129)

## *I*

**Imagery** The formation of picture-like representations; a process known to aid memory. (p. 108)

**Implicit memory task** A memory task that does not require a subject to consciously remember a previous event. (p. 109)

**Independent variables** The variables that are manipulated within an experimental study. (p. 506)

**Individual time** The time in an individual's life at which an event occurs. (p. 321)

**Information-processing approach** A perspective in cognitive psychology that suggests that the human mind functions in a manner similar to that of a computer. (p. 92)

**Interindividual differences** The different patterns of developmental change that may be observed between different adults. (p. 3)

**Interiority** Neugarten's description of the increased sensitivity of older adults to their inner experiences. (p. 310)

**Interitem reliability** The extent to which measurements on one-half of the items on a test are predictable from the measurements of the other half. (p. 497)

**Intermediate (ordinary) nursing care** A level of nursing care which is less intensive than that which is provided in a skilled nursing facility. (p. 422)

**Internal validity** The extent to which an independent variable determines the outcome of an experiment. (p. 509)

**Interrater reliability** The assessed amount of agreement between two or more observers who make independent observations in behavioral studies. (p. 497)

**Intraindividual change** Different patterns of developmental change observed within individual adults. (p. 3)

**Intrinsic motivation** The initiative and maintenance of an activity or behavior for its own reward rather than any external achievement. (p. 260)

**Invariant movement** A criteria of developmental stages; suggests that individuals must progress through developmental stages in an unchangeable manner. (p. 163)

## *K*

**Kinesthesis** The ability to sense the position of one's body parts in space. (p. 83)

**Korsakoff's syndrome** A disorder, typified by severe memory loss, manifested by chronic alcoholics. (p. 400)

**Kugelberg-Welander's disease** A progressive spinal muscular atrophy that does not affect cognitive functioning. (p. 458)

## *L*

**Late-onset alcoholism** Emerges in middle to late life, usually in response to multiple stressors such as loss of loved ones; currently underdiagnosed. (p. 400)

**Leisure** Descriptive account of a person's activities during free time and may include work for some people, recreation for others, or a state of mind for others. (p. 265)

**Life-events framework** A view that suggests that life events produce taxing circumstances for individuals, forcing the individuals to change their personality; it is important to consider the sociohistorical circumstances in which those events are occurring. (pp. 318, 336)

**Life expectancy** How long, on the average, one is expected to live. (pp. 26, 29)

**Life management** The integration and application of both assimilative and accommodative processes used to protect the aging self in the face of the cumulative effects of developmental change and preserve positive self-evaluation and well-being. (p. 350)

**Life review** A looking-back process that is set in motion by nearness to death and that potentially proceeds toward personality reorganization; the attempts to make sense of one's own life and experiences through reflection. (p. 299)

**Life satisfaction** An individual's general perception or feeling about the quality of their life. (p. 45)

**Life structure** Levinson's theoretical construct that defines the context in which adult development occurs, including the people, the places, the work, and the situations through which people choose to define themselves. (p. 301)

**Limbic system** A part of the brain that controls memory and emotional responsiveness. (p. 69)

**Lipofuscin** A pigment that accumulates in progressive fashion with age in specific organ systems of the body. (p. 73)

**Living will** A document in which an individual identifies for a physician and/or family members the specific conditions under which life-sustaining measures may be implemented or withdrawn. (p. 451)

**Lobes** A name used to describe different areas of the cortex of the brain. (p. 69)

**Longevity** The theoretical upper limits of the life span that is genetically fixed and species-specific. (p. 29)

**Longevity difference** The difference between the number of years individuals live when compared to the number of years they are expected to live based on their age, race, and sex. (p. 31)

**Longitudinal study** A research design in which data is collected from the same group of individuals on multiple occasions. (p. 512)

**Long-term memory** The processes involved in the storage, retrieval, and access of information over a lengthy period of time (e.g., hours, months, and years). (pp. 105, 106)

## *M*

**Magnetic resonance imaging (MRI)** A noninvasive procedure used to study the structure of the brain. (p. 75)

**Male climacteric** The decline of sexual potency that usually begins when men are in their sixties and seventies and progresses at a much slower rate than female menopause. (p. 232)

**Mean** The statistical procedure used to determine the arithmetic average. (p. 502)

**Mechanics of mind** The basic operations of our human information-processing system. Mental hardware such as sensation, perception, and memory. (p. 186)

**Mechanistic paradigm** The model that suggests that adults are passive machines that merely react to environmental events. (p. 15)

**Median** The value in the exact middle of a distribution of scores. (p. 502)

**Medicaid** Federal and state supported health care program for low-income persons. (p. 428)

**Medical directive** An explicit written statement of a person's wishes to accept or reject particular forms of medical intervention which might arise in key situations; it preserves the rights of persons to self-determination when they become incompetent or unable to make decisions or unable to express their wishes. (p. 451)

**Medicare** Federal health insurance for adults 65 and older and the disabled regardless of age which provides short-term in-patient hospital care and limited skilled care at home or in a nursing home. (p. 430)

**Menopause** The permanent cessation of menstruation and the ability to bear children. (p. 229)

**Mental rotation** The representational process of transforming mental images. (p. 104)

**Mentor** An adult who guides or advises another, typically younger, adult about personal, social, or occupational goals. (p. 262)

**Metamemory** Knowing about one's own memory abilities. Being able to accurately assess your own memory abilities and to accurately report what you know are examples. (p. 113)

**Mode** The most frequently appearing score in a distribution of scores. (p. 502)

**Morbidity** The incidence or prevalence of disease in a population group. (p. 28)

**Mortality** The death rate in a population group. (p. 28)

**Most efficient design** The complex design that allows investigators to separate out the specific effects of age, time of testing, and cohort. (p. 517)

**Mourning** The overt, behavioral expression of grief and bereavement that is heavily influenced by cultural patterns. (p. 476)

**Multidirectional versus unidirectional change** The notion that developmental changes in a given type of functioning may decline, stabilize, or improve within or between individuals; versus the notion that developmental change in a given function follows the same trajectory in all individuals. (p. 7)

**Mutation theory** The theory that aging is due to changes in the DNA of the cells in vital organs of the body. (p. 53)

**Mutual pretense** The strategy of coping in which friends, family, and medical personnel avoid coming to terms with the dying individual by pretending that the individual's disease may improve. (p. 469)

**Myelin sheath** The fatty covering surrounding the axons. (p. 74)

## *N*

**Naturalism vs. control dimension** Data collection strategies which employ naturally occurring events in environments (naturalism) compared to those artificially constructed situations such as experiments which investigators employ (control). (pp. 500–501)

**Negative correlation** A pattern of association between two variables in which higher scores on one variable are related to lower scores on another. (p. 503)

**Neurofibrillary tangles** Intertwined fibers that interfere with normal neuronal functioning. (p. 358)

**Neuroticism** One of the personality traits in Costa and McCrae's Five-Factor Model of adult personality. (p. 311)

**Neurotransmitter** A chemical substance used to send messages across a synapse. (p. 71)

**Nonnormative life events** Influences on development that are related to chancelike factors. (p. 8)

**Normative age-graded factors** Influences on developmental change that are closely related to an individual's chronological age. (p. 8)

**Normative history-graded factors** Influences on development that are closely related to societal events. (p. 8)

## *O*

**Obesity** A condition in which an individual weighs more than 20 percent over normal skeletal and physical requirements. (p. 66)

**Occipital lobe** The portion of the cortex involved in visual perception. (p. 71)

**Old-age dependency ratio** The ratio of the number of retired individuals 65 years-of-age and older to every 100 of working age. (p. 33)

**Ontogeny** The study of maturation of the individual. The term ontogeny can be contrasted with phylogeny which refers to the study of species development. (p. 3)

**Openness to experience** One of the personality traits that comprises Costa and McCrae's Five-Factor Model of adult personality. (p. 311)

**Ordinary creativity** Creativity exhibited by "ordinary adults" in everyday situations. (p. 151)

**Organic disorders** Psychological dysfunction caused by biological factors. (p. 355)

**Organismic paradigm** The model that views development as genetically programmed and following a set progression of qualitatively discontinuous stages. (p. 16)

**Organization** A strategy useful in enhancing memory performance. (p. 106)

**Organ of Corti** The organ in the inner ear that transforms sound vibrations into nerve impulses. (p. 80)

**Osteoporosis** The thinning and weakening of the bones due to calcium deficiency in older people, especially women. (p. 59)

## *P*

**Palliative treatment** A treatment that focuses on the symptoms rather than the cause of a disease. (p. 365)

**Paradigm** Refers to a theoretical approach or perspective that helps researchers organize and interpret their observations. (p. 15)

**Parental imperative** According to Guttman, the tendency of the birth of a child to trigger heightened sex-role differentiation between mother and father in order to assist with the division of labor. (p. 43)

**Parietal lobe** A portion of the cortex involved in short-term memory and the representation of spatial relationships. (p. 71)

**Parkinson's disease** A neurological disorder caused by decreased levels of dopamine that results in involuntary muscle tremors and rigid movements. (p. 74)

**Passive accommodative mastery style (passive mastery)** According to Guttman, a style of coping that varies by age and sex in which individuals fit themselves to the environment rather than try to change the external environment. (p. 42)

**Passive euthanasia** Inducing a natural death by withdrawing some life-sustaining therapeutic effort such as turning off a respirator or heart-lung machine. (p. 457)

**Pearson product moment correlation coefficient** Abbreviated as *r* this computes the quantitative strength of a correlation on a scale of –1.00 to +1.00. (p. 504)

**Perception** The process of experiencing incoming sensory information in a coherent organized, and meaningful fashion. (p. 93)

**Persistent vegetative state** A clinical condition of complete unawareness of the self and the environment, accompanied by sleep-wake cycles but no evidence of purposeful or voluntary behavioral responsiveness to environmental stimuli, no language comprehension or expression, no bowel or bladder control. It lasts for at least one month following degenerative or metabolic disorders. (p. 448)

**Personality** The distinctive patterns of behavior, thought, and emotion that characterize each person's adaptation to the situations of his/her life. (p. 293)

**Personologists** Personality theorists who argue for consistency and stability of traits over time. (p. 308)

**Philosophical wisdom** Refers to an understanding of the abstract relationship between one's self and the rest of humanity. (p. 185)

**Physiological theories** Theories or proposals about the nature of biological aging that give explanatory emphasis to breakdowns in particular organ systems and to the mechanisms that control such systems. (p. 54)

**Plasticity** Refers to the range of function that can be observed in individuals. The term plasticity is frequently used to refer to the extent to which cognitive or physical performance can be improved by practice or training. (p. 7)

**Positive correlation** An association between variables such that high scores on one variable are related to high scores on another variable. (p. 503)

**Positron–emission tomography (PET SCAN)** A noninvasive method of measuring the metabolic activity of the brain. (p. 75)

**Postconventional level** The last two stages within Kohlberg's theory of moral development; at this level, individuals are capable of generating moral rules that are based on universal principles of justice. (p. 325)

**Postformal operations** The generic term used to describe qualitative changes in thinking beyond Piaget's stage of formal operations, characterized by an acceptance of relativity, dialectic thinking, and problem-finding. (p. 171)

**Potential life span** The maximum age that could be attained if an individual were able to avoid or be successfully treated for all illnesses and accidents. (p. 29)

**Practical wisdom** Refers to the ability to display superior judgment with regard to important matters of real life. (p. 185)

**Pragmatics of mind** The mental software that encompasses the general system of factual and strategic knowledge accessible to members of a particular culture, the specialized systems of knowledge available to individuals within particular occupations and avocations, and an understanding of how to effetively activate these different types of knowledge within particular contexts to aid problem solving. (p. 186)

**Preconventional level** The first two stages in Kohlberg's theory of moral development; characterized by the construction of moral rules that are based on the fear of punishment and the desire for pleasure. (p. 323)

**Preoperational stage** The second stage in Piaget's theory of cognitive development; characterized by illogical thinking that is marked by irreversibility as well as the inability to distinguish fantasy from reality. (p. 164)

**Presbycusis** The general term used to describe age-related problems in hearing, especially high-pitched sounds. (p. 80)

**Presbyopia** The reduction in the efficacy of near vision; usually first observed during middle-adulthood. (p. 77)

**Presbystasis** Loss of balance and equilibrium. (p. 84)

**Primary appraisal** The process of choosing whether an event is stressful and requires the implementation of coping strategies. (p. 339)

**Primary mental abilities** Thurstone's belief that intelligence consisted of the following mental abilities: verbal comprehension, word fluency, number, space, associative memory, perceptual speed, and induction. (p. 127)

**Prior-to-need (or pre-need) burial** The practice of arranging funeral expenses well before the need arises, when the individual is healthy and well. (p. 478)

**Problem finding** Arlin's description of a fundamental feature of adult cognition, the identification and construction of sophisticated problems to resolve. (p. 156)

**Problem-focused coping** The determination that a stressful life event requires changing the event or obtaining additional information about the event in order to cope successfully. (p. 344)

**Proprietary homes** A type of nursing home, operated by a private company, designed to make a profit. (p. 422)

**Psychological age** An individual's ability to adapt to changing environmental demands in comparison to the adaptability of other individuals of identical chronological age. (p. 14)

**Psychometric approach** An approach to adult intellectual development that involves the administration of standardized adult intelligence tests such as the WAIS and PMA. (p. 126)

**Psychomotor slowing** The age-related slowing of behavior. (p. 83)

**Psychosexual development** The study of how individuals of different ages deal with pleasurable body sensations. (p. 294)

**Psychosocial development** The study of the lifelong relationship between the developing individual and the social system of which she or he is a part. (p. 294)

**P300 brain wave** A unique pattern of brain activity associated with the identification of novel stimuli. (p. 76)

## *Q*

**Qualitative change** The unique change in the type or quality of thinking that occurs as individuals move from one specific stage to another. (pp. 5, 163)

**Quantitative change** The differences in amount rather than kind that occur in development. (p. 5)

**Quasi-experiments** Studies that resemble true experiments in design and analysis but contain an independent variable that cannot be manipulated. (p. 508)

## *R*

**Random assignment** The technique of assigning individuals to exposure conditions on a random basis in order to evenly distribute extraneous factors. (p. 508)

**Range** The simplest measure of variability; revealed by the lowest and the highest score in a set. (p. 503)

**Reaction-time tasks** Experimental assessments of the time elapsed between the appearance of a signal and a person's responding movement. (p. 495)

**Reactivity** The way in which an individual reacts to being tested/observed within a psychological study; a threat to the internal validity of an experiment or quasi-experiment. (p. 500)

**Recognition test** A basic strategy for assessing memory ability. (p. 108)

**Reliability** The consistency of the results of a test in the same person(s) from one time to another. (p. 496)

**Representative sample** A sample of a population that has the same characteristics as the entire population. (p. 519)

**Reserve capacity** The amount of resources available to the individual for responding to physical or psychological challenges. The amount of reserve capacity, or the range of plasticity, of particular physiological systems may become limited with aging. (p. 7)

**Residential care facility** A nursing home that provides routine care and personal assistance in providing routine care for day-to-day needs. (p. 423)

**Respite care** Temporary assistance to relieve family members of the physical, emotional, and social responsibility of caring for an older person at home. Such caring-giving assistance is often provided by volunteers, friends, relatives, or through community agencies including adult day care programs. (p. 368)

**Retrieval deficit** Memory impairment due to the inability to successfully access stored information. (p. 118)

## *S*

**Sati** The ancient Hindu practice of burning a dead man's widow to increase his family's prestige and establish her image as a goddess in his memory. (p. 476)

**Schaie-Thurstone adult mental abilities test** A standardized test of adult intelligence which is adapted from Thurstone's Primary Mental Abilities Test. (p. 127)

**Secondary appraisal** The person's assessment of available resources and the "cost" of such resources when faced with a stressful life event. (p. 339)

**Selection** A threat to internal validity when the procedures used to select individuals for research result in extraneous or unintended differences in the groups selected for study, e.g., young vs. old subjects may differ not only on education but also in terms of health. (p. 509)

**Selective attention** A type of attention in which we ignore irrelevant information while focusing on relevant information (e.g., ignoring a television program while listening to a friend). (p. 98)

**Selective dropout** The tendency for particular individuals to drop out of longitudinal studies, e.g., the infirm, the less able, those who move from the area, and thus skew the results in a biased fashion. (p. 141)

**Selective optimization with compensation** A technique by which older adults alter their behavior in such a way as to preserve (and perhaps enhance) specific cognitive, behavioral, or physical abilities. (p. 191)

**Self-report inventories** The use of specific questionnaires in which participants are required to report their opinions, feelings, or activities on a wide range of topics. (p. 311)

**Semantic elaboration** A strategy used to enhance memory. (p. 108)

**Semantic memory** Use of acquired knowledge about the world. When we use semantic memory, we can think about the meanings of words or concepts without reference to when or how we acquired such knowledge. (p. 102)

**Senescence** All of the changes that are associated with the normal process of aging. (pp. 52, 356)

**Senile plaques** The accumulation of spherical masses of amyloid surrounded by degenerating axons and dendrites; senile plaques prevent normal communication between neurons. (p. 73)

**Senility** An outdated term referring to abnormal deterioration of mental functions in old people. (p. 356)

**Sensation** The reception of physical stimuli at a sense organ and the translation of this stimulation to the brain. (p. 76)

**Sensorimotor development** The growth and coordination of sensory and motor processes. (p. 88)

**Sensorimotor stage** The first stage in Piaget's theory of cognitive development in which the child discovers the world using the senses and motor activity. (p. 164)

**Sex role** The behaviors that are expected of individuals because they are either male or female. (p. 41)

**Short-term memory** Information that is stored and retained for a brief period, usually less than sixty seconds. (p. 106)

**Single-task performance** Performance that does not entail dividing one's attention. (p. 99)

**Skilled nursing facility** The most highly intensive form of nursing-home care. (p. 422)

**Social age** Refers to the social roles and social expectations people have for themselves as well as those imposed by others in society. (p. 14)

**Social clock** The internalized sense of timing that tells people whether they are progressing too fast or too slow in terms of social events. (p. 56)

**Social cognition** Cognitive development that is focused on the individual's reasoning about social and interpersonal matters. (p. 178)

**Social convoy** The network of close relationships that accompany an individual throughout life. (p. 200)

**Soma** The cell body of a neuron. (p. 71)

**Source memory** The ability to remember the context in which a particular piece of information was learned. (p. 112)

**Spatial frequency** The number of cycles of bars of light imaged within a specific area of the retina. (p. 78)

**Spending down** Depletion of an individual's income and assets to meet the eligibility requirements for Medicaid. (p. 430)

**Stage theory** A theory that suggest that development consists of a series of abrupt changes in psychological functions and processes, marked by qualitative change at each stage. (p. 6)

**Standard deviation** A common measure of variability that reveals the extent to which the individual scores deviate from the mean of a distribution. (p. 503)

**Standardization** The establishment of fixed procedures for administration, scoring, and norms for age, grade, race, sex and so on. (p. 501)

**Standard phase** Gibbs's term that refers to the first four stages in Kohlberg's theory of moral development. (p. 329)

**Statistical significance** A mathematical procedure to determine the extent to which differences in performance between groups of subjects are due to chance factors or the independent variable. (p. 506)

**Structured wholeness** A criteria for determining developmental stages; implies that individuals' cognitions are consistent with their current stage of development. (p. 164)

**Substantia nigra** A structure in the base of the brain responsible for the production of dopamine. (p. 71)

## *T*

**Temporal lobe** The portion of the cortex involved in audition, language, and long-term memory. (p. 69)

**Terminal drop** A decline in psychological functioning, revealed in standardized tests, that precedes death by about five years. (p. 143)

**Testing** A threat to internal validity that is based on the readministration of the same instrument on more than one occasion. (p. 510)

**Test-retest reliability** The degree of predictability that measurements taken on one test on one occasion will be similar to those taken on another occasion. (p. 496)

**Thematic apperception test (TAT)** A standardized projective test, consisting of a series of ambiguous pictures, developed by Henry Murray used to assess personality and individual character traits. (p. 259)

**Time-sequential design** A complex research design that allows an investigator to disentangle age effects from time-of-testing effects. (p. 515)

**Tinnitus** A constant high-pitched or ringing sound in the ears reported in about 10 percent of older adults. (p. 80)

**Trait theorists** Personality theorists who believe that there is some consistency and stability to human personality over time. (p. 308)

**Trajectory of life** According to Pattison, our anticipated life span and the plan we make for the way we will live out our life. (p. 468)

**Transient ischemic attack (TIA)** A temporary, reversible minor stroke. (p. 373)

**Transitions** According to Levinson, the periods that overlap one era with another; transitions last for approximately five years. (p. 303)

**Type A behavior style** Behavior reflecting excessive competitiveness, accelerated pace of normal activities, time-urgency, hostility, and aggressiveness. (p. 67)

**Type B behavior style** Behavior reflective of the absence of Type A Behavior Style; behavior indicative of a relaxed, less-hurried, and less-preoccupied life-style. (p. 67)

## *U*

**Unfinished business** Completing and resolving, where possible, the interpersonal problems created in personal relationships; the desire for a dying person to bring closure to the different dimensions of their life. (p. 464)

**Universal progression** A criteria for the presence of developmental stages; the belief that all individuals in all cultures progress through all stages in the same invariant sequence. (p. 164)

**Uplifts** Those small, positive experiences we encounter in daily living that counterbalance the hassles that occur in everyday life. (p. 340)

**Upswing hypothesis** The contention that there is an increase in marital satisfaction when children leave home. (p. 205)

## *V*

**Validity** The soundness of measurements in terms of measuring what they are intended to measure. (p. 498)

**Variability** The statistical description of distribution scores; includes range and standard deviation. (p. 503)

**Variable** Anything that may change and influence behavior. (p. 503)

**Visual acuity** The ability to accurately see small details in the visual field under maximal amounts of contrast. (p. 78)

**Voluntary nonprofit nursing homes** Nursing homes that establish rates that do not generate excess capital (i.e., a profit); are usually designed for individuals with a specific religious, fraternal, or union affiliation. (p. 422)

## *W*

**Wechsler adult intelligence scale (WAIS)** A standard test of adult intelligence that provides both a verbal IQ and performance IQ as well as an overall IQ score. (p. 130)

**Widower's syndrome** The tendency for men, after a long period of time following the loss of a spouse, to develop an incomplete penile erection when presented with the opportunity for sexual intercourse. (p. 235)

**Wisdom** An expert knowledge system in the fundamental pragmatics of life permitting exceptional insight, judgment, and advice involving complex and uncertain matters of the human condition. (p. 162)

**Within-subjects manipulations** Experimental design in which each subject is administered each level of an independent variable. (p. 508)

**Working memory** According to Baddeley, the active manipulation of information in short-term memory. (p. 103)

## *Y*

**Young-age dependency ratio** The number of individuals seventeen years-of-age and younger for every one hundred people of working age. (p. 33)

# REFERENCES


## A

Achete, K., & Karha, E. (1986). Some psychodynamic aspects of the presuicidal syndrome with special reference to older persons. *Crisis, 1,* 24–32.

Adams, S. L., & Waskel, S. A. (1993). Late onset alcoholism: Stress or structure. *Journal of Psychology, 127* (3), 329–334.

Adler, T. (1992, Feb.). For depressed elderly, drugs advised. *The APA Monitor,* pp. 16–17.

Adrain, M. J. (1981). Flexibility in the aging adult. In E. L. Smith & R. C. Serfass (Eds.), *Exercise and aging: The scientific basis.* Hillsdale, NJ: Enslow.

Ahrons, C. R., & Rodgers, R. H. (1987). *Divorced families: A multidisciplinary view.* New York: Norton.

Albert, M. S., & Moss, M. B. (Eds.). (1988). *Geriatric neuropsychology.* New York: Guilford.

Albert, M. S., & Stafford, J. L. (1988). Computed tomography studies. In M. S. Albert & M. B. Moss (Eds.), *Geriatric neuropsychology* (pp. 211–227). New York: Guilford.

Albert, S. M. (1991). Cognition of caregiving tasks: Multidimensional scaling of the caregiver task domain. *The Gerontologist, 31,* 726–734.

Aldridge, D., & Aldridge, G. (1992). Two epistemologies: Music therapy and medicine in the treatment of dementia. *Arts in Psychotherapy, 19,* 243–255.

Aldwin, C. M., Spiro, A., Bosse, R., & Levenson, M. R. (1989). Longitudinal findings from the normative aging study: 1. Does mental health change with age? *Psychology and Aging, 4,* 295–306.

Allen, P. A. (1992) On mental multiplication and age. *Psychology and Aging,* 7, 536–545.

Allport, G. W. (1961). *Pattern and growth in personality.* New York: Holt, Rinehart & Winston.

Alpaugh, P., & Birren, J. E. (1977). Variables affecting creative contributions across the life span. *Human Development, 20,* 240–248.

Altman, L. K. (1992). Alzheimer's dilemma: Whether to tell people they have the disease. *NY Times,* Tuesday, April 7, C3.

American Association of Retired Persons. (1986). A profile of older Americans. Brochure, AARP, Washington, DC.

American Association of Retired Persons. (1988). Cemetery goods and services. Brochure, AARP, Washington, DC.

American Association of Retired Persons. (1992). Pre-paying your funeral? *Product Report, 2*(2), AARP, Washington, DC.

American Association of Retired Persons. (1992). *A profile of older Americans.*

American Association of Retired Persons. (1993a). *Understanding Senior Housing.* (D13899). Washington, DC.

American Association of Retired Persons. (1993b). *A perfect fit.* (D14823). Washington, DC.

American College Testing Program. (1993). *Discover for colleges and adults.* Hunt Valley, MD: American College Testing Program, Educational Testing Center.

American Psychiatric Association. (1987). *Diagnostic and Statistical Manual of Mental Disorders-Third Edition-Revised.*

Anders, T. R., Fozard, J. L., & Lillyquist, T. D. (1972). Effects of age upon retrieval from short-term memory. *Developmental Psychology, 6,* 214–217.

Anderson, L., & Stevens, N. (1993). Associations between early experiences with parents and well-being in old age. *Journal of Gerontology: Psychological Sciences, 48,* P109–116.

Anderson, S. A., Russell, C. S., & Schumm, W. R. (1983). Perceived marital quality and family life-cycle categories: A further analysis. *Journal of Marriage and the Family, 45,* 127–139.

Anderson, T. B., & McCulloch, B. J. (1993). Conjugal support: Factor structure for older husbands and wives. *Journal of Gerontology: Psychological Sciences, 48,* P109–116.

Angel, J., & Hogan, D. P. (1992). The demography of minority aging populations. *Journal of Family History, 16,* 95–114.

Annas, G. J. (1990). Nancy Cruzan and the right to die. *New England Journal of Medicine, 323,* 670–673.

Anthony, J. C., & Aboraya, A. (1992). The epidemiology of selected mental disorders in later life. In J. E. Birren, R. B. Sloane, G. D. Cohen, N. R. Hooyman, B. Leibowitz, M. H. Wykle, & D. E. Deutchman, *Handbook of mental health and aging* (2nd ed.). San Diego: Academic Press.

Anthony-Bergstone, C. R., Zarit, S. H., & Gatz, M. (1988). Symptoms of psychological distress among caregivers of dementia patients. *Psychology and Aging, 3,* 245–248.

Antonucci, T. C. (1990). Social supports and social relationships. In R. H. Binstock & K. K. George (Eds.), *Handbook of aging and the social sciences* (3rd ed.). New York: Academic Press.

Antonucci, T. C., & Akiyama, H. (1987). Social networks in adult life and a preliminary examination of the convoy model. *Journal of Gerontology, 42,* 519–527.

Antonucci, T. C., & Akiyama, H. (1991a). Social relationships and aging well. *Generations, 15,* 39–44.

Antonucci, T. C., & Akiyama, H. (1991b). Convoys of social support: Generational issues. *Marriage and Family Review, 16,* 103–123.

Argyle, M., & Beit-Hallahmi, B. (1975). *The social psychology of religion.* London: Routledge & Kegan Paul.

Arlin, P. K. (1975). Cognitive development in adulthood: A fifth stage. *Developmental Psychology, 11,* 602–606.

———. (1984). Adolescent and adult thought: A structural interpretation. In M. L. Commons, F. A. Richards, & C. Armon (Eds.), *Beyond formal operations: Late adolescent and adult cognitive development.* New York: Praeger.

———. (1989). Problem solving and problem finding in young artists and young scientists. In M. L. Commons, J. D. Sinnott, F. A. Richards, & C. Armon (Eds.), *Adult development, Vol. 1: Comparisons and applications of developmental models.* New York: Praeger.

Armon, C. (1991). *The development of reasoning about the good life.* Paper presented at the Sixth Adult Development Symposium of the Society for Research in Adult Development, Boston, MA, July.

Ascher, B. (1993). *Landscape without gravity.* New York: Delphinivar Books.

Atchley, R. C. (1976). *The sociology of retirement.* Cambridge, MA: Schenkman.

———. (1983). *Aging: Continuity and change.* Belmont, CA: Wadsworth.

Athelstan, G. T. (1981). Psychosocial adjustment to chronic disease and disability. In W. C. Stolov & M. R. Clowers (Eds.), *Handbook of severe disabilities.* Washington, DC: U.S. Department of Education.

Atkinson, J. H., & Schuckit, M. A. (1981). Alcoholism and over-the-counter and prescription drug misuse in the elderly. In C. Eisdorfer (Ed.), *Annual review of gerontology and geriatrics* (Vol. 2.) New York: Springer.

Atkinson, R. M., Ganzini, L., & Bernstein, M. J. (1992). Alcohol and substance-use disorders in the elderly. In J. E. Birren, R. B. Sloane, and G. D. Cohen (Eds.), *Handbook of mental health and aging* (2nd ed.). San Diego, CA: Academic Press.

Attig, T. (1992). Person-centered death education. *Death Studies, 16,* 357–370.

Ausubel, D. P. (1968). *Educational psychology.* New York: Holt, Rinehart & Winston.


## *B*


Bäckman, L., Mantyla, T., & Herlitz, A. (1990). Psychological perspectives on successful aging: The optimization of episodic remembering in old age. In P. B. Baltes & M. M. Baltes (Eds.), *Successful aging* (pp. 118–163). New York: Cambridge University Press.

Baer, D. M. (1970). An age-irrelevant concept of development. *Merrill Palmer Quarterly of Behavior and Development, 16,* 238–245.

Bahrick, H. P., Bahrick, P. O., & Wittlinger, R. P. (1975). Fifty years of memory for names and faces: A cross-sectional approach. *Journal of Experimental Psychology: General, 104,* 54–75.

Bailey, K. D. (1987). *Methods of social research.* New York: Free Press.

Baillie, P. H., & Danish, S. J. (1992, March). Understanding the career transition of athletes. *Sport Psychologist, 6,* 77–98.

Baird, J. (1976). The funeral industry in Boston. In E. Shneidman (Ed.), *Death: Current perspectives.* Palo Alto: Mayfield Press.

Baltes, P. B. (1987). Theoretical propositions of life-span developmental psychology: On the dynamics between growth and decline. *Developmental Psychology, 23,* 611–626.

———. (1993). The aging mind: Potential and limits. *The Gerontologist, 33,* 580–594.

Baltes, P. B., & Baltes, M. (1990). Psychological perspectives on successful aging: The model of selective optimization with compensation. In P. B. Baltes & M. Baltes (Eds.), *Longitudinal research and the study of successful (optimal) aging* (pp. 1–49). Cambridge England: Cambridge University Press.

Baltes, P. B., & Kliegel, R. (1986). On the dynamics between growth and decline in the aging of intelligence and memory. In K. Poeck, H. J. Freund, & H. Ganshirt (Eds.), *Neurology.* Heidelberg, West Germany: Springer-Verlag.

Baltes, P. B., & Kliegel, R. (1990). Testing-the-limits research suggests irreversible aging loss in memory based on mental imagination. *Developmental Psychology, 28,* 121–125.

Baltes, P. B., & Kliegel, R. (1992). Further testing of limits of cognitive plasticity: Negative age differences in a mnemonic skill are robust. *Developmental Psychology, 28,* 121–125.

Baltes, P. B., & Lindenberger, U. (1990). On the range of cognitive plasticity in old age as a function of experience: Fifteen years of intervention research. *Behavior Therapy, 19,* 283–300.

Baltes, P. B., Reese, H. W., & Lipsitt, L. P. (1980). Life-span developmental psychology. *Annual Review of Psychology, 31,* 65–110.

Baltes, P. B., & Staudinger, U. (1993). The search for a psychology of wisdom. *Current Directions in Psychological Science, 2,* 75–80.

Baltes, P. B., Sowarka, D., & Kliegel, R. (1989). Cognitive training research on fluid intelligence in old age: What can older adults achieve by themselves? *Psychology and Aging, 4,* 217.

Bandura, A. (1982). Self-efficacy in human agency. *American Psychologist, 37,* 122–137.

Bandura, A. L. (1989). Human agency in social cognitive theory. *American Psychologist, 44,* 1175–1184.

Banzinger, G., & Roush, S. (1983). Nursing homes for the birds: A control-relevant intervention with bird feeders. *The Gerontologist, 23,* 527–531.

Bardwick, J. (1990). Where we are and what we want: A psychological model. In R. A. Nemiroff & C. A. Colarusso (Eds.), *New dimensions in adult development* (pp. 186–213). New York: Basic Books.

Baron, R. S., Cutrona, C. E., Hicklin, D., Russell, D. W., & Lubaroff, D. M. (1990). Social support and immune function among spouses of cancer patients. *Journal of Personality and Social Psychology, 59,* 344–352.

Barringer, F. (1992). Prospects for the elderly differ widely by sex. *The New York Times,* November 10.

Barron, S. A., Jacobs, L., & Kirkei, W. R. (1976). Changes in size of normal lateral ventricles during aging determined by computerized tomography. *Neurology, 26,* 1011–1013.

Bart, P. (1971). Depression in middle-aged women. In V. Gornick & B. K. Moran (Eds.), *Women in sexist society.* New York: New American Library.

———. (1973). Portnoy's mother's complaint. In H. Z. Lopata (Ed.), *Marriages and families.* New York: Van Nostrand Reinhold.

Bart, W. M. (1971). The factor structure of formal operations. *British Journal of Educational Psychology, 41,* 40–77.

Bartoshuk, L. M., Rifkin, B., Marks, L. E., & Bars, P. (1986). Taste and aging. *Journal of Gerontology, 41,* 51–57.

Bashore, T. R. (1993). Differential effects of aging on the neurocognitive functions subserving speeded mental processing. In J. Cerella, J. M. Rybash, W. J. Hoyer, & M. L. Commons (Eds.), *Adult information processing: Limits on loss* (pp. 37–76). San Diego: Academic Press.

Basseches, M. (1984). *Dialectic thinking.* Norwood, NJ: Ablex.

Bastida, E. (1987). Sex-typed age norms among older Hispanics. *The Gerontologist, 27,* 59–65.

Baum, C., Edwards, D. F., & Morrow-Howell, N. (1993). Identification and measurement of productive behaviors in servile dementia of the Alzheimer type. *Journal of Gerontology, 33,* 403–408.

Baum, M., & Page, M. (1991). Caregiving and multi-generational families. *The Gerontologist, 31,* 762–769.

Bedford, V. H. (1992). Memories of parental favoritism and the quality of parent-child ties in adulthood. *Journal of Gerontology: Social Sciences, 47,* S149–155.

Begley, S. (1993). The puzzle of genius. *Newsweek,* June 28, 46–50.

Bekker, L., DeMoyne, L., & Taylor, C. (1966). Attitudes toward the aged in a multigenerational sample. *Journal of Gerontology, 21,* 115–118.

Beland, F. (1984). The decision of elderly persons to leave their homes. *The Gerontologist, 24,* 179–185.

———. (1987). Living arrangement preferences among elderly people. *The Gerontologist, 27,* 797–803.

Belasco, J. A. (1991). *Teaching the elephant to dance: The manager's guide to empowering change.* New York: Plume & Penguin Books.

Belbin, R. M. (1983). The implications of gerontology for new work roles in later life. In J. E. Birren et al. (Eds.), *Aging: A challenge to science and society.* New York: Oxford University Press.

Bell, A. P., & Weinberg, M. S. (1978). *Homosexualities.* New York: Simon & Schuster.

Bell, A. P., Weinberg, M. S., & Mannersmith, S. K. (1981). *Sexual preference: Its development in men and women.* New York: Simon & Schuster.

Bell, J. (1992). In search of a discourse on aging: The elderly on television. *The Gerontologist, 32,* 305–311.

Bell, R. R., & Bell, P. L. (1972). Sexual satisfaction among married women. *Medical Aspects of Human Sexuality, 6,* 136–144.

Bell, R. R., & Lobsenz, N. (1979, September). Married sex: How uninhibited can a woman dare to be? *Redbook,* pp. 75–78.

Belsky, J. (1981). Early human experience: A family perspective. *Developmental Psychology, 17,* 3–23.

Belsky, J. (1987a). *Mother care, not together care, other care, and infant-parent attachment security.* Paper presented at the annual meeting of the American Psychological Association, New York.

Belsky, J. (1987b). Risks remain. *Zero to Three, 7,* 22–24.

Belsky, J. (1987c). *Science, social policy, and day care: A personal odyssey.* Paper presented at the annual meeting of the Society for Research in Child Development, Baltimore, MD.

Bem, S. L. (1974). The measurement of psychological androgyny. *Journal of Consulting and Clinical Psychology, 42,* 155–162.

Bem, S. L. (1977). On the utility of alternative procedures for assessing psychological androgyny. *Journal of Consulting and Clinical Psychology, 45,* 196–205.

Bem, S. L. (1981). Gender schema theory: A cognitive account of sex typing. *Psychological Review, 88,* 354–364.

Bengtson, V. L. (1985). Diversity and symbolism in grandparental roles. In V. L. Bengtson & J. Robertson (Eds.), *Grandparenthood.* Beverly Hills, CA: Sage.

Bengtson, V. L., Mangen, D. G., & Landry, T. J., Jr. (1984). Multigenerational family: Concepts and findings. In V. Garmsholova, E. M. Horning, & D. Schaffer (Eds.), *Intergenerational relationships.* Lewiston, NY: Hogrefe.

Bengtson, V. L., Reedy, M., & Gordon, C. (1985). Aging self conceptions: Personality processes and social context. In J. E. Birren & K. W. Schaie (Eds.), *Handbook of the psychology of aging* (second edition). New York: Van Nostrand Reinhold.

Ben-Sira, Z. (1991). *Regression, stress, and readjustment in aging.* New York: Praeger.

Beresford, T. P., Blow, F. C., Brower, K. J., Adams, K. M., & Hall, R. C. (1988). Alcoholism and aging in the general hospital. *Psychosomatics, 29,* 61–72.

Berg, C. A., Hertzog, C., & Hunt, E. (1982). Age differences in the speed of mental rotation. *Developmental Psychology, 18,* 95–107.

Berg, C. A., & Sternberg, R. J. (1992). Adults' conceptions of intelligence across the adult life span. *Psychology and Aging, 7,* 221–231.

Berkelman, R. L., & Hughes, J. M. (1993). The conquest of infectious diseases: Who are we kidding? *Annals of Internal Medicine, 119,* 426–427.

Bernard, J. (1975). Notes on changing lifestyles: 1970–1974. *Journal of Marriage and the Family, 37,* 582–593.

Berndt, T. J. (1982). The features and effects of friendship in early adolescence. *Child Development, 53,* 1447–1460.

Berscheid, E. (1988). Some comments on love's anatomy: Or whatever happened to old-fashioned lust? In R. J. Sternberg & M. L. Barnes (Eds.), *Anatomy of love.* New Haven: Yale University Press.

Berzonsky, M. D. (1978). Formal reasoning in adolescence: An alternative view. *Adolescence, 13,* 279–290.

Betz, N. E., & Fitzgerald, L. E. (1987). *The career psychology of women.* San Diego: Academic Press.

Betz, N. E., & Fitzgerald, L. E. (1993). Individuality and diversity: Theory and research in counseling psychotherapy. *Annual review of psychology, 44,* 343–381.

Biegel, D. E., & Blum, A. (Eds.). 1990. *Aging and caregiving: Theory, research and policy.* Newbury Park, CA: Sage.

Birren, J. E. (1965). Age changes in speed of behavior: Its central nature and physiological correlates. In A. T. Welford & J. E. Birren (Eds.), *Behavior, aging, and the nervous system* (pp. 191–216). Springfield, IL: Charles C Thomas.

Birren, J. E. (1988). A contribution to the theory of aging: As a counterpart of development. In J. E. Birren & V. L. Bengtson (Eds.), *Emergent theories of aging* (pp. 153–176). New York: Springer.

Birren, J. E., & Birren, B. A. (1990). The concepts, models, and history of the psychology of aging. In J. E. Birren & K. W. Schaie (Eds.), *Handbook of the psychology of aging* (3rd edition, pp. 3–20). San Diego: Academic Press.

Birren, J. E., & Renner, J. V. (1977). Research on the psychology of aging: Principles and experimentation. In J. E. Birren and K. W. Schaie (Eds.), *Handbook of the psychology of aging.* New York: Van Nostrand Reinhold.

Birren, J. E., & Sloane, R. B. (Eds.). (1980). *Handbook of mental health and aging.* Englewood Cliffs, NJ: Prentice-Hall.

Black, P. M. (1983a). Clinical problems in the brain death standards. *Archives of Internal Medicine, 143,* 121–123.

Black, P. M. (1983b). Guidelines for the diagnosis of brain death. In A. H. Ropper, S. K. Kennedy, & N. T. Zervas (Eds.), *Neurological and neurosurgical intensive care.* Baltimore: University Park Press.

Black, S. M., & Hill, C. E. (1984). The psychological well-being of women in their middle years. *Psychology of Women Quarterly, 8,* 282–292.

Blakely, B. E., & Dolon, R. (1991). The relative contributions of occupation groups in the discovery and treatment of elder abuse and neglect. *Journal of Gerontological Social Work, 17,* 183–199.

Blakely, B. E., Dolon, R., & May, D. D. (1993). Improving the responses of physicians to elder abuse and neglect: Contributions of a model program. *Journal of Gerontological Social Work, 19,* 35–47.

Blanchard-Fields, F., & Irion, J. C. (1988). The relation between locus of control and coping in two contexts: Age as a moderator variable. *Psychology and Aging, 3,* 197–203.

Blanchard-Fields, F., & Robinson, S. L. (1987). Age differences in the relation between controllability and coping. *Journal of Gerontology, 42,* 497–501.

Blazer, D. (1982). *Depression in late life.* St. Louis: Mosby.

Blazer, D. G., Bacher, J. R., & Manton, K. G. (1986). Suicide in later life: Review and commentary. *Journal of the American Geriatrics Society, 34,* 519–525.

Blenkner, M. (1965). Social work and family relationships in later life with some thoughts on filial maturity. In E. Shanas & G. Streib (Eds.), *Social structure and the family.* Englewood Cliffs, NJ: Prentice-Hall.

Block, M. R., Davidson, J. L., & Grambs, J. D. (1981). *Women over forty.* New York: Springer.

Bloom, A. (1993). The death of eros. *New York Times Magazine,* May 23, 26.

Blueband-Langner, M. (1977). The meanings of death to children. In H. Feifel (Ed.), *New meanings of death.* New York: McGraw-Hill.

Blumenthal, J. A., Emery, C. F., Madden, D. J., Schniebolk, S., Walsh-Riddle, M., George, L. K., McKee, D. C., Higgenbotham, M. B., Cobb, F. R., & Coleman, R. E. (1991). Long-term effects of exercise on psychological functioning in older men and women. *Journal of Gerontology: Psychological Science, 46,* P352–361.

Boehm, T., & Ihlanfeldt, K. (1986). The improvement expenditures of urban home owners: An empirical analysis. *AREVEA Journal, 14,* 48–60.

Bolles, R. N. (1988). *What color is your parachute?* Berkeley, CA: Ten Speed Press.

Booth-Kewley, S., & Friedman, H. (1987). Psychological predictors of heart disease: A quantitative review. *Psychological Bulletin, 101,* 343–362.

Bortz, W. M. (1980). Effects of exercise on aging—effects of aging on exercise. *Journal of the American Geriatric Society, 28,* 49–51.

Borup, J. H. (1983). Relocation mortality research: Assessment, reply, and the need to refocus on the issues. *The Gerontologist, 23,* 235–242.

Bosse, R., Aldwin, C. M., Levenson, M. R., Spiro, A., & Mroczek, D. K. (1993). Change in social support after retirement: Longitudinal findings from the normative aging study. *Journal of Gerontology: Psychological Sciences, 48,* P210–217.

Bosse, R., Aldwin, C. M., Levenson, M. R., Workman-Daniels, K., & Ekerdt, D. J. (1990). Differences in social support among retirees and workers: Findings from the Normative Aging Study. *Psychology and Aging, 5,* 41–47.

Boston Women's Health Book Collective. (1976). *Our bodies, ourselves* (2nd ed.). New York: Simon & Schuster.

Botwinick, J. (1977). Intellectual abilities. In J. E. Birren & K. W. Schaie (Eds.), *Handbook of the psychology of aging.* New York: Van Nostrand Reinhold.

Botwinick, J., & Storandt, M. (1974). *Memory-related functions and age.* Springfield, IL: Charles C Thomas.

Bould, S., Sanborn, B., & Reif, L. (1989). *Eighty-five plus: The oldest old.* Belmont, CA: Wadsworth.

Bowlby, J. (1969). *Attachment and loss* (Vol. 1.) London: Hogarth (New York: Basic Books).

Bowlby, J. (1980). Loss: Sadness and depression. In J. Bowlby (Ed.), *Attachment and loss* (Vol. 6). New York: Basic Books.

Bowles, N. L. (1993). Semantic processes that serve picture naming. In J. Cerella, J. M. Rybash, W. J. Hoyer, & M. A. Commons (Eds.), *Adult information processing: Limits on loss* (pp. 303–326). San Diego: Academic Press.

Boyd, P. (1969). The valued grandparent: A changing social role. In W. Donahue, J. Kornbluth, & B. Powers (Eds.), *Living in the multigenerational family.* Ann Arbor, MI: Institute of Gerontology.

Bradsher, J. E., Longino, C. F., Jackson, D. J., & Zimmerman, R. S. (1992). Health and geographic mobility among the recently widowed. *Journal of Gerontology: Social Sciences, 47,* S261–268.

Brainerd, C. J. (1978). The stage question in cognitive developmental theory. *Behavioral and Brain Sciences, 1,* 173–214.

Braithwaite, V. A., Gibson, D. M., and Bosly-Craft, R. (1986). An exploratory study of poor adjustment styles among retirees. *Social Science and Medicine, 23,* 493–499.

Bram, S. (1985–1987). Parenthood or nonparenthood: A comparison of intentional families. *Lifestyles, 8,* 69–84.

Branch, L. G. (1987). Continuing care retirement communities: Self-insuring for long-term care. *The Gerontologist, 27,* 4–8.

Branch, L. G., Friendman, D. J., Cohen, M. A., Smith, N., & Socholitzky, E. (1988). Impoverishing the elderly: A case study of the financial risk of spending down among Massachusetts' elderly. *The Gerontologist, 28,* 648–658.

Brandtstadter, J., & Renner, G. (1992). Coping with discrepancies between aspirations and achievements in adult development: A dual-process model. In L. Montada, S. H. Filipp, & M. Lerner (Eds.), *Crises and experiences of loss in adulthood* (pp. 301–319). Hillsdale, NJ: Lawrence Erlbaum.

Brandtstadter, J., Wentura, D., & Greve, W. (1993). Adaptive resources of the aging self: Outlines of an emergent perspective. *International Journal of Behavioral Development, 16,* 323–350.

Brennan, P. L., Moos, R. H. (1992). Life stressors social resources and late life problem drinking. *Psychology and Aging, 7*(4), 653.

Brickel, C. M. (1980–1981). A review of the roles of pet animals in psychotherapy and with the elderly. *International Journal of Aging and Human Development, 12,* 119–128.

Brickel, C. M. (1982). Pet-facilitated psychotherapy: A theoretical explanation via attention shifts. *Psychological Reports, 50,* 71–74.

Brickel, C. M. (1985). Initiation and maintenance of the human-animal bond: Familial roles from a learning perspective. *Marriage and the Family Review, 8,* 31–48.

Brim, G. (1992). *Ambition: How we manage success and failure throughout our adult lives.* New York: Basic Books.

Brim, O. G., Jr., & Ryff, C. D. (1980). On the properties of life events. In P. B. Baltes & O. G. Brim, Jr. (Eds.), *Life-span development and behavior* (Vol. 3). New York: Academic Press.

Brink, S. (1993). Elderly empowerment. *U.S. News and World Report,* April 26, 65–70.

Brody, E. M. (1985). Parent care as a normative family stress. *The Gerontologist, 25,* 19–29.

Brooks, J. B. (1981). Social maturity in middle-age and its developmental antecedents. In D. Eichorn, N. Haan, J. Clausen, M. Honzik, & P. Mussen (Eds.), *Present and past in middle life.* New York: Academic Press.

Burchinal, M., & Appelbaum, M. I. (1991). Estimating individual developmental functions: Methods and their assumptions. *Child Development, 62,* 23–43.

Burkhauser, R. V., & Salisbury, D. L. (Eds.). (1993). *Pensions in a changing economy.* Employee Benefit Research Institute, Washington, D.C. and Syracuse University.

Bureau of Justice Department Statistics. (1987). *Special report: Elderly victims.* Washington, DC: Bureau of Justice.

Burrus-Bammel, L. L., & Bammel, G. (1985). Leisure and recreation. In J. E. Birren & K. W. Schaie (Eds.), *Handbook of the psychology of aging* (2nd ed.). New York: Van Nostrand Reinhold.

Burt, J. J., & Meeks, L. B. (1985). *Education for sexuality: Concepts and programs for teaching* (3rd ed.). Philadelphia: Saunders College.

Burton, L. C., German, P. S., Rovner, B. W., Brant, L. J., & Clark, R. D. (1992). Mental illness and the use of restraints in nursing homes. *The Gerontologist, 32,* 164–170.

Buss, T., & Redburn, F. S. (1983). Unpublished and untitled manuscript. Center for Urban Studies, Youngstown State University, Youngstown, Ohio.

Butcher, L. L. & Woolf, N. J. (1986). Central cholinergic systems: Synopsis of anatomy and overview of physiology and pathology. In A. B. Scheibel, A. F. Wechsler, & M. A. B. Brazier (Eds.), *The biological substrates of Alzheimer's disease.* New York: Academic Press.

Butler, R. N. (1963). The life review: An interpretation of reminiscence in the aged. *Psychiatry, 26,* 65–76.

Butler, R. N., Lewis, M., & Sunderland, T. (1991). *Aging and mental health* (4th ed.). New York: Macmillan.

## *C*

Caine, E. D., & Grossman, H. (1992). Neuropsychiatric assessment. In J. E. Birren, R. B. Sloane, & G. D. Cohen (Eds.), *Handbook of mental health and aging* (2nd ed., pp. 603–641). San Diego: Academic Press.

Cairl, R. E., & Kosberg, J. I. (1993). The interface of burden and level of task performance in caregivers of Alzheimer's disease patients: An examination of clinical profiles. *Journal of Gerontological Social Work, 19,* 133–151.

Calasanti, T. M. (1988). Participation in a dual economy and adjustment to retirement. *International Journal of Aging and Human Development, 26,* 13–27.

Callan, M. (1990). *Surviving AIDS.* New York: HarperCollins.

Callan, V. J. (1984). Childlessness and marital adjustment. *Australian Journal of Sex, Marriage, and the Family, 5,* 210–214.

———. (1987). Personal and marital adjustment of voluntary and nonvoluntary childless wives. *Journal of Marriage and the Family, 49,* 847–856.

Campbell, D. T., & Stanley, J. C. (1963). *Experimental and quasi-experimental designs for research.* Chicago: Rand McNally.

Campbell, M. K., Bush, T. L., & Hale, W. E. (1993). Medical conditions associated with driving cessation in community-dwelling ambulatory elders. *Journal of Gerontology: Social Sciences, 48,* S230–234.

Campbell, S., & Silverman, P. R. (1987). *Widower.* Englewood Cliffs, NJ: Prentice-Hall.

Capitani, E., Della Sala, S., Lucchelli, F., Soave, P., & Spinnler, H. (1988). Perceptual attention in aging and dementia measured by Gottschaldt's Hidden Figures Test. *Journal of Gerontology: Psychological Sciences, 43,* P157–163.

Caracci, G., & Miller, N. S. (1991, July). Epidemiology and diagnosis of alcoholism in the elderly (A review). *International Journal of Geriatric Psychiatry, 6,* 511–515.

Carey, R. G. (1977). The widowed: A year later. *Journal of Counseling Psychology, 24,* 125–131.

Carlin, V. F., & Mansberg, R. (1984). *If I live to be 100 . . . Congregate housing for later life.* West Nyack, NY: Parker.

Carp, F. M. (1976). Housing and living environments of older people. In R. H. Binstock & E. Shanas (Eds.), *Handbook of aging and the social sciences.* New York: Van Nostrand Reinhold.

Cartwright, A., Hockey, L., & Anderson, J. L. (1973). *Life before death.* London: Routledge and Kegan Paul.

Cartwright, W., Huang, L. F., & Hu, T. (1988). Social science index: The economic costs of senile dementia in the United States. In *Public Health Reports* (Vol. 1, pp. 3–7). Washington, DC: U.S. Government Printing Office.

Carver, C. S., Scheier, M. F., & Weintraub, J. K. (1989). Assessing coping strategies: A theoretically based approach. *Journal of Personality and Social Psychology, 56,* 267–283.

Catania, J. A., Turner, H., Kegeles, S. M., Stall, R., Pollack, L., & Coates, T. J. (1989). Older Americans and AIDS transmission risks and primary prevention research needs. *The Gerontologist, 29,* 373–381.

Cattell, R. B. (1971). *Abilities: Their structure, growth, and action.* Champaign, IL: IPAT.

Cavanaugh, J. C. (1993). *Adult development and aging.* Pacific Grove, CA: Brooks Cole.

Ceci, S. J., & Liker, J. K. (1986). A day at the races: A study of IQ, expertise, and cognitive complexity. *Journal of Experimental Psychology: General, 115,* 255–266.

Centers for Disease Control. (1992, January 3). Sexual behavior among high school students—United States, 1990. *Morbidity and Mortality Weekly Report, 40,* 885–888.

Cerella, J. (1985). Age-related decline in extrafoveal letter perception. *Journal of Gerontology, 40,* 727–736.

Cerella, J. (1990). Aging and information processing rate. In J. E. Birren & K. W. Schaie (Eds.), *Handbook of the psychology of aging* (3rd ed., pp. 201–221). New York: Academic Press.

Cerella, J. (1991). Age effects may be global, not local: Comment on Fisk and Rogers (1991). *Journal of Experimental Psychology: General, 120,* 215–223.

Cerella, J., Hoyer, W. J., Rybash, J. M., & Commons, M. A. (Eds.). (1993). *Adult information processing: Limits on loss.* New York: Academic Press.

Cerella, J., Poon, L., & Fozard, J. L. (1981). Mental rotation and age reconsidered. *Journal of Gerontology, 38,* 447–454.

Chalke, H. D., Dewhurst, J. R., & Ward, C. W. (1958). Loss of sense of smell in old people. *Public Health, 72,* 223–230.

Chappell, N. L., & Novak, M. (1992). The role of support in alleviating stress among nursing assistants. *The Gerontologist, 32,* 351–359.

Charness, N. (1981). Search in chess: Age and skill differences. *Journal of Experimental Psychology: Human Perception and Performance, 7,* 467–476.

———. (1985). *Age and expertise: Responding to Talland's challenge.* Paper presented at the George A. Talland Memorial Conference on Aging and Memory, Cape Cod, MA.

———. (1988). Expertise in chess, music, and physics: A cognitive perspective. In L. K. Obler & D. A. Fein (Eds.), *The neuropsychology of talent and special abilities.* New York: Guilford Press.

Charness, N., & Bosman, E. A. (1992). Human factor and age. In Fergus I. M. Craik & Timothy A. Salthouse (Eds.), *Handbook of aging and cognition* (pp. 495–551). Hillside, NJ: Lawrence Erlbaum & Associates.

Charness, N., & Campbell. (1988). Acquiring skill at mental calculation in adulthood: A task decomposition. *Journal of Experimental Psychology: General, 117,* 115–129.

Chen, Y. P. (1987). Making assets out of tomorrow's elderly. *The Gerontologist, 27,* 410–416.

Cherlin, A., & Furstenberg, F. (1985). Styles and strategies of grandparenting. In V. L. Bengtson & J. Robertson (Eds.), *Granparenthood.* Beverly Hills, CA: Sage.

Cherlin, A., & Furstenberg, F. (1986). Grandparents and family crisis. *Generations, 10,* 26–28.

Chiarello, C. (1994). Semantic memory. In V. S. Ramachandran (Ed.), *Encyclopedia of human behavior,* Volume 4. San Diego: Academic Press.

Chiarello, C., & Hoyer, W. J. (1988). Adult age differences in implicit and explicit memory: Time course and encoding effects. *Psychology and Aging, 3,* 358–366.

Chiriboga, D. A. (1982a). Adaptations to marital separation in later and earlier life. *Journal of Gerontology, 37,* 109–114.

Chiriboga, D. A. (1982b). An examination of life events as possible antecedents to change. *Journal of Gerontology, 37,* 595–601.

Church, D. K., Siegel, M. A., & Foster, C. D. (1988). *Growing old in America.* Wylie, TX: Information Aids.

Cicirelli, V. G. (1981). *Helping elderly parents: The role of adult children.* Boston: Auburn House.

Cicirelli, V. G. (1992). *Family caregiving.* Newbury Park, CA: Sage Library of Social Research (Vol. 186).

Clairfield, A. M. (1988). The reversible dementias: Do they really reverse? *Annals of Internal Medicine, 109,* 476–486.

Clancy, S. M., & Hoyer, W. J. (1988). Effects of age and skill on domain specific search. In V. L. Paterl, & G. J. Groen (Eds.), *Proceedings of the tenth conference of the Cognitive Science Society* (pp. 398–404). Hillsdale, NJ: Earlbaum.

Clancy, S. M., & Hoyer, W. J. (1993). Skill and hemispheric specialization in detecting featural differences in visual images. *Brain and Cognition, 21,* 192–202.

Clancy, S. M., & Hoyer, W. J. (1994). Age and skill in visual search. *Developmental Psychology.*

Clausen, J. A. (1981). Men's occupational careers in the middle years. In D. H. Eichorn, J. A. Clausen, N. Haan, M. Honzik, & P. Mussen (Eds.), *Present and past in middle life.* New York: Academic Press.

Clayton, V., & Birren, J. E. (1980). Age and wisdom across the life-span: Theoretical perspectives. In P. B. Baltes & O. G. Brim, Jr. (Eds.), *Life-span development and behavior: Vol. 3.* New York: Academic Press.

Clebone, B. L., & Taylor, C. M. (1992, February). Family and social attitudes across four generations of women or maternal lineage. *Psychological Reports, 70,* 268–270.

Clipp, E. C., & George, L. K. (1990). Psychotropic drug use among caregivers of patients with dementia. *Journal of the American Geriatrics Society, 38,* 227–235.

Coelrick, E. J., & George, L. J. (1986). Predictors of institutionalization among caregivers of Alzheimer's patients. *Journal of the American Geriatrics Society, 34,* 493–498.

Cohen, C. I., Teresi, J. A., Holmes, D., & Roth, E. (1988). Survival strategies of older homeless men. *The Gerontologist, 28,* 58–65.

Cohen, D., & Eisdorfer, C. (1986). *The loss of self.* New York: Norton.

Cohen, D., & Eisdorfer, C. (1989). Depression in family members caring for a relative with Alzheimer's Disease. *Journal of the American Geriatrics Society, 36,* 385–389.

Cohen, F., Bearison, D. J., & Muller, C. (1987). Interpersonal understanding in the elderly: The influence of age-integrated and age-segregated housing. *Research on Aging, 9,* 79–100.

Cohen, G. D. (1988). *The brain in human aging.* New York: Springer.

———. (1989). The interface of mental and physical health phenomena in later life: New directions in geriatric psychiatry. *Gerontology and Geriatrics Education, 9,* 27–38.

———. (1990). Psychopathology and mental health in the mature and elderly adult. In J. E. Birren & K. W. Schaie (Eds.), *Handbook of the psychology of aging* (3rd ed., pp. 359–374). New York: Academic Press.

Cohen, J. (1957). The factorial structure of the WAIS between early adulthood and old age. *Journal of Consulting Psychology, 21,* 283–290.

Cohen, M. A., Tell, E. J., Batten, H. L., & Larson, M. J. (1988). Attitudes toward joining continuing care retirement communities. *The Gerontologist, 28,* 637–643.

Cohen, R. A., Van Nostrand, J. F., & Furner, S. E. (1993). *Chartbook on health data on older Americans, U.S. 1992,* Series 3 (No. 28) PHS 93-1413. Washington, DC: National Center for Health Statistics, U.S. Govt. Printing Office.

Cohen, S., & Syme, S. L. (1985). *Social support and health.* New York: Academic Press.

Cohen-Mansfield, J., Droge, J. A., & Billig, N. (1992). Factors influencing hospital patients' preferences in the utilization of life-sustaining treatments. *The Gerontologist, 32,* 89–95.

Cohen-Mansfield, J., Werner, P., Marx, M. S., & Freedman, L. (1991). Two studies of pacing in the nursing home. *Journal of Gerontology, 46,* 77–83.

Cohler, B. J., & Grunebaum, H. V. (1981). *Mothers, grandmothers, and daughters: Personality and child-care in three-generation families.* New York: John Wiley.

Colby, A., & Kohlberg, L. (Eds.). (1987). *The measurement of moral judgment, Vol. 1: Theoretical foundations and research validation.* New York: Cambridge University Press.

Colby, A., Kohlberg, L., Gibbs, J. C., & Lieberman, M. (1983). A longitudinal study of moral development. *Monographs of the Society for Research in Child Development, 48* (4), 1–124.

Coleman, J. (1988). Intimate relationships, marriage, and families. New York: Macmillan.

Coleman, L., & Antonucci, T. (1983). Impact of working women at midlife. *Developmental Psychology, 19,* 290–294.

Coleman, P. D., & Flood, D. G. (1987). Neuron numbers and dendritic extent in normal aging and Alzheimer's disease. *Neurobiology of Aging, 8,* 521–545.

Collaborative Study. (1977). An appraisal of the criteria of cerebral death: A summary statement. *Journal of the American Medical Association, 237,* 982–986.

Colletta, N. D. (1978). *Divorced mothers at two income levels: Stress, support, and childrearing practices.* Unpublished master's thesis. Ithaca, NY: Cornell University.

Comfort, A. (1980). Sexuality in later life. In J. E. Birren & R. B. Sloane (Eds.), *Handbook of mental health and aging.* New York: Van Nostrand Reinhold.

Commons, M. L., Richards, F. A., & Armon, C. (1984). Applying the general stage model. In M. L. Commons, F. A. Richards, & C. Armon (Eds.), *Beyond formal operations: Late adolescent and adult cognitive development.* New York: Praeger.

Commons, M. L., Sinnott, J. D., Richards, F. A., & Armon, C. (1989). *Adult development, Vol. 1: Comparisons and applications of developmental models.* New York: Praeger.

Congressional Caucus for Women's Issues. (1987). *The American woman: 1987–1988.* Washington, DC: Report.

Conley, J. J. (1985). Longitudinal stability of personality traits. *Journal of Personality and Social Psychology, 54,* 1266–1282.

Connelly, S. L., & Hasher, L. (1993). Aging and inhibition of spatial location. *Journal of Experimental Psychology: Human Perception and Performance, 19,* 1238–1250.

Connidis, I. A. (1989). The subjective experience of aging: Correlates of divergent views. *Canadian Journal of Aging, 8,* 7–18.

Connidis, I. A., & Davies, L. (1990a). *Family ties and aging.* Toronto: Butterworths.

Connidis, I. G., & Davies, L. (1990b). Confidants and companions in later life: The place of friends and family. *Journal of Gerontology: Social Sciences, 45,* S141–149.

Connolly, J. (1992). Participatory versus lecture/discussion preretirement education: A comparison. *Educational Gerontology, 18,* 365–379.

Connolly, N. K., & Williams, M. E. (1993). Plagues and tangles in approaching dementia. *Journal of Gerontology, 33,* 133–136.

Conrad, P. (1990). Qualitative research on chronic illness: A commentary on method and conceptual development. *Social Science Medicine, 30,* 1257–1263.

Constantinople, A. (1976). Masculinity-femininity: An exception to a famous dictum. In F. Denmark (Ed.), *Women: A PDI research reference work* (Vol. I.). New York: Psychological Dimensions.

Cool, L., & McCabe, J. (1983). The "scheming hag" and the "dear old thing": The anthropology of aging women. In J. Sokolovsky (Ed.), *Growing old in different societies: Cross cultural perspectives.* Belmont, CA: Wadsworth.

Cooney, T. M., Schaie, K. W., & Willis, S. L. (1988). The relationship between prior functioning on cognitive and personality dimensions and subject attrition in longitudinal research. *Journal of Gerontology: Psychological Science, 43,* P12–P17.

Corbin, J. N. (1974). *The effects of counselor-assisted exploratory activity on career development.* Unpublished doctoral dissertation. New York: Columbia University.

Corby, N., & Solnick, R. (1980). Psychosocial and physiological influences on sexuality in the older adult. In J. E. Birren & R. B. Sloane (Eds.), *Handbook of mental health and aging.* Englewood Cliffs, NJ: Prentice-Hall.

Cornelius, S. W., & Capsi, A. (1987). Everyday problem solving in adulthood and old age. *Psychology and Aging, 2,* 144–153.

Corso, J. F. (1977). Auditory perception and communication. In J. E. Birren & K. W. Schaie (Eds.), *Handbook of the psychology of aging* (2nd ed.). New York: Van Nostrand Reinhold.

Corso, J. F. (1981). *Aging, sensory systems, and perception.* New York: Praeger.

Costa, P. T., Jr. (1986). *The scope of individuality.* Paper presented at the meeting of the American Psychological Association, Washington, DC.

Costa, P. T., Jr., & McCrae, R. R. (1977). Age differences in personality structure revisited: Studies in validity, stability, and change. *Aging and Human Development, 8,* 261–275.

———. (1978). Objective personality assessment. In M. Storandt, I. C. Siegler, & M. P. Elias (Eds.), *The clinical psychology of aging.* New York: Plenum.

———. (1980). Still stable after all these years: Personality as a key to some issues of adulthood and old age. In P. B. Baltes & O. G. Brim, Jr. (Eds.), *Life-span development and behavior* (Vol. 3). New York: Academic Press.

———. (1982). An approach to the attribution of aging: Period and cohort effects. *Psychological Bulletin, 92,* 238–250.

———. (1985). Personality as a lifelong determinant of well-being. In C. Malatesta & C. Izard (Eds.), *Affective processes in adult development and aging.* New York: Sage.

———. (1986). Cross-sectional studies of personality in a national sample: I. Development and validation of survey measures. *Psychology and Aging, 1,* 140–143.

Costa, P. T., & McCrea, R. R. (1988). Personality in adulthood: A six-year longitudinal study of self reports and spouse rating in the NEO personality inventory. *Journal of Personality and Social Psychology, 54,* 853–863.

Cote, L. (1981). Aging of the brain and dementia. In E. R. Kandel & J. H. Schwartz (Eds.), *Principles of neural science.* New York: Elsevier-North Holland.

Cotrell, M., & Schulz, R. (1993). The perspective of the patient with Alzheimer's disease: A neglected dimension of dementia research. *The Gerontologist, 33,* 205–211.

Couldrick, A. (1992). Optimizing bereavement outcome: Reading the road ahead. *Social Science and Medicine, 35,* 1521–1523.

Covey, H. C. (1988). Historical terminology used to represent older people. *The Gerontologist, 28,* 291–297.

Cowgill, D., & Holmes, L. D. (1972). *Aging and modernization.* New York: Appleton-Century-Crofts.

Coyle, J. T., Price, D. L., & DeLong, M. R. (1983). Alzheimer's disease: A disorder of cortical cholinergic innervation. *Science, 219,* 1184–1190.

Craik, F. I. M. (1977). Age differences in human memory. In J. E. Birren & K. W. Schaie (Eds.), *Handbook of the psychology of aging.* New York: Van Nostrand Reinhold.

———. (1983). On the transfer of information from temporary to permanent memory. *Philosophical Transactions of the Royal Society, B302,* 341–359.

Craik, F. I. M., Byrd, M., & Swanson, J. M. (1987). Patterns of memory loss in three elderly samples. *Psychology and Aging, 2,* 79–86.

Craik, F. I. M., & Jennings, J. (1992). Human memory. In F. I. M. Craik & T. A. Salthouse (Eds.), *Handbook of aging and cognition* (pp. 51–110). Hillsdale, NJ: Erlbaum.

Craik, F. I. M., Morris, L. W., Morris, R. G., & Loewen, E. R. (1990). Relations between source amnesia and frontal lobe functioning in older adults. *Psychology and Aging, 5,* 148–151.

Craik, F. I. M., & Simon, E. (1980). Age differences in memory: A framework for memory research. *Journal of Verbal Learning and Verbal Behavior, 11,* 671–684.

Cristofalo, V. J. (1986). The biology of aging: An overview. In M. J. Horan, G. M. Steinberg, J. B. Dunbar, & E. C. Hadley (Eds.), *NIH, Blood pressure regulation and aging: Proceedings from a symposium.* New York: Biomedical Information Corporation.

Crohan, S. E., & Antonucci, T. C. (1989). Friends as a source of social support in old age. In R. Adams & R. Blieszner (Eds.), *Older adult friendship: Structure and process.* Beverly Hills, CA: Sage.

Cross, S., & Markus, H. (1991). Possible selves across the lifespan. *Human Development, 34,* 230–255.

Crystal, S., Shea, D., & Krioshnaswami, S. (1992). Educational attainment, occupational history, and stratification: Determinants of later-life outcomes. *Journal of Gerontology: Social Sciences, 47,* S213–S221.

Cuba, L., & Longino, C. F. (1991). Regional retirement migration: The case of Cape Cod. *Journal of Gerontology: Social Sciences, 46,* S33–S42.

Cude, R. L., & Jablin, F. M. (1992). Retiring from work: The paradoxical impact of organizational commitment. *Journal of Managerial Issues, 4* (1), 31–45.

Cumming, E., & Henry, W. (1961). *Growing old.* New York: Basic Books.

Cumming, E., & Henry, W. (1961). *Growing old.* New York: Basic Books.

Cunningham, W. R., & Owens, W. A., Jr. (1983). The Iowa study of the adult development of intellectual abilities. In K. W. Schaie (Ed.), *Longitudinal studies of adult psychological development.* New York: Guilford Press.

Curran, J., Jaffe, H., Hardy, A., Morgan, W., Selik, R., & Dondero, T. (1988). Epidemiology of HIV infection and AIDS in the United States. *Science, 239,* 610–616.

Curtis, Geller, Stokes, & —-. (1989). J. American Geriatrics Society. p. 593.

Cutler, S. J., & Hendricks, J. (1990). Leisure time use across the life course. In R. H. Binstock, & L. K. George (Eds.), *Handbook of aging and social sciences* (3rd ed.). New York: Academic Press.

Cutter, M. A. G. (1991). Euthanasia: Reassessing the boundaries. *Journal of National Institute of Health Research, 3,* 59–61.

## D

Dannefer, D., & Perlmutter, M. (1990). Development as a multidimensional process: Individual and social constraints. *Human Development, 33,* 108–137.

Davis, H. P., Cohen, A., Gandy, M., Colombo, P., VanDusseldorp, G., Simolke, N., & Romano, J. (1990). Lexical priming deficits as a function of age. *Behavioral Neuroscience, 104,* 288–297.

Davis, K. E. (1985). Near and dear: Friendship and love compared. *Psychology Today, 19,* 22–30.

DeAngelis, T. (1989, January). Mania, depression, and genius: Concert, talks inform public about manic-depressive illness. *American Psychological Association Monitor, 20* (1), 24.

Deci, E. (1975). *Intrinsic motivation.* New York: Plenum Press.

Deci, E. L., & Ryan, R. M. (1985). *Intrinsic motivation and self-determination.* New York: Plenum Press.

———. (1987). The support of autonomy and the control of behavior. *Journal of Personality and Social Psychology, 51,* 1024–1037.

Deets, H. B. (1993). Americans still believe 'Home is where the heart is.' *American Association of Retired Persons Bulletin, 34,* 3.

DeGenova, M. K. (1992). If you had your life to live over again: What would you do differently? *International Journal of Aging and Human Development, 34,* 135–143.

deGroot, A. (1965). *Thought and choice in chess: The Hague:* Mouton.

DeLongis, A., Coyne, J. C., Dakof, S., Folkman, S., & Lazarus, R. S. (1982). Relationship of daily hassles, uplifts, and major life events to health status. *Health Psychology, 1,* 119–136.

Demaris, A. (1984). A comparison of remarriages with first marriages on satisfaction in marriage and its relationship to prior cohabitation. Special Issue: Remarriage and stepparenting. *Family Relations Journal of Applied Family and Child Studies, 33,* 443–449.

Demetriou, A. (1990). Structural and developmental relations between formal and postformal capacities: Towards a comprehensive theory of adolescent and adolescent cognitive development. In M. L. Commons, C. Armon, L. Kohlberg, F. A. Richards, T. A. Groetzer, & J. D. Sinnott (Eds.), *Adult development, Vol. 2: Models and methods in the study of adolescent and adult thought.* New York: Praeger.

Denney, N. W. (1982). Aging and cognitive changes. In B. J. Wolman (Ed.), *Handbook of developmental psychology.* Englewood Cliffs, NJ: Prentice-Hall.

Denney, N. W. (1984). A model of cognitive development across the life span. *Developmental Review, 4,* 171–191.

Dennis, W. (1966). Creative productivity between the ages of twenty and eighty years. *Journal of Gerontology, 21,* 1–18.

———. (1968). Creative productivity between the ages of twenty and eighty years. In B. L. Neugarten (Ed.), *Middle age and aging.* Chicago: University of Chicago Press.

DePaola, S. J., Neimeyer, R. A., Lupfer, M. B., & Fiedler, J. (1992, Nov./Dec.). Death concern and attitudes toward the elderly in nursing home personnel. *Special issue: Death attitudes. Death Studies, 16,* 537–555.

Department of Health and Human Services. (1990). *Program announcement: Research on the prevention of alcohol abuse in the older population (RFP).* Catalog of Federal Domestic Assistance No. 13, 273, p. 2, Washington, DC: U.S. Superintendent of Documents.

Depner, C. E., & Ingersoll-Dayton, B. (1988, December). Supportive relationships on later life. *Psychology and Aging, 3,* 348–357.

Derogatis, L. R., Meyer, J., & King, K. M. (1981). Psychopathology in individuals with sexual dysfunction. *American Journal of Psychiatry, 138,* 757–763.

DeSpelder, L. A., & Strickland, A. L. (1992). *The last dance: Encountering death and dying* (3rd ed.). Mountainview, CA: Mayfield Publishers.

deVries, B., Bluck, S., & Birren, J. E. (1993). The understanding of death and dying in a lifespan perspective. *The Gerontologist, 33,* 366–372.

Diamond, E. E. (1988). *Women's occupational plans and decisions: An introduction.* 97–102.

Dickinson, G. E. (1992). First childhood death experiences. *Omega Journal of Death and Dying, 25,* 169–182.

Dittmann-Kohli, F., & Baltes, P. B. (1988). Toward a neofunctionalist conception of adult intellectual development: Wisdom as a prototypical case of intellectual growth. In C. Alexander, E. Langer, & R. Oetzel (Eds.), *Higher stages of human development.* New York: Oxford University Press.

Dittmann-Kholi, F., Lachman, M. E., Kliegel, R., & Baltes, P. B. (1991). Effects of cognitive training and testing on intellectual efficacy beliefs in elderly adults. *Journal of Gerontology: Psychological Sciences, 46,* P162–164.

Dixon, R. A., & Baltes, P. B. (1986). Toward life-span research on the functions and pragmatics of intelligence. In R. J. Sternberg & R. K. Wagner (Eds.), *Practical intelligence: Origins of competence in the everyday world.* New York: Cambridge University Press.

Dixon, R. A., Kurzman, D., & Friesen, I. C. (1993). Handwriting performance in younger and older adults: Age, familiarity, and practice effects. *Psychology and Aging, 8,* 360–370.

Dobbs, A. R., & Rule, B. G. (1990). Adult age differences in working memory. *Psychology and Aging, 4,* 500–503.

Doddridge, R., Schumm, W. R., & Bergen, M. B. (1987). Factors related to decline in preferred frequency of sexual intercourse among young couples. *Psychological Reports, 60,* 391–395.

Dohrenwend, B. S., & Dohrenwend, B. P. (1978). Some issues in research on stressful life events. *Journal of Nervous and Mental Disease, 166,* 7–15.

Dohrenwend, B. S., Krasnoff, L., Askensay, A., & Dohrenwend, B. P. (1978). Exemplification of a method of scaling life events: The PERI life-events scale. *Journal of Health and Social Behavior, 19,* 205–229.

Doka, K. J., & Mertz, M. E. (1988). The meaning and significance of great-grandparenthood. *Gerontologist, 28,* 192–197.

Donaldson, G. (1981). Letter to the editor. *Journal of Gerontology, 36,* 634–636.

Dorfman, L. T. (1992, June). Academics and the transition to retirement. *Educational Gerontology, 18,* 343–363.

Douglas, K. W., & Arenberg, D. (1978). Age changes, cohort differences, and cultural change on the Guilford-Zimmerman temperament survey. *Journal of Gerontology, 33,* 737–747.

Douvan, D. (1983). Listening to a different drummer. *Contemporary Psychology, 28,* 261–262.

Duncan, G. J., & Smith, K. R. (1989). The rising affluence of the elderly: How far, how fair, and how frail? *Annual Review of Sociology, 15,* 261–28.

Durlak, J. A., & Riesenberg, L. A. (1991). The impact of death education. *Death Studies, 15,* 39–58.

Dywan, J., & Jacoby, L. (1990). Effects of aging on source monitoring: Differences in susceptibility to false fame. *Psychology and Aging, 5,* 379–387.

## *E*

Edmonds, S., & Hooker, K. (1992). Perceived changes in life meaning following bereavement. *Omega Journal of Death and Dying, 25,* 307–318.

Edwards, J. N., & Booth, A. (1976). The cessation of marital intercourse. *American Journal of Psychiatry, 133,* 1333–1336.

Edwards, M. (1977). Coupling and uncoupling vs. the challenge of being single. *Personnel and Guidance Journal, 55,* 542–545.

Eichorn, D., Clausen, J., Haan, N., Honzik, M., & Mussen, P. (1981). (Eds.), *Past and present in middle life.* New York: Academic Press.

Eisdorfer, C. (1993). Three overviews of mental health and aging. *The Gerontologist, 33* (4), 570–571.

Eisdorfer, C., & Wilkie, F. (1973). Intellectual changes with advancing age. In L. F. Jarvik, C. Eisdorfer, & J. E. Blum (Eds.), *Intellectual functioning in adults.* New York: Springer.

Ekerdt, D. J. (1986). The busy ethic: Moral continuity between work and retirement. *The Gerontologist, 26,* 239–244.

Ekerdt, D. J., Bosse, R., & Levkoff, S. (1985). An empirical test for phases of retirement: Findings from the normative aging study. *Journal of Gerontology, 40,* 95–101.

Ekerdt, D. J., & DeViney, S. (1990). On defining persons as retired. *Journal of Aging Studies, 4,* 211–229.

Ekerdt, D. J., & DeViney, S. (1993). Evidence for a pre-retirement process among older male workers. *Journal of Gerontology: Social Sciences, 48,* S535–S543.

Ekstrom, R. B., French, J. W., & Harman, M. H. (1979). Cognitive factors: Their identification and replication. *Multivariate Behavior Research Monographs* (No. 79.2).

Elder, G. (1981). *Present and past in middle life.* San Diego: Academic Press.

Elder, G. H., & Pavalko, E. K. (1993). Work careers in men's later years: Transitions, trajectories, and historical change. *Journal of Gerontology: Social Sciences, 48,* S180–191.

Elder, G. H., Shanahan, M. J., & Clipp, E. C. (1994). When war comes to men's lives: Life-course patterns in family, work, and health. *Psychology and Aging, 9,* 5–16.

Elias, C. J., & Inui, T. S. (1993). When a house is not a home: Exploring the meaning of shelter among chronically homeless elderly men. *The Gerontologist, 33,* 396–402.

Elias, M. F., Elias, J. W., & Elias, P. K. (1990). Biological and health influences on behavior. In J. E. Birren & K. W. Schaie (Eds.), *Handbook of the psychology of aging* (3rd ed., pp. 80–102). San Diego: Academic Press.

Endroczi, E. (1991). *Stress and adaptation.* Adademiai Kiado, Budapest, Hungary.

Engen, T. (1977). Taste and smell. In J. E. Birren & K. W. Schaie (Eds.), *Handbook of the psychology of aging* (2nd ed.). New York: Van Nostrand Reinhold.

Ericsson, K. A., & Charness, N. (1994). Expert performance: Its structure and acquisition. *American Psychologist, 49,* 725–747.

Ericsson, K. A., & Crutcher, R. J. (1990). The nature of exceptional performance. In P. B. Baltes, D. L. Featherman, & R. Lerner (Eds.), *Life-span development and behavior* (Vol. 10, pp. 187–217). New York: Academic Press.

Ericsson, K. A., & Simon, H. A. (1984). *Protocol analysis.* Cambridge, MA: Harvard University Press.

Erikson, E. H. (1963). *Childhood and society* (2nd ed.). New York: Norton.

———. (1968). *Identity, youth and crisis.* New York: Norton.

———. (1969). *Gandhi's truth.* New York: Norton.

———. (1982). *The life cycle completed: A review.* New York: Norton.

Erikson, E. H., Erikson, J. M., & Kivnick, H. Q. (1986). *Vital involvement in old age.* NY: Norton.

Erikson, R., & Ekert, K. (1977). The elderly poor in downtown San Diego hotels. *The Gerontologist, 17,* 440–446.

Essex, M. J., & Nam, S. (1987). Marital status and loneliness among older women: The differential importance of close family and friends. *Journal of Marriage and the Family, 49,* 93–106.

Eth, S., & Leong, G. B. (1992). Forensic and legal issues. In J. E. Birren, R. B. Sloane, & G. D. Cohen (Eds.), *Handbook of mental health and aging* (2nd ed., pp. 853–871). San Diego, CA: Academic Press.

## *F*

Fackelmann, F. A. (1992). Anatomy of Alzheimer's disease. *Science News, 142,* 394–396.

Farberow, N. L., Gallagher-Thompson, D., Gilewski, M., & Thompson, L. (1992). Changes in grief and mental health. *Journal of Gerontology: Psychological Sciences, 47,* P357–366.

Farkas, M. S., & Hoyer, W. J. (1980). Processing consequences of perceptual grouping in selective attention. *Journal of Gerontology, 35,* 207–216.

Farrell, M. P., & Rosenberg, S. D. (1981). *Men at midlife.* Boston: Auburn House.

Fassinger, R. E. (1985). A causal model of college women's career choice. *Journal of Vocational Behavior, 27,* 123–153.

Featherman, D. L. (1983). The life-span perspective in social science research. In P. B. Baltes & O. G. Brim, Jr. (Eds.), *Life-span development and behavior* (Vol 5., pp. 1–59). New York: Academic Press.

Featherman, D. L., & Petersen, T. (1986). Markers of aging: Modeling the clocks that time us. *Research on Aging, 8,* 339–365.

Federal Trade Commission, Bureau of Consumer Protection. (1978). *Funeral industry practices.* Washington, DC: U.S. Superintendent of Documents.

Feifel, H., & Nagy, T. (1981). Another look at fear of death. *Journal of Consulting and Clinical Psychology, 49,* 278–286.

Ferraro, K. F., & LaGrange, R. L. (1992). Are older people afraid of crime? Reconsidering age differences in fear of victimization. *Journal of Gerontology: Social Sciences, 47,* S233–244.

Field, D. (1991). Continuity and change in personality in old age—Evidence from five longitudinal studies: Introduction to a special issue. *Journal of Gerontology: Psychological Sciences, 46,* P271–274.

Field, D., & Millsap, R. E. (1991). Personality in advanced old age: Continuity or change. *Journal of Gerontology: Psychological Sciences, 46,* P299–308.

Field, D., & Minkler, M. (1988). Continuity and change in social support between young-old and old-old or very-old age. *Journal of Gerontology: Psychological Sciences, 43,* P100–106.

Field, D., Minkler, M., Falk, R. F., & Leino, E. V. (1993).The influences of health and family contacts and family feelings in advanced old age: A longitudinal study. *Journal of Gerontology: Psychological Sciences, 48,* P18–28.

Finch, C. E. (1991). New models for new perspectives in the biology of senescence. *Neurobiology of aging, 12,* 625–634.

Finch, C. E., & Morgan, D. G. (1990). RNA and protein metabolism in the aging brain. *Annual Review of Neuroscience, 13,* 75–87.

Fischer, K. W. (1980). A theory of cognitive development: The control and construction of hierarchies of skills. *Psychological Review, 87,* 477–531.

Fisk, A. D., & Rogers, W. (1991). Toward an understanding of age-related memory and visual search effects. *Journal of Experimental Psychology: General, 120,* 131–149.

Fiske, M. L. (1980). Changing hierarchies of commitment in adulthood. In N. J. Smelser & E. Erikson (Eds.), *Theories of love and work in adulthood.* Cambridge, MA: Harvard University.

Fitzgerald, J. M. (1984). Autobiographical memory across the life span. *Journal of Gerontology, 39,* 692–699.

———. (1988). Vivid memories and the reminiscence phenomenon: The role of a self-narrative. *Human Development, 31,* 260–270.

Fitzgerald, J. M., & Lawrence, R. (1984). Autobiographical memory across the life-span. *Journal of Gerontology, 39,* 692–699.

Fitzgerald, L. E., & Betz, N. E. (1984). Astin's model in theory and practice: A technical and philosophical critique. *Counseling Psychologist, 12,* (3–4), 135–138.

Flavell, J. H. (1977). *Cognitive development.* Englewood Cliffs, NJ: Prentice-Hall.

———. (1985). *Cognitive development* (2nd ed.). Englewood Cliffs, NJ: Prentice-Hall.

Fletcher, W. L., Hansson, R. O., & Bailey, L. (1992, December). Assessing occupational self-efficacy among middle-aged and older adults. *Journal of Applied Gerontology, 11,* 489–501.

Flint, A. J., Black, S. E., Campbell-Taylor, I., Gailey, G. F., et. al. (1992, September). Acoustic analysis in the differentiation of Parkinson's disease and major depression. *Journal of Psycholinguistic Research, 21,* 383–399.

Folkman, S. L., & Lazarus, R. S. (1980). An analysis of coping in a middle-aged community sample. *Journal of Health and Social Behavior, 21,* 219–239.

Folkman, S. L., Lazarus, R. S., Dunkel-Schetter, C., DeLongis, A., & Gruen, R. J. (1986). The dynamics of a stressful encounter: Cognitive appraisal, coping, and encounter outcomes. *Journal of Personality and Social Psychology, 50,* 992–1003.

Folkman, S. L., Lazarus, R. S., Gruen, R., & DeLongis, A. (1986). Appraisal, coping, health status, and psychological symptoms. *Journal of Personality and Social Psychology, 50,* 571–579.

Folkman, S. L., Lazarus, R. S., Pimley, S., & Novacek, J. (1987). Age differences in stress and coping processes. *Psychology and Aging, 2,* 171–184.

Ford, A. B., Haug, M. R., Roy, A. W., Jones, P. K., & Folmar, S. J. (1992). New cohorts of urban elders: Are they in trouble? *Journal of Gerontology: Social Sciences, 47,* S297–303.

Fozard, J. L. (1990). Vision and hearing in aging. In J. E. Birren & K. W. Schaie (Eds.), *Handbook of the psychology of aging* (3rd ed., pp. 150–170). San Diego: Academic Press.

Franceschi, C., & Fabris, N. (1993). Human longevity: The gender difference. *Aging: Clinical and Experimental Research, 5,* 333–335.

Francis, D. (1990). The significance of work friends in late life. Special Issue: Process, change, and social support. *Journal of Aging Studies, 4,* 405–424.

Franks, M. M., & Stephens, M. A. P. (1992). Multiple roles of middle-generation caregivers: Contextual effects and psychological mechanisms. *Journal of Gerontology: Social Sciences, 47,* S123–S129.

Frazier, L., & Hoyer, W. J. (1992). Object recognition by component features: Adult age differences. *Experimental Aging Research, 18,* 9–15.

Fredrick, J. E. (1983–1984). The biochemistry of bereavement: Possible bias for chemotherapy. *Omega, 13,* 295–303.

Freuchen, P. (1961). *Book of the Eskimos.* Cleveland: World Press.

Freud, S. (1949). *An outline of psychoanalysis.* New York: W. W. Norton.

Friedman, M., & Rosenman, R. M. (1974). *Type A behavior and your heart.* New York: Knopf.

Friedmann, E., & Havighurst, R. J. (1954). *The meaning of work and retirement.* Chicago: University of Chicago Press.

Friedmann, E., Katcher, A. H., Lynch, J. J., & Thomas, S. A. (1980). Animal companions and one-year survival of patients after discharge from a coronary care unit. *Public Health Reports, 95,* 307–312.

Fries, J. F. (1990). Medical perspectives upon successful aging. In P. B. Baltes & M. M. Baltes (Eds.), *Successful aging* (pp. 35–49). New York: Cambridge University Press.

Fries, J. F., & Crapo, L. M. (1981). *Vitality and aging.* San Francisco: Freeman.

Frisancho, A. R. (1984). New standards of weight and body composition by frame size and heights for assessment of nutritional status of adults and the elderly. *American Journal of Clinical Nutrition, 84,* 808–819.

Fromm, E. (1955). *The sane society.* New York: Fawcett Books.

Fulton, R., & Owen, G. (1987–1988). Death and society in twentieth century America: Special issue: Research in thantology: A critical appraisal. *Omega Journal of Death and Dying 18* (4). 379–395.

## G

Galinsky, E. (1993). *National study of the changing work force.* New York: Families and Work Institute.

Gallagher, D., & Thompson, L. W. (1983). Depression. In P. Lewinsohn & L. Teri (Eds.), *Clinical geropsychology: New directions in assessment and treatment.* New York: Pergamon Press.

Gallagher, D., Thompson, L. W., & Breckenridge, J. S. (1986). Efficacy of three modalities of individual psychotherapy: One-year follow-up results. *The Gerontologist, 26,* 214.

Gallagher, W. (1993). Midlife myths. *Newsweek,* May, 51–68.

Gambert, S. R. (Ed.). (1987). *Handbook of geriatrics.* New York: Plenum Medical Book Company.

Gardner, H. (1983). *Frames of mind: The theory of multiple intelligences.* New York: Basic Books.

———. (1985). *The mind's new science.* New York: Basic Books.

———. (1993). *Creating minds.* New York: Basic Books.

Garret, H. E. (1957). *Great experiments in psychology* (3rd ed.). New York: Appleton-Century-Crofts.

Gatz, M., Bengtson, V. L., & Blum, M. J. (1990). Caregiving families. In J. E. Birren & K. W. Schaie (Eds)., *Handbook of the psychology of aging* (3rd ed., pp. 404–426). New York: Academic Press.

Gatz, M., Smyer, M. A., & Lawton, M. P. (1980). The mental health system and the older adult. In L. W. Poon (Ed.), *Aging in the 1980's: Psychological issues.* Washington, DC: American Psychological Association.

Geer, J. T., O'Donohue, W. T., & Schorman, R. H. (1986). Sexuality. In M. G. H. Coles, F. Donchin, & S. Porges (Eds.), *Psychophysiology: Systems, processes, applications.* New York: Guilford Press.

Gelman, R. (1979). Preschool thought. *American Psychologist, 34,* 900–904.

George, L. K. (1980). *Role transition in later life.* Belmont, CA: Wadsworth.

George, L. K. (1989). Social and economic factors. In E. W. Busse & D. G. Blazer (Eds.), *Geriatric psychiatry* (pp. 203–234). Washington, DC: Geriatric Press.

George, L. K. (1990a). Social structure, social processes, and social-psychological states. In R. H. Binstock & L. K. George (Eds.), *Handbook of aging and the social sciences* (3rd ed., pp. 186–204). San Diego, CA: Academic Press.

George, L. K. (1990b). Caregiver stress studies: There really is more to learn. *The Gerontologist, 30,* 580–581.

George, L. K. (1992a). Community and home care for mentally ill older adults. In J. E. Birren, R. B. Sloane, & G. D. Cohen (Eds.), *Handbook of mental health and aging* (2nd ed., pp. 793–813). San Diego, CA: Academic Press.

George, L. K., & Gwyther, L. P. (1986). Caregiver well-being: A multidimensional examination of family caregivers of demented adults. *The Gerontologist, 26,* 253–259.

Gerhardt, V. (1990). Qualitative research on chronic illness: The issue and the story. *Social Science Medicine, 30,* 1149–1159.

Gibbons, F. X., & Gerrard, M. (1991). Downward comparisons and coping with threat. In J. Suls & T. A. Wills (Eds.), *Social comparison: Contemporary theory and research* (pp. 317–346). Hillsdale, NJ: Lawrence Erlbaum.

Gibbs, J. C. (1977). Kohlberg's stages of moral development: A constructive critique. *Harvard Educational Review, 47,* 43–61.

———. (1979). Kohlberg's moral stage theory: A Piagetian revision. *Human Development, 22,* 89–112.

Gibbs, J. C., Arnold, K. D., & Burkhart, J. E. (1984). Sex differences in the expression of moral judgment. *Child Development, 55,* 1040–1044.

Gilhooly, M. L. M. (1984). The impact of caregiving on caregivers: Factors associated with the psychological well-being of people supporting a demented relative in the community. *British Journal of Medical Psychology, 57,* 544–547.

Gilley, D. W., Wilson, R. S., Bennett, D. A., Stebbins, G. T., Bernard, B. A., Whalen, M. E., & Fox, J. H. (1991). Cessation of driving and unsafe motor vehicle operation by dementia patients. *Archives of Internal Medicine, 15,* 941–946.

Gilligan, C. (1977). In a different voice: Women's conceptions of self and morality. *Harvard Educational Review, 47,* 481–517.

———. (1982). *In a different voice: Psychological theory and women's development.* Cambridge, MA: Harvard University Press.

———. (1985). *Response to critics.* Paper presented at the Biennial Meeting of the Society for Research in Child Development, Toronto.

Gilligan, C., & Belenky, M. F. (1980). A naturalistic study of abortion decisions. *New Directions for Child Development* (No. 7, pp. 69–90). San Francisco: Jossey-Bass.

Ginzberg, E. (1971). *Career guidance.* New York: McGraw-Hill.

———. (1972). Toward a theory of occupational choice: A restatement. *Vocational Guidance Quarterly, 20,* 169–176.

Glaser, B. G., & Strauss, A. L. (1965). *Awareness of dying.* Chicago: Aldine.

Glass, J. C., Jr. (1990). Changing death anxiety through education in the public schools. *Death Studies, 14,* 31–52.

Glass, S. P., & Wright, T. L. (1985). Sex differences in type of extramarital involvement and marital dissatisfaction. *Sex-roles, 12,* 1101–1120.

Glick, P. C. (1984). How American families are changing. *American Demographics, 6,* 20–25.

Glick, P. C., & Carter, H. (1976). *Marriage and divorce: A social and economic study* (2nd ed.). Cambridge, MA: Harvard University Press.

Glick, P. C., & Ling-Lin, S. (1986). Recent changes in divorce and remarriage. *Journal of Marriage and the Family, 48,* 737–747.

Golan, N. (1986). *The perilous bridge: Helping clients through midlife transitions.* New York: Free Press.

Goleman, D. (1987). Personality: Major traits found stable through life. *New York Times,* March 24, pp. C1, C14.

Goleman, D. (1988). Erickson, in his own old age, expands his view of life. *New York Times,* June 14, pp. C1, C14.

Goodman, M., Rubinstein, R. L., Alexander, B. B., & Luborsky, M. (1991). Cultural differences among elderly women in coping with the death of an adult child. *Journal of Gerontology: Social Sciences, 46,* S321–329.

Gorman, D. G., Benson, F., Vogel, D. G., & Vinters, H. V. (1992, February). Creutzfeldt-Jakob disease in a pathologist. *Neurology, 42,* 463.

Gottleib, G. L. (1992). Economic issues and geriatric mental health. In J. E. Birren, R. B. Sloane, & G. D. Cohen (Eds.), *Handbook of mental health and aging* (2nd ed). (pp. 873–890). San Diego, CA: Academic Press.

Gould, R. L. (1972). *Transformations: Growth and change in adult life.* New York: Simon & Schuster.

Gould, R. L. (1980). Transformation tasks in adulthood. In *The course of life, Vol. 3: Adulthood and aging process.* Bethesda, MD: National Institute of Mental Health.

Greenbook. (1992). Background material and data on programs within the jurisdiction of the U.S. Senate Committee on Ways and Means. U.S. Senate. Washington, DC: U.S. Government Printing Office.

Greene, V. L. (1983). Substitution between formally and informally provided care for the impaired elderly in the community. *Medical Care, 21,* 609–619.

Greene, V. L., & Monahan, D. J. (1987). The effects of a professionally guided caregiver support and education group on institutionalization and care receivers. *The Gerontologist, 27,* 716–721.

Greer, G. (1992). *The change: Women, aging, and menopause.* New York: Knopf.

Griese. (1987). p. 369.

Gresser, G., Wong, P., & Reker, G. (1987–88). Death attitudes across the lifespan: The development and validation of the death attitude profile (DAP). *Omega, 18,* 113–128.

Griffin, L. W., & Williams, O. J. (1992). Abuse among African-American elderly. *Journal of Family Violence, 7,* 19–35.

Grober, E., & Buschke, H. (1987). Genuine memory deficits in dementia. *Developmental Neuropsychology, 3,* 13–36.

Gubrium, J. F. (1975). *Living and dying at Murray Manor.* New York: St. Martin's Press.

Guilford, J. P. (1959a). *Personality.* New York: McGraw-Hill.

———. (1959b). Three faces of intellect. *American Psychologist, 14,* 469–479.

———. (1967). *The nature of human intelligence.* New York: McGraw-Hill.

Guralnik, J. M., Lacroix, A. S., Everett, D. F., et al. (1989).

Guralnick, J. M., & Simonsick, E. M. (1993). Physical disability in older Americans. *Journal of Gerontology, 48 (Special Issue),* 3–10.

Gurland, B. J. (1976). The comparative frequency of depression in various adult age groups. *Journal of Gerontology, 31,* 283–292.

———. (1980). The assessment of the mental status of older adults. In J. E. Birren & R. B. Sloane (Eds.), *Handbook of mental health and aging.* Englewood Cliffs, NJ: Prentice-Hall.

Gurland, B. J., & Cross, P. S. (1982). Epidemiology of psychopathology in old age. In L. F. Jarvik & G. W. Small (Eds.), *Psychiatric clinics of North America.* Philadelphia: W. B. Saunders.

Gutmann, D. L. (1975). Parenthood, key to the comparative study of the life cycle. In N. Datan & L. Ginsberg (Eds.), *Life-span developmental psychology: Normative life crises.* New York: Academic Press.

———. (1977). The cross-cultural perspective: Notes toward a comparative psychology of aging. In J. E. Birren & K. W. Schaie (Eds.), *Handbook of the psychology of aging* (1st ed.) New York: Van Nostrand Reinhold.

Gutmann, D. L. (1987). *Reclaimed powers: Toward a new psychology of men and women in later life.* New York: Basic Books.

Gutmann, D. L. (1992). Culture and mental health in later life. In J. E. Birren, R. B. Sloane, and G. D. Cohen (Eds.), *Handbook of mental health and aging* (2nd ed., pp. 75–97). San Diego: Academic Press.

Gwyther, L. P. (1992). Proliferation with pizzazz. *The Gerontologist, 33,* 865–867.


## H


Haber, P. A. L. (1987). Nursing homes. In G. L. Maddox (Ed.), *Encyclopedia of aging.* New York: Springer.

Habermas, J. (1971). *Knowledge and human interests.* Boston: Beacon Press.

Hagberg, B., Samuelsson, G., Lindberg, B., & Dehlin, O. (1991). Stability and change of personality in old age and its relation to survival. *Journal of Gerontology: Psychological Sciences, 46,* P285–291.

Hagberg, J. M. (1987). Effects of training on the decline of $VO_2$ max with aging. *Federation Proceedings, 46,* 1830–1833.

Hagestad, G. O. (1982). Divorce: The family ripple effect. *Generations: Journal of the Western Gerontological Society,* Winter, 24–31.

———. (1985). Continuity and connectedness. In V. L. Bengtson & J. Robertson (Eds.), *Grandparenthood.* Beverly Hills, CA: Sage.

Halevy, A., & Brody, B. (1993). Brain death reconciling definitions, criteria, and tests. *Annals of Internal Medicine, 119,* 519–525.

Haley, W. E. (1991). Caregiver intervention programs: The moral equivalent of free haircuts. *The Gerontologist, 31,* 7–8.

Hall, D. T., & Rabinowitz, S. (1988). Maintaining employee involvement in a plateaved career. In M. London & E. Mone (Eds.), *Career management and human resources.* New York: Quorum.

Hall, G. S. (1922). *Senescence: The last half of life.* New York: Appleton.

Hamdani, R. J. (1974). *Exploratory behavior and vocational development among disadvantaged inner-city adolescents.* Unpublished doctoral dissertation. New York: Columbia University.

Hammer, B. J. (1974). *Effects of two treatments designed to foster vocational development in disadvantaged inner-city adolescents.* Unpublished doctoral dissertation. New York: Columbia University.

Hannon, D. J., & Hoyer, W. J. (1994). Mechanisms of visual-cognitive aging: A neural network account. *Aging and Cognition, 1.*

Hardy, M. A. (1985). Occupational structure and retirement. In Z. B. Blau (Ed.), *Current perspectives on aging and the life cycle: Work, retirement, and social policy.* Greenwich, CT: JAI.

Harkins, S. W., Price, D. D., & Martinelli, M. (1986). Effects of age on pain perception. *Journal of Gerontology, 41,* 58–63.

Harkness, S., Edwards, C. P., & Super, C. (1981). Social roles and moral reasoning: A case study in a rural African village. *Developmental Psychology, 17,* 595–603.

Harma, M. I., Hakola, T., & Laitinen, J. (1992). Relation of age of circadian adjustment to night work. Fifth US-Finnish Joint Symposium on Occupational Safety and Health: Occupational epidemics on the 1990s. *Scandinavian Journal of Work, Environment and Health, 18,* Suppl. 2, 116–118.

Harris, L. (1976). *The myth and reality of aging in America.* Washington, DC: National Council on Aging.

Hart, R. P., Kwentus, J. A., Hamer, R. M., & Taylor, J. R. (1987). Selective reminding procedures in depression and dementia. *Psychology and Aging, 2,* 111–115.

Hartley, A. A. (1992). Attention. In F. I. M. Craik & T. A. Salthouse (Eds.), *The handbook of aging and cognition* (pp. 3–49). Hillsdale, NJ: Erlbaum.

Hasher, L., Stoltzfus, E. R., Zacks, R. T., & Rypma, B. (1991). Age and inhibition. *Journal of Experimental Psychology: Learning, Memory and Cognition, 17,* 163–169.

Hasher, L., & Zacks, R. (1988). Working memory, comprehension, and aging: A review and a new view. In G. H. Bower (Ed.), *The psychology of learning and motivation* (Vol. 22, pp. 193–225). New York: Academic Press.

Hatch, L. R. (1992). Gender differences in orientation toward retirement from paid labor. *Gender and Society, 6,* 66–85.

Havighurst, R. J. (1972). *Developmental tasks and education* (3rd ed.). New York: David McKay.

———. (1982). The world of work. In B. J. Wolman (Ed.), *Handbook of developmental psychology.* Englewood Cliffs, NJ: Prentice-Hall.

Havighurst, R. J., McDonald, W. J., Perun, P. J., & Snow, R. B. (1976). *Social scientists and educators: Lives after sixty.* Chicago: Committee on Human Development, University of Chicago.

Hawkins, H. L., Kramer, A. F., & Capaldi, D. (1992). Aging, exercise, and attention. *Psychology and Aging, 7,* 643–653.

Hayflick, L. (1980). The cell biology of human aging. *Scientific American, 242,* 58–65.

Hayslip, B., Jr., & Leon, J. (1988). *Geriatric case practice in hospice settings.* Beverly Hills, CA: Sage.

Heald, J. E. (1977). Midlife career influence. *Vocational Guidance Quarterly, 25,* 309–312.

Heath, H. A., & Orbach, J. (1963). Reversibility of the Necker cube: IV. Responses of older people. *Perceptual and Motor Skills, 17,* 625–626.

Heckhausen, J., Dixon, R. A., & Baltes, P. B. (1989). Gains and losses in development throughout adulthood as perceived by different adult age groups. *Developmental Psychology, 25,* 109–121.

Heidrich, S. M., & Ryff, C. D. (1993). The role of social comparisons. Processes in the psychological adaptation of elderly adults. *Journal of Gerontology: Psychological Sciences, 48,* P127–136.

Henderson, J. N., Gutierrez-Mayka, M., Garcia, J., & Boyd, S. (1993). A model for Alzheimer's disease support group development in African-American and Hispanic populations. *The Gerontologist, 33,* 409–414.

Hendricks, C. D., & Hendricks, S. (1983). *Living, loving, and relating.* Monterey, CA: Brooks/Cole.

Henretta, J. C., Chan, C. G., & O'Rand, A. M. (1992). Retirement reason versus retirement process: Examining the reasons for retirement typology. *Journals of Gerontology: Social Sciences, 47,* S1–S7.

Hertzog, C., & Schaie, K. W. (1988). Stability and change in adult intelligence: 2. Simultaneous analysis of longitudinal means and covariance structures. *Psychology and Aging, 3,* 122–130.

Herz, D. E. (1988, September). Employment characteristics of older women. *Monthly Labor Review, 111,* 3–9.

Hess, B. (1971). *Amicability.* Unpublished doctoral dissertation. New Brunswick, NJ: Rutgers University.

Hess, L. A. (1988). *The depiction of grandparents and their relationships with grandchildren in recent children's literature: Content analysis.* Unpublished master's thesis. State College, PA: Penn State University.

Heston, L. L., & White, J. A. (1983). *Dementia: A practical guide to Alzheimer's disease and related illnesses.* New York: W. H. Freeman.

Hetherington, E. M. (1979). Divorce: A child's perspective. *American Psychologist, 34,* 851–858.

Hetherington, E. M., Cox, M., & Cox, R. (1978). The aftermath of divorce. In J. H. Stevens & M. Mathews (Eds.), *Mother-child/father-child relations.* Washington, DC: National Association for the Education of Young Children.

Hetherington, E. M., Stanley-Hagan, M., & Anderson, E. R. (1989). Marital transitions: A child's perspective. *American Psychologist, 44,* 303–312.

Heumann, L., & Boldy, D. (1982). *Housing for the elderly: Policy and planning formulations in Western Europe and North America.* London: Croon Helm.

Hickey, T., Akiyama, H., & Rakowski, W. (1991). Daily illness characteristics and health care decisions of older people. *Journal of Applied Gerontology, 10,* 169–184.

High, D. M. (1991). A new myth about families of older people. *The Gerontologist, 31,* 611–618.

———. (1993). Advance directives and the elderly: A study of intervention strategies to increase use. *The Gerontologist, 33,* 342–349.

Hill, R. D., Storandt, M., & Malley, M. (1993). The impact of long-term exercise training on psychological function in older adults. *Journal of Gerontology: Psychological Sciences, 48,* P12–17.

Hillman, D. (1985). Artificial intelligence. *Human Factors, 27,* 21–31.

Hinrichsen, G. A., & Ramirez, M. (1992). Black and white dementia caregivers: A comparison of their adaptation, adjustment and service utilization. *The Gerontologist, 32,* 375–381.

Hinton, J. M. (1972). *Death* (2nd ed.). Baltimore: Penguin Books.

———. (1979, January 6). Comparison of places and policies for terminal care. *Lancet, 8106,* 29–32.

Hirsch, C. H., Davies, H. D., Boatwright, F., & Ochango, G. (1993). Effects of a nursing-home respite admission on veterans with advanced dementia. *The Gerontologist, 33*(4), 523–528.

Hoch, C. C., Buysse, D. J., Monk, T. H., & Reynolds, C. F., III. (1992). Sleep disorders and aging. In J. E. Birren, R. B. Sloane, & G. D. Cohen (Eds.), *Handbook of mental health and aging* (2nd ed., pp. 557–581). San Diego, CA: Academic Press.

Hocker, W. (1988). Parental loss of an adult child. In O. S. Margolis, A. H. Kutscher, E. R. Marcus, H. C. Raether, V. R. Pine, I. B. Seeland, and D. J. Cherico (Eds.), *Grief and loss of an adult child.* NY: Praeger.

Hoffman, L. W. (1979). Maternal employment. *American Psychologist, 34,* 859–865.

———. (1982). Social change and its effects on parents and children: Limitations to knowledge. In P. W. Berman & E. R. Ramey (Eds.), *Women: A developmental perspective.* Washington, DC: U.S. Department of Health and Human Services, Public Health Services, National Institute of Health Publication No. 82-2298.

———. (1986). Work, family, and the child. In M. S. Pallak & R. O. Perloff (Eds.), *Psychology and work: Productivity, change, and unemployment.* Washington, DC: American Psychological Association.

Holland, J. L. (1973). *Making vocational choices.* Englewood Cliffs, NJ: Prentice-Hall.

———. (1985). *Making vocational choices: A theory of vocational personalities and work environments* (2nd ed.). Englewood Cliffs, NJ: Prentice-Hall.

Holmes, T. H., & Rahe, R. H. (1967). The social readjustment rating scale. *Journal of Psychosomatic Research, 11,* 213–218.

Holte, A. (1978). *The interaction of social-cognitive and physiological determinants of peri-menopausal symptoms.* Paper presented at workshop on sociological, psychological, and anthropological aspects of the menopause. Second international Congress on the Menopause, Jerusalem, Israel.

Hooker, K. (1991). Change and stability in self during the transition to retirement: An intraindividual study using P-technique factor analysis. *International Journal of Behavioral Development, 14,* 209–233.

Hooker, K., & Kaus, C. R. (1992). Possible selves and health behaviors in later life. *Journal of Aging and Health, 4,* 390–411.

Hooker, K., & Kaus, C. R. (1994). Health-related possible selves in young and middle adulthood. *Psychology and Aging, 9,* 126–133.

Hooker, K., & Ventis, G. (1984). Work ethic, daily activities and retirement satisfaction. *Journal of Gerontology, 39,* 478–484.

Horn, J. C., & Meer, J. (1987). The vintage years. *Psychology Today, 21,* 76–84.

Horn, J. L. (1970). Organization of data on life-span development of human abilities. In L. R. Goulet & P. B. Baltes (Eds.), *Life-span developmental psychology: Research and theory.* New York: Academic Press.

———. (1982a). The aging of human abilities. In B. B. Wolman (Ed.), *Handbook of developmental psychology.* Englewood Cliffs, NJ: Prentice-Hall.

———. (1982b). The theory of fluid and crystallized intelligence in relation to concepts of cognitive psychology and aging in adulthood. In F. I. M. Craik & S. Trehub (Eds.), *Aging and cognitive processes* (Vol. 8). New York: Plenum.

Horn, J. L., & Donaldson, G. (1976). On the myth of intellectual decline in adulthood. *American Psychologist, 31,* 701–709.

Hornstein, G. A., & Wapner, S. (1985). Modes of experiencing and adapting to retirement. *International Journal of Aging and Human Development, 21,* 291–315.

Horowitz, A., Silverstone, B. M., & Reinhardt, J. P. (1991). A conceptual and empirical exploration of personal autonomy issues within family caregiving relationships. *The Gerontologist, 31*(1), 23–31.

Horvath, T. B., & Davis, K. L. (1990). Central nervous system disorders in aging. In E. L. Schneider & J. W. Rowe (1990). *Handbook of the biology of aging* (3rd ed., pp. 306–329). San Diego: Academic Press.

*Hospital Law Manual, 2.* (1982). Dying, death, and dead bodies (pp. 39–41). Gaithersburg: Aspen Systems Corporation.

Howard, D. V. (1988). Implicit and explicit assessment of cognitive aging. In M. L. Howe & C. J. Brainerd (Eds.), *Cognitive development in adulthood: Progress in cognitive development research* (pp. 3–37). New York: Springer-Verlag.

Howard, D. V., Fry, A. F., & Brune, C. M. (1991). Aging and memory for new associations: Direct versus indirect measures. *Journal of Experimental Psychology: Learning, Memory, and Cognition, 17,* 779–792.

Howard, D. V., & Wiggs, C. L. (1993). Aging and learning: Insights from implicit and explicit tests. In J. Cerella, W. J. Hoyer, J. M. Rybash, & M. L. Commons (Eds.), *Adult information processing: Limits on loss* (pp. 511–527). San Diego: Academic Press.

Hoyer, W. J. (1985). Aging and the development of expert cognition. In T. M. Shlechter & M. P. Toglia (Eds.), *New directions in cognitive science.* Norwood, NJ: Ablex.

Hoyer, W. J. (1986). Toward a knowledge-based conceptualization of adult intellectual development. In C. Schooler & K. W. Schaie (Eds.), *Cognitive functioning and social structures over the life course.* Norwood, NJ: Ablex.

Hoyer, W. J., & Hannon, D. J. (1993). Aging and individual differences in visual information processing: Toward a formal model. In D. Detterman (Ed.), *Current topics in human intelligence* (Volume 3, pp. 55–81). Norwood, NJ: Ablex.

Hoyer, W. J., Labouvie-Vief, G., & Baltes, P. B. (1973). Modification of response speed deficits and intellectual performance in the elderly. *Human Development, 16,* 233–242.

Hoyer, W. J., & Plude, D. J. (1980). Attentional and perceptual processes in the study of cognitive aging. In L. W. Poon (Ed.), *Aging in the 1980s: Psychological issues.* Washington, DC: American Psychological Association.

Hoyer, W. J., Rebok, G. W., & Sved, S. M. (1979). Effects of varying irrelevant information on adult age differences in problem solving. *Journal of Gerontology, 34,* 553–560.

Hoyer, W. J., & Rybash, J. M. (1992). Knowledge in visual perception: In R. L. West & J. D. Sinnott (Eds.), *Everyday memory and aging: Current research and methodology* (pp. 79–98). New York: Springer-Verlag.

Hoyer, W. J., & Rybash, J. M. (1992a). Knowledge factors in everyday visual perception. In R. L. West & J. D. Sinnott (Eds.), *Everyday memory and aging: Current research and methodology* (pp. 215–222). New York: Springer-Verlag.

Hoyer, W. J. & Rybash, J. M. (1992b). Age and visual field differences in computing visual-spatial relations. *Psychology and Aging, 7,* 339–342.

Hoyer, W. J., & Rybash, J. M. (1994). Characterizing adult cognitive development. *Adult Development, 1,* 7–12.

Hoyer, W. J., Rybash, J. M., & Roodin, P. A. (1989). Cognitive change as a function of knowledge access. In M. L. Commons, J. Sinnott, F. A. Richards, & C. Armon (Eds.), *Beyond formal operations: Comparisons and applications of adolescent and adult models.* New York: Praeger.

Hoyert, D. L. (1991). Financial and household exchange between generations. *Research on Aging, 13,* 205–225.

Hultsch, D. F. (1971). Adult age differences in free classification and free recall. *Developmental Psychology, 4,* 338–342.

Hultsch, D. F., & Dixon, R. A. (1990). Learning and memory and aging. In J. E. Birren & K. W. Schaie (Eds.), *Handbook of the psychology of aging* (3rd ed., pp. 258–274). San Diego: Academic Press.

Hultsch, D. F., Hammer, M., & Small, B. J. (1993). Age differences in cognitive performance in later life: Relationship to self-reported health and activity life style. *Journal of Gerontology: Psychological Sciences, 48,* P1–11.

Hultsch, D. F., Hertzog, C., & Dixon, R. A. (1987). Age differences in metamemory: Resolving the inconsistencies. *Canadian Journal of Gerontology, 41,* 193–208.

Hultsch, D. F., Masson, M. E. J., & Small, B. J. (1991). Adult age differences in direct and indirect tests of memory. *Journal of Gerontology: Psychological Sciences, 46,* P22–30.

Hultsch, D. F., & Plemons, J. K. (1979). Life events and life-span development. In P. B. Baltes & O. G. Brim, Jr. (Eds.), *Life-span development and behavior* (Vol. 2). New York: Academic Press.

Human Capital Initiative. (1993). *Vitality for life: Psychological research for productive aging.* Washington, DC: American Psychological Society.

Hunt, E. (1993). What we need to know about aging. In J. Cerella, J. Rybash, W. Hoyer, & M. L. Commons (Eds.), *Adult information processing: Limits on loss* (pp. 587–589). San Diego, CA: Academic Press.

Hunt, M. (1974). *Sexual behavior in the seventies.* Chicago: Playboy Press.

Hunt, M., & Hunt, B. (1977). *The divorce experience.* New York: McGraw-Hill.

Hutchison, T. D., & Scherman, A. (1992, July/August). Didactic and experiential death and dying training: Impact upon death anxiety. *Death Studies, 16,* 317–330.

Huyck, M. H. (1990). Gender differences in aging. In J. E. Birren & K. W. Schaie (Eds.), *Handbook of the psychology of aging* (3rd ed., pp. 124–132). San Diego: Academic Press.

Huyck, M. H., & Hoyer, W. J. (1982). *Adult development and aging.* Belmont, CA: Wadsworth.

## I

Iaffaldano, M. T., & Muchinsky, P. M. (1985). Job satisfaction and job performance: A meta-analysis. *Psychological Bulletin, 97,* 251–271.

Ingersoll-Dayton, B., & Antonucci, T. C. (1988). Reciprocal and nonreciprocal social support: Contrasting sides of intimate relationships. *Journal of Gerontology: Social Sciences, 43,* S65–S73.

Inhelder, B., & Piaget, J. (1958). *The growth of logical thinking from childhood to adolescence.* New York: Basic Books.

Insurance Institute for Highway Safety. (1992). *Status report 12,* 1–7. Arlington, VA.

## J

Jackson, J. S. (1988). *The black American elderly.* New York: Springer.

Jacobs, J. A. (1989). *Revolving doors: Sex segregation in women's careers.* Stanford, CA: Stanford University Press.

Jacoby, L. L., Kelley, C., Brown, J., & Jasechko, J. (1989). Becoming famous overnight: Limits on the ability to avoid unconscious influences of the past. *Journal of Personality and Social Psychology, 56,* 326–338.

James, A., James, W. L., & Smith, H. L. (1984). Reciprocity as a coping strategy of the elderly: A rural Irish perspective. *The Gerontologist, 24,* 483–489.

James, W. (1890). *Principles of psychology.* New York: Henry Holt.

Janowsky, J. S., Shimamura, A. P., & Squire, L. R. (1989). Source memory impairment in patients with frontal lobe lesions. *Neuropsychologia, 27,* 1043–1056.

Jarvik, L. (1987). *The aging of the brain: How to prevent it.* Paper presented at the annual meeting of the Gerontological Society of America, Washington, DC.

Jecker, N. S. (1990). The role of intimate others in medical decision-making. *The Gerontologist, 30,* 65–71.

Johnson, C., Lahey, P. P., & Shore, A. (1992). An exploration of creative arts therapeutic group work on an Alzheimer's unit. *Arts in Psychotherapy, 19,* 269–277.

Johnson, C. L. (1988). Grandparenting options in divorcing families: An anthropological perspective. In V. L. Bengtson & J. Robertson (Eds.), *Grandparenthood.* Beverly Hills, CA: Sage.

Johnson, S. J., & Rybash, J. M. (1993). A cognitive neuroscience perspective on age-related slowing: Developmental changes in the functional architecture. In J. Cerella, J. M. Rybash, W. J. Hoyer, & M. L. Commons (Eds.), *Adult information processing: Limits on loss* (pp. 143–175). San Diego, CA: Academic Press.

Jones, H. E., & Conrad, H. S. (1933). The growth and decline of intelligence: A study of a homogeneous group between the ages of ten and sixty. *Genetic Psychology Monographs, 13,* 223–294.

Jorm, A. F. (1990). *The epidemiology of Alzheimer's disease and related disorders.* London: Chapman and Hall.

Jung, C. G. (1933). Modern man in search of a soul. New York: Harcourt, Brace, & World.

## *K*

Kagan, J. (1979). Family experience and the child's development. *American Psychologist, 34,* 886–891.

Kahana, B. (1992). Theoretical and methodological issues in the study of extreme stress in later life. In M. Wykle (Ed.), *Stress and health among the aged* (pp. 151–171). New York: Springer.

Kahana, B., & Kahana, E. (1970). Grandparenting from the perspective of the developing grandchild. *Developmental Psychology, 3,* 98–105.

Kahana, E., Stange, K., & Kahana, B. (1993). Stress and aging: The journey from what, to how, to why. *The Gerontologist, 33,* 423–426.

Kahneman, D. (1973). *Attention and effort.* Englewood Cliffs, NJ: Prentice-Hall.

Kalish, R. (1976). Death and dying in a social context. In R. Binstock & E. Shanas (Eds.), *Handbook of aging and the social sciences* (pp. 483–507). NY: Van Nostrand Reinhold.

———. (1981). *Death, grief, and caring relationships.* Monterey, CA: Brooks-Cole.

———. (1985). The social context of death and dying. In R. H. Binstock & E. Shanas (Eds.), *Handbook of aging and the social sciences* (2nd ed.). New York: Van Nostrand Reinhold.

———. (1987). Death. In G. L. Maddox (Ed.), *Encyclopedia of aging.* New York: Springer.

Kalish, R. A., & Reynolds, D. K. (1981). *Death and ethnicity: A psychosocial study.* Farmingdale, NY: Baywood. (Original work published 1976).

Kanner, A. D., Coyne, J. C., Schaefer, C., & Lazarus, R. S. (1981). Comparison of two modes of stress measurement: Daily hassles and uplifts versus major life events. *Journal of Behavioral Medicine, 4,* 1–39.

Kaplan, H. S. (1974). *The new sex therapy.* New York: Brunner/Mazel.

Kapp, M. B. (1991). Health care decision-making by the elderly: I get by with a little help from my family. *The Gerontologist, 31,* 619–623.

Kaprio, J., Kosenvuo, M., & Rita, H. (1987). Mortality after bereavement: A prospective study of 95,647 widowed persons. *American Journal of Public Health, 77,* 283.

Karoly, P. (1993). Mechanisms of self-regulation: A systems view. *Annual Review of Psychology, 44,* 23–52.

Kaslow, F. W., & Schwartz, L. I. (1987). *The dynamics of divorce: A life cycle perspective.* New York: Brunner/Mazel.

Kasper, J. D. (1988). Aging alone: Profiles and projections. *Report of the Commonwealth Fund Commission: Elderly People Living Alone.* Baltimore: Commonwealth Fund Commission.

Kastenbaum, R. (1969). Death and bereavement in later life. In A. H. Kutscher (Ed.), *Death and bereavement.* Springfield, IL: Charles C Thomas.

———. (1981). *Death, society, and human experience* (2nd ed.). Palo Alto, CA: Mayfield.

———. (1985). Death and dying: A life-span approach. In J. E. Birren & K. W. Schaie (Eds.), *Handbook of the psychology of aging* (2nd ed.). New York: Van Nostrand Reinhold.

———. (1992). *The psychology of death* (2nd ed.). New York: Springer.

Kastenbaum, R., & Norman, C. (1990). Deathbed scenes imagined by the young and experienced by the old. *Death Studies, 14,* 201–217.

Katchadourian, H. (1987). *Fifty: Midlife in perspective.* New York: W. H. Freeman.

Katzman, R. (1986). Alzheimer's disease. *New England Journal of Medicine, 314,* 964–973.

Kaufman, H. H., & Lynn, J. (1986). Brain death: Perspectives on neurological practice. *Neurosurgery 19,* 850–855.

Kay, D. W. K., & Bergmann, K. (1980). Epidemiology of mental disorders among the aged in the community. In J. E. Birren & R. B. Sloane (Eds.), *Handbook of mental health and aging.* Englewood Cliffs, NJ: Prentice-Hall.

Keith, P. M. (1981–1982). Perceptions of time remaining and distance from death. *Omega, 12,* 307–318.

Kelley, J. B. (1982). Divorce: The adult perspective. In B. J. Wolman (Ed.), *Handbook of developmental psychology.* New York: Van Nostrand Reinhold.

Kemp, B. (1985). Rehabilitation and the older adult. In J. E. Birren & K. W. Schaie (Eds.), *Handbook of the psychology of aging* (2nd ed.). New York: Van Nostrand Reinhold.

Kemp, B. J., & Mitchell, J. M. (1992). Functional assessment in geriatric mental health. In J. E. Birren, R. B. Sloane, & G. D. Cohen (Eds.). *Handbook of mental health and aging* (2nd ed., pp. 671–719). San Diego, CA: Academic Press.

Kendig, H. L. (1990). Comparative perspectives on housing, aging, and social structure. In R. H. Binstock and L. K. George (Eds.), *Handbook of aging and the social sciences* (3rd ed.). New York: Academic Press.

Kendig, N. E., & Adler, W. H. (1990). The implications of acquired immunodeficiency syndrome for gerontology research and geriatric medicine. *Journal of Gerontology: Medical Sciences, 45,* M77–81.

Kennedy, S., Kiecolt-Glaser, J. K., & Glaser, R. (1990). Social support, stress, and the immune system. In B. R. Sarason, I. G. Sarason, & G. R. Pierce (Eds.), *Social support: An interactional view* (pp. 253–266). New York: Wiley.

Kenshalo, D. R. (1977). Age changes in touch, vibration, temperature, kinesthesis, and pain sensitivity. In J. E. Birren & K. W. Schaie (Eds.), *Handbook of the psychology of aging* (2nd ed.). New York: Van Nostrand Reinhold.

Kerlikowske, K., Grady, D., Barclay, J., Sickles, E. A., Eaton, A., & Ernster, V. (1993). Positive predictive value of screening mammography by age and family history of breast cancer. *Journal of the American Medical Association, 270,* 2444–2450.

Kessler, R. C., Foster, C., Webster, P. S., & House, J. S. (1992). The relationship between age and depressive symptoms in two national surveys. *Psychology and Aging, 7,* 119–126.

Kety, S. (1980). Foreword: Bringing knowledge to bear on the mental dysfunctions associated with aging. In J. E. Birren & R. B. Sloane (Eds.), *Handbook of mental health and aging.* Englewood Cliffs, NJ: Prentice-Hall.

Kidd, A. H. & Feldman, B. M. (1981). Pet ownership and self-perceptions of older people. *Psychological Reports, 48,* 867–875.

Kiecolt-Glaser, J. K., Fisher, L. D., Ogrocki, P., Stout, J. C., Speicher, C. E., & Glaser, R. (1987). Marital quality, marital disruption, and immune function. *Psychosomatic Medicine, 49,* 13–34.

Kiecolt-Glaser, J. K., Glaser, R., Shuttleworth, E. C., Dyer, C. S., Ogrocki, P., & Speicher, C. E. (1987). Chronic stress and immunity in family caregivers of Alzheimer's disease victims. *Psychosomatic Medicine, 49,* 523–535.

Kiesler, C. A. (1992). U.S. mental health policy: Doomed to fail. *American Psychologist, 47,* 1077–1081.

Kiline, D. W., Kline, T., Fozard, J. L., Kosnik, W., Scheiber, F. & Sekuler, R. (1992). Vision, aging and driving: The problems of older drivers. *Journal of Gerontology: Psychological Sciences, 47,* P27–P34.

Kiloh, L. G. (1961). Pseudodementia. *Acta Psychiatrica Scandanavica, 37,* 336–351.

Kimura, D. (1992). Sex differences in the brain. *Scientific American, 267,* 118–125.

King, P. M., Kitchener, K. S., Davison, M. L., Parker, C. A., & Wood, P. K. (1983). The justification of beliefs in young adults: A longitudinal study. *Human Development, 26,* 106–116.

King S. (1989). Sex differences in a causal model of career maturity. *Job Counseling and Development, 68,* 208–215.

Kingson, E. R., & O'Grady-LeShane, R. (1993). The effects of caregiving on women's social security benefits. *The Gerontologist, 33,* 230–239.

Kinicki, A. J. (1989). Predicting occupational role choices after involuntary job loss. *Journal of Vocational Behavior, 35,* 204–218.

Kinicki, A. J., & Latack, C. J. (1990). Explication of the construct of coping with involuntary job loss. *Journal of Vocational Behavior, 36,* 339–360.

Kinney, H. C., Korein, J., Panigraphy, A., Dikkers, P., & Goode, R. (1994). Neuropathological findings in the brain of Karen Ann Quinlan. *New England Journal of Medicine, 330* (#21), 1469–1475.

Kinoshita, Y., & Kiefer, C. W. (1993). *Refuge of the honored: Social organization in a Japanese retirement community.* Berkeley, CA: University of California Press.

Kinsey, A. C., Pomeroy, W. B., & Martin, C. (1948). *Sexual behavior in the human male.* Philadelphia: W. B. Saunders.

Kitch, D. L. (1987). Hospice. In R. J. Corsini (Ed.), *Concise encyclopedia of psychology.* New York: Wiley.

Kitchener, K. S., & King, P. M. (1981). Reflective judgment: Concepts of justification and their relationship to age and education. *Journal of Applied Developmental Psychology, 2,* 89–111.

Kitchener, K. S., & Wood, P. K. (1987). Development of concepts of justification in German university students. *International Journal of Behavioral Development, 10,* 171–186.

Kivela, S. L. (1985). Relationship between suicide, homicide, and accidental death among the aged in Finland in 1951–1979. *Acta Psychiatrica Scandinavica, 72,* 155–160.

Kivnick, H. Q. (1983). Dimensions of grandparental meaning: Deductive conceptualization and empirical derivation. *Journal of Personality and Social Psychology, 44,* 1056–1068.

Klass, D. (1988). *Parental grief: Solace and resolution.* New York: Springer.

Kleemeier, R. W. (1972). Intellectual change in the senium. *Proceedings of the Social Statistics Section of the American Statistical Association, 1,* 290–295.

Kliegel, R. (1990). *On the triangulation of adult age differences in developmental reserve capacity.* Paper presented at the annual meetings of the Cognitive Aging Society, Atlanta.

Kliegel, R., Smith, J., & Baltes, P. B. (1989). Testing-the-limits and the study of adult age differences in cognitive plasticity of a mnemonic skill. *Developmental Psychology, 25,* 247–256.

Kliegel, R., Smith, J., & Baltes, P. B. (1990). On the locus and process of magnification of age differences during mnemonic training. *Developmental Psychology, 26,* 894–904.

Kline, D. W., Kline, T. J. B., Fozard, J. L., Kosnik, W., Schieber, F., & Sekuler, R. (1992). Vision, aging, and driving: The problems of older drivers. *Journal of Gerontology: 47,* P27–34.

Kline, T. J. B., Ghali, L. M., Kline, D. W., & Brown, S. (1990). Visibility distance of highway signs among young, middle-aged, and older observers. *Human Factors, 32,* 609–619.

Knesek, G. E. (1992). Early versus regular retirement: Differences in measures of life satisfaction. *Journal of Gerontological Social Work, 19,* 3–34.

Knight, B. G., Lutzky, S. M., & Macofsky-Urban. (1993). A meta-analytic review of interventions for caregiver distress: Recommendations for future research. *The Gerontologist, 33,* 240–248.

Knox, D. (1985). *Choices in relationships.* St. Paul, MN: West.

Kobasa, S. C. (1979). Stressful life events, personality, and health: An inquiry into hardiness. *Journal of Personality and Social Psychology, 37,* 1–11.

Koenig, H. G., & Blazer, D. G. (1992). Mood disorders and suicide. In J. E. Birren, R. B. Sloane, & G. D. Cohen (Eds.), *Handbook of mental health and aging* (2nd ed., pp. 380–409). San Diego, CA: Academic Press.

Koff, T. H. (1981). *Hospice: A caring community.* Cambridge, MA: Winthrop.

Kogan, N. (1990). Personality and aging. In J. E. Birren, & K. W. Schaie (Eds.), *Handbook of the psychology of aging* (3rd ed., pp. 330–346). San Diego, CA: Academic Press.

Kohlberg, L. (1958). *The development of mode of moral thinking and choice in the years ten to sixteen.* Unpublished doctoral dissertation, University of Chicago.

———. (1969). Stage and sequence: The cognitive-developmental approach to socialization. In D. Goslin (Ed.), *Handbook of socialization theory and research.* Chicago: Rand McNally.

———. (1976). Moral stages and moralization: The cognitive-developmental approach. In T. Lickona (Ed.), *Moral development and behavior: Theory, research, and social issues.* New York: Holt, Rinehart & Winston.

———. (1987). The development of moral judgment and moral action. In L. Kohlberg (Ed.), *Child development and childhood education: A cognitive-developmental view.* New York: Longman Press.

———. (1990). Which postformal levels are stages? In M. L. Commons, C. Armon, L. Kohlberg, F. A. Richards, T. A. Groetzer, & J. D. Sinnott (Eds.), *Adult development, Vol. 2: Models and methods in the study of adolescent and adult thought.* New York: Praeger.

Kohlberg, L., & Candee, D. (1984). The relationship of moral judgment to moral action. In W. M. Kurtines & J. L. Gewirtz (Eds.), *Morality, moral behavior, and moral development.* New York: Wiley.

Kohlberg, L., & Kramer, R. B. (1969). Continuities and discontinuities in childhood and adult moral development. *Human development, 12,* 93–120.

Kolata, G. (1985). Down's syndrome—Alzheimer's disease linked. *Science, 230,* 1152–1153.

Kolb, B. & Whishaw, I. Q. (1992). *Fundamentals of human neuropsychology* (2nd ed.). New York: W. H. Freeman.

Koplowitz, H. (1984). A projection beyond Piaget's formal operations stage: A general system stage and a unitary stage. In M. L. Commons, F. A. Richards, & C. Armon (Eds.), *Beyond formal operations: Late adolescent and adult cognitive development.* New York: Praeger.

Korchin, S. J., & Basowitz, H. (1956). The judgment of ambiguous stimuli as an index of cognitive functioning in aging. *Journal of Personality, 25,* 81–95.

Kosik, K. S. (1992). Alzheimer's disease: A cell biological perspective. *Science, 256,* 780–783.

Kosnik, W., Winslow, L., Kline, D., Rasinski, K., & Sekuler, R. (1988). Visual changes in daily life throughout adulthood. *Journal of Gerontology: Psychological Sciences, 43,* P63–70.

Kosnik, W. D., Sekuler, R., & Kline, D. W. (1990). Self-reported visual problems of older drivers. *Human Factors, 32,* 597–608.

Kosslyn, S. M. (1987). Seeing and imagining in the cerebral hemispheres: A computational approach. *Psychological Review, 94,* 148–175.

Kotary, L., & Hoyer, W. J. (1995). Age and the ability to inhibit distractor information in visual selective attention. *Experimental Aging Research, 21.*

Kozol, J. (1988). *Rachel and her children: Homeless families in America.* New York: Fawcett.

Kral, K. (1962). Senescent forgetfulness: Benign and malignant. *Canadian Medical Association Journal, 86,* 257–260.

Kramer, D. A. (1983). Postformal operations: A need for further conceptualization. *Human Development, 26,* 91–105.

Kramer, D., Kahlbaugh, P. E., & Goldston, R. B. (1992). A measure of paradigm beliefs about the social world. *Journal of Gerontology: Psychological Sciences, 47,* P180–189.

Kraus, R. (1978). *Recreation and leisure in modern society* (2nd ed.). Santa Monica, CA: Goodyear.

Krause, N. (1991a). Stress and isolation from close ties in later life. *Journal of Gerontology: Social Sciences, 46,* S183–194.

———. (1991b). Stress, religiosity, and abstinence from alcohol. *Psychology and Aging, 6,* 134–143.

———. (1993). Early parental loss and personal control in later life. *Journal of Gerontology: Psychological Sciences, 48,* P100–108.

Krout, J. A. (1988). Rural vs. urban differences in elderly parents; contacts with their children. *The Gerontologist, 28,* 198–203.

Krueger, J., & Heckhausen, J. (1993). Personality development across the adult life span.: Subjective conceptions vs cross-sectional constraints. *Journal of Gerontology: Psychological Sciences, 48,* P100–108.

Kübler-Ross, E. (1969). *On death and dying.* New York: Macmillan.

———. (1974). *Questions and answers on death and dying.* New York: Macmillan.

———. (1981). *Living with dying.* New York: Macmillan.

Kuhn, D., Langer, J., Kohlberg, L., & Haan, N. (1977). The development of formal operations in logical and moral thought. *Genetic Psychology Monographs, 95,* 97–188.

Kuhn, T. S. (1962). *The structure of scientific revolutions.* Chicago: University of Chicago Press.

Kurdek, L. A. (1981). An integrative perspective on children's divorce adjustment. *American Psychologist, 36,* 856–866.

Kurdek, L. A., & Schmitt, J. P. (1985–1986). Relationship quality of gay men in closed or open relationships. *Journal of Homosexuality, 12,* 85–99.


## *L*


Labouvie-Vief, G. (1982). Dynamic development and mature autonomy. *Human Development, 25,* 161–191.

———. (1984). Logic and self-regulation from youth to maturity. In M. L. Commons, F. A. Richards, & C. Armon (Eds.), *Beyond formal operations: Late adolescent and adult cognitive development.* New York: Praeger.

Labouvie-Vief, G. (1985). Intelligence and cognition. In J. E. Birren & K. W. Schaie (Eds.), *Handbook of the psychology of aging* (2nd ed.), New York: Van Nostrand Reinhold.

Labouvie-Vief, G., & Schell, D. A. (1982). Learning and memory in later life. In B. B. Wolman (Ed.), *Handbook of developmental psychology.* Englewood Cliffs, NJ: Prentice-Hall.

Lachman, M. E. (1986). Personal control in later life: Stability change, and cognitive correlates. In M. M. Baltes & P. B. Baltes (Eds.), *Aging and the psychology of control.* Hillsdale, NJ: Erlbaum.

Lachman, M. E., & Burak, O. R. (1993). Planning and control processes across the lifespan: An overview. *International Journal of Behavioral Development, 16,* 131–143.

Lack, S., & Buckingham, R. W. (1978). *First American hospice:Three years of home care.* New Haven, CT: Hospice, Inc.

Lamberson, S. D., & Fischer, K. W. (1988). Optimal and functional levels in cognitive development: The individual's developmental range. *Newsletter of the International Society for the Study of Behavioral Development, 2,* 1–4.

Lambert, P., Gibson, J. M., & Nathanson, P. (1990). The values history: An innovation in surrogate decision-making. *Law, Medicine, and Health Care, 18,* 202–212.

Langer, E. J., & Rodin, J. (1976). The effects of choice and enhanced personal responsibility for the aged: A field experiment in an institutionalized setting. *Journal of Personality and Social Psychology, 34,* 191–198.

Langer, E. J., Rodin, J., Beck, P., Weinman, C., & Spitzer, L. (1979). Environmental determinants of memory improvement in late adulthood. *Journal of Personality and Social Psychology, 37,* 2003–2013.

Larsen, M. E. (1973). Humbling cases for career counselors. *Phi Delta Kappan, 54,* 374.

Larson, E. B. (1993). Illnesses causing dementia in the very elderly. *New England Journal of Medicine, 328,* 203–205.

Larson, R., Zuzanek, J. & Mannel, R. (1985). Being alone versus being with people: Disengagement in the daily experience of older adults. *Journal of Gerontology, 40,* 375–381.

LaRue, A., Dessonville, C., & Jarvik, L. F. (1985). Aging and mental disorders. In J. E. Birren & K. W. Schaie (Eds.), *Handbook of the psychology of aging* (2nd ed.). New York: Van Nostrand Reinhold.

Lau, E. E., & Kosberg, J. I. (1979). Abuse of the elderly by informal care providers. *Aging,* September/October, 11–15.

Lavigne-Pley, C., & Levesque, L. (1992). Reactions of the institutionalized elderly upon learning of the death of a peer. *Death Studies, 16,* 451–461.

Lawton, M. P. (1977). The impact of the environment on aging and behavior. *Handbook of the psychology of aging.* New York: Van Nostrand Reinhold.

———. (1980). *Environment and aging.* Monterey, CA: Brooks/Cole.

———. (1985). Housing and living arrangements of older people. In R. A. Binstock & E. Shanas (Eds.), *Handbook of aging and the social sciences* (2nd ed.). New York: Van Nostrand Reinhold.

———. (1986). Functional assessment. In L. Teri & M. P. Lewinsoh (Eds.), *Geropsychological assessment and treatment: Selected topics* (pp. 39–84). NY: Springer.

Lawton, M. P. (1990). Residential environment and self-directedness among older people. *American Psychologist, 45*(5), 638–640.

Lawton, M. P., Brody, E. M., & Saperstein, A. R. (1991). *Respite care for caregivers of Alzheimer patients: Research and practice.* New York: Springer.

Lawton, M. P., Moss, M., Kleban, M. H., Glicksman, A., & Rovine, M. (1991). A two-factor model of caregiving appraisal and well-being. *Journal of Gerontology: Psychological Sciences, 46,* P181–189.

Lawton, M. P., & Nahemow, L. (1973). Ecology and the aging process. In C. Eisdorfer & M. P. Lawton (Eds.), *The psychology of adult development and aging.* Washington, DC: American Psychological Association.

Lazarus, R. S., & DeLongis, A. (1983). Psychological stress and coping in aging. *American Psychologist, 38,* 245–254.

Lazarus, R. S., & Folkman, S. (1984). *Stress, appraisal, and coping.* New York: Springer.

Lee, G. R. (1978). Marriage and morale in late life. *Journal of Marriage and the Family, 40,* 131–139.

Lee, G. R., Dwyer, J. W., & Coward, R. T. (1993). Gender factors in parent care: Demographic factors and same-gender preferences. *Journal of Gerontology: Social Sciences, 48,* S9–S16.

Lefebvre-Pinard, M. (1984). Taking charge of one's cognitive activity: A moderator of competence. In E. Neimark (Ed.), *Moderators of competence.* Hillsdale, NJ: Erlbaum.

Legh-Smith, J., Wade, D. T., & Hewer, L. (1986). Driving after stroke. *Journal of the Royal Society of Medicine, 79,* 200–203.

Lehman, H. C. (1953). *Age and achievement.* Princeton, NJ: Princeton University Press.

———. (1960). The age decrement in outstanding scientific creativity. *American Psychologist, 15,* 128–134.

Lentzner, H. R., Pamuk, E. R., Rhodenhiser, E. P., Rothberg, R., & Powell-Griner, E. (1992). The quality of life in the year before death. *American Journal of Public Health, 82,* 1093–1098.

Lepper, M. R., & Greene, D. (1975). Training play into work: Effects of adult surveillance and extrinsic rewards on children's intrinsic motivation. *Journal of Personality and Social Psychology, 31,* 479–486.

Lerner, M. (1970). When, why, and where people die. In O. G. Brim, H. E. Freeman, S. Levine, and N. A. Scotch (Eds.), *The dying patient.* New York: Russell Sage Foundation.

Lerner, M. J., Somers, D. G., Reid, D., Chiriboga, D., & Tierney, M. (1991). Adult children as caregivers: Egocentric biases in judgments of sibling contributions. *The Gerontologist, 31,* 746–755.

Lerner, R. M. (1984). *On the nature of human plasticity.* New York: Cambridge University Press.

———. (1991). Changing organism-context relations as the basic process of development: A developmental contextual perspective. *Developmental Psychology, 27,* 27–32.

Letzelter, M., et al. (1986). Swimming performance in old age. *Zeitschrift für Gerontologie, 19,* 389–395.

Levenson, R. W., Carstensen, L. L., & Gottman, J. M. (1993). Long-term marriage: Age, gender, and satisfaction. *Psychology and Aging, 8,* 301–313.

Leventhal, E. A., Leventhal, H., Schaefer, P., & Easterling, D. (1993). Conservation of energy, uncertainty reduction and swift utilization of medical care among the elderly. *Journal of Gerontology: Psychological Sciences, 48,* P78–86.

Leventhal, H., Leventhal, E. A., & Schaefer, P. M. (1991). Vigilant coping and health behavior: A life span problem. In M. Ory & R. Abeles (Eds.), *Aging, health, and behavior* (pp. 109–140). Baltimore: Johns Hopkins.

Levine, P., Janda, J. K., Joseph, J. A., Ingram, D. K., & Roth, G. S. (1981). Dietary restriction retards the age-associated loss of rat striatal dopaminergic receptors. *Science, 214,* 516–562.

Levinger, G. (1970). Husbands' and wives' estimates of coital frequency. *Medical Aspects of Human Sexuality, 4,* 42–57.

Levinson, D. J. (1978). *The seasons of a man's life.* New York: Knopf.

———. (1980). Toward a conception of the adult life course. In N. J. Smelser & E. H. Erikson (Eds.), *Themes of work and love in adulthood.* Cambridge, MA: Harvard University Press.

———. (1986). A conception of adult development. *American Psychologist, 41,* 3–13.

———. (1987). *The seasons of a woman's life.* Paper presented at the annual meeting of the American Psychological Association, New York.

———. (1990). A theory of life structure in adult development. In C. N. Alexander & E. J. Langer (Eds.). *Higher stages of human development: Perspectives on adult growth* (pp. 35–53). New York: Oxford University Press.

———. (in press). *Seasons of a woman's life.* New York: Alfred Knopf.

Levinson, R. J. (1987). Euthanasia. In G. L. Maddox (Ed.), *The encyclopedia of aging.* New York: Springer.

Lew, E. A., & Garfinkel, L. (1979). Variations in mortality by weight among 750,000 men and women. *Journal of Chronic Diseases, 32,* 563–576.

Lewis, D. A., & Salem, G. (1986). *Fear of crime incivility and the production of a social problem.* New Brunswick, NJ: Transaction.

Li, T., & Liu, S. (1991). *Moving from moral moratorium in Chinese youth: Equilibrium effect of experiencing estranging events.* Paper presented at the Sixth Adult Development Symposium of the Society for Research in Adult Development, Boston, MA, July.

Liberto, J. G., Oslin, D. W., & Ruskin, P. E. (1992). Alcoholism in older persons: A review of the literature. *Hospital and Community Psychiatry, 43,* 975–984.

Lichter, D. T. (1989). Race, employment hardship, and inequality in the American non-metropolitan south. *Rural Sociology, 54,* 509–532.

Lieberman, M. A. (1992). A re-examination of the adult life crises: Spousal loss in mid and late life. In G. H. Pollock (Ed.), *The course of life.* New York: International Press.

Lieberman, M. A., & Peskin, H. (1992). Adult life crises. In J. E. Birren, R. B. Sloane, & G. D. Cohen (Eds.), *Handbook of mental health and aging* (2nd ed., pp. 119–143). San Diego: Academic Press.

Lieberman, Heller, & Mullan. (1990). In J. E. Birren & R. B. Sloane (Eds.), *Handbook of Mental Health and Aging* (2nd ed.). San Diego: Academic Press.

LifePlans. (1990). Financing long-term care: The impact of alternative government programs and the potential of private insurance. Boston University, Department of Economics (June). Boston: Mass.

Lifson, A. (1988). Do alternative models for transmission of HIV exist? *Journal of the American Medical Association, 259,* 1353–1356.

Lifton, R. J. (1977). The sense of immortality: On death and the continuity of life. In H. Feifel (Ed.), *New meanings of death.* New York: McGraw-Hill.

Light, E., Niederehe, G., & Lebowitz, B. (Eds.). (1994). *Stress effects on family caregivers of Alzheimer's patients: Research and interventions.* New York: Springer.

Light, L. L. (1991). Memory and aging: Four hypotheses in search of data. *Annual Review of Psychology, 42,* 333–376.

Light, L. L., & Singh, A. (1987). Implicit and explicit memory in young and older adults. *Journal of Experimental Psychology: Learning, Memory, & Cognition, 13,* 531–541.

Lindenberger, U., & Baltes, P. B. (1994). Sensory functioning and intelligence in old age: A strong connection. *Psychology and Aging, 9.*

Lindenberger, U., Kliegel, R., & Baltes, P. B. (1992). Professional expertise does not eliminate age differences in imagery-based memory performance during adulthood. *Psychology and Aging, 7,* 585–593.

Lindenberger, U., Mayr, U., & Kliegel, R. (1993). Speed and intelligence in old age. *Psychology and Aging, 8,* 207–220.

Lindmann, E. (1944). Symptomatology and management of acute grief. *American Journal of Psychiatry, 101,* 141–148.

Linquist, J. H., & Duke, J. M. (1982). The elderly victim at risk: Explaining the fear-victimization paradox. *Criminology, 20,* 115–126.

Lipowski, Z. J. (1980). *Delerium.* Springfield, IL: Charles C Thomas.

Liptzin, B. (1992). Nursing home care. In J. E. Birren, R. B. Sloane, & G. D. Cohen (Eds.), *Handbook of mental health and aging* (2nd ed., pp. 833–852). San Diego, CA: Academic Press.

Litz, B. T., Zeiss, A. M., & Davies, H. T. (1990). Sexual concerns of male spouses of female Alzheimer's disease patients. *The Gerontologist, 30,* 113–116.

Livson, N., & Peskin, H. (1981). Psychological health at age forty: Prediction from adolescent personality. In D. M. Eichorn, J. Clausen, H. Haan, M. Honzik, & P. Mussen (Ed.), *Present and past at midlife.* New York: Academic Press.

Lonky, E., Kaus, C., & Roodin, P. A. (1984). Life experience and mode of coping: Relation to moral judgment in adulthood. *Developmental Psychology, 20,* 1159–1167.

Lopata, H. Z. (1979). *Widowhood in an American city.* Cambridge, MA: Schenkman.

———. (1987a). Widowhood. In G. L. Maddox (Ed.), *Encyclopedia of aging.* New York: Springer.

———. (1987b). *Widows: The Middle East, Asia, and the Pacific.* Durham, NC: Duke University Press.

Lopez-Bushnell, F. K., Tyra, P. A., & Futrell, M. (1992). Alcoholism and the Hispanic older adult. Special Issue: Hispanic aged mental health. *Clinical Gerontologist, 11(3-4),* 123–130.

Loveridge-Sanonmatsu, J. (1994, April). *Personal communication.* Oswego, NY: SUNY College at Oswego, Department of Communication.

Lowenthal, M., Turnher, M., & Chiriboga, D. (1975). *Four stages of life: A comparative study of women and men facing transitions.* San Francisco: Jossey-Bass.

Ludeman, K. (1981). The sexuality of the older person: Review of the literature. *The Gerontologist, 21,* 203–208.

Lyons, N. (1983). Two perspectives: On self, relationships, and morality. *Harvard Educational Review, 53,* 125–145.

## *M*

Macklin, E. (1980). Nontraditional family forms: A decade of research. *Journal of Marriage and the Family, 42,* 905–922.

Mackworth, N. H. (1965). Originality. *American Psychologist, 20,* 51–66.

Madden, D. J. (1986). Adult age differences in the attentional capacity demands of visual search. *Cognitive Development, 1,* 335–363.

Madden, D. J., & Plude, D. J. (1993). Selective preservation of selective attention. In J. Cerella, J. M. Rybash, W. J. Hoyer, & M. A. Commons (Eds.), *Adult information processing: Limits on loss.* San Diego: Academic Press.

Maddi, S. (1986). *The great stress-illness controversy.* Paper presented at the meeting of the American Psychological Association, Washington, DC.

Mages, N. L., & Mendelsohn, G. A. (1979). Effects of cancer on patients' lives: A personological approach. In G. C. Stone, F. Cohen, & N. E. Adler (Eds.), *Health psychology.* San Francisco: Jossey-Bass.

Malfetti, J. (Ed.) (1985). *Drivers 55 plus.* Falls Church, VA: AAA Foundations of Traffic Safety.

Manton, K. G., Corder, L. S., & Stallard, E. (1993). Estimates of change in chronic disability and institutional incidence and prevalence rates in the U.S. elderly population from the 1982, 1984, and 1989 National Long Term Care Survey. *Journal of Gerontology: Social Sciences, 48,* S153–S166.

Markus, H. R., & Nurius, P. (1986). Possible selves. *American Psychologist, 41,* 954–969.

Markus, H. R., & Herzog, A. R. (1992). The role of the self-concept in aging. In K. W. Schaie & M. P. Lawton (Eds.), *Annual review of gerontology and geriatrics* (Vol. 11, pp. 110–143).

Marottoli, R. A., Ostfeld, A. M., Merrill, S. S., Perlman, G. D., Foley, D. J., & Cooney, L. M. (1993). Driving cessation and changes in mileage drivers among elderly individuals. *Journal of Gerontology: Social Sciences, 48,* S255–260.

Marshall, V. W. (1980). *Last chapters: A sociology of aging and dying.* Monterey, CA: Brooks/Cole.

Marsiglio, W., & Donnelly, D. (1991). Sexual relations in later life: A national survey of married persons. *Journal of Gerontology: Social Sciences, 46,* S338–344.

Martin, J. The trauma of homlessness. (1990). *International Journal of Mental Health 20(2),* 17–27.

Martino-Saltzman, D., Blasch, B. B., Morris, R. D., & McNeal, L. W. (1992). Travel behavior of nursing home residents perceived as wanderers and non-wanderers. *The Gerontologist, 31,* 666–672.

Mason, S. E., & Smith, A. D. (1977). Imagery and the aged. *Experimental Aging Research, 3,* 17–32.

Masoro, E. J. (1988). Food restriction in rodents: An evaluation of its role in the study of aging. *Journal of Gerontology: Biological Sciences, 43,* B59–64.

Masters, H. H., Johnson, V. E., & Kolodny, R. C. (1991). *Human sexuality.* Boston: Little, Brown.

Masters, W. H., & Johnson, V. E. (1970). *Human sexual inadequacy.* Boston: Little, Brown.

Mathews, S. H., Werkner, J. E., & Delaney, P. J. (1989). Relative contributions of help by employed and nonemployed sisters to their elderly parents. *Journal of Gerontology: Social Sciences, 44,* S536–544.

Matthews, K. A., Wing, R. R., Kuller, L. H., Meilhn, E. N., Kelsey, S. F., Costello, E. J., & Caggiula, A. W. (1990). Influence of natural menopause on psychological characteristics and symptoms of middle-aged women. *Journal of Consulting and Clinical Psychology, 58,* 345–351.

Maymi, C. R. (1982). Women in the labor force. In P. W. Berman & E. R. Ramey (Eds.), *Women: A developmental perspective* (National Institute of Health Publication #82–2298). Washington, DC: Department of Health and Human Services.

Mayr, U., & Kliegel, R. (1993). Sequential and coordinative complexity: Age based processing limitations in figural transformations. *Journal of Experimental Psychology: Learning, Memory, and Cognition, 19,* 1297–1320.

McAdams, D. P., de St. Aubin, E., & Logan, R. L. (1993). Generativity among young, midlife and older adults. *Psychology and Aging, 8,* 221–230.

McAuley, E. (1992). Understanding exercise behavior: A self-efficacy perspective. In G. C. Roberts (Ed.), *Understanding motivation in exercise and sport* (pp. 107–128). Champaign, IL: Human Kinetics.

McAuley, E., Courneya, K. S., & Lettunich, J. (1991). Effects of acute and long-term exercise on self-efficacy responses in sedentary, middle-aged males and females. *The Gerontologist, 31,* 534–542.

McAuley, E., Lox, L., & Duncan, T. E. (1993). Long-term maintenance of exercise, self-efficacy, and physiological change in older adults. *Journal of Gerontology: Psychological Sciences, 48,* P218–224.

McAvoy, L. (1979). The leisure preferences, problems, and needs of the elderly. *Journal of Leisure Research, 11,* 40–47.

McCain, G., & Segal, E. M. (1988). *The game of science* (5th ed.). Pacific Grove, CA: Brooks/Cole.

McCain, N. L., & Gramling, L. F. (1992). Living with dying: Coping with HIV disease. Issues in *Mental Health Nursing, 13,* 271–284.

McCartney, J., Izemen, H., Rogers, D., & Cohen, N. (1987). Sexuality in the institutionalized elderly. *Journal of the American Geriatrics Society, 35,* 331–333.

McClelland, D., Constanian, C., Regaldo, D., & Stone, C. (1978). Making it to maturity. *Psychology Today, 12,* 42–53, 114.

McClelland, D. C. (1951). *Personality.* New York: McGraw-Hill.

McClelland, D. C., Atkinson, J. W., Clark, R. W., & Lowell, E. L. (1953). *The achievement motive.* New York: Appleton-Century-Crofts.

McCracken, A. L., & Gerdsen, L. (1991, December). Sharing the legacy: Hospice care principles for terminally ill elders. *Journal of Gerontological Nursing, 17* (12), 4–8.

McCrae, R. R., Arenberg, D., & Costa, P. T., Jr. (1987). Declines in divergent thinking with age: Cross-sectional, longitudinal, and cross-sequential analyses. *Psychology and Aging, 2,* 130–137.

McCrae, R. R., & Costa, P. T., Jr. (1984). *Emerging lives and enduring dispositions: Personality in adulthood.* Boston: Little, Brown.

McCrae, R. R., & Costa, P. T., Jr. (1987). Validation of the five-factor model of personality across instruments and observers. *Journal of Personality and Social Psychology, 52,* 81–90.

McCrae, R. R., & Costa, P. T. (1990). *Personality in adulthood.* New York: Guilford Press.

McDonald, R. T. (1981). The effect of death education on specific attitudes toward death in college students. *Death Education, 3,* 59–66.

McDowd, J. M., & Birren, J. E. (1990). Attention and aging. In J. E. Birren & K. W. Schaie (Eds.), *Handbook of the psychology of aging* (3rd ed., pp. 222–233). San Diego: Academic Press.

McDowd, J. M., & Craik, F. I. M. (1988). Effects of aging and task difficulty on divided attention performance. *Journal of Experimental Psychology: Human Perception and Performance, 14,* 267–280.

McDowd, J. M., Oseas-Kreger, D. M., & Filion, D. L. (1994). Inhibitory processes in selective attention and aging. In F. Dempster (Ed.), *New perspectives on interference and inhibition in cognition.* New York: Academic Press.

McEvoy, G. M., & Cascio, W. F. (1989). Cumulative evidence of the relationship between employee age and job performance. *Journal of Applied Psychology, 74*(1), 11–17.

McGowin, D. F. (1993). *Living in the labyrinth: A personal journey through Alzheimer's disease.* New York: Delacorte Press.

McIntyre, J. S., & Craik, F. I. M. (1987). Age differences in memory for item and source information. *Canadian Journal of Psychology, 41,* 175–192.

McLachlan, D. R. C. (1982). Cellular mechanisms of Alzheimer's disease. In F. I. M. Craik & S. Trehub (Eds.), *Cognitive processes and aging* (Vol. 8). New York: Plenum.

McLaughlin, D. K., & Jensen, L. (1993). Poverty among older Americans: The plight of non-metropolitan elders. *Journal of Gerontology, 48,* S44–54.

McLay, P. (1989). The Parkinsonian and driving. *International Disability Studies, 11,* 50–51.

McLoyd, V. C. (1989). Socialization and development in a changing economy: The effects of paternal job and income loss on children. *American Psychologist, 44*(2), 293–302.

McNeil, J. K., LeBlanc, E. M., & Joyner, M. (1991). The effects of exercise on depressive symptoms in the moderately depressed elderly. *Psychology and Aging, 6,* 487–488.

Medical consultants on the diagnosis of death for the study of ethical problems in medicine and biomedical research: President's commission. (1981). *Journal of the American Medical Association, 246,* 2184–2186.

Metzger, A. M. (1979). A Q-methodological study of the Kübler-Ross stage theory. *Omega, 10,* 291–302.

Meyers, G. C. (1990). Demography of aging. In R. H. Binstock and L. K. George (Eds.), *Handbook of aging and the social sciences* (3rd ed.). San Diego, CA: Academic Press.

Mikelson, M. (1990). *Special tabulations from the 1987 National American Housing Survey.* Washington, DC: The Urban Institute.

Miles, S. H., & Irvine, P. (1992). Deaths caused by physical restraints. *The Gerontologist, 32,* 762–766.

Miller, D., Staats, S. R., & Partlo, C. (1992, December). Discriminating positive and negative aspects of pet interaction: Sex differences in the older population. *Social Indicators Research, 27,* 363–374.

Miller, P. H. (1983). *Theories of developmental psychology.* San Francisco: Freeman Press.

Mirowsky, J., & Ross, C. E. (1992). Age and depression. *Journal of Health and Social Behavior, 33,* 187–205.

Mischel, W. (1981). *Introduction to personality* (3rd ed.). New York: Holt, Rinehart & Winston.

Mishra, S. (1992). Leisure activities and life satisfaction in old age: A case study of retired government employees living in urban areas. *Activities, Adaptation and Aging, 16,* 7–26.

Mitchell, D. B. (1989). How many memory systems? Evidence from aging. *Journal of Experimental Psychology: Learning, Memory, & Cognition, 15,* 31–49.

Mitford, J. A. (1963). *The American way of death.* New York: Simon & Schuster.

Moeller, G. L. (1989). Fear of victimization: The effects of neighborhood racial composition. *Sociological Inquiry, 59,* 208–221.

Monat, A., & Lazarus, R. S. (Eds.). (1985). *Stress and coping* (2nd ed.). New York: Columbia University.

Montgomery, R. J. V., Kosloski, & Borgatta, (1990). Service use and the caregiving experience: Does Alzheimer's disease make a difference? In D. E. Biegel and A. Blum (Eds.), *Aging and caregiving: Theory, research, and policy.* Newbury Park, CA: Sage.

Moon, A., & Williams, D. (1993). Perception of elder abuse and help-seeking patterns among African-American, Caucasian American, and Korean American elderly women. *The Gerontologist, 33,* 386–395.

Moos, R. H., Mertens, J. R., & Brennan, P. L. (1993). Patterns of diagnosis and treatment among late middle-aged and older substance abuse patients. *Journal of Studies on Alcohol, 54*(4), 479–487.

Mor, V. (1982). *The national hospice study: Progress reports.* Providence, RI: School of Medicine, Brown University.

Mor-Barak, M. E., Scharlach, A. E., Birba, L., & Sokolov, J. (1992). Employment, social networks, and health in the retirement years. *International Journal of Aging and Human Development, 35,* 145–159.

Morgan, D. G. (1992). Neurochemical changes with aging: Predisposition toward age-related mental disorders. In J. E. Birren, R. B. Sloane, & G. D. Cohen (Eds.), *Handbook of mental health and aging* (2nd ed., pp. 175–199). San Diego, CA: Academic Press.

Morgan, D. L., Schuster, T. L., & Butler, E. W. (1991). Role reversals in the exchange of social support. *Journal of Gerontology: Social Sciences, 46,* S278–287.

Morgan, S. (1978). *Hysterectomy.* New York: Healthright.

Moritz, D. J., Kasl, V., & Berkman, L. F. (1989). The health impact of living with a cognitively impaired elderly spouse: Depressive symptoms and social functioning. *Journal of Gerontology: Social Sciences, 44,* S17–S27.

Morris, J. (1982). *Technical reports: National hospice study.* Boston, MA: Hebrew Home for the Rehabilitation of the Aged: Social Gerontology Research Unit.

Morrow, D., Leirer, V., Alteri, P. & Fitzsimmons, C. (1992). *When expertise reduces age differences in performance.* Annual Meeting of the Psychonomics Society, St Louis, MO.

Morse, W. C., & Weiss, R. S. (1968). The function and meaning of work and the job. In D. G. Zytowski (Ed.), *Vocational behavior.* New York: Holt, Rinehart & Winston.

Moscovitch, M., & Winocur, G. (1992). The neuropsychology of memory and aging. In F. I. M. Craik & T. A. Salthouse (Eds.), *The handbook of aging and cognition* (pp. 315–372). Hillsdale, NJ: Erlbaum.

Moscovitch, M., Wincour, G., & McLachlan, D. (1986). Memory as assessed by recognition and reading time in normal and memory-impaired people with Alzheimer's disease and other neurological disorders. *Journal of Experimental Psychology: General, 115,* 331–347.

Moss, M., & Lawton, M. P. (1982). Time budgets of older people: A window on four lifestyles. *Journal of Gerontology, 37,* 115–123.

Moss, M. S., Lawton, M. P., Kleban, M. H., & Duhamel, L. (1993). Time use of caregivers of impaired elders before and after institutionalization. *Journal of Gerontology: Social Sciences, 48,* S102–S111.

Moss, M. S., & Moss, S. Z. (1983–1984). The impact of parental death on middle-aged children. *Omega,* 74–80.

Multi-Society Task Force on Persistent Vegetative State. (1994). Medical aspects of the persistent vegetative state. *New England Journal of Medicine, 330* (#21), 1499–1508.

Mumford, M. D., & Gustafson, S. B. (1988). Creativity syndrome: Integration, application, and innovation. *Psychological Bulletin, 103,* 27–43.

Murstein, B. I. (1982). Marital choice. In B. B. Wolman (Ed.), *Handbook of developmental psychology.* Englewood Cliffs, NJ: Prentice-Hall.

Muschel, I. J. (1984). Pet therapy with terminal cancer patients. *Social Casework, 65,* 451–458.

Must, A., Jacques, P. F., Dallal, G. E., Bajema, C. J., & Dietz, W. H. (1992). Long-term morbidity and mortality of overweight adolescents. *The New England Journal of Medicine, 327,* 1350–1355.

Myers, J. E., & Shelton, B. (1987). Abuse and older persons: Issues and implications for counselors. *Journal of Counseling and Development, 65,* 376–380.

Myerson, J., & Hale, S. (1993). General slowing and age-invariance in cognitive processing: The other side of the coin. In J. Cerella, J. M. Rybash, W. J. Hoyer, & M. C. Commons (Eds.), *Adult information processing: Limits on loss* (pp. 115–141). San Diego: Academic Press.

Myerson, J., Hale, S., Wagstaff, D., Poon, L. W., & Smith, G. A. (1990). The information loss model: A mathematical theory of age-related cognitive slowing. *Psychological Review, 97,* 475–487.

## *N*

Nagy, M. (1948). The child's theories concerning death. *Journal of Genetic Psychology, 73,* 3–27.

Nahemow, N. R. (1984). Grandparenthood in transition. In K. A. McCluskey & H. W. Reese (Eds.), *Life-span developmental psychology: Historical and generational effects.* New York: Academic Press.

———. (1985). The changing nature of grandparenthood. *Medical Aspects of Human Sexuality, 19,* 81–92.

National Center for Health Statistics. (1987a). *Characteristics of the populations below the poverty level.* (Current Population Reports, Series P-60, No. 152). Washington, DC: U.S. Government Printing Office.

National Center for Health Statistics. (1987b). *Use of nursing homes by the elderly: Preliminary data from the national nursing home survey.*

National Center for Health Statistics (1992). *Chartbook on health data on older Americans: United States, 1992.* Series 3–29.

National Center for Health Statistics. (1993). *Common beliefs about the rural elderly: What do national data tell us?* Series 3 (No. 28) PHS 93-1412. Washington, DC: U.S. Govt. Printing Office.

National Institute of Aging. (1980). Senility reconsidered. *Journal of the American Medical Association, 244,* 259–263.

National Institute on Aging. (1982). *Toward an independent old age: A national plan for research on aging: Report of the National Research on Aging Planning Panel. U.S. Department of Health and Human Services.* Public Health Services, National Institutes of Health, National Institute on Aging. Washington, DC: U.S. Government Printing Office, #447-H-1.

National Institutes of Health. (1988, September). *Health benefits of pets.* National Institutes of Health Technology Assessment Workshop. U.S. Department of Health and Human Services, Washington, DC: U.S. Government Printing Office.

National Research Council. (1988). *Transportation in an aging society.* Washington, D.C. Transportation Research Board.

———. (1992). Committee for the study of improving mobility and safety for older persons. *Transportation in an aging society* (Vol. 1). Washington, DC: Transportation Research Board.

Neimark, E. D. (1975). Intellectual development during adolescence. In F. D. Horowitz (Ed.), *Review of child development research* (Vol. 4). Chicago: University of Chicago Press.

———. (1982). Adolescent thought: Transition to formal operations. In B. B. Wolman (Ed.), *Handbook of developmental psychology.* Englewood Cliffs, NJ: Prentice-Hall.

Nelson, L. D., & Nelson, C. C. (1973). *Religion and death anxiety.* Presentation to the annual joint meeting, Society for the Scientific Study of Religion and Religious Research Association, San Francisco. As cited in Kalish, R. A., (1985). The social context of death and dying. In J. E. Birren and K. W. Schaie (Eds.), *Handbook of the psychology of aging* (2nd ed.). New York: Van Nostrand Reinhold.

Nesselroade, J. R. (1991). The warp and the woof of the developmental fabric. In R. Downs, L. Liben, & D. Palermo (Eds.), *Visions of aesthetics, the environment, and development: The legacy of Joachim F. Wohlwill* (pp. 213–240). Hillsdale, NJ: Erlbaum.

Neugarten, B. L. (1964). *Personality in middle and late life.* New York: Atherton Press.

———. (1968). *Personality in middle and late life* (2nd ed.). New York: Atherton Press.

———. (1973). Personality change in late life: A developmental perspective. In C. Eisdorfer & M. P. Lawton (Eds.), *The psychology of adult development and aging.* Washington, DC: American Psychological Association.

———. (1977). Personality and aging. In J. E. Birren & K. W. Schaie (Eds.), *Handbook of the psychology of aging.* New York: Van Nostrand Reinhold.

———. (1980a). Act your age: Must everything be a midlife crisis? In *Annual editions: Human development, 1980/1981* (pp. 289–290). Guilford, CT: Dushkin Publishers.

———. (1980b, February). Must everything be a midlife crisis? *Prime Time.*

———. (1989). Policy issues for an aging society. *The psychology of aging.* Washington, DC: American Psychological Association.

Neugarten, B. L., & Datan, N. (1973). Sociological perspectives on the life cycle. In P. B. Baltes & K. W. Schaie (Eds.), *Life-span developmental psychology.* New York: Academic Press.

Neugarten, B. L., & Gutmann, D. L. (1968). Age-sex roles and personality in middle age. In B. L. Neugarten (Ed.), *Middle age and aging.* Chicago: University of Chicago Press.

Neugarten, B. L., Havighurst, R. J., & Tobin, S. S. (1968). Personality and patterns of aging. In B. L. Neugarten (Eds.), *Middle age and aging.* Chicago: University of Chicago Press.

Neugarten, B. L., & Neugarten, D. A. (1987). The changing meanings of age. *Psychology Today, 21,* 29–33.

Neugarten, B. L., & Weinstein, K. K. (1984). The changing American grandparent. *Journal of Marriage and the Family, 26,* 199–204.

Neugebauer, R., Rabkin, J. G., Williams, J. B., Remien, R. H., et. al. (1992). Bereavement reactions among homosexual men experiencing multiple losses in the AIDS epidemic. *American Journal of Psychiatry, 149,* 1374–1379.

Neulinger, J. (1981). *The psychology of leisure.* Springfield, IL: Charles C Thomas.

Newman, B. M. (1982). Midlife development: In B. B. Wolman (Ed.), *Handbook of developmental psychology.* Englewood Cliffs, NJ: Prentice-Hall.

New York State Department of Health. (1988). *Do-not-resuscitate orders: A guide for patients and families.* Albany, NY: New York State Department of Health.

Niederehe, G. (1986). Depression and memory impairment in the aged. In L. W. Poon (Ed.), *Handbook for clinical memory assessment of older adults* (pp. 226–237). Washington, DC: American Psychological Association.

Nissen, M. J., & Bullemer, P. (1987). Attentional requirements of learning: Evidence from performance measures. *Cognitive Psychology, 19,* 1–32.

Noble, B. P. (1993). Dissecting the '90's workplace. *New York Times,* Sunday, September 19, F21.

Noelker, L. S., & Bass, D. M. (1989). Home care for elderly persons: Linkages between formal and informal caregivers. *Journal of Gerontology: Social Sciences, 44,* S63–S70.

Nord, W. R. (1977). Job satisfaction reconsidered. *American Psychologist, 32,* 1026–1036.

Nordin, B. E. C., & Need, A. G. (1990). Prediction and prevention of osteoporosis. In M. Berener, M. Ermini, & H. B. Stahelin (Eds.), *Challenges of aging.* New York: Academic Press.

Norris, F. H., & Murrel, S. A. (1990). Social support, life events, and stress as modifiers of adjustment to bereavement by older adults. *Psychology and Aging, 5,* 429–436.

Nystrom, E. P. (1974). Activity patterns and leisure concepts among the elderly. *American Journal of Occupational Therapy, 28,* 337–345.

## *O*

Ochs, A. L., Newberry, J., Lenhardt, M. L., & Harkins, S. W. (1985). Neural and vestibular aging associated with falls. In J. E. Birren & K. W. Schaie (Eds.), *Handbook of the psychology of aging* (2nd ed.). New York: Van Nostrand Reinhold.

O'Connor, P. (1993). Same gender and cross-gender friendships among the frail elderly. *The Gerontologist, 33,* 24–30.

Okun, B. F., & Rappaport, L. J. (1980). *Working with other families: An introduction to family therapy.* North Scituate, MA: Duxbury.

Olshansky, S. J., Carnes, B. A., & Cassel, C. K. (1993). The aging of the human species. *Scientific American, 268,* 46–52.

Orgel, L. E. (1973). Aging of clones of mammalian cells. *Nature, 243,* 441–445.

Ornstein, R., & Thompson, R. F. (1984). *The amazing brain.* Boston: Houghton Mifflin.

Ornstein, S., & Isabella, L. (1990). Age vs. stage models of career attitudes of women: A partial replication and extension. *Journal of Vocational Behavior, 36,* 1–19.

Ortega, S. L., & Myles, J. L. (1987). Race and gender effects on the fear of crime: An interactive model with age. *Criminology, 25,* 133–152.

Ory, M. G., & Goldberg, E. L. (1983). Pet possession and well-being in elderly women. *Research on Aging, 5,* 389–409.

Osgood, N. J. (1992). Suicide in the elderly: Etiology and assessment. *International Review of Psychiatry, 4,* 217–223.

Osipow, S. H. (1983). *Theories of career development.* Englewood Cliffs, NJ: Prentice-Hall.

———. (1987). Counseling psychology: Theory, research, and practice in career counseling. *Annual Review of Psychology, 38,* 257–278.

Osterweis, M., Solomon, F., & Green, M. (1984). *Bereavement reactions, consequences, care.* Washington, DC: National Academy of Sciences.

Ostrow, A. C. (1980). Physical activity as it relates to the health of the aged. In N. Data & N. Lohmann (Eds.), *Transitions of aging.* New York: Academic Press.

Over, R. (1989). Age and scholar impact. *Psychology and Aging, 4,* 222–225.

Overton, W. F. (1991). The structure of developmental theory. In H. Reese (Eds.), *Advances in Child Development and Behavior* (pp. 1–37). New York: Academic Press.

Owens, W. A., Jr. (1966). Age and mental abilities: A second adult follow-up. *Journal of Educational Psychology, 51,* 311–325.

Owsley, C., Sekuler, R., & Siemsen, D. (1983). Contrast sensitivity throughout adulthood. *Vision Research, 23,* 689–699.

## P

Paffenbarger, R. S. (1993). The association of changes in physical activity level and other lifestyle characteristics with mortality among men. *The New England Journal of Medicine, 328,* 538–545.

Palmore, E. (1982). Predictors of the longevity difference: A twenty-five year follow-up. *The Gerontologist, 22,* 513–518.

Palmore, E., & Maeda, D. (1985). *The honorable elders revisited: A revised cross-cultural analysis of aging in Japan.* Durham, NC: Duke University Press.

Palmore, E. B. (1990). *Ageism: Negative and positive.* NY: Springer.

———. (1984). Consequences of retirement. *Journal of Gerontology, 39,* 109–116.

Palmore, E. B., Burchett, B. M., Fillenbaum, G. C., George, L. K., & Wallman, L. M. (1985). *Retirement: Causes and consequences.* New York: Springer.

Palmore, E. B., George, L. K., & Fillenbaum, G. G. (1982). Predictors of retirement. *Journal of Gerontology, 37,* 733–742.

Paloma, M., Pendelton, B. F., & Garland, T. N. (1982). Reconsidering the dual-career marriage: A longitudinal approach. In J. Aldous (Ed.), *Two paychecks: Life in dual-earner families.* Beverly Hills, CA: Sage.

Panepito, W. C., & Fulton, P. A. (1988). Alcoholism day treatment programs: Myths and reality. *Alcoholism Treatment Quarterly 5* (3–4), 23–35.

Papalia, D., & Bielby, P. (1974). Cognitive functioning in middle and old age adults: A review of research on Piaget's theory. *Human Development, 17,* 424–443.

Parasuraman, R., Greenwood, P. G., Haxby, J. V., & Grady, C. L. (1992). Visuospatial attention in dementia of the Alzheimer's type. *Brain, 115,* 711–733.

Parkes, C. M. (1964). The effects of bereavement on physical and mental health—A study of the medical records of widows. *British Medical Journal, 2,* 274–279.

———. (1970). Seeking and finding a lost object. *Social Science and Medicine, 4,* 187–201.

———. (1972). *Bereavement: Studies of grief in adult life.* New York: International University Press.

Parmelee, P. A., Katz, I. R., & Lawton, M. P. (1991). The relation of pain to depression among institutionalized aged. *Journal of Gerontology: Psychological Sciences, 46,* P15–21.

———. (1992). Depression and mortality among institutionalized aged. *Journal of Gerontology: Psychological Sciences, 47,* P3–10.

Parmelee, P., & Lawton, M. P. (1990). The design of special environments for the aged. In J. E. Birren & K. W. Schaie (Eds.), *Handbook of the psychology of aging* (3rd ed.). New York: Academic Press.

Parnes, H. W., Crowley, J. E., Haurin, R. J., Less, L. J., Morgan, W. R., Mott, F. L., & Nestel, G. (1985). *Retirement among American men.* Lexington, KY: Lexington Books.

Pattison, E. M. (1977). *The experience of dying.* Englewood Cliffs, NJ: Prentice-Hall.

Paveza, G., Cohen, D., Eisdorfer, C., Freels, S., Semla, T., Ashford, J. W., Gorelick, P., Hirschman, R., Luchins, D., & Levy, P. (1992). Severe family violence and Alzheimer's disease: Prevalence and risk factors. *The Gerontologist, 32*(4), 493–497.

Pearlin, L. I. (1985). Life strains and psychological distress among adults. In A. Monat & R. S. Lazarus (Eds.), *Stress and coping: An anthology* (2nd ed.). New York: Columbia University Press.

Pearlin, L. I., & Lieberman, M. A. (1977). Social sources of emotional distress. In R. Simmons (Ed.), *Research in community mental health.* Greenwich, CT: J. A. I. Press.

Pearlin, L. I., Mullan, J. T., Semple, S. J., & Staff, M. M. (1990). Caregiving and the stress process: An overview of concepts and their measures. *The Gerontologist, 30,* 583–594.

Pearlman, R. A. (1991). Clinical fallout from the Supreme Court decision on Nancy Cruzan: Chernobyl or Three Mile Island? *Journal of American Geriatrics Society, 39,* 92–97.

Pepper, L. G. (1976). Patterns of leisure and adjustment to retirement. *The Gerontologist, 16,* 441–446.

Peretti, P. O., & Majecen, K. G. (1991). Emotional abuse among the elderly: Affecting behavior variables. *Social Behavior and Personality, 19,* 255–261.

Perkins, K. (1992). Psychosocial implications of women and retirement. *Social Work, 37,* 526–532.

Perlmutter, M. (1978). What is memory aging the aging of? *Developmental Psychology, 14,* 330–345.

Perlmutter, M. (1980). An apparent paradox about memory aging. In L. W. Poon, J. L. Fozard, L. S. Cermak, D. Arenberg, & L. W. Thompson (Eds.), *New directions in memory and aging.* Hillsdale, NJ: Erlbaum.

———. (1986). A life-span view of memory. In P. B. Baltes, D. Featherman, & R. Lerner (Eds.), *Advances in life-span development and behavior* (Vol. 7). Hillsdale, NJ: Erlbaum.

Perlmutter, M., Metzger, R., Nezworski, T., & Miller, K. (1981). Spatial and temporal memory in twenty- and sixty-year-olds. *Journal of Gerontology, 36,* 59–65.

Perlmutter, M., & Mitchell, D. B. (1982). The appearance and disappearance of age differences in adult memory. In F. I. M. Craik & S. Trehub (Eds.), *Aging and cognitive processes* (pp. 127–144). New York: Plenum.

Perry, W. B. (1968). *Forms of intellectual and ethical development in the college years: A scheme.* New York: Holt, Rinehart & Winston.

Persson, D. (1993). The elderly driver deciding when to stop. *The Gerontologist, 33,* 88–91.

Petit, T. L. (1982). Neuroanatomical and clinical neuropsychological changes in aging and senile dementia. In F. I. M. Craik & S. Trehub (Eds.), *Aging and cognitive processes,* (Vol. 8). New York: Plenum.

Petruzzello, S. J., Landers, D. M., Hatfield, B. D., Kubitz, K. A., & Salazar, W. (1991). A meta-analysis on the anxiety-reducing effects of acute and chronic exercise. *Sports Medicine, 11,* 143–182.

Pfeiffer, E. (1983). Health, sexuality, and aging. In J. E. Birren et al. (Eds.), *Aging: A challenge to science and society, Vol. 3.* New York: Oxford University Press.

Pfeiffer, E., Verwoerdt, A., & Davis, G. C. (1974). Sexual behavior in midlife. In E. Palmore (Ed.), *Normal aging II: Reports from the Duke longitudinal studies, 1970–1973.* Durham, NC: Duke University Press.

Phillips, D., McCartney, K., & Scarr, S. (1987). Child-care quality and children's social development. *Developmental Psychology, 23,* 537–543.

Piaget, J. (1954). *The construction of reality in the child.* New York: Basic Books.

———. (1970). Piaget's theory. In P. H. Mussen (Ed.), *Carmichael's manual of child psychology* (3rd ed., Vol. 1). New York: Wiley.

———. (1972). Intellectual evolution from adolescence to adulthood. *Human Development, 15,* 1–12.

Piaget, J., & Inhelder, B. (1969). *The psychology of the child.* (H. Weaver, trans.). New York: Basic Books (Original work published 1932).

Pillemer, K. A. (1986). The dangers of dependency: New findings on domestic violence against the elderly. *Social Problems, 33,* 147–156.

Pillemer, K. A., & Finkelhor, D. (1988). The prevalence of elder abuse: A random sample survey. *The Gerontologist, 28,* 51–57.

Pillemer, K. A., & Wolf, R. S. (1986). *Elder abuse.* Dover, MA: Auburn House.

Pincus, L. (1976). *Death and the family: The importance of mourning.* New York: Pantheon Books.

Pinkus, R. L. (1984). Families, brain death, and traditional medical excellence. *Journal of Neurosurgery, 60,* 1192–1194.

Pitts, B. J., Popovich, M. N., & Bober, A. T. (1986). *Life after football: A survey of former NFL players.* (Unpublished manuscript). Cited in M. Shahnasarian (1992). Career development after professional football. *Journal of Career Development, 18,* 299–304.

Plomin, R. (1990). The role of inheritance in behavior. *Science, 248,* 183–188.

Plomin, R., Lichtenstein, P., Pederson, N. L., McClearn, G., & Nesselroade, J. R. (1990). Genetic influences on life events during the last half of the life span. *Psychology and Aging, 5,* 25–30.

Plude, D. J., & Hoyer, W. J. (1981). Adult age differences in visual search as a function of stimulus mapping and processing load. *The Journal of Gerontology, 36,* 598–604.

Plude, D. J., & Hoyer, W. J. (1985). Attention and performance: Identifying and localizing age deficits. In N. Charness (Ed.), *Aging and human performance* (pp. 47–99). London: Wiley.

Plude, D. J., & Hoyer, W. J. (1986). Aging and the selectivity of visual information processing. *Psychology and Aging, 1,* 1–9.

Plude, D. J., Kaye, D. B., Hoyer, W. J., Post, T. A., Saynisch, M. J., & Hahn, M. V. (1983). Aging and visual search under consistent and varied mapping. *Developmental Psychology, 19,* 508–512.

Pollack, G. (1961). Mourning and adaptation. *International Journal of Psychoanalysis, 42,* 341–361.

———. (1978). Processes and affect: Mourning and grief. *International Journal of Psychoanalysis, 59,* 255–276.

Ponds, R. W., Brouwer, W. H., & van Wolffelaar, P. C. (1988). Age differences in divided attention in a simulated driving task. *Journal of Gerontology, 43,* P151–156.

Porcino, J. (1985). Psychological aspects of aging in women. *Women and Health, 10,* 115–122.

Pratt, M. W., Golding, G., & Kerig, P. (1987). Life-span differences in adult thinking about hypothetical and personal moral issues: Reflection or regression? *International Journal of Behavioral Development, 10,* 359–376.

Price, R. W., Sidtis, J., & Rosenblum, M. (1988). The AIDS dementia complex: Some current questions. *Annals of Neurology 23* (Supplement), S27–S33.

Pritchard, K., Hoyer, W. J., & Kotary, L. (1994, June). *Toward an object-based model of age related differences in visual selective attention.* Poster presented at the American Psychological Society meetings, Washington, DC.

Prosen, S., & Farmer, J. (1982). Understanding stepfamilies: Issues and importance for counselors. *Personnel and Guidance Journal, 60,* 393–397.

## *Q*

Quam, J. K., & Whitford, G. S. (1992). Adaptation and age-related expectations of older gay and lesbian adults. *The Gerontologist, 32,* 367–374.

Quinn, J. F., & Smeeding, T. M. (1993). The present and future economic well-being of the aged. In D. Salisbury & R. B. Burkenhauser (Eds.), *Pensions in a changing economy.* Washington, DC: Employee Benefit Research Institute.

Quinn, M., & Tomita, S. (1986). *Elder abuse and neglect: Causes, diagnosis, and intervention strategies.* New York: Springer.

## R

Rabins, P. V. (1992). Schizophrenia and psychotic states. In J. E. Birren, R. B. Sloane, & G. D. Cohen (Eds.), *Handbook of mental health and aging* (2nd ed., pp. 463–475). San Diego, CA: Academic Press.

Rabkin, J. G., & Struening, E. L. (1976). Life events, stress, and illness. *Science, 194,* 1013–1020.

Rakfedlt, J., Rybash, J. M., & Roodin, P. A. (in press). Affirmative coping as a marker of success in adult therapeutic intervention. In M. L. Commons, C. Goldberg, & J. Demick (Eds.), *Clinical approaches to adult development.* Norwood NJ: Ablex Publishers.

Rakfeldt, S., Rybash, J. M., & Roodin, P. A. (in press). Affirmative coping as a marker of adult therapeutic intervention. In M. L. Commons, F. A. Richards, & C. Armon (Eds.), *Adult development. Vol. 4: Longitudinal and case approaches.* New York: Praeger.

Rando, T. A. (Ed.). (1986). *Parental loss of a child.* Champaign, IL: Research Press.

Raskind, M. A., & Peskind, E. R. (1992). Alzheimer's disease and other dementing disorders. In J. E. Birren, R. B. Sloane, & G. D. Cohen (Eds.), *Handbook of mental health and aging* (2nd ed., 477–513). San Diego, CA: Academic Press.

Ratner, H. H., Schell, D. A., Crimmins, A., Mittleman, D., & Baldinelli, L. (1987). Changes in adults' prose recall: Aging or cognitive demands. *Developmental Psychology, 23,* 521–525.

Read, D. E. (1987). Neuropsychological assessment of memory in the elderly. *Canadian Journal of Psychology, 41,* 158–174.

Rebok, G. W. (1987). *Life-span cognitive development.* New York: Holt, Rinehart & Winston.

Reedy, M. N., Birren, J. E., & Schaie, K. W. (1981). Age and sex differences in satisfying love relationships across the adult life span. *Human Development, 24,* 52–66.

Regnier, V., & Pynoos, J. (1992). Environmental intervention for cognitively impaired older persons. In J. E. Birren, R. B. Sloane, & G. D. Cohen (Eds.), *Handbook of mental health and aging* (2nd ed., pp. 763–792). San Diego, CA: Academic Press.

Rehmar, M. I. (1988). Sensitizing practitioners, families, and elderly persons. *Pride Institute Journal of Long Term Home Health Care, 7,* 22–29.

Reinberg, J., & Hayslip, B. (1991). *The effect of elder abuse education on persons with experienced childhood violence.* Paper presented at annual meetings of Gerontological Society of America, San Francisco.

Reisberg, B. (1981). *Brain failure.* New York: Free Press.

———. (1986). Dementia: A systematic approach to identifying reversible causes. *Geriatrics, 41,* 30–46.

———. (1987, October). *Classification of the various stages of Alzheimer's disease.* Paper presented at the conference on Alzheimer's Update: Translating Theory into Practice, Utica, NY.

Reisberg, B., & Bornstein, J. (1986). Clinical diagnosis and assessment. *Drug Therapy, 16,* 43–59.

Reisberg, B., Ferris, S. H., deLeon, M. J., & Crook, T. (1985). Age associated cognitive decline and Alzheimer's disease: Implications for assessment and treatment. In M. Berganer, M. Ermini, & H. B. Stahelin (Eds.), *Thresholds in aging.* London: Academic Press.

Reisberg, B., Ferris, S. H., & Franssen, E. (1985). An ordinal functional assessment toll for Alzheimer's-type dementia. *Hospital and Community Psychiatry, 36,* 593–595.

Reitzes, D. C., Mutran, E., & Pope, H. (1991). Location and well-being among retired men. *Journal of Gerontology: Social Sciences, 46,* S195–S203.

Remafedi, G. (1987a). Adolescent homosexuality: Psychosocial and medical implications. *Pediatrics, 79,* 331–337.

———. (1987b). Male homosexuality: The adolescent's perspective. *Pediatrics, 79;* 326–330.

Reschovsky, J. D. (1990). Residential immobility of the elderly: An empirical investigation. *AREVEA Journal, 18,* 160–183.

Reschovsky, J. D., & Newman, S. J. (1991). Home upkeep and housing quality of older home owners. *Journal of Gerontology, 46,* S288–297.

Reskin, B. F., & Roos, P. A. (1990). *Job queues, gender queues: Explaining women's inroads into male occupations.* Philadelphia, PA: Temple University Press.

Reveron, D. (1982, February). Aged are a mystery to most psychologists. *American Psychological Association Monitor,* p. 9.

Reynolds, D. K., & Kalish, R. A. (1974). Anticipation of futurity as a function of ethnicity and age. *Journal of Gerontology, 29,* 224–231.

Rhodes, S. L. (1977). A developmental approach to the life cycle of the family. *Social Casework, 58,* 301–311.

Rhodes, S. R. (1983). Age-related differences in work attitudes and behavior: A review and conceptual analysis. *Psychological Bulletin, 93,* 328–367.

Richardson, V., & Kilty, K. M. (1992). Retirement intentions among Black professionals: Implications for practice with older Black adults. *The Gerontologist, 32,* 7–16.

Riddick, C. C. (1985). Health, aquariums, and the noninstitutionalized elderly. *Marriage and the Family Review, 8,* 163–173.

Riegel, K. F. (1976). The dialectics of human development. *American Psychologist, 31,* 689–700.

Riegel, K. F., & Riegel, R. M. (1972). Development, drop, and death. *Developmental Psychology, 6,* 306–319.

Rikli, R., & Busch, S. (1986). Motor performance of women as a function of age and physical activity level. *Journal of Gerontology, 41,* 645–649.

Riley, M. W. (1985). Age strata and social systems. In R. H. Binstock & E. Shanas (Eds.), *Handbook of aging and the social sciences* (Vol. 3, pp. 369–411). New York: Van Nostrand Reinhold.

Riley, M. W., & Riley, J. W. (1994). Age integration and the lives of older people. *The Gerontologist, 34,* 110–115.

Rinaldi, A., & Kearl, M. C. (1990). The hospice farewell: Ideological perspectives of its professional practitioners. *Omega, Journal of Death and Dying, 21*(4), 283–300.

Rivers, P. C., Rivers, L. S., & Newman, D. L. (1991). Alcohol and aging: A cross-gender comparison. *Psychology of Addictive Behaviors, 5,* 41–47.

Rivlin, A. M., & Weiner, J. M. (1988). *Caring for the elderly: Who will pay?* Washington, DC: Brookings Institution.

Roadberg, A. (1981). Perceptions of work and leisure among the elderly. *The Gerontologist, 21,* 142–145.

Robbins, R. A. (1992). Death competency: A study of hospice volunteers. Special Issue: Death attitudes. *Death Studies, 16*(6), 557–569.

Roberts, P., & Newton, P. M. (1987). Levinsonian studies of women's adult development. *Psychology and Aging, 2,* 154–163.

Robertson, J. (1976). Significance of grandparents: Perceptions of young adult grandchildren. *The Gerontologist, 16,* 137–140.

Rockstein, M., & Sussman, M. (1979). *Biology of aging.* Belmont, CA: Wadsworth.

Rodin, J. (1986). Aging and health: Effects of the sense of control. *Science, 233,* 1271–1276.

———. (1990). Control by any other name: Definitions, concepts, and processes. In J. Rodin, C. Schooler, & K. W. Schaie (Eds.), *Self-directedness cause and effects throughout the life course* (pp. 1–17). Hillsdale, NJ: Lawrence Erlbaum.

Rodin, J., & McAvay, G. (1992). Determinants of change in perceived health in a longitudinal study of older adults. *Journal of Gerontology, 47,* P373–384.

Roediger, H. L., Weldon, M. S., & Challis, B. A. (1989). Explaining dissociations between implicit and explicit measures of retention: A processing account. In H. L. Roediger & F. I. M. Craik (Eds.), *Varieties of memory and consciousness: Essays in honor of Endel Tulving* (pp. 3–41). Hillsdale, NJ: Erlbaum.

Rogers, Watkins, & Woodward. (1990). p. 610.

Rollins, B. C., & Feldman, H. (1970). Marital satisfaction over the life cycle. *Journal of Marriage and the Family, 32,* 20–28.

Rollins, B. C., & Gallagher, R. (1978). The developing child and marital satisfaction. In R. Lerner & G. Spanier (Eds.), *Child influences on marital interaction: A life-span perspective.* New York: Academic Press.

Romaniuk, J. G., & Romaniuk, M. (1981). Creativity across the life span: A measurement perspective. *Human Development, 24,* 366–381.

Roodin, P. A., Rybash, J. M., & Hoyer, W. J. (1984). Affect in adult cognition: A constructivist view of moral thought and action. In C. Malatesta & C. Izard (Eds.), *The role of affect in adult development and aging.* Beverly Hills, CA: Sage.

———. (1985). *Qualitative dimensions of social cognition in adulthood.* Paper presented at meetings of Gerontological Society of America, New Orleans.

Rook, K. S. (1987). Reciprocity of social exchange and social satisfaction among older women. *Journal of Personality and Social Psychology, 52,* 145–154.

Rose, C., & Bell, B. (1971). *Predicting longevity.* Lexington, MA: Heath.

Rosen, J. L., & Neugarten, B. L. (1964). Ego functions in the middle and later years: A thematic apperception study. In B. L. Neugarten (Ed.), *Personality in middle and late life.* New York: Atherton.

Rosenbloom, C. A., & Whittington, F. J. (1993). The effects of bereavement on eating behaviors and nutrient intakes in elderly widowed persons. *Journal of Gerontology, 48,* S223–229.

Rossi, A. (1977). A biosocial perspective on parenting. *Daedalus, 106,* 1–31.

Rossi, A. (1984). Gender and parenthood. *American Sociological Review, 49,* 1–19.

Roth, S., & Cohen, L. J. (1986). Approach, avoidance, and coping with stress. *American Psychologist, 41,* 813–819.

Rowe, J. W., & Kahn, R. L. (1987). Human aging: Usual and successful. *Science, 237,* 143–149.

Rowse, T. (1988). *Cemetery goods and services.* Washington, DC: American Association of Retired Persons #PF4087 (488). D13162.

Roy, D. J., Verret, D., & Roberge, C. (1986). Death, dying, and the brain: Ethical moments in critical care medicine. *Critical Care Clinics, 2,* no. 1, 168–169.

Rubenstein, C., & Shaver, P. (1981). The experience of loneliness. In L. A. Peplau & D. Perlman (Eds.), *Loneliness: A source book of current theory, research, and therapy.* New York: Wiley Interscience.

Rubenstein, R. L., Alexander, B. B., Goodman, M., & Luborsky, M. (1991). Key relationships of never married, childless older women: A cultural analysis. *Journal of Gerontology: Social Sciences, 46,* S270–277.

Rubin, R. M., & Koelln, K. (1993). Out-of-pocket health expenditure differentials between elderly and nonelderly households. *The Gerontologist, 33,* 596–602.

Rubin, Z. (1970). Measurement of romantic love. *Journal of Personality and Social Psychology, 16,* 265–273.

Rubin, Z. (1973). *Liking and loving: An invitation to social psychology.* New York: Holt, Rinehart & Winston.

———. (1979, October). Seeking a cure for loneliness. *Psychology Today, 13,* 82–91.

Ruchlin, H. S., & Morris, J. N. (1992, February). Deteriorating health and the cessation of employment among older workers. *Journal of Aging and Health, 4,* 43–57.

Ruggles, P. (1992). *Income and poverty among the elderly.* Paper presented at the National Academy on Aging and Executive Seminar on Poverty and Income Security. Washington DC., June.

Ruth, J. E., & Birren, J. E. (1985). Creativity in adulthood and old age: Relations to intelligence, sex, and mode of testing. *International Journal of Behavioral Development, 8,* 99–109.

Rybash, J. M. (in press). A taxonomy of priming: Implications for aging. In D. J. Herrmann, M. K. Johnson, C. L. McEvoy, C. Hertzog, & P. T. Hertel (Eds.) *Basic and applied memory: Research on practical aspects of memory.* Hillsdale, NJ: Erlbaum

Rybash, J. M. (in press). Aging and implicit memory: A cognitive neuropsychological perspective.

Rybash, J. M. (1994). Aging, test awareness, and associative priming. *Aging and Cognition, 1,* 158–173.

Rybash, J. M., Deluca, K., & Rubenstein, L. (1994, July). *Conscious and unconscious influences on remembering information from the near and distant past: A developmental analysis.* Third Practical Aspects of Memory Conference, College Park, MD.

Rybash, J. M., Hoyer, W. J., & Roodin, P. A. (1986). *Adult cognition and aging: Developmental changes in processing, knowing, and thinking.* New York: Pergamon.

Rybash, J. M., & Roodin, P. A. (1989). A comparison of formal and post formal modes of health care decision-making competence. In M. L. Commons, J. D. Sinnott, F. A. Richards, & C. Armon (Eds.), *Adult development: Vol. 1. Comparisons and applications of developmental models,* (pp. 217–235). New York: Praeger.

Rybash, J. M., & Roodin, P. A. (1989). The framing heuristic influences judgments about younger and older adults' decisions to refuse medical treatment. *Applied Cognitive Psychology, 3,* 171–180.

Rybash, J. M., Roodin, P. A., & Hoyer, W. J. (1983). Expressions of moral thought in later adulthood. *The Gerontologist, 23,* 254–260.

Rybash, J. M., Roodin, P. A. & Hoyer, W. J. (1986). Adult morality: A Neo-Piagetian perspective on cognition and affect. *Genetic Epistemologist, 14,* 24–29

Ryff, C. D. (1991). Possible selves in adulthood and old age: A tale of shifting horizons. *Psychology and Aging, 6,* 286–295.

Ryff, C. D., & Essex, M. J. (1991). Psychological well-being in adulthood and old age: Descriptive markers and explanatory processes. In K. W. Schaie & M. Powell Lawton (Eds.), *Annual review of gerontology and geriatrics,* (Vol. 11, pp. 144–171). New York: Springer.

## *S*

Sahler, O. J. (1978). *The child and death.* St. Louis: Mosby.

Salthouse, T. A. (1984). Effects of age and skill in typing. *Journal of Experimental Psychology: General, 113,* 345–371.

———. (1985). Spread of behavior and its implications for cognition. In J. E. Birren & K. W. Schaie (Eds.), *Handbook of the psychology for aging* (2nd ed.). New York: Van Nostrand Reinhold.

Salthouse, T. A. (1988). Initiating and formalization of theories of cognitive aging. *Psychology and Aging, 3,* 3–16.

———. (1990). Speed of behavior and its implications for cognition. In J. E. Birren & K. W. Schaie (Eds.), *The handbook of the psychology of aging* (2nd ed., 400–426). New York: Van Nostrand Reinhold.

Salthouse, T. A., Babcock, R. L., Skovronek, E., Mitchell, D., & Palmon, R. (1990). Age and experience effects in spatial visualization. *Developmental Psychology, 26,* 128–136.

Salthouse, T. A., Mitchell, D., & Palmon, R. (1989). Memory and age differences in spatial manipulation ability. *Psychology and Aging, 4,* 480–486.

Salthouse, T. A., & Prill, K. A. (1988). Effects of aging on perceptual closure. *American Journal of Psychology, 101,* 217–238.

Salthouse, T. A., & Somberg, B. L. (1982). Skilled performance: Effects of adult age and experience on elementary processes. *Journal of Experimental Psychology: General, 111,* 176–207.

Sampson, J. P., Jr., Reardon, R. C., & Lenz, J. G. (1991). Computer assisted career guidance: Improving the design and use of systems. *Journal of Career Development, 17,* 185–190.

Sande, M. A. (1986). Transmission of AIDS: The case against casual contagion. *New England Journal of Medicine, 314,* 380–382.

Sandler, I. N., West, S. G., Baca, L., Pillov, D. R., et. al. (1992, Aug.). Linking empirically based theory and evaluation: The Family Bereavement Program. *American Journal of Community Psychology, 20,* 491–521.

Sands, L. P., & Meredith, W. (1992). Blood pressure and intellectual function in late midlife. *Journal of Gerontology: Psychological Sciences, 47,* P81–84.

Sandvik, L., & Erikssen, J. (1993). Physical fitness as a predictor of mortality among healthy middle-aged Norwegian men. *The New England Journal of Medicine, 328,* 533–537.

Santrock, J. W., & Warshak, R. A. (1979). Father custody and social development in boys and girls. *Journal of Social Issues, 35,* 112–125.

Sarason, I. G., Sarason, B. R., & Pierce, G. R. (1989). *Social support: An interactional view.* NY: Wiley.

Sarason, I. G., & Speilberger, C. D. (1980). *Stress and anxiety* (Vol. 7). Washington, DC: Hemisphere.

Sarrell, L., & Sarrell, P. (1974). The college subculture. In M. S. Calderone (Ed.), *Sexuality and human values.* New York: Association Press.

Sati: A pagan sacrifice. (1987, October). *India Today,* pp. 58–61.

Sauber, M., & Corrigan, E. M. (1970). *The six-year experience of unwed mothers as parents.* New York: Community Council of Greater New York.

Saunders, C. (1977). Dying to live: St. Christopher's Hospice. In H. Feifel (Ed.), *New meanings of death.* New York: McGraw-Hill.

Schacter, D. L. (1987). Implicit memory: History and current status. *Journal of Experimental Psychology: Learning, Memory and Cognition, 13,* 501–518.

Schacter, D. L. (1994). Priming and multiple memory systems: Perceptual mechanisms of implicit memory. In D. L. Schacter, D. L., & E. Tulving, (Eds.). *Memory systems 1994.* Cambridge, MA: MIT Press.

Schacter, D. L., Kasniak, A., Kihlstrom, J., & Valdiserri, M. (1991). The relation between source memory and aging. *Psychology and Aging, 6,* 559–568.

Schacter, D. L., Kihlstrom, J. F., Kaszniak, A. W., & Valdiserri, M. (1993). Preserved and impaired memory functions in elderly adults. In J. Cerella, J. M. Rybash, W. J. Hoyer, & M. A. Commons (Eds.), *Adult information processing: Limits on loss* (pp. 327–350). San Diego: Academic Press.

Schaie, K. W. (1965). A general model for the study of developmental problems. *Psychological Bulletin, 64,* 92–107.
———. (1977). Quasi-experimental research designs in the psychology of aging. In J. E. Birren & K. W. Schaie (Eds.), *Handbook of the psychology of aging.* New York: Van Nostrand Reinhold.
———. (1979). The primary mental abilities in adulthood: An exploration in the development of psychometric intelligence. In P. B. Baltes & O. G. Brim, Jr. (Eds.), *Life-span development and behavior* (Vol. 2). New York: Academic Press.
———. (1983). Consistency and changes in cognitive functioning of the young-old and old-old. In M. Bergner, U. Lehr, E. Lang, & R. Schmidt-Scherzer (Eds.), *Aging in the eighties and beyond.* New York: Springer.
———. (1985). *Manual for the Schaie-Thurstone Adult Mental Abilities Test (STAMAT).* Palo Alto, CA: Consulting Psychologists Press.
———. (1990). The optimization of cognitive functioning in old age: Prediction based on cohort-sequential and longitudinal data. In. P. B. Baltes & M. Baltes (Eds.), *Longitudinal research and the study of successful (optimal) aging* (pp. 94–117). Cambridge, England: Cambridge University Press.
———. (1993). The Seattle longitudinal studies of adult intelligence. *Current Directions in Psychological Science, 2,* 171–174.
Schaie, K. W. (1994). The course of adult intellectual development. *American Psychologist, 49,* 304–313.
Schaie, K. W., & Hertzog, C. (1983). Fourteen-year cohort-sequential studies of adult intelligence. *Developmental Psychology, 19,* 531–543.
Schaie, K. W., & Hertzog, C. (1985). Toward a comprehensive model of adult intellectual development: Contributions of the Seattle longitudinal study. In R. J. Sternberg (Ed.), *Advances in human intelligence* (Vol. 3). New York: Academic Press.
Schaie, K. W., & Labouvie-Vief, G. (1974). Generational versus ontogenetic components of change in adult cognitive behavior: A fourteen-year cross-sequential study. *Developmental Psychology, 10,* 305–320.
Schaie, K. W., & Parham, I. A. (1976). Stability of adult personality traits: Fact or fable? *Journal of Personality and Social Psychology, 34,* 146–158.
Schaie, K. W., & Willis, S. L. (1986). *Adult development and aging* (2nd ed.). Boston: Little, Brown.
———. (1991). Adult personality and psychomotor performance: Cross-sectional and longitudinal analyses. *Journal of Gerontology: Psychological Sciences, 46,* P275–284.
———. (1993). Age difference patterns of psychometric intelligence in adulthood: Generalizability within and across ability domains. *Psychology and Aging, 8,* 44–55.
Schaie, K. W., Willis, S. L., Hertzog, C., & Schulenberg, J. E. (1987). Effects of cognitive training on primary mental ability structure. *Psychology and Aging, 2,* 233–242.
Scharff, V. (1991). *Taking the wheel: Women and the coming of the motor age.* New York: Free Press.
Schatz, B. D. (1986). *Grief of mothers.* In T. A. Rando (Ed.), Parental loss of a child. Champaign, IL: Research Press.
Scheibel, A. B., & Wechsler, A. F. (Eds.). (1986). *The biological substrates of Alzheimer's disease.* New York: Academic Press.
Scheidt, R. J. (1985). The mental health of the aged in rural environments. In R. T. Coward & G. R. Lee (Eds.), *The elderly in rural society.* New York: Springer.
Schieber, F. (1992). Aging and the senses. In J. E. Birren, R. B. Sloane, & G. D. Cohen (Eds.), *Handbook of mental health and aging* (second edition, pp. 252–306). San Diego: Academic Press.
Schiffman, S. (1977). Food recognition by the elderly. *Journal of Gerontology, 32,* 586–592.
Schleifer, S. J., Keller, S. E., Camerino, M., Thornton, J. C., & Stein, M. (1983). Suppression of lymphocyte stimulation following bereavement. *Journal of the American Medical Association, 250,* 374–377.
Schmitt, N. Gogate, J., Rothert, M., Rovner, D., Holmes, M., Talarcyzk, G., Given, B., & Kroll, J. (1991). Capturing and clustering women's judgment policies: The case of hormonal therapy for menopause. *Journal of Gerontology: Psychological Sciences, 46,* S92–101.
Schmitz-Secherzer, R. (1976). Longitudinal change in leisure behavior of the elderly. *Contributions to Human Development, 3,* 127–136.
———. (1979). Aging and leisure. *Society and Leisure, 2,* 377–396.
Schneider, E. L., & Guralnik, J. M. (1990). The aging of America: Impact on health care costs. *JAMA, 263,* 2335–2340.
Schnelle, J. F., Simmons, S. F., & Ory, M. G. (1992). Risk factors that predict staff failure to release nursing home residents from restraints. *The Gerontologist, 32,* 767–770.
Schurr, P., Vaillant, C. O. & Vaillant, G. E. (1990). Predicting Exercise in late middle life from young adult personality. *International Journal of Aging and Human Development 30(2),*153–160.
Schonfield, A. E. D., & Robertson, B. A. (1966). Memory storage and aging. *Canadian Journal of Psychology, 20,* 228–236.
Schroots, J. J. F., & Birren, J. E. (1990). Concepts of time and aging in science. In J. E. Birren & K. W. Schaie (Eds.), *Handbook of the psychology of aging* (3rd ed., pp. 45–64). New York: Academic Press.
Schuckit, M. A., Morrissey, E. R., & O'Leary, M. R. (1979). Alcohol problems in elderly men and women. In D. M. Peterson (Ed.), *Drug use among the aged.* New York: Spectrum.
Schultz, N. R., Jr., Elias, M. F., Robbins, M. A., Streeten, D. P. H., & Blakeman, N. (1986). A longitudinal comparison of hypertensives and normotensives on the Wechsler Adult Intelligence Scale: Initial findings. *Journal of Gerontology, 41,* 169–175.
Schulz, R., & Alderman, D. (1974). Clinical research and the stages of dying. *Omega, 5,* 137–143.

Schulz, R., Biegel, D., Morycz, R., & Visintainer, P. (1989). Psychological paradigms for understanding caregiving. In E. Light & B. D. Leibowitz (Eds.), *Alzheimer's disease treatment and family stress: Directions for research.* National Institutes on Mental Health (DHHS Publication No. ADM89-1569): Washington, DC.

Schulz, R., & Curnow, C. (1988). Peak performance and age among superathletes: Track and field, swimming, baseball, tennis, and golf. *Journal of Gerontology: Psychological Sciences, 43,* 1113–1120.

Schulz, R., Musa, D., Staszewski, J., & Siegler, R. S. (1994). The relation between age and major league baseball performance: Implications for development. *Psychology and Aging, 9.*

Schwartzman, A. E., Gold, D., Andres, D., Arbuckle, T. Y., & Chiakelson, J. (1987). Stability of intelligence: A forty-year follow-up. *Canadian Journal of Psychology, 41,* 244–256.

Seeman, T. E., Guranick, J. M., Kaplan, G. A. & Knudsen, L., et al (1989). The health consequences of multiple morbidity in the elderly: The Alameda County Study. *Journal of Aging and Health 1*(1), 50–66.

Selkoe, D. J. (1992). Aging, brain, and mind. *Scientific American, 267,* 134–143.

Selkoe, D. J., Bell, D. S., Podlisny, M. B., Price, D. L., & Cork, L. C. (1987). Conservation of brain amyloid proteins in aged mammals and humans with Alzheimer's disease. *Science, 235,* 873–877.

Selkoe, D. J., Bell, D. S., Podlisny, M. B., Price, D. L., & Cork, I. C. (1987). Conservation of brain amyloid proteins in aged mammals and humans. *Science, 235,* 873–877.

Selye, H. (1956). *The stress of life.* New York: McGraw-Hill.

Selye, H. (1980). *Selye's guide to stress research.* New York: Van Nostrand.

Shahnasarian, M. (1992). Career development after professional football. *Journal of Career Development, 18,* 299–304.

Shanan, J. (1991). Who and how: Some unanswered questions in adult development. *Journal of Gerontology: Psychological Sciences, 46,* P309–316.

Sharps, M. J., & Gollin, E. S. (1987). Speed and accuracy of mental image rotation. *Journal of Gerontology, 42,* 342–344.

Shaughnessy, J. J., & Zechmeister, E. B. (1990). *Research methods in psychology* (2nd ed.). New York: McGraw-Hill.

Sheehy, G. (1976). *Passages: The predictable crises of adult life.* New York: Dutton.

———. (1981). *Pathfinders.* New York: Dutton.

Sheridan, C. (1993). *Failure-free activities for the Alzheimer's patient.* San Francisco: Elder Books.

Sherwood, S., Ruchlin, H. S., & Sherwood, C. C. (1989). CCRC's: An option for aging in place. In D. Tillson & C. J. Fahey (Eds.), *Support for the frail elderly in residential environments.* Glenview, IL: Scott Foresman.

Shi, L. (1993). Family financial and household support exchange between generations: A survey of Chinese rural elderly. *The Gerontologist, 33,* 468–480.

Shields, S. A. (1973). *Personality trait attribution and reproductive role.* Unpublished master's thesis, Pennsylvania State University, University Park.

Shimamura, A. P., & Squire, L. R. (1991). The relationship between fact and source memory: Findings from amnesic patients and normal subjects. *Psychobiology, 19,* 1–10.

Shirom, A., & Mazeh, T. (1988). Periodicity in seniority-job satisfaction relationship. *Journal of Vocational Behavior, 33,* 38–49.

Shneidman, E. (1973). *Deaths of man.* New York: Quadrangle/ New York Times.

———. (1980). *Voices of death.* New York: Harper & Row.

———. (1992). *Death: Current perspectives* (3rd ed.). Mountain View, CA: Mayfield.

Shupe, D. R. (1985). In J. E. Birren & J. Livingston (Eds.), *Cognition, stress, and aging.* Englewood Cliffs, NJ: Prentice-Hall.

Siegler, I. C. (1983). Psychological aspects of the Duke longitudinal studies. In K. W. Schaie (Ed.), *Longitudinal studies of adult psychological development.* New York: Guilford Press.

Siegler, I. C., & Costa, P. T., Jr. (1985). Health behavior relationships. In J. E. Birren & K. W. Schaie (Eds.), *Handbook of the psychology of aging* (2nd ed.). New York: Van Nostrand Reinhold.

Silverstein, M., & Waite, L. J. (1993). Are blacks more likely than whites to receive and provide social support in middle and old age? Yes, no, and maybe so. *Journal of Gerontology: Social Sciences, 48,* S212–222.

Simms, L. M., Jones, S. J., & Yoder, K. K. (1982). Adjustment of older persons in nursing homes. *Journal of Gerontological Nursing, 8,* 383–386.

Simon, J. L., & Burstein, P. (1985). *Basic research methods in social science* (3rd ed.). New York: Random House.

Simon, S. (1980). The neuroses, personality disorders, alcoholism, drug use and misuse, and crime in the aged. In J. E. Birren, & R. B. Sloane (Eds.), *Handbook of mental health and aging.* Englewood Cliffs, NJ: Prentice-Hall.

Simonton, D. K. (1988). Age and outstanding achievement: What do we know after a century of research? *Psychological Bulletin, 104,* 251–267.

———. (1990). Creativity and wisdom in aging. In. J. E. Birren & K. W. Schaie (Eds.), *Handbook of the psychology of aging* (3rd ed., pp. 320–329). San Diego, CA: Academic Press.

Sinnott, J. D. (1981). The theory of relativity: A metatheory for development? *Human Development, 24,* 293–311.

———. (1984). Postformal reasoning: The relativistic stage. In M. L. Commons, F. A. Richards, & C. Armon (Eds.), *Beyond formal operations: Late adolescent and adult cognitive development.* New York: Praeger.

———. (1989). Life-span relativistic postformal thought: Methodology and data from everyday problem-solving studies. In M. L. Commons, J. D. Sinnott, F. A. Richards, & C. Armon (Eds.), *Adult Development, Vol. 1: Comparisons and applications of developmental models.* New York: Praeger.

Sinnott, J. D., & Cavanaugh, J. C. (Eds.). (1991). *Bridging paradigms: Positive development in adulthood and cognitive aging.* New York: Praeger.

Sixsmith, A. J., & Sixsmith, J. A. (1991). Transitions in home experience in later life. *Journal of Architectural Planning and Research, 8,* 181–191.

Skinner, B. F. (1990). Can psychology be a science of mind? *American Psychologist, 45,* 1206–1210.

Skolnick, E. (1986). *The intimate environment: Exploring marriage and family* (4th ed.). Boston: Little, Brown.

Slomka, J. (1992). The negotiation of death: Clinical decision making at the end of life. *Social Science and Medicine, 35,* 251–259.

Small, G. W. (1992). Editorial. *Journal of American Medical Association,* November 11.

Small, G. W., & Jarvik, L. F. (1982). The dementia syndrome. *The Lancet, 2,* 1443–1446.

Smeeding, T., Torrey, B., & Rainwater, L. (1993). Going to extremes: Income inequality, poverty, and the U.S. aged from an international perspective. Mimeo. Syracuse, NY: Syracuse University.

Smith, A. D. (1977). Adult age differences in cued recall. *Developmental Psychology, 13,* 326–331.

Smith, B. B. (1992, Summer). Treatment of dementia: Healing through cultural arts. *Pride Institute Journal of Long Term Home Health Care, 11,* 37–45.

Smith, J., & Baltes, P. B. (1990). Wisdom-related knowledge: Age/cohort differences in response to life-planning problems. *Developmental Psychology, 26,* 494–505.

Smith, J. S., & Kiloh, I. G. (1981). The investigation of dementia: Results in 200 consecutive admissions. *The Lancet, 1,* 824–827.

Snarey, J. (1985). Cross-cultural universality of socio-moral development: A critical review of Kohlbergian research. *Psychological Bulletin, 97,* 202–232.

Snyder, D. C. (1993). The economic well-being of retired workers by race and Hispanic origin. In D. Salisbury & R. B. Burkenhauser (Eds.), *Pensions in a changing economy* (pp. 67–78). Employee Benefit Research Institute: Washington, DC.

Soares, C. J. (1985). The companion animal in the context of the family system. *Marriage and the Family Review, 8,* 49–62.

Society for the Right to Die. (1987). *A living will.* New York: Society for the Right to Die.

Sokolovsky, J. (1986). *Growing old in different societies: Cross-cultural perspectives.* Belmont, CA: Wadsworth.

Soldo, B. J., & Agree, E. M. (1988). America's elderly population. *Population Bulletin, 43,* 1–53.

Solnick, R. E., & Corby, N. (1983). Human sexuality and aging. In D. S. Woodruff & J. E. Birren (Eds.), *Aging: Scientific perspectives and social issues* (2nd ed.), Monterey, CA: Brooks-Cole.

Sommers, I., Baskin, D., Specht, D., & Shively, M. (1988). Deinstitutionalization of the elderly mentally ill: Factors affecting discharge to alternate living arrangements. *The Gerontologist, 28* (5), 653–658.

Sorenson, A., & McLanahan, S. (1987). Married women's economic dependency, 1940–1980. *American Journal of Sociology, 93,* 659–687.

Souza, P., & Hoyer, W. J. (1994). *Adaptive strategies for compensating for hearing loss in old age.* Communication and Aging Conference, Toronto.

Spanier, G., & Glick, P. (1981). Marital instability in the United States: Some correlates and recent changes. *Family Relations, 31,* 329–338.

Spanier, G. B., & Margolis, R. L. (1983). Marital separation and extramarital sexual behavior. *Journal of Sex Research, 19,* 23–48.

Speare, A., & Avery, R. (1993). Who helps whom in older parent-child families. *Journal of Gerontology, 48,* 564–573.

Spearman, C. (1927). *The abilities of man.* New York: Macmillan.

Speece, M. W., & Brent, S. B. (1984). Children's understanding of death: A review of three components of a death concept. *Child Development, 55,* 1671–1686.

Spence, J. T. (1979). *Achievement and achievement-related motives.* Paper presented at the meeting of the American Psychological Association, New York.

Spence, J. T., & Helmreich, R. L. (1978). *Masculinity and femininity: Their psychological dimensions.* Austin, TX: University of Texas Press.

Spencer, W. D., & Raz, N. (1994). Memory for facts, source, and context: Can frontal lobe dysfunction explain age-related differences. *Psychology and Aging, 9,* 149–159.

Spicer, J., & Hampe, G. (1975). Kinship interaction after divorce. *Journal of Marriage and the Family, 28,* 113–119.

Spitze, G., Logan, J. R., & Robinson, J. (1992). Family structure and changes in living arrangements among elderly nonmarried parents. *Journal of Gerontology, 47*(6), S289–296.

Squire, L. R. (1992). Memory and the hippocampus: A synthesis of findings with rats, monkeys, and humans. *Psychological Review, 99,* 195–231.

Stagner, R. (1985). Aging in industry. In J. E. Birren & K. W. Schaie (Eds.), *Handbook of the psychology of aging* (2nd ed.). New York: Van Nostrand Reinhold.

Stall, R., Catania, J., & Pollack, L. (1988). AIDS as an age-defined epidemic. The social epidemiology of HIV infection among older Americans. *Report to the National Institute of Aging.* Unpublished document.

Staudinger, U. M., Smith, J., & Baltes, P. B. (1992). Wisdom-related knowledge in a life review task: Age differences and the role of professional specialization. *Psychology and Aging, 7,* 271–281.

Stearns, H. L., Barrett, G. V., and Alexander, R. A. (1985). Accidents and the aging individual. In J. E. Birren and K. W. Schaie (Eds.), *Handbook of the psychology of aging* (2nd ed.). New York: Van Nostrand Reinhold.

Steenland, S. (1987). *Prime time women: An analysis of older women on entertainment television.* Washington, DC: National Commission on Working Women.

Steger, H. G. (1976). Understanding the psychological factors in rehabilitation. *Geriatrics, 31,* 68–73.

Stein, J. A., Newcomb, M. D., & Bentler, P. M. (1990). The relative influence of vocational behavior and family involvement on self-esteem: Longitudinal analyses of young adult women and men. *Journal of Vocational Behavior, 36,* 320–328.

Stein, S., Linn, M. W., & Stein, E. M. (1985). Patient's anticipation of stress in nursing home care. *The Gerontologist, 25,* 88–94.

———. (1986). *Patient's perceptions of nursing home stress related to quality of care.* Unpublished report, VA Health Services Research Grant (#547). Miami, FL: University of Miami Medical School.

Steinmetz, S. (1978). Battered parents. *Society, 15,* 54–55.

Steinmetz, S. (1981). Elder abuse. *Aging,* January/February, 6–10.

Stephens, J. (1976). *Loners, losers, and lovers: Elderly tenants in a slum hotel.* Seattle: University of Washington Press.

Stephens, M. A. P., Crowther, J. H., Hobfoll, S., & Tennenbaum, D. (1990). *Stress and coping in later life families.* New York: Hemisphere.

Stephens, M. A. P., Norris, V. K., Kinney, J. M., Ritchie, S. W., & Grotz, R. C. (1988). Stressful situations in caregiving: Relations between caregiver coping and well-being. *Psychology and Aging, 3,* 208–209.

Stephenson, J. S. (1985). *Death, grief, and mourning: Individual and social realities.* New York: Free Press.

Sternberg, R. J. (1985). *Beyond IQ: A triarchic theory of human intelligence.* New York: Cambridge University Press.

———. (1986). *Intelligence applied: Understanding and increasing your intellectual skills.* New York: Harcourt Brace Jovanovich.

Sternberg, S. (1969). The discovery of processing stages: Extensions of donders' method. *Acta Psychologica, 30,* 276–35.

Stevens-Long, J., & Commons, M. L. (1992). *Adult life* (4th ed.). Mountain View, CA: Mayfield.

St. George-Hyslop, P. H., Tanzi, R. E., Polinsky, R. J., Haines, J. L., Nee, L., Watkins, P. C., Myers, R. H., Feldman, R. G., Pollen, D., Drachman, D., Growdon, J., Bruni, A., Foncin, J. F., Salmon, D., Frommelt, P., Amaducci, L., Sorbi, S., Piacentini, S., Steward, G. D., Hobbs, W. J., Conneally, P. M., & Gusella, J. F. (1987). The genetic defect causing familial Alzheimer's disease maps on chromosome 21. *Science, 235,* 885–889.

Stillion, J., and Wass, H. (1979). Children and death. In H. Wass (Ed.), *Dying: Facing the facts.* New York: McGraw-Hill.

Stine, E. A. L. (1990). On-line processing of written text by younger and older adults. *Psychology and Aging, 5,* 68–78.

Strawbridge, W. J., Camacho, T. C., Cohen, R. D., & Kaplan, G. A. (1993). Gender differences in factors associated with change in physical functioning in old age: A 6-year longitudinal study. *The Gerontologist, 33,* 603–609.

Stuck, A. E., Van Gorp, W. G., Josephson, K. R. & Morgenstern, H., et al (1992). Multidimensional risk assessment versus age as criterion for retirement of airline pilots. *Journal of the American Geriatrics Society, 40*(5), 526–532.

Stuck, Van Gorp, Josephson, et al. (1992). J. American Geriatric Society. p. 415.

Stull, D. E., & Hatch, L. R. (1984). Unraveling the effects of multiple life changes. *Research on Aging, 6,* 560–571.

Suitor, J., & Pillemer, K. (1993). Support and interpersonal stress in the social networks of married daughters caring for parents with dementia. *Journal of Gerontology, 48*(1), S1–8.

Summers, R., et al., (1986). Oral tetrahydroaminoacridine in long-term treatment of senile dementia, Alzheimer's type. *New England Journal of Medicine, 315,* 1241–1245.

Super, D. E. (1969). Vocational developmental theory: Persons, positions, and processes. *The Counseling Psychologist, 1,* 2–8.

———. (1975). *The psychology of careers.* New York: Harper & Row.

———. (1980). A life-span, life-space approach to career development. *Journal of Vocational Behavior, 16,* 282–298.

Super, D. E., Kowalski, R., & Gotkin, E. (1967). *Floundering and trial after high school.* Unpublished manuscript, Columbia University, New York.

Sussman, M. B. (1985). Family life of old people. In R. H. Binstock & E. Shanas (Eds.), *Handbook of aging and the social sciences* (2nd ed.). New York: Van Nostrand Reinhold.

Svenson, O. (1981). Are we all less risky and more skillful than our fellow drivers? *Acta Psychologica, 47* (2), 143–148.

Swanson, B. M. (1989). *Careers in mental health.* Lincolnwood, IL: VGM Career Horizons.

Swanson, E. A., & Bennett, T. F. (1982–1983). Degree of closeness: Does it affect the bereaved's attitudes toward selected funeral practices? *Omega, 13,* 43–50.

Szinovacz, M., & Washo, C. (1992). Gender differences in exposure to life events and adaptation to retirement. *Journals of Gerontology, 47,* S191–S196.

## T

Taking the "Iliad" on the road. (1994, April 27). *Chronicle of Higher Education, 40,* no. 34.

Takman, A. (1992). Nonpharmacologic treatment of behavioral symptoms. *Acta Neurologica Scandinavica, 85,* Suppl. 81–83.

Tamir, L. M. (1989). *Modern myths about men at mid-life: An assessment.* Newbury Park, CA: Sage.

Tangri, & Jenkins. (1992). The women's lifepaths study: The Michigan Graduates of 1967. In D. Shuster & K. Hulbert (Eds.), *Women's lives through time: Educated American women of the 20th century* (pp. 22–35). San Francisco: Jossey Bass.

Tanzi, R. E., et al. (1987). Amyloid B protein gene: cDNA, mRNA distribution, and genetic linkage near the Alzheimer locus. *Science, 219,* 1184–1190.

Taylor, R. J., & Chatters, L. M. (1988). Correlates of education, income, and poverty among aged blacks. *The Gerontologist, 28,* 435–441.

Taylor, S. E. (1983). Adjustment to threatening events: A theory of cognitive adaptation. *American Psychologist, 38,* 1161–1173.

———. (1990). Health psychology: The science and the field. *American Psychologist, 45,* 40–50.

Taylor, S. E., & Brown, J. D. (1988). Illusions and well-being: A social psychological perspective on mental health. *Psychological Bulletin, 103,* 193–210.

Taylor, S. E., Kemeny, M. E., Aspinwall, L. G., Schneider, S. G., Rodriguez, R., & Heubert, M. (1992). Optimism, coping, psychological distress, and high-risk sexual behavior among men at risk for Acquired Immunodeficiency Syndrome (AIDS). *Journal of Personality and Social Psychology, 63,* 460–473.

Taylor, S. E., & Lobel, M. (1989). Social comparison activity under threat: Downward evolution and upward contacts. *Psychology Review, 96,* 569–575.

Tell, E. J., Cohen, M. A., Larson, M. J., & Batten, H. L. (1987). Assessing the elderly's preferences for life-care retirement options. *The Gerontologist, 27,* 503–509.

Teltsch, K. (1991). New study of older workers finds they can become good investments. *New York Times,* Tuesday, May 21, A16.

Tesch, S., Whitbourne, S. K., & Nehrke, M. F. (1981). Friendship, social interaction, and subjective well-being of older men in an institutional setting. *International Journal of Aging and Human Development, 13,* 317–327.

Thomae, H. (1992). Emotion and personality. In J. E. Birren, R. B. Sloane, & G. D. Cohen (Eds.), *Handbook of mental health and aging* (2nd ed., pp. 355–375). San Diego, CA: Academic Press.

Thomas, J. (1986a). Gender differences in satisfaction with grandparenting. *Psychology and Aging, 1,* 215–219.

———. (1986b). Age and sex differences in perceptions of grandparenting. *Journal of Gerontology, 41,* 417–423.

Thomas, L. E. (1977). Midlife career changes: Self-selected or externally mandated? *Vocational Guidance Quarterly, 25,* 320–328.

Thomas, L. W., & Gallagher, D. (1985). Depression and its treatment in the elderly. *Aging, 348,* 14–18.

Thompson, E. H., Futterman, A. M., Gallagher-Thompson, D., Rose, J. M., & Lovett, S. B. (1993). Social support and caregiving burden in family caregivers of frail elders. *Journal of Gerontology: Social Sciences, 48,* S245–S254.

Thompson, L., & Spanier, G. (1983). The end of marriage and acceptance of marital termination. *Journal of Marriage and the Family, 45,* 103–114.

Thompson, R. A., Tinsley, B. R., Scalora, M. J., & Parke, R. D. (1989). Grandparents' visitation rights. *American Psychologist, 44,* 1217–1222.

Thompson, R. F. (1993). *The brain: An introduction to neuroscience.* New York: W. H. Freeman.

Thompson, R. F. (1986). *The brain: An introduction to neuroscience.* New York: W. H. Freeman.

Thurstone, L. L. (1938). *Primary mental abilities.* Chicago: University of Chicago Press.

TIAA (1992). *Long term care.* New York: Teachers Insurance and Annuity Association.

Tietjen, A. M., & Walker, L. J. (1985). Moral reasoning and leadership among men in a Papua, New Guinea society. *Developmental Psychology, 21,* 982–992.

Tinsley, B. J., & Parke, R. D. (1987). Grandparents as interactive and socialization agents. In M. Lewis (Ed.), *Beyond the dyad.* New York: Plenum.

Tipper, S. P. (1991). Less attentional selectivity as a result of declining inhibition in older adults. *Bulletin of the Psychonomic Society, 29,* 45–47.

Tipper, S. P., Bourque, T. A., Anderson, S. H., & Brehaut, J. C. (1989). Mechanisms of attention: A developmental study. *Journal of Experimental Child Psychology, 48,* 353–378.

Tobin, J. J. (1987). The American idealization of old age in Japan. *The Gerontologist, 27,* 53–58.

Tobin, S. S. (1978). Old people. In H. Mass (Ed.), *Review of research in the social services.* New York: National Association of Social Workers.

Tobin, S. S., & Lieberman, M. (1976). *Last home for the aged.* San Francisco: Jossey-Bass.

Tomlinson-Keasey, C. (1972). Formal operations in females from eleven to fifty-four years of age. *Developmental Psychology, 6,* 364.

Tomlinson-Keasey, C., & Keasey, C. B. (1974). The mediating role of cognitive development in moral judgment. *Child Development, 45,* 291–298.

Troll, L. E. (1971). The family of later life: A decade review. *Journal of Marriage and the Family, 33,* 263–290.

———. (1983). Grandparents: The family watchdogs. In T. Brubaker (Ed.), *Family relationships in later life.* Beverly Hills, CA: Sage.

Trunzo, C. E. (1982). Solving the age-old problem. *Money, 11,* 70–80.

Tryban, G. M. (1985). Effects of work and retirement within long-term marital relationships. *Lifestyles, 7,* 207–223.

Tulving, E. (1993). What is episodic memory? *Current Directions in Psychological Science, 6,* 67–70.

Tulving, E., & Schacter, D. L. (1990). Priming and human memory systems. *Science, 247,* 301–306.

## *U*

Uhlenberg, P., Cooney, T., & Boyd, R. (1990). Divorce for women after midlife. *Journal of Gerontology, 45,* S3–S11.

United Nations Department of Economic and Social Affairs. (1956). *The aging of populations and its economic and social implications.* (Population Studies, No. 26). New York: United Nations.

U.S. Bureau of the Census. (1983). *U.S. census of population and housing, 1980: Summary* (Vol. 2). Washington, DC: U.S. Government Printing Office.

U.S. Bureau of the Census. (1985). *Statistics.* Washington, DC: U.S. Government Printing Office.

U.S. Bureau of the Census. (1986). *Statistics.* Washington, DC: U.S. Government Printing Office.

U.S. Bureau of the Census. (1990). Household and family characteristics. (Current Population Reports) Washington, DC: U.S. Government Printing Office.

U.S. Bureau of the Census. (1990). *Modified and actual age, sex, race, and Hispanic origin data.* (Census of Population and Housing, Series CPH-L-74). Washington, DC: U.S. Government Printing Office.

U.S. Bureau of the Census. (1992). Poverty in the United States: 1991. *Current population reports Series P-60, No. 81.* U.S. Government Printing Office: Washington, DC.

U.S. Congress, House Committee on Ways and Means. (1992). *Green book: Background material and data on programs within the jurisdiction of the Committee on Ways and Means.* Washington, DC: U.S. Government Printing Office.

U.S. Dept. of Commerce, Bureau of the Census. (1989). *American housing survey for the United States in 1987* (Current housing reports, H 150-187). Washington, DC: U.S. Government Printing Office.

U.S. Department of Health and Human Services (1992). *Income of the aged chartbook, 1990.* (Social Security Administration Publication No. 13-11727). Washington, DC: U.S. Government Printing Office.

U.S. Department of Labor. (1987, August). *United States Department of Labor News,* 87–345.

U.S. Department of Labor. (1989, January). *Labor market problems of older women.* Report of the Secretary. Washington, DC: United States Department of Labor.

*U.S. News and World Report.* (1993, June 14). Grief re-examined. pp. 81–87.

U.S. Select Committee on Aging (1991, June). Long-term care costs. (Hearings). U.S. House of Representatives. Washington, DC: U.S. Government Printing Office.

U.S. Veterans Administration (1985). *Dementia guidelines for diagnosis and treatment.* Washington DC: Department of Medicine and Surgery Office of Geriatrics and Extended Care.

## *V*

Valliant, G. (1977). *Adaptation to life.* Boston: Little, Brown.

Valliant, G. E., & Valliant, C. O. (1981). Natural history of male psychological health, X: Work as a predictor of positive mental health. *American Journal of Psychiatry, 138,* 1433–1440.

Van Hoose, W. H., & Worth, M. (1982). *Adulthood in the life cycle.* Dubuque, IA: Wm. C. Brown.

Van Nostrand, J. (1993a). *Health data on older Americans.* U.S. Department of Health and Human Services. Series 3, #7 (PHS), 93-1411.

———. (1993b). Common beliefs about the rural elderly: What do the national data tell us. *Series 3 (No. 28) PHS 93-1412, U.S. Department of Health and Human Services.* Washington, DC.

Van-Tilburg, T. (1992). Support networks before and after retirement. *Special issue: Social networks. Journal of Social and Personal Relationships, 9,* 433–445.

Vasudev, J. (1987). *Maturity in adulthood: A cross-cultural perspective.* Paper presented at the Third Beyond Formal Operations Symposium Held at Harvard: Positive Development During Adolescence and Adulthood. Cambridge, MA, July.

Vatican Congregation for the Doctrine of the Faith. (1980). Vatican declaration on euthanasia. *Origins, 10,* 154–157.

Veatch, R. M. (1981). *A theory of medical ethics.* New York: Basic Books.

Veevers, J. E. (1980). *Children by choice.* Toronto, Canada: Butterworth.

Verrillo, R. (1980). Age-related changes in sensitivity to vibration. *Journal of Gerontology, 35,* 185–193.

Vinton, L. (1991). An exploratory study of self-neglectful elderly. *Journal of Gerontological Social Work, 18(1–2),* 55–68.

Vinton, L. (1992, Mar.). Battered women's shelters and older women: The Florida experience. *Journal of Family Violence, 7,* 63–72.

Vitaliano, P. P., Russo, J., Young, H. M., Teri, L., & Maivro, R. D. (1991). Predictors of burden in spouse caregivers of individuals with Alzheimer's disease. *Psychology and Aging, 6,* 392–402.

Vondareck, F. W., Lerner, R. M., & Schulenberg, J. E. (1986). *Career development: A life-span developmental approach.* Hillsdale, NJ: Erlbaum.

## *W*

Waldrop, M. M. (1984). The necessity of knowledge. *Science, 223,* 1279–1283.

Walford, R. L. (1986). *The 120-year diet.* New York: Simon & Schuster.

Walker, A. J., Martin, S. S. K., & Jones, L. L. (1992). *Journal of Gerontology: Social Sciences, 47,* S130–139.

Walker, L. J. (1986). Experiential and cognitive sources of moral development in adulthood. *Human Development, 29,* 113–124.

Walker, L. J., deVries, B., & Trevethan, S. D. (1987). Moral stages and moral orientations in real-life and hypothetical dilemmas. *Child Development, 58,* 842–858.

Walker, P. F. (1991). The older driver. *Human Factors, 33,* 499–505.

Wallerstein, J. S., & Blakeslee, S. (1988). *Second chances: Men, women, and children a decade after divorce.* Boston: Ticknor & Fields.

Ward, R., Logan, J., & Spitze, G. (1992). The influence of parent and child needs on co-residence in middle and later life. *Journal of Marriage and the Family, 54,* 209–221.

Warr, P. (1992). Age and occupational well-being. *Psychology and Aging, 7,* no. 1, 37–45.

Weale, R. A. (1986). Aging and vision. *Vision Research, 26,* 1507–1512.

Wechsler, D. (1939). *Measurement of adult intelligence.* Baltimore: Williams & Wilkins.

———. (1958). *The measurement and appraisal of adult intelligence.* Baltimore: Williams & Wilkins.

———. (1972). "Hold" and "don't hold" tests. In S. M. Chown (Ed.), *Human aging.* New York: Penguin.

Weinberger, D. A., & Schwartz, G. E. (1990). Distress and restraint on superordinate dimensions of adjustment: A typological perspective. *Journal of Personality, 58*(2), 381–417.

Weiner, M. B. (1992). Treating the older adult: A diverse population. Special issue: Psychoanalysis of the mid-life and older patient. *Psychoanalysis and Psychotherapy, 10,* 66–76.

Weiner, M. F. (ed.). (1991). *The dementias: Diagnosis and management.* Washington, DC: American Psychiatric Press.

Weir, R. F. (Ed.). (1986). *Ethical issues in death and dying.* New York: Columbia University Press.

Weisberg, R. W. (1986). *Creativity.* New York: W. H. Freeman.

Weisman, A. T. (1972). *On dying and denying: A psychiatric study of terminality.* New York: Behavioral Publications.

Weiss, L., & Lowenthal, M. (1975). Life course perspectives on friendship. In M. Lowenthal, M. Turnher, & D. Chiriboga (Eds.), *Four stages of life.* San Francisco: Jossey-Bass.

Weiss, R. S. (1973). *Marital separation.* New York: Basic Books.

Wenger, G. C. (1984). *The supportive network coping with old age.* London: George Allen and Unwin.

Wertheimer, M. (1945). *Productive thinking.* New York: Harper & Row.

Wertman, E., Speedie, L., Shemesh, Z., Gilon, D., et. al. (1993, January). Cognitive disturbances in Parkinsonian patients with depression. *Neuropsychiatry, Neuropsychology, and Behavioral Neurology, 6,* 31–37.

West, R. L., & Sinnott, J. D. (Eds.). (1992). *Everyday memory and aging: Current research and methodology.* New York: Springer-Verlag.

Westoff, C. F., & Westoff, L. A. (1971). *From now to zero: Fertility, contraception, and abortion in America.* Boston, MA: Little, Brown.

Wheaton, B. (1985). Models of stress-buffering functions of coping resources. *Journal of Health and Social Behavior, 26,* 352–364.

Whitbourne, S. K. (1985a). *The aging body.* New York: Springer-Verlag.

Whitbourne, S. K. (1985b). The psychological construction of the lifespan. In J. E. Birren & K. W. Schaie (Eds.), *The psychology of aging* (2nd ed., pp. 594–618). New York: Van Nostrand.

White, N., & Cunningham, W. R. (1988). Is terminal drop pervasive or specific? *Journal of Gerontology: Psychological Sciences, 44,* P141–P144.

Whitehouse, P. J. (1993). Autopsy. *The Gerontologist, 33,* 436–437.

Wickens, C. D., Braune, R., & Stokes, A. (1987). Age differences in the speed and capacity of information processing: A dual-task approach. *Psychology and Aging, 2,* 70–78.

Wiffenbach, J. M., Cowart, B. J., & Baum, B. J. (1986). Taste sensitivity and aging. *Journal of Gerontology, 41,* 460–468.

Wiggins, J. D., & Lederer, D. A. (1984). Differential antecedents of infidelity in marriage. *American Mental Health Counselors Association Journal, 6,* 152–161.

Wilkie, F., & Eisdorfer, C. (1971). Intelligence and blood pressure in the aged. *Science, 172,* 959–962.

———. (1973). *Intellectual change: A fifteen-year follow-up of the Duke sample.* Paper presented at the meeting of the Gerontological Society of America.

Williamson, G. M., & Schulz, R. (1991). Pain, activity restriction, and symptoms of depression among community-residing elderly adults. *Journal of Gerontology, 46,* 367–372.

Williamson, G. M., & Schulz, R. (1992). Pain, activity restriction, and symptoms of depression among community residing elderly adults. *Journal of Gerontology, 47*(6), pp. 367–372.

Williamson, J. B., Munley, A., & Evans, I. (1980). *Aging and society: An introduction to social gerontology.* New York: Holt, Rinehart and Winston.

Willis, S. L. (1985). Towards an educational psychology of the adult learner. In J. E. Birren & K. W. Schaie (Eds.), *Handbook of the psychology of aging* (2nd ed.). New York: Van Nostrand Reinhold.

Willis, S. L., & Schaie, K. W. (1985). Practical intelligence in later adulthood. In R. J. Sternberg & R. K. Wagner (Eds.), *Intelligence in the everyday world.* New York: Cambridge University Press.

Willis, S. L., & Schaie, K. W. (1986). Training the elderly on the ability factors of spatial orientation and inductive reasoning. *Psychology and Aging, 2,* 239–247.

Winch, R. F. (1974). Complementary needs and related notions about voluntary mate selection. In R. F. Winch & G. B. Spanier (Eds.), *Selected studies in marriage and the family.* New York: Holt, Rinehart and Winston.

Wise, P. M. (1993, June). Hormone regulation during aging. *Paper presented at the NIA Conference on Experimental Psychology of Aging.* University of Michigan.

Wisocki, P. A., & Averill, J. R. (1987). The challenge of bereavement. In L. L. Cartensen & B. A. Edelstein (Eds.), *Handbook of clinical gerontology* (pp. 312–321). New York: Pergamon Press.

Wiswell, R. A. (1980). Relaxation, exercise, and aging. In J. E. Birren & R. B. Sloan (Eds.), *Handbook of mental health and aging.* Englewood Cliffs, NJ: Prentice-Hall.

Wohlwill, J. F. (1973). *The study of behavioral development.* New York: Academic Press.

Wolfson, C., Handfield-Jones, R., Glass, K. C., McClaran, J., & Keyserlingk, E. (1993). Adult children's perception of their responsibility to provide care for their elderly parents. *The Gerontologist, 33,* 315–323.

Women's Medical Center. (1977). *Menopause.* Washington, DC: Women's Medical Center.

Wood, J. V., Taylor, S. E., & Lichtman, R. R. (1985). Social comparison in adjustment to breast cancer. *Journal of Personality and Social Psychology, 49,* 1169–1183.

Woodruff-Pak, D. (1988). *Psychology and Aging.* Englewood Cliffs, NJ: Prentice-Hall.

———. (1993). Neural plasticity as a substrate for cognitive adaptation in adulthood and old age. In J. Cerella, J. M. Rybash, W. J. Hoyer, & M. C. Commons (Eds.), *Adult information processing: Limits on loss* (pp. 13–35). San Diego: Academic Press.

Worden, J. W. (1982). *Grief counseling and grief therapy: A Handbook for the mental health practitioner.* New York: Springer.

Wright, J. W. (1982). *The American almanac of jobs and salaries.* New York: Avon.

Wright, L. L., & Elias, J. W. (1979). Age differences in the effects of perceptual noise. *Journal of Gerontology, 34,* 704–708.

Wurtman, R. J. (1985). Alzheimer's disease. *Scientific American, 252,* 62–74.

## Y

Yalom, I. D., & Lieberman, M. A. (1991). Bereavement and heightened existential awareness. *Psychiatry, 54*(4), 334–345.

Yankelovich, D. (1982, April). New rules in American life: Searching for self-fulfillment in a world turned upside down. *Psychology Today,* 35–91.

Yin, P. (1985). *Victimization and the aged.* Springfield, IL: Charles C Thomas.

York, K. L., & John, O. P. (1992). The four faces of Eve: A typological analysis of women's personality at midlife. *Journal of Personality and Social Psychology, 63,* 494–508.

## Z

Zabrucki, K., & Moore, D. (1994). Contributions of working memory and evaluation and regulation of understanding to adults' recall of texts. *Journal of Gerontology: Psychological Sciences, 49, 201–212.*

Zarit, S. H., Anthony, C. R., & Boutselis, M. (1987). Intervention with caregivers of dementia patients: Comparison of two approaches. *Psychology and Aging, 2,* 225–232.

Zarit, S. H., Cole, K. D., & Guilder, R. J. (1981). Memory-training strategies and subjective memory complaints in the aged. *The Gerontologist, 21,* 158–164.

Zarit, S. H., Eiler, J., & Hassinger, M. (1985). Clinical assessments. In J. E. Birren & K. W. Schaie (Eds.), *Handbook of the psychology of aging* (2nd ed.). New York: Van Nostrand Reinhold.

Zarit, S. H., Orr, N. K., & Zarit, J. M. (1985). *The hidden victims of Alzheimer's disease: Families under stress.* New York: New York University Press.

Zarit, S. H., Todd, P. A., & Zarit, J. M. (1986). Subjective burden of husbands and wives as caregivers: A longitudinal study. *The Gerontologist, 26,* 260–266.

Zarit, S. H., & Zarit, J. M. (1983). Cognitive impairment. In P. M. Lewinsohn & L. Teri (Eds.), *Clinical geropsychology: New directions in assessment and treatment.* New York: Pergamon Press.

Zarit, S. H., & Zarit, J. M. (1983b). Cognitive impairment. In P. M. Lewinsohn & L. Teri (Eds.), *Clinical geropsychology: New directions in assessment and treatment.* New York: Pergamon Press.

Zelnick, M., & Kanter, J. (1977). Sexual and contraceptive experience of young unmarried women in the United States. *Family Planning Perspectives, 9,* 55–71.

Zimmerman, R. S., Jackson, D. J., Longino, C. F., & Bradsher, J. E. (1993). Interpersonal and economic resources as mediators of the effects of health decline on the geographic mobility of the elderly. *Journal of Aging and Health 5*(1), 37–57.

Zisook, S. (1987). Adjustment to widowhood. In S. Zisook (Ed.), *Biopsychosocial aspects of grief and bereavement.* Washington, DC: American Psychiatric Press.

Zisook, S., Shuchter, S. R., & Lyons, L. E. (1987). Predictors of psychological reactions during the early stages of widowhood. *Psychiatric Clinics of North America, 10,* 355–368.

Zweibel, N. R., & Cassel, C. K. (1989). Treatment choices at the end of life: A comparison of decisions by older patients and their physician-selected proxies. *The Gerontologist, 29,* 615–621.

# CREDITS

## Line Art

*Chapter 3*

**Fig. 3.2:** From J. Stevens-Long and M. L. Commons, *Adult Life,* 4th ed. Copyright © 1992 Mayfield Publishing Co., Mountain View, CA. Reprinted by permission. **Fig. 3.6:** From K. G. Manton, L. S. Corder, and E. Stallard, "Estimates of Change in Chronic Disability and Institutional Incidence and Prevalence Rates in the U.S. Elderly Population from the 1982, 1984, and 1989 National Long-Term Care Survey" in *Journal of Gerontology: Social Sciences,* 48:153–166. Copyright © 1993 The Gerontological Society of America. Additional data from Riley and Riley, 1994. **Fig. 3.8b:** Reprinted with permission from *Annals of Neurology,* 21(6):533, 1987.

*Chapter 4*

**Fig. 4.1:** From W. J. Hoyer, "Aging and the Development of Expert Cognition" in *New Directions in Cognitive Science,* T. M. Shlechter and M. P. Poglia (eds.). Copyright © 1985 Ablex Publishing Corp., Norwood, NJ. Reprinted by permission. **Fig. 4.2b:** Copyright © Gerald H. Fisher, University of Newcastle upon Tyne, United Kingdom. Reprinted by permission. **Fig. 4.2e,f:** Douglas A. Bernstein, Alison Clarke-Stewart, Edward J. Roy, Thomas K. Srull, and Christopher D. Wickens, *Psychology,* Third Edition. Copyright © 1994 by Houghton Mifflin Company. Reprinted with permission. **Fig. 4.3:** From T. A. Salthouse and B. L. Somberg, "Effects of Adult Age and Experiences on Elementary Processes" in *Journal of Experimental Psychology: General,* III:176–207. Copyright 1982 by the American Psychological Association. Reprinted by permission. **Fig. 4.4:** From J. L. Fozard, T. R. Anders, and T. D. Lilyquist, "The Effects of Age upon Retrieval from Short-Term Memory" in *Developmental Psychology,* 6:214–217. Copyright 1972 by the American Psychological Association. Reprinted by permission. **Fig. 4.6:** From L. W. Poon and J. L. Fozard, "Mental Rotation and Age Reconsidered" in *Journal of Gerontology,* 36:620–624. Copyright © 1981 The Gerontological Society of America. **Fig. 4.7:** Copyright (1966) Canadian Psychological Association. Reprinted by permission. **Fig. 4.A:** From G. G. Murdock, Jr., "Recent Developments in Short-Term Memory" in *British Journal of Psychology,* 58:421–433. Copyright © 1967 The British Psychological Society, Leicester, England. Reprinted by permission. **Fig. 4.8:** From H. P. Bahrick, P. O. Bahrick, and R. P. Wittlinger, "Fifty Years of Memory for Names and Faces: A Cross-Sectional Approach" in *Journal of Experimental Psychology,* 104:54–75. Copyright 1975 by the American Psychological Association. Reprinted by permission. **Fig. 4.10:** From F. I. M. Craik, M. Byrd, and J. M. Swanson, *Psychology and Aging,* 2:79–86. Copyright 1987 by the American Psychological Association. Reprinted by permission.

*Chapter 5*

**Fig. 5.1:** From J. L. Horn, G. Donaldson, and R. Engstrom, *Research on Aging,* 3:40. Copyright © Sage Publications, Inc., Thousand Oaks, CA. **Fig. 5.2:** From K. W. Schaie and S. L. Willis, "Age Difference Patterns of Psychometric Intelligence in Adulthood: Generalizability Within and Across Ability Domains" in *Psychology and Aging,* 8:44–55. Copyright 1993 by the American Psychological Association. Reprinted by permission. **Box Fig. 5.A:** From P. B. Baltes and M. Baltes (eds.), "Psychological Perspectives on Successful Aging: The Model of Selective Optimization with Compensation" in *Longitudinal Research and the Study of Successful (Optimal) Aging.* Copyright © 1990 Cambridge University Press, New York, NY. Reprinted with the permission of Cambridge University Press. **Fig. 5.6:** From K. W. Schaie, *The Seattle Longitudinal Studies of Adult Psychological Development.* Copyright © 1983 The Guilford Press, New York, NY. Reprinted by permission. **Fig. 5.7:** From U. Lindenberger and R. Kliegel, "Speed and Intelligence in Old Age" in *Psychology and Aging,* 8:207–220. Copyright 1993 by the American Psychological Association. Reprinted by permission. **Fig. 5.10a:** Reprinted by permission of Jack Botwinick from *Cognitive Processes in Maturity and Old Age,* published 1967 by Springer Publishing Company, Inc. Copyright © by Jack Botwinick. **Fig. 5.10b:** Reprinted by permission of Jack Botwinick from *Cognitive Processes in Maturity and Old Age,* published 1967 by Springer Publishing Company, Inc. Copyright © by Jack Botwinick.

*Chapter 6*

**Fig. 6.1:** From M. D. Berzonsky, "Formal Reasoning in Adolescence: An Alternative View" in *Adolescence,* 13:279–290. Copyright © 1978 Libra Publishers, Inc., San Diego, CA. Reprinted by permission. **Fig. 6.2:** From D. Kramer, P. E. Kahlbaugh, and R. B. Goldston, "A Measure of Paradigm Beliefs about the Social World" in *Journal of Gerontology: Psychological Sciences,* 47:180–189. Copyright © 1992 The Gerontological Society of America. **Fig. 6.3:** From P. B. Baltes and U. Staudinger, "The Search for a Psychology of Wisdom" in *Current Directions in Psychological Science,* 2:75–80. Copyright © 1993 Cambridge University Press, New York, NY. Reprinted by permission. **Fig. 6.4:** From P. B. Baltes and R. Kliegl, "Further Testing of Limits of Cognitive Plasticity: Negative Age Differences in a Mnemonic Skill Are Robust" in *Developmental Psychology,* 28:121–125. Copyright 1992 by the American Psychological Association. Reprinted by permission.

*Chapter 7*
**Fig. 7.2:** From M. N. Reedy, J. E. Birren, and K. W. Schaie, "Age and Sex Differences in the Life Span" in *Human Development,* 24:52–66. Copyright © 1981 S. Karger AG, Basel, Switzerland. Reprinted by permission. **Extract, p. 213:** From G. O. Hagestad, "Continuity and Connectedness" in *Grandparenthood,* V. Bengston and J. Robertson (eds.). Copyright © 1985 by Sage Publications, Inc. Reprinted by permission of Sage Publications, Inc. **Outline list in Research Focus 7.4:** Adapted from P. A. Lichtenberg and D. M. Strzepek, "Assessments of Institutionalized Dementia Patients' Competencies to Participate in Intimate Relationships" in *The Gerontologist,* 30:117–120. Copyright © 1990 The Gerontological Society of America.

*Chapter 8*
**Fig. 8.6:** From Robert C. Atchley, *The Social Forces in Later Life: An Introduction to Social Gerontology,* 2d ed. Copyright © 1977 Wadsworth Publishing Co., Belmont, CA. Reprinted by permission.

*Chapter 9*
**Fig. 9.3:** Reproduced by permission from the publisher, Psychological Assessment Resources, Inc., from the NEO PI-R Professional Manual, Copyright 1985, 1989, 1992 by PAR, Inc. Further reproduction prohibited without written permission from the publisher. **Fig. 9.4:** From D. Field and R. E. Millsap, "Personality in Advanced Old Age: Continuity or Change" in *Journal of Gerontology: Psychological Sciences,* 46:299–308. Copyright © 1991 The Gerontological Society of America. **Fig. 9.C:** From B. Hagbery, G. Samuelson, R. Lindberg, and O. Dehlin, "Stability and Change of Personality in Old Age and Its Relation to Survival" in *Journal of Gerontology: Psychological Sciences,* 46:285–291. Copyright © 1991 The Gerontological Society of America. **Fig. 9.5:** From D. F. Hultsch and J. K. Plemons, "Life Events and Life Span Development" in *Life Span Development and Behavior,* P. B. Baltes and O. G. Brim, Jr. (eds.). Copyright © 1979 Academic Press. Reprinted by permission.

*Chapter 10*
**Fig. 10.1:** From S. K. Whitbourne, "The Psychological Construction of the Life-Span" in *Handbook of the Psychology of Aging,* 2d ed., J. E. Birren and K. W. Schaie (eds.). Copyright © 1985 Van Nostrand Reinhold Company, New York, NY. Reprinted by permission. **Fig. 10.2:** From S. K. Whitbourne, "The Psychological Construction of the Life-Span" in *Handbook of the Psychology of Aging,* 2d ed., J. E. Birren and K. W. Schaie (eds.). Copyright © 1985 Van Nostrand Reinhold Company, New York, NY. Reprinted by permission. **Fig. 10.3:** From Braudtstadter, Wenture, and Greve, "Adaptive Resources of the Aging Self: Outlines of an Emergent Perspective" in *International Journal of Behavioural Development,* 2:323–349. Copyright © Lawrence Erlbaum Associates Ltd., East Sussex, England. Reprinted by permission of *International Journal of Behavioural Development.* **Extract, p. 366:** From A. LaRue, et al., "Aging and Mental Disorders" (data from DSM-III) in *Handbook of the Psychology of Aging,* 2d ed., J. E. Birren and K. W. Schaie (eds.). Copyright © 1985 Van Nostrand Reinhold Company, New York, NY. Reprinted by permission. **Extract, p. 380:** "Excerpts" from *Living in the Labyrinth: A Personal Journey* by Diana Friel McGowin. Copyright © 1993 by Elder Books. Used by permission of Dell Books, a division of Bantam Doubeday Dell Publishing Group, Inc. **Fig. 10.4:** Copyright © 1988 by The New York Times Company. Reprinted by permission. **Box 10.5:** From T. Adler, "For Depressed Elderly, Drugs Advised" in *APA Monitor,* February 1992:16–17. Copyright 1992 by the American Psychological Association. Reprinted by permission. **Fig. 10.5:** From Patricia L. McCall, *Journal of Gerontology: Social Sciences,* 46(1):43–51. Copyright © 1991 The Gerontological Society of America.

*Chapter 11*
**Fig. 11.1:** From J. E. Birren, R. B. Sloane, and D. Cohen, *Handbook of Mental Health and Aging.* Copyright © Academic Press, Orlando, FL. Reprinted by permission. **Fig. 11.2:** From D. W. Kline, T. J. B. Kline, and J. L. Fozard, "Vision Aging and Driving: The Problems of Older Drivers" in *Journal of Gerontology: Psychological Sciences,* 47(1):27–34. Copyright © 1992 The Gerontological Society of America. **Fig. 11.5:** Source: E. L. Schneider and J. M. Guralnik, "The Aging of America: Impact on Health Care Costs" in *Journal of the American Medical Association,* 263:2335–2340, 1990. **Fig. 11.9:** From M. P. Lawton and L. Nahemow, "Ecology and the Aging Process" in *The Psychology of Adult Development and Aging,* C. Eisdorfer and M. P. Lawton (eds.). Copyright 1973 by the American Psychological Association. Reprinted by permission. **Fig. 11.10:** Source: Data from Luxembourg Income Study. **Fig. 11.11:** From *Long-Term Care—A Guide for the Educational Community.* Copyright © 1992 Teachers Insurance and Annuity Association (TIAA), New York, NY. Reprinted by permission. **Fig. 11.13:** From V. Regnier and J. Pynoos, "Environmental Intervention for Cognitively Impaired Older Persons" in J. E. Birren, R. B. Sloane, and G. D. Cohen (eds.), *Handbook of Mental Health and Aging,* 2d ed. Copyright © 1992 Academic Press, Orlando, FL. Reprinted by permission. **Fig. 11.15:** From D. Martino-Saltzman, B. B. Blasch, R. D. Morris, and L. W. McNeal, "Travel Behavior of Nursing Home Residents Perceived as Wanderers and Non-Wanderers" in *The Gerontologist,* October 31, (5):666–672. Copyright © 1992 The Gerontological Society of America.

*Chapter 12*
**Box 12.1:** From "Guidelines for the Determination of Death: Report of the Medical Consultants on the Diagnosis of Death to the President's Commission for the Study of Ethical Problems in Medicine and Biomedical and Behavioral Research" in *Journal of the American Medical Association,* 246:2184–2186. Copyright 1981, American Medical Association. Reprinted by permission. **Fig. 12.1:** Reprinted by permission of Choice In Dying (formerly Society for the Right to Die), 200 Varick Street, NY, NY 10014. **Page 479–480:** From *Death, Grief, and Caring Relationships,* by R. A. Kalish. Copyright © 1981 by Wadsworth, Inc. Reprinted by permission of Brooks/Cole Publishing Company, Pacific Grove, CA. **Extract, p. 494:** From *Death, Grief, and Caring Relationships,* by R. A. Kalish. Copyright © 1981 by Wadsworth, Inc. Reprinted by permission of Brooks/Cole Publishing Company, Pacific Grove, CA.

## Illustrator

***Bensen Studios***
Figures: 2.1, 3.1, 3.2, 3.3, 3.4, 3.5, 3.6, 3.7, 3.8, 3.10, 3.12, 4.1, 4.4, 4.6, 4.7, 5.2, 5.7, 6.2, 6.3, 6.4, 6.5, 7.4, 7.5, 8.3, 8.4, 8.5, 9.4, 10.3, 10.5, 11.1, 11.2, 11.3, 11.4, 11.5, 11.6, 11.7, 11.10, 11.11, 11.12, 11.13, 11.14, 11.15; Box figures: 5.A, page 139; 9.A & 9.B, page 316; 9.C, page 317; and 11.A, page 449.

## Photo

*Chapter 1*
**Opener:** © Gail Meese/Meese Photo Research; **p. 12, top:** © Allen Zak/Meese Photo Research; **p. 13, left, right:** © Gail Meese/Meese Photo Research; **p. 15:** AP/Wide World Photos

*Chapter 2*
**Opener:** © Quiel Begonia/Meese Photo Research; **p. 29:** © Toni Michaels/The Image Works; **p. 32:** © Martha Tabor/Meese Photo Research; **p. 43, left, right:** © Gail Meese/Meese Photo Research; **p. 46:** Courtesy of Patricia M. Peterson

*Chapter 3*
**Opener:** © Earl Dotter/Meese Photo Research; **p. 57:** © Allen Zak/Meese Photo Research; **p. 58, left, right:** AP/Wide World Photos; **3.11:** © CNRI/Science Photo Library/Photo Researchers, Inc.; **p. 81:** National Archives; **p. 82:** © Gail Meese/Meese Photo Research

*Chapter 4*
**Opener:** © Bob Daemmrich/The Image Works; **p. 93:** © Cathy Watterson/Meese Photo Research; **4.2d:** Bettmann Archive; **p. 99:** © Allen Zak/Meese Photo Research; **p. 114:** © Gail Meese/Meese Photo Research

*Chapter 5*
**Opener:** © Martha Tabor/Meese Photo Research; **p. 142, top:** © Martha Tabor/Meese Photo Research; **p. 142, bottom:** © James Shaffer; **p. 146:** AP/Wide World Photos; **p. 147:** © Allen Zak/Meese Photo Research

*Chapter 6*
**Opener:** © Bedrich Grumzweig/Photo Researchers, Inc.; **p. 168:** © Gail Meese/Meese Photo Research; **p. 173:** © Tim Davis/Photo Researchers, Inc.; **p. 181:** AP/Wide World Photos; **p. 189:** © Martha Tabor/Meese Photo Research

*Chapter 7*
**Opener:** © Allen Zak/Meese Photo Research; **p. 204:** © Gale Zucker/Meese Photo Research; **p. 206:** © Gail Meese/Meese Photo Research; **p. 215:** © Peter A. Silva/Meese Photo Research; **p. 221:** © Gail Meese/Meese Photo Research

*Chapter 8*
**Opener:** © Catherine Green/Meese Photo Research; **p. 242:** © James Shaffer; **p. 270:** © Julie O'Neil; **p. 274:** © James Shaffer; **p. 283:** © Yamada-Lapides/Meese Photo Research

*Chapter 9*
**Opener:** © Art Phaneuf/Meese Photo Research; **p. 293:** Reuters/Bettmann; **p. 307, left:** © David Grossman/Photo Researchers, Inc.; **p. 307, right:** © Dion Ogust/The Image Works; **p. 310:** © Karen Preuss/The Image Works; **p. 331:** © The National Geographic Society/courtesy of Supreme Court Historical Society

*Chapter 10*
**Opener:** © Owen Franken/Stock, Boston; **p. 347:** AP/Wide World Photos; **p. 376:** © Rebecca Bryant Lockridge/Meese Photo Research

*Chapter 11*
**Opener:** © Gail Meese/Meese Photo Research; **p. 403:** © Allen Zak/Meese Photo Research; **p. 407:** © Michael Hayman/Photo Researchers, Inc.; **p. 417:** © Martha Tabor/Meese Photo Research; **p. 444, top:** © David Strickler/Meese Photo Research

*Chapter 12*
**Opener:** © Jim Mahoney/The Image Works; **p. 484, top:** © Toni Michaels/The Image Works; **p. 484, bottom:** © Joseph Nettis/Photo Researchers, Inc.; **p. 488:** © Etter/Anthro-Photo; **p. 491, 497:** © Gail Meese/Meese Photo Research

# NAME INDEX

## C



## D

## *H*



## *I*



## *J*



## *K*

## N



## O



## P

## Q



## R



## S

## T



## U



## V



## W

## Y



## Z

# *SUBJECT INDEX*

## A



## B

## C



## D

## *E*



## *F*



## *G*

## M



## N



## O

## P



## Q



## R

## S



## T

## *U*



## *V*



## *W*



## *Y*